Comparing Cultures

*Readings on Contemporary Japan
for American Writers*

Comparing Cultures

Readings on Contemporary Japan for American Writers

Merry I. White
Boston University and Harvard University

Sylvan Barnet
Tufts University

Bedford Books *of* St. Martin's Press • Boston

For Bedford Books
President and Publisher: Charles H. Christensen
General Manager and Associate Publisher: Joan E. Feinberg
Managing Editor: Elizabeth M. Schaaf
Developmental Editor: Stephen A. Scipione
Production Editor: Lori Chong
Production Associate: Heidi Hood
Copyeditor: Cynthia Benn
Cover Design: Diane Levy
Cover Photograph: Nicholas De Vore III, *Man in Winter Street, Shimukappu, Japan.*
Photographers/Aspen.

Library of Congress Catalog Card Number: 94–65173

Manufactured in the United States of America.

9   8   7   6   5
f   e   d   c   b   a

For information, write: St. Martin's Press, Inc.
175 Fifth Avenue, New York, NY 10010

Editorial Offices: Bedford Books *of* St. Martin's Press
75 Arlington Street, Boston, MA 02116

ISBN: 0–312–10620–3

Acknowledgments
Anne Allison, "The Hostess Club: A Type of Routine" is excerpted from *Nightwork* and appears courtesy of The University of Chicago Press, © 1994 The University of Chicago Press.
Ikuo Amano, "The Examination Hell" appears courtesy of The Pennsylvania State University Press, © 1989 The Pennsylvania State University Press. An earlier version of this essay originally appeared in *The Japan Foundation Newsletter,* Vol. 13, No. 5 (March 1986).
Walter L. Ames, "*Yakuza* and the Police" originally appeared in the *Japan Society Newsletter* and is reprinted courtesy of The Japan Society, © PHP Institute of America, Inc.
Elizabeth Andoh, "The Japanification of American Fast Food" originally appeared in *Mangajin* and appears courtesy of the author, © Elizabeth Andoh.
Harumi Befu, "Gift Giving" is reprinted from the *Kodansha Encyclopedia of Japan,* Vol. 3, and appears courtesy of the Kodansha Institute.

Acknowledgments and copyrights are continued at the back of the book on pages 469–471, which constitute an extension of the copyright page. It is a violation of the law to reproduce these selections by any means whatsoever without the written permission of the copyright holder.

Preface for Instructors

CASSIUS: *Tell me, good Brutus, can you see your face?*
BRUTUS: *No, Cassius, for the eye sees not itself*
But by reflection, by some other things.
—William Shakespeare, *Julius Caesar*

A knowledge of one other culture should sharpen our ability to scrutinize more steadily, to appreciate more lovingly, our own.
—Margaret Mead, *Coming of Age in Samoa*

The Aim of the Book

Comparing Cultures is designed for composition courses—that is, for courses in which students write essays, instructors (and often other students) read the essays, and instructors and students discuss them. It contains multi-disciplinary readings about a contemporary culture—modern Japan—in eleven chapters. The organization of the chapters and the editorial apparatus seek to promote thoughtful, nuanced comparisons with America.

This last point needs to be explained a bit, although the quotations from Mead and Shakespeare tip our hand. We use a single culture, Japan, as an aid or foil to enable students to think and write about America with a fresh perspective. Japan—like us in being democratic, patriarchal, and capitalistic but emphatically *not* Western—is an ideal cultural mirror for the United States. By reading intensively about Japanese culture and by testing their new knowledge of Japan against their existing knowledge of American culture, students learn to think critically (which is chiefly to say that they learn to examine their assumptions and to evaluate evidence) about what may be distinctively American in their own disparate experiences and subcultures.

These fifty-six readings (ranging from academic analyses to popular journalism, from entries in reference works to personal accounts, from fiction to song lyrics) are offered, then, not in order to assist students to become experts on Japan, but in order to assist them to examine thoughtfully their own experiences as Americans. By providing students with the chance to read one culture against another, these readings about a contrasting culture help students to think about what Americans have in common as well as how they differ. (This is not to say that students will not learn a great deal about Japan—they will, as will their instructors, who we hope will welcome the challenge and the opportunity to learn along with their students.)

The Two-Part Organization

Part One, with eight readings in two chapters on cross-cultural analysis and on critical reading and writing practices, introduces students to comparative thinking and writing. In these chapters we try to adapt some of the insights of anthropologists and social scientists in a way that will be useful in a composition course where students are thinking and writing about culture.

Part Two contains forty-eight readings arranged into nine categories that social scientists consider most germane to the study of modern industrialized societies. Because these categories include social institutions as well as stages of life, personal experiences as well as ethnographic description, the readings include such matters as material culture, growing up, work, leisure, crime, and notions of nation.

The Editorial Apparatus

Because this is a text for courses in composition, we have included apparatus designed not only to enable students to think rigorously and to read thoughtfully, but also to write effectively. The apparatus continuously connects the readings with the aims of the composition course.

- **Chapter assignments,** called "Explorations," reinforce the cultural and comparative lessons of Part One and, in Part Two, prompt students to examine their own cultural assumptions.

- **Chapter introductions** in Part Two present overviews of the topics.

- **Two sets of discussion and writing assignments after each selection,** called "Thinking About the Text" and "Thinking About Culture," prompt students to examine the content and rhetoric of the selection, and also to explore larger cultural connections between the readings (and other readings) and their own experiences. The overall aim is to encourage students to produce writing that draws on both personal experience and on critical thinking.

- **Footnotes** for each selection provide biographical and background information and gloss Japanese and cross-cultural terms and concepts.

- The **appendix,** "Doing Research," equips students to perform library and field research as they write and document research papers in the MLA style.

- Our **instructor's manual,** titled *Editors' Notes to Accompany COMPARING CULTURES,* provides commentary on and teaching suggestions for every chapter and selection, as well as an annotated bibliography of works on cultural analysis and on Japan.

Acknowledgments

"The last thing one discovers composing a work," Blaise Pascal said three hundred years ago, "is what to put first." Still true. We could not have written this preface before we finished the rest of the manuscript. But the first thing we discovered, almost as soon as we met with our publisher to talk about the project, was what we are putting last in the preface, our massive debt to those who helped us.

First, we must name three people at Bedford Books: publisher Charles H. Christensen, general manager and associate publisher Joan E. Feinberg, and development editor Stephen A. Scipione. These three shapers of many first-rate textbooks assumed (not entirely accurately) that we wanted frank criticism, rather as if we shared Emily Dickinson's request (in a letter to T. W. Higginson) for an honest appraisal: "Will you tell me my faults frankly as to yourself, for I had rather wince, than die. Men do not call the surgeon to commend the bone, but to set it, Sir." When they did not play the role of surgeon, cutting into our manuscript and setting its bones, they played the role of chiropractor, straightening out the kinks and putting in a few good twists of their own. Much of what we think is good in the book is because Chuck, Joan, and Steve always found time to follow our progress and to suggest sensible improvements. They were, so to speak, just what the doctor ordered.

In the later stages of working on the book, we became deeply indebted to yet another group at Bedford Books: managing editor Elizabeth Schaaf, production editor Lori Chong, copyeditor Cynthia Benn, and production associate Heidi Hood made many valuable suggestions. And between the beginning—with the searching and shaping lunch talks with Chuck, Joan, and Steve—and the end—with the detailed critical appraisals of Elizabeth, Lori, Cynthia, and Heidi—as we worked on this book *on* culture *for* writers, we were indebted to colleagues who read drafts and shared their experience and ideas about using our material in composition courses. We are glad, then, to be able to thank Glenn Blalock, University of North Carolina at Chapel Hill; George Bozzini, George Washington University; Kathy Hutnick, Indiana University; Sonia Maasik, University of California, Los Angeles; David Porter, Southern University of Baton Rouge; Barbara Sloan, Santa Fe Community College; and Irwin Weiser, Purdue University.

Contents

Part Two

Readings for Cultural Comparison

Appendix Doing Research 439

A Note on
Names and Pronunciation

Japanese Names

In Japan, the family name is given first, but to avoid any confusion, we use the Western style, personal name first, throughout this book. An exception to this is made for historical figures such as the tenth-century diarist Sei Shonagon, who is always referred to in this manner.

Pronouncing Japanese Words

Japanese words are pronounced approximately as they are written in English, which is more than you can say about English words. (Consider *rough*, *bough*, and *through*, for instance; or *you* and *ewe*, which are pronounced identically even though they do not share a single letter. It has been aptly said of English spelling that the consonants count for very little, and the vowels for nothing at all.)

When Japanese words are written in a romanized script, the vowels are pronounced more or less as in English or Italian, thus:

a as in "f*a*ther"

e as in "g*e*t"

i as in "mar*i*ne"

o as in "n*o*"

u as in "r*u*le"

The consonants are pronounced as is usual in English, but note that *g* is always hard as in "get," never soft as in "gem." The *f* (as in *Fuji*) is pronounced somewhere between *f* and *h*—that is, the sound is somewhat like what is produced when one blows out a match—but the English *f* will do.

All the letters are pronounced. Thus, Professor Chie Nakane's given name has two syllables (Chi-e), and her family name has three (Na-ka-ne).

Part One

Thinking and Writing About Culture

Chapter 1

Thinking About Culture

Japan, modern but not Western, provides a mirror for America. Looking in this mirror we see a society that is highly developed, perhaps even more than ours: The outward trappings—including high-speed public transportation, high-rise office buildings, countrywide communications and media, a booming economy supporting a postindustrial work and life-style—are matched with democratic principles and practices, a superior educational system, and a rational, egalitarian legal code. Remember, however, that when mirrors reflect an image, they reverse and in other ways change the object in reflection. You may have noticed that the rearview mirror of a car may bear the message, "Caution: Objects seen in the mirror are closer than they appear." Mirrors are quite wonderful: They show us something that is and is not ourselves. (This sense of wonder is inherent in the word itself, which comes from the Latin *mirus,* "wonderful.")

Observing: Insiders and Outsiders

The perceptions of an observer, especially of one who is an outsider, are not of course as clearly reflective as a mirror. When reporting our observations, we try to mirror the original accurately, but in fact most of us observe, or "mirror," from a distorting angle. Understanding the angle is an important part of observing.

Here is a brief extract from a book by an American woman who visited Japan, where she taught English at a women's university. Let's see what she saw. (We reprint another selection from the same book, *36 Views of Mount Fuji,* on p. 215.)

Cathy N. Davidson

A Teacher Learns

After summer break, I require students in beginning Oral English for Non-Majors to give a brief presentation on what they've done over the vacation. It's designed to be simple, to ease them back into the term. They've been in Oral English since April, the beginning of the Japanese school year. They have had six weeks off for the summer, and now must return to classes for three more weeks before the grueling end-of-semester exams in late September.

I call on the first student.

"I was constipated most of the way to Nikko," a lovely young woman in a Kenzo flower-print jumper begins her talk.

I set my face like a Japanese mask, careful to express no emotion, and steal glances around the room. No one seems even remotely surprised at this beginning except me, and I know that it is absolutely mandatory that I act as if this is the most ordinary opening in the world.

"I was with the tennis club, and my *sensei*° made sure I ate *konnyaku*   5
for my constipation."

At this point she gets flustered. She is obviously embarrassed.

"It's okay," I jump in hastily, searching for my most soothing and encouraging Japanese. "You're doing very well. Please go on."

"It's just," she stammers, also in Japanese, "I don't know the English for *konnyaku*. Do you know?"

I assure her that there's no American equivalent. *Konnyaku* is a glutinous substance, made from the root of a plant that seems to grow only in Japan. In America, I tell her, most people eat bran to cure constipation or we take over-the-counter medicines such as Ex Lax.

"Ecks Racks," she repeats solemnly, then breaks into giggles (American-   10
style). So does everyone.

The word sounds so funny. It becomes the class joke for the next few weeks. If anyone forgets a word in English, someone else inevitably whispers to a friend, loud enough for the rest of us to hear, "Ecks Racks!"

Three or four other speeches that morning give blow-by-blow reports of near gastrointestinal crises and how they were averted, usually by the wise intervention of some *sensei*.

What surprises me most about the morning is how embarrassed *I* am, although I think I've concealed it pretty well. These students would wilt with shame if they had any inkling that this is not something we would talk about in America, and I find myself in a quandary. They trust me to tell them

sensei: Mentor. [Editors' note]

about Western culture, but I know that if I tell them it's not considered polite to talk about one's bowel movements in Western society, it will destroy the easy camaraderie I've worked so hard to foster this year. But if I don't tell them, I'm violating a trust.

I decide to resolve this by keeping a list of things they bring up that wouldn't be acceptable in the West. All semester I've been working to correct certain Japanese misconceptions and stereotypes, especially their idea that English is a completely logical and direct language, and that Americans always say exactly what they mean, regardless of social status or power relationships. Often my students say things that sound very rude because they've been taught that English lacks the politeness levels of Japanese. These are topics we discuss all the time, so it will work just fine to devote the last week of the semester to lecturing, in my comical Japanese, about misconceptions and cultural differences that I've discovered during my year in Japan. I can tell them about how surprised I was the first time I used a public restroom that turned out to be coed or about bathing Japanese-style with a group of women I barely knew or having a male colleague slip around a corner on the way home from a party. I started to follow, then realized he was taking a quick pee. I know I can act out my own surprise, making my Westerner's prudishness about bodily functions seem funny but also relevant. This is as close as I can come to having my pedagogical cake and eating it too.

Davidson's experience—of being a bit discombobulated by her encounter with persons from a culture other than her own—is a more comic version of something that all of us have occasionally experienced. For instance, although colleges seek to ease the transition from high school to college (and perhaps from life at home to life at college) by means of orientation programs, our first days at college are almost inevitably disconcerting. Consider the kind of culture shock that you may experience in a composition course. In the first place, although the catalog may have listed the course as an "English" course, it probably is very unlike your past English courses; you have to revise your expectations accordingly. In the second place, you may be in a class with students from various ethnic backgrounds, from different parts of the country or perhaps from other countries, and from all walks of life. People may be saying things you have never heard said before and perhaps behaving in ways you have never seen. You and your fellow students are gathered in a classroom that has become what some scholars call a "contact zone," a place where cultural interchanges go on like crazy and where even the role of the teacher may shift. Cathy Davidson, you may recall, was supposed to be the teacher, but she learned a great deal—and not only about the Japanese. She learned about herself. For instance, in the next-to-last paragraph she says, "What surprises me most about the morning is how embarrassed *I* am . . . ," and in the final paragraph she mentions several episodes that caused her to become aware of her "Westerner's prudishness about bodily functions. . . ."

Representing—and Misrepresenting—Others

We all like to think of ourselves as open-minded, but we probably all have our share of misconceptions, especially misconceptions derived from overgeneralizing. If we are Yankees and have spent a week in North Carolina, we may find ourselves saying, "You know, Southerners are . . ." A week in California may produce another set of generalizations. We need not spend even a week in North Carolina or in California to formulate stereotypes; we may have picked them up from our parents, or we may have based them on a next-door neighbor. In short, we probably stereotype more than we are aware of. As the nineteenth-century humorist Josh Billings said, "Lots of our problems come from the things we know that aren't true."

You may know from your own experience that when people encounter another culture—even if only in an ethnic restaurant—they tend to react in one of two extreme ways: "This is wonderful, the most marvelous food I have ever tasted, and the waiter is so polite!" or "You mean they eat rattlesnake!!! And did you see the waiter's fingernails!!!" At least at first, we may idealize another culture, or we may demonize it. Either way, we may unknowingly be endorsing stereotypes or overgeneralizing. For instance, when Europe first encountered what for it was the New World, some explorers wrote enthusiastically about the nobility of the people they encountered ("courageous," "honest," "handsome") whereas others regarded them with loathing ("cowardly," "deceitful," "deformed"). By the way, the reaction of the first Europeans who encountered the Japanese, in the middle of the sixteenth century and on into the early seventeenth, was along similar lines. In the extract printed on page 12, a Spanish missionary wrote that the Japanese "are as prudent as could be desired and are governed by reason just as much as, or even more than, Spaniards," but an English merchant who spent ten years in Japan took a different view:

> I doe protest unto yow I am sick to see their proceadinges, and canot eate a bit of meate that doth me good, but cast it up as sowne as I have eaten it. God send me well once out of this cuntrey, yf it be His blessed will.

For other extracts from the earliest Western visitors to Japan, see page 12.

If you think about your own encounters with other cultures and the experiences of your friends, you may distinguish two extreme views, which we call (admittedly with some element of caricature) The Unvarying Heart and The Unknowable Other.

The belief that people are all pretty much the same, in all places and in all times, can be called The Unvarying Heart. Parental love, for instance, might be cited as evidence to support this belief. The idea is that under an ancient Chinese robe, under a medieval knight's armor, and under a modern Japanese business suit there beats a heart—a mind, we mean—that resembles our own. This view recognizes that customs differ from culture to culture or group to group (some eat with knives and forks, some with chopsticks, some with their fingers), but it holds that the obvious differences are trivial when compared with universal similarities.

People who subscribe to the contrasting view, The Unknowable Other, believe that it is impossible for an outsider ever to read another culture accurately. According to this view, although we may think we understand completely, we get the words but not the tune. It may be a delusion, if we are, say, middle-class whites, to believe that we can understand even middle-class African Americans. This is a point made jestingly by the motto on T-shirts worn by some African Americans: "It's a black thing; you wouldn't understand." As an example of our inability to perceive another culture accurately, think of the centuries of talk about "the discovery of America." How European! America, with its people, was here all the while; only a European could have talked of "discovering" America and of calling it the New World (it is as old as Europe) or, for that matter, of calling it America— that is, of imposing a European name on this "other" and thereby seeking to absorb the unfamiliar into the familiar. In this perspective, any exploration and "discovery" is seen as hegemonic—not as a discovery (an uncovering) but as a projection or extension of one nation's own authority over others.

Consider, for a moment, the dilemma faced by an American museum when it exhibits an object from another culture—a Japanese tea bowl or an African cup, for example. The museum can place the object in a showcase, illuminate it effectively, and leave it for viewers who will admire its beauty. The implication of such display is that everyone can enjoy this work of art and that standards of beauty are universal because the human heart is unvarying. Or the museum can instead exhibit the object with a detailed label on the wall explaining its use and perhaps with photographs or even with an audiovisual accompaniment showing *how the object was used within its own culture.* The African cup, let's say, held wine used in an enthronement ceremony. It must (in this view) *not* be seen as a mere object of beauty. To see it as a mere object of beauty is to deprive it of its cultural uniqueness. Rather, the object must be recognized as something that functioned in a particular way and that held particular meaning for persons in a particular society—and an outsider cannot achieve empathy with this meaning. The idea that outsiders cannot fully respond is easily demonstrated every day: Objects that we can't bring ourselves to throw away—pictures of our beloved, deceased grandparents or dried, pressed roses from the high school prom—are just so much junk to outsiders.

As noted, the two views contrasted here are extreme. Most of us believe that we can get some insight into the behavior of others and that, when we understand others, we also gain insight into ourselves. We may come to see, for instance, that our own cherished views are not as reasonable as we had thought.

In reading about Japanese culture we will not only be broadening our horizons but acquiring a lens through which we might view our own culture freshly, rather as Cathy Davidson came to learn things not only about the Japanese but about her own culture. By "thinking Japanese" we may get a glimpse of ourselves as others see us, and we may increase our understanding of what is distinctively American in our behavior, in our culture. Before we consider this point, let's examine the idea of *culture* in some detail.

Speaking Culture

In Molière's comedy *Le Bourgeois Gentilhomme,* the chief character, a newly rich but ignorant upstart, is terribly pleased with himself when, upon learning the distinction between poetry and prose, he realizes that he has been speaking prose all his life. And without even trying! Similarly, it is sometimes a surprise to discover that there is *culture* in everything that we do and experience. True, in one sense of the word, "culture" refers to what *The American Heritage Dictionary* calls "a high degree of taste and refinement," but the same dictionary gives other meanings. The first meaning, in fact, is "the totality of socially transmitted behavior patterns . . . and all other products of human work and thought." In short, culture informs— gives form to or is the informative principle of—all human activity. This kind of culture shapes the way we give change in a shop (in Japan, money is almost always put on a tray, not handed directly to the customer), how we take a bath (in a Japanese-style bath, one soaps and rinses oneself *outside* of the tub, then gets into the tub and soaks, keeping the water clean for the next person), or how we express love for another person (no need for explanatory details here).

No one is born fully acculturated, fully instructed in the culture of a particular society, but culture happens to you immediately thereafter. Even the way you enter the world is culturally determined: Newborns are bathed, swaddled, and nursed according to beliefs, rationales, and practices that differ by culture. Those born in modern, highly technologized hospitals are of course subject to the culture of modern Western medicine and the institution of the hospital. And institutions such as hospitals are shaped by the dominant culture—meaning the culture of the group with the greatest political and economic power—of their society as well.

If culture is virtually identical with the life we live, we will of course have difficulty in seeing it clearly. Just as Molière's bourgeois gentleman was unaware that he spoke something called prose, we are unaware that actions we consider "natural" (or at least second nature) are, in fact, shaped by culture. We may be no more aware of them than we are of the air we breathe. Usually we become aware of the air we breathe only when it takes on a new scent or becomes foul—that is, when the situation becomes unusual or unnatural. In *Mirror for Man* (1949), anthropologist Clyde Kluckhohn put it this way: "It would hardly be a fish who discovered the existence of water."

Take, for instance, the concept of adolescence. Americans consider adolescence (generally concurrent with the teen years) to be an inevitable phase in the life course, and teens themselves can see it as "natural" if sometimes painful. Teenagers know that they are "supposed" to rebel or at least to resist adults; they are "supposed" to crave the rights and freedoms of adult life, such as a driver's license, the right to drink, and other evidence of maturity. But until very recently, such a marked stage did not exist in Japan: People went from childhood to adulthood without much emotional turbulence. Japanese culture was unencumbered by the cultural beliefs and expectations that defined American adolescence; but of course Western observers, assuming that certain kinds of adolescent behaviors were universal, looked for the expected symptoms. Incidentally, the twentieth-century American conception of adolescence did not exist in earlier America, either, but that's another matter.

Working with Concepts of Culture

Now we want to come up with a working definition of culture, one we can use as a tool in critical thinking, especially in thinking about *our own* culture. That is, we will read about Japanese culture—Japanese life, we might say—and we will test what we find against our own experiences, which is also to say that we will test American culture in all its diversity against Japanese culture.

"Culture" may be simply but usefully defined as *the beliefs, ideas, and practices (customs) of a group of people.* Thus, because the Japanese customarily give presents to their colleagues on returning from a trip, we can say that this practice is an aspect of Japanese culture. Another definition holds that *culture includes tools and symbols as well as strategies employed to construct a society.* In this second definition, culture has a more aggressive, instrumental nature: Culture includes the ways in which one is persuaded, even pressured, to give those gifts and the ways in which doing so establishes status, maintains cohesion, and even preempts choice-making within the group. Culture thus is also seen as a managed construct: Not just a medium like the water fish move through, or the air we breathe, it is also *created by people and by institutions*—for instance, by laws and markets—to arrange power and status in the community. And, to continue the liquid and air analogies, the flow may be directed or channeled.

Thus, even the pervasive notion of homogeneity in Japan—the insistence by the Japanese that they are one racially pure group—can be seen not as the assertion of a social truth, the assertion of a reality, but as a deliberately fostered idea, perhaps even a piece of propaganda, created, constructed, or cultivated by leaders in the nineteenth century who were eager to establish, in the most efficient way possible, a modern nation-state, a coherent unit that could stand next to the things called England, Germany, and the United States.[1]

Not Getting Lost
in the Translation

As indicated in the case of American sociologists hunting in vain for American-style adolescence in prewar Japan, it is very difficult—perhaps impossible—to perceive another culture as the insider perceives it. For one thing, the words and concepts of one culture may misrepresent the realities of another. You may have read accounts of eighteenth-century foreign visitors to the United States who, since they themselves lived in monarchies, spoke of George Washington as the king of the United States. Ridiculous, of course—but all of us project our familiar ideas onto the unfamiliar just as the visitors did whose languages had no convenient term for someone called a "president." Indeed, journalists today speak of Mohammedans, a term that wrongly suggests that Moslems (the proper name for followers of Islam) regard Mohammed in the way that Christians regard Christ. Mohammed was Allah's prophet but was not himself a divinity to be worshipped. Thus one can properly speak of Christians, worshippers of Christ, but one cannot properly speak of Mohammedans, worshippers of Mohammed. It is this sort of unconscious thinking, and the use of one's own words and concepts, laden with one's own culture, that makes it so difficult to understand others—and to understand ourselves.

In his satirical work of fiction, *Gulliver's Travels* (1726), Jonathan Swift gives an amusing version of the lack of comprehension with which one culture earnestly examines another. Gulliver has been shipwrecked in Lilliput, a land whose inhabitants are six inches tall. Here is part of the account a committee of Lilliputians wrote, describing a strange object they found in Gulliver's possession.

> We directed him to draw out whatever was at the end of that
> chain; which appeared to be a globe, half silver, and half of some
> transparent metal: for on the transparent side we saw certain
> strange figures circularly drawn, and thought we could touch

[1] Frank K. Upham, *Law and Social Change in Postwar Japan* (Cambridge: Harvard UP, 1987).

them, until we found our fingers stopped with that lucid substance. He put this engine to our ears, which made an incessant
noise like that of a watermill. And we conjecture it is either some
unknown animal, or the god that he worships: but we are more
inclined to the latter opinion, because he assured us (if we understood him right, for he expressed himself very imperfectly), that
he seldom did anything without consulting it. He called it his
oracle, and said it pointed out the time for every action of his
life.

The object is in fact a pocket watch attached to a chain. In thinking that
Gulliver's watch is the god he worships, the Lilliputians—outsiders so far
as English or European culture goes—are marvelously wrong; but they are
also marvelously right in seeing something that Gulliver himself can't see
because he is swimming in his natural element. Only an outsider can see
that indeed the Englishman worships time and in effect is enslaved to it,
voluntarily, unknowingly, but nevertheless enslaved. (When you read Horace
Miner's essay "Body Ritual Among the Nacirema" on p. 29, you may well
feel that you are reading the report of a Lilliputian describing Gulliver and
his watch.)

Four Suggestions for Thinking About Culture

When thinking about the behavior of people in a culture other than
your own, try to do the following:

- Pay attention to the *context* in which the particular behavior or belief
  occurs.

- Examine *your own cultural baggage,* the context that predisposes you
  to hold the beliefs you do on this particular matter.

- Use language very carefully in describing the other culture, understanding that words and concepts are culture-bound too.

- Allow your perceptions to guide you to the commonalities as well as
  to the differences.

Alessandro Valignano, Cosme de Torres,
and Francesco Carletti

Reports of the Earliest Western Visitors to Japan

Alessandro Valignano, S.J.: "Unlike Any Other People"

They also have rites and ceremonies so different from those of all the other nations that it seems they deliberately try to be unlike any other people. The things which they do in this respect are beyond imagining and it may truly be said that Japan is a world the reverse of Europe; everything is so different and opposite that they are like us in practically nothing. So great is the difference in their food, clothing, honors, ceremonies, language, management of the household, in their way of negotiating, sitting, building, curing the wounded and sick, teaching and bringing up children, and in everything else, that it can be neither described nor understood.

Now all this would not be surprising if they were like so many barbarians, but what astonishes me is that they behave as very prudent and cultured people in all these matters. To see how everything is the reverse of Europe, despite the fact that their ceremonies and customs are so cultured and founded on reason, causes no little surprise to anyone who understands such things. What is even more astonishing is that they are so different from us, and even contrary to us, as regards the senses and natural things; this is something which I would not dare to affirm if I had not had so much experience among them. Thus their taste is so different from ours that they generally despise and dislike the thing that we find most pleasing; on the other hand, we cannot stand the things which they like.

Cosme de Torres, S.J.: "Governed by Reason"

These Japanese are better disposed to embrace our holy Faith than any other people in the world. They are as prudent as could be desired and are governed by reason just as much as, or even more than, Spaniards; they are more inquisitive than any other people I have met. No men in the wide world more like to hear sermons on how to serve their Creator and save their souls.

The first Westerners to encounter Japan were Portuguese sailors and merchants, beginning in 1543. Catholic missionaries reached Japan in 1549 and were active there for the rest of the century. The extracts reprinted here are observations made by these earliest visitors, some of whom were Jesuits, or members of the Society of Jesus (hence the initials S.J. after their names).

Their conversation is so polite that they all seem to have been brought up in the palaces of great nobles; in fact, the compliments they pay each other are beyond description. They grumble but little about their neighbors and envy nobody. They do not gamble; just as theft is punished by death, so also gambling. As a pastime they practice with their weapons, at which they are extremely adept, or write couplets, just as the Romans composed poetry, and most of the gentry occupy themselves in this way. They are very brave and put much faith in their weapons; boys over the age of thirteen carry a sword and dagger, and never take them off. They have every kind of weapon, both offensive and defensive, and some are of great value; you may even find swords worth 1,500 *cruzados*. They do not have any kind of guns because they declare that they are for cowards alone. They are the best archers I have seen in this world. They look down on all other nations.

They run their universities with the greatest strictness and peace; there are no licentiates in them, nor bachelors, nor proctors, nor notaries, nor constables, neither do they have any lawsuits or claims—a most surprising state of affairs. They just as readily execute a man for stealing one farthing as for stealing a hundred thousand, because they maintain that a man who takes one thing will take a hundred if he gets the chance. The nobles are well served and venerated by their servants, for a man of whatever rank may have his servant put to death for his slightest act of disobedience; for this reason servants obey their masters diligently, and when they speak to them they always bow their heads and place both hands on the ground.

Alessandro Valignano, S.J.: "Prudent and Discreet"

They are very prudent and discreet in all their dealings with others and they never weary anybody by recounting their troubles or by complaining or grumbling as people do in Europe. When they go visiting, their etiquette demands that they never say anything which might upset their host. And so they never come and talk about their troubles and grievances, because as they claim to suffer much and always to show courage in adversity, they keep their troubles to themselves as best they can. When they meet or go to visit somebody, they always appear cheerful and in good spirits, and they either do not refer to their troubles at all, or, if they do, at most they just mention them with a laugh as if they did not worry about such unimportant matters. As they are so opposed to every kind of gossip, they never talk about other people's affairs or grumble about their princes and rulers, but instead they speak on topics in keeping with the times and circumstances, dwelling on them only for as long as they think they can afford pleasure and content to their hosts.

For this reason (and also in order not to become heated in their dealings with others), they observe a general custom in Japan of not transacting any important or difficult business face to face with another person, but instead

5

they do it all through messages or a third person. This method is so much in vogue that it is used between fathers and their children, masters and their servants, and even between husbands and wives, for they maintain that it is only prudent to conduct through a third person such matters which may give rise to anger, objections, or quarrels. As a result they live in such peace and quietness that even the children forbear to use inelegant expressions among themselves, nor do they fight or hit each other like European lads; instead, they speak politely and never fail to show each other respect. In fact they show such incredible gravity and maturity that they seem more like solemn men than children.

Francesco Carletti:
"Most Shameless Immorality"

They do not, however, hold in equal esteem the virtue of their daughters and sisters; or rather they take no account of this at all. Indeed it often happens that a girl's own father, mother, or brothers—without any feeling of shame on the part of any of those concerned—will without hesitation sell her as a prostitute before she is married, for a few pence, under the pressure of poverty, which is very severely felt throughout the whole country. And this poverty is the cause of the most shameless immorality—an immorality which is so gross and which takes such different and unusual forms, as to pass belief.

But the Portuguese are my witnesses and cannot be gainsaid—especially those who come year by year from China, that is, from the island of Macao. The ships on which they travel are laden with silk and other textile materials, as well as pepper and cloves (used for making dyes) and many other kinds of merchandise, which they sell here at great profit, doing their bargaining in this town and harbor of Nagasaki, where they lie for eight or nine months, until they are able to finish their business. As soon as ever these Portuguese arrive and disembark, the pimps who control this traffic in women call on them in the houses in which they are quartered for the time of their stay, and inquire whether they would like to purchase, or acquire in any other method they please, a girl, for the period of their sojourn, or to keep her for so many months, or for a night, or for a day, or for an hour, a contract being first made with these brokers, or an agreement entered into with the girl's relations, and the money paid down. And if they prefer it they will take them to the girl's house, in order that they may see her first, or else they will take them to see her on their own premises, which are usually situated in certain hamlets or villages outside the city. And many of these Portuguese, upon whose testimony I am relying, fall in with this custom as the fancy takes them, driving the best bargain they can for a few pence. And so it often happens that they will get hold of a pretty little girl of fourteen or fifteen years of age, for three or four *scudi,* or a little more or less, according to the time during which they wish to have her at their disposal, with no other responsibility beyond that of sending her back home when done with. Nor does this practice in any way interfere with a girl's chances of marriage.

Indeed many of them would never get married, if they had not by this means acquired a dowry, by accumulating thirty or forty *scudi,* given to them from time to time by these Portuguese, who have kept them in their houses for seven or eight months on end, and who have in some cases married them themselves. And when these women are hired by the day, it is enough to give them the merest trifle, nor do they ever refuse to be hired on account of a variation in the price, which is hardly ever refused by their relations, or by those who keep them as a sort of stock in trade for these purposes in their houses, and to whom the money is paid—the women being in effect all slaves sold for these purposes. And there are, moreover, some of them who, by agreement with the brokers, ask for no more than their food and clothing—neither of which costs much—while the whole of their earnings go to the men who keep them.

To sum up, the country is more plentifully supplied than any other with these sort of means of gratifying the passion for sexual indulgence, just as it abounds in every other sort of vice, in which it surpasses every other place in the world.

Thinking About the Text

1. In his second sentence, Cosme de Torres says that the Japanese are "governed by reason," and he goes on to say that "they just as readily execute a man for stealing one farthing [a trifling amount] as for stealing a hundred thousand, because they maintain that a man who takes one thing will take a hundred if he gets the chance" (para. 4). Assuming the accuracy of his report about punishment in sixteenth-century Japan, do you agree that the system of punishment is an example of the reign of "reason"? Should the system be adopted in the United States? Or does the example prove that society should *not* be governed by "reason"?

2. Do some research on reports of the early encounters of Europeans with Native Americans. What similarities and differences do you note between these reports and those of European missionaries in Japan?

   You may want to begin your research on visitors to America by looking at one or more of the following titles: Hugh Honor, *The New Golden Land: European Images of America from the Discoveries to the Present Time* (1975); Jay A. Levenson, ed., *Circa 1492: Art in the Age of Exploration* (1991). (The first book listed is a good introduction to the topic, with many attractive illustrations. The second book is a massive art book with superb illustrations and several short but excellent essays that are relevant. Both books include illustrations made by the early visitors.) Samuel Eliot Morison, *The European Discovery of America: The Northern Voyages, A.D. 500–1600* (1971); Djelal Kadir, *Columbus and the Ends of the Earth* (1993); Irving Rouse, *The Tainos* (1993); Peter Hulme and Neil Whitehead, eds., *Wild Majesty* (1993); Philip Boucher, *Cannibal Encounters* (1993).

Thinking About Culture

3. In his first paragraph Carletti explains that "the pressure of poverty" causes adults to sell girls into prostitution, but he nonetheless unequivocally condemns the practice. In fact, his view of sixteenth-century Japan is that the country "abounds in . . . vice." Do you suppose that an outsider visiting the United States—perhaps someone from the former Soviet Union or from any culture that you believe is distinct from ours—might regard some aspect of our accepted practice—for instance, the plight of the uninsured under our current system of medical coverage or the large number of people in our prisons—as equally vicious?

4. These accounts were written about four hundred years ago. Brainstorm a list of traits that you associate with Japan and the Japanese. How much of what the early European visitors to Japan reported conforms to your own impressions of contemporary Japan?

5. Probably outsiders inevitably simplify, or "naturalize," making the unfamiliar familiar, by seeing it in terms of their own culture. Write an account of some aspect of American culture, for instance life on an American campus, or life at evening classes, as might be written by a person from a very different culture. You may want to imagine that you are one of the sixteenth-century Europeans who visited Japan and are now, by means of a time capsule, visiting a neighborhood in the United States in the late twentieth century.

James Fallows

The Japanese Are Different from You and Me

Japan is turning me into Mrs. Trollope. She was the huffy Englishwoman who viewed the woolly American society of the 1820s and found it insufficiently refined. ("The total and universal want of good, or even pleasing, manners, both in males and females, is so remarkable, that I was constantly endeavoring to account for it," and so forth.) Her mistake, as seems obvious in retrospect, was her failure to distinguish between things about America

James Fallows, Washington editor for the Atlantic Monthly, *lived for several years in Japan. He is the author of a book about Asia,* Looking at the Sun *(1994), and also of a book about the differences between Japan and the United States,* More Like Us: Making America Great Again *(1990). This selection appeared in the September 1986 issue of the* Atlantic Monthly.

that were merely different from the ways of her beloved England and things that were truly wrong. The vulgar American diction that so offended her belongs in the first category, slavery in the second.

I will confess that this distinction—between different and wrong—sometimes eludes me in Japan. Much of the time I do keep it in mind. I observe aspects of Japanese life, note their difference from standard practice in the West, and serenely say to myself, who cares? Orthodontia has never caught on in Japan, despite seemingly enormous potential demand, because by the local canon of beauty overlapping and angled-out teeth look fetching, especially in young girls. It was barely a century ago that Japanese women deliberately blackened their teeth in the name of beauty. The delicate odor of decaying teeth was in those days a standard and alluring reference in romantic poetry. This is not how it's done in Scarsdale, but so what? For their part, the Japanese can hardly conceal their distaste for the "butter smell" that they say wafts out of Westerners or for our brutish practice of wearing the same shoes in the dining room and the toilet.

Similarly, child psychologists and family therapists have told me that the Japanese parent's way of persuading his children to stop doing something is not to say "It's wrong" or "It's unfair" but rather to tell the child, "People will laugh at you." This is not my idea of a wholesome childrearing philosophy, but I'm not preparing my children for membership in a society that places such stress on harmonious social relations. Several American psychologists have recently claimed that the Japanese approach may in fact equip children for more happiness in life than American practices do. Americans are taught to try to control their destiny; when they can't, they feel they've failed. Japanese children, so these psychologists contend, are taught to adjust themselves to an externally imposed social order, which gives them "secondary control"—that is, a happy resignation to fate.

Now that Japan has become so notoriously successful, American visitors often cannot help feeling, This is different—and better. Practically anything that has to do with manufacturing and economic organization falls into this category. Recently I toured a Nissan factory an hour outside Tokyo, escorted by a manager who seemed almost embarrassed by the comparisons I asked him to make between his company's standards and GM's or Ford's. Yes, Nissan did insist on a higher grade of steel for its cars. No, the foreign companies had not matched its level of automation. Yes, the gap between managers' earnings and those of assembly workers was tiny compared with that in Detroit. No, the company did not expect trouble surmounting the challenge of the higher yen.

From what I have seen, a tight-knit, almost tribal society like Japan is   5
better set up for straightforward productive competition than is the West. It places less emphasis on profit than on ensuring that every company and every worker will retain a place in the economic order. (Apart from raw materials and American movies, most Japanese would be content, I think, if the country imported nothing at all. Who cares about high prices, as long

as everyone is at work?) Its politics is ridden with factions—because of certain peculiarities of the electoral system, politicians can win seats in the Diet with only 10 or 12 percent of their district's vote. (Each district elects several representatives to the Diet, but each voter has only one vote. In a four-member district, for example, the leading candidate might get 35 percent of the total vote, and the next three might get 15, 12, and 8 percent. All four of them would be winners.) But there are few seriously divisive political issues, and the country has a shared sense of national purpose, as the United States last did between 1941 and 1945.

Even beyond the measurable signs of its productive success, Japan seems different and better in those details of daily life that reflect consideration and duty. During my first week here another American journalist told me that only when I had left would I realize how thoroughly Japan had had me. At the time, I was still reeling from exchange-rate shock and thought she was crazy. But I am beginning to understand what she meant. A thousand times a day in modern society your life is made easier or harder, depending on the care with which someone else has done his job. Are the newspapers delivered on time? Are vending machines fixed when they break? Are the technocrats competent? Do the captains of industry really care about their companies, not just about feathering their own nests? In general, can you count on others to do their best? In Japan you can. Mussolini gave trains that ran on time a bad name. After seeing Japan, I think that on this one point Mussolini had the right idea.

From bureaucrats at the Ministry of Foreign Affairs (who, I am told, average six hours of overtime a *day*) to department-store package-wrappers, the Japanese seem immune against the idea that discharging their duty to others might be considered "just a job." Tipping is virtually unknown in Japan; from the Japanese perspective it seems vulgar, because it implies that the recipient will not do his best unless he is bribed. The no-tipping custom is something you get used to very quickly, because it seems so much more dignified and honorable, not—at least in Japan—because it's a way of gypping the working class. Japan is famous for the flatness of its income distribution. Year in and year out more than 90 percent of the Japanese tell pollsters that they think of themselves as "middle class"—and here the perception seems accurate, not a delusion as it might be in the United States. Indeed, from the Japanese perspective America seems fantastically wrapped up in and bound by class. American commercials are basically targeted along class lines: One kind of person drinks Miller beer, another buys Steuben glass. Japanese commercials are not—or so I am told by people who produce them. They may aim at different age groups—new mothers, teenage boys, and so forth—but otherwise they address the Japanese as one.

I can't say exactly, but I would bet that 100,000 people live within half a mile of the apartment where I live with my family. Yet in the evening, when I walk home through the alleyways from the public baths, the neighborhoods are dead quiet—unless my own children are kicking a can along the pavement or noisily playing tag. The containedness and reserve of Japanese life can seem suffocating if you're used to something different, but they are also admirable, and necessary, if so many people are to coexist so harmoniously in such close quarters. Because the Japanese have agreed not to get on one another's nerves (and because so much of Tokyo is built only two or three stories high), the city, though intensely crowded, produces nothing like the chronic high-anxiety level of New York. The very low crime rate obviously has something to do with this too. "Is this not, truly, Japan's golden age?" one American businessman exclaimed, spreading his arms in non-Japanese expansiveness and nearly knocking over the passersby, as we walked near the Imperial Palace on a brilliant sunny day recently. Everyone was working, Japan was taking a proud place in the world, there were no serious domestic divisions, and the drugs, dissoluteness, and similar disorders that blight the rest of the world barely existed here. Wasn't it obvious that Japan had figured out what still puzzled everybody else?

On the whole, I had to agree. What most Americans fear about Japan is precisely that it works so well. Foreigners who have lived for years in Japan tell me that the legendary Japanese hospitality toward visitors suddenly disappears when you stop being an "honored guest" and slide into the "resident alien" category. In effect, the country is like an expensive, very well run hotel, making the guest comfortable without ever tempting him to think he's found a home. But while it lasts, the hospitality is a delight. Those I interview at least feign more attention and courtesy than their counterparts in the United States have done. A few people have moved beyond the tit-for-tat ritualistic exchange of favors to displays of real generosity. Still, after making all appropriate allowances for the debts I owe them, and all disclaimers about the perils of generalizing after a few months on the scene, I find that two aspects of Japanese life bring out the Mrs. Trollope in me.

One is the prominence of pornography in daily life. I realize that no one   10
from the land that created *Hustler* and *Deep Throat* can sound pious about obscene material. The difference is the degree of choice. In the United States pornography did not enter my life unless I invited it in, and I had no trouble keeping it from my grade-school children. Here it enters unbidden all the time.

Like most other residents of Tokyo, I spend a lot of time on the trains—about three hours a day. There I am surrounded not just by people but also by printed matter—advertising placards all over the trains, and books, magazines, and newspapers in everyone's hands. The dedicated literacy of Japan is yet another cause for admiration, but the content of the reading matter—especially on the trains, where no one knows his neighbor and in principle everyone is unobserved—is not. Some of the men are reading books, but more are reading either "sports papers" or thick volumes of comics, the size of telephone books, known as *manga*. What these two media have in common is the porno theme. Sports papers carry detailed coverage of baseball games or sumo tournaments on the outside pages and a few spreads of nearly nude women inside. (The only apparent restriction is that the papers must not display pubic hair.) The comic books, printed on multicolored paper and popular with every segment of the population, are issued weekly and sell in the millions. They run from innocent kids' fare to hard-core pornography.

To some degree the sports papers and the more prurient *manga* exist to display female bodies, no more and no less, and they differ from their counterparts in other cultures only in the carefree spirit with which men read them in public. I don't know whether Japanese men consume any more pornography than American ones, but in the United States men look guilty as they slink out of dirty movies, and they rarely read skin magazines in front of women. Japanese men are far less inhibited—perhaps because of the anonymity of the crowded train car, or perhaps because their society is, as often claimed, more matter-of-fact about sex. In any case, the trains and subways are awash in pornography, as are television shows starting as early as 8 P.M. My sons, ages nine and six, very quickly figured out this new aspect of Japanese culture. On train rides they stare goggle-eyed at the lurid fare now available to them.

In addition to its pervasiveness, Japanese subway pornography differs from the *Playboy*s and *Penthouse*s of the West in the graphic nastiness of its themes. Voyeurism plays a big part in the *manga* and in a lot of advertisements too. One new publication recently launched a huge advertising campaign billing itself as "the magazine for watchers." Its posters showed people peeping out from under manhole covers or through venetian blinds. In the comics women—more often, teenage girls—are typically peeped up at, from ground level. A major weekly magazine recently published two pages of telephoto-lens shots of couples in advanced stages of love-making in a public park. Most of the teenage girls in Japan spend their days in severe, dark, sailor-style school uniforms, with long skirts. As in Victorian-era fantasies, in the comics the skirts are sure to go. But before the garments are ripped off, the girls are typically spied upon by ecstatic men.

The comics are also quite violent. Women are being accosted, surprised, tied up, beaten, knifed, tortured, and in general given a hard time. Many who are so treated are meant to be very young—the overall impression is as if the Brooke Shields of [1981] had been America's exclusive female sexual icon, with no interference from Bo Derek or other full-grown specimens. One advertising man, who has been here for ten years and makes his living by understanding the Japanese psyche, says that everything suddenly fell into place for him when he thought of a half-conscious, low-grade pedophilia as the underlying social motif. It affects business, he said, where each year's crop of fresh young things, straight out of high school, are assigned seats where the senior managers can look at them—until the next year, when a newer and younger crop are brought in. It affects TV shows and commercials, which feature girls with a teenage look. The most sought-after description in Japan is *kawaii,* or "cute" (as opposed to "beautiful" or "sexy"), often pronounced in a way equivalent to "Cuu-uuuute!" The *kawaii* look is dominant on television and in advertising, giving the impression that Japanese masculinity consists primarily of yearning for a cute little thing about fifteen years old. "A director can shoot an act of sodomy or rape for a TV drama programmed for the dinner hour with impunity so long as he allows no pubic hair to be shown," a recent article by Sarah Brickman in the *Far Eastern Economic Review* said. "He is, of course, particularly assured of immunity from legal repercussions if the female star of the scene is prepubescent."

A few years ago Ian Buruma, a Dutch writer who had lived here for years and has a Japanese wife, published *Behind the Mask,* a wonderful book that closely analyzed the *manga,* soap operas, low-brow movies, and other aspects of Japanese popular culture. He richly illustrated how the Japanese, in many ways so buttoned up and contained, sought outlandish fantasy releases. Buruma attempted to trace the oddities of *manga*-style fantasy to the deep bond between Japanese boys and their mothers, who typically raise their children with little help from the father. I don't know enough to judge Buruma's theory, or otherwise to make sense of Japan's standards of pornographic display. My point is that they rest on theories and values at odds with the West's. According to the *Far Eastern Economic Review* article, the director-general of Japan's Agency for Cultural Affairs once endorsed physical exercise this way: "When asked my reasons for jogging, I used to answer 'although it is shameful for a gentleman to rape a woman, it is also shameful for a man not to have the physical strength necessary to rape a woman!' "

In the United States, more and more people are claiming that pornography contributes to sex crimes. If you look at Japan—with its high level of violent stimulation but reportedly low incidence of rape and assault—you have your doubts. But even if it leads to few indictable offenses, and even if Japanese women themselves do not complain, the abundance of violent pornography creates an atmosphere that gives most Westerners the creeps.

The other off-putting aspect of Japan is the ethnic—well, racial—exclusion on which the society is built. I hesitated to say "racial" or "racist," because the terms are so loaded and so irritating to the Japanese. I can understand why they are annoyed. In their dealings with the West, the Japanese have traditionally seen themselves as the objects of racial discrimination—the little yellow men looked down on by the great white fathers. A new book by the historian John W. Dower, called *War Without Mercy,* provides hair-raising illustrations of the racism with which both Japanese and Japanese-

Americans were viewed during the war. For instance, Ernie Pyle explained to the readers of his famous battlefront column that the difference between the Germans and the Japanese was that the Germans "were still people."

Rather than talking about race—as white Americans did when enslaving blacks and excluding "inferior" immigrants—the Japanese talk about "purity." Their society is different from others in being purer; it consists of practically none but Japanese. What makes the subject so complicated is the overlap between two different kinds of purity, that of culture and that of blood.

That the Japanese have a distinct culture seems to me an open-and-shut case. Some economists here have given me little speeches about the primacy of economic forces in determining people's behavior. Do the Japanese save more, stick with their companies longer, and pay more attention to quality? The explanations are all to be found in tax incentives, the "lifetime-employment" policy at big firms, and other identifiable economic causes. I'm sure there is something to this outlook, but I am also impressed by what it leaves out. We do not find it remarkable that the past 250 years of American history, which include revolution, settling the frontier, subjugating Indians, creating and then abolishing slavery, and absorbing immigrant groups, have given the United States a distinctive set of values. Is it so implausible that 2,500 years of isolation on a few small islands might have given the Japanese some singular traits?

Japan is different from certain "old" Western cultures because it has been left to itself so much. In the same 2,500 years the British Isles were invaded by Romans, Angles, Saxons, and Normans—and after that the British themselves went invading and exploring. Blood was mixed, and culture was opened up. During all that time the Japanese sat at home, uninvaded and disinclined to sail off to see what the rest of the world might hold. The effect of this long isolation was a distinctive culture *and* the isolation of a "pure" racial group, which tempted people to think that race and culture were the same.

I'm sure that someone could prove that the Japanese are not really monoracial, or not clearly separate from the Koreans or the Chinese. The significant point is that as far as the Japanese are concerned, they *are* inherently different from other people, and are all bound together by birth and blood. The standard Japanese explanation for their horror of litigation and their esteem for consensus is that they are a homogenous people, who understand one another's needs. When I've asked police officials and sociologists why there is so little crime, their explanations have all begun, "We are a homogenous race . . ." Most people I have interviewed have used the phrase "We Japanese . . ." I have rarely heard an American say "We Americans . . ."

The Japanese sense of separateness rises to the level of race because the Japanese system is closed. The United States is built on the principle of voluntary association; in theory anyone can become an American. A place in Japanese society is open only to those who are born Japanese.

20

When I say "born," I mean with the right racial background, not merely on rocky Japanese soil. One of Japan's touchiest problems is the second- or even third-generation Koreans, descended from people who were brought to Japan for forced labor in the fascist days. They are still known as Koreans even though they were born here, speak the language like natives, and in many cases are physically indistinguishable from everyone else. They have long-term "alien residence" permits but are not citizens—and in principle they and their descendants never will be. (Obtaining naturalized Japanese citizenship is not impossible but close to it.) They must register as aliens and be fingerprinted by the police. The same prospect awaits the handful of Vietnamese refugees whom the Japanese, under intense pressure from the United States, have now agreed to accept for resettlement.

The Japanese public has a voracious appetite for *Nihonjinron*—the study of traits that distinguish them from everyone else. Hundreds of works of self-examination are published each year. This discipline involves perfectly reasonable questions about what makes Japan unique as a social system, but it easily slips into inquiries about what makes the Japanese people special as a race. Perhaps the most lunatic work in this field is *The Japanese Brain*, by a Dr. Tadanobu Tsunoda, which was published to wide acclaim and vast sales in the late 1970s. The book contends that the Japanese have brains that are organized differently from those of the rest of humanity, their internal wiring optimized for the requirements of the Japanese language. (Tsunoda claims that all non-Japanese—including "Chinese, Koreans, and almost all Southeast Asian peoples"—hear vowels in the right hemispheres of their brains, while the Japanese hear them in the left. Since the Japanese also handle consonants in the left hemisphere, they are able to attain a higher unity and coherence than other races.)

I haven't heard anyone restate the theory in precisely this form. And in fairness, during the war British scientists advanced a parallel unique-Japanese-brain theory (as John Dower points out), asserting that Japanese thought was permanently impaired by the torture of memorizing Chinese characters at an early age. But British scientists don't say this any longer, while Tsunoda is still a prominent, nonridiculed figure in Japan. Whatever the Japanese may think of his unique-brain theory, large numbers of them seem comfortable with the belief that not just their language but also their thoughts and emotions are different from those of anyone else in the world.

The Japanese language is the main evidence for this claim. It is said to foster the understatement for which the Japanese are so famous, and to make them more carefully attuned to nuance, nature, unexpressed thoughts, and so forth, than other people could possibly be. Most of all, it is a convenient instrument of exclusion. Mastering it requires considerable memory work. Japanese businessmen posted to New York or London often fret about taking their children with them, for fear that three or four years out of the Japanese school system will leave their children hopelessly behind. It's not that the overall intellectual standards are so different but that in Japan children spend much of their time memorizing the Chinese characters, *kanji*, necessary for full literacy—and for success on the all-important university-entrance tests.

Until a few years ago, only a handful of foreigners had bothered to become fully fluent in Japanese, and they could be written off as exceptions proving the general rule: that Japanese was too complicated and subtle for non-Japanese to learn. Now the situation is changing—many of the Americans I meet here are well into their Japanese-language training—but the idea of uniqueness remains. Four years ago an American linguist named Roy Andrew Miller published a splenetic book titled *Japan's Modern Myth*, designed to explode the idea that Japanese was unique, any more than Urdu or German or other languages are. Edward Seidensticker, a renowned translator of Japanese literature, makes the point concisely: " 'But how do you manage the nuances of Japanese?' the Japanese are fond of asking, as if other languages did not have nuances, and as if there were no significance in the fact that the word 'nuance' had to be borrowed from French."

As Roy Miller pointed out, the concept of an unlearnable language offers a polite outlet for a more deeply held but somewhat embarrassing belief in racial uniqueness. In a passage that illustrated his book's exasperated tone but also his instinct for the home truth, Miller wrote:

> Japanese race consists in using the Japanese language. But how does one become a member of the Japanese race? By being born into it, of course, just as one becomes a member of any other race. . . . But what if someone not a Japanese by right of race . . . does manage to acquire some proficiency in the Japanese language? Well, in that case, the system literally makes no intellectual provision at all for his or her very existence. Such a person is a nonperson within the terms and definitions of Japanese social order. . . . The society's assumption [is] that the Japanese-speaking foreigner is for some unknown reason involved in working out serious logical contradictions in his or her life. . . . He or she had better be watched pretty carefully; obviously something is seriously amiss somewhere, otherwise why would this foreigner be speaking Japanese?

As applied to most other races of the world—especially other Asians, with whom the Japanese have been in most frequent contact—the Japanese racial attitude is unambiguous: Southeast Asians and Koreans are inferior to Japanese. Koreans are more closely related to the Japanese than are any other Asians, but they are held in deep racial contempt by the Japanese. (A hilarious, long-running controversy surrounds excavations in central Honshu that seemed to indicate that the Imperial Family was originally . . . Korean! The digs were soon closed up, for reasons that are continually debated in the English-language but not, I am told, the Japanese-language press.) Recent opinion polls show that the nation the Japanese most fear is not the United

States, on which they depend for their export market, nor the Soviet Union, which still occupies four of their northern islands, but Korea—which threatens to beat them at their own hard-work game and which fully reciprocates Japan's ill will. China—the source of Japan's written language and the model for much of its traditional culture—presents a more difficult case. The Australian journalist Murray Sayle offers the model of China as the "wastrel older brother," who forfeited his natural right of prominence through his dissolute behavior, placing the family burden on the steadfast younger brother, Japan. This is one reason why stories of Chinese opium dens were so important in prewar Japan: The older brother had gone to hell and needed the discipline of Japanese control.

For Westerners the racial question is more confusing than even for the   30
Chinese. For a few weeks after arrival I seized on the idea that being in Japan might, for a white American, faintly resemble the experience of being black in America. That is, my racial identity was the most important thing about me, and it did not seem to be a plus.

I am just beginning to understand how complicated the racial attitude toward Westerners really is. Whereas Southeast Asians in Japan are objects of unrelieved disdain, Westerners are seen as both better and worse than the Japanese. One timeless argument in Japan is whether the Japanese feel inferior to Westerners, or superior to them, or some combination of the two. Feeling equal to them—different in culture, but equal as human beings—somehow does not emerge as a possibility, at least in the talks I have had so far.

There is evidence for both propositions—that the Japanese feel superior to Westerners, and that they feel inferior to them. On the one hand, Japanese culture is simply awash in Western—mainly American—artifacts. The movies and music are imported straight from America; the fashion and commercial models are disproportionately Caucasian; the culture seems to await its next signal from the other side of the Pacific. A hundred years ago, Japan began its Meiji-era drive to catch up with the West's industrial achievements. Prominent figures urged Japanese to interbreed with Westerners, so as to improve the racial stock, and to dump the character-based Japanese language in favor of English, which was the mark of a more advanced race. To judge by the styles they affect and the movies and music they favor, today's young Japanese seem to take Europe as the standard of refinement and America as the source of pop-cultural energy. Even when nothing earthshaking is happening in America, the TV news has extensive what's-new-in-New-York segments.

Herbert Passin, a professor of sociology at Columbia University, who came to Japan during the Occupation and has been here off and on ever since, contends that the sense of inferiority is so deep-seated that a few years of economic victories cannot really have dislodged it. The longer I have been here, and the better I've gotten to know a few Japanese, the more frequently I've seen flashes of the old, nagging fear of inferiority. Americans often talk, with good reason, about the defects of their "system." Many Japanese take pride in their economic and social system but still act as if something is wrong with them as a race. I talked with a group of teenage entrepreneurs, who had set up a mildly rebellious magazine. We talked about Japan's economic success, and then one of them burst out: "We're just like a bunch of ants. We all teem around a biscuit and carry it off. That's the only way we succeed." A famous scientist who has directed successful research projects for the Ministry of International Trade and Industry—precisely the kind of man American industrialists most fear—described Japan's impressive scientific work-in-progress. Then he sighed and said, "Still, my real feeling is, Everything new comes from the States. We can refine it and improve it, but the firsts always come from outside."

On the other hand, many Japanese can barely conceal their disdain for the West's general loss of economic vigor. Many people I have interviewed have talked about the United States the way many Americans talk about England: It had its day, but now that's done. One influential businessman in his early forties told me that members of his generation were not even daunted by the wartime defeat. Our fathers were beaten, he told me with a fierce look—not us. This is shaping up as the year of "economic-adjustment" plans: Every week a new ministry comes out with a scheme for reducing Japan's trade surplus. I have yet to see the word *fairness* in the English versions of these documents. Instead they are all designed to promote "harmony." The stated premise is that Japan has to give foreigners a break, so that it doesn't make needless enemies overseas. The unstated but obvious corollary is that Japan could crush every indolent Western competitor if it tried. Even the things some Japanese still claim to admire about America suggest racial condescension. Among the American virtues that Japanese have mentioned to me are a big army, a sense of style and rhythm, artistic talent and energy, and raw animal (and supposedly sexual) strength. In their eyes we are big, potent, and hairy.

The Japanese have obviously profited, in purely practical terms, from   35
their racial purity. Many of the things that are most admirable about the society—its shared moral values, its consideration for all its members' interests, the attention people pay to the collective well-being as well as to their own—are easier to create when everyone is ethnically the same. Three years ago, at a commemoration for those killed by the atomic bomb at Hiroshima, Prime Minister Nakasone made this point as crudely as possible. He said, "The Japanese have been doing well for as long as 2,000 years because there are no foreign races."

I have always thought that, simply in practical terms, the United States had a big edge because it tried so hard, albeit inconsistently and with limited success, to digest people from different backgrounds and parts of the world. Didn't the resulting cultural collisions give us extra creativity and resilience? Didn't the ethnic mixture help us at least slightly in our dealings with other countries? The Japanese, in contrast, have suffered grievously from their lack of any built-in understanding of foreign cultures. Sitting off on their own, it is easy for them to view the rest of the world as merely a market—an attitude harder to hold if your population contains a lot of refugees and immigrants. This perspective has as much to do with "trade frictions" as does their admirable management style. I am exaggerating for effect here— the most cosmopolitan Japanese I have met have a broader view than most people I know in America—but in general a homogeneous population with no emotional ties to the rest of the world acts even more narcissistically than do others. When the United States threatened to drown the world in its trade surpluses, it started the Marshall Plan.° The Japanese, to put it mildly, have been less eager to share their wealth.

Practicalities aside, the United States, like the rest of Western society, has increasingly in the twentieth century considered it morally "right" to rise above differences of race, inconvenient and uncomfortable as that may sometimes be. Few Western societies, and few people, may succeed in so rising—but they feel guilty when they fail. The Japanese do not.

The integrationist dream has few supporters in this half of the globe. The Japanese are unusual in having so large a population with so little racial diversity, but their underlying belief that politics and culture should run on racial lines is held in many other parts of Asia. Directly or indirectly, the politics of most Asian countries revolve around racial or tribal divisions, especially those between the numerous Chinese expatriates and the Malays, Vietnamese, Indonesians, and others among whom the Chinese live. It's hard to think of a really stable or happy multiracial Asian state. Asians look at the Hindu-Moslem partition of India and see acquiescence to fate. Japanese look at America and see a mongrel race.

Edward Seidensticker, now a professor at Columbia, lived here for many years after the war—and then, in 1962, announced his intention to depart. "The Japanese are just like other people," he wrote in a *sayonara* newspaper column. "But no. They are not like other people. They are infinitely more clannish, insular, parochial, and one owes it to one's self-respect to preserve a feeling of outrage at the insularity. To have the sense of outrage go dull is to lose the will to communicate; and that, I think, is death. So I am going home."

I've just gotten here, but I think I understand what Seidensticker was   40
talking about. And it is connected with my only real reservation about the Japanese economic miracle. Even as Japan steadily rises in influence, the idea that it should be the new world model is hard for me to swallow. I know it is not logical to draw moral lessons from economics. But everyone does it—why else did Richard Nixon brag to Nikita Krushchev about our big refrigerators—and the Japanese are naturally now drawing lessons of their

Marshall Plan: The 1947 aid program was instrumental in the economic recovery of war-torn Europe. [Editors' note]

own. Their forty-year recovery represents the triumph of a system and a people, but I think many Japanese see it as the victory of a *pure* people, which by definition no inferior or mixed-blood race can match. The Japanese have their history and we have ours, so it would not be fair to argue that they "should" be a multiracial, immigrant land. Most of the world, with greater or lesser frankness, subscribes to the Japanese view that people must be ethnically similar to get along. But to me, its ethic of exclusion is the least lovable thing about this society. And I hope, as the Japanese reflect upon their victories, that they congratulate themselves for diligence, sacrifice, and teamwork, not for remaining "pure."

Thinking About the Text

1. In what ways, if any, are Fallows's impressions of the Japanese similar to those of the Jesuits (p. 12)? In what ways, if any, are they different?

2. Fallows observes that "American commercials are basically targeted along class lines: One kind of person drinks Miller beer, another buys Steuben glass" (para. 7). Do you agree with Fallows's comment? How might you go about supporting or disproving it?

3. Suppose someone argued along the following lines: "Fallows is mistaken in his view of Japanese pornography (paras. 10–16); pornography provides a release, through fantasy, and thus it acts as a safety valve, protecting society from physical assaults on women. Fallows himself offers some support for this argument when he says that Japan reportedly has a "*low* incidence of rape and assault" (para. 16, emphasis added). How acceptable do you find this view? Why?

4. Fallows always assumed that in the United States "cultural collisions give us extra creativity and resilience" (para. 36). One often hears this idea, but do you believe it? How might one try to support or refute it?

5. Fallows offers many generalizations about America. Make a list of those you disagree with. Choose one from the list and write a letter to Fallows, in which you (temperately) take him to task. Explain what you disagree with, and give your reasons. Your job is to change his opinion, not to prove him wrong.

Thinking About Culture

6. In his introductory paragraph Fallows explains that Mrs. Trollope, an Englishwoman who surveyed American culture early in the nineteenth century, failed to distinguish between things in America that were merely different from those in her beloved England (such as speech) and things that were truly wrong (such as slavery). Look back on your experience

with a culture other than your own—perhaps an ethnic group in the United States, or, if you have been abroad, the people of another country—and reflect on whether you too have failed to make this distinction. Or perhaps you have encountered people who have failed to make this distinction in commenting on *your* culture. In either case, report your findings.

7. In paragraph 21 Fallows points out that Americans rarely speak of themselves as "we Americans" in the way that the Japanese refer to themselves as "we Japanese." Is this true? As an exercise, go through Fallows's essay and make a list of the issues he discusses, for example, Japanese attitudes toward pornography, violence against women, the Japanese language. Then try to formulate what the "American" attitude is to the same issues. In each case is there a dominant attitude? Discuss with your classmates.

8. "I seized on the idea that being in Japan might, for a white American, faintly resemble the experience of being black in America. That is, my racial identity was the most important thing about me, and it did not seem to be a plus" (para. 30). What is your response to this statement by Fallows? Do you think you might equally substitute some other group for African American?

9. Fallows claims that the Japanese take Europe as the standard of refinement, and America as the source of pop-cultural energy (para. 32). Can you think of any foreign cultures that Americans look to for standards? or any ethnic groups within America? If so, what are they? Take one, and evaluate the popular view.

Horace Miner

Body Ritual Among the Nacirema

The anthropologist has become so familiar with the diversity of ways in which different peoples behave in similar situations that he is not apt to be surprised by even the most exotic customs. In fact, if all of the logically possible combinations of behavior have not been found somewhere in the world, he is apt to suspect that they must be present in some yet undescribed tribe. This point has, in fact, been expressed with respect to clan organization by Murdock (1949: 71). In this light, the magical beliefs and practices of the

Horace Miner was a professor of anthropology at the University of Michigan. He conducted research on French-speaking Canada and other areas of the world. He also served with U.S. counterintelligence in World War II. He published the following essay in 1956, and to his death, in 1993, he was still receiving requests for information on visiting the Nacirema.

Nacirema present such unusual aspects that it seems desirable to describe them as an example of the extremes to which human behavior can go.

Professor Linton first brought the ritual of the Nacirema to the attention of anthropologists twenty years ago (1936: 326), but the culture of this people is still very poorly understood. They are a North American group living in the territory between the Canadian Cree, the Yaqui and Tarahumare of Mexico, and the Carib and Arawak of the Antilles. Little is known of their origin, although tradition states that they came from the east. According to Nacirema mythology, their nation was originated by a culture hero, Notgnih-saw, who is otherwise known for two great feats of strength—the throwing of a piece of wampum across the river Pa-To-Mac and the chopping down of a cherry tree in which the Spirit of Truth resided.

Nacirema culture is characterized by a highly developed market econ-omy which has evolved in a rich natural habitat. While much of the people's time is devoted to economic pursuits, a large part of the fruits of these labors and a considerable portion of the day are spent in ritual activity. The focus of this activity is the human body, the appearance and health of which loom as a dominant concern in the ethos of the people. While such a concern is certainly not unusual, its ceremonial aspects and associated philosophy are unique.

The fundamental belief underlying the whole system appears to be that the human body is ugly and that its natural tendency is to debility and disease. Incarcerated in such a body, man's only hope is to avert these characteristics through the use of the powerful influences of ritual and cere-mony. Every household has one or more shrines devoted to this purpose. The more powerful individuals in the society have several shrines in their houses, and, in fact, the opulence of a house is often referred to in terms of the number of such ritual centers it possesses. Most houses are of wattle and daub construction, but the shrine rooms of the more wealthy are walled with stone. Poorer families imitate the rich by applying pottery plaques to their shrine walls.

While each family has at least one such shrine, the rituals associated   5
with it are not family ceremonies but are private and secret. The rites are normally only discussed with children, and then only during the period when they are being initiated into these mysteries. I was able, however, to establish sufficient rapport with the natives to examine these shrines and to have the rituals described to me.

The focal point of the shrine is a box or chest which is built into the wall. In this chest are kept the many charms and magical potions without which no native believes he could live. These preparations are secured from a variety of specialized practitioners. The most powerful of these are the medicine men, whose assistance must be rewarded with substantial gifts. However, the medicine men do not provide the curative potions for their clients, but decide what the ingredients should be and then write them down in an ancient and secret language. This writing is understood only by the medicine men and by the herbalists who, for another gift, provide the required charm.

The charm is not disposed of after it has served its purpose, but is placed in the charm-box of the household shrine. As these magical materials are specific for certain ills, and the real or imagined maladies of the people are many, the charm-box is usually full to overflowing. The magical packets are so numerous that people forget what their purposes were and fear to use them again. While the natives are very vague on this point, we can only assume that the idea in retaining all the old magical materials is that their presence in the charm-box, before which the body rituals are conducted, will in some way protect the worshipper.

Beneath the charm-box is a small font. Each day every member of the family, in succession, enters the shrine room, bows his head before the charm-box, mingles different sorts of holy water in the font, and proceeds with a brief rite of ablution. The holy waters are secured from the Water Temple of the community, where the priests conduct elaborate ceremonies to make the liquid ritually pure.

In the hierarchy of magical practitioners, and below the medicine men in prestige, are specialists whose designation is best translated "holy-mouth-men." The Nacirema have an almost pathological horror of and fascination with the mouth, the condition of which is believed to have a supernatural influence on all social relationships. Were it not for the rituals of the mouth, they believe that their teeth would fall out, their gums bleed, their jaws shrink, their friends desert them, and their lovers reject them. They also believe that a strong relationship exists between oral and moral characteristics. For example, there is a ritual ablution of the mouth for children which is supposed to improve their moral fiber.

The daily body ritual performed by everyone includes a mouth-rite. 10 Despite the fact that these people are so punctilious about the care of the mouth, this rite involves a practice which strikes the uninitiated stranger as revolting. It was reported to me that the ritual consists of inserting a small bundle of hog hairs into the mouth, along with certain magical powders, and then moving the bundle in a highly formalized series of gestures.

In addition to the private mouth-rite, the people seek out a holy-mouth-man once or twice a year. These practitioners have an impressive set of paraphernalia, consisting of a variety of augers, awls, probes, and prods. The use of these objects in the exorcism of the evils of the mouth involves almost unbelievable ritual torture of the client. The holy-mouth-man opens the client's mouth and, using the above mentioned tools, enlarges any holes which decay may have created in the teeth. Magical materials are put into these holes. If there are no naturally occurring holes in the teeth, large sections of one or more teeth are gouged out so that the supernatural substance can be applied. In the client's view, the purpose of these ministrations is to arrest decay and to draw friends. The extremely sacred and traditional character of the rite is evident in the fact that the natives return to the holy-mouth-men year after year, despite the fact that their teeth continue to decay.

It is to be hoped that, when a thorough study of the Nacirema is made, there will be careful inquiry into the personality structure of these people. One has but to watch the gleam in the eye of a holy-mouth-man, as he jabs an awl into an exposed nerve, to suspect that a certain amount of sadism is involved. If this can be established, a very interesting pattern emerges, for most of the population shows definite masochistic tendencies. It was to these that Professor Linton referred in discussing a distinctive part of the daily body ritual which is performed only by men. This part of the rite involves scraping and lacerating the surface of the face with a sharp instrument. Special women's rites are performed only four times during each lunar month, but what they lack in frequency is made up in barbarity. As part of this ceremony, women bake their heads in small ovens for about an hour. The theoretically interesting point is that what seems to be a preponderantly masochistic people have developed sadistic specialists.

The medicine men have an imposing temple, or *latipso*, in every community of any size. The more elaborate ceremonies required to treat very sick patients can only be performed at this temple. These ceremonies involve not only the thaumaturge but a permanent group of vestal maidens who move sedately about the temple chambers in distinctive costume and headdress.

The *latipso* ceremonies are so harsh that it is phenomenal that a fair proportion of the really sick natives who enter the temple ever recover. Small children whose indoctrination is still incomplete have been known to resist attempts to take them to the temple because "that is where you go to die." Despite this fact, sick adults are not only willing but eager to undergo the protracted ritual purification, if they can afford to do so. No matter how ill the supplicant or how grave the emergency, the guardians of many temples will not admit a client if he cannot give a rich gift to the custodian. Even after one has gained admission and survived the ceremonies, the guardians will not permit the neophyte to leave until he makes still another gift.

The supplicant entering the temple is first stripped of all his or her clothes. In everyday life the Nacirema avoids exposure of his body and its natural functions. Bathing and excretory acts are performed only in the secrecy of the household shrine, where they are ritualized as part of the body-rites. Psychological shock results from the fact that body secrecy is suddenly lost upon entry into the *latipso*. A man, whose own wife has never seen him in an excretory act, suddenly finds himself naked and assisted by a vestal maiden while he performs his natural functions into a sacred vessel. This sort of ceremonial treatment is necessitated by the fact that the excreta are used by a diviner to ascertain the course and nature of the client's sickness. Female clients, on the other hand, find their naked bodies are subjected to the scrutiny, manipulation, and prodding of the medicine men.

Few supplicants in the temple are well enough to do anything but lie on their hard beds. The daily ceremonies, like the rites of the holy-mouth-men, involve discomfort and torture. With ritual precision, the vestals awaken their miserable charges each dawn and roll them about on their beds of pain while performing ablutions, in the formal movements of which the maidens are highly trained. At other times they insert magic wands in the supplicant's mouth or force him to eat substances which are supposed to be healing. From time to time the medicine men come to their clients and jab magically treated needles into their flesh. The fact that these temple ceremonies may not cure, and may even kill the neophyte, in no way decreases the people's faith in the medicine men.

There remains one other kind of practitioner, known as a "listener." This witch-doctor has the power to exorcise the devils that lodge in the heads of people who have been bewitched. The Nacirema believe that parents bewitch their own children. Mothers are particularly suspected of putting a curse on children while teaching them the secret body rituals. The counter-magic of the witch-doctor is unusual in its lack of ritual. The patient simply tells the "listener" all his troubles and fears, beginning with the earliest difficulties he can remember. The memory displayed by the Nacirema in these exorcism sessions is truly remarkable. It is not uncommon for the patient to bemoan the rejection he felt upon being weaned as a babe, and a few individuals even see their troubles going back to the traumatic effects of their own birth.

In conclusion, mention must be made of certain practices which have their base in native esthetics but which depend upon the pervasive aversion to the natural body and its functions. There are ritual fasts to make fat people thin and ceremonial feasts to make thin people fat. Still other rites are used to make women's breasts larger if they are small, and smaller if they are large. General dissatisfaction with breast shape is symbolized in the fact that the ideal form is virtually outside the range of human variation. A few women afflicted with almost inhuman hypermammary development are so idolized that they make a handsome living by simply going from village to village and permitting the natives to stare at them for a fee.

Reference has already been made to the fact that excretory functions are ritualized, routinized, and relegated to secrecy. Natural reproductive functions are similarly distorted. Intercourse is taboo as a topic and scheduled as an act. Efforts are made to avoid pregnancy by the use of magical materials or by limiting intercourse to certain phases of the moon. Conception is actually very infrequent. When pregnant, women dress so as to hide their condition. Parturition takes place in secret, without friends or relatives to assist, and the majority of women do not nurse their infants.

Our review of the ritual life of the Nacirema has certainly shown them   20
to be a magic-ridden people. It is hard to understand how they have managed to exist so long under the burdens which they have imposed upon themselves. But even such exotic customs as these take on real meaning when they are viewed with the insight provided by Malinowski when he wrote (1948: 70):

Looking from far and above, from our high places of safety in the developed civilization, it is easy to see all the crudity and irrelevance of magic. But without its power and guidance early man could not have mastered his practical difficulties as he has done, nor could man have advanced to the higher stages of civilization.

References Cited

Linton, Ralph. 1936. *The Study of Man.* New York: D. Appleton-Century Co.

Malinowski, Bronislaw. 1948. *Magic, Science, and Religion.* Glencoe: The Free Press.

Murdock, George P. 1949. *Social Structure.* New York: The Macmillan Co.

Thinking About the Text

1. What do you suppose is Miner's chief point? to entertain? to show the limitations of anthropological study? or something else?

2. Miner pretends to be writing as someone who is outside of Nacirema culture, but of course he is himself a Nacirema. Do you find any evidence in the text that he is in fact a culture-bound Nacirema? What, if any, cultural baggage do you detect?

Thinking About Culture

3. Miner did not get around to writing about the eating habits of the Nacirema. Write a 500-word essay on the topic. If you are familiar with a particular group within the Nacirema—perhaps an ethnic subgroup or an age-group—consider writing about the eating habits of this group.

4. Miner wrote his essay in 1956. Rewrite a section of the essay from the perspective of someone studying the Nacirema in the 1990s.

Explorations

1. If you have visited another country—or another cultural setting within your own country—did certain apparent similarities turn out, on inspection, to reveal significant differences? If so, explain.

2. Look around you as you read this. First, imagine your immediate surroundings (or the people near you, or your clothing, etc.) as someone from another century, but of your own culture, might see it. Second,

imagine it from the perspective of someone from another culture. For instance, might your clothing appear indecent to another culture? or your food repellent?

3. Find a popular textbook on child-rearing, such as those written by Dr. Benjamin Spock, Dr. T. Berry Brazelton, Dr. Haim Ginott, or Dr. Penelope Leach. Open the book to any page and try to discern what elements in the advice or directions might be culture-specific. Try to discern a point of view by looking at specific details as well as at the preface or introduction.

4. Anthropologists place a high value on interviewing informants without directing them in any way, without leading the answers through value- or culture-bound questioning. Interview a student from another country or a student whose family practices a religion or celebrates holidays differently from your own. Ask him or her about this religion, or this holiday, and attempt to frame your questions using neutral, culture-free terms. Were your questions culture-free? How might your questions affect the responses?

5. Did you ever have an "idealizing" or "demonizing" response to another culture? (See the discussion on p. 6.) If so, describe the experience. Have your responses changed since then? If so, how? To what do you attribute the change?

6. Off the top of your head, indicate in your journal whether you subscribe to "The Unvarying Heart" belief or to the "The Unknowable Other" belief—that is, do you believe people are basically the same everywhere, or fundamentally different and unknowable? (See pp. 6–8.)

   Having recorded your initial response, think further about what "cultural influences" may have affected your answer (e.g., family, friends, schooling, job, the media). *How* have they affected your response?

7. In your journal, brainstorm a definition of "culture." Now look at the list of meanings in an unabridged dictionary, such as *The Random House Dictionary of the English Language,* 2nd ed. (1987) or *Webster's Third New International Dictionary of the English Language* (1986). Which meanings did you overlook? List the ones that you overlooked, and try to come up with illustrative examples from your own experience to help clarify these meanings for you.

8. If possible, watch a non-English-language version of a type of television show that you are familiar with in the United States. For instance, on a cable network you may be able to catch a South American soap opera or a French Canadian talk show or newscast. (You may want to turn the sound down on these shows, so that you can better focus on the

unspoken signals and contextual differences.) How do the on-screen characters differ? the sets? the commercials?

Alternatively, you may want to compare an original foreign movie with its American remake. What do the differences suggest about the two cultures you are comparing?

Chapter 2

Thinking About Texts

Most of the essays in this book seem to be chiefly expository, seeking to provide information, but in fact most of them also seek to persuade the reader to hold certain beliefs and even (as a consequence of holding these beliefs) to act in certain ways. You are reading them partly to acquire information, of course, but the reason you want to acquire information is that you want to live a wise, interesting, useful life. You will, in short, make *use* of your reading—but you want first of all to be sure that you know what the writer is saying. You may go on to disagree, but you ought to have an accurate idea of what you are disagreeing with. Even from the first sentence onward you will be interacting with the author, mentally saying such things as "Hey, wait a minute" or "I don't quite follow this" or "I don't believe it" or "Exactly my thoughts" or "I'd go even further," but in fairness to that author, and also as part of your own education, you will want to be sure you know what the author is saying.

If you own the newspaper, magazine, or book that you are reading, a good way to help you get a writer's gist is to **underline or highlight key passages,** those passages that seem to you to provide clues to the writer's main points. Writers themselves often indicate their main points, saying such things as "The three chief problems are . . . ," or "Although no solution will be acceptable to all parties, the best solution probably is . . . ," or "Most important. . . ." By underlining or highlighting the sentences that the author emphasized and then reviewing the marked material, you can probably get the author's gist.

Thinking Big: Eating Whales

Here is a short essay, published in *Time* magazine in February 1988, with a student's annotations. Later in this chapter we will talk about summarizing the essay and about analyzing it.

Let Them Eat Beef

Starting in January, Japan joined an international moratorium on all commercial whaling. But last week a small <u>Japanese expedition began killing minke whales</u> off the coast of Antarctica. The goal: a catch of 300 whales. U.S. Commerce Secretary William Verity immediately declared Japan in violation of its agreement to observe the moratorium. Under U.S. law, Verity may recommend that President Reagan impose trade sanctions on Japan. If that happens, the president must either impose the sanctions or explain to Congress why such action is not warranted. Japanese officials called Verity's pronouncement "extremely regrettable" and expressed hope that the issue would not heighten tensions between the two countries, already entangled in trade disputes over products ranging from beef to semiconductors.

a claim   Japan <u>contends</u> that the whale hunt is for <u>scientific purposes</u> allowed under the moratorium. The minke whales, which are not on the endangered-species list, will be dissected to determine their age and reproductive history. Fair enough, but the <u>whale meat produced will</u> *a fact* turn up at restaurants in Japan. And that, says Commerce Department spokesman Brian Gorman, "gives rise to concerns that this may be a *can't one culture understand another?* thinly veiled commercial hunt." The Japanese people cannot understand why killing an unendangered species should cause such a ruckus. "Americans eat beef," they say. "Why can't we eat whale?"

American law specifies <u>two actions that the president can take.</u> He can ban <u>Japanese fishing vessels</u> from U.S. waters, but that would *(1)symbolic banning (pointless)* merely be <u>symbolic</u>, since, for conservation reasons, the Japanese do not currently have American fishing rights. An <u>alternative would be to restrict imports of Japanese fish products,</u> which amount to more than *(2)restrict imports but we would suffer* <u>$300 million annually.</u> That could backfire, however, since <u>Japan might retaliate against fish imports from the United States worth some $1.4 billion a year.</u>

Thinking About the Text

1. Reread the essay and consider how your underlinings and annotations might differ from those in the text.

2. Does the title sound at all familiar to you? If so, how might you annotate it? If it doesn't sound familiar, how does it strike you? (Jot down a phrase or two indicating your response.)

Thinking Small: Summarizing

A second way of helping yourself to take in the author's ideas is to write a **summary** of the material, that is, to restate it in very brief form. (Summaries have other purposes too; for instance, if you are writing a book review, you will probably want to include a brief summary in order to help a reader who is unfamiliar with the book. And in a research paper you probably will include brief summaries—perhaps only a sentence or two long—of some of the significant essays that you have read or lectures that you have heard.) Your summary may be as short as a sentence or two or (if the original is, say, ten pages or more) as long as a paragraph or a page. Here are some points about writing a summary.

1. A summary is an *objective* brief restatement of the original. It represents the original author's points as accurately as possible, and it does not evaluate the material.

2. The brevity of a summary is achieved largely by concentrating on main points, and by omitting supporting details, such as examples. If, for instance, the original begins with several examples—perhaps anecdotes offered as evidence from which some sort of inductive conclusion will be drawn—your summary will probably begin with the conclusion that the author draws from these examples.

3. The organization of a summary need not follow the organization of the original. In fact, if the original is poorly organized (point 10 of the original belonging instead to point 2, for example), a summary will reorganize the material. The idea is to give the author's point concisely, not to reproduce the weaknesses in the writing.

4. It's usually helpful to make the first sentence of your summary an assertion of the author's main point, even though the author didn't make this point until the tenth paragraph. (Persuasive essays, which argue a case, may be easier to summarize than expository essays, such as "Let Them Eat Beef," which are devoted chiefly to offering information, because the point of the persuasive essay may be a single assertion supported by lots of evidence, whereas the point of the expository essay may be the abundant detail that it offers.)

5. In preparing to write a summary of an essay, read the essay carefully, highlighting or underlining (if you own the text) what seem to be key points. Then *reread* the essay. During this second reading, now that you have a sense of where the author will be going, it's a very good idea to jot down a sentence or a phrase or two summarizing each paragraph, or each group of closely related paragraphs. You now have

a very brief version of the essay, something that may be useful in reviewing for an examination or in preparing a research paper.

6. Look over the sentences that you have jotted down and see if any of them in itself summarizes the gist of the essay. (Because authors frequently summarize their case in their concluding paragraph, your one-sentence summary of the author's concluding paragraph may be such a sentence.) If you find a sentence that seems to summarize the essay, you may want to use this sentence as the opening sentence of a summary that you will include in your own essay. Next, look at your summarizing notes and ignore those sentences that simply amplify or support the writer's basic point(s), and see what's left. In preparing to write a summary, keep your own purpose in mind. If, for instance, your purpose is to use the summary in an essay, where you want to inform your reader that X said such-and-such, whereas Y said this-and-that, and Z said something-very-different, you may want to summarize X, Y, and Z in only a couple of sentences. If, however, your essay is largely a response only to X, you may want to set forth X's views in somewhat greater length, say in a paragraph.

We have said that a summary may be useful in a research paper, where you occasionally have to inform your reader of the gist of something that you have read or heard, and you don't want to quote extensively. If you think you may want to include a summary in your paper and the essay consists of three paragraphs, in your preliminary notes you might write something along the following lines. (It happens that the three paragraphs— especially the first—contain a fair number of facts. Different people doubtless will offer slightly different summaries.)

```
1. February 1988: Japan resumed killing minke whales.
   The president may have to impose sanctions or ex-
   plain to Congress why sanctions are not warranted.

2. Japan says the hunt is for scientific purposes, but
   the whales will end up in restaurants.

3. The president can ban Japanese fishing vessels from
   U.S. waters--but they aren't here anyway--or he can
   restrict imports of fish, but this would backfire
   since we import from Japan only $300 million annu-
   ally, and we annually export to Japan $1.4 billion
   of fish.
```

Is this summary **objective?** We can pause for a moment to agree that of course someone else's summary will be slightly different. Another reader might think, for example, that the summary ought to mention that the Japanese call attention to the fact that Americans eat beef. Still, though we can disagree about some details, we can probably agree that this summary is objective, accurately stating (given the limitations of space) the gist of the article. It does not misrepresent or distort what the writer for *Time* had to say.

Now suppose we want to reduce this material to a couple of sentences, for use in our research essay on the media's coverage of the whaling conflict. Perhaps we'll find ourselves writing something like this:

```
Time, on February 22, 1988, reported that when
the Japanese resumed whaling, they said that the
purposes were scientific--though the whales
would end up in restaurants. The president,
Time reported, can ban the Japanese fleet from
American water--an idle threat, since the boats
are not here anyway--or he can restrict the im-
porting of Japanese fish products, but this
might backfire since we annually import only
$300 million whereas we annually export $1.4
billion of fish products.
```

Again, another student's summary might be a little different; it might for instance omit the bit about symbolically banning the fleet, since such an action would be of no importance anyway. Or a summary might specify the number of whales the Japanese fleet planned to harvest. Still, it's hard to imagine a useful and accurate summary that is much different from what we have given.

Thinking Responsively: Keeping a Journal

Your instructor may require you to keep a journal, in which you write (for instance) at least twice a week about what you have been reading, the weekly entries totaling at least 250 words. But even if your instructor does not require you to keep a journal, you may find it useful to record your responses to your reading. Although a journal is not a diary ("Today I read an essay about whaling"), it is better to make such an entry in your journal than to write nothing at all. Similarly, although entries in a journal ought (by their thoughtfulness) to go beyond offering summaries of your reading, one good way to stimulate responses to a text is to write a brief summary. You will probably find that the act of summarizing an essay sets you to thinking about what the essay says and what it omits. But chiefly a journal is a place to record reactions. Some of these may generate thoughts that later provide the germs of essays.

Here are four sample entries from the journals of students who read "Let Them Eat Beef" (p. 38).

> What <u>are</u> minke whales, anyway? And how come
> they are not on the endangered-species list?
> Why are some whales on the list and others not?
> Because certain varieties were hunted more vig-
> orously? Why were certain varieties especially
> hunted? Maybe for oil? Or because they are
> bigger and thus provide more meat? Or is it a
> matter of breeding habits? (Maybe begin by
> checking the article on whales in an encyclo-
> pedia.)
>
> > --William Geraghty
>
> How do I feel about eating whales? To tell the
> truth, I'd like to try. I don't quite see the
> argument against it, if they really aren't en-
> dangered. Maybe I'm hard-hearted, but I also
> don't see the fuss about catching dolphins in
> nets set out for tuna. If we kill millions of
> tuna to eat them, why is it so terrible if we
> also kill some dolphins along with the tuna?
> The answer can't be that dolphins are mammals or
> are more intelligent than tuna, since we kill
> plenty of other mammals for food.
>
> > --Sheila Artson
>
> As a Hindu I don't eat beef--most Westerners
> know that the cow is sacred in India, but they
> don't know that one reason is that the cow was
> created on the same day as the god Brahma and
> (in our eyes) to kill a cow is like killing a
> Brahmin. In fact, I can't understand the West's
> craving for beef or for any other kind of meat.
> I don't think that I'm missing anything by not

eating any meat. I try to tell my friends that
vegetables, nuts, fruit, rice, etc. offer a varied and tasty diet, so why would I kill an animal or have anyone else kill it for me? The
animal rights movement has a somewhat different
basis from my vegetarianism, but at least we
agree that it is wrong to kill animals.

                                    --S. Nagarajan

I don't think I could eat whale meat, partly because of the fact that many species are endangered but also partly because I don't like to
try new foods. Why don't I like to try them? I
realize that foreign foods are loved by those
who are brought up on them, but to me they always look unappetizing or they smell funny. I
imagine that the reasons we like or don't like
some foods depend on our experiences when we
were children, and that when we become adults,
we invent rationalizations to explain why we
like or dislike certain foods. Anyway, when I
was in a Japanese restaurant in Los Angeles, the
only thing that I felt like eating was the fried
shrimp because it seemed pretty much like what
we have at home. The breading was a little different, but it wasn't bad. I certainly couldn't
dream of ordering the raw fish or even the
cooked eel.

                                --Bobbianne MacDonald

As each example indicates, the writer is responding to the text. Your response
can, of course, take many forms. You may, for instance, indicate your uncertainty about what the writer is getting at, or even your uncertainty about
the meaning of a word; you may express your doubt about the writer's
assumptions or definitions; you may report a personal experience that supports or departs from the writer's argument. But in any case, an entry in a
journal records your reaction to some aspect of your reading.

   You may find it interesting to note that keeping journals as part of
course work is customary in Japanese schools from elementary school through

secondary schools. A teacher will introduce a new concept briefly and then will ask the class members to write their reactions in journals, to be discussed individually at a later time. Japanese pedagogy assumes that a student's own ideas and reactions are an important part of learning and should be actively engaged.

Thinking Critically: Analyzing

We have seen that an entry in a journal differs from a summary in two obvious ways: Whereas a summary is impersonal and seeks to set forth the gist of the whole, an entry in a journal (1) usually expresses a personal response, and (2) it usually concerns only a part of the essay. An **analysis** in some ways draws on the two other forms. Like a summary, an analysis keeps the whole in mind, but essentially it is a study of the relation of the parts to the whole, or of one part to the whole. And like a journal, an analysis is rooted in the writer's response to what he or she reads; in short, it concerns the relationships as you perceive them.

Let's begin by analyzing the structure of the essay as a whole—the way in which the anonymous author arranged the material. Almost all readers of "Let Them Eat Beef" would probably agree that the relationships between the parts of this three-paragraph essay are pretty obvious: The first paragraph summarizes the current situation, the second gives the Japanese point of view, and the third gives the American options. (The *Time* essay itself thus is both a summary and an analysis—a summary of the events and an analysis of possible American responses.) An analysis of the *Time* essay might go along these lines:

> The essay in <u>Time</u> consists of three para-
> graphs. The first paragraph sets forth the cir-
> cumstances: Japan has resumed killing minke
> whales, the commerce secretary has declared
> Japan in violation of its agreement to observe
> the moratorium, and the Japanese are nervous
> that the dispute may heighten tensions that have
> already been engendered by trade disputes con-
> cerning various products. The second paragraph
> gives the Japanese point of view (the expedition
> is basically scientific, and in any case Ameri-
> cans eat meat too), and the third gives two
> American options: (a) The president can ban the
> Japanese from U.S. waters (a symbolic but mean-

ingless gesture since the Japanese whalers
aren't in these waters anyway), or (b) he can
restrict the importing of fish products, but
such an action might backfire since we annually
import from Japan only $300 million but we ex-
port $1.4 billion.

What is especially interesting in the _Time_
article is that the second and third paragraphs
are not parallel. The second is devoted to the
Japanese attitude ("What's the fuss?"), but the
third is _not_ devoted to the American attitude.
Rather, it is devoted to the American dilemma:
We can do two things, one an ineffectual symbolic gesture and the other an action that might
backfire. The implication of the _Time_ article
is twofold: (1) The American attitude isn't
worth discussing (beyond what is conveyed by
saying that the secretary of commerce has
declared Japan to be in violation of the
agreement), and (2) we are on the horns of a
dilemma.

This seems to us an acceptable analysis of the _Time_ essay; the analysis takes the essay apart and shows something of how it works. In one respect, however, this analysis is atypical. Normally an analysis will name the author, but because the _Time_ essay is anonymous, the analyst is forced to speak of "the essay in _Time_" and of "the _Time_ article."

Now readers who know more about whaling might be able to analyze the article further, perhaps pointing out, for instance, that _Time_ fails to mention such-and-such important action that the president can take. We should therefore slightly amend our comment that an analysis reveals how the parts work to make up a whole. _An analysis can also point out that an important part is missing._ And of course the "parts" are not always the paragraphs of an essay. One might—still speaking of an essay—analyze such things as the use of statistics, or the use of emotional appeals, or the trustworthiness of the evidence, or the soundness of generalizations based on only a few samples. And going now beyond an essay, one might analyze the three or five or ten causes of a problem and the merits of a dozen proposed solutions. One might analyze the connection—if there is a connec-tion—between our concern for a ban on whaling and our concern for dolphins killed by fishermen. The whales are said to be endangered, but dolphins are not endangered. Are the issues related?

Here is a short analysis by a student—a journalism major—examining a small part of the essay: the title "Let Them Eat Beef."

Most readers of Time probably assume that the magazine's chief concern is to give the week's news. In all probability, however, the magazine's editors are as concerned with entertaining or at least with drawing the audience's interest as they are with informing it. That's why so many of the titles of the articles in Time are what journalists call a hook, a device to catch the reader. This concern with immediately getting attention is evident in the title of the Time essay, "Let Them Eat Beef."

The title echoes a famous line attributed to Marie Antoinette, the last queen of France. Legend has it that when she heard the poor people of France had no bread to eat, she said, "Let them eat cake." This statement is taken to show her ignorance of what it was like to be poor in France before the French Revolution since, of course, if the people had no bread they certainly did not have any cake. Time changes the line, but probably the writer expects the reader to remember the original and to smile at Marie Antoinette's stupidity. Once we get into the article, we realize that the joke is on us: When we say of the Japanese, "Let them eat beef" (rather than eat whale meat), we are like Marie Antoinette, ignorant of the people we are talking about.

But of course the joke is not harsh; Time wishes to amuse us, not offend us. Still, the reader does feel the jab or pinprick, and it sets one thinking. Is our position (if we have one) quite as sensible as we think it is?

Of course other readers may have other things to say about the title. You may want to take a minute to respond to this analysis, first by annotating it and then, stimulated by your annotations, by writing a paragraph or two in which you set forth your view of the function of the title.

Analyzing Cultural Differences: Looking at Two Essays

We have already seen, from the *Time* account of whaling, how cultures can clash. Let's look at two additional essays on the subject, the first from a newspaper and the second (a more meditative piece) from a book by John Elder.

Andrew Pollock

They Eat Whales, Don't They?

As he surveyed his restaurant one recent preholiday evening, Kiyoo Tanahashi was proud that almost all the wooden chairs and *tatami* mats were occupied by office workers or college students partaking of the house specialities— whale steak, whale bacon, fried whale, smoked whale, raw whale, and whale soup containing slivers of whale tongue.

But Mr. Tanahashi, who dishes out the equivalent of two whales a year, turns sour when he thinks of the ban on commercial whaling that is making restaurants like his Kujiraya, which means whale store, an endangered species. "I am rather angry that outside countries would tell us what food we should or should not eat," he said.

The freedom to eat what one chooses has become a rallying cry among whaling supporters on the eve of a crucial meeting of the International Whaling Commission, the thirty-nine-nation group that regulates whaling.

The annual meeting, which will be held in Kyoto from May 10 to May 14, comes when the moratorium on commercial whaling that has been in effect since 1986 shows signs of cracking.

Iceland has withdrawn from the commission, though it has not started   5
whaling, and Norway announced last year that it would resume whaling, although it will remain a member of the commission. Now Japan, with the meeting on its home turf, will push—against long odds—to have the ban lifted.

Andrew Pollock writes for the New York Times, *where this article appeared on May 3, 1993.*

The Opposing Arguments

Japan and Norway argue that the moratorium, initially put in place to revive stocks that had been depleted by decades of excessive whaling, is no longer needed for certain types of whales. The whaling commission's scientific committee has estimated that there are 760,000 minkes, a relatively small whale, in the Southern Hemisphere. Japan says that catching 2,000 a year would have no effect on the population.

Those opposed to whaling say that whales in general are still in such a precarious state that even the minke whales should continue to be protected.

But now the issue is becoming whether whales, which many people consider majestic creatures with high intelligence, should be hunted at all, even if their numbers permit.

Some countries, including Australia and New Zealand, already have said whaling should never resume and the United States is also strongly in the antiwhaling camp. France has proposed that the entire Antarctic region south of 40 degrees latitude be made into a whale sanctuary. The idea, supported by the United States, will be a major item on the agenda in Kyoto.

"If we were using whale meat to offset the hunger of the third world   10
it might be permitted," said Dr. Michael F. Tillman, acting assistant administrator for fisheries at the United States National Oceanic and Atmospheric Administration and the leader of the American delegation to the Kyoto conference. "But that's not what's happening. It's going to the most expensive restaurants in the largest cities in the world."

Japanese officials argue that the idea of a whale sanctuary represents the imposition of one nation's morals on another and is, in a sense, a form of Japan-bashing. Why, they ask, should Western nations be allowed to kill cows and pigs and Japan not allowed to kill whales.

"We should not make a new religion of whale-ism," said Kazuo Shima, Japan's commissioner on the whaling body and deputy director general of the government's Fisheries Agency. "We believe science and we believe scientists. We should not permit religious arguments in this field."

Japanese officials say they want to take a stand to insure that other species, like dolphins and different types of trees, also do not come under protection for what they say are irrational reasons.

Last year, the International Whaling Commission approved a computerized formula for calculating the permissible yearly catches for some types of whales. But it said it would not allow any whaling to resume until it approves other necessary measures, like monitoring and inspecting whaling ships.

At this year's meeting, Japan and Norway will push for approval of   15
such plans, thereby clearing the way for whaling to begin. But it is considered unlikely that the commission will complete the work this year, especially since countries opposed to whaling will delay the process as much as possible.

"The longer this thing drags out the more people in Japan will forget about eating whale meat," said an official of an American environmental group.

Norway has said it will resume whaling this summer, even if the commission does not allow it.

Japan, however, is not expected to take such a bold move or to withdraw from the whaling commission. Despite its tough words now, it is unlikely the nation would risk the enmity of the United States and many European nations for the sake of a whaling industry that, in terms of Japan's overall economy, is insignificant.

The nation has been trying for years to reverse a poor environmental image that stems from its history of industrial pollution and its reluctance to cease trading in whales and other endangered species like tortoises. Even though it has stopped commercial whaling, Japan continues to catch about 300 whales a year for research purposes, with the meat ending up at restaurants and food stores.

Japan now has only four boats with twenty-eight crew members active 20 in catching a few types of small whales that are not protected, according to the Fisheries Agency.

"The industry's gone," said Kunio Yonezawa, an adviser to the Japanese government on the whaling issue. "We are fighting for a cause, not for economic interests. We have to insure the principle of rational use of ocean resources."

Let's begin our examination of cultural differences by questioning a point Pollock makes in paragraph 8:

> But now the issue is becoming whether whales, which many
> people consider majestic creatures with high intelligence, should
> be hunted at all, even if their numbers permit.

We might ask ourselves lots of questions. First, we might ask ourselves why we consider certain creatures majestic. Is it because of their size? Does this mean that big creatures—let's say whales and elephants—should not be hunted but smaller creatures—let's say lions and tigers—may be hunted? Or are lions and tigers big enough to be majestic, whereas goats are not? Why is size relevant? Or is "majesty" a matter of behavior, say of voice or gait? Does the roar of a lion or the walk of a tiger make it majestic? And therefore does the hippitty-hop of a rabbit make it fair game for hunters and butchers? What preconceptions, what cultural practices, are we bringing when we make such assertions?

Second, we might ask why "high intelligence" is relevant? And what if it turns out that rats are more intelligent than whales? Do we stop ridding houses of rats? If one believes that all life is sacred, it may make sense to say that no life should be taken, including the lives of mosquitoes, but does it make sense to say that we can take some lives—let's say of cows and pigs—but not those of "majestic creatures" with "high intelligence"? What in our culture may bring us to such conclusions?

Now let's look closely at some of the issues that are raised in Pollock's article about Japanese attitudes toward whaling.

Thinking About the Text

1. If the statistics given in paragraph 6 are true, is the antiwhaling position untenable? (Paragraph 8 offers a response. How convincing do you find it?)
2. In paragraph 10 the argument against whaling is that the food is *not* alleviating the hunger of the so-called Third World. How relevant do you find this argument?

Thinking About Culture

3. In paragraph 2 Kiyoo Tanahashi is quoted as saying, "I am rather angry that outside countries would tell us what food we should or should not eat." In your opinion, does this statement end the argument? (Think of the old idea "There's no disputing taste.") Can we offer moral judgments about aspects of culture? Why, or why not? What implications does the phrase "outside countries" have, in this statement?
4. What answer, if any, can you make to the Japanese response (see para. 11) that Western nations slaughter cows and pigs, and that therefore the Japanese should be allowed to slaughter whales? (John Elder touches on this issue in the next essay.)
5. When Shima suggests that "whale-ism" is a "religion" in the United States, what does he imply? Might Americans similarly criticize Japanese resistance to importing American rice as an aspect of a "religion of rice"? What kind of "science" lies behind American campaigns to "save the whales"?

John Elder

Whale Meat

An unanticipated benefit of having our children attend Kiyomizushogakko was the hot lunch they were served there every day. We had been startled by the high price of food in Japan, so that when Rachel, Matthew, and Caleb

John Elder, a professor of English and environmental studies at Middlebury College in Vermont, spent a year in Kyoto with his family and then wrote a book about his experience. This essay comes from Following the Brush *(1993).*

returned from school that first week describing the huge bowls of rice they helped carry up to the classrooms from the kitchen, the fish or prawns served with it, and the cartons of milk all around, we began to hope that we might just be able to afford this year after all. But one winter's day our children came home unhappy about the stew they had been served. They had consumed their bowls of food before realizing what that red, chewy meat was, then were distressed to learn they too had now eaten whale. A Japanese friend from Tokyo was amazed when we told him about this incident, not because of the ethical or political controversies swirling around whaling, but simply because he found it hard to believe a neighborhood elementary school had actually served something so *expensive.* The fact remained, though, that even with whale meat running from thirty to seventy-five dollars per pound, the school authorities had made the decision to expose Japanese children to this traditional food. For Japanese and Americans alike, Japan's decision to continue whaling is a symbolically charged fact. It is also an area in which even sympathetically inclined citizens of our two countries often have a particularly hard time understanding one another.

The Japanese aesthetic of nature has enriched my own terrain for me since our family's return to Vermont. Hiking along the spur of the Green Mountains which lies to the east of our village, I perceive the woods differently for having walked the temple grounds of Kyoto. In Vermont, too, we have rock gardens. Each winter, frost heaves boulders up out of the bony soil that drove so many settlers west after the Civil War and turned the hill farms back to woods. Beeches bend their roots around these rocks. Red oaks, toppling in high winds along the ridge, lift up half-circles of interwoven roots, with stones as big as loaves or basketballs exposed among them, glinting in the new light.

Stone walls and abandoned cellar holes keep being tumbled by the respiring earth, too, until they subside into the elegant scatter of the garden at Ryoanji.° Like that celebrated garden's fifteen stones, these relics are ringed with moss. The rhythm of gray and green, dry and wet, leads an onlooker into a cycle of perception as fruitful and mysterious as the genesis of soil. The gardens I admired in Kyoto were designed in the period between six hundred and two hundred years ago by artist-monks who derived much of their inspiration from the tradition of black-and-white landscape painting originating in southern China. The compositions scattered through the woods above our Vermont village date both from the much longer history of geological collisions along this ridge and from the relatively recent convulsions of settlement and emigration in this state. But the Japanese gardeners' eyes have

Ryoanji: The temple in Kyoto that contains Japan's most famous Zen garden. The garden consists of a rectangle of raked gravel with fifteen rocks. There are no trees, shrubs, or grasses; the only vegetation is some moss at the base of the rocks. The garden is surrounded on three sides by a low, mottled, earthen wall; the viewer contemplates the garden from a veranda on the fourth side. [All notes are the editors'.]

nonetheless helped mine to recognize an elusive order in woods where they never walked, to discover a natural value unintentionally parallel to theirs.

The Japanese tradition of sensitivity to nature has often intensified our Western experience. Japanese poetry, architecture, and gardening, as well as cabinet-making, paper-making, and textiles, have been powerful influences on present-day culture in America and Europe. An appreciation of asymmetry and of natural forms and textures has been helpful to Western artists wanting to escape from closed or geometrical design and from the oppressiveness of heavily worked or sealed surfaces. Japan's poetry, where natural details have not been subordinated to the ego and its logical propositions, has also become a chosen tradition for many writers around the world, just as the Zen which influenced *haiku*° poets like Basho has become a point of reference for environmentalists who want to abdicate the Western sense of patriarchal warrant of dominion over nature.

But over the past couple of decades, many of those Westerners most attracted to the Japanese tradition of nature have been surprised, distressed, and increasingly outraged by the rapacity of Japan's exploitation of the natural world. In part, the environmental destructiveness of Japanese practices reflects that country's economic growth. As their economy has come to rival and, in some important regards, to surpass that of the United States, so too have the ecological disasters perpetrated on the world by Japanese become similar to those enacted by us Americans. Like ours, theirs is an oil-driven economy, with a standard of living, according to a recent United Nations report, higher than ours. And, as a manufacturing giant with few natural resources, they have become ravenous for the materials growing on or lying beneath the surface of other lands.

Beyond the major threat posed by their manufacturing machine to global forests and the atmosphere, though, Japan has also isolated itself dramatically as the nation most resistant to the elimination of whaling. In 1981, when the International Whaling Commission (IWC) voted twenty-five to one to institute a moratorium on sperm whaling, Japan's was the sole dissenting vote. They persisted in hunting sperm whales until 1988, even though that species was endangered. And although in that year they finally acceded to the IWC's 1982 moratorium on all commercial whaling, they have exploited a loophole in the IWC document that allows limited whaling for "research" purposes. Annual sales of meat from the hundreds of minke whales brought home by Japanese whalers under this program amount to billions of yen.

Japan's persistence about whaling has done much to tarnish that nation's image in Europe and the United States, especially given incidents like the collision between one of their boats and a Greenpeace vessel during a recent

haiku: A traditional form of poetry that consists of three lines (respectively five, seven, and five syllables long).

Antarctic whaling season. In view of the facts that international trade is the basis for Japanese wealth, and that, with their scarcity of natural resources at home, they are particularly vulnerable to anti-Japanese backlash among world consumers, it has been hard to understand why the government has been determined to protect a whaling industry which makes up so minuscule a fraction of their nation's fisheries.

The question of why Japan should take such an inflexible stance is a troubling one. On the surface, it seems to have little to do with economic or political self-interest, and on a deeper level it appears to violate the sensitivity to nature that has always been one of the principal elements of Japanese culture. For us in the West, especially those of us with a sympathetic interest in Japan, it thus represents a source of confusion as well as a conflict. As an environmentalist and a nature writer, I find myself asked how I can square my own continuing enthusiasm for Japanese culture with that nation's continued whaling.

One simple yet significant fact is that the Japanese like the taste of whale meat much more than most Europeans or Americans do. The Japanese Whaling Association ran a survey which reported that 80 percent of the respondents wanted to eat whale meat, while 70 percent said that commercial whaling should be continued. A common statement, as reported by the surveyors, was that people liked to include whale in their diets because Japanese had done so since ancient times. The fact that Americans don't generally eat whale meat and Japanese do thus affects our differing views of the whaling moratorium. Perception is always colored by desire, as seen in the conflicting views of antismoking ordinances often held by smokers and nonsmokers.

A recent statement by Japan's representative to the IWC expressed   10
anger at other nations' "ethnocentrism concerning food habits." He went on to argue that Japan should be granted special permission to take and eat whales, just as certain Eskimo groups in Alaska are allowed to continue taking bowhead whales for their own villages' consumption. This analogy between remote villages in Alaska and the economic and technological juggernaut that is Japan would strike most non-Japanese as ludicrous. But I believe that it may accurately reflect the Japanese self-image of being both isolated and culturally distinct, as well as a people for whom, despite all outward signs of economic dominance, subsistence is a daily concern. In this regard, the way Japan clings to whaling resembles its insistence on subsidizing domestic rice farmers, even though people could eat much less expensively if American and Thai rice were allowed to come readily into their markets. If there were ever a nation that lived by trade, Japan is it. But in such highly symbolic areas as whaling and rice farming, at least, they want to control their own destiny.

In some ways, the Japanese intransigence about whaling is simply the most dramatic example of a general resentment of foreign interference in

Japan's economic and political systems. The aggravation many Japanese felt about the recent trade talks with the United States focused on one point: In order to continue with the international commerce that the Japanese economy requires, they were being forced to rearrange their domestic system of distribution. From the Western point of view, this is simple fairness—cutting through the web of middlemen who effectively seal non-Japanese goods out of the market. For the Japanese it means substituting bigger stores for the numerous, tiny neighborhood operations that have made big cities feel more like villages and that have often supported the elderly. It is a hateful imposition on their Japanese ways of doing business.

It's important to recognize that, despite the surprise and distress of Western environmentalists, neither Japan's appetite for whale meat nor its desire to maintain national sovereignty come into essential conflict with that culture's traditional love of nature. Rather, they accord with distinctively Japanese beliefs about the spiritual and aesthetic meaning of the physical world. At its heart, the Japanese love of nature is microcosmic. This fact is evident both in the garden at Ryoanji and in many little details of modern life.

On a street near our apartment in Kyoto was a shop specializing in local spices and condiments. Different blends were packed in individual sections of bamboo, with a little wooden plug to be removed for shaking some of the mixture out onto a steaming bowl of noodles. In one of the little showcases the shop owner displayed a venerable *bonsai* tree. Half of it was a plum, the other half, grafted onto the same trunk, a cherry. It was old, to judge from the gnarly bark, even though the total height of tree and branches was not over eighteen inches. The *bonsai* was planted in a rectangular ceramic container, flat and green. When the plum trees on our street bloomed, so did the plum within the window. The blossoms were as big as those on the full-size tree, but looked much larger on those boughs no thicker than a chopstick. There was a week, as the cherries in Maruyama Park were just beginning to flower, when the tree in the shop window was full of pink-purple plum blossoms on one side and cherry blossoms, white with a tinge of pink near the center, on the other. Then the plum faded into its leaves and the cherry held the stage of spring.

The Japanese have always loved art that magnifies the small, from *bonsai* to *haiku*, by identifying the particular with the universal. They have discovered within local expressions the largest forces of nature. There's another side to this: The same dynamic has allowed Japanese culture to control those vast forces, to make the large small. The intensity of response to nature has derived its sharpness from the often frightening face of Japanese nature over the centuries. *Tsunami*° have swept the coastal villages. Earthquakes have tumbled down houses, despite an architecture of wooden posts set on stones to maximize the buildings'

---

tsunami: Large tidal waves.

flexibility and their capacity to absorb shock. Given the traditional building materials of wood, paper, and straw, Japanese homes have always been particularly vulnerable to typhoons and fire, as well. Wherever they looked, the Japanese have seen forces threatening to eradicate their settlements.

It seems to me that eating whales may actually typify the pleasure of rendering the vast and fearsome small. Cubing a whale for stew, or slicing it fine for *sashimi,*° is the most striking reduction of scale, and hence the most impressive demonstration of control. Eating is, on a symbolic level as well as a physical one, a process of internalization. This metaphor of digestion and absorption is much more central to the Japanese vision of nature than it is to the Western view. We in America, especially, take pleasure in the notion of "wilderness." Our Wilderness Act of 1964 uses the adjectives "pristine," "vast," and "untrammelled" to distinguish such wilderness from the settled landscape. The value of such terrain is taken to be its separateness, a place over against human culture where people can go to escape our social roles and experience the world on a different level. Wilderness, from such a perspective, is the wild heart of nature.

By contrast, the Japanese find intense natural pleasure through enfolding nature within history and culture. Basho took special enjoyment in visiting scenes his poetic model Saigyo was associated with, just as that twelfth-century predecessor had planned *his* travels so as to see places visited by his own hero Kukai over three centuries before that. A Zen garden like the one at Ryoanji is walled in on three sides. On the fourth is a wooden viewing platform, from which one looks into the garden as into a painting. In this way, the garden continues the tradition of Sung Dynasty paintings, where the artist and his friends entered imaginatively into the mountains and forests of the ink and paper, wandering in the image and then returning refreshed to mundane reality. Art and nature, venturing forth and pulling the world back into oneself, become in this fashion indistinguishable. On the one hand, such an attitude has guarded against the dichotomies between spirit and matter, subjective and objective, by which Western culture has been plagued. On the other, it may contribute to the apparent difficulty the Japanese are experiencing today in grasping the reality of extinction or to the heedlessness with which they, as a nation rooted in the worship of trees, are depleting the world's forests. Just as we in the West need the delicacy and integration of their natural celebrations, they need, perhaps, a sense of nature more *separable* from their own sensibilities and microcosms.

There must be continuing international pressure upon Japan to give up whaling. It may already be too late to stop the blue whales and sperm whales from drifting into extinction, but we must try, much as we have tried, apparently successfully, to restore the population of peregrine falcons in the

sashimi: Raw fish.

eastern United States. Such commitments to the survival of other species, like the development of a wilderness ethic, are basic tests of humanity's capacity for maturity and humility. They are important indications as to whether we will finally be able to survive in a healthy, balanced biosphere. But we in Europe and America must realize that in asking Japanese to give up whaling we are asking them to make what they feel to be a radical change in their cultural practice. Are we prepared to undertake as fundamental a critique of our own preferences in food?

In John David Morley's novel *Pictures from the Water Trade* (1985) a young Englishman sits in a bar sampling tiny red slivers of whale meat. His Japanese comrades are concerned about the Western furor over whaling, and they ask this Westerner why killing whales for meat is any different from killing cows and pigs. He replies that cows and pigs can be bred, while whales cannot. It's a good answer, as far as it goes, but does not address the morality or the ecological consequences of our non-Japanese choices about food—the sorts of questions that the Japanese rightly raise given the sort of pressure now being brought to bear on them. American practices of feedlots, animals injected with hormones and antibodies, and egg factories where chickens never touch the ground are pretty hard to affirm as alternative "traditions" of food production. More to the point, the American taste for fast-food hamburgers, now successfully transplanted to Japan, is a major influence in destroying the world's rainforests. Hundreds of thousands of acres are being bulldozed in order to raise the beef for our drive-through lunches. Are we prepared, then, in asking the Japanese to give up their eating preferences and a measure of their national autonomy, to sacrifice some of our own antiecological habits? For that matter, if we are truly serious about forcing an end to whaling, can we bring ourselves to carry out a boycott that might mean giving up some of the ingenious and delightful electronic devices which we so avidly buy from the Japanese? The 1984 bilateral agreement with Japan suggested that we were willing to weaken the whaling moratorium because of our own perceived trade interests. Unless we demonstrate a willingness to sacrifice, we can scarcely expect the Japanese to regard our outrage about their whaling very seriously.

Finally, Japan and America alike are called upon to reinterpret our traditions and revise our practices in relation to the natural world. One irony of the recent trade tensions and of the conflict between our two countries over the issue of whaling is that precisely in our traditional love of nature we have much to offer one another. In both countries there has been a collision between a powerful tradition of natural sensitivity and a rapacious, technology-driven economy. It is not so much that we have lost our way as that dangers inherent in our cultures from the start have been disclosed by our new power to bend the physical processes of the earth to our desires. The emergence of America's National Park system, the development of our wilderness ethic, and the growth of the genre of personal, reflective nature writing that flourishes in the United States today are all inextricably related to the industrial boom that began after the Civil War. In Japan, too, sensitivity to nature has often been entwined with less benign social facts.

Flower arrangement, poetry, the tea ceremony, and landscape architec-   20
ture, those arts through which the Japanese love of nature has been so strikingly expressed, all reached new levels of refinement under the Ashikaga *shoguns°* in the fourteenth and fifteenth centuries. Visiting the Gold and Silver Pavilions in Kyoto one is reminded of the exquisite sensibilities of their builders, the *shogun* Yoshimitsu and his grandson Yoshimasa. Yet under the Ashikaga the people of the city experienced nothing but misery. Plague and warfare ravaged the city as the *shoguns* shut themselves up within their gardens, planning new and even more splendid artistic endeavors. The love of nature in microcosm was a hermetic pleasure for them, and was no more attentive to the sufferings of the people then than it has proven to be to the plight of the whales today.

But Basho, in the latter part of the seventeenth century, showed another way to appreciate the microcosmic arts of nature. Although he too was a lover of the tea ceremony, gardens, and painting, Japan's most famous poet embedded his *haiku* in a life of traveling the length of Honshu. Rather than acting out a selfish fantasy of refinement and immortality, he pushed out along the road in all weathers, experiencing his own frailty and discovering compassion for other creatures, human and nonhuman alike. One of our challenges, in all of the industrialized countries, is willingly to accept more discomfort in our lives, rather than destroy the atmosphere and water through the pollutions of our hermetic transportation and living arrangements. Basho welcomed discomfort as a bond with other forms of life:

> Early winter shower—
> Even the shivering monkey wants
>   A straw raincoat.
>   (trans. R. H. Blyth)

We are entering an era in which those of us in the industrialized world will have to give up some of the comfort which so much of human history has devoted itself to attaining. This is a very difficult road to double back on. Only because the suffering of our planet, including millions of the human victims of drought and famine, is expressing itself more and more clearly can we even contemplate such change. The microcosmic love of nature may also offer one source of strength and consolation now, allowing us to bring into focus saving forces that have been blurred in the larger devastations of our landscapes. An artist like Basho suggests how we may integrate such moments with a passage outward into sympathy with other forms of life.

---

shogun: One in a line of military generals who governed Japan until the revolution of 1867–68.

Models are available to us in the Western tradition, too. St. Francis, recently declared the patron saint of ecology, has been proposed as a corrective to Genesis's emphasis on "dominion." His was a comprehensive view of nature, finding sisters and brothers throughout creation. Our American ancestor Thoreau can help us as well. In *Walden* and his other writings he suggests the limitations of an abstractly transcendentalist view, which holds nature to be simply a staging ground for human thought and spirituality. Thoreau says that we need instead to "have intelligence with the earth." In the confusions of wealth and power nations need, not to abandon traditions, but rather to enter into them more fully, following the examples of the poets and authentic spiritual leaders. At such a time Americans, like the rest of the world, can also continue to draw strength from the traditional Japanese vision of nature. After all, whales, enormous as they are, are themselves microcosms, capturing in their pulsing mystery both the chemistry of the sea and this evolutionary moment when all of humanity is challenged to expand our sense of identification and responsibility.

Elder's essay nicely illustrates the uses of several kinds of writing. For instance, he begins with a **narrative,** a few sentences telling a little story, in this case about how his children unwittingly ate whale stew and how they then became distressed when they learned what they had eaten. He follows this little narrative with another, still in the first paragraph, telling how a Japanese friend from Tokyo responded to the first narrative.

But Elder's point is *not* to tell stories. His book is in part a narrative of his year in Japan, but we imagine that he would be deeply disappointed if readers told him that they enjoyed hearing about his experiences—and that was all. What *is* Elder's point, for instance, in this chapter? We take it that he is offering an argument, writing a persuasive essay, trying to make his readers share his views about the Japanese view of nature, the American view of nature, and, most important of all, what we must all do in order to preserve the environment.

You may find it helpful to reread the essay and to jot down, as we suggested early in this chapter, a sentence for each of Elder's paragraphs or for each group of related paragraphs. In any case, we suggest that you reread the essay and try to formulate a **thesis sentence,** a sentence that sets forth Elder's essential point. (You may, or you may not, find that Elder himself has written such a sentence.)

Next, you may want to analyze the essay or some aspects of it. For instance, you may want to write a paragraph in which you consider such a topic as the way(s) in which Elder convinces his reader that he is a man of goodwill, not a Japan-basher and not an indiscriminate Japan-lover. Or you may want to analyze the structure of the essay. Elder indicates certain units of thought by putting extra space between certain paragraphs. Are these units meaningful? (One way to try to answer this question would be to try to write a single sentence summarizing each unit, and then to see if the sentences revealed a structure.) Or you might examine the role of narratives in the argument. How effective are they? We have already said that Elder begins with narratives, and you doubtless noticed that he doesn't offer explicit arguments until fairly late in the essay. What does he gain by this structure? Are there any disadvantages?

Thinking About the Text

1. In paragraph 17 Elder says, "There must be continuing international pressure upon Japan to give up whaling." Do you accept this view? Why, or why not?

2. Elder points out that, ethically, American methods of food production—"feedlots, animals injected with hormones and antibodies, and egg factories where chickens never touch the ground" (para. 18)—are just as questionable as Japan's whale-eating. In fact, he notes that "the American taste for fast-food hamburgers . . . is a major influence in destroying the world's rainforests." Do you agree with Elder that these issues are relevant in a discussion of Japan's attitude toward whaling? Why, or why not?

3. Elder speaks of "the love of nature in microcosm" and "the microcosmic arts of nature" (paras. 20–21). Suppose a classmate told you that he or she didn't quite understand this business about the microcosm. Write a paragraph or two in which you explain what Elder means.

4. Those of us who live in "the industrialized countries" must be willing, according to Elder, "to accept more discomfort in our lives" (para. 21). In a paragraph or two explain to your classmates why you think that Elder has or has not made a convincing case for this point.

Thinking About Culture

5. In class, discuss what Elder means when he calls whaling and rice farming "highly symbolic areas" for the Japanese (para. 10). With your classmates try to produce a list of "highly symbolic areas" for Americans. Why might they be highly symbolic? What sort of cultural preoccupations might they reflect?

6. Elder generalizes about what "we in America" feel about nature (para. 15). With your classmates, discuss whether you accept his generalization. Then write a brief essay in which you state your opinion about his generalization, supporting your argument with examples and evidence from your own experience and from the class discussion.

Comparing and Contrasting

Comparing and contrasting are ways of getting to know things, ways of thinking that can produce knowledge. (A comparison emphasizes similarities, a contrast emphasizes differences—but in common speech both processes are called comparison. We will use the one word for both.) Confronted with the unfamiliar, we study it to see if in some ways it resembles the familiar. Similarly, we may study the familiar—let's say our own culture—by setting it against the unfamiliar in order to see details that we may have overlooked until now, because nothing stimulated us to notice them. Obviously much in this book will help readers to understand something of Japan, but it will also help readers deepen their understanding of the United States by comparing it with Japan.

Comparing and contrasting are ways of getting to know things, but they are also ways of communicating that knowledge to others. In your writing you may wish to present comparisons to help your readers better understand a topic. We'll begin, then, with a few comments about organizing a comparison. Briefly, the two chief methods are subject-by-subject and point-by-point.

A **subject-by-subject comparison** takes one subject (let's say, arguments on behalf of whaling), talks about various aspects of the subject (ecological implications of whaling, significance of whales as a source of food, significance of whaling as a source of employment, and so forth), and then turns to the second subject (arguments against whaling) and probably talks about the same aspects.

Or, to take another (but a related) topic, consider Japanese food. One might talk about various aspects (the ingredients, the methods of cooking, the presentation of the food on the plate, the sequence of courses, and so forth), and then by way of comparison turn to a second subject (let's say American cooking, leaving aside for now the point that "American" food includes a wide range of cuisines), and probably talk about the same aspects. A bare-bones outline of such an essay might look like this:

American food
    ingredients
    methods of cooking
    presentation
    sequence
    strengths
    weaknesses
Japanese food
    ingredients
    methods of cooking

presentation

sequence

strengths

weaknesses

Concluding paragraph (synthesis)

Of course the topics we have listed (ingredients, methods of cooking, etc.) are rather arbitrarily chosen here, simply as examples. Depending on one's purpose, one might discuss expense, amount of time required for preparation, degree of skill required, nutritional value, or some other point.

The danger of this organization is that the comparison may break into two parts. The writer may, in effect, produce two essays—in this case, an essay on American food and an essay on Japanese food—with little relation between the two. Fortunately, this danger is easily avoided if the second half of the comparison occasionally looks back to the first, by means of such expressions as "In contrast to a typical American family-style meal, with large serving dishes passed around the table, Japanese food is presented in small individual portions, arranged in front of each diner" and "from the point of view of seasonings and spice, Japanese food can be said to be less interesting than American foods, which derive from several spicier sources such as Mexican, Chinese, and Italian cuisines" and so forth. In general, a subject-by-subject comparison is not only easy to write but is also easy to read—*if* when writing the second half the author refers back to the first half of the comparison and reminds the reader of the relationships.

The danger, of course, is that in a very long paper some of the force of the comparison will be lost because a reader, in the second half, will not sufficiently recall the details of the first half. And this is why some writers prefer a **point-by-point comparison.** A point-by-point comparison takes a given point—let's say ingredients—and discusses one half of the comparison (America) and then the other (Japan). It then takes the second point (methods of cooking) and similarly discusses one part of the comparison and then the second, thus:

Ingredients (in which you might choose to compare the Japanese emphasis on seasonality with the American emphasis on quantity)

America

Japan

Methods of cooking (in which you might compare the Japanese emphasis on a right way of doing it with the more casual American emphasis on improvising)

America

Japan

Presentation (again, you could stress the point that Japanese food is to be enjoyed with the eyes as well as the taste buds, while in America—at least in home-style cooking—design and appearance are less important)

America

Japan

and so on.

A point-by-point organization is usually effective in a paper that is essentially an argument replying to other arguments. For instance, if you want to argue against whaling, you may (after introducing the issue) proceed thus: Present the first opposing argument (for instance, a paragraph arguing that certain species of whales are not endangered) and then follow it with a paragraph or two of refutation; then present the second argument (a paragraph or two arguing that whaling is part of Japanese culture), and then a refutation of this argument, and so on.

In a very short paper, however, where perhaps the sentences alternate from A to B, a point-by-point comparison may produce a distracting Ping-Pong effect, turning the reader's head in opposite directions every few seconds. This organization *can* be used successfully even in a short paper, but be sure to reread what you hope is the finished version to make certain that it doesn't seem to proceed by fits and starts. If you ask a friend to read your draft (many instructors encourage peer review, a process in which students exchange drafts and offer suggestions), be sure to ask your reviewer if the comparison is effectively organized.

You need not, of course, slavishly use either of these organizing patterns. Many writers find them useful, both as ways of getting ideas and as ways of communicating ideas to readers, but the patterns are aids or tools, not ends in themselves. After all, the point of a comparison (or a comparison/contrast) is not simply to describe two things. Comparison is an analytic tool, not an end in itself; we compare so that we can come to a better understanding of the things that seem to differ but that (on close inspection) may reveal interesting similarities; and we contrast things that seem to resemble each other but that (again, on close inspection)—may reveal interesting differences.

When we begin our analysis—for instance, when we start making lists of similarities or differences, or perhaps as we underline, if we are comparing two essays—we probably don't quite know how things will turn out. But during the course of our work, we begin to see a pattern, and we find we are developing a **thesis,** a point, an argument. Of course, we may have started with a thesis, and the investigation may support it, but it's not at all unusual for a writer to find, partly through the process of taking notes and preparing a draft, that the thesis changes. As we investigate, we may be surprised to find unexpected resemblances—or differences. Thus, in thinking about a particular ethnic cuisine, we make discoveries, and the underlying discovery will probably serve as our thesis: for instance, that Chinese food emphasizes contrasts and freshness, whereas Indian food emphasizes a palette of color and the alchemical blending of spices. The thesis—the point—should permeate the essay, so that the reader learns more than simply four things about X and four things about Y; the reader is guided, throughout the essay, to see X and Y as the writer sees them.

In the following essay, by Donald Richie, you will read about Japanese food. This essay is primarily an **exposition** (an explanation of what Japanese food is), but of course it is also **argument** (an attempt to persuade the reader to see things the way the author sees them). In his attempt to explain to Westerners what Japanese food is, Richie almost inevitably makes comparisons with Western food. He also includes a few comparisons with Chinese food, *not* because he is writing for a Chinese audience—he certainly isn't— but because he knows that his audience of Westerners is more familiar with Chinese food. This point about the writer's audience is worth emphasizing, even at the cost of briefly delaying our look at Richie's essay.

An audience is a writer's best friend, at least as a stimulus for ideas. First, imagine an audience (probably your classmates) and ask yourself what this audience already knows about the topic. Next, ask yourself what you know and what you want the audience to know or believe. A sense of audience is especially important in writing a comparison. Why? Because comparing is a way of teaching—and when you write, you are a teacher. (It's a mistake to think that you are writing for the teacher; *you* are the teacher.) You know from your experience as a student that we all learn by connecting unfamiliar material to familiar material. And so, when you write a comparison, your purpose will be to teach by connecting the unfamiliar with the familiar. As you will see, this is what Richie does.

Donald Richie

Introduction to A Taste of Japan

> *The dinner tray seems a picture of the most delicate order: It is a frame containing, against a dark background, various objects (bowls, boxes, saucers, chopsticks, tiny piles of food, a little gray ginger, a few shreds of orange vegetable, a background of brown sauce), and since these containers and these bits of food are slight in quantity*

Donald Richie, born in Ohio in 1924, a graduate of Columbia University, and a former curator of film at the Museum of Modern Art (New York), has lived much of his life in Japan. Among his books are The Japanese Cinema *(1990),* The Films of Akira Kurosawa *(1984),* The Japanese Tattoo *(1990),* A Lateral View *(1992, from which on*

*but numerous, it might be said that these trays fulfill the definition
of painting. . . . However, such an order, delicious when it appears,
is destined to be undone, recomposed according to the very rhythm
of eating . . . the painting was actually a palette.*

—Roland Barthes

The cuisine of Japan is in many ways different from those of other countries. Different kinds of food, different ways of cooking, of serving—different ways too of thinking about food, eating, meals.

Where to begin among all the differences? Well, most cuisines emphasize the large—big portions, healthy helpings; only in Japan, and in Japanese-inspired styles such as *la nouvelle cuisine,* is the small considered satisfying. Small but lots, however; a traditional meal is made up of a variety of little portions. Not then the mighty American steak, the French stew, or the Chinese fish, but something much smaller.

And something usually already cut up or in some way made instantly edible as, say, the sizzling steak is not. In the West, indeed, a part of culinary pleasure comes from the ritual dismembering of the roast or the standing crown of ribs. In China as well, the moment of the crumbling of the charcoal-broiled carp, the opening of the clay-baked fowl, are part of the gustatory experience.

Not so in Japan. Here the portions arrive already cut up into bite-sized pieces or are small enough to be easily broken at the table. One of the reasons given for this is that the Japanese use chopsticks, instruments not ideal for cutting and slicing. But then, so do the Chinese and many another Asian country as well, and these cuisines do not insist on small portions being cut into bite-sized pieces before being served.

The reason is not chopsticks. It is, I think, a great concern for the presentation of the food, its appearance. To be sure, food everywhere must be presentable. Things must look, in the Western phrase, "good enough to eat." But there the matter usually ends. Not, however, in Japan. It is enough, in America and Europe, that a steak look like a steak, a chicken like a chicken. In Japan, while fish should look like fish, the fish dish ought also to look like something more. It ought to reflect within its composition another concern, one the West considers aesthetic. The effect should be as pleasing to the eye as the taste is to the tongue. At the same time, there is a canon of presentation, a system of culinary aesthetics to be satisfied.

This, then, is one of the reasons for small portions and plate preparation in the kitchen. The food is to be looked at as well as eaten. The admiration to be elicited is more, or other, than gustatory. This appeal has its own

5

---

p. 133 we reprint an essay on kissing), and A Taste of Japan *(1993, from which the present essay is taken).*

satisfactions, and it may be truly said that in Japan the eyes are at least as large as the stomachs. Certainly the number of rules involving modes and methods of presentation indicate the importance of eye appeal.

The colors, for example, must be artfully opposite. The pink of the tuna *sashimi*° ought to be contrasted with the light green of the grated *wasabi* (horseradish) and the darker green of the *shiso*° leaf upon which the slices rest. And the slices themselves are, despite their casual appearance, carefully arranged.

There are five types of arrangement *(moritsuke)* of food on dishes. The most common is *yamamori,* a mountainlike mounded arrangement. There is also *sugimori,* a standing or slanting arrangement, like the cedar *(sugi)* that gives the style its name. Then there is *hiramori,* a flat arrangement used for foods such as *sashimi.* And there are *ayamori* (woven arrangements) and *yosemori* (gathered arrangements) as well.

Asymmetrical aesthetics also apply in the way in which food is placed in relation to the surface area of the dish itself. Let us say something round-ish—a fillet or *teriyaki*-style fish—is to be served. It will appear on a long, narrow, flat dish. Resting against the fish and extending the length of the dish will be a single stalk of pickled ginger. An asymmetrical balance has been created in which the negative space (the empty part of the dish) serves as balance to the positive (fish-filled) and is accentuated by the single line (pickled ginger), which intensifies the emptiness and, of course, by so doing also intensifies the succulence of the fish.

That such aesthetic considerations should extend to food surprises the   10
West. One is used to Japanese concepts of negative space in such arts as *sumi-e* (black ink painting) or *ikebana* (flower arranging), but to see such ideas in the kitchen strikes us as odd—as though Poussin's ideas on the golden rectangle° should be made apparent in the way a quiche is sliced.

But this just goes to show how very different Japanese ideas on food are. And there are many more aesthetic considerations common in Japanese cuisine as well. For instance, there is a general law of opposites, which has nothing in common with food presentation elsewhere. Foods that are round-ish in shape (small dumplings, ginkgo nuts, small fillets) are served, as we have seen, in dishes having straight lines, while foods which are straight (square-sliced vegetables, blocks of *tofu*) are always served in round dishes.

At the same time, the dishes themselves are rotated during the year, because each of the four seasons calls for special ware—glass dishes, for example, are associated with summer, and bowls considered appropriate for

---

sashimi: Slices of raw fish.   **shiso:** A flavorful green.   **Poussin's . . . golden rect-angle:** Nicolas Poussin (1594–1665) was a French painter. Some of his paintings employ a composition based on a ratio called the "golden section": The ratio between the two divisions of a line (for instance, trees at the left and open country in the center and at the right) is such that the ratio of the smaller is to the larger as the larger is to the sum of the two—roughly 3 to 5. [All notes are the editors'.]

spring could not be used in the autumn. This is particularly true for the natural containers of which Japanese cuisine is fond—seasonal leaves serving as a base on the plate, actual clam shells for seafood, and so on.

Such rotation reflects, or mirrors, the larger seasonal concern in the food itself. The West observes season only insofar as availability and safety (no oysters in "r"-less months) is concerned. In Japan, however, the season must be reflected in all food. Even in these days of year-round fresh hothouse produce, the seasonal aspect of Japanese cuisine is kept strong.

Eggplant is best savored in summer, while spinach and other greens are considered winter fare. The only time to find and eat the *matsutake* mushroom is early autumn; trout is a spring and the troutlike *ayu* an early summer fish; and no *nabemono* (one-pot meal) is edible in the summer. The diet itself is controlled by the seasons, and the garnishes are seasonal as well. In spring, for example, a single fiddlehead may be nibbled at; in the fall, a scattering of baby maple leaves (inedible) may be found on the appropriate plate beside the appropriate food.

Whoever said Japanese cuisine was all presentation and no food was,   15
of course, quite wrong, but one can at the same time understand how such a statement came to be made, particularly if one comes from a country where it is simply enough that food looks decent and tastes all right.

Actually, the presentational ethos so much a part of the Japanese cuisine continues right into the mouth. Is there any other cuisine, I wonder, which makes so much of texture, as divorced from taste? The West, of course, likes texture, but only when it is appropriate and never when it is tasteless. Consequently, the feel of the steak in the mouth, the touch of the clam on the tongue are part of the Western eating experience, but they are not enjoyed for their own sakes. Rather these sensations are enjoyed as harbingers of taste.

Japan, is again, quite different. There are, in fact, not a few foods that are used for texture alone. *Konnyaku* (devil's tongue jelly) has no taste to speak of though it has an unforgettable texture. *Tororo* (grated mountain yam) again has much more feel than flavor. *Udo* looks like and feels much like celery but it tastes of almost nothing at all. *Fu,* a form of wheat gluten, has no taste, except the flavor of whatever surrounds it. Yet all are prized Japanese foods.

The reason is that the Japanese appreciate texture almost as much as they appreciate taste. The feel of the food, like its appearance, is of prime importance. The West, on the other hand, does not like extreme textures. Those few Westerners who do not like *sushi°* or *sashimi* never say that it does not taste good. Rather, it is the texture they cannot stand—the very feel of the food.

---

sushi: Rice flavored with vinegar and then shaped and topped with fish or seaweed.

Not only do the Japanese like textures, they have turned their consideration into one more aesthetic system governing the cuisine. Textures, runs the unwritten rule, ought to be opposite, complementary. The hard and the soft, the crisp and the mealy, the resilient and the pliable. These all make good and interesting combinations and these, too, have their place within this presentational cuisine.

There are other aesthetic considerations as well but this is a good place   20
to stop and take stock of what we have so far observed. For review let us take a very simple dish, a kind of elemental snack, something to eat while drinking, a Japanese canapé. Let us see how it contrives to satisfy the aesthetic demands of Japanese cuisine.

The dish is *morokyu,* baby cucumber with *miso* (bean paste), usually consumed with *sake,* more often nowadays with beer. Let us look at its qualities. First, the colors are right; fresh green and darkish red is considered a proper combination. Second, the portions are small enough so that their patterns can be appreciated—the dish consists of just one small cucumber cut up into sticks and a small mound of *miso.* Third, the arrangement and plate complement each other. The round mound of *miso* (*yamamori*) is considered operative, so the dish is served on a long, flat, narrow plate, thus emphasizing the very roundness of the bean paste. The length of the cucumber—and it is always cut along its length, never its width—stretches away from the *miso* and emphasizes the emptiness and again, by contrast, the fullness of the food. Fourth, the dish should be redolent of summer, since *morokyu* is mainly eaten in warm weather. So the dish should be untextured, unornamented, of a light color—white, pale blue, or a faint celadon green—thus emphasizing the seasonal nature of *morokyu* itself. Fifth, the textures are found to blend. The cool crispness of the cucumber complements perfectly the mealy, soft, and pungent *miso.*

Let's see, is there anything else? Oh, yes, almost forgot—the taste. Well, *morokyu* tastes very good indeed, the firm salty *miso* fitting and complementing the bland and watery flavor of the cucumber. But it is perhaps telling that, with so much going on in this most presentational of cuisines, it is the taste that one considers last. Perhaps it is also fitting. The taste of this cuisine lingers.

Naturally, one cannot compare the taste of a few slices of fresh fish and almost raw vegetables with, let us say, one of the great machines of the French cuisine, all sauces and flavors. And yet, because it is made of so little, because there is so little on the plate, because what there is is so distinctly itself, Japanese cuisine makes an impression that is just as distinct as that of the French.

This is because the taste is so fresh, because the taste is that of the food itself and not the taste of what has been done to it. The sudden freshness of Japanese cuisine captures attention as does a whisper in the midst of shouts. One detects, in presentation and in flavor, authenticity. Things are introduced and eaten in varying degrees of rawness, nothing is overcooked; one feels near the food in its natural state. Indeed, one *is* often very near it because so much Japanese food (cut bite-sized in the kitchen and arranged on plates before being brought out) is cooked or otherwise prepared at the table, right in front of you.

Japanese cuisine is, finally, unique in its *attitude* toward food. This   25
ritual, presentational cuisine, which so insists upon freshness and naturalness, rests upon a set of assumptions concerning food and its place in life. Eventually, the cuisine itself depends upon the Japanese attitude toward the environment, toward nature itself.

These assumptions are many. First, one will have noticed that the insistence upon naturalness implies a somewhat greater respect for the food than is common in other cuisines. At the same time, however, it is also apparent that respect consists of doing something to *present* naturalness. In other words, in food as in landscape gardens and flower arrangements, the emphasis is on a presentation of the natural rather than the natural itself. It is not what nature has wrought that excites admiration but what man has wrought with what nature has wrought.

Thus Japanese cuisine is as anthropomorphic as most cuisines are, but it is anthropomorphic in a different way. Man in Japan includes the natural more than does man in other countries perhaps because the Japanese sees himself as an adapter, an ameliorator, a partner. He does not see himself so completely lord of the universe that he could design a formal Italian garden or prepare *tripes à la mode de Caen,* a dish featuring four or more kinds of tripe simmered with a cow's foot and various vegetables in the dry cider of Normandy for fourteen hours.

Certainly nothing, food included, gets into the Japanese world without becoming Japanified. This is true of other cuisines as well. Most Western food is eaten by most Japanese—eaten every day as a matter of fact—but it is changed, sometimes subtly, sometimes not—to the satisfaction of the native palate.

The Western breakfast, for example, is now very popular, particularly in the cities, but it is understood that the eggs always be sunny-side up and served cold and that a small salad (often using cabbage) is necessary if the meal is to be authentic.

Or, there are some dishes which we foreigners think of as being com-   30
pletely Japanese since they occur nowhere else, for example, chicken rice, curry rice, and *hayashi* rice. Yet all are adaptations which have suffered a great change in Japan. Chicken rice is a ketchup-flavored cross between pilaf and fried rice; curry rice was obviously once Indian; *hayashi* rice was, despite its native name, perhaps once North American—*hayashi* is how the Japanese originally understood "hashed."

The Japanese, of course, think of such food as being originally imported, though it has now become in an honorary sense Japanese. Though they are omnivorous as far as cuisines go, a great distinction is thus made between the Japanese and all the others. (And not only in food. The rigid division between things Japanese and things otherwise is to be observed in all fields of human endeavor in Japan.)

Restaurants serving Japanese food, for example, serve only Japanese food and those serving Western food serve only Western food. It is only in the lowly *shokudo* (something like the Western station buffet) that the categories are mixed. (In those and in the smart avant-garde eateries among which *nouvelle cuisine* got its start, where there are such miscegenous dishes as raw tuna over avocado and pasta with sea urchin roe.) One of the reasons (there are many more) is that Japanese food Japanese-style has for the Japanese a special character, more so than does, for example, American-style American food for the American.

Though Japanese-style food is usually eaten at least once a day by all Japanese (so great are the inroads of Western-style food and now the fast and/or junk foods), it is never taken for granted the way that a Big Mac (or *Châteaubriand,* for that matter) could be taken for granted.

Rice was the food of the gods and even now the Japanese meal, centered as it is around rice, retains something of a sacerdotal character. Certainly, to be served such food (Japanese home-cooking) in someone's house is an honor. Visiting foreigners are also often steered to authentically Japanese food. (And the Japanese feel that even such landed cuisines, as, say, *tonkatsu°* are not Japanese enough for such presentation.) *Real* Japanese food remains both something very homelike and something at the same time rather special.

If nowadays the home table tends to be a bit mixed (*sashimi* and salad,   35 something sweet and sticky at the end), it is not perhaps that Japan has become so Westernized as that things Western in Japan have been so Japanified.

At the same time there exists a concern for the purity of the Japanese cuisine as it has evolved, and Japan remains one of the countries (France is another) where food represents a lineage, going back into history. Where, indeed, the cuisine is rightly viewed as one of the cultural adjuncts of the country itself. Thus, an understanding and appreciation of Japanese cuisine implies a certain understanding and appreciation of the Japanese themselves.

Thinking About the Text

1. Compare Richie's essay with Elder's (on page 50). One way to begin thinking about the issue is to ask yourself: Did one essay interest you more than the other? If so, why? Was it because of the subject, the style, the author's position on an issue?

---

tonkatsu: Pork cutlet, breaded and fried and served with shredded cabbage.

Thinking About Culture

2. Richie mentions (para. 5) the Japanese "canon of presentation," and in the next few paragraphs he gives examples. Can a case be made that other cultures too—perhaps including that of traditional American restaurants—also follow a "canon of presentation"? Explain your response, using comparisons where they are helpful.

3. In his final sentence Richie says that "an understanding and appreciation of Japanese cuisine implies a certain understanding and appreciation of the Japanese themselves." Write an essay of 500–750 words in which, with the aid of comparisons, you argue that an understanding of American cuisine (or any other cuisine of your choice) implies an understanding of the culture.

Explorations

1. From a weekly newsmagazine (such as *Time, Newsweek, U.S. News & World Report*), select a brief report on a current event in another country and examine it for evidence of American cultural assumptions and biases. Summarize the article and explain whether or not you detect any such evidence.

2. Try to find a report on the same event in a concurrent issue of another weekly newsmagazine. How do the two reports differ, in their assumptions and their styles? How are they similar? Write a comparison of the two accounts in which you set forth your findings.

3. If you are keeping a journal (for a class or just for yourself), analyze one of your earliest entries. Jot down why it was written (was it in response to an assignment, to record something you thought was important, or to explain something to yourself?) and whether you would now change anything in it (have you revised your opinion?). Then analyze the entry as a piece of writing: How is it organized? Is there a thesis statement? What about the language? Finally, imagine how you might now rewrite it for a different purpose and for a different audience; and then rewrite it. If you don't keep a journal, try the same exercise with another example of your writing, such as a letter or an essay or paper that you wrote for another class.

4. Submit an essay to someone from another country who is willing to read your writing and discuss what (if anything) is characteristically "American" about it. Summarize the results of your discussion in a brief essay.

5. Pair up with a classmate or friend with whom you share a deep and informed interest in something (for instance a particular hobby, a television program or movie or book, a social organization, a college course). Working independently of each other, draw up a list of what you find most and least interesting about that thing in which you share an interest. Then compare your lists and discuss the differences and similarities. Finally, write a report in which you compare and contrast your responses and come to some conclusion about your findings.

6. Write an essay based on one of the assignments at the end of Chapter 1. For example, you may want to base your paper on Assignment 8 and write a paper in which you compare a foreign film with its American remake.

Part Two

Readings for
Cultural Comparison

Chapter 3

Growing Up

Children are the focus of culture wherever they grow up. In fact, of course, the root meaning of both "culture" and "cultivation" is the same. But the cultivation of children, unlike that of garden vegetables, is also socialization, the learning of a society's system of beliefs and behaviors. Cultivation means giving a child what he or she needs to learn to survive, prosper, and reproduce, whether for his or her own good, the good of the family, or the good of society. In both the United States and Japan, there have been changes in social mores as well as broader change affecting the results of this cultural learning.

Learning takes place in many areas of our lives: primarily at home and in school, but also (less formally) among peers, at work, and in the streets. What is expected to occur, and what really does occur, is a topic of controversy among parents, teachers, and the wider population. Take schools for example: Increasingly, what schools do is under scrutiny. In Japan, critics claim that schools, especially at the secondary level, serve only as part of a process of distributing credentials, prerequisites for a successful career and status. In the United States, schools have had to do more than educate students and distribute credentials; they have been forced, in lieu of other agencies, to take on a variety of tasks—providing supervision during parents' work hours, hot breakfasts, psychological screening and treatment, health and sex counseling, and day care for students' children as well as enforcing weapons bans and providing legal advice. Learning as the job of schooling sometimes seems pushed aside in both countries by these different functions.

What happens in schools is a reflection of the wider society's needs as well as our views of children's developmental and social demands. But these influences are experienced even earlier, in the home and family.

We humans receive our first cultural input at birth, when our active learning begins, as Ruth Benedict points out in the essay on page 78. While her description of infant care and training is somewhat outdated (for example, fewer houses now have the open fire pit and *tatami* matting she describes, very few mothers would wean a baby in this definitive way, indeed fewer mothers may breastfeed their children that long to begin with, and multiple siblings are a rarity), still the underlying cultural values such as early social learning and early training in gender-specific roles are relevant today.

It has been said that the Japanese mother looks at her newborn child and sees a being who has separated from her and who needs to be reconnected to her in order to grow up healthy and to learn. Closeness and what we Americans would call excessive dependency are encouraged, and mothers of young children are rarely apart from them, usually carrying infants *onbu* style, strapped closely to their backs. This desired physical closeness is given a Japanese-English name, *skinship,* meaning skin-to-skin proximity. On the other hand, the American mother is said to see her newborn infant as born dependent, needing to be made independent as quickly as possible. Thus an American family will, if possible, set aside a separate room for the baby while a Japanese family (even those with space available for a room for the baby) will see this as cruel and unnecessary, bad for the child.

What a society encourages in its young children previews societal expectations for them in later life. Japanese schools and families agree that learning provides not only necessary credentials and skills but also character, and that interdependent learning helps rather than impedes healthy development. So, for example, in elementary schools, as Merry White observes in the selection on page 95, children often work in teams to solve problems, and mothers' involvement as "home coach" is not seen as a threat to the autonomy of the individual child. American classrooms tend to value individual work over cooperative learning; the *han* (team) system of the Japanese school might be encouraged only in the younger grades, since the approved developmental trajectory is toward greater individuation with maturity. Doing one's own work is valued in America, while collaboration is considered unhelpful to a child and may even be seen as cheating.

Still, individuation is tolerated in Japan, though in different forms. Trusting that a child's intentions are inherently good, antisocial behavior is tolerated much more in Japan than in the United States, where a child's inherent nature may be viewed with more suspicion. In describing the "naughty" child Hiroki, Joseph Tobin (p. 89) points out that a very different interpretation of his "bad" behavior is given by Japanese teachers than would be given by American teachers.

The outcomes of our at-home and in-school learning seem to indicate that American children are at risk, while Japanese children are at promise. This, however, is too simple a formulation, and education reformers in both countries tell us to look beyond the test scores to see what children really need, and get, from families and schools. The fact that 90 percent of Japanese high school students do as well in math and science as the top 10 percent of American youth should not distract us from considering other measures of success and failure.

In Japan, critics like Ikuo Amano (p. 109) note the lack of attention to individual learning styles, the lack of encouragement for creative genius, the lack of flexibility in the system, and the existence of only one significant measure for success. In the United States, critics worry about the lack of discipline and order, the higher rate of dropping out, and the alienation from the joy of learning. The family in both countries is alternately seen as the cause and the victim of the damage done to youth.

In the past ten years, looking at Japanese schools has become an industry among American educators, and, as Merry White notes, attempts to encapsulate, package, and import ideas from Japanese education have been matched by a view of Japanese successes as being not only unfair but based in practices we would find unproductive and ultimately inhumane.

Adolescent young people of course are not only members of families and learners, but, according to their culture's lights, may be seen as members of something else—the stage of life called "teen age" (the American word "teenager" is borrowed as *cheenayja* in Japan).

This idea of a stage of life set apart, neither adult nor child, is a recent phenomenon in America, having appeared as a time for experimentation and the sowing of one's wild oats only in the past sixty years or so. In Japan, too, youth is even more recently seen as a time of life in which one's behavior, clothing, activities, and other aspects of one's identity (at least out of school) are influenced more by peers than by adults. The teenager was created in Japan primarily as a market for goods, music, media, and even foods, isolated first in the late 1960s, and fully developed as an audience and consumer industry target in the 1980s. In fact, it is so recent a construct that older people are quite left out, and when asked, "What is a teenager?," many don't even know the word.

The idea of distinct generations, as Shinobu Yoshioka (p. 119) points out, is not at all new in Japan. Clothing styles and behavior, like other aspects of life, are generally age-graded, and among the more traditional, even the colors one should wear at different ages are prescribed. In this sense, a young person leaping ahead of schedule or an older person holding on to younger styles is unseemly. Of course, even a college professor may wear blue jeans in certain environments, and many businessmen in their off-hours will wear the latest sports clothes, but when an older man tints his hair black (women, of course, can do this until they are quite old), it may be seen as undignified.

It is not just age and stage that differentiate people but also history. The idea of the generation as a group or cohort with whom one has shared historical experiences is quite prominent in Japan as a source of identity. The prewar generation, like the generation born during World War II, is said to have special characteristics and personality, and the two or three (depending on how you count them) postwar generations also are said to be identifiable. The current labeling of people as members of cohorts such as the "baby boomers" or "Generation X" in America similarly characterizes generations in terms of historical, social, and economic conditions.

And of course, in both countries, the older generation looks to the younger and says, "Young people are going to the dogs—in *my* generation, we didn't do that. . . ." The younger generation may respond with "What a rotten world you are leaving us."

Explorations

1. What do infants and small children learn at home in America? What kinds of behaviors and expectations for relationships do parents teach? What do children learn from siblings and other relatives? Are these lessons similar to those learned in school (nursery school, kindergarten, elementary and secondary schools)? Explain.

2. Some critics of American schooling say that too much time is taken up in U.S. schools with nonacademic matters and that schoolchildren in other countries have more "time on task." What other things go on in American classrooms besides content learning? How might you argue that some of these things are valuable activities and that education in other countries might benefit by emulating them?

3. Young people in both America and Japan are target audiences for media and marketing of consumer goods. Choose a product (or magazine, movie, or musician or musical group) that is primarily targeted to young people and note what images of youth are invoked in the marketing of this youth-focused item.

4. Since the 1950s, American adults have been concerned with adolescence as a "problem stage." With your classmates, explore the psychological, social, and economic conditions that have made a four-letter word of "teen." Begin by comparing experiences, and then continue with library research. For example, your class may want to break into groups, each of which explores popular homemaking, parenting, and "teen" magazines of a particular decade from the 1950s to the 1990s.

Ruth Benedict

The Child Learns

Japanese babies are not brought up in the fashion that a thoughtful Westerner might suppose. American parents, training their children for a life so much less circumspect and stoical than life in Japan, nevertheless begin immediately

---

Ruth Benedict (1887–1948), a professor of anthropology at Columbia University, was the author of two of the most famous works in anthropology, Patterns of Culture *(1934) and* The Chrysanthemum and the Sword *(1946). The latter, which we excerpt here, is notable in that Benedict's data is drawn from interviews with Japanese immigrants in America, since no fieldwork was possible in wartime. Today her work is seen as out of date in some respects and overdrawn but is still cited frequently for its insights and detail.*

to prove to the baby that his own little wishes are not supreme in this world. We put him immediately on a feeding schedule and a sleeping schedule, and no matter how he fusses before bottle time or bedtime, he has to wait. A little later his mother strikes his hand to make him take his finger out of his mouth or away from other parts of his body. His mother is frequently out of sight and when she goes out he has to stay behind. He has to be weaned before he prefers other foods, or if he is bottle fed, he has to give up his bottle. There are certain foods that are good for him and he must eat them. He is punished when he does not do what is right. What is more natural for an American to suppose than that these disciplines are redoubled for the little Japanese baby who, when he is a finished product, will have to subordinate his own wishes and be so careful and punctilious an observer of such a demanding code?

The Japanese, however, do not follow this course. The arc of life in Japan is plotted in opposite fashion to that in the United States. It is a great shallow U-curve with maximum freedom and indulgence allowed to babies and to the old. Restrictions are slowly increased after babyhood till having one's own way reaches a low just before and after marriage. This low line continues many years during the prime of life, but the arc gradually ascends again until after the age of sixty men and women are almost as unhampered by shame as little children are. In the United States we stand this curve upside down. Firm disciplines are directed toward the infant and these are gradually relaxed as the child grows in strength until a man runs his own life when he gets a self-supporting job and when he sets up a household of his own. The prime of life is with us the high point of freedom and initiative. Restrictions begin to appear as men lose their grip or their energy or become dependent. It is difficult for Americans even to fantasy a life arranged according to the Japanese pattern. It seems to us to fly in the face of reality.

Both the American and the Japanese arrangement of the arc of life, however, have in point of fact secured in each country the individual's energetic participation in his culture during the prime of life. To secure this end in the United States, we rely on increasing his freedom of choice during this period. The Japanese rely on maximizing the restraints upon him. The fact that a man is at this time at the peak of his physical strength and at the peak of his earning powers does not make him master of his own life. They have great confidence that restraint is good mental training *(shuyo)* and produces results not attained by freedom. But the Japanese increase of restraints upon the man or woman during their most active producing periods by no means indicates that these restraints cover the whole of life. Childhood and old age are "free areas."

A people so truly permissive to their children very likely want babies. The Japanese do. They want them, first of all, as parents do in the United States, because it is a pleasure to love a child. But they want them, too, for reasons which have much less weight in America. Japanese parents need children, not alone for emotional satisfaction, but because they have failed in life if they have not carried on the family line. Every Japanese man must have a son. He needs him to do daily homage to his memory after his death at the living-room shrine before the miniature gravestone. He needs him to perpetuate the family line down the generations and to preserve the family honor and possessions. For traditional social reasons the father needs his son almost as much as the young son needs his father. The son will take his father's place in the on-going future and this is not felt as supplanting but as insuring the father. For a few years the father is trustee of the "house." Later it will be his son. If the father could not pass trusteeship to his son, his own role would have been played in vain. This deep sense of continuity prevents the dependency of the fully grown son on his father, even when it is continued so much longer than it is in the United States, from having the aura of shame and humiliation which it so generally has in Western nations.

A woman too wants children not only for her emotional satisfaction   5
in them but because it is only as a mother that she gains status. A childless wife has a most insecure position in the family, and even if she is not discarded she can never look forward to being a mother-in-law and exercising authority over her son's marriage and over her son's wife. Her husband will adopt a son to carry on his line but according to Japanese ideas the childless woman is still the loser. Japanese women are expected to be good childbearers. . . .

Childbirth is as private in Japan as sexual intercourse and women may not cry out in labor because this would publicize it. A little pallet bed has been prepared for the baby with its own new mattress and bedcover. It would be a bad omen for the child not to have its own new bed, even if the family can do no more than have the quilt covers and the stuffing cleaned and renovated to make them "new." The little bed quilt is not as stiff as grown-ups' covers and it is lighter. The baby is therefore said to be more comfortable in its own bed, but the deeply felt reason for its separate bed is still felt to be based on a kind of sympathetic magic: A new human being must have its own new bed. The baby's pallet is drawn up close to the mother's, but the baby does not sleep with its mother until it is old enough to show initiative. When it is perhaps a year old, they say the baby stretches out its arms and makes its demand known. Then the baby sleeps in its mother's arms under her covers.

For three days after its birth the baby is not fed, for the Japanese wait until the true milk comes. After this the baby may have the breast at any time either for food or comfort. The mother enjoys nursing too. The Japanese are convinced that nursing is one of a woman's greatest physiological pleasures and the baby easily learns to share her pleasure. The breast is not only nourishment: It is delight and comfort. For a month the baby lies on his little bed or is held in his mother's arms. It is only after the baby has been taken to the local shrine and presented there at the age of about thirty days that his life is thought to be firmly anchored in his body so that it is safe to carry him around freely in public. After he is a month old, he is carried on his mother's back. A double sash holds him under his arms and under his behind and is passed around the mother's shoulders and tied in front at the waist. In cold weather the mother's padded jacket is worn right over the baby. The older children of the family, both boys and girls, carry the baby, too, even at play when they are running for base or playing hopscotch. The villagers and the poorer families especially depend on child nurses, and "living in public, as the Japanese babies do, they soon acquire an intelligent, interested look, and seem to enjoy the games of the older children upon whose backs they are carried as much as the players themselves."[1] The spread-eagle strapping of the baby on the back in Japan has much in common with the shawl-carrying common in the Pacific Islands and elsewhere. It makes for passivity and babies carried in these ways tend to grow up, as the Japanese do too, with a capacity for sleeping anywhere, anyhow. But the Japanese strapping does not encourage as complete passivity as shawl and bag carrying. The baby "learns to cling like a kitten to the back of whoever carries it. . . . The straps that tie it to the back are sufficient for safety; but the baby . . . is dependent on its own exertions to secure a comfortable position and it soon learns to ride its bearer with considerable skill instead of being merely a bundle tied to the shoulders."[2]

The mother lays the baby on its bed whenever she is working and carries it with her wherever she goes on the streets. She talks to it. She hums to it. She puts it through the etiquette motions. If she returns a greeting herself, she moves the baby's head and shoulders forward so that it too makes salutation.° The baby is always counted in. Every afternoon she takes it with her into the hot bath and plays with it as she holds it on her knees.

. . . When the baby is three or four months old, the mother begins his nursery training.° She anticipates his needs, holding him in her hands outside the door. She waits for him, usually whistling low and monotonously, and the child learns to know the purpose of this auditory stimulus. Everyone agrees that a baby in Japan, as in China too, is trained very early. If there are slips, some mothers pinch the baby but generally they only change the tone of their voices and hold the hard-to-train baby outside the door at more frequent intervals. If there is withholding, the mother gives the baby an enema or a purge. Mothers say that they are making the baby more comfortable; when he is trained he will no longer have to wear the thick uncomfortable diapers. It is true that a Japanese baby must find diapers unpleasant, not only because they are heavy but because custom does not decree that they be changed whenever he wets them. The baby is nevertheless too young to perceive the connection between nursery training and getting rid of uncomfortable diapers. He experiences only an inescapable routine

---

If she returns a greeting . . . salutation: When the mother bows in greeting, the baby strapped to her back perforce bows.   **nursery training:** Toilet training. [Editors' notes]

[1] Alice Mabel Bacon, *Japanese Women and Girls,* p. 6.

[2] Op. cit., p. 10.

implacably insisted upon. Besides, the mother has to hold the baby away from her body, and her grip must be firm. What the baby learns from the implacable training prepares him to accept in adulthood the subtler compulsions of Japanese culture.[3]

The Japanese baby usually talks before it walks. Creeping has always   10 been discouraged. Traditionally there was a feeling that the baby ought not to stand or take steps till it was a year old and the mother used to prevent any such attempts. The government in its cheap, widely circulated *Mother's Magazine* has for a decade or two taught that walking should be encouraged and this has become much more general. Mothers loop a sash under the baby's arms or support it with their hands. But babies still tend to talk even earlier. When they begin to use words the stream of baby talk with which adults like to amuse a baby becomes more purposive. They do not leave the baby's acquiring of language to chance imitation; they teach the baby words and grammar and respect language, and both the baby and the grown-ups enjoy the game.

When children can walk they can do a lot of mischief in a Japanese home. They can poke their fingers through paper walls, and they can fall into the open fire pit in the middle of the floor. Not content with this, the Japanese even exaggerate the dangers of the house. It is "dangerous" and completely taboo to step on the threshold. The Japanese house has, of course, no cellar and is raised off the ground on joists. It is seriously felt that the whole house can be thrown out of shape even by a child's step upon the threshold. Not only that, but the child must learn not to step or to sit where the floor mats join one another. Floor mats are of standard size and rooms are known as "three-mat rooms" or "twelve-mat rooms." Where these mats join, children are often told, the samurai of old times used to thrust their swords up from below the house and pierce the occupants of the room. Only the thick soft floor mats provide safety; even the cracks where they meet are dangerous. The mother puts feelings of this sort into the constant admonitions she uses to the baby: "Dangerous" and "Bad." The third usual admonition is "Dirty." The neatness and cleanness of the Japanese house is proverbial and the baby is admonished to respect it.

Most Japanese children are not weaned till shortly before a new baby is born, but the government's *Mother's Magazine* has in late years approved of weaning the baby at eight months. Middle-class mothers often do this, but it is far from being the common custom in Japan. True to the Japanese feeling that nursing is a great pleasure to the mother, those circles which are gradually adopting the custom regard the shorter nursing period as a mother's sacrifice to the welfare of her child. When they accept the new dictum that "the child who nurses long is weak," they blame the mother for her self-indulgence if she has not weaned her baby. "She says she can't wean her

[3] Geoffrey Gorer has also emphasized the role of Japanese toilet training in *Themes in Japanese Culture*, Transactions of the New York Academy of Science, vol. 5, pp. 106–124, 1943.

baby. It's only that she hasn't made up her own mind. She wants to go on. She is getting the better part." With such an attitude, it is quite understandable that eight-month weaning has not become widespread. There is a practical reason also for late weaning. The Japanese do not have a tradition of special foods for a just-weaned baby. If he is weaned young, he is fed the water in which rice has been boiled, but ordinarily he passes directly from his mother's milk to the usual adult fare. Cow's milk is not included in Japanese diet and they do not prepare special vegetables for children. Under the circumstances there is a reasonable doubt whether the government is correct in teaching that "the child who nurses long is weak."

Children are usually weaned after they can understand what is said to them. They have sat in their mother's lap at the family table during meals and been fed bits of the food; now they eat more of it. Some children are feeding problems at this time, and this is easy to understand when they are weaned because of the birth of a new baby. Mothers often offer them sweets to buy them off from begging to nurse. Sometimes a mother will put pepper on her nipples. But all mothers tease them by telling them they are proving that they are mere babies if they want to nurse. "Look at your little cousin. He's a man. He's little like you and he doesn't ask to nurse." "That little boy is laughing at you because you're a boy and you still want to nurse." Two-, three-, and four-year-old children who are still demanding their mother's breast will often drop it and feign indifference when an older child is heard approaching.

This teasing, this urging a child toward adulthood, is not confined to weaning. From the time the child can understand what is said to it, these techniques are common in any situation. A mother will say to her boy baby when he cries, "You're not a girl," or "You're a man." Or she will say, "Look at that baby. He doesn't cry." When another baby is brought to visit, she will fondle the visitor in her own child's presence and say, "I'm going to adopt this baby. I want such a nice, good child. You don't act your age." Her own child throws itself upon her, often pommeling her with its fists, and cries, "No, no, we don't want any other baby. I'll do what you say." When the child of one or two has been noisy or has failed to be prompt about something, the mother will say to a man visitor, "Will you take this child away? We don't want it." The visitor acts out his role. He starts to take the child out of the house. The baby screams and calls upon its mother to rescue it. He has a full-sized tantrum. When she thinks the teasing has worked, she relents and takes back the child, exacting its frenzied promise to be good. The little play is acted out sometimes with children who are as old as five and six.

Teasing takes another form too. The mother will turn to her husband and say to the child, "I like your father better than you. He is a nice man." The child gives full expression to his jealousy and tries to break in between his father and mother. His mother says, "Your father doesn't shout around the house and run around the rooms." "No, no," the child protests, "I won't either. I am good. *Now* do you love me?" When the play has gone on long enough, the father and mother look at one another and smile. They may tease a young daughter in this way as well as a young son.

Such experiences are rich soil for the fear of ridicule and of ostracism which is so marked in the Japanese grown-up. It is impossible to say how soon little children understand that they are being made game of by this teasing, but understand it they do sooner or later, and when they do, the sense of being laughed at fuses with the panic of the child threatened with loss of all that is safe and familiar. When he is a grown man, being laughed at retains this childhood aura.

The panic such teasing occasions in the two- to five-year-old child is the greater because home is really a haven of safety and indulgence. Division of labor, both physical and emotional, is so complete between his father and mother that they are seldom presented to him as competitors. His mother or his grandmother runs the household and admonishes the child. They both serve his father on their knees° and put him in the position of honor. The order of precedence in the home hierarchy is clear-cut. The child has learned the prerogatives of elder generations, of a male as compared with a female, of elder brother as compared with younger brother. But at this period of his life a child is indulged in all these relationships. This is strikingly true if he is a boy. For both girls and boys alike the mother is the source of constant and extreme gratifications, but in the case of a three-year-old boy he can gratify against her even his furious anger. He may never manifest any aggression toward his father, but all that he felt when he was teased by his parents and his resentments against being "given away" can be expressed in tantrums directed against his mother and his grandmother. Not all little boys, of course, have these tantrums, but in both villages and upper-class homes they are looked upon as an ordinary part of child life between three and six. The baby pommels his mother, screams, and, as his final violence, tears down her precious hair-do. His mother is a woman and even at three years old he is securely male. He can gratify even his aggressions.

To his father he may show only respect. His father is the great exemplar to the child of high hierarchal position, and, in the constantly used Japanese phrase, the child must learn to express the proper respect to him "for training." He is less of a disciplinarian than in almost any Western nation. Discipline of the children is in the woman's hands. A simple silent stare or a short admonition is usually all the indication of his wishes he gives to his little children, and these are rare enough to be quickly complied with. He may make toys for his children in his free hours. He carries them about on occasion long after they can walk—as the mother does too—and for his

---

serve his father on their knees: In traditional Japanese style, meals are eaten while kneeling or sitting on the floor around a low table. Thus, the whole family is kneeling, not just the women. [Editors' note]

children of this age he casually assumes nursery duties which an American father ordinarily leaves to his wife.

Children have great freedom with their grandparents, though they are also objects of respect. Grandparents are not cast in the role of disciplinarians. They may take that role when they object to the laxness of the children's upbringing, and this is the occasion of a good deal of friction. The child's grandmother is usually at hand twenty-four hours of the day, and the rivalry for the children between father's mother and mother is proverbial in Japanese homes. From the child's point of view he is courted by both of them. From the grandmother's point of view, she often uses him in her domination of her daughter-in-law. The young mother has no greater obligation in life than satisfying her mother-in-law and she cannot protest, however much the grandparents may spoil her children. Grandmother gives them candies after Mother has said they should not have any more, and says pointedly, "*My* candies aren't poison." Grandmother in many households can make the children presents which Mother cannot manage to get them and has more leisure to devote to the children's amusements.

The older brothers and sisters are also taught to indulge the younger children. The Japanese are quite aware of the danger of what we call the baby's "nose being put out of joint" when the next baby is born. The dispossessed child can easily associate with the new baby the fact that he has had to give up his mother's breast and his mother's bed to the newcomer. Before the new baby is born the mother tells the child that now he will have a real live doll and not just a "pretend" baby. He is told that he can sleep now with his father instead of his mother, and this is pictured as a privilege. The children are drawn into preparations for the new baby. The children are usually genuinely excited and pleased by the new baby but lapses occur and are regarded as thoroughly expectable and not as particularly threatening. The dispossessed child may pick up the baby and start off with it, saying to his mother, "We'll give this baby away." "No," she answers, "it's our baby. See, we'll be good to it. It likes you. We need you to help with the baby." The little scene sometimes recurs over a considerable time but mothers seem to worry little about it. One provision for the situation occurs automatically in large families: The alternate children are united by closer ties. The oldest child will be favored nurse and protector of the third child and the second child of the fourth. The younger children reciprocate. Until children are seven or eight, what sex the children are generally makes little difference in this arrangement.

All Japanese children have toys. Fathers and mothers and all the circle of friends and relatives make or buy dolls and all their appurtenances for the children, and among poorer people they cost practically nothing. Little children play housekeeping, weddings, and festivals with them, after arguing out just what the "right" grown-up procedures are, and sometimes submitting to mother a disputed point. When there are quarrels, it is likely that the mother will invoke *noblesse oblige* and ask the older child to give in to the

20

younger one. The common phrase is, "Why not lose to win?" She means, and the three-year-old quickly comes to understand her, that if the older child gives up his toy to the younger one the baby will soon be satisfied and turn to something else; then the admonished child will have won his toy back even though he relinquished it. Or she means that by accepting an unpopular role in the master-servants game the children are proposing, he will nevertheless "win" the fun they can have. "To lose to win" becomes a sequence greatly respected in Japanese life even when people are grown-up.

Besides the techniques of admonition and teasing, distracting the child and turning his mind away from its object has an honored place in child-rearing. Even the constant giving of candies is generally thought of as part of the technique of distraction. . . .

Except among the upper classes children do not wait to go to school before they play freely with other children of the neighborhood. In the villages they form little play gangs before they are three and even in towns and cities they play with startling freedom in and out of vehicles in the crowded streets. They are privileged beings. They hang around the shops listening to grown-ups, or play hopscotch or handball. They gather for play at the village shrine, safe in the protection of its patron spirit. Girls and boys play together until they go to school, and for two or three years after, but closest ties are likely to be between children of the same sex and especially between children of the same chronological age. These age-groups (donen), especially in the villages, are lifelong and survive all others. In the village of Suye Mura, "as sexual interests decrease parties of donen are the true pleasures left in life. Suye (the village) says, 'Donen are closer than a wife.' "[4]

These preschool children's gangs are very free with each other. Many of their games are unabashedly obscene from a Western point of view. The children know the facts of life both because of the freedom of grown-ups' conversation and because of the close quarters in which a Japanese family lives. Besides, their mothers ordinarily call attention to their children's genitals when they play with them and bathe them, certainly to those of their boy children. The Japanese do not condemn childish sexuality except when it is indulged in the wrong places and in wrong company. Masturbation is not regarded as dangerous. The children's gangs are also very free in hurling criticisms at each other—criticisms which in later life would be insults—and in boasting—boasts which would later be occasions of deep shame. "Children," the Japanese say, their eyes smiling benignantly, "know no shame (haji)." They add, "That is why they are so happy." It is the great gulf fixed between the little child and the adult, for to say of a grown person, "He knows no shame" is to say that he is lost to decency.

Children of this age criticize each other's homes and possessions and   25

4 John F. Embree, Suye Mura, p. 190.

they boast especially about their fathers. "My father is stronger than yours," "My father is smarter than yours" is common coin. They come to blows over their respective fathers. This kind of behavior seems to Americans hardly worth noting, but in Japan it is in great contrast to the conversation children hear all about them. Every adult's reference to his own home is phrased as "my wretched house" and to his neighbor's as "your august house"; every reference to his family, as "my miserable family," and to his neighbor's as "your honorable family." Japanese agree that for many years of childhood—from the time the children's play gangs form till the third year of elementary school, when the children are nine—they occupy themselves constantly with these individualistic claims. Sometimes it is, "I will play overlord and you'll be my retainers." "No, I won't be a servant. I will be overlord." Sometimes it is personal boasts and derogation of the others. "They are free to say whatever they want. As they get older they find that what they want isn't allowed, and then they wait till they're asked and they don't boast any more." . . .

The serious business of fitting a boy into the circumspect patterns of adult Japanese life does not really begin till after he has been in school for two or three years. Up to that time he has been taught physical control, and when he was obstreperous, his naughtiness has been "cured" and his attention distracted. He has been unobtrusively admonished and he has been teased. But he has been allowed to be willful, even to the extent of using violence against his mother. His little ego has been fostered. Not much changes when he first goes to school. The first three grades are coeducational and the teacher, whether a man or a woman, pets the children and is one of them. More emphasis at home and in school, however, is laid on the dangers of getting into "embarrassing" situations. Children are still too young for "shame," but they must be taught to avoid being "embarrassed." The boy in the story who cried "Wolf, wolf" when there was no wolf, for instance, "fooled people. If you do anything of this kind, people do not trust you and that is an embarrassing fact." Many Japanese say that it was their schoolmates who laughed at them first when they made mistakes—not their teachers or their parents. The job of their elders, indeed, is not, at this point, themselves to use ridicule on the children, but gradually to integrate the fact of ridicule with the moral lesson of living up to giri-to-the-world.° Obligations which were, when the children were six, the loving devotion of a faithful dog . . . now gradually become a whole series of restraints. "If you do this, if you do that," their elders say, "the world will laugh at you." The rules are particularistic and situational and a great many of them concern what we should call etiquette. They require subordinating one's own will to the ever-increasing duties to neighbors, to family, and to country. The child must restrain himself,

---

giri-to-the-world: Social debts; repayment for favors or gifts received from persons outside one's immediate family. [Editors' note]

he must recognize his indebtedness. He passes gradually to the status of a debtor who must walk circumspectly if he is ever to pay back what he owes.

Thinking About the Text

1. Consider "the arc of life" (para. 2), a poetic term that Benedict applies to Americans and (with a difference) to Japanese. Do you think this metaphor stimulates thought, by wisely perceiving a pattern under what might at first glance seem to be the chaos of experience? Or does it perhaps hinder thought by falsely imposing a pattern? Would it be equally or even more fruitful to speak of, say, the spiral of life, or the maze of life, or the zigzag of life? Explain.

2. Benedict asserts (para. 9) that the baby learns the importance of predictable routines through the methods of nursery training. She goes on in this paragraph to relate toilet training to adult behavior. Do her assertions strike you as reasonable? How might they be verified? Or are they unverifiable? Explain.

Thinking About Culture

3. The number of children in a Japanese family has greatly decreased in the last twenty years, to the point where many children have no siblings. How might family dynamics and parental attention be different in a one-child family? Similarly there are fewer three-generation households now: What differences might there be in the so-called New Family?

4. The transition from childhood to adulthood as Benedict describes it among Japanese in the 1940s was fairly sharp. To a young person in the United States, growing up often means acquiring rights and freedoms, symbolized by the driver's license, the working permit, and the freedom to drink alcohol. For this reason, many young people want to grow up as fast as possible. How would you characterize the meaning of adulthood, coming of age, for the Japanese people in Benedict's study?

5. Benedict's first paragraph offers a concise statement of how an American baby (or at least a middle-class white Anglo-Saxon baby) was treated in the 1940s. Try your hand at writing a comparable paragraph describing the treatment of babies either in the 1990s or in the decade when you were a baby. You may want to make it clear that you are not talking about "American babies" but about babies of a particular subculture of the United States. And you may want to develop a comparison between middle-class white customs and those of another culture with which you are especially familiar.

Joseph Tobin

Dealing with a Difficult Child

On the day we videotaped at Komatsudani, Hiroki started things off with a flourish by pulling his penis out from under the leg of his shorts and waving it at the class during the morning welcome song. During the workbook session that followed, Hiroki called out answers to every question the teacher asked and to many she did not ask. When not volunteering answers, Hiroki gave a loud running commentary on his workbook progress ("now I'm coloring the badger, now the pig . . .") as he worked rapidly and deftly on his assignment. He alternated his play-by-play announcing with occasional songs, entertaining the class with loud, accurate renditions of their favorite cartoon themes, complete with accompanying dancing, gestures, and occasional instrumental flourishes. Despite the demands of his singing and announcing schedule, Hiroki managed to complete his workbook pages before most of the other children (of course, those sitting near him might have finished their work faster had they a less distracting tablemate).

Work completed, Hiroki threw his energies wholeheartedly into his comedy routine, holding various colored crayons up to the front of his shorts and announcing that he had a blue, then a green, and finally a black penis. We should perhaps mention at this point that penis and butt jokes were immensely popular with four-year-old children in nearly every school we visited in [Japan, the United States, and China]. The only noticeable difference was that such humor was most openly exhibited in Japan, where the teachers generally said nothing and sometimes even smiled, whereas American teachers tended to say something like "We'd rather not hear that kind of talk during group time," and in China such joking appeared to have been driven largely underground, out of adult view.

As the children lined up to have Fukui-sensei check their completed work, Hiroki fired a barrage of pokes, pushes, and little punches at the back of the boy in front of him, who took it all rather well. In general, as Hiroki punched and wrestled his way through the day with various of his male classmates, they reacted by seeming to enjoy his attentions, by becoming irritated but not actually angry, or, most commonly, by shrugging them off with a "That's Hiroki for you" sort of expression. The reaction of Satoshi,

---

Joseph Tobin teaches in the College of Education and the Center for Youth Research at the University of Hawaii at Manoa. He is the coauthor of Preschool in Three Cultures: Japan, China, and the United States *(1989), the source of the excerpt reprinted here, and he is the editor of* Re-Made in Japan *(1992), a collection of scholarly essays on the transformation of foreign (borrowed) culture in Japanese material culture.*

who cried when Hiroki hit him and stepped on his hand, was the exception to this rule.

During the singing of the prelunch song, Hiroki, who was one of the four daily lunch monitors, abandoned his post in front of the organ to wrestle with a boy seated nearby. While eating, Hiroki regaled his classmates with more songs and jokes. Finishing his lunch as quickly as he had his workbook, Hiroki joined other fast diners on the balcony, where he roughhoused with some other boys and then disrupted a game by throwing flash cards over the railing to the ground below. The other children seemed more amused than annoyed by these antics, although one girl, Midori, ran inside to tattle to the teacher, who was by now sweeping up under the tables. Fukui-sensei sent Midori back to the balcony with some instructions. A few minutes later Fukui-sensei walked out to the balcony, looked over the railing, and said, "So that's where the cards are going." Soon several of the children, with the conspicuous exception of Hiroki, ran down the steps to retrieve the fallen cards. This proved to be a losing battle as Hiroki continued to rain cards down upon them. It was now that Hiroki (purposely) stepped on Satoshi's hand, which made him cry. Satoshi was quickly ushered away from the scene by Midori, the girl who had earlier reported the card throwing. Midori, arm around Satoshi's neck, listened very empathetically to his tale of woe and then repeated it several times with gestures to other girls who came by: "Hiroki threw cards over the balcony and then he stepped on Satoshi's hand, and then he punched Satoshi like this." The girls then patted Satoshi on the back, suggesting that in the future he find someone other than Hiroki to play with.

Lunch over and the room cleaned up, Fukui-sensei returned to the balcony where, faced with the sight of Hiroki and another boy involved in a fight (which consisted mostly of the other boy's being pushed down and climbed on by Hiroki), she said neutrally, "Are you still fighting?" Then she added, a minute later, in the same neutral tone, "Why are you fighting anyway?" and told everyone still on the balcony, "Hurry up and clean up [the flash cards]. Lunchtime is over. Hurry, hurry." Hiroki was by now disrupting the card clean-up by rolling on the cards and putting them in his mouth, but when he tried to enter the classroom Fukui-sensei put her hand firmly on his back and ushered him outside again. Fukui-sensei, who by now was doing the greatest share of the card picking-up, several times blocked Hiroki from leaving the scene of his crime, and she playfully spanked him on the behind when he continued to roll on the cards.

The rest of the day wound down for Hiroki in similar fashion. At one point in the afternoon Komatsudani's assistant principal, Higashino-sensei, came over to Hiroki and talked softly but seriously to him for three or four minutes, presumably about his behavior. During the free playground period that ends the day, Hiroki played gently with a toddler and more roughly with some of the older boys. He was finally picked up shortly before 6:00 by his father, making him one of the last children to go home.

When we showed Fukui-sensei and her supervisors the film we made in her classroom, we were most curious to see if Fukui-sensei would be at all defensive about the way the film depicted her dealing with—and seeming not to deal with—Hiroki's misbehavior. Both Fukui-sensei and her supervisors told us they were very satisfied with the film and felt that it adequately captured what they are about. Indeed, they said, the way Fukui-sensei dealt with Hiroki in the film, including ignoring his most provocatively aggressive and exhibitionistic actions, reflected not negligence but just the opposite, a strategy worked out over the course of countless meetings and much trial and error.

Japanese preschool teachers and, to a lesser extent, preschool administrators generally are pragmatists rather than ideologues, and thus their discipline and classroom-management techniques tend to be eclectic, focusing on what works. And for most Japanese teachers, for most situations, what seems to work best is a nonconfrontational, energetic, friendly, yet affectively neutral approach. After viewing the tape, we discussed their strategy:

> HIGASHINO: Dealing with Hiroki is really a problem. We've had him here two years now, since he was less than three. You should have seen him before if you think he's something now. We've tried just about everything we could think of to deal with Hiroki. But we've found that especially for a boy like Hiroki the techniques you saw Fukui-sensei using in the film work best. Hiroki has one more year here in our school, so we have one more year to help him straighten himself out, to get over his problem, before he begins primary school.
> TOBIN: Do you ever punish Hiroki?
> HIGASHINO: What do you mean? Like tie him up or hit him or something?
> TOBIN: Well, no. I was thinking of time-outs—for instance, making him sit alone on a chair in a corner for a while.
> HIGASHINO: We've tried that sort of approach a bit and some other approaches as well, but with Hiroki, he misbehaves so often we must overlook the little things or we'd be yelling at him and making him sit in the corner all day. He's got pride. He gets easily offended; his pride gets hurt a lot when we punish him. He gets [physically] punished at home.

Komatsudani's teachers are careful not to isolate a disruptive child from the group by singling him out for punishment or censure or excluding him from a group activity. Similarly, whenever possible, they avoid direct confrontations with children. As Higashino-sensei told us, "The moment a teacher raises her voice or begins to argue or plead with a child, the battle is already lost." Catherine Lewis (1984) suggests that Japanese teachers think their most powerful source of influence over children is their being viewed unambivalently as benevolent figures; teachers are therefore careful to avoid interacting with children in unpleasant, stressful, emotionally complex ways. (Of course this is an ideal: Teachers in Japan, as in other countries, occasionally lose their tempers and say and do things they later regret.) Lewis also suggests that teachers maintain order without intervening directly in children's disputes and misbehavior by encouraging in various ways other children to deal with their classmates' troubles and misdeeds.

Fukui-sensei's approach to dealing with Hiroki illustrates each of these   10
Japanese strategies of discipline and classroom management. She scrupulously avoided confronting or censuring Hiroki even when he was most provocative. (Indeed, she remained composed even during those moments when it was all we could do not to drop our camera and our posture of scholarly neutrality and tell Hiroki to cut it out.)

Fukui-sensei encouraged the other children in the class to take responsibility for helping Hiroki correct his behavior—for instance, when she told Midori to go do something herself about Hiroki's throwing cards. And Fukui-sensei diligently avoided excluding Hiroki from the group in any way. In fact, she insisted he participate in the balcony clean-up to the bitter end, though his presence clearly made the others' task much more difficult.

Another strategy Fukui-sensei employed to remain a benevolent figure to Hiroki was to allow Higashino-sensei to play the role of heavy and give Hiroki a stern talking to (by Japanese preschool standards). This is a strategy we observed in many Japanese preschools; for example, the teacher would tell the children that if they did not clean up, the principal would be cross. Principals, who are often men in this world of women and children, generally appear to be willing and well suited to play this role. They periodically give assembled groups of children lectures on comportment, on the need to work and play hard, to wake up early during vacation just as they do during the school year, to eat well and get plenty of exercise, and to be respectful of their elders and mindful of the feelings of others.

Intelligence and Behavior

Why does Hiroki misbehave? Dana Davidson, who has a background working in assessment and in gifted and talented programs, speculated that Hiroki's behavior problems might be related to his being intellectually gifted and easily bored. When we returned to Komatsudani to talk with the staff about our tape, Davidson suggested to Fukui-sensei and Higashino-sensei that Hiroki might be quicker and smarter than the other children and that this "giftedness" (which proved to be a very difficult concept for us to express in Japanese) might provide at least a partial explanation for Hiroki's behavior in the classroom. Fukui and Higashino looked a bit confused and even taken aback by this suggestion:

> HIGASHINO: Hiroki's intelligence is about average, about the same as most other children, I would say.

DAVIDSON: But he finishes his work so quickly. And he looks like he knows the words to so many songs. He just seems so bright, gifted.

HIGASHINO: What do you mean by "gifted"?

DAVIDSON: Well, by "gifted" in the United States we mean someone who is exceptionally talented in some area, like intelligence. Like Hiroki who seems to be so smart, so quick. He has such a bright look in his eyes. We would say that a boy like this has a lot of energy and is so bright that he is quickly bored by school. To me, it seems that his incidents of misbehavior occur when he has finished his work before the other children. He provokes his teacher and the other children in an attempt to make things more exciting, better matched to the pace and level of stimulation he needs.

HIGASHINO: It seems to me that Hiroki doesn't necessarily finish his work first because he is smarter than the other children. Speed isn't the same thing as intelligence. And his entertaining the other children by singing all those songs is a reflection not so much of intelligence as it is of his great need for attention.

The different perspectives that are apparent in this discussion suggest important cultural differences between Americans and Japanese, not only in definitions of and attitudes toward intelligence, but also in views of character, behavior, and inborn dispositions and abilities.

One possible explanation for Higashino's insistence that Hiroki is of only average intelligence might lie in the great value Japanese teachers and contemporary Japanese society place on equality and on the notion that children's success and failure and their potential to become successful versus failed adults has more to do with effort and character and thus with what can be learned and taught in school than with raw inborn ability. Thus, even if we were to assume, for the moment, that Hiroki is in fact of exceptional intelligence, his Japanese teachers would be hesitant to acknowledge this special gift because of their reluctance to explain or excuse behavior in terms of differences in abilities. We suspect that many Japanese preschool teachers and administrators we talked with found our questions about giftedness hard to understand in part because of their distaste for the notion of inborn abilities and their suspicion that the identification of children as having unequal abilities would inevitably lead to an unequal allocation of educational effort, resources, and opportunity.

The Japanese do, of course, recognize that children are born with 15 unequal abilities and that some children have special gifts, but Japanese society in general and teachers in particular view the role of education and perhaps especially of primary and preschool education as to even out rather than sort out or further accentuate these ability differences. Thus one Japanese preschool teacher responded to our description of programs for gifted children in American preschools by saying, "How sad that by age three or four a child might already be labeled as having less chance for success than some of his classmates." . . .

When Japanese preschool teachers do talk about inborn differences in ability, it is usually in the context of praising a child of less than average ability for struggling to keep up with his classmates. For instance, on school sports days it is not unusual to hear a teacher say: "Look at him go! His legs are shorter than everyone else's, but he sure is trying hard." When Fukui-sensei watched the section of our film that shows Kuniko, a pudgy, slowish sort of girl, struggling to make an origami ball with her fat, uncooperative fingers, the teacher said, "Things never come easily to Kuniko, but she really gives it her best."

The Japanese, in contrast to Americans, seldom view intelligence in a young child as a value-free trait that can be used to good or bad result (LeVine and White, 1986). Rather, Japanese tend to view intelligence as closely linked to moral action and to associate the terms *oriko* (smart) and *atama ga ii* (intelligent), when applied to young children, with traits such as *kashikoi* (obedient, well behaved), *erai* (praiseworthy), *ki ga tsuku* (sensitive to others), and *wakareru* (understanding). Intelligence or smartness in a child in America is just as likely to be associated with asocial (naughty) as with desirable behaviors, as can be seen in such expressions as "smart-alec," "too smart for her own good," and "don't get smart with me, young man." But in Japan misbehavior is more likely to be associated with being not smart enough (lacking understanding). Lewis gives the example of the teacher who explains her young charges' misbehavior on an outing (throwing rocks at carp) by saying, "If they *understood* it was wrong, they wouldn't do it" (1984, p. 77).

One often hears Japanese preschool teachers and Japanese adults in general use the word "smart" to compliment preschool-aged children for a variety of socially approved actions, including behaviors Americans might consider indicative of intelligence but also behaviors that to Americans have little or nothing to do with intelligence, such as helping to clean up. In these situations the words "smart" and "intelligent" are used more or less synonymously with the words "well behaved" and "praiseworthy."

These linguistic and cultural factors make it difficult for Hiroki's teachers to think of him as especially intelligent. Their reasoning would go, "If he is so smart, why doesn't he understand better? If he understood better, he would behave better."

Thinking About the Text

1. Social learning is an important component of the early years of schooling in Japan. In your own experience and observations, what are the social lessons of American schools and how are they taught?

Thinking About Culture

2. In another part of his book, Tobin speculates that he focused on Hiroki because the child's bad behavior fascinated him, noting that the Japanese teachers were not as involved with Hiroki as a problem as was the American observer. Others have said that Americans are more apt to "reward" bad behavior with attention and that doing so *encourages* the child to continue misbehaving. Compare our ideas about and reactions to "bad behavior" with those of Japanese teachers as illustrated here.

3. "Giftedness" and "talent" may be seen as different from other forms of ability. Discuss the differences between American and Japanese ideas of ability and its sources—in the genes, in the individual personality, in sheer effort, and so on—and their outcomes in our teaching goals and methods.

Merry I. White

Japanese Education: How Do They Do It?

Japan has become the new reference point for the developing nations and the West, and comparisons with Japan cause increasing wonder and sometimes envy. Travel agents continue to profit from the curiosity of Americans, particularly businessmen, who take regular tours of Japan seeking the secrets of Japanese industry. They come back with photographs and full notebooks, convinced they have learned secrets that can be transplanted to their own companies.

Even the Japanese have entered the pop-sociological search for the secrets of their own success; their journalists suggest that they emphasize problem *prevention* while Americans make up for their lack of prescience and care through *remediation* (in the case of cars, recalls for flawed models). The explanation given by a European Economic Community report—that the Japanese are workaholics willing, masochistically, to live in "rabbit hutches" without complaint—was met with amused derision in Japan. But it seems that those who do not look for transportable "secrets" are nonetheless willing to believe that the source of Japanese success is genetic, and thus completely

Merry I. White, a sociologist specializing in Japan, teaches at Boston University and is a researcher at Harvard's Edwin O. Reischauer Institute of Japanese Studies. She has written several books on Japanese society, including The Japanese Educational Challenge *(1986),* The Japanese Overseas *(1987), and* The Material Child: Coming of Age in Japan and America *(1993). This essay appeared in* The Public Interest *(Summer 1984).*

untransferable. There are alternatives to these positions, and an examination of Japanese education provides us with a backdrop for considering them.

The Social Consensus

The attention given to the decline of both American industry and American education has not yet led to an awareness here of the close relationship between the development of people and the development of society, an awareness we see everywhere in Japanese thought and institutions, and whose effects we can see in the individual achievements of Japanese children. If Americans realized how powerful the relationship is between Japanese school achievement and social and economic successes we might see the same kind of protectionist language aimed at the Japanese educational system that we see directed at their automobile industry. ("The Japanese must stop producing such able and committed students because *it isn't fair*.")

The Japanese understand how important it is to have not just a high level of literacy (which they have had since well before modernization), but also a high level of education in the whole population. It has been said that the Japanese high school graduate is as well educated as an American college graduate, and indeed it is impressive that any worker on the factory floor can be expected to understand statistical material, work from complex graphs and charts, and perform sophisticated mathematical operations. This consensus that education is important, however simple it may sound, is the single most important contributor to the success of Japanese schools. Across the population, among parents, at all institutional and bureaucratic levels, and highest on the list of national priorities, is the stress on excellence in education. This is not just rhetoric. If the consensus, societal mobilization, and personal commitment—all focused on education—are not available to Americans, the reason is not genetic, nor are we locked in an immutable cultural pattern. We simply have not mobilized around our children.

There are clear advantages to being a Japanese child: a homogeneous population focused on perpetuating its cultural identity; an occupational system where selection and promotion are based on educational credentials; a relatively equal distribution of educational opportunities; a universal core curriculum; highly trained and rewarded teachers; and families, especially mothers, devoted to enhancing the life chances of children and working cooperatively with the educational system. Finally, there are high standards for performance in every sector, and a carefully graded series of performance expectations in the school curriculum.

It is clear from these assertions that the measurable cognitive achievements of Japanese education represent only part of the picture. The American press stresses these achievements and accounts for them in terms of government expenditures, longer school years, and early use of homework. While the International Association for the Evaluation of Educational Achievement (IEA) test scores certainly indicate that Japanese children are testing higher than any children in the world (especially in math and science), and while some researchers have even claimed that Japanese children on average score eleven points more than American children on IQ tests, the social and psychological dimensions of Japanese education are similarly impressive and are primary contributors to cognitive achievement. The support given by family and teachers to the emotional and behavioral development of the child provides a base for the child's acquisition of knowledge and problem-solving skills. But beyond this, the Japanese think a major function of education is the development of a happy, engaged, and secure child, able to work hard and cooperate with others.

Inside the Japanese School

In order to understand the context of the Japanese educational system, some basic information is necessary:

1. Education is compulsory for ages six to fifteen, or through lower secondary school. (Age is almost always correlated with grade level, by the way, because only rarely is a child "kept back" and almost never "put ahead.") Noncompulsory high school attendance (both public and private) is nearly universal, at 98 percent.

2. There is extensive "nonofficial" private education. Increasing numbers of children attend preschools. Currently, about 95 percent of the five-year-olds are in kindergarten or nursery school, 70 percent of the four-year-olds, and 10 percent of three-year-olds. Many older children attend *juku* (after school classes) as well. These are private classes in a great variety of subjects, but most enhance and reinforce the material to be learned for high school or college entrance examinations. There are also *yobiko* (cram schools) for those taking an extra year between high school and college to prepare for the exams.

3. While competition for entrance to the most prestigious universities   10 is very stiff, nearly 40 percent of the college-age group attend college or university. (The rates are slightly higher for women, since many attend two-year junior colleges.)

4. Japanese children attend school 240 days a year, compared to 180 in the United States. Many children spend Sundays in study or tutoring, and vacation classes are also available. Children do not necessarily see this as oppressive, and younger children often ask their parents to send them to *juku* as a way of being with their friends after school. Homework starts in first grade, and children in Japan spend more time in home study than children in any other country except Taiwan. In Japan, 8 percent of the high school seniors spend less than five hours per week on homework, compared to 65 percent of American seniors.[1]

[1] Thomas Rohlen, *Japan's High Schools* (Berkeley: University of California Press, 1983), p. 277.

5. Primary and lower secondary schools provide what we would call a core curriculum: a required and comprehensive course of study progressing along a logical path, with attention given to children's developmental levels. In elementary and lower secondary school, language learning dominates the school curriculum, and takes up the greatest number of classroom hours, particularly from second to fourth grade. The large number of characters to be learned requires an emphasis on memorization and drill that is not exhibited in the rest of the curriculum. Arithmetic and math are next in number of class hours, followed by social studies. The curriculum includes regular physical education and morning exercise as part of a "whole-child" program. In high school all students take Japanese, English, math, science, and social studies each year, and all students have had courses in chemistry, biology, physics, and earth sciences. All high school students take calculus.

6. Computers and other technology do not play a large role in schools. The calculator is used, but has not replaced mental calculations or, for that matter, the abacus. There is no national program to develop high-technology skills in children. Americans spend much more money on science and technology in the schools; the Japanese spend more on teacher training and salaries.

These features should be seen in the context of a history of emphasis on education in Japan. To begin with, an interest in mass (or at least widespread) education greatly antedated the introduction of Western schools to Japan. Literacy, numeracy, and a moral education were considered important for people of all classes. When Western style universal compulsory schooling was introduced in 1872, it was after a deliberate and wide-ranging search throughout the world that resulted in a selection of features from German, French, and American educational systems that would advance Japan's modernization and complement her culture. While uniform, centralized schooling was an import, it eventually brought out Japan's already refined powers of adaptation—not the ability to adapt to a new mode as much as *the ability to adapt the foreign mode to Japanese needs and conditions.*

Also striking was the rapidity with which Japan developed a modern   15
educational system and made it truly universal. In 1873, one year after the Education Act, there was 28 percent enrollment in primary schools, but by 1904 enrollment had already reached 98 percent—one percent less than the current rate. The rush to educate children was buttressed both by the wish to catch up with the West and by a cultural interest in schooling.

A Truly National System

Tradition, ideology, and international competition are not, however, the only motive forces in Japanese education: Other factors are as significant. First, Japan has a relatively homogeneous population. Racially and economically there is little variety. Minority groups, such as Koreans and the former outcastes, exist and do suffer some discrimination, but all children have equal access to good schooling. Income is more evenly distributed in Japan than in America and most people (96 percent in a recent Prime Minister's Office poll) consider themselves middle class. There are few remaining regional differences that affect the educational system, except perhaps local accents.

Second, educational financing and planning are centralized. While American educational policy sees the responsibility for schooling as a local matter, Japanese planners can rely on a centralized source of funding, curriculum guidance, and textbook selection. In terms of educational spending as a percentage of total GNP, the United States and Japan are not so far apart: The United States devotes 6.8 percent of its GNP to education, and Japan devotes 8.6 percent. But in Japan about 50 percent of this is national funding, while in the United States the federal government provides only 8 percent of the total expenditure on education, most of which is applied to special education, not to core schooling. Moreover, in the United States there exist no national institutions to build a consensus on what and how our children are taught. The most significant outcome of centralization in Japan is the even distribution of resources and quality instruction across the country. National planners and policymakers can mobilize a highly qualified teaching force and offer incentives that make even the most remote areas attractive to good teachers.

Third (but perhaps most important in the comparison with the United States), teachers enjoy respect and high status, job security, and good pay. More than in any other country, teachers in Japan are highly qualified: Their mastery of their fields is the major job qualification, and all have at least a bachelor's degree in their specialty. Moreover, they have a high degree of professional involvement as teachers: 74 percent are said to belong to some professional teachers' association in which teaching methods and curriculum are actively discussed.[2]

Teachers are hired for life, at starting salaries equivalent to starting salaries for college graduates in the corporate world. Elementary and junior high school teachers earn $18,200 per year on the average, high school teachers $19,000. Compared to other Japanese public sector workers, who earn an average of $16,800, this is a high salary, but it is less than that of managers in large companies or bureaucrats in prestigious ministries. In comparison with American teachers, whose salaries average $17,600, it is an absolutely higher wage. The difference is especially striking when one considers that over all professions, salaries are lower in Japan than in the United States. In fact, American teachers' salaries are near the bottom of the scale of jobs requiring a college degree. Relative status and prestige correlate with salary in both countries. Japanese teachers' pay increases, as elsewhere in

[2] William Cummings, *Education and Equality in Japan* (Princeton: Princeton University Press, 1980), p. 159.

Japan, are tied to a seniority ladder, and older "master teachers" are given extra pay as teacher supervisors in each subject.[3]

Japanese teachers see their work as permanent: Teaching is not a waysta-   20
tion on a path to other careers. Teachers work hard at improving their skills and knowledge of their subject, and attend refresher courses and upgrading programs provided by the Ministry of Education. While there are tendencies, encouraged by the Teachers' Union, to downplay the traditional image of the "devoted, selfless teacher" (since this is seen as exploitative), and to redefine the teacher as a wage laborer with regular hours, rather than as a member of a "sacred" profession, teachers still regularly work overtime and see their job's sphere extending beyond classroom instruction. Classes are large: The average is about forty students to one teacher. Teachers feel responsible for their students' discipline, behavior, morality, and for their general social adjustment as well as for their cognitive development. They are "on duty" after school hours and during vacations, and supervise vacation play and study. They visit their students' families at home, and are available to parents with questions and anxieties about their children. The Teachers' Union protests strongly against this extensive role, but both teachers and parents reinforce this role, tied as it is to the high status of the teacher.

Fourth, there is strong ideological and institutional support for educa-tion because the occupational system relies on schools to select the right person for the right organization. Note that this is not the same as the "right job" or "slot": A new company recruit, almost always a recent graduate, is not expected to have a skill or special identity, but to be appropriate in general educational background and character for a company. The company then trains recruits in the skills they will need, as well as in the company style. Of course, the basic skill level of the population of high school and college graduates is extremely high. But the important fact is that the social consensus supports an educational system that creates a committed, produc-tive labor force. And although the emphasis seems to be on educational credentials, the quality of graduates possessing these credentials is indisput-ably high.

Mom

The background I have presented—of national consensus, institutional cen-tralization, and fiscal support—alone does not explain the successes of Japa-nese education. There are other, less tangible factors that derive from cultural conceptions of development and learning, the valued role of maternal support,

[3] There is a debate in Japan today concerning rewarding good teachers with higher pay: Professor Sumiko Iwao, of Keio University, reports that when quality is measured in *yen*, the commitment of teachers to good teaching declines. [Editors' note: The statistics were for 1983. Salaries of course are now higher both in Japan and in the United States.]

and psychological factors in Japanese pedagogy, and which distinguish it from American schooling.

The role of mothers is especially important. The average Japanese mother feels her child has the potential for success: Children are believed to be born with no distinguishing abilities (or disabilities) and can be mobilized to achieve and perform at high levels. Effort and commitment are required, and, at least at the beginning, it is the mother's job to engage the child. One way of looking at Japanese child development is to look at the words and concepts related to parental goals for their children. A "good child" has the following, frequently invoked characteristics: He is *otonashii* (mild or gentle), *sunao* (compliant, obedient, and cooperative), *akarui* (bright, alert), and *genki* (energetic and spirited). *Sunao* has frequently been translated as "obedient," but it would be more appropriate to use "open minded," "nonresistant," or "authentic in intent and cooperative in spirit." The English word "obedience" implies subordination and lack of self-determination, but *sunao* assumes that what we call compliance (with a negative connotation) is really cooperation, an act of affirmation of the self. A child who is *sunao* has not yielded his personal autonomy for the sake of cooperation; cooperation does not imply giving up the self, but in fact implies that working with others is the appropriate setting for expressing and enhancing the self.

One encourages a *sunao* child through the technique, especially used by mothers and elementary school teachers, of *wakaraseru,* or "getting the child to understand." The basic principle of child-rearing seems to be: Never go against the child. *Wakaraseru* is often a long-term process that ultimately engages the child in the mother's goals, and makes her goals the child's own, thus producing an authentic cooperation, as in *sunao*. The distinction between external, social expectations and the child's own personal goals becomes blurred from this point on. An American might see this manipulation of the child through what we would call "indulgence" as preventing him from having a strong will of his own, but the Japanese mother sees long-term benefits of self-motivated cooperation and real commitment.

Japanese mothers are active teachers as well and have a real curriculum for their preschool children: Games, teaching aids, ordinary activities are all focused on the child's development. There are counting games for very small babies, songs to help children learn new words, devices to focus the child's concentration. Parents buy an average of two or three new books every month for their preschoolers, and there are about forty monthly activity magazines for preschoolers, very highly subscribed. The result is that most, at least most urban children, can read and write the phonetic syllabary before they enter school and can do simple computations.

Maternal involvement becomes much more extensive and "serious" once she and the child enter the elementary school community. In addition to formal involvement in frequent ceremonies and school events, PTA meetings and visiting days, the mother spends much time each day helping the child with homework (sometimes to the point at which the teachers joke that they are really grading the mothers by proxy). There are classes for mothers, called *mamajuku,* that prepare mothers in subjects their children are studying. Homework is considered above all a means for developing a sense of responsibility in the child, and like much in early childhood education, it is seen as a device to train character.

The Japanese phenomenon of maternal involvement recently surfaced in Riverdale, New York, where many Japanese families have settled. Schoolteachers and principals there noted that each Japanese family was purchasing two sets of textbooks. On inquiring, they found that the second set was for the mother, who could better coach her child if she worked during the day to keep up with his lessons. These teachers said that children entering in September with no English ability finished in June at the top of their classes in every subject.

The effort mothers put into their children's examinations has been given a high profile by the press. This is called the *kyoiku mama* syndrome—the mother invested in her children's progress. In contrast to Western theories of achievement, which emphasize individual effort and ability, the Japanese consider academic achievement to be an outgrowth of an interdependent network of cooperative effort and planning. The caricature of the mother's over-investment, however, portrays a woman who has totally identified with her child's success or failure, and who has no separate identity of her own. The press emphasizes the negative aspects of this involvement with accounts of maternal nervous breakdowns, reporting a murder by a mother of the child next-door, who made too much noise while her child was studying. But the press also feeds the mother's investment by exhorting her to prepare a good work environment for the studying child, to subscribe to special exam-preparation magazines, to hire tutors, and to prepare a nutritious and exam-appropriate diet.

High-schoolers from outlying areas taking entrance exams in Tokyo come with their mothers to stay in special rooms put aside by hotels. They are provided with special food, study rooms, counselors, and tension-release rooms, all meant to supply home-care away from home. The home study-desk bought by most parents for their smaller children symbolizes the hovering care and intensity of the mother's involvement: All models have a high front and half-sides, cutting out distractions and enclosing the workspace in womblike protection. There is a built-in study light, shelves, a clock, electric pencil sharpener, and built-in calculator. The most popular model includes a push-button connecting to a buzzer in the kitchen to summon mother for help or for a snack.

"How Do You Feel About Cubing?"

Not much work has been done yet to analyze the relationship between the   30
strongly supportive learning atmosphere and high achievement in Japan. In the home, mothers train small children in a disciplined, committed use of

energy through what Takeo Doi° has called the encouragement of "positive dependency"; in the schools as well there is a recognition that attention to the child's emotional relationship to his work, peers, and teachers is necessary for learning.

A look at a Japanese classroom yields some concrete examples of this. Many Westerners believe that Japanese educational successes are due to an emphasis on rote learning and memorization, that the classroom is rigidly disciplined. This is far from reality. An American teacher walking into a fourth-grade science class in Japan would be horrified: children all talking at once, leaping and calling for the teacher's attention. The typical American's response is to wonder, "Who's in control of this room?" But if one understands the content of the lively chatter, it is clear that all the noise and movement is focused on the work itself—children are shouting out answers, suggesting other methods, exclaiming in excitement over results, and not gossiping, teasing, or planning games for recess. As long as it is the result of this engagement, the teacher is not concerned over the noise, which may measure a teacher's success. (It has been estimated that American teachers spend about 60 percent of class time on organizing, controlling, and disciplining the class, while Japanese teachers spend only 10 percent.)

A fifth-grade math class I observed reveals some elements of this pedagogy. The day I visited, the class was presented with a general statement about cubing. Before any concrete facts, formulae, or even drawings were displayed, the teacher asked the class to take out their math diaries and spend a few minutes writing down their feelings and anticipations over this new concept. It is hard for me to imagine an American math teacher beginning a lesson with an exhortation to examine one's emotional predispositions about cubing (but that may be only because my own math training was antediluvian).

After that, the teacher asked for conjectures from the children about the surface and volume of a cube and asked for some ideas about formulae for calculation. The teacher asked the class to cluster into its component *han* (working groups) of four or five children each, and gave out materials for measurement and construction. One group left the room with large pieces of cardboard, to construct a model of a cubic meter. The groups worked internally on solutions to problems set by the teacher and competed with each other to finish first. After a while, the cubic meter group returned, groaning under the bulk of its model, and everyone gasped over its size. (There were many comments and guesses as to how many children could fit inside.) The teacher then set the whole class a very challenging problem, well over their heads, and gave them the rest of the class time to work on it. The class ended without a solution, but the teacher made no particular

---

Takeo Doi: A noted Japanese psychoanalyst. [Editors' note]

effort to get or give an answer, although she exhorted them to be energetic. (It was several days before the class got the answer—there was no deadline but the excitement did not flag.)

Several characteristics of this class deserve highlighting. First, there was attention to feelings and predispositions, provision of facts, and opportunities for discovery. The teacher preferred to focus on process, engagement, commitment, and performance rather than on discipline (in our sense) and production. Second, the *han:* Assignments are made to groups, not to individuals (this is also true at the workplace) although individual progress and achievement are closely monitored. Children are supported, praised, and allowed to make mistakes through trial and error within the group. The group is also pitted against other groups, and the group's success is each person's triumph, and vice versa. Groups are made up by the teacher and are designed to include a mixture of skill levels—there is a *hancho* (leader) whose job it is to choreograph the group's work, to encourage the slower members, and to act as a reporter to the class at large.

Japanese teachers seem to recognize the emotional as well as the intellectual aspects of engagement. Japanese pedagogy (and maternal socialization) are based on the belief that effort is the most important factor in achievement, and that the teacher's job is to get the child to commit himself positively and energetically to hard work. This emphasis is most explicit in elementary school, but persists later as a prerequisite for the self-discipline and effort children exhibit in high school. 35

American educational rhetoric does invoke "the whole child," does seek "self-expression," and does promote emotional engagement in "discovery learning." But Japanese teaching style, at least in primary schools, effectively employs an engaging, challenging teaching style that surpasses most American attempts. In the cubing class, I was struck by the spontaneity, excitement, and (to American eyes) "unruly" dedication of the children to the new idea, and impressed with the teacher's ability to create this positive mood. It could be a cultural difference: We usually separate cognition and emotional affect, and then devise artificial means of reintroducing "feeling" into learning. It is rather like the way canned fruit juices are produced—first denatured by the preserving process and then topped up with chemical vitamins to replace what was lost.

The Role of Competition

The frequent accusation that Japanese education involves children in hellish competition must also be examined. In the elementary school classroom, competition is negotiated by means of the *han.* The educational system tries to accommodate both the ideology of harmony and the interest in hierarchy and ranking. The introduction of graded, competitive Western modes of education into societies where minimizing differences between people is valued has often produced severe social and psychological dislocation (as in

Africa and other parts of the Third World). In Japan, the importance of the modern educational system as a talent selector and the need to preserve harmony and homogeneity have produced complementary rather than conflicting forces. The regular classroom is a place where the individual does not stick out, but where individual needs are met and goals are set. Children are not held back nor advanced by ability: The cohesion of the age-group is said to be more important. Teachers focus on pulling up the slower learners, rather than tracking the class to suit different abilities. For the most part, teachers and the school system refuse to engage in examination preparation hysteria. Part of the reason for this is pressure from the Teachers' Union, a very large and powerful labor union which consistently resists any moves away from the egalitarian and undifferentiating mode of learning. Turning teachers into drill instructors is said to be dehumanizing, and the process of cramming a poor substitute for education.

So where is the competitive selection principle served? In the *juku*. *Juku* are tough competitive classes, often with up to five hundred in one lecture hall. The most prestigious are themselves very selective and there are examinations (and preparation courses for these) to enter the *juku*. Some *juku* specialize in particular universities' entrance exams, and they will boast of their rate of admission into their universities. It is estimated that one-third of all primary school students and one-half of all secondary school students attend *juku*, but in Tokyo the rate rises to 86 percent of junior high school students. The "king of *juku*," Furukawa Noboru, the creator of a vast chain of such classes, says that *juku* are necessary to bridge the gap of present realities in Japan. He says that public schools do not face the fact of competition and that ignoring the reality does not help children. The Ministry of Education usually ignores this nonaccredited alternative and complementary system, and permits this functional division to take the pressure off the public schools. While there is considerable grumbling by parents, and while it is clear that the *juku* introduce an inegalitarian element into the process of schooling (since they do cost money), they do, by their separation from the regular school, permit the persistence of more traditional modes of learning, while allowing for a fast track in the examinations.

It is important to note that in Japan there really is only one moment of critical importance to one's career chances—the entrance examination to college. There are few opportunities to change paths or retool. Americans' belief that one can be recreated at any time in life, that the self-made person can get ahead, simply is not possible in Japan—thus the intense focus on examinations.

The Problems—in Context

This rapid tour through the Japanese educational system cannot neglect the   40
problems. However, two things must be kept in mind when considering these well-publicized difficulties: One is that although problems do exist, the

statistical reality is that, compared to the West, Japan still looks very good indeed. The other is that the Japanese themselves tend to be quite critical, and educational problems are given attention. But this attention should be seen in context: Not that people are not truly concerned about real problems, but that the anxiety seems related to a sense of national insecurity. The Japanese focus on educational issues may emanate from a sense of the importance of intellectual development in a society where there are few other resources. Any educational problem seems to put the nation truly at risk.

Japanese parents are critical and watchful of the schools and are not complacent about their children's successes. There was a telling example of this in a recent comparative study of American and Japanese education. Mothers in Minneapolis and in Sendai, roughly comparable cities, were asked to evaluate their children's school experiences. The Minneapolis mothers consistently answered that the schools were fine and that their children were doing well, while the Sendai mothers were very critical of their schools and worried that their children were not performing up to potential. Whose children were, in objective tests, doing better? The Sendai group—in fact so much better that the poorest performer in the Japanese group was well ahead of the best in the American group. Mothers in Japan and the United States have very different perspectives on performance: Japanese mothers attribute failure to lack of effort while American mothers explain it as lack of ability. Japanese children have an external standard of excellence to which they can aspire, while an American child normally can only say he will "do his best."

Problems have surfaced, of course. Psychotherapists report a syndrome among children related to school and examination pressure. School phobia, psychosomatic symptoms, and juvenile suicide are most frequently reported. Japan does lead the world in school-related suicides for the fifteen- to nineteen-year-old age-group, at about three hundred per year. Recently, the "battered teacher" and "battered parent" syndromes have received much attention. There are cases where teenagers have attacked or killed parents and teachers, and these have been related to examination pressure. The numbers involved in these cases are very small—at least in comparison with American delinquency patterns and other juvenile pathologies. Dropouts, drug use, and violent juvenile crimes are almost nonexistent in Japan. The crimes reported in one year among school-age children in Osaka, for example, are equal to those reported in one day in New York.

Criticism leveled at Japanese education by Western observers focuses on what they regard as a suppression of genius and individuality, and a lack of attention to the development of creativity in children. The first may indeed be a problem—for the geniuses—because there is little provision for tracking them to their best advantage. There has been discussion of introducing tracking so that individual ability can be better served, but this has not been implemented. The superbright may indeed be disadvantaged.

On the other hand, creativity and innovation *are* encouraged, but their manifestations may be different from those an American observer would expect. We must look at our own assumptions, to see if they are too limited. Americans see creativity in children as a fragile blossom that is stifled by rigid educational systems or adult standards. Creativity involves a necessary break with traditional content and methods, and implies the creation of a new idea or artifact. Whether creativity is in the child or in the teaching, and how it is to be measured, are questions no one has answered satisfactorily. Why we emphasize it is another question, probably related to our theories of progress and the importance we attach to unique accomplishments that push society forward. The fact is that, if anything, our schools do less to encourage creativity than do the Japanese, especially in the arts. All children in Japan learn two instruments and how to read music in elementary school, have regular drawing and painting classes, and work in small groups to create projects they themselves devise. It is true, though, that if everyone must be a soloist or composer to be considered creative, then most Japanese are not encouraged to be creative.

It is not enough to claim that the Japanese have been successful in   45
training children to take exams at the expense of a broader education. And it is not at all appropriate to say that they are unable to develop children's individuality and create the geniuses who make scientific breakthroughs. The first is untrue and the second remains to be shown as false by the Japanese themselves, who are now mobilizing to produce more scientists and technologists. In fact, the scales are tipped in favor of Japan, and to represent it otherwise would be a distortion.

The success of the Japanese model has led to its use in other rapidly developing countries, including South Korea, Taiwan, and Singapore. There, education is seen as the linchpin for development, and attention to children has meant the allocation of considerable resources to schools. The results are similar to those seen in Japanese schools: highly motivated, hard-working students who like school and who have achieved very high scores on international achievement tests.

Seeing Ourselves Through Japanese Eyes

What *America* can learn from Japan is rather an open question. We can, to begin with, learn more *about* Japan, and in doing so, learn more about ourselves. Japanese advancements of the past twenty years were based on American principles of productivity (such as "quality control"), not on *samurai* management skills and *zen* austerities. Looking for Japanese secrets, or worse, protesting that they are inhuman or unfair, will not get us very far. They have shown they can adjust programs and policies to the needs and resources of the times; we must do the same. We need to regain the scientific literacy we lost and reacquire the concrete skills and participatory techniques we need. We should see Japan as establishing a new standard, not as a model to be emulated. To match that standard we have to aim at general excellence, develop a long-term view, and act consistently over time with regard to our children's education.

Thinking About the Text

1. What does White say about Japanese education that you already knew or believed, and what does she say that is new or surprising? What familiar, and what surprising, things does she say about American education?

2. White makes a number of generalizations about democracy, egalitarianism, individualism, and creativity. How do American young people experience such principles in daily classroom life? In thinking about this topic, draw upon your own experiences in school.

3. White discusses learning as an interdependent activity, describing examples of team and cooperative learning and parental homework coaching. Do these practices strike you as inappropriate for American schools? Why? If you have participated in team learning or worked with your parents on homework, draw on those experiences to support your answer.

4. Both White and Joseph Tobin (p. 89) focus on elementary school education. Compare the two essays, noting points of agreement and contradiction. Summarize your findings.

Thinking About Culture

5. Studies indicate that Japanese children, as a whole, enjoy school more than children in other nations do. From reading this essay, and from your own school experiences, how would you explain this finding? Discuss aspects of school you liked and why.

6. In class, drawing on the readings by Joseph Tobin (p. 89), Merry White, and Ikuo Amano (the next selection), discuss the key, bottom-line, concrete differences between the United States and Japan that affect our educational systems and outcomes.

7. White notes that neither harsh critiques nor slavish emulation are appropriate in American educators' views of Japanese schooling. She suggests that we look at Japan not as a blueprint, but as a mirror, to reflect on our own practices. What can we learn about ourselves by looking at Japan?

Ikuo Amano

The Examination Hell

The most immediate reason why reform is necessary now is the troubled relationship between the children who are the main actors in the educational process and the system itself. A reexamination of that relationship, not so much of educational institutions or of education's role in society, is the key issue.

Student dissatisfaction with the education system began to take concrete form around the beginning of the 1970s. As in other industrialized countries, student activism in the universities was vigorous, even violent. Strikes and sit-ins were common, and the fever of protest showed signs of spreading even to the high schools. Eventually the situation returned to normal, but "antischool" attitudes and behavior began to surface among junior and senior high school students. Disillusionment and dislike of school, refusal to attend school, violence, lapses in scholastic performance, and dropouts are manifestations of that protest.

Of course, it is true that the situation still seems to be far less serious than in some other advanced nations, especially the United States. Only 3 percent of Japanese students drop out of high school. The yearly averages for incidences of school vandalism are 0.3 cases per junior high school and 0.15 cases per senior high school. Some have pointed out that increasing numbers of students have difficulty keeping up with the curriculum, but Japanese students continue to score better than their peers from other countries on international scholastic aptitude tests.

Nonetheless, a sense of crisis is widely felt toward education, not only among those directly involved in the system, but among the general public as well. The strong support for reform derives from the totally new perception of the changes occurring in children on the one hand and of the relationship between children and the education system on the other. At first, people regarded the new developments as transient or due to some kind of minor friction. It was when they realized that the situation resulted from structural problems in Japanese society and the educational system itself that the reform movement gained public support.

Initially, examinations began with elementary school. The academic progress of children and their eligibility for higher grades or for graduation were constantly tested in a continuous stream of examinations. The same was true for secondary school and universities. Graduation rolls listed the

5

Ikuo Amano is a professor of educational sociology at Tokyo University. An earlier version of this essay was published in The Japan Foundation Newsletter, *vol. 13, no. 5 (March 1986).*

names in order of achievement, and seating in the classroom was determined by the students' marks. This endless succession of tests was done away with at the elementary school level in the early twentieth century but remained at other levels.

The distinguishing feature of the examination system in Japan, however, is the entrance examination. It has become standard practice for individual secondary schools and universities to prepare their own entrance examinations, a system that is the exception rather than the rule in Europe. The "examination hell," as it is known today, existed in Japan as early as the 1920s, but the cause was not competition to enter higher grades or to graduate, but rather to gain entrance to schools and universities.

Examinations were also introduced for public service and for the professions, including medicine, law, and school teaching. In other words, certification in most of the professions was granted only to people who could demonstrate, through tests, a certain level of knowledge, skill, or competence. Similarly, only those who passed the government examinations were eligible to become senior public servants. These screening tests were closely linked with the education system, moreover, and only students whose school background was sufficiently outstanding were exempted from taking them. Some of the tests were open only to university students.

The graduates of the Imperial universities, founded in 1886 to train the bureaucratic corps for the central government, were a case in point. Graduates from these universities (there were seven in 1945) enjoyed various advantages in finding employment. Special consideration was gradually extended, in varying degrees, to graduates of some other higher and secondary educational institutions.

Educational Credentialism

The custom whereby the state granted various privileges to the graduates of certain prestigious institutions of secondary and higher education eventually gave rise to the phenomenon that is known today as *gakureki shugi,* or what I shall call "educational credentialism." Essentially it refers to the high priority placed on a person's academic background by government organizations, companies, and society in general.

Educational credentialism became entrenched first in the civil service. In 1887, when the Japanese government established its system for hiring public officials, the factors given the greatest weight were the school from which the candidate had graduated and his results in the civil service examinations. While the basic idea was to ensure that middle- and high-ranking bureaucrats were selected fairly through open and competitive government-sponsored examinations, certain candidates were exempted from the exams if their educational credentials were sufficiently illustrious. Educational credentials, especially if they included graduation from an Imperial university, also had an important effect on pay and promotion after hiring.

Educational background was crucial for those who sought to enter the medical profession or become secondary school teachers; if the candidates had graduated from certain government-accredited schools, they were exempted from the qualifying exams and automatically granted professional certification. However, educational credentialism did not take root in society simply because it was the norm in hiring public servants or certifying professionals. Only when it became important in the hiring of white-collar workers in the private sector did it become an overwhelming concern.

The new jobs in the bureaucracy, the professions, and private businesses were created in the process of Japan's modernization and industrialization. They carried high prestige and provided access to wealth and power. The fact that educational credentials were the basic qualification for engaging in these occupations goes far to explain why a person's educational background is still considered a major indicator of his social standing even outside officialdom and the corporate world.

The words *gakureki shugi* and *gakureki shakai* ("educational credential society") only came into common use in the 1960s. But the phenomenon had existed since the early part of the 1920s, and had become one of the most important ways of defining a person's status and prestige in Japanese society.

Equality of Opportunity

In examining the relationships between the education system, the examination system, and educational credentialism, a key element to keep in mind is equality of opportunity. Examinations may be decisive in employment and promotion. But without equal access to education, the education system would be incapable of inspiring young people or functioning as a ladder up to the higher rungs of society. Fortunately, the far-reaching changes brought about by the Meiji Restoration of 1868 and later by Japan's defeat in 1945 contributed to making the system more open.

The first change, made in the wake of the Meiji Restoration, was the dismantling of the country's feudal status hierarchy. Schooling was made available to all, regardless of class or lineage. Of course, education at the advanced levels was still very expensive. On the other hand, even the children of the wealthiest families could not enter the higher level schools, particularly the government-run higher schools or universities that promised elite careers, unless they passed the grueling entrance examinations. It was this rigorous system of entrance examinations which made access to education equitable. After the defeat in World War II, during the period of the Allied Occupation, Japan underwent its second great social transformation. The social structure became more fluid as a result of pervasive land reform and the dismantling of the *zaibatsu* (business combines). Under the slogan of "democratization of education," the authorities introduced the new "6–3–3–4" education system (six years of elementary school, three years of junior high school,

15

another three years of senior high school, and four years of university education). Compulsory education was extended from six to nine years. The prewar secondary schools, which had been organized in a multitrack system, were rationalized and merged into three-year senior high schools. The higher education system, which had consisted of a few universities and many other short-term institutions, was also reformed into a new system of four-year universities and two-year junior colleges. Universities, which had totaled only 48 in the year 1945, increased to 201 by 1950. This made the education system even more open and provided more opportunities for access.

Obtaining this passport required some financial wherewithal. But the prime requirement was intellectual ability and individual effort. It was possible for an intelligent child, diligent and strongly motivated but born into a poor family, to eventually acquire distinguished educational credentials. In the early stages of rapid modernization and industrialization, many people did in fact rise to the highest levels of society in just this way. The examination system stimulated their aspirations, and the intensity of their desire to succeed in turn supported the diligence and hard work required for academic achievement.

The school as a competitive arena was regarded by society, and particularly by enterprises and government offices, as a highly effective system for training and selecting able manpower. As long as the children's achievements were gauged impartially and objectively by the schools, there was no need to measure their ability again upon hiring. Educational credentials provided an indicator of an individual's diligence and ability and both industry and the government placed great weight on these credentials in basic personnel policy. This had the effect of intensifying competition within the school system.

The Japanese education system was very effective in meeting the needs of modernization and industrialization and is often portrayed as one of the country's greatest successes. When the competition generated by the examination system for acquisition of academic credentials became overheated, however, the dark side of the system began to reveal itself.

Entrance Examinations and Educational Credentialism

In Japan, competition at all levels of school education was already severe in the 1890s. This was the reason that entrance examinations and examinations for eligibility to higher grades were eliminated in the nation's elementary schools at the beginning of the 1900s. That was as far as the reform went, however. Schools educating students who would occupy the top rungs of the social ladder considered examinations an unavoidable gauntlet that students must run to separate the able from the rest.

The most serious problem involved the entrance examinations. Japan   20 had borrowed the examination system from Europe, but not without changes. In Europe, students who score acceptably on national standardized exams given at the conclusion of one level of education are automatically guaranteed admittance to the next level. The emphasis, in other words, is not on *entrance* examinations. In Japan, however, individual schools began to use examinations to select which students could enter their halls.

In the days when the education system was still not yet well established, some schools found that they were not receiving a sufficient number of students whose ability was above a certain level from the lower levels of education, and they introduced entrance examinations as a "temporary" means of selecting students to meet their standards. This practice continued even after the education system took firm root, eventually becoming one of the key characteristics of the Japanese education system. The importance of entrance examinations was further inflated because the quantitative expansion of the secondary and higher education was not rapid enough to accommodate the sudden large increase of students who sought to proceed to higher levels.

Although education was an important tool for achieving rapid industrialization and modernization, the government could devote only limited human and material resources to the building of the system. Emphasis was placed on achieving universal compulsory elementary education, and this goal was rapidly achieved (by 1902, over 90 percent of eligible children were enrolled). On the other hand, too few secondary schools and universities and colleges were built to respond to the rapidly growing demand for education advancement that was the natural outcome of universal elementary education.

In addition, in an effort to allocate its limited resources effectively, the government supported secondary schools and universities on a selective basis, according to the degree of their importance to the modernization and industrialization effort. This created great disparities in human and material resources among educational institutions which, at least on paper, were at the same level. This, in turn, made people discriminate among schools in accordance with this allocation of resources, and as a consequence a clear hierarchical system based on social prestige came into being. Among universities, for example, the Imperial universities ranked highest, followed by other government-run universities, and then by the private universities.

These two factors—the paucity of institutions of secondary and higher education and their stratification—ensured that an increasingly competitive entrance examination system would remain a permanent feature of Japanese education. The system has produced phenomena that surely exist only in Japan, such as large numbers of students who failed in one try to pass the university entrance exams to the school of their choice and who are studying for another try (known as *ronin,* after the masterless samurai of old), the proliferation of less selective private schools, and the flourishing cram-school industry.

These distortions produced by overcompetition were already apparent 25 in the 1920s. The government, concerned about programs that laid too much importance on preparation for entrance examinations, directed all schools to be more moderate. In 1927, entrance exams for secondary schools were done away with and an attempt was made to introduce basic reforms into the entrance exam system for universities and colleges.

However, the flames of desire for educational credentials and higher social status had been fanned; as long as they remained alight, it would be impossible to eliminate the entrance examinations. The obstacles posed by the heavy reliance on educational credentials in industry and the government became a social problem in the 1920s, and carried over without resolution to the postwar period.

Far from cooling down, the excessive competition grew even more intense after World War II. A series of social reforms implemented by the occupation authorities brought mobility back to Japan's social structure. This mobility, together with the reformed education system emphasizing democracy and equality, provided further motivation for people to seek better educational credentials and aim for the upper rungs of the social ladder.

The recovery and rapid growth of Japan's economy was partly responsible for the sharp increase of the numbers of students going on to senior high school or college. Japan's industrial structure underwent enormous changes during the process of rapid economic growth, and these were accompanied by great strides in technological innovation. Private enterprises, especially in the secondary sector, experienced remarkable growth, and the demand for university graduates increased rapidly. Opportunities to enter the upper strata of society were abundant. Defeated in World War II and in the throes of revolutionary changes in the educational system and other aspects of its society, Japan once again became a "land of opportunity," and there were many success stories, just as there had been after the Meiji Restoration.

This new wave of rising aspirations made the competition in the entrance examinations even more intense than before the war. First of all, the number of competitors tremendously increased. In 1935, 19 percent of those who had completed compulsory education (six years of schooling) went on to secondary school. Only 3 percent of those who had completed compulsory schooling went on to college. The competition then was among a very small elite. After the war, the scale expanded tremendously: The corresponding figures for 1960 were 58 percent and 10 percent respectively, and for 1980, 94 percent and 37 percent.

Even when nearly 95 percent of junior high school graduates go on   30
to senior high school, they must take entrance exams, and this means an unavoidable ordeal for virtually every fifteen-year-old. The same may be said for almost all of the 70 percent of students at general high schools (those schools which emphasize academic subjects, as opposed to commercial and technical ones). The curriculum offered at general high schools, moreover, is designed in such a way that the main emphasis is on preparation for

university entrance examinations. Passing the university entrance exams is the chief educational concern of most senior high schools.

Another important reason why the competition has grown more fierce than it was before the war is that the stratified structure of secondary schools and universities has remained basically unchanged. In fact, despite the postwar reform of the educational system, stratification became even more rigid as more and more senior high schools and universities were built to meet the rapidly increasing number of students seeking higher education. The progress of stratification was particularly marked in the case of universities and colleges, their numbers jumping from 48 in 1945 to 201 in 1950. In 1980 there were 446 four-year universities and colleges in Japan. Most of these newly founded institutions are private. Often they are insufficiently endowed and possess few sources of income other than the tuition paid by the students. These schools form the bottom strata of higher education.

After the war, all universities, old and new, were officially ranked equally. Corporations, too, abolished the practice of starting-pay differentials determined by the rank of the school or university of the new employee. Nevertheless, the ranking of universities has not disappeared. A small group of prestigious universities with traditions going back to before the war, including the former Imperial universities, continue to occupy the top of the hierarchy. Most of the institutions established after the war, therefore, suffer from very low social regard.

The personnel policy of businesses—the most important employers of university graduates after the war—has contributed largely to maintaining and expanding the stratification of higher education. The starting-pay differentials may have been dropped, but corporations adopted the policy of preferring graduates of certain first-class or prestige universities in hiring new workers. This forged an explicit connection between first-class universities and top-ranking corporations.

In Japan there is a very close correlation between the size of a corporation and the wages its employees receive, as well as their career stability and social prestige. It is natural, then, that people seek employment at large corporations. Moreover, thanks to the connection just mentioned, the competition for jobs at these large companies begins with the race to enter the prestigious universities at the top of the educational hierarchy. The entrance exams of the universities, then, are part, a kind of first phase, of the scramble to secure a stable career.

The End of Rapid Economic Growth

Even after the end of the postwar period of rapid economic growth, the structure of interrelationships between the overheated "examination hell," stratified educational institutions, and educational credentialism has not fundamentally changed. But the attitudes of the children and young people who

35

are being educated and who take part in the examination competition have changed greatly. In particular, it would seem that their aspirations to receive a good education and climb the ladder of success are weakening. Paradoxically, it was the remarkable economic growth that began in the 1960s that is responsible for this change.

Rapid economic growth brought to Japan affluence such as it had never before experienced. Moreover, this prosperity was enjoyed not just by a few but by all the people. It is well known that of the advanced nations Japan is among the top in terms of equality in the areas of income, consumption, and education. Egalitarianism pervades the popular consciousness, so much so that today by far the majority of Japanese people believe they are members of the middle class.

The affluence, needless to say, is a product of the effort and hard work of people who fervently aspired toward more income and higher social status. But, as attitudinal surveys have shown, the signs of declining aspirations became apparent once Japan became affluent in the mid-1970s. The aspirations of parents, teachers, businessmen—those who belong to the older generations—remain as high as before. They prize hard work and diligence as important virtues and expect their children and young people to follow suit. Many young Japanese are still eager to do so, but the statistics show that their numbers are steadily decreasing.

The more affluent and egalitarian a society becomes—one might say the less hungry the people are—the weaker their motivation for success becomes. After the oil crisis of 1973, it became apparent that rapid economic growth was coming to an end and that Japan was in the process of becoming a mature society. This meant that opportunities to move into higher social classes would grow fewer. It gradually became clear that hard work was not always sure to gain the expected reward. For the first time in its one-hundred-year history of modernization, Japan is ceasing to be a land of opportunity and success stories, and young Japanese keenly feel this change.

In the past, a university diploma ensured its holder prestige, power, and much higher wages than the average (although the degree of these benefits differed according to the university in question). Now that nearly 40 percent of young people go on to college, prestige and privilege is no longer at the disposal of every university graduate. Already there is a growing number of very well-educated college graduates who will not receive promotion to managerial positions, or who cannot even find white-collar jobs.

A university education, particularly at a prominent university, is still   40
an effective passport to employment in a large corporation, of course, but having entered such a corporation no longer necessarily ensures a stable career with lifetime employment and promotion and wage increases by seniority. With the economy in a phase of slow growth, competition among corporations has become fierce both domestically and internationally. The struggle for survival is intensifying not only among corporations but also within them. The white-collar employees and engineers of large corporations, who by now

are almost all college graduates, face a severe battle for a few managerial posts, and the chances of winning are getting slimmer.

In other words, the rewards promised by academic credentials are no longer certain. As it is becoming clear that higher wages, greater prestige and power do not necessarily follow from academic credentials, young people's aspiration[s] to aim for the upper rungs of society or to undergo the grueling competition for academic credentials are naturally cooling down.

The "Cooling Down" Phenomenon

Despite weakening aspirations, no basic change has occurred in the educational structure so far. With few exceptions, students still have to pass entrance exams to enter senior high schools or universities. Because of the stratification of senior high schools and universities, moreover, the schools cannot revamp their curriculums, which are designed to prepare students for entrance exams and to put as many students into the good senior high schools or universities as possible. Parents will not let the schools do that. But children and young people are of another mind.

Of course, there are still many children who will study very hard to pass the exams to a prestigious school in hopes of gaining a high position in society. And school education takes it for granted that children are strongly oriented to upward mobility. As a whole, however, such children are becoming a minority.

The existence of a pyramid, the top of which is occupied by a handful of first-rate, prestigious universities, is a fact of life. But the number of places at the top is limited, and the race to gain one of them is harsh. Many children enter the competition with alacrity, and many parents encourage them at every step of the way. But as they proceed through each stage, battling their way from elementary school to junior high school, and then to senior high school, the aspirations of many young people and their parents as well may suddenly cool, for the toll they must pay is heavy.

In order to enter a first-rate university, it is most advantageous to enter   45
a six-year privately run secondary school. Such schools are something like prep schools in the United States or public schools in Britain. The competition to enter them is among the most severe. Another option is to attend one of the few high schools, run by the local governments or privately, that are well known for producing graduates who pass the entrance exams to the top universities. The competition to enter these schools is also fierce.

The children who attend such schools not only study very hard exclusively to prepare for entrance exams; they also repeatedly take mock exams prepared by the exam-preparation companies. The results of these tests are scored by computer and sent to the children and their parents. Like it or not, the computer data tell them exactly where the child's level of academic ability stands in comparison with other children. Many students give up the idea of going to a good university if their showing in such exams is poor.

The examination system, which once greatly encouraged the aspirations of children and parents, has begun to play the role of "cooling down" their hopes. Ironically, the more emphasis the teachers and the schools place on examination-centered curriculums and the harder they push children to study to beat the competition for entrance to better schools, the lower the children's aspirations are becoming.

As long as children want to go to a senior high school or college, they cannot avoid taking part in the entrance examination competition. Not only do their teachers and parents expect them to participate, the school education system itself gives top priority to that eventuality. Students who have little desire to gain better marks or acquire higher academic credentials suffer a serious dilemma at school, and this is the source of the problems that are endemic in junior and senior high schools today, especially the former. Well over 90 percent of junior high school graduates go on to senior high school today, which means almost every junior high school graduate is on track to take entrance exams.

One of the reasons, and probably the greatest reason, for the pathological phenomena occurring in the schools today, including violence and "bullying," is the gap between the changed values and attitudes of young people and the unchanged orientation of the older generation. The educational system and institutions, which are maintained and run by the latter, have changed little.

Children's aspirations are no longer directed solely at gaining academic   50
credentials and higher ranks in the social hierarchy. What the schools must do now is to establish new objectives for education that will nurture and encourage other aspirations. Reforms in the basic structure of the school and educational system are clearly needed, for without them, little improvement can be made in the examination system centered around entrance exams or in the problems of academic credentialism.

Thinking About the Text

1. Outline and summarize Amano's essay. What are his main points? What is his thesis?

2. Compare Amano's account of the development of secondary and college education in Japan with an account in a general encyclopedia, such as the *Encyclopedia Americana* or *Encyclopedia Britannica*. How do the two accounts differ? How might you account for the differences?

3. Amano appears to emphasize the negative factors in Japanese education, while Merry White (p. 95) emphasizes the positive ones. Why do you think this is so? In class, debate the strengths and weaknesses of the Japanese educational system, with half of the class representing Amano's point of view and half representing White's.

Thinking About Culture

4. Amano is largely concerned with the Japanese demand for accreditation. But *our* society too requires members of some professions (for instance, physicians and lawyers) to pass state qualifying exams, or at least (in the case of elementary and secondary school teachers) to have completed certain kinds of degree programs. Do you think we would be a healthier society if these requirements were abolished? Or does it depend on the field? For instance, should physicians and electricians have to pass qualifying examinations, but not teachers? Why?

5. Amano asserts that in Japan "passing the university entrance exams is the chief educational concern of most senior high schools" (para. 30). What was the chief educational concern in your high school? By the way, although colleges and universities in the United States do not have their own entrance exams, most of them do have academic requirements of some sort, and they take into account such criteria as an applicant's SAT scores and rank in class. Explain whether such requirements shaped the educational concern of your school, and if they did, whether it was for better or for worse.

6. Amano claims, "The more affluent and egalitarian a society becomes—one might say the less hungry the people are—the weaker their motivation for success becomes" (para. 38). Discuss this statement in terms of both societies, and determine what evidence we would need to bear this out. What evidence does Amano provide to support his claim for Japan? Do you think the statement is true of the United States? Support your opinion.

Shinobu Yoshioka

Talkin' 'bout
My Generation

Whenever I hear someone mention Japan's baby boomers (known in Japan as the *dankai*, or group, generation), I think back to a conversation I had many years ago.

It was the summer of 1976 at a rock concert in fashionable Shibuya. The band had the latest sound equipment, but its talent was no match for its technology. Bored, I left my seat and wandered out to the lobby, where

Shinobu Yoshioka, born in 1948, is a member of the post–World War II baby boom generation. He is a well-known essayist in his country. This selection originally appeared in the April 1993 issue of Look Japan, *a government-sponsored magazine.*

I struck up a conversation with two young girls who had found the concert as thrilling as I had.

They had attended the same high school in Sendai, a town about 350 kilometers north of Tokyo. They had run away from home in their second year, they said, because they were sick of school, and had come to Tokyo in search of adventure.

When I met them, the two had been in Tokyo for three months. They had lied about their ages to get part-time jobs, were sharing a tiny apartment, and from time to time went out to concerts like the one we were at.

I told them I thought they must be having the time of their lives.   5

Safety Net

"Your generation had it good," one of the girls answered. "When you ran away from home, there was rock music, underground theater, demonstrations, all kinds of things—you could do whatever you wanted.

"Our generation has to walk a tightrope," she continued. "And there's nothing to catch us if we fall. We lose our balance, we die. You guys might have walked a tightrope too, but you had a safety net below. If you didn't like it up on the rope, you could always dive down and let yourself be caught in midair. You could do whatever you wanted to."

She had hit home. So *that's* how we look in the eyes of someone ten years younger, I thought.

My generation, of course, had an entirely different understanding of itself. The *dankai*—those 11 million born from 1947 to 1950—had many names, some of which are probably familiar: the baby boomers, the Beatles generation, the anti-Vietnam generation. We were also dubbed the Zenkyoto generation, named after a student organization active in the antiwar and antiestablishment movements of the 1960s.

The Zenkyoto demonstrations did much to discredit the established   10
political system, but our generation was more than just a new political force. We began new trends in music, theater, art, and social customs, trends that defied the existing structure of authority and social conventions. In those days, nothing was worse than a willingness to capitulate to the "system" and adopt its narrow expectations.

Consequently, we tried our hands at everything. Singers of traditional *enka*,° who had had to put in years of hard work climbing the rigid, hierarchical ladder before they were allowed to perform publicly, suddenly found themselves displaced by our barely rehearsed bands and spontaneous concerts. Some put on plays in renovated basements or tents set up in vacant lots, ridiculing the empty and imitative formalism of Japan's commercial theater.

---

enka: Sentimental songs. [Editors' note]

Others in my generation took off nearly penniless to wander about in foreign countries—their adventurousness helped make travel abroad commonplace.

The two girls were saying that these experiences, of which most of us are secretly proud, were only possible because we had a safety net underneath us. It might have looked like we were performing a dangerous tightrope routine, but a fall would have done us no harm.

The girls had a point. When the *dankai* generation was growing up, the chaos and confusion of the early postwar years had given way to spectacular economic growth. Japanese-made textiles, toys, cameras, and transistor radios had easy access to wide-open American and South Asian markets. This period of economic growth engendered confidence in liberal politics and democratic government, and it also created a willingness to forgive the unruliness of the younger generation.

Dropping out—of school or society—was nothing to fear. During antiwar demonstrations, we might clash with the riot police, but even if we were arrested it did not worry us much. If we did not fit the groove, so much the better.

I still clearly recall the first issue of *Arubaito News,* a daily listing of part-time jobs. Founded when the antiwar and Zenkyoto movements were at their zenith, the magazine's perusers—for we rarely bought it—were mostly students and dropouts. We optimistically assumed that we did not have to go to the trouble of finding a real job to feed ourselves. 15

The runaway girls told me that the age of such optimism was over. Indeed, one of the best-selling novels that year depicted the social disarray that would occur when our generation had grown old. The phrase "*dankai* generation" was taken from the title of this book, and the phrase became the newest name for our generation.

Do Watchya Want

One of the girls continued: "I want to hurry up and get married. When I realize that I'm just enjoying myself and not doing what everybody else is doing, it's scary. Our generation does not want to be left behind. If you get married, you're doing what everybody else is, so you can feel secure."

From the late 1970s through the 1980s, "high tech" and "rapid growth" were the watchwords of the Japanese economy. Japan was an internationally recognized economic power; the majority of its people considered themselves middle class. These girls were growing up in an economic environment that should have given them even more freedom than we had.

But instead of doing whatever they wanted, they worried about being "left behind." People only ten years younger than I were indifferent to politics, even slightly conservative. They traveled abroad on package tours or with a closed group of friends. Their music and drama did not aim to change society, but instead were exaggerations of commercialized, social trends.

Between my generation and the next, attitudes toward change took a 20

180-degree turn. For us, changes in society and the individual were exciting and intrinsically valuable. For the younger generation, however, change is frightening and the source of insecurity.

Of course, they have good reason to regard change with fear. The authorities responded to our antiwar demonstrations with arrests by the thousand, to all intents and purposes snuffing out the movement. Control over junior high and high school students reached new heights. Rules were laid down for everything, from what the students could bring to school to what they could wear and how they could cut their hair.

Infighting erupted among and within factions of student movements, and the senseless violence that ensued convinced the younger generation that no matter how hard they tried things would not change. Their fear of committing themselves to political principles begins to make sense, too.

Both generations grew up under favorable economic conditions, but it is our attitudes toward change that divide us.

In talking about change, the U.S. presidential election comes to mind. Younger voters were particularly strong supporters of Bill Clinton, choosing his emphasis on change over Bush's defense of the status quo.

If a man like Bill Clinton had run for public office in Japan, he would   25
not have won, and would certainly not have appealed to Japan's younger voters. To them, the status quo is essential; change is simply not on their agenda.

The Gap Narrows

The new generation tends to see change, in society and themselves, as dangerous. But actually, our generation was not much different. We, the antiwar generation, the Zenkyoto generation—we, who joined in demonstrations and meetings and even took over university buildings—we too preferred the status quo.

I attended a private university in Tokyo. There were about fifty students in my foreign language class, but only five participated in the antiwar or student movements. It seems that the whole generation has been characterized by the activities of 10 percent. The radical and highly visible minority overshadowed the rest of the dankai; but now that we have grown older, the majority has won out.

The *dankai* generation, now in their forties, has adapted to the system, and is invested in maintaining the status quo. But this shift did not occur overnight; it was the other side of our character from the beginning.

I believe the *dankai* generation has shed its rebellious outer layer and has put its faith again in the world's rules and conventions. The number of posts available—whether in business or the bureaucracy—cannot keep up with the sheer size of the *dankai* generation, and the competition among us is fierce.

Our life changes have tremendous influence over the rest of the popula-   30 tion. In each stage in our lives, we have been targeted as a huge consumer market. As teenagers, we were the jeans market. Later, we were the "new family" market, and the household furniture industry, the interior design industry, and family-style restaurants flourished because of us. Even now we are seen as a huge population of middle-aged consumers with large disposable incomes and a willingness to spend.

In the 1980s, another issue suddenly grabbed Japan's attention—the problem of an aging society. In 1970, the average lifespan for Japanese men was 69.3 years; for women, 74.7. Now the numbers are 76.1 for men and 82.1 for women.

Everybody is asking whether Japan will be able to hold on to its vitality when the *dankai* generation, the largest segment of the population, reaches old age in the twenty-first century. Sick and bedridden senior citizens are a serious drain on financial resources, and when the huge *dankai* generation enters the ranks of the elderly, the problem will worsen.

Just the other day, I received a questionnaire in the mail from a think tank asking me, as one of those who will contribute to Japan's top-heavy elderly population, how I planned to get along in my old age. It was the tenth time I'd received one of those things. I crumpled this one into a ball and tossed it into the wastebasket.

"What a stupid question," I mumbled to myself. "Look at the U.S. Look at India. Aging of the population has had nothing to do with the weakening of those societies."

But as I stared at the wastebasket, a more rebellious thought hit me.   35

Just watch, I thought. We were never ones to take things lying down, even if we *have* become more conventional in recent years. And no matter what they say about old folks being bedridden, we never before took affronts to our freedom lying down. I doubt if we are going to take our old age lying down, either.

Thinking About the Text

1. Overall, what seems to be Yoshioka's attitude toward the younger generation exemplified by the two young women with whom he talks? Cite specific passages in the text to support your opinion.

2. In reading Yoshioka's description of "his generation," did you find yourself making comparisons to American "baby boomers"? Explain.

Thinking About Culture

3. Yoshioka discusses the idea of generation (as in the *dankai*, or "group," generation) as it is popularly conceived in Japan. Americans similarly invoke

the idea of generation, usually for marketing purposes, as in Generation X. What if anything characterizes your generation? What might be some problems with characterizing all members of a generation this way?

4. Yoshioka describes the revolutionary period of his youth with some nostalgia. Your parents are likely to be in that generation—interview them, or others of that generation, and compare the tone of their memories with Yoshioka's.

Chapter 4

Courtship, Love, and Marriage

"Love and marriage," a midcentury American song lyric says, "go together like a horse and carriage." But horses and carriages were no longer in use even when the song was popular, and even in horse-and-buggy days this combination was not inevitable. In America, love is seen both as a kind of social glue keeping families together and as an arena for individual self-fulfillment. These contradictions have never been resolved.

For various cultural, historical, and religious reasons, Americans have come to see romantic love, sex, and marriage as a kind of package. In the mid–nineteenth century, when the middle-class home represented a sanctuary from the chaotic industrializing world, the husband-wife relationship grew ever more important as the extended, three-generation family yielded to the two-generation nuclear family. The romantic notions of courtly love, borrowed from the medieval and Renaissance courts of Europe, were never intended to represent marital love, but these conventions were adapted to the socially approved monogamous and legal relationship which became the bedrock of the family in America. The restriction of love, and sex, to the marriage bond was also supported by religious and cultural codes, though the codes never completely resembled the reality of people's lives.

A recent issue of *CanCam,* a teenage girls' magazine published in Japan, focused its monthly pull-out manual on sexual technique and performance. It included an article on how to enjoy a love hotel (mostly discreet, upscale, luxurious houses of assignation with by-the-hour rental rooms in a variety of styles and fantasies, rather like love theme parks). Detailed discussions of female orgasms, sensual methods for applying condoms, and ways of prolonging one's partner's excitement are also included. Nothing about "just saying no," or "saving virginity for the wedding night," nor is there much about the emotional aspects of sexual relationships. A month or so later, the pull-out manual in the same magazine featured a specialized discussion of modern forms of *o-miai,* the formal meeting between prospective spouses, leading to what used to be called an "arranged marriage." (Very few marriages today are said to be arranged, and almost all young couples say they married for love—even if love followed a meeting of this sort.) The assumption is that busy professional people have little time to date or socialize, and that *o-miai* are necessary—rather like dating services in the United States, or blind dates set up by mutual friends. How to conduct oneself, what to wear, how to appraise the gentleman and his family—and how to use computer *o-miai* services (also described in the article by Ito, Murray, and Loveless on p. 139) in lieu of more traditional go-betweens, are the stuff of this thorough treatment.

Neither description is what an American would expect of Japanese society, yet *both* are representative of trends in love and marriage in modern Japan. Our images of shy, virginal Japanese women and parentally induced marriages, where the hierarchical power of the father is transferred to the husband, are very far from the realities, in spite of the popularity of love songs like Masashi Sada's "The Lordly Marriage Declaration" (p. 145).

While magazines such as *CanCam* may not reflect everyone's realities, they (like American magazines) are created in an interactive relationship with their readers, based on editorial views of what readers can relate to as well as on marketing views of what consumers can be persuaded, and titillated, to want. The content of Japanese magazines in particular is based on deep research on their audience's life-style and aspirations, and the apparent contradiction between open sexuality and modern "arranged" marriage is easily assimilated and noncontroversial among young readers. There are also magazines for and by gay young people in Japan, equally straightforward. The excerpt by Neil Miller (p. 147) provides a brief historical overview of gay and lesbian relationships in Japan, which explains distinctive straight attitudes toward gays and lesbians.

In ancient Japan, at least among the elites, there was a similarly liberal attitude toward sexuality, and court intrigues were based on the assumptions that love is open, available, and fleeting, as we see in the extracts from Sei Shonagon's diary on page 129. (In Europe and America, as in ancient Japan, the elite—and the very poor—were customarily and by economic reality exempted from the morality of common people.)

Before attempting a more thorough description of love and marriage among the young today, it is instructive to see how much these matters have changed in Japan during the living memory of parents and grandparents of the youth targeted as the market for contemporary magazines.

Couples now in their fifties and sixties, who were children during World War II, were most likely introduced by go-betweens (*nakhodo*), who were often friends of their families or employers. Although in urban middle-class families the young people were usually consulted as to their wishes, in more traditional rural families both the young man and the young woman were expected to comply with their parents' choice. In such families, the object of marriage was the perpetuation of the family through the male line, in what anthropologists call the "stem family"—a household ideally composed of an older couple, their eldest son and his wife and children, and any unmarried children of the older couple. This is the "main" family. The younger sons traditionally did not share in the inheritance of the house and land, but instead were established elsewhere in "branch" families. In a land-poor society, this primogeniture functioned to keep family holdings intact through each generation.

What this meant for marriages was that eldest sons' wives were crucial as both future household managers and producers of heirs to the *ie,* or family establishment. They were brought to their husbands' households and trained by their mothers-in-law to the ways of their new families. Often a marriage would not even be recorded in the family register (*koseki*) until the new bride had produced an heir, thus proving her worth to the family.

In the late twentieth century, however, such families are very few, and farmers in particular have a difficult time finding brides willing to endure arduous farm work and dictatorial mothers-in-law. Women are saying no to extended (three-generation) households, and the preferred family is now one without a mother-in-law, or one where the mother-in-law is happy to baby-sit while her daughter-in-law engages in modern white-collar (or pink-collar) employment, away from the farm.

Urban families too have changed. Since—as in the United States—more young people now complete college, the notion of the right age for marriage has been pushed up to accommodate college and several years of work before marriage, and it is common now to wait to marry until one's late twenties. "Marriage credentials" now include both higher education and good employment tracks for men and higher education, some work experience, and a range of artistic and social skills for women.

Young men and women now date, but usually after the high school years, and dating is not necessarily the path to marriage. Some young women, with a pragmatic attitude toward their social life, assemble a "stable" of young men. They say that it is good to have an *asshi-kun* ("leg man") to run errands, a *kaa-man* ("car man") who has wheels to drive her around, and a *kawaikochan* ("cute guy") to be seen with in popular spots. Most young people today (depending on age, region, and social class) have had some sexual experience (by which is meant anything from heavy petting to full sexual intercourse) by the end of high school or early in college years, a vast change from the experience of those now in their later twenties, who in their youth usually did not. American young people too are said to be much more sexually experienced, at much younger ages, than previous generations. While one should be cautious about accepting at face value data based on individuals' reporting their own sexual behavior—particularly in America where some might report more, and others less, than the truth—it is clear that there is a sharp rise in sexual activity, particularly among younger teens, and a concomitant rise in teen pregnancy in America. It is interesting to note that, while the rates of reported sexual activity among teens in America are roughly similar to those of several western European countries, the rates of teen pregnancy in those countries are very much lower than in America. In Japan, a rise in reported sexual activity has not been followed by a rise in reported teen pregnancy. This difference has been related to the fact that American young people also receive much less school-based sex education than do their European counterparts, who are also said to live in less puritanical cultures, where talking about sex is less restricted. Sex education in Japanese schools, however, is limited, and young people now learn about sex from the straightforward curriculum presented in their magazines.

Japan is not, and never has been, a puritanical society with regard to sex. Social relationships may be highly organized, but sexual ones are left to the freedom of privacy (as long as they are not paraded in public). Sexual expressiveness has been part of literature and romance as far back as written history in Japan. There are some limits though, choices which may appear inconsistent to Americans. For instance, there is a taboo against kissing in public, whereas co-bathing with members of the opposite sex (especially within the family) is common. Similarly, there is a prohibition against publishing photographs showing pubic hair, but aggressive sadomasochistic pornography can be bought easily from vending machines in the streets. Of course, Japanese view Western customs and taboos as similarly inconsistent and Americans appear to have made strange choices. While Americans allow magazines to show pubic hair, we see mixed bathing or mixed sleeping arrangements as at least potentially sexual activities and, thus, would find such practices in families doubtful for children's healthy development.

Also, while middle-class Americans expect a blend of emotional, familial, and sexual satisfactions within one relationship—ideally with one's spouse—in Japan, sexual relationships need not be romanticized and love may be separate from marriage (and both men and women may have extramarital romances, though of course discreetly).

As in American society, there are many mixed messages and contradictions in the realm of love and marriage in Japan.

Explorations

1. Define—as they are exhibited in relationships in America, both ideal and real—romance, sexuality, and marriage. Give examples of each, perhaps using a couple you know as evidence for each or all together.

2. A Japanese woman said to her American friend, "Why do Americans always have to be in love?" Do you agree with her observation? Why do you think she made it, and what might you infer about her perspective—and perhaps her experience—from this question?

3. What "mixed messages" did you receive as a child and adolescent from

your parents or other sources about love and marriage, and what might you yourself say to a young person you would advise, for instance to a child of your own?

4. The rules and regulations of dating and sex vary by family, generation, and ethnic group in America. What differences have you noticed among your friends and others of your acquaintance? What is approved for people your age that was not for your parents at this age, or perhaps was not even for an older sibling?

Sei Shonagon

Love in the Tenth Century

To Meet One's Lover

To meet one's lover, summer is indeed the right season. True, the nights are very short, and dawn creeps up before one has had a wink of sleep. Since all the lattices have been left open, one can lie and look out at the garden in the cool morning air. There are still a few endearments to exchange before the man takes his leave, and the lovers are murmuring to each other when suddenly there is a loud noise. For a moment they are certain that they have been discovered; but it is only the caw of a crow flying past in the garden.

In the winter, when it is very cold and one lies buried under the bedclothes listening to one's lover's endearments, it is delightful to hear the booming of a temple gong, which seems to come from the bottom of a deep well. The first cry of the birds, whose beaks are still tucked under their wings, is also strange and muffled. Then one bird after another takes up the call. How pleasant it is to lie there listening as the sound becomes clearer and clearer!

Captain Narinobu

One rainy evening, when the Empress had said that we must all spend the night in the Palace, Shikibu no Omoto and I went to bed in the southern

---

Almost nothing is known about Sei Shonagon, other than that she served as lady-in-waiting to the empress in the last decade of the tenth century, and that she kept a journal that is now called The Pillow Book of Sei Shonagon. *The pillows used in her day were actually headrests made of wood or wicker. Their hollow centers were often used for storing diaries and other personal items. We reprint from* The Pillow Book *a few excerpts concerned with love.*

anteroom. Presently there was a loud knocking at the door. We agreed that it would be a nuisance to have a visitor, and pretended to be asleep. But then someone called my name loudly and I heard the Empress say, "Go and wake her, I'm sure she's only pretending." Lady Hyobu came in and tried to wake me, but I did not stir. Hyobu reported this to the Empress and then went out to the veranda and began a conversation with my visitor. I did not think this would last very long, but the night wore on and still they were chatting away. It seemed fairly certain that the visitor was Narinobu. What on earth could they be discussing all that time? I lay in bed, chuckling to myself—something that the couple on the veranda could hardly have suspected. When dawn came, my visitor finally went home.

"What a terrible man!" I thought, "If he ever comes again, I shall refuse to speak to him. What can they have found to say to each other all night?" Just then Hyobu pushed open the sliding door and came in.

On the following morning she heard Shikibu and me talking in our anteroom and joined us. "A man who comes in such a heavy rainstorm to visit a woman deserves some sympathy," she declared. "However much he may have made her worry and suffer during the past days, surely she should forgive him when he arrives with his clothes all drenched." 5

I wondered what gave her such an idea. If a man has been visiting one night after night and then comes again despite a heavy downpour, it shows that he cannot bear to be separated for even a single evening and one has good reason to be impressed. If, on the other hand, he has made one worry by letting several days go by, one is bound to question his sincerity even if he should choose to appear on a stormy night. But no doubt people have different feelings about these matters.

Narinobu is in fact devoted to a woman who has quick wits and a mind of her own, and who also impresses him as being kindhearted. But he has several other attachments, not to mention his wife, and he cannot come very often. If he chooses such a terrible night to visit the woman, it can only be because he knows people will talk and praise him for his devotion. Of course, if he had no feeling for her at all, he would not bother to invent such stratagems.

Hateful Things

A lover who is leaving at dawn announces that he has to find his fan and his paper. "I know I put them somewhere last night," he says. Since it is pitch dark, he gropes about the room, bumping into the furniture and muttering, "Strange! Where on earth can they be?" Finally he discovers the objects. He thrusts the paper into the breast of his robe with a great rustling sound; then he snaps open his fan and busily fans away with it. Only now is he ready to take his leave. What charmless behavior! "Hateful" is an understatement.

Equally disagreeable is the man who, when leaving in the middle of the night, takes care to fasten the cord of his headdress. This is quite unnecessary; he could perfectly well put it gently on his head without tying the cord. And why must he spend time adjusting his cloak or hunting costume? Does he really think someone may see him at this time of night and criticize him for not being impeccably dressed?

A good lover will behave as elegantly at dawn as at any other time. He   10
drags himself out of bed with a look of dismay on his face. The lady urges him on: "Come, my friend, it's getting light. You don't want anyone to find you here." He gives a deep sigh, as if to say that the night has not been nearly long enough and that it is agony to leave. Once up, he does not instantly pull on his trousers. Instead he comes close to the lady and whispers whatever was left unsaid during the night. Even when he is dressed, he still lingers, vaguely pretending to be fastening his sash.

Presently he raises the lattice, and the two lovers stand together by the side door while he tells her how he dreads the coming day, which will keep them apart; then he slips away. The lady watches him go, and this moment of parting will remain among her most charming memories.

Indeed, one's attachment to a man depends largely on the elegance of his leave-taking. When he jumps out of bed, scurries about the room, tightly fastens his trouser-sash, rolls up the sleeves of his Court cloak, over-robe, or hunting costume, stuffs his belongings into the breast of his robe and then briskly secures the outer sash—one really begins to hate him.

A Young Bachelor

A young bachelor of an adventurous nature comes home at dawn, having spent the night in some amorous encounter. Though he still looks sleepy, he immediately draws his inkstone to him and, after carefully rubbing it with ink, starts to write his next-morning letter. He does not let his brush run down the paper in a careless scrawl, but puts himself heart and soul into the calligraphy. What a charming figure he makes as he sits there by himself in an easy posture, with his robe falling slightly open! It is a plain unlined robe of pure white, and over it he wears a cloak of rose-yellow or crimson. As he finishes his letter, he notices that the white robe is still damp from the dew, and for a while he gazes at it fondly.

Then he makes arrangements for delivering his letter. Instead of calling one of the ladies in attendance, he takes the trouble to get up and select a page boy who seems suitable for the task. Summoning the boy to his side, he whispers his instructions and hands over the letter. The page leaves for the lady's house, and for some time the gentleman watches him disappear in the distance. As he sits there, he quietly murmurs some appropriate passage from the sutras.

Now one of his servants comes to announce that his washing water   15
and morning gruel have been prepared in the neighboring wing. The gentleman goes there, and soon he is leaning against the reading desk and looking

at some Chinese poems, from which he now and then reads out a passage that he has particularly enjoyed—altogether a charming sight.

Presently he performs his ablutions and changes into a white Court cloak, which he wears without any trousers. Thus attired, he starts reciting the sixth scroll of the Lotus Sutra from memory. A pious gentleman indeed—or so one might think, except that at just this moment the messenger returns (he cannot have had far to go) and nods encouragingly to his master, who thereupon instantly interrupts his recitation and, with what might strike one as sinful haste, transfers his attention to the lady's reply.

Annoying Things

A woman is angry with her lover about some trifle and refuses to continue lying next to him. After fidgeting about in bed, she decides to get up. The man gently tries to draw her back, but she is still cross. "Very well then," he says, feeling that she has gone too far. "As you please." Full of resentment, he buries himself under his bedclothes and settles down for the night. It is a cold night and, since the woman is wearing only an unlined robe, she soon begins to feel uncomfortable. Everyone else in the house is asleep, and besides it would be most unseemly for her to get up alone and walk about. As the night wears on, she lies there on her side of the bed feeling very annoyed that the quarrel did not take place earlier in the evening when it would have been easy to leave. Then she begins to hear strange sounds in the back of the house and outside. Frightened, she gently moves over in bed toward her lover, tugging at the bedclothes, whereupon he annoys her further by pretending to be asleep. "Why not be stand-offish a little longer?" he asks her finally.

Thinking About the Text

1. Write an entry of your own, such as Shonagon might write today.

Thinking About Culture

2. Shonagon wrote a thousand years ago. Judging from the entries that we reprint, would you say that human nature has not changed much over the centuries, or that it does not differ much from one side of the globe to the other? Explain.

3. Take one of Shonagon's entries and adapt it to the United States in the 1990s.

Donald Richie

The Japanese Kiss

More than 100 years ago, May 31, 1883, to be exact, the brothers Goncourt wrote in their journal that dinner conversation had been about kissing and that "somebody who had lived for many years in Japan said that the kiss did not exist in Japanese love-making." This early, then, the West knew of Japan's odd relation to the kiss.

Nowadays, of course, Japan is full of it. Just look around—billboards, magazines, TV itself, lots of kissing . . . and more. But this was not always so and even now the kiss in Japan does not quite mean what it does in the West.

To begin with, there wasn't any kissing—at least, not officially. In Japan, as in China, the kiss was invisible. Lovers never kissed in public; family members never kissed. The touching of the lips never became the culturally encoded action it has for so long been in Europe and America.

Nonetheless, some people kissed. One knows this from the erotic prints. Yet, even here, the full kiss is rare. It is almost as though it were an occasional practice, a further perversion, rather than the standard fare it is in the West. Certainly, it was something one did only when carried away by passion itself. And, of a consequence, the kiss remained only, singularly, sexual.

Imagine then the surprise felt by early Japanese abroad who found   5 mothers kissing children and fathers kissing mothers, and all in public. Yukichi Fukuzawa, the later statesman and educator, in the United States in 1860 as a member of the retinue of the Shogun's envoy, has mentioned this surprise in his journals.

As befits a statesman and diplomat, he realized that he was viewing a cultural aberration. This indiscriminate pressing together of mouths did not shock him. He viewed the odd practice somewhat as Americans of the period were viewing Eskimo nose-rubbing.

At the same time, however, kissing was not among the foreign customs introduced into the rapidly modernizing country. Still, kissing was so much a part of the Western world that it kept intruding itself. For example, in modern novels being translated into Japanese. Donald Keene writes of one

---

Donald Richie, born in Ohio in 1924, a graduate of Columbia University, and a former curator of film at the Museum of Modern Art (New York), has lived much of his life in Japan. Among his books are Japanese Cinema: An Introduction *(1990);* The Films of Akira Kurosawa *(1984);* The Japanese Tattoo *(1990);* A Taste of Japan *(1993), from which we reprint an essay on p. 63; and* A Lateral View *(1992), from which this essay, written in 1983, is taken.*

such example in the early translation of Bulwer-Lytton's *Ernest Maltravers*—
fittingly Japanized as *A Springtime Tale of Blossoms and Willows.*

In it the hero speaks of his satisfaction "if I could get one kiss from
those coral lips." This the translator, doubtless after some thought, translated
as "if I could get one lick of your red lips." Though there existed in the new
dictionaries a word for "kiss," the translator preferred *hitoname* (literally,
"one lick"), doubtless feeling that licking was, after all, a more decent activity
than kissing.

In the event, Alice, she of the coral lips, "hid her face with her hands."
In Japanese, however, Arisu "hid her face with her sleeve and though she
would speak could find no words," so affected was she by what had nearly
transpired.

Though the practice of kissing doubtless continued in private, its ap-   10
pearance in public remained condemned. It was even made a statutory
offense, punishable by fine or detention if "committed" in public. What
outrage had occurred to make such a law necessary is not recorded, but it
remained on the books from the early 1920s through 1945, when it was
finally rescinded by the Occupation authorities.

While it was in force it was also invoked. There was a famous incident
in the 1930s when Rodin's celebrated *Le Baiser* was to be exhibited. This
sculpture is of a completely nude couple in the act of kissing. The police
promptly prohibited the proposed exhibition.

The Japanese authorities were scandalized that such a thing would be
shown; the French authorities were scandalized that it would not be. Diplomatic pressure was brought to bear and the police themselves suggested a
solution. As social critic Kimpei Shiba has told it, the authorities said that
the nudity was, of course, permissible—therefore the work might be shown
if just the heads were in some way muffled, perhaps if a cloth were wrapped
around them.

It was not until after the Pacific War that the Rodin was seen in Japan.
Now it is on permanent display, to be seen anytime by anyone, on the plaza
in front of the Tokyo Museum of Western Art in Ueno. Its appearance,
however, should not be taken as indication that the kiss in Japan has (in
Western terms) been entirely normalized.

Indeed, kissing has only with difficulty become even a semiaccepted
convention. Take, for example, the difficulties occasioned by its public
debut—in the movies.

Before the war, of course, all kissing scenes were routinely cut from   15
foreign films—at great peril to their continuity. Hero and heroine would
look deeply into each other's eyes. They would move closer and closer
together. Then they would snap apart with a suddenness that ought to have
set their teeth rattling.

Now, however, post-1945, with Western ways loose, indeed rampant,
within the country, the time of the kiss had come. In 1946 the Daiei Motion
Picture Company planned "the first kiss scene in any Japanese film." It was
to be included in a picture appropriately named *A Certain Night's Kiss.* At

the last moment, however, Daiei lost its nerve. The director made obscure the important event by having his heroine coyly open her umbrella at the crucial point.

The honors consequently went to a Shochiku film, *Twenty-Year-Old Youth,* where there was an appropriately shameless kiss, right on the lips. An indication of how little kissing was accepted is seen in the degree of sensation which this osculation occasioned. The press wrote of nothing else. Was this kiss "merely commercial" or was it "artistically motivated"? Was it "hygienic"? Did it have a "sexual motive"? And, was it "Japanese or not"?

No agreement was possible but a majority decided against its being hygienic. For some time after, kiss scenes were faked, and shot from an angle where the fakery would not be apparent. Or, if that proved impossible, then the principals would wear touched up gauze over the lips for the dirty event.

Even now there is the feeling, in public entertainments at any rate, that the kiss is somehow not entirely Japanese. It is telling that the only thoroughly accepted screen kiss in the postwar era was a "foreign" one. This was in a film called *A Brilliant Revenge.* The long on-screen kiss was occasioned by the performance of a foreign drama. Since all Japanese were pretending to be foreigners it was perfectly proper, in fact in character, for them to spend periods of time with their lips glued to each other.

The discrimination continues. There is, for example, a perfectly good 20 Japanese word for "kiss." It is *seppun.* Yet, it is rarely heard. Instead, most young Japanese (those doing most of the kissing) use *kissu,* if they talk about it at all. It is felt that the use of English sanitizes by endistancing. The word becomes a euphemism. It is like (in all languages) calling the toilet a hand-washing place. It indicates that though a word is somehow necessary, the designated action is not quite socially acceptable.

The reason that we in the West need not feel funny about kissing and that the Japanese do is that we have a much larger kissing repertoire. We have, as it were, domesticated the act.

We kiss just everyone. Mother, father, brother, sister, wife, children—no one is safe. The Japanese, however, still think of the kiss as an exotic adjunct to the act of making love. For a couple to kiss in public would be for them to publicly indulge in foreplay. And as for kissing Mom at train station or airport lobby, well. . . .

Thus the social role that kissing takes in Japan is narrow. It does not mean affection or reverence or sorrow or consolation or any of the other things it can mean in the West. It means just one thing and that is the reason for the ambivalence which surrounds it.

Thinking About the Text

1. How would you characterize Richie's tone? Is it academic, heavy-handed, genial, ironic, or something else? Don't confine yourself to a one-word description. Point to specific passages that led you to your characterization.

2. Write a brief essay—in Richie's style, if you wish—on "The American Kiss."

3. Do you think there should be limits to what is accepted in the way of public erotic kissing or other erotic behavior? For instance, does any behavior of any rock groups, or individual stars, strike you as inappropriate? Why?

Thinking About Culture

4. Writing in 1945, Emil Ludwig in *Of Life and Love* said, "The kiss in a motion picture, in close-up, impresses one as even more repellent than the showing of the sexual act. Lovers, sitting next to each other and watching such things from orchestra seats, will in embarrassment unclasp their hands" (p. 32). Is it conceivable that anyone today would respond thus to a filmed kiss? But what about other erotic actions? How liberated in fact are we? (Have you seen in films or television programs erotic actions that you think are better left unshown?) How are the lines drawn between PG-13, G, and R movies?

5. In paragraph 22 Richie says, "We kiss just everyone. Mother, father, brother, sister, wife, children—no one is safe." Probably even within America, ethnic groups vary in the amount of social kissing. How acceptable is it, in your group, for a mother to kiss her college-age son at the airport? For a father to do so? For a grandmother or grandfather? How about relatives kissing a college-age daughter or granddaughter?

6. Are you familiar with any culture that today regards public erotic kissing more or less as the Japanese (according to Richie's essay) regarded it? If so, indicate what sorts of kissing, if any, are acceptable, and what sorts are not.

Takashi Watanabe

Young Japanese Confront Social Taboos

While Japanese society is often characterized as profoundly conservative, some taboos are fading rapidly—for example, the traditional aversion to public displays of private feelings.

Takashi Watanabe is a staff writer for the Nikkei Weekly, *where this article on social taboos appeared. The* Nikkei *is a daily national newspaper focused on business and the economy, similar to the* Wall Street Journal. *The weekly edition summarizes trends.*

On street corners, at station ticket barriers, and even on trains, kissing couples are becoming an increasingly common sight in Japan. Some observers suggest the growing number of love scenes appearing on television and in magazines may be influencing real life.

Among the various schools of thought about such behavior, there are those who encourage people to openly express affection for each other. However, many Japanese still find such public displays distasteful, while others dismiss the trend as just another passing fad.

For the time being, Japanese society seems divided over the question of whether such inhibitions are dying a permanent death, or just being temporarily shelved. Many young people, in particular, have developed very different attitudes from those of their parents.

Lack of Embarrassment

Koji Nishihara (a pseudonym), twenty-six, and Yukie Kawashima (also a pseudonym), twenty-two, both office employees, have been dating for over a year now. As they both have flexible working hours, one sees the other off to work almost every morning.

At 9:00 A.M., they meet near their offices in the trendy shopping area of Shibuya in Tokyo for a stroll through the park. On one such morning, Kawashima starts work earlier, so it is her boyfriend's turn to walk her to the office. At an intersection just before the company's main entrance, they kiss.

The good-bye kiss has become an important part of their everyday routine together. Kawashima admits that, at first, she was a little surprised by Koji's lack of embarrassment, but now she feels that it would be strange to say good-bye without kissing. Although they both know their work colleagues may see them kissing, the young couple says the risk is part of the thrill.

"The fact that he is prepared to risk being seen by his colleagues proves to me how much he loves me," she explains.

University student, Ryoichi Aida (a pseudonym), twenty-one, is not bothered in the least by the idea that people might be watching—as far as he is concerned, showing affection by kissing is perfectly natural. Aida's relaxed attitude may have something to do with the seven-and-a-half years he spent studying in the United States. He says he finds something strange in the Japanese attitude toward kissing.

"The reason why some Japanese are offended by couples kissing in public is that they automatically equate it with sex. In the end, I really don't think it matters what other people think."

When it comes to public displays of affection, another traditional characteristic of Japanese society—for men to lead and women to follow—is also being challenged.

Take twenty-year-old Terumi Miyashita (a pseudonym), who says: "If, say, we are waiting on a train platform and I feel like kissing my boyfriend, then I go ahead and kiss him."

Ordinarily, it bothers Miyashita if people stare at her in a public place. But when she is with her boyfriend, she says, "it's as if we're cut off from the rest of the world—I just don't see other people around us."

Reflecting this more liberated attitude, the recent flood of Japanese videos, television dramas, and commercials featuring sizzling kissing scenes has portrayed women in more assertive roles. In one such commercial, a girl turns to her boyfriend and asks him outright to kiss her.

Michiko Shimamori, editor of an advertising industry magazine, be-   15
lieves such commercials have heavily influenced the recent trend for kissing in public.

"The advertisement where the girl asks her boyfriend to kiss her draws a lot of sympathy from female audiences, as it comes very close to capturing the feelings of an ordinary girl," she says.

"Messages like that, which are now appearing in all kinds of media, are eroding resistance to the idea of kissing in public," the editor adds.

Takashi Tomita, assistant professor at Shirayuri Women's College in Tokyo, attributes the phenomenon to the flow of Western culture into Japan and the relative anonymity of urban life.

Exposure to the West through movies and overseas travel has caused younger Japanese, at least, to lose their inhibitions, says Tomita.

Furthermore, the high degree of urbanization in Japan means many   20
people live surrounded by others whom they do not know and whose opinions, therefore, do not really count.

Another factor, according to Tomita, is the "exhibitionist" nature of some young Japanese. "When young people kiss in front of others, they hope to embarrass those around them. By provoking a reaction, they can say to themselves that they are different from the rest."

In other words, she says, kissing in public can be a form of narcissism, no different in psychological terms from youth gangs who show off by racing cars or motorbikes up and down main streets.

Superficial Trends

Just as with many other trends in youth culture, older generations can be extremely critical of couples who display their affection in public. Says one middle-aged man: "It's a horrible thing to watch. It really makes me wonder where the Japanese sense of aesthetics has gone. If my daughter behaved like that, I would hate it."

Tomita said she believes that while public displays of affection may increase among younger Japanese, it will not necessarily change basic values.

Despite the trappings of Western culture which have entered the coun-   25
try, the trends they generate in Japanese social behavior are only superficial

imitations, says Tomita, who maintains they are unlikely to substantially alter the Japanese mind-set.

Thinking About the Text

1. What do you think Watanabe's attitude is toward the young Japanese he describes?

2. Donald Richie (p. 133) and Watanabe both focus on kissing as a cultural practice. Compare and contrast how they write about the subject, taking into consideration such factors as tone and audience.

3. Yukie Kawashima says that the risk of being seen by colleagues is "part of the thrill" of kissing on the street (paras. 7 and 8). Do you imagine that most young Americans might say something similar? (See also paras. 21 and 22 on exhibitionism.)

Thinking About Culture

4. Watanabe talks about the influence of Japanese advertisements showing couples kissing. Try to recall images of kissing in American magazine, TV, or billboard advertisements. Do you think that kissing in American ads influences behavior? (By the way, how prevalent is kissing in American ads?)

5. Think about some common gesture (such as a greeting, or a handshake, or a hug) or behavior (preparing for bed, waiting for a friend, or waiting for class to begin) and reflect on how you perform it. What cultural influences do you note (e.g., family, friends, school, the media?)

T. K. Ito, Virginia Murray, and R. U. Loveless

Computerized Matchmaking

It's almost impossible to pick up a Japanese magazine now without finding at least one full-page ad [showing] a picture of an attractive young woman and/or young man, with copy such as:

This essay is reprinted from Mangajin *("comic-book people"), a magazine created for those teaching and learning Japanese. It covers contemporary popular culture and literature, especially* manga *(comic books), which form the largest segment of the publishing industry in Japan.*

> How many people of the opposite sex will I be able to meet during
> my marriageable years?

Along with the ad there is always a postage-paid questionnaire card which, in addition to the basic personal information (age, height, weight, blood type, occupation, income, education), includes ten or so "personality profile" questions covering topics such as degree of importance placed on lucky/ unlucky days of the Buddhist calendar, opinions on professional boxing, level of confidence in one's own sense of fashion, etc. One of the most common "personality tests" involves ranking several colors by degree of preference.

You fill out the card, mail it in, and it's run through a computer. About a week later you're sent information on the potential partners you can meet through that service—but first, you have to pay a registration fee ranging from 20,000 yen to 300,000 yen,° or more.

There are an estimated 5,000 businesses in Japan classified as *kekkon joho sabisu* ("marriage information services"), many of them large and reputable firms. Many use *kekkon joho* in the company name, while others (some of which may be more along the lines of dating services) use names with endings like *Bunka Senta* (Cultural Center), *Pasonaru Senta* (Personal Center), or *Yusu Senta* (Youth Center). As might be expected, there is a lot of *katakana°* in these names since they are positioned as alternatives to the traditional *o-miai* "arranged marriages."

When an ad of any type continues to run for a long period of time, one can assume that it is getting results. Ads such as . . . these . . . have been running regularly in the Japanese media since the 1980s so they must be doing something right, or filling some kind of need.

The copy used in the ads provides some clues. For example, the young   5
singles in the OMMG ad . . . are asking "How many people . . . will I be able to meet?" For some people, these services are simply a way of increasing their options. In addition to informal socializing at work (usually rather limited), they may try the occasional *o-miai,* and also join a *kekkon joho* service, just to see what's available.

Although ads targeted at women, or unisex ads such as the OMMG ad . . . are not unusual, the bulk of the advertising seems to be targeted at men. There are several factors involved here.

There is definitely social pressure on Japanese men to get married. Until a man takes on the responsibility of a wife and family, he is not considered to be a real adult. This attitude is the basis for an OMMG ad showing a young couple (in Japanese dress) with the copy *Kekkon shite, hajimete ichinin-mae. Sono imi ga sukoshi wakaru toshi ni natta.* ("It's only

---

20,000 yen to 300,000 yen: $200 to $300.   **katakana:** A syllabary used to write words from Western languages. [All notes are the editors'.]

after you marry that you become a real adult. I've reached the age where I understand a little about what that means.") Being single past age thirty can hurt a man's career, especially in a big corporation. This attitude is reflected in the copy of another OMMG ad which shows a young man saying, "*Boku no tekireiki wa boku ga kimeru, to wa itta mono no, seken ga ki ni naru.*" ("I said I would decide when I was of marriageable age, but I'm concerned about what people think.")

The situation is changing for Japanese women. They have more career options than they used to, and are better able to provide for themselves without having to rely on a husband. While remaining single still carries a certain social stigma, it does not bring the mandatory sentence of economic hardship that it once did. In addition, there have been reports in the Japanese press that more and more Japanese women feel that this world (the present environment) is just not a suitable place to bring up a child. Add to this the fact that there are about 1.5 times more single men than women in the marriageable twenty to thirty-nine age range, and it's easy to see why Japanese women are becoming choosier about their marriage partners. It's not that they don't want to get married, they are just more likely to hold out for what's called *sanko* "the three highs"—a man who is tall, has a "high" academic background (graduated from a good school), and has a high income.

This makes it tough on the average young salaryman, especially those in occupations such as engineering, who put in long hours in a mostly male workplace. In the past, one recourse for a young man reaching marriageable age in such a situation was to ask his boss to help him find a bride. That is, the superior acted as *nakodo* "go-between" in an *o-miai*. Now, the bosses claim that they are under too much business pressure and don't have time to help out their young charges. As a countermeasure, many large corporations have set up in-house agencies, usually referred to as *kekkon sodan-jo* ("Marriage Consulting Offices"). The membership fee is typically one-tenth of what ordinary commercial *kekkon joho* services charge, and because male employees of major "first-rate corporations" (*ichi-ryu kigyo*—Mitsubishi/Mitsui/Sumitomo, etc.) are considered highly desirable catches, women outnumber men in these groups 2:1. The "success rate" of completed marriages, however, is only about 10 to 15 percent, perhaps due to the fact that membership is restricted to employees of these corporations or affiliated companies. So this is not a complete solution to the problem.

The concept of *nanpa*, sometimes translated as "picking up girls on   10
the street". . . , does exist in Japan, but for most Japanese men it's not a viable option for meeting women, much less a way to find a prospective marriage partner. In fact, there really aren't even any establishments in Japan that would be called singles bars.

Gokon ("mixers"—drinking parties for two monosex groups, these started as college functions, but are now popular on and off campus) provide a chance to meet that special someone, but the word from those who know their *gokon* is "If you can't find a girlfriend elsewhere, chances are you won't be able to find one at a *gokon.*" *Naruhodo.*°

For those who are feeling workplace, peer, parental, or self-imposed pressure to get married, *kekkon joho* services can at least provide hope. "Industry" sources claim that there are currently 250,000 people registered with *kekkon joho* services all over the country. This figure was zero back in 1978 when Altmann, the pioneer, set up shop in Japan. Altmann had started as an introduction service in post-WWII West Germany, and sensed that there was yen to be made by providing a similar service in Japan.

"Compatibility diagnosis—determining how suitable a particular man is for a particular woman—is very different in Japan and in Europe," reflects the Altmann founder (now in the securities business). "For example, there is the question of religion in Europe. Catholics and Protestants tend to avoid each other when they look for partners. In Japan, this is a very minor issue. We spent a long time developing a diagnostic structure fitted to the Japanese culture."

The heads of many of the major *kekkon joho* services now in Japan got their start with Altmann, and as a result, most companies offer pretty much the same fare. The industry leaders like OMMG, Sun Mark Life Creation, Altmann, SULC, Eternal Bridal, and Academic Unicharm all charge in the neighborhood of 300,000 yen for a two-year membership.

Members are entitled to a monthly list of prospective partners as deter-   15
mined by a computer analysis of their responses to a compatibility diagnosis questionnaire completed when they join the service. The list includes names and basic personal data for these prospects. If any of these look good on paper, the member can go down to the agency office and look at photos. If still interested, the agency will contact the other party to see if the interest is mutual, and if all goes well, the initiator will receive a phone call or letter a few days later.

In addition, all major *kekkon joho* services hold dance parties, trips, and other functions every month to help members find partners on their own. At the parties held by Academic Unicharm, members wear a name tag, and are provided with a set of fifteen name cards for use only at the party. The cards give first name, blood type, astrological sign, and membership number. Participants give the cards to people they like, and after the party, members can tell the staff the names of three people they would like to meet again. The staff then determines if the feelings are mutual. Members may also bypass this process and make dates on their own.

As the former president of Altmann notes, "The biggest problem with this system is that it works best for people who need no help. If a *sanko*—tall,

Naruhodo: "Of course."

good education, high income—man joins the service, he will enjoy plenty of chances, but such a man doesn't need this system."

According to an Altmann staff member, many women specify on their application that they are looking for a man with an annual income of over 10 million yen ($74,000).° "When we tell them that very few members have that high an income, they look disappointed and select the next lower category, which is 6 million yen ($44,000), but in fact, only 13.3 percent of all male Altmann members claim an annual income of 6 million yen or more."

Concerning the male members, our Altmann staff contact comments, "Many of the young men who use our service are insensitive and mechanical. One type has absolutely no sense of the romantic—they look filthy and seem to be totally unconcerned about their personal appearance. Another type blindly follows 'love manuals' from men's magazines like *Popeye* and *Hot Dog Press*. They don't know what to do when things don't go as they expect."

A female member of Academic Unicharm complains, "I think men using this service have no passion—they are not assertive enough. Even when I meet a nice man at a party, we somehow wind up going out with a bunch of friends, not one-on-one." 20

Although all major services assign a counselor to each member, there are no lessons in romance or the art of communication. Even so, the services that disclose their "success ratio" claim that 25 to 35 percent of their members wind up finding a partner through the service.

All through the 1980s the *kekkon joho* services enjoyed rapid growth, but that phase seems to have come to an end. One reason is that a small number of unscrupulous operators have created image problems for the entire "industry." In 1990, an "ultra-exclusive introduction agency" called *Rodan no Mori* (Rodin's Forest) which offered an absolute guarantee of marriage in exchange for a membership fee of 10 million yen ($74,000) was charged with fraud by the Tokyo Metropolitan Police. There have been cases of agencies which employed bar hostesses to pose as partner-seekers, and numerous complaints have been registered about being charged for supposedly free consultations, receiving too few introductions, and being unable to get out of expensive contracts. In December of 1990, twelve of the largest services formed an industry association to establish basic policies and standards.

Fraud is not the only problem facing these companies. Among the younger generation, there is a stigma attached to any kind of arranged marriage. The much-publicized romance in which the present emperor Akihito met his bride on the tennis court at Karuizawa, a fashionable resort, captured the imagination of the younger generation of the time and did much to promote the image of the "love marriage" as opposed to the traditional "arranged marriage." An Altmann staff member comments

---

$74,000: The figure today would be about $100,000.

"Things are changing, but many people still hide from their friends the fact that they are using a *kekkon joho* service. If they find a partner and get married, they make up a story of a romantic encounter to tell their family and friends."

What does the future hold for computerized matchmaking in Japan? It's hard to predict, but like the computers that make the system possible, it seems certain that computerized matchmaking is here to stay.

Thinking About the Text

1. As you read the article, what details and information interested you most? Why? Did your classmates find the same things interesting? Explain.

2. Based on the descriptions in the article, and any other essay you have read in this book, design a Japanese personal ad. You may want to work with a group of your classmates. Discuss the results with the rest of the class.

Thinking About Culture

3. The first paragraph says that ads for computerized matchmaking services are found in virtually all Japanese magazines. How common are such ads in the United States? Are they found chiefly in specialized magazines? If so, how would you characterize these magazines? What other services function in the United States in this way? (You may want to examine the "personals" ads in a range of magazines.)

4. According to paragraph 6, the Japanese ads are chiefly targeted at men. Are American ads for comparable services chiefly aimed at one sex or the other?

5. "Until a man takes on the responsibility of a wife and family, he is not considered to be a real adult" (para. 7). Do some or most of your adult acquaintances share this view? What, for instance, do you think would be the view of your parents? Your grandparents? Do you think that members of your group (determined by country of origin or religion or some other criterion) hold a view on this matter that distinguishes them from members of other groups?

6. Do you think that a Japanese-style computerized matchmaking company (see especially paras. 15–16) would do much business in your community? Explain.

Masashi Sada

The Lordly Marriage Declaration
(Kampaku Sengen)

1. Before I take you as my wife,
   There's something I want to say;
   Some of my words may be rather harsh,
   But you better know what's on my mind.

   You mustn't go to bed before I do,
   And you mustn't get up after I do.
   Be a good cook and always look beautiful:
   Do what you can and it'll be okay.

   Don't forget that if a man can't do his work well,
   There's no way he can take care of his family;
   There are things only you can do,
   But aside from those, don't butt in:
   Just be obedient and follow me.

2. There's no difference between your parents and mine:
   Take care of mine as you would your own.
   Get along with my mother and sisters:
   It should be easy as long as you love them.

   Don't speak ill of people behind their backs,
   Don't listen to such talk,
   And don't give way to silly jealousy.

   I won't be unfaithful,
   Perhaps I won't be,
   There's a good chance I won't be;
   Well, anyway, get yourself a bit ready for such things.

In 1979 Masashi Sada composed and sang the song we reprint here. His ballad became one of Japan's top-selling records, perhaps partly because (according to informal polls of men and women of various ages) it accurately expressed the ideal marriage—a strong husband who takes care of his wife, and a devoted wife who obeys her husband.

The title is a bit hard to translate. Sengen is easy enough ("declaration," "proclamation"), but kampaku *means (a) "chief advisor to the emperor," and (b) "a self-confident husband." The translator, James McLendon, catches something of both meanings in "Lordly."*

Happiness is created by two people;
It is not something to be built through the pains of one alone.
You are coming to my place, casting your own home away,
So think that you have nowhere to return to:
From now on, I am your home.

3. After our children are grown and we are old,
   You mustn't die before I do;
   Even one day later is okay,
   But you mustn't die sooner than I do.

The only thing I'll need from you when I die,
Will be for you to take my hand and shed some tears,
And I will say I lived a good life because of you,
I will definitely say it.

Don't forget you'll always be the only woman I love,
The only woman I'll ever love,
The only woman I'll ever love is you,
The only one.

Thinking About the Text

1. In the biographical footnote we mention that *kampaku* can be translated as "a self-confident husband." But "The Arrogant Husband's Proclamation" would also do as a translation of the title. In any case, the song is to be imagined as sung or spoken by a particular kind of person. Describe the character of the imagined speaker, and compare your response to those of your classmates.

2. Think of a current or traditional popular song about love or marriage (or both), and compare its ideals or values to those of *"Kampaku Sengen."*

Thinking About Culture

3. *"Kampaku Sengen"* was a hit song in 1979. If you have read the essays on women by Watanabe, Iwao, and Greenfeld in Chapter 5, speculate on whether the song would be popular with Japanese women if it were released today.

Neil Miller

In and Out of the Closet

Japan was a culture of hierarchies, of compartments, of rooms within rooms. These characteristics often made it seem impervious to analysis or understanding. "They say a Japanese man has six faces," a Canadian woman who lived in Tokyo told me. "You never see every one of them. In fact, you are lucky to see three." There was a rigid demarcation between public and private, between the outer facade of social convention *(tatemae)* and one's inner feelings *(honne)*. They were expected to be separate. You followed the rules and otherwise thought or did what you wished; in exchange, people (and society) left you alone. As a Japanese academic put it, "Japan is a country of double standards, of multistandards, really. You can say you are straight in public and be gay in private. That is acceptable."

For many Japanese gays and lesbians that meant there was no urgency to come out and to tell family or friends about one's sexual orientation; it also meant there was no need to avoid marriage. You could divide your life. You could have sex behind a screen in a public place, and people were supposed to pretend it wasn't happening, as long as when the screen was removed you were sitting there perfectly composed with your tie on straight. . . .

Japanese culture has a long historical tradition of male-male sexual relations. During the feudal period, *samurai* warriors pledged themselves to one another in "brotherhood bonds," in the manner of ancient Sparta. The Buddhist clergy was rife with homosexual relations: Saint Francis Xavier, the first Portuguese missionary to Japan, wrote in the sixteenth century that, among Buddhist monks, "the abominable vice against nature is so popular that they practice it without any feeling of shame." Among the urban classes of the Tokugawa, or Edo, period (1603–1868), a "cheerful bisexuality" was the norm, according to American historian Gary Leupp.

As in Thailand, traditional Japanese same-sex relations never implied a gay identity. The closest word the Japanese language offered was *"nanshoku-zuki"*—"lover of *nanshoku*"—*nanshoku* being what Leupp calls the "role-structured male homosexual behavior" that flourished during the Edo period

---

After graduating in 1967 from Brown University, Neil Miller traveled in the Middle East and then taught English to Moroccan and Iraqi children in Israel. When he returned to the United States he became the news editor of the Gay Community News, *and later a feature writer for the* Boston Phoenix. *Miller is the author of* In Search of Gay America *(1989) and of* Out in the World: Gay and Lesbian Life from Buenos Aires to Bangkok *(1993), the source of our selection. (The title of the selection is ours.)*

and whose culture centered around *nanshoku* teahouses and the Kabuki theater. In a society characterized by often loveless arranged marriages, *nanshoku* offered the possibility of romantic love. Given the rigorously hierarchical social structure, male homosexual relationships in Edo Japan were almost exclusively between older men and boys, and often involved a difference in social status as well. And in view of the patriarchal character of that social structure, there appears to have been little or no outlet for lesbian relations—or at least no writing or records to document them.

If, in seventeenth- and eighteenth-century Japan, male-male relationships were an accepted part of the sexual landscape, that began to change with the accession to power of the Westernizing Meiji dynasty in 1868. *Nanshoku* was increasingly regarded as an embarrassment, a feudal holdover in an era when Japan desperately wanted to industrialize and catch up with the West. Negative Western medical views about homosexuality became influential. Even the laws began to reflect this change in perception: Anal intercourse between consenting males was briefly prohibited, between 1874 and 1882. (Homosexual sex has been legal since then, however.)

By the mid–twentieth century, the traditional *nanshoku* had faded from public view. A new word became part of the language: *doseiai*, or "same-sex love." "*Doseiai*" applied to both men and women, so it had fewer connotations of pederasty than "*nanshoku*" had. But *doseiai* was still *shumi*—a "hobby," or "pastime," or "personal interest," something that could be taken on and put off at will. It wasn't serious and certainly didn't constitute an identity. For women, *doseiai* was "*S*"—nonsexual schoolgirl crushes, which involved holding hands and exchanging love letters. *S*—the letter stood for "sister"—received wide attention in the Japanese press in the 1930s after a series of suicides among infatuated schoolgirls. By and large, *S* involvements ended when school was over, and young women yielded to parental and societal pressure to marry.

By the late 1980s, a concept of gay and lesbian identity began to emerge. In part, this was the result of Western cultural influence. Postwar Japan imported dress, music, and youth culture from Europe and North America. Why not ideas about sexuality, as well? As a result of increasing affluence, many young people were no longer forced to live with their families. Women began to enjoy a degree of economic independence and social freedom. The proliferation of gay bars, following the 1964 Tokyo Olympics, and the emergence of gay magazines enabled gay men to feel less isolated, to communicate with one another, and hinted at the possibility of community. In the mid- to late 1980s, the first gay organizations were established in Tokyo: Mr. Minami's ILGA/Japan; a gay youth group, OCCUR; and a lesbian organization, Regumi Studio. "Dyke weekends," started by a group of Western lesbians living in Japan, were held four times a year at a women's educational center near Tokyo. Because of the still unequal status of women in Japanese society, lesbians have lagged far behind gay men in developing a sense of identity and community. But that was changing, as well.

Nonetheless, in contemporary Japan the overwhelming majority of gays and lesbians remained in the closet. In Tokyo and Osaka and other major cities, there were no gay neighborhoods; no one on the streets or subways appeared visibly gay or lesbian; few, if any, businesses apart from the bars, sex establishments, and variety stores of Ni-chome, catered to a gay or lesbian community.

Homosexuality remained a subject unsuitable for academic study. The media continued to equate male homosexuality with transvestism; lesbians were ignored completely. Although there were few signs of overt hostility, Japan remained an extremely homogeneous society, with little tradition of tolerance for minority groups. As one Osaka lesbian put it, "The policy of our society regarding something it doesn't like or feels uncomfortable with is to ignore it. People don't criticize it or say it's bad. They just pretend it isn't there. Japanese don't think about themselves or examine themselves. They don't ask the question, 'Who am I?' So it is hard to develop a sense of identity. And without a sense of identity, a minority group cannot survive."

As a result, to many Japanese, homosexuality was still an alien concept, 10 something that belonged to the West, not to modern-day Japan. One Japanese woman told me that when she had made some mention of Ni-chome's gay bars to a friend, the friend said, "No Japanese go there, right? Only foreigners!"

The formation of gay identity, Japanese-style, was precisely what was going on one Sunday afternoon in my newly adopted living room—the ILGA office. "I Flat," as everyone called the place, was sleek and high-tech, with a computer, a TV, a conference table, and neat rows of audiotapes and videotapes. It was located in a neighborhood of fake brick- and stucco-fronted residences on a little lane down from a Baskin-Robbins ice cream parlor; at night you heard crickets and air conditioners and the chanting of Buddhist prayers in living room shrines.

The occasion was a discussion group on homosexuality, attended by a handful of young Japanese men and led by a mild-mannered American named Michael. Michael was assigning reading—an early account of the U.S. gay liberation movement and an academic-sounding Canadian tome that was unfamiliar to me. He had been in Japan for ten years and taught history at a university in Tokyo. Today he lectured in English, primarily for my benefit.

In Japan, Michael said, sexuality as a category that defined a group of people was a new idea. "I don't say to my friends that I am gay," he noted. "I say, 'I like men.' One of the problems in Japan is this lack of definition. To most people, saying 'I'm gay' is like saying 'I masturbate.' It still represents an act, not an identity." This was "troublesome" when it came to gay liberation. "For this reason, Japan is a laboratory for the social construction of homosexuality," he said.

While in the United States, Michael went on, there was a "gut reaction" against homosexuality that led to gay bashing, in Japan, this wasn't the case.

"There is no feeling of hatred against gays," he contended. "What there is is discomfort. The main Japanese concern is 'How should I act?' So when it comes to homosexuality, it is not that they hate gays but that they are afraid of embarrassing themselves. They are uneasy; they prefer not to talk about it."

In Japan, Michael said, "the cowardly thing is to be yourself. Conformity is considered the strong thing to do, the admirable thing."   15

Most of the Japanese in attendance were silent as Michael talked. He was the professor, after all. Then someone spoke up—a tall man dressed in blue jeans and an epauletted denim jacket, with plastic bangles hanging from his wrist. "Michael is right when he says that Japanese people don't say homosexuals should be killed or anything like that," he said. "They don't bash them. If anything they find them funny. Not immoral or evil, but cute!" He added, with a trace of bitterness in his voice, "As cute as dogs."

The speaker's name was Masonari Kanda and he was fierce. He was argumentative and critical of everything. In fact, he behaved in such an "un-Japanese" manner that he admitted people found him rather "scary." He was proud of that, except that it made for difficulties in finding a boyfriend. "Japanese people want everything to be calm and quiet," he maintained. "They don't want to do or say anything that is different, shocking, confrontational." I thought Kanda would be happier in North America, in an organization like ACT UP or Queer Nation, than he was in Japan, where compromise and consensus ruled. . . .

AIDS was a factor in Japan—and then again, it wasn't. When I asked Mr. Minami what ILGA's greatest achievement had been, he paused and responded, "AIDS services." The AIDS crisis had played a role in gay community-building; Tokyo's gay and lesbian organizations had been founded shortly after the first cases of AIDS were reported in Japan in 1985. That was no coincidence. For many people, including many gays themselves, the arrival of AIDS was the first indication that there actually were homosexuals in Japan.

Yet the reality was that, thus far, Japan—and the country's gay community in particular—had been spared the worst of the AIDS epidemic. Most of the reported cases were among hemophiliacs, infected by blood products imported from the United States. Forty percent of the nation's hemophiliacs were estimated to be HIV-positive; a group of hemophiliacs was suing the government and five pharmaceutical companies for $1.6 billion in damages. As of April 1990, a total of only thirty-eight homosexual men had been diagnosed with AIDS, and another seventy-nine had tested postive for HIV infection in a country of 120 million people. A study of the prevalence of HIV among gay men in Tokyo from 1985 to 1989 had found an infection rate of 3 percent; half of those who tested positive were *gaijin*.° A similar

---

gaijin: Foreigner. The word is short for *gaikokujin,* or "person from another country." [Editors' note]

study of gay men in cities other than Tokyo revealed a rate of infection of less than 1 percent.

The effect of these numbers was that the overwhelming majority of   20
Japanese gays didn't personally know anyone infected with HIV. No gay man in Japan had gone public to offer himself as a "role model" for living with the disease. In my conversations with Japanese gays, the subject of AIDS never came up unless I raised it. AIDS just wasn't viewed as a serious problem. As a result, there was little awareness of safe sex among gay men. Gay saunas barred Westerners (but not other Asians), and that was viewed as all that was needed to combat AIDS. Safe sex was sex with another Japanese— whatever his sexual practices or however many times he had traveled abroad. Although Japan had the highest rate of condom use in the world (condoms were the leading method of birth control in the country), gay men weren't exactly lining up at drugstore counters. . . .

. . . In a country with little manifest antihomosexual prejudice, where gays were "cute as dogs" and AIDS was primarily a disease of hemophiliacs, marriage remained the central issue for Japanese homosexuals. The formation of lesbian and gay identity was inextricably linked with it. It was unclear which created more problems—to be gay or to refuse to marry. "The sole obstacle Japanese gays would face in coming out is the marriage system," as one gay man put it. "You can live with things as they are, as long as you clear up the question of marriage with family and bosses."

Although still strong, the marriage system was beginning to weaken. *Miai kekkon*, or arranged marriage, was in decline, particularly in the cities. Japanese were marrying later than in the past; today the average age was twenty-five for women and twenty-eight for men. A survey of Japanese men had shown that one-third wanted to postpone marriage, while another third didn't want to marry at all. "The whole social mood is changing," one woman told me. These changes—particularly the delay in the marriage age—presented gay men and women with a little more room to maneuver, a window of time in which to take control of their lives and stave off marriage, if not avoid it completely.

In Japan, gay men and lesbians were suddenly discovering that lover relationships, long-term partnerships, were possible, instead of the "hobbies" of a previous era. "Right now, one of the major changes is that people want to have *koibito*, a lover," OCCUR's Niimi told me. A Tokyo lesbian named Minako made the same point. "Today, it is the hottest thing—to have a lover," she said. "Before, it was difficult. There wasn't a real community. You were in a heterosexual world, and your lover might become lovers with a man. You were no match for that. You were in a tug of war and you were on one side and the rest of the world was on the other side. So you let her go. Now, it is lover, lover. Everyone is talking about *koibito, koibito*."

A gay academic related that when he was at university ten years before, he and a male friend tried to rent an apartment together and found it wasn't possible. At that time, students were expected to live in dormitories; the idea of two unmarried men sharing a flat was not well accepted. Today, living with a roommate was increasingly common, especially in the large apartment buildings run by absentee company landlords. "You have to understand that the idea of gay couples is really a new idea," the academic added. "The traditional combination was a rich older man, usually married, and a younger man. And the younger man was replaceable—the older man could always find someone else. These were short-time relationships. Today, it's different. Relationships are possible that are *real* relationships."

Nonetheless, it was easy to overestimate change. In Japan, there was   25
always the tension between *tatemae* and *honne,* between the outward acquiescence to social convention and one's inner feelings. Sometimes, the facade one presented to the world was sleek and high-tech and seemingly Western, and at other times it was traditional. But what people really thought and felt—the *honne*—was often quite different and difficult to fathom. So, while long-standing social arrangements appeared to be undergoing change, at the same time deference to the wishes of one's parents remained a powerful countervailing force. Young people were extremely hesitant to offend parents or to make them unhappy in any way. . . .

"At my bank, no one says that unless you get married, you're fired," Kato told me. "But the pressure is there. It's just unspoken. When we have drinks after work or in ordinary conversations during lunch, people ask, 'Why are you not married? Are you not interested in this girl, that girl?' There are some people who remain single, although it is not clear if they are gay or not. And they are not treated well. They are not promoted as high."

Besides the issue of homosexuality, Kato emphasized, "All gay people face one problem—the problem of marriage."

One reason the bank cared so much about marriage was because a major task of its employees was to negotiate with officials from companies with which the bank had financial dealings. The negotiators on both sides of the table were almost always men. "In Japan, it is very hard for men to take part in negotiations or just to talk in a friendly manner if they are not married," Kato said. "Single men are not considered grown-ups. The banks want to send people to negotiate who look capable in their jobs and capable in other parts of their lives, like taking care of their families."

For his first seven years at the bank, Kato's job had been to engage in such negotiations. But recently, he had been shifted to another area. "I am now one of those who take care of odd jobs, paperwork," he noted. "So now I really don't have to talk with people from different companies." He emphasized that in his bank it was not uncommon for employees to be moved from one area to another. "I have not been demoted," he insisted.

How would his coworkers react if they knew he was gay?   30

"Some of them know," he said. "I was constantly being asked, 'Why are you not married?' and 'Aren't you interested in any girl in this company?' I was sick and tired of this. So, one day at lunch, I just said it—'I'm gay!' "

After that revelation, some coworkers stopped bothering him. But others either didn't understand what he was talking about or thought it was simply irrelevant. They continued asking the same question as before: "Kato, tell us, when are you going to get married?"

For Japanese lesbians, the formation of identity and relationships—to say nothing of the avoidance of marriage—was a far more difficult process than for gay men. Japan, after all, was a society only fifty years away from the time when women were expected to stay behind their husbands when walking down the street. Despite the advances women had made, they were less economically independent than men and far more susceptible to family and social pressures. For many, being a lesbian was just not a viable option, even today. As Mr. Minami put it, "For women, before taking the position of a lesbian, they have to take a position as a woman. And, in Japan, the position of women is weak."

Nonetheless I had an easier time meeting lesbians in Japan than anywhere outside the West. This probably had to do with the higher status of women there, at least compared to the rest of Asia. Perhaps it was simply that my contacts were better. In Boston, I had been introduced to a Japanese lesbian who had met a woman named Yoko at Regumi Studio, the Tokyo lesbian group. The Boston acquaintance, who was barely twenty and rather meek, found the women at Regumi intimidating. But she didn't feel that way about Yoko.

I took the subway out to the quiet Tokyo neighborhood where Yoko   35
lived with her New Zealand lover of five years, a photographer. Their apartment was a typical Japanese fusion and confusion of East and West: *tatami* mats for Japanese guests to sit on and Western-style tables and chairs for *gaijin*.

Yoko was forty and taught physical education at a university outside Tokyo. She had her hair cut short and and insisted she never wore a dress or makeup. "My students say, 'You are like a man,' " she told me. "I say, 'So what!' Students understand that you have the right to your freedom." She added, "Of course, there are some who won't talk to me at all." Yoko looked robust and healthy, as a physical education instructor should. In white shorts and a lavender polo shirt, she might have been off for a morning at the tennis court.

She painted a rather dreary picture of being a lesbian in Japan. You couldn't come out, she said, or you'd lose your job and friends. Most lesbians with little education wound up marrying men. Others, who refused to marry and became involved with another woman, often wound up taking on the stereotypical roles of heterosexual couples, with one partner playing the "husband" and the other the "wife."

Yoko had had a long struggle to accept herself as a lesbian. While at university, she had a lesbian relationship that lasted for four years. "We always quarreled," she said. "It was because of this feeling of sin every day—that we should not be doing this. We were miserable. We felt that everything we did was the result of sin!"

She went off to England, where she lived for nine years. There, she was involved in a relationship with another woman; they were constantly debating whether or not to have sex. They never did.

Back in Japan, she met an American lesbian who told her it was "good to be gay." Yoko visited her in Honolulu, spending time at the women's center there; in that environment she felt comfortable with her sexuality for the first time. Shortly after she returned home, she met her current lover.

Within the past four years, there had been significant changes in Japan, she said. The lesbian group, Regumi Studio, had started up in Tokyo; in Osaka, the country's third-largest city, there was a women's coffeehouse. The first book about lesbians in Japan was published; this documentation of a previously hidden subject enabled greater numbers of women to consider the possibility that they might be gay.

The four times yearly "Dyke Weekends" were instrumental in the creation of a sense of lesbian solidarity and community, as well. "I remember that first weekend so well," said Yoko. "Women were crying. It was like a new world had opened." The weekends, which attracted sixty to seventy women—half *gaijin* and half Japanese—were still rather clandestine. The women's educational center where the events took place refused to allow the organizers to use the term "lesbian." They called it the "International Women's Conference" instead.

Networking was in a relatively rudimentary state. Yoko showed me a telephone tree ("Dyke Denwa," *denwa* being Japanese for "telephone") that was used to organize dinners and social events. One person would telephone someone else, who in turn would call the next person on the tree. One woman was the link to Osaka; she made the call that activated the Dyke Denwa in that city.

I noted that most of the twenty or so names on the list were foreign women.

"That's true," said Yoko gloomily. "Most Japanese lesbians are isolated and alone. They find a lover and they stay by themselves."

Despite her own five-year lover relationship and the evolving support system, Yoko admitted that even now she couldn't totally accept herself as a lesbian. "Some part of me resists," she said.

Sometimes, she would go and have a drink with a male colleague who had repeatedly asked her to marry him. "I ask myself why am I going out with him," she said. "I won't marry him. But I feel it's bad not to. I can't get rid of this cultural feeling that I should marry, that I shouldn't be a lesbian. I am getting better, but I still feel this way to some extent."

She wanted to tell her mother that she was gay but just couldn't manage it. "If I told her, she would be desperate," Yoko said. "I am ready to tell her. Really I am. But she is relying on me. I just can't do it."

Living abroad throughout most of her twenties had enabled Yoko to resist pressure to marry. She believed that being involved in a relationship with a foreigner was helpful, too. Japanese had an "inferiority complex" regarding *gaijin,* she said. Living with a Westerner afforded Yoko a degree of status that somewhat counterbalanced the stigma of being an unmarried woman (to say nothing of being a lesbian). And the fact that she had lived in England for nine years also made it more understandable to colleagues and neighbors why she might live in a way that appeared unconventional by Japanese standards.

"Actually, I am quite lucky," she said. "I live with my lover. I work at   50
a university. My behavior is that which is expected of a physical education teacher. I have friends who have to put on makeup and dresses for their jobs. I don't have to do that." Still, she said, "being a lesbian is not easy in this country." She wanted to leave Japan and move to New Zealand with her lover. She was studying osteopathy at night school in order to enhance herself professionally and thus make emigration easier.

Whatever her conflicts about her sexuality, Yoko, as she herself pointed out, was in a far better position than Japanese lesbians of her generation who had less education and fewer skills. "Their parents are powerful, and so these women get married and then divorced," she said. "They wind up working at the supermarket checkout counter. It isn't surprising they want another woman to be their 'husband.' Or maybe they wind up remarrying with a man. That is the lesbian pattern. There are a few brave ones who won't marry and keep on working at the supermarket."

Thinking About the Text

1. If you found this essay of interest, what do you think are some of the things that make it interesting? Is it the topic itself, the use of narratives, the writer's tone, or some other aspect?

2. In paragraph 13 the point is made, or, rather, repeated, that the Japanese do not see being gay as "an identity." The implication is that being gay (or lesbian) *is* "an identity" in the United States. If a woman is a doctor and a Latina and a lesbian, does she have three identities, or is she a person who happens to be a doctor, a Latina, and a lesbian? Is it your impression that most gays and lesbians find their primary identity in their sexuality? Is this more likely to be true of homosexual persons than heterosexual? Explain.

Thinking About Culture

3. In the first two paragraphs Miller suggests that because the Japanese distinguish between *tatemae* and *honne,* there is in Japan "no urgency to come

out and to tell your family or friends about one's sexual orientation." But doesn't much of American society also accept a form of *tatemae* and *honne*? We scarcely speak our minds on all issues and in all contexts. What accounts for the "urgency" in the United States "to come out and to tell family or friends about one's sexual orientation"? (By the way, how widespread is the urgency to talk about one's sexuality? Do heterosexuals for the most part "come out and tell" about the particular sexual practices they engage in?)

4. "The policy of our society regarding something it doesn't like or feels uncomfortable with is to ignore it," comments a Japanese lesbian (para. 9). Can something similar be said of American society, at least in regard to some things—let's say alcoholism among the clergy, or (until recently) sexual infidelity among political figures, faculty-student sexual relationships, and child molestation?

5. Miller quotes a Japanese lesbian who says, "You couldn't come out . . . or you'd lose your job and friends" (para. 37). To what degree, if any, is this statement also applicable in the United States?

Chapter 5

Women's Roles

Twenty years ago a standard Japanese joke went thus: Heaven is an English home, a Chinese chef, an American salary, and a Japanese wife; Hell is a Japanese home, an English chef, a Chinese salary, and an American wife. The joke—perhaps always more amusing to men than to women—has only slight resonance today, for Japanese women are not what they were once thought to be. And the tales of Japan as an ancient matriarchal society in which up to half of the early emperors were women also belie the idea of a cultural rock base of male power.

Two images of the new Japanese woman contend: the quiet revolutionary, as Sumiko Iwao (p. 180) describes her, and the victim of the system, as others have observed. The old idea of *ryosai kembo,* or the "good wife, wise mother" model of womanhood, may never have been more than an ideal propagated by leaders, even in the days of patriarchal households and domineering mothers-in-law.

As observers influenced by Western perspectives, we must also contend with our own lenses. Many would say that Japanese women are indeed oppressed and exploited, prevented from the full realization of their potential. We see in Japan no "unisex" model for life chances, and we see that gender does explicitly define roles and opportunities for both women and men. Japanese society therefore seems to us to be male dominated and constraining for women, and perhaps exploiting women for the sake of national economic goals, as Kazuko Watanabe suggests in the second selection of this chapter.

There may, however, be other views. A Japanese man told one of us he would rather have been born a woman, with the freedom not to be a wage slave, and a Japanese woman once commented that it is American women who suffer: "We may be economically dependent on men," she said, "but we are not emotionally dependent—we wouldn't ever sit by a telephone waiting for a guy to call." Her perspective is supported by those who see even the Japanese housewife whose tasks keep her largely at home as a woman with her own sphere of authority and decision-making, with very secure social credit for her accomplishments as a woman. Such women—especially middle-aged housewives—also say that they wouldn't want their husbands' narrow, workaholic "salaryman" lives. Their expression for the separation of roles is "The good husband is healthy and absent."

On the other hand, young women about to enter the work force and blue-collar women express themselves somewhat differently. Young women today, raised with expectations other than home and children, hope for careers or at least satisfying work, and are taking a longer time to decide what it is they will do with their lives. Many young women are now waiting until well past the age of *tekireiki,* or the optimal years for marriage. The expression for such "old maids" used to be "parsley" (something left on the plate) or "Christmas cake" (a commodity no longer desired after the 25th, as in her twenty-fifth birthday). Some young women are also saying no to children, or desire only one child, causing consternation among leaders and economic planners, who foresee a severe labor shortage in the near future. Blue-collar women workers are acutely affected by the lack of upward mobility as "permanent temporaries," working without benefits and security. It may be only elite women who have a choice.

Sigmund Freud once asked: "What do women want?" Our question is a trifle more modest: What do Japanese and American women want? Freedom of choice is clearly only part of the picture, and it is evident that women in Japan are making choices. Not only when to marry, but whom, as the older practice of arranged marriage has in its traditional form all but disappeared. Educational options are also available, as increasing numbers of young women choose four-year universities, when twenty years ago, the usual choice was a two-year junior college. Employment is also nearly universal among women, as one out of three employees is female and nearly 60 percent of the female work force are housewives, revealing that marriage no longer drives women out of wage labor. In 1986, Japan's Equal Employment Opportunity Act created a base for future initiatives in equal pay for equal work and hiring equity—though, in its present form, the law is weak and scarcely enforceable. In schools, both boys and girls study home economics and shop. It has become fashionable for men to attend cooking schools. Young women are beginning to postpone marriage and childbearing; some are even saying no to marriage or children altogether. While government officials are deeply concerned that women are having on average only 1.46 children, young women, at least for a time, are saying as Karl Taro Greenfeld (p. 195) puts it, that they want to have fun. The fact is, however, that maintenance of a middle-class life-style demands two salaries in a family and most women who work *must* work.

American women, too, see great change, but perhaps not for all women. Most continue to lead complicated lives, juggling work, children, marriage, a home, and other relationships and responsibilities. They may not be so different from their Japanese counterparts, for combining roles is difficult in any society.

Some changes in Japan focus on image and identity: There are campaigns to stop depicting women as sexual slaves and victims of physical violence in pornographic comic books, and there are recent court cases upholding a woman's right to keep her own name after marriage. Compared to the issues that confront American women, such as rape (acquaintance or random), domestic abuse, and other violent crimes, Japanese women's issues seem less immediate. Women have begun to organize to protect themselves against sexual harassment in Japan, but the more violent crimes are both less prevalent and less publicly discussed. The overall safety of Japanese society allows women much more physical freedom.

As might be expected, feminism has taken different forms and has had different agendas in Japan from its counterpart in the West.

In America in the 1960s, the civil rights movement gave impetus to a revival of feminism. While earlier campaigns to promote equality for women (as in the suffrage movement, birth control campaigns, etc.) had provided at least legal support for women's equality, after the mid-1960s, cultural and attitudinal issues came forward as well as many new legal demands. In the 1960s, the women's liberation movement stressed "full participation" for women, access to traditionally male career ladders, and the denunciation of gender-role stereotyping of women as wives and mothers. While Japanese feminism (for the most part) has favored seeking a separate-but-equal notion of female options, American feminists have sought not just equality, but a gender-neutral definition of work and family, which—not to oversimplify her argument—is the contention of Yoko Kirishima as well, in her essay "Liberation Begins in the Kitchen" (p. 161).

In the "second stage" of feminism as defined by Betty Friedan, some feminists have promoted a different model. Since the early 1980s, feminists in America have asked for changes in the workplace, such as flexible schedules, family-leave plans, and the office-at-home, for everyone, with the assumption that the male model of work is good for no one.

The furor in the United States over Felice N. Schwartz's 1989 revelation of the "mommy track" (a not always intentional strategy by management that forces women to choose between motherhood and career) became a focal point of discussion in management and women's groups. It brought out into the open a silent conspiracy, in which American women knew they were either constrained from professional progress by their wishes for a family or constrained from the satisfactions of child-rearing by their hope for a professional identity. The crucial childbearing and rearing years are, of course, also the crucial career-building years. Women have known that employers were watching them for signs of conflict between their goals of domesticity and of professionalism, but after Schwartz's article appeared, the discussions became more open. Young women in America today are not all involved in such discussions and campaigns, but most are involved in the choices opened by the several waves of feminist debate. Women of the earlier generation of activists, however, are concerned that younger women are not fully aware of the continuing need to confront sociocultural bias and may be ignorant of the battles won, and still to be won.

In Japan, while there are (as in the United States) radical feminists who favor complete separation and the repudiation of men, recent feminist agenda are more continuous with those of the 1970s. They maintain that women's values are more humane and conducive to a peaceful, harmonious society than are men's, and they hope to promote stronger families with more male domestic participation, as the workplace becomes a healthier environment through its adoption of female principles.

In the 1970s, Japanese women organized in several women's groups and movements, the most public of which was Chupiren, a group founded initially to support the legalization of the birth control pill, but which took on other women's causes as well. For example, Chupiren members donned pink hard hats and descended on the offices of philandering or neglectful husbands to shame them into treating their wives better. While similarly angry groups exist in the United States, the expectation that "shame" would be a powerful weapon is much stronger in Japan.

Groups for studying women's issues were formed as well, including the International Group for the Study of Women, based in Tokyo and funding research and fellowships for research on women's lives. Over six million women belong to housewives' organizations, grass-roots groups chiefly functioning as consumer groups, investigating the safety and quality of products, but also becoming active in other political movements as well.

While birth control has become an aspect of the women's movement in Japan, abortion has not. Abortion there is legal, not a major religious or political concern, and relatively safe. Many of today's middle-aged women underwent multiple abortions in their younger years; though later generations tend to use other forms of birth control, abortion is still a socially acceptable method. Abortion recently has become something of an issue for other reasons, however, as William R. LaFleur (p. 200) reports, and women who have had abortions may be susceptible to what he sees as the guilt-producing and costly exploitation by some religious groups.

Young women seeking a full identity as career women in Japan do have an uphill battle: From their families, they may hear voices of dismay as they turn down suggestions of marriage; from employers, they may hear that they are not promotable; from their friends, they may feel excluded by the engrossing demands of child-rearing and homemaking. Young women are now seeking work in new kinds of employment, however, ones that welcome their unique talents, such as *katakana* jobs in media, fashion, marketing, and publishing. (*Katakana* is the syllabary used for writing words borrowed from foreign languages; thus used in this extended sense, the word implies modern cultural or technological borrowings.) These are modern, glamorous, and potentially less hierarchical and male-dominated than other more mainstream jobs.

Gender-based social divisions have not disappeared altogether in Japan, but rather than using legal and public means to combat these issues, most young women choose private campaigns of their own to produce a realistic, contemporary life for themselves.

Explorations

1. As in our discussion of youth and sexuality, the topic of women in contemporary America and Japan may be subject to "mixed messages." What are some of these with regard to gender-role separation and the question of social value for women as women in both societies? What if an American woman is an exceptionally good cook, for example, and her husband is not: Is she labeled "feminine" if she does all the cooking? What about male gender-role stereotyping? How can we—or, for that matter, should we—separate task from role identity? Is this a particularly American goal?

2. American young married men are said on the whole to be proud of their involvement with children and household tasks, noting that they are doing more than their fathers did. American women are said to be dissatisfied with their domestic performance, as they compare themselves with their mothers, who did more than they now do. How are your goals and activities different from those of your same-sex parent? What message would you pass on to your own children or to other younger people?

3. In the 1950s, television and movies and advertising encouraged women to think of themselves as homemakers, and the most common image (apart from the sexy pinups) was the woman in an apron. What images of women do you see in today's American media and advertising? What do you imagine advertisers use as images in Japan? If you can find any Japanese popular magazines (in a Japanese grocery store, for example, or perhaps at the library), see what the photographs and illustrations tell you about these images. If you are familiar with the advertising images of women in some other culture, characterize those images.

Yoko Kirishima

Liberation Begins in the Kitchen

"What are you working on now?"

"I'm doing a book on cooking," I answer, and get a very suspicious look in return.

Yoko Kirishima was a popular commentator writing for and about contemporary Japanese women when this essay appeared in the May 1975 issue of Chuo koron. *The translation by Wayne R. Root and Takechi Manabu is from the Autumn 1975 edition of* Japan Interpreter.

"You mean cooking *food?*"

"Well, is there any other kind?"

"Knowing you, Kirishima-san, I thought you might be writing about   5
how to cook men." (Laughter)

"In a way, you might say that cooking has to do with 'handling men,'
but only indirectly. Cooking actually is a very important art."

"That doesn't sound at all like you. I thought you were strong on
women's liberation."

"Maybe, but I'm not a member of an activist women's group. Still, any
person with common sense must realize that women should be liberated and
free."

"But to claim that cooking is important is somewhat reactionary, isn't
it?"

"What do you mean?"   10

Devastated Kitchen

"Just think about it. Women's lib is supposed to help women develop their
talents and competence, free themselves and build a positive, creative sense
of identity, but when they no longer bother to learn how to cook because
it's too 'insignificant,' they are no better than most men, who are completely
hopeless when it comes to preparing food. Women are actually beginning
to lose their freedom to cook well! They are no longer the masters of their
kitchens. *That* is reactionary, and I think it means a crisis is coming in the
women's movement. That is why I began my own campaign. The book I'm
writing now is the first step; to me, this issue is important. And it is International Women's Year!

"Even without seeing that skeptical look on your face, I know it seems
presumptuous of me to write a cookbook. But no matter how odd it seems,
I am, in fact, a better cook than the average woman today. When I was living
in the United States I was able to make some money by teaching cooking
to groups of housewives. At the time I thought the reason I could get by
that way was because Americans are such bad cooks, but when I came back
to Japan, I found that things are worse here. The only food worth eating
nowadays is in restaurants; the quality of home cooking is dismal. To give
a new twist to the Chinese poem that Governor Minobe[1] once quoted,
'Because the kitchen is devastated, I will go back to it now.' "

"If I understand you correctly, you think women's liberation means
that women should go back to the kitchen and learn how to be good cooks."

"In part, yes, but I don't expect them to stay in the kitchen forever. If

---

[1] Tokyo's Governor Ryokichi Minobe once prematurely announced that he would not run for
a third term but would leave politics and retreat to the academic world. At that time he quoted
the following passage from a poem by T'ao Yüan-ming, "Because the fields are devastated, I
will go back to them now." [Translators' note]

someone wants to sleep she goes to bed, but only so she can get up and go out to work again. Sleeping and cooking are part of everyone's life, but they are certainly not all there is to it. Everyone has her own individual talents, which it is her responsibility to use wisely and well. Otherwise she will be wasting what she has."

"It seems to me that working outside the home—using one's individual   15 talents—is what women's liberation is saying women should do. Aren't doing domestic chores and developing one's own talents somehow incompatible?"

"Of course there may be conflicts in terms of time and energy, but not as far as ability is concerned. I am convinced that the superior woman is a superior cook. And conversely, the woman who is a poor cook is most likely a dull person."

"That's a pretty harsh statement. Do you really believe that?"

"Certainly. It may offend some, but the people whom I like and think highly of are all good cooks. Being disliked by anyone else doesn't bother me. The women who are highly competent in their jobs are good cooks as well. It is the sticky-sweet feminine types with nothing on their minds but marriage who, more often than not, are poor cooks. And they never get any better even if they study at cooking schools. I think that cooking is somehow a 'masculine' art. But because men discriminate, and shut women out from the 'masculine' world, women become more 'feminine' and are therefore terrible cooks."

"But talk about women being confined to their own world—hasn't their situation improved vastly recently?"

"You must remember that in the past the role of women was much   20 more 'masculine' than it is now. At one time the home was a woman's battlefield, the place where she fought the daily fight like a warrior. But now the household, with the women and children, has been pushed way behind the lines."

"Behind the lines?"

"Exactly. And you poor husbands go out to battle every day so that you can bring back the dough at night. But you frequently eat out on company business, so naturally even when you come back to camp behind the lines, you think nothing of eating institutional food."

"I don't like institutional food at all. But I agree with you that most home-cooked food tastes exactly like school lunches. Or worse, like dog food. Whenever I eat with my kids we always have spaghetti. We look like a group of ponies lined up at the trough!"

"No doubt. It's a rather pathetic scene."

"I don't like to say this, but you know, I can still remember the taste   25 of my mother's cooking with much fondness. But I don't think the reason my wife can't cook is because she is more feminine than my mother. I don't think that any woman could be more feminine than my mother."

I don't think this man got the point of my argument. Some confusion seems to have arisen, largely from our different ways of using the words "masculine" and "feminine." Differences in individual character and ability are not determined by sex differences. I have no sympathy with the primitive way of thinking that places human beings, before all else, into male and female categories. Words like *dansei-teki* (masculine) and *josei-teki* (feminine), *otoko-rashii* (manly) and *onna-rashii* (womanly) are so closely associated with old stereotypes and patterns of discrimination that they should not even be used, so I want to make clear that I use these words only for convenience, but I mean them to describe something beyond simple sexual differences. When I say that a "feminine" woman is a poor cook, I am using the word as an adjective that can be applied as easily to men as to women, just as "snobbish" or "naive" can apply to anyone. "Feminine" is convenient because it is broad and flexible. It may cause confusion, but I can't think of a better word for the same thing.

When the word "feminine" is used positively it can mean gentle, lovely, and pliable, but when used demeaningly it can mean cowardly, weak, and indecisive. "Masculine" is another general term, but it does not have as much fluidity as the word "feminine," and it is relatively fixed as a word of praise. It conveys many of the same qualities that the word "feminine" does when used in a good sense, such as gentleness and pliability, and so "masculine" has come to connote the most desirable features of a human being. When a man is called "feminine" it is an insult, but to use "masculine" to describe a woman is usually not as derogatory. This use of words is truly insulting to women, but if we make a fuss about it, there would be no end. I simplify the problem by accepting the fact that the word "masculine" is used positively while "feminine" has negative connotations, and use the adjectives accordingly.

Of all the qualities that are considered desirable, I am convinced that those most closely associated with the word "masculine" are essential to the superior cook. Think of the terms used to describe men considered to be the most "manly": having "the ability to make decisions and act on them," "a bold and flexible imagination," "clearheadedness," "keen insight," "natural coordination and robust physical strength," "steadfast, cool powers of judgment," "unyielding tenacity and a sense of responsibility," "broadmindedness," and "a plain, unpretentious outlook." These are exactly what the ideal cook needs among his or her personal characteristics. First, cooking is a series of decisions and actions. The "feminine" housewife gets weary of thinking up menus and will usually ask her husband in the morning, just after he has filled himself with breakfast, "What do you want for supper?" He gets annoyed at her. Then she watches TV cooking programs but gets discouraged at the complicated directions. She goes out shopping, gets tired of having to decide what to buy, and at last brings back some frozen *shumai.*°

If one has a bold and flexible imagination, it is nothing to think up a

---

shumai: Meat- and vegetable-filled dumplings. [Editors' note] new menu for each of the three hundred and sixty-five days of the year. We have no idea of when we might be confronted with a food crisis, but at least right now the markets are filled to overflowing with all kinds of things. I can't sympathize with people who say that they can't afford what they want. Prices for perishables are always changing, so if you look carefully, you can almost always find something reasonable. If women would go about planning menus in this way, it would be so easy. However, they try to do things just as they are told by the cookbooks and TV programs. Take salad, for example. Most people assume that salad has to be made with lettuce and tomatoes. They insist on buying green, tasteless tomatoes in the winter that may cost as much as two hundred yen apiece. They don't know that spinach, radishes, mushrooms, yams, or so many other things will do for a delicious salad.

The same applies to meat. Japanese housewives will only buy neatly   30 sliced meat. Shanks, tails, and various internal organs are cheap and can be very good depending on how they are cooked, but they are usually bought only by the foreigners who live here.

If you say that this is probably natural since the custom of eating meat is still new to Japanese, then what about fish? Today, who is really good at cleaning fish except the fishing buffs, who are usually men? Women have come to dislike the job; they hate to get their hands dirty and find it repulsive, so they leave it up to the fishmonger. And so they usually throw away the bony parts of the fish, which can be used for delicious soup. I find it even more surprising that most housewives do not use the portion around the central backbone of the bonito, and they refuse to use abalone liver. What they come back with is sliced raw fish. What a waste, but what good luck for me! Chuckling inside like an introverted hyena, I go and get what they leave behind, at a fraction of what they paid.

In order to get through the difficulties that pollution and the natural resources problem have posed, we need insight about safety, nutrition, and ways of economizing on food. It is not unusual these days to see someone throw away a large part of a *daikon* (radish) into the garbage. The moment you decide to buy the radish, you should be thinking quickly of how it will be used, the first day for *daikon oroshi* (grated use), the next day for *furofuki* (steamed then garnished with miso), and on the third day it can be cut into fine strips and used in miso soup.

From now on the trend will probably be toward buying food in large quantities, for a week at a time, perhaps. Then one will need to be able to think like a computer in order to calculate and plan a menu for seven days, combining what is on hand with the foodstuffs in the market and leftovers. "Feminine" consumers buy their groceries without any forethought, and consequently the refrigerator is crowded with leftovers that have no place in the next day's menu. Then the kitchen becomes a bother to them.

Cooking is not only an intellectually demanding pastime, it also requires physical effort, which means a natural coordination and robust physical strength. Those who operate in slow motion or are in poor physical condition cannot prepare good food. Moving the body quickly and energetically, one should be able to handle as many jobs as the number of fingers on one's hand. A "feminine" cook cannot do even two jobs at the same time, so while she is frying one thing, what she is boiling will be burned. She hasn't developed steadfast and cool judgment and does not know how to take emergency measures, so she stands there vacantly. When black smoke rises out of the skillet, she breaks into complete panic. "Feminine" people are overly excitable, as was demonstrated by the toilet paper panic° a couple of years ago.

She panics again when someone comes to visit. When her husband   35
brings his friends for an evening at home, she is far from delighted. She looks sullen and keeps saying, "Sorry, but we have nothing to give you." There are very few houses where there is really *nothing* to eat in the kitchen. There should at least be some eggs, *nori* (dried laver), *katsuo-bushi* (dried bonito), *negi* (onion), some other vegetables, and cold rice. With these alone, some dishes can be produced that go well with sake, and it should be easy to make *zosui* (rice and vegetable soup) and other things as well. "Feminine" housewives lack the agility to move with circumstances, and they hate to receive unexpected guests. They hate to have guests even when they know in advance. For several days ahead they are bothered, not knowing what to prepare, and in the worst cases, when they have not been able to decide even by the time the guest comes, they order something from a caterer. In short, they dislike serving any guests. Handing out the same limited fare day after day to their immediate family is about all contemporary housewives can do. They have lost the broadmindedness of the housewife of former times who quite easily coped with a houseful of people of all ages, as well as a few freeloaders.

What about the need for a "plain, unpretentious outlook"? One of the first things you usually notice about "feminine" cooking is its ostentation. Every once in a while when she gets wound up the "feminine" cook is eager to make something showy like hors d'oeuvres, a dish that makes you think you are at a hotel banquet. Neat notches are made in hard boiled eggs, and an apple slice is cut in such a way that the peel sticks up to look like a rabbit's ear. These are cheap tricks with decoration — the energy would be better used in making the food taste better.

Don't misunderstand me: Decoration is an important element in cooking, but the "feminine" cook feels uneasy unless she does everything, including decoration, exactly as told, for she has no confidence in her imagination.

She seems to think it would spoil the atmosphere if the dishes served at home did not look exactly like the plastic displays in the dusty show windows of restaurants. Somehow omelettes always have the specified blob of ketchup on them, asparagus in a salad seems always to have an identical

---

toilet paper panic: A media-inspired run on the shops for toilet paper, said to be in short supply in the early 1970s. [Editors' note]

twist of mayonnaise wrapped around it. There is always the same red spaghetti with hamburger, fried prawns always come with potato salad, and of course the ever-present sprig of parsley, which no one is supposed to eat in Japan. Why is the "feminine" person always so uncouth and so ready to follow everyone else? The rough and makeshift cooking of a man on a fishing trip or camping is much more gallant and appealing to the appetite.

Daily Self-expression in Cooking

There seems to be no end to the discussion once we begin talking about how "femininity" in the kitchen destroys the art of cooking. What should be done to make cooking more "masculine"? Bringing more "masculine" men into the kitchen is one answer, of course, but it is still very difficult to make men suddenly join in the kitchen work. Almost all men have grown up in a society where work is divided between male and female, and they have been completely cut off from the kitchen. Changing that is going to require steady training for several generations.

In this sense, the female who has been at home in the kitchen since   40 she was small is better prepared to take care of herself. I want women to realize that they have this advantage over males. Yet, girls are losing this advantage as the number of overly protective mothers increases. Not only boys, but girls as well are being kept out of the kitchen and sent into the world lacking in housework ability. That was practically the only area where women clearly had the advantage over men. Why is it that women, who are in general so tenacious and possessive in other areas, so easily abandon the practical skills they held firmly for thousands of years?

I am grateful for the difficult circumstances in which I grew up. It was my mother who was the main support of a family diminished by World War II, and it was only natural that the small children in the family did their best to help. There were no electric appliances, so when we made rice we had to collect firewood on a hill in back of our house and draw water from a well. Bread, pickles, jam, and everything else was almost always homemade. Vegetables, too, we grew in our garden. We improved on these most basic techniques for living and so we have no trouble doing housework today with all the modern electrical appliances.

From the time that I was a child, I have always felt it natural to do housework at home and study at school, so when I became an adult, it seemed just as natural to work outside my home and to do housework as well. It strikes me as very strange that so many women torture themselves by a self-imposed choice—whether to do housework at home or work outside.

But among the women of my generation there are still many who have fewer hangups in their attitude toward housework. They do not consider housework a painful process, as most younger women do, but have mastered housework casually and with ease. With this as a basis, they work outside and take the same attitude to their work as men do. They choose the work that makes it possible for them to use their talents best. These women have been working ever since they graduated from school. Some are married, others are not, but they are all housewives, for they manage the camp called the household.

To the best of my knowledge, capable workers are capable housewives. The time they give to housework is short because they are busy, but in that time they do their work quickly and energetically, like compressed air coming out of a pump. They handle it much better than women who lazily stay home all day. Housework for them is not like the ponderous rock in the myth of Sisyphus, but a kind of sport or recreational activity. Above all they think of cooking as creative, an art in which their individuality and talents are enlivened. Cooking, if not any other job at home, is something they would never willingly give up.

You are lucky if you constantly have a chance to express yourself, and it is even better if you have a family, lover, or friends who appreciate your ability at self-expression. Other human needs and desires fade away, but the desire for food remains as long as you do not have some serious illness. Sharing a passion for creative work with food and establishing communication through the medium of food can lead you to the easiest-made and longest-lasting of human relationships. 45

However, to develop the power of expression is very difficult if one stays in the kitchen. Absorbing the excitement and the trials of the outside world, one's cooking skills grow, too. Among all of my women friends, not one ever went to a cooking school. While they were busy in their studies, their work, their travels and loves, they developed an ability to prepare food almost without knowing it.

Nothing makes me happier than being with these friends now, in the prime of life. We really enjoy our dinner parties. We invite each other to our homes and entertain with meals we make ourselves. It is natural to all of us, and the food is superb. All of these friends enjoy expressing themselves, and if they cannot prepare an outstanding meal impossible to find anywhere else, they do not feel satisfied when entertaining.

It's discouraging when someone praises your cooking by comparing it with some restaurant, but anyone who thinks in those terms is convinced that restaurant cooking is better than home cooking. My proud friends work hard in their kitchens just because they want to do what restaurants cannot. The food that we prepare is made purely for pleasure, unrelated to profit or loss, so we would not be happy with the kind of food that restaurants put out. Although none of these people is rich, they have their own incomes and can spend what they need to prepare a gourmet meal. Sometimes it feels extravagant, but in the long run they actually get more for their money than someone eating in a back-street drinking place.

They can also use their abundant knowledge and experience, along with their money. Working outside the home, one has a chance to eat in many different places. These women are very enterprising, and when they eat something they fully enjoy, they study the ingredients and how to make it, and add it to their repertoire. When one of my friends comes back from abroad we wait with mouths watering to see what new addition she has made to her cooking abilities. It seems that we are among the few people in Japan who eat cod from the shores of Portugal, couscous from Algeria, or moussaka eggplant from Greece.

Some of us are interested in classical cooking and have tried to recreate 50 cooking from ages long past: the kind of omelette that Napoleon had after he awoke, the vegetable soup Yang Kuei-fei° used to maintain her fabulous beauty, and the bisque that Hirobumi Ito° used to sip at the Rokumeikan.°

Good conversation at the table is an important element that we have also developed. Any of the trivial topics of conversation, which usually center around children, are absolutely forbidden at our table—that would be like mixing sweet ketchup with a good wine.

Whenever I spend time with these intelligent and capable women I become convinced that they come closest to the ideal of the integrated human being. Generally, men are more reliable and fun to be with than women. But there are those women, like my friends, who are all that and more. They are androgynous; they have the good points of both men and women. If there were more such people, regardless of gender, the world would be a much pleasanter and easier place to live in.

It would be unfortunate if women's lib encouraged women to discard the abilities that they have maintained for so long, only to be on a par with the contemporary male. Even if all women were to advance so far that they became unable to get along without employing a male housekeeper, that would represent little improvement over the present situation; it would only mean that the negative and positive aspects of today's comfortless society, with its division of labor by sex, would be reversed.

A women's movement that has discarded such fundamental skills of human life as cooking and household management is on shaky ground indeed. I have had a few chances to see some communes in the United States and found that in groups where most of the women hated housework, daily life had all but collapsed. These communes felt somehow corrupt, rank, and decayed. But the communes were vigorous where the women were lively and enjoyed cooking and housework. They made you feel hopeful for the future of the women's movement.

One thing that I keep repeating is that one loses nothing by being good 55 at cooking. Some reply that you do. By obediently learning how to cook,

---

Yang Kuei-fei: The famous Chinese courtesan, concubine of the great T'ang emperor Hsüan Tsung (eighth century A.D.). **Hirobumi Ito:** The preeminent statesman of the Meiji period (1868–1912), architect of Japan's first constitution, and prime minister for four terms. **Rokumeikan:** A meeting hall and catering service introducing Western food and customs to Japan in the Meiji era. [Editors' notes]

women allow men to take their labor for granted. They also say equality for women should start by abandoning the housework that has oppressed them. But I suspect the able woman feels that since men grow up only partially formed, they are to be pitied, and it would be better not to fuss over trivial matters that are so easy to take care of.

While men cannot yet do the jobs that women can, women are increasingly mastering the jobs traditionally given to men. What is needed if we are to attain equality is not that the women catch up to a group of people who are deformed, but that "deformed" men catch up with the superior women—the women who have developed within themselves the good points of both sexes.

What I have written so far may give the impression that I am pushing a personal fetish too far. Honestly speaking, I often get exhausted and even wish sometimes I had a wife to do my housework for me. In a society where labor is divided, as in ours, it is not as easy to hold down a job and maintain a household as it is to talk about doing so. But we should not yield to the rules of a society that are wrong. We have to be stubborn and work with a spirit two or three times as strong as that of the ordinary person, otherwise we can never change anything.

Keeping our noses to the grindstone won't get us anywhere, so we must manage household affairs more rationally, using a free "masculine" approach; we have to rule our kitchens with wisdom to create a more comfortable method of doing things. What I want to write is a cookbook that will help to achieve that. I was asked by my publisher to write something on a philosophy of life for young women, but there are already too many books about love and marriage. Thinking about putting out another one only bores me.

I informed the publisher that I wanted to write a book on cooking, and that I thought it would be more useful to young women. The publisher's agent did not appear to be very enthusiastic about this idea. That was probably natural, for most women who buy my books are those who are dissatisfied with the traditional female roles and who want to live much freer and more interesting lives. Those who react against having housework forced on them would probably pay no attention to a cookbook. But that is exactly the kind of woman who needs to learn to love cooking. If cooking is a partner that one must go through life with, it is better to hold fast and love the partner than to bear it like some fearsome burden. If you can do that you will have a life that is much more interesting and free.

Thinking About the Text

1. Summarize Kirishima's argument. Do you agree with her reasoning and conclusions? Why, or why not?

2. Examine the remark "Women are actually beginning to lose their freedom

to cook well!" (para. 11) in context, and then explain exactly what Kirishima means. Might the same be said of American women? Explain.

3. How might Kazuko Watanabe (see the next selection) reply to Kirishima? How might Sumiko Iwao (p. 180)?

Thinking About Culture

4. In an effort to elevate eating beyond a trivial or "fueling" activity, Kirishima asks her friends to focus on nontrivial conversation at table. Eating together has many different meanings and moods, from the Last Supper to food fights. Examine three different kinds of meals in your experience, characterizing them by their focus on food, ritual, communication, simple maintenance, or other foci. Some examples: a holiday meal, such as Thanksgiving; a tête-à-tête at a romantic restaurant; a camping meal outdoors by a fire; an airplane meal at 30,000 feet.

5. "A women's movement," Kirishima says in paragraph 54, "that has discarded such fundamental skills of human life as cooking and household management is on shaky ground indeed." Do you agree? And is it your impression that the women's movement in the United States has discarded these skills? Support your answers with evidence.

Kazuko Watanabe

The New Cold War with Japan: How Are Women Paying for It?

The tension between Japan and the United States, which has been building for years, is at fever pitch: Business executives and politicians in each country are expressing their resentment toward the economic policies of the other country; *The Coming War with Japan*, a book by a U.S. author, has become a Japanese best-seller; a recent poll revealed that many Japanese now believe the United States is as much a threat to Japan's security as was the Soviet Union. "Japan-bashing" from Washington to Hollywood has unnerved the

Kazuko Watanabe teaches women's studies and American literature at Kyoto Sangyo University. She is an adviser to Kyoto City on issues especially related to women, and she founded the Kyoto International Women's Club. This article, based in part on an interview with Nancy Lee Koschmann, originally appeared in the November/December 1991 issue of Ms. *magazine.*

Asian American community, and businesspeople fear that cultural misunderstandings will damage what the Commission on U.S.-Japan Relations for the Twenty-First Century calls "the single most important bilateral relationship in the world."

The rhetoric of this nascent cold war on both sides of the Pacific is the same—it is by, for, and about men. In Japan, in our factories, offices, farms, and homes are the women who constitute the invisible army, drafted for a war not of their making. The irony is familiar: As our economy expands, victory is claimed—and women are left to count their losses.

I never realized the extent of Japan's economic growth until I visited the United States, since in Japan we feel few benefits from it. Despite economic development, we suffer from inflation, overcrowding, and high costs of housing, education, and everyday goods (Tokyo is among the world's most expensive cities).

Most women work hard to make ends meet for their families. Women usually control family businesses and their husbands' salaries, and are responsible for their children's education. They believe educational success guarantees economic success, which eventually will lead to spiritual happiness. Therefore, they struggle so that their children will get into prestigious universities; there is a special desk some children have, with a buzzer that alerts their mothers to bring them snacks so they won't have to interrupt their studying.

Most families are, figuratively speaking, fatherless. Men are never home   5
because jobs demand long hours of overtime. The average male employee has little private life and can be transferred at any time. Figures from 1986 reveal that husbands of full-time employed women spend fifteen minutes a day on household chores, while the employed women spend four and a half hours. On the surface the family is stable, but married couples become estranged, and affairs are common. More couples divorce in later years, especially after the husband's retirement—when the wife's suppressed resentment explodes.

The economic giants make a big show of plans to increase free time and encourage vacations. But smaller companies, which employ the majority of women workers, find it difficult to compete. If an employee takes a holiday, dedication is suspect and a promotion is jeopardized. There is a new concern with *karoshi,* or "death by overwork": A recent poll showed that over 25 percent of workers are afraid of dying on the job. This year the family of a woman who allegedly died of *karoshi* sued the bank that had employed her.

Behind the Affluence:
Women Workers on the Margins

Japan's labor shortage, a result of accelerated economic development, has brought more women into the work force. But men and a male-centered society haven't changed much. A government survey this year on sex roles showed that more than a third of all men still support traditional roles, while only a quarter of women do. A Japanese newspaper reported that the number of women who favor the single life rose from 4 percent in 1984 to 14 percent in 1989.

Such changes in women's attitudes have had a growing influence on our economics, politics, and culture. But in many cases, women's increased access to education and employment is only an adaptation of the traditional mother-wife role to the needs of Japan's expanding economy (which we are told is owed entirely to men).

Women's roles in the economy are seldom recognized, nor are the ways Japan's "bubble economy" is sacrificing women workers—Japanese and migrant—as marginal labor. Shortly after the passage of the Equal Employment Opportunity Law (EEOL) in 1986, one of my best women students was hired to work in the international office of Minolta, one of the most popular companies for young women job hunters. But when she visited me a few months later, she told me she had nothing to do at work except when she was sent out to get snacks. When she asked her boss to give her real work, he was astonished and said nothing. The young woman eventually quit, saying she'd have more rewarding work at home. When I related her story to an executive men's group, they told me that they did not want to waste money and time to seriously train female workers because women lacked "motivation."

Due in large part to the EEOL, women now make up 40.4 percent of the work force and 70 percent of married women with teenage children work outside the home. But their jobs are the lowest paid, and less than 10 percent are in management. There are increasing calls for a review of the EEOL, which forbids discrimination on the basis of sex but has no penalties for companies that fail to comply. Married women are tax-deductible dependents only if they earn less than one million yen (U.S. $7,300) annually, which makes women's economic independence impossible. One-quarter of all employed women are part-time workers, and women earn only 50.3 percent of men's wages.

The situation is worse for the estimated 150,000 migrant women who come to Japan yearly, some recruited supposedly to work in a factory or as a waitress, who find themselves virtually indentured servants. Most come to Japan in search of work because they have to feed families back in Thailand, Malaysia, or the Philippines; but when they arrive, the employer confiscates their passports, threatens them with court action for working on a tourist visa, often forces them into sex work, and subtracts "expenses" from their paychecks.

Japanese corporations have also started to move overseas in search of cheap labor. The role of these corporations in exploiting Asian women workers will be among the central issues of the second Asia-wide Women's Conference to be held in Japan in April 1992. The conference will also focus on sexual violence, women in development, and trafficking in women.

(Feminists have notified the UN antidiscrimination committee about a card game produced by the Takara Company, Ltd., called "Human Trash," in which players compete to make money by selling women.) The Asian Women Workers' Exchange Center in Tokyo has been working on these issues and supporting labor unions in other Asian countries.

Women workers in Japanese factories and corporations, at home and abroad, report pervasive sexual harassment—which is only beginning to emerge as a public issue. The term *seku hara,* for sexual harassment, was recently coined from the English, and the first lawsuit against sexual harassment was filed in 1989.

Japanese feminists are increasingly initiating legal action, surveys, and media attention. The Japan Pacific Resource Network (JPRN), a Berkeley, California–based educational organization, monitors cases of sexual harassment of women workers by Japanese employers in both Japan and the United States, and conducted a nationwide public education campaign in Japan last May.

Outspoken journalist Yayori Matsui founded the Asian Women's Association to help the thousands of Asian women exploited by "sex tours" of Japanese men to South Korea, Thailand, and the Philippines. A recent incident has particularly incensed women's groups: In a deal with the Tokyo government, the Sogo Department Store opened a branch in the new, billion-dollar Tokyo Metropolitan Government Building, rent-free. When Sogo built another branch in Indonesia last year, the store invited employees, clients, and business connections for opening day, and entertained them with sex tours. Women's groups have protested the store's policy—which might have been ignored as one of thousands of such "tours," except that Sogo happened to receive special benefits from the Tokyo government. 15

The Cult of Motherhood

To really understand the complexity of Japanese women's lives, more attention should be paid to the cultural factors that influence female decision-making. A survey revealed that 77 percent of women employees assume a company will request their retirement upon the birth of a child, although most companies do not have any written policies on such matters. But in Japan, where the cultural images of motherhood are ubiquitous, the pressure of socialization invariably limits women's goals.

The image of "mother" can only be understood in terms of the Japanese concept of self; it is significantly different from the Western view, and thus differentiates our feminist strategy. Japanese culture is antiego, in that it applies sanctions to those who stand out. One is supposed to compete and do well, but only to contribute to the collectivity of the family, school, company, or country. For the individual, self-assertion suggests selfishness, and is shameful. Women gain self-respect and the admiration of others only through the performance of their designated female role—self-sacrifice.

Because women are considered the regulators of behavior, the immaturity and dependence of those who are cared for by mothers—men and children—are reinforced. Given this situation, relationships between women and men cannot develop on equal terms; they remain mother-son relationships. This may explain why the study of incest in Japan focuses primarily on sons as victims and mothers as initiators, not on fathers and daughters—as in reality. The myth of son-as-victim is readily believed because of the dominant maternal culture.

Feminist historians argue that "maternalism" has dangerous political aspects—the clearest example being the emperor system, the root of Japanese patriarchy. The emperor is characterized in terms of *motherhood*. He is sentimentally respected for his self-sacrifice for the nation; Japanese soldiers internalized his image as a mother and died for it during wartime.

Like women the world over, we also have the duty of caring for the   20
elderly. Life expectancy is among the longest in the world—nearly 82 years for women and 76 years for men according to 1990 statistics—and the declining birthrate means that adults will soon have even fewer siblings with whom to share the burden. The cultural ideal is the son's devotion to his mother, but 80 percent of caretakers for the elderly are daughters or daughters-in-law. Today, more women quit jobs to care for parents than to care for children. The EEOL supposedly equalized retirement benefits, but most women can't work long enough to take advantage of them.

Economics and Reproduction

Japan's economy will stagnate by the first decade of the twenty-first century, partly because of the decreasing birthrate. The Committee for Twenty-First-Century Economic Planning predicts a labor shortage because of Japanese women's "refusal" to bear enough children to maintain a population growth rate. The birthrate in 1990 dropped to its lowest level on record, 1.53 percent.

The government has reacted by quickly passing a new law granting up to a year's leave for both parents, and announced last March that it would pay women 5,000 yen ($38) per month for each preschool-age child, and double that for a third child. Some Japanese leaders have also suggested that the government discourage women from continuing their education (see *Ms.*, September/October 1990). All of this has outraged Japanese women, whose average marriage age is now 25.8, the highest on record in Japan (for men it's 28.5). And women's groups are protesting a recent government decision to reduce the legal abortion period from 24 to 22 weeks.

Men's desperation for childbearing mates is also leading to an increase in "mail-order bride" schemes. Few Japanese women are now willing to live in agricultural regions, so farmers "buy" wives from the Philippines and Thailand through international marriage brokers. They pay a large fee, which sometimes goes to the woman's family, but usually ends up in the broker's pocket. What was once a rural phenomenon is becoming an urban one.

Greater numbers of blue-collar workers and merchants are sending for women from Korea, Taiwan, the Philippines, Thailand, and Malaysia, in that order.

In Politics and Education,
a Mixed Picture

Although Takako Doi eventually resigned as head of the Socialist Party in April 1991, she made her mark. She became the first woman leader of a major political party in the wake of numerous disclosures of corruption among Diet (parliament) members.

Doi also inspired ordinary women to become interested in politics. Increasing numbers of women have run for local government posts and the Diet, and with women supporters—some labeling themselves "full-time, activist housewives"—they won seats; the victory last April of Harue Kitamura as the first woman mayor of Ashiya City (and in all of Japan) was due to their energy.

During the April elections women broke records around the country: 82 (from 52) to prefectural assemblies; 61 (from 39) to major city assemblies; 1,157 to city councils; and 791 to town and village assemblies. Each political party now has more women than before; in the minor parties, women have doubled the number of their seats. Still, all this is far behind feminists' aim of achieving a 30 percent representation in local government by 1999.

In education, one must also look twice at the recent numbers. In 1989, for the first time, more women (36.8 percent) entered colleges and universities than men (35.8 percent). But two-thirds of female students are in women's junior colleges (established to promote traditional, domestic roles for women), whereas 80 percent of male students are in four-year universities.

Only 14 percent of women entered four-year universities in 1989—and they usually majored in home economics, nutrition, or literature. Such a postsecondary education becomes an asset for a marriage partner, the way the study of flower arrangement and tea ceremonies did in years past. Very few major in political science, engineering, or biology, although recently, more have focused on law and economics. The proliferation of women's studies in higher education has helped politicize students, but few women go on to graduate school. Most female academics are relegated to lecturer positions and introductory courses.

Today's Wars and Yesterday's Victims

Whereas statistics tell one story, the dramatic increase in activist groups tells another—and is most indicative of the changes in women's consciousness. Prior to the Gulf War, thousands of women demonstrated in Tokyo against sending "defensive" personnel to the gulf, and against the proposed law permitting the first post–World War II dispatch of Japanese troops overseas (which would have violated the constitution's prohibition on Japan having an army).

All over Japan, thousands of women are involved in campaigns around   30
the environment, pornography, disability issues, violence in the family, racism, economic exploitation, peace, and lesbian issues. (The second Asian Lesbian Conference is planned for May 1992, organized by the only national lesbian group, Regumi.) The antiwar Delta Women's Group in Hiroshima is organized by women—who, along with children, comprised the majority of victims of the atomic bombs dropped by the United States on Hiroshima and Nagasaki on August 6 and 9, 1945.

The Delta group, which includes women from all over Japan, works together with Hibakusha women, who are survivors of the bombs. Many of these women have leukemia and cancers caused by their exposure to nuclear radiation, and have a high incidence of miscarriage and children with birth defects; others live in constant fear of latent disease for themselves and their children. Thousands of women who were disfigured were abandoned by their husbands. All of these women have suffered from discrimination in marriage and employment. They can get some health insurance benefits, if they identify themselves as Hibakusha, which they are often reluctant to do. But in an effort to contribute to the peace movement, more Hibakusha have courageously started to reveal their experiences to young people who visit Hiroshima, and some of their stories were finally told in a Japanese TV documentary last summer.

Women's groups have also been working together with Korean Japanese women to unearth the tragic stories of more than 200,000 women, the majority of them Korean, who were conscripted by the Japanese army and sent to the front to have forced sex with soldiers during World War II. Called "comfort women," they were made to take the place of Japanese prostitutes, too many of whom suffered from venereal diseases. Some killed themselves to avoid humiliation, and others were murdered; few returned home. Women's groups have appealed to the government to officially apologize to these women, to compensate them and their parents, and to put their stories in history textbooks.

Fighting racism has been the goal of Mieko Chikkap, an active Ainu feminist. The Ainu, an indigenous ethnic minority, migrated from the Asian continent to Japan in prehistoric times and live in Hokkaido. Chikkap has been trying to resurrect Ainu crafts and culture, traditionally preserved by women. She helped organize a campaign called "People's Plan Twenty-First Century," which brought indigenous minority groups from all over the world to Hokkaido.

Deciphering Official Feminism

After Japan ratified the United Nations Convention for the Elimination of All Forms of Discrimination Against Women (CEDAW) in 1985, each local government was instructed to create a Women's Action Plan based on the convention; as a result, women's bureaus and centers were established all over the country.

Many women attend courses and workshops at the centers because   35 they are organized by the government—not by radical feminists or "women's lib" people. As feminists, some of us used to be suspicious of these centers, but we've learned that many of their programs are valuable.

But there are reasons why the government has increasingly committed resources to these centers: It wants to keep women's energy from erupting in a more rebellious way. The government is also afraid of international criticism; it wants to make sure it has something to show as a signatory to the convention.

Still, women can use the government's sensitivity regarding its international reputation. Japanese companies need pressure from the outside to reform their sexist and racist practices. Such pressure might have discouraged corporate developers, who were pushing for the 1998 Winter Olympics to be in Japan, from ordering Japanese women athletes to wear kimonos and serve tea while lobbying the International Olympic Committee (the male athletes wore blazers). We need our sisters in the West—and everywhere— and hope they understand that *we* are not adversaries; the patriarchy is our mutual problem.

Meanwhile, at home, it is time to look at our economy from a more global perspective, and be concerned with *real* growth—which would include recognition of the human rights of women. But I am encouraged by the past decade's progress. Increasing numbers of Japanese and other Asian women are creating our own vision for the twenty-first century, making the kinds of international contacts businessmen only dream of. According to Akiko Yosano (1878–1942), one of Japan's most celebrated woman poets:

> The day when the mountain will move is coming.
> When I say this, no one believes me,
> The mountains have been asleep only temporarily.
> In antiquity, mountains, all aflame, moved about.
> No one need believe this.
> But, all of you, believe this.
> All the women who had been asleep
> Have now awakened and are on the move.

Thinking About the Text

1. Summarize the main points of Watanabe's essay. Has she convinced you that Japan and the United States are in a new "cold war" and that Japanese women are "paying for it"?

2. Watanabe presents a wide-ranging feminist analysis and critique of many elements of Japanese society. Try on Watanabe's perspective and reread one of the other selections in this book. How does the selection change?

3. In addition to Watanabe, several authors—including Ruth Benedict (p. 78), Merry I. White (p. 95), and Sumiko Iwao (the next selection)—discuss the importance of mothers in Japan. Compare the various claims and try to sum up their similarities and differences.

Thinking About Culture

4. According to Watanabe, Japanese corporations in search of cheap foreign labor are "exploiting Asian women" (para. 12). How would you define exploitation? If a Japanese corporation in Thailand pays the prevailing wage—a wage far below the wage for a comparable job in Japan—is the corporation exploiting the Thai worker? If you believe that Japanese businesses do exploit foreign workers, do you also believe we should therefore not buy Japanese goods manufactured in other Asian countries? Explain.

   Furthermore, do American corporations exploit Mexican and Asian workers by establishing factories in Mexico and in Asia? And do we exploit Mexican and Mexican American migrant workers in this country? (Again, you will have to construct a definition of exploitation in order to think usefully about this question.) If you believe that we do indeed exploit migrant workers, what, as an individual, do you intend to do about it?

5. Watanabe expresses unhappiness with the idea that in Japan "one is supposed to compete and do well, but only [in order] to contribute to the collectivity of the family, school, company, or country" (para. 17). Leaving aside the question of whether or not most Japanese feel this way, does this strike you as an utterly un-American ideal? Does it strike you as a good or a bad ideal? Explain.

6. Watanabe refers to a "maternal" emperor in a "patriarchal" system (para. 19). Takeo Doi, a Japanese psychoanalyst, has also referred to the prewar emperor as evoking the kind of dependency experienced in a baby's relationship with the mother. Let us assume Watanabe is *not* confusing "matriarchy" and "patriarchy" but rather is explaining Japanese *society* as structurally patriarchal, and the *emperor* as a "mother." How would you characterize the American people's relation to their society and to their president?

Sumiko Iwao

The Quiet Revolution:
Japanese Women Today

The past fifteen years have been an era of profound change—a time of what I call inconspicuous revolution—for Japanese women. While the central organizations and groups that make up Japanese society are still almost exclusively staffed and controlled by men, opportunities for women to work and seek fulfillment outside the home have increased, giving them a whole new range of freedoms.

This development has led to a reversal of freedoms, as it were. Once it was women who were chained, responsible for family and household while men were free to pursue power, wealth, and adventure outside the home. But now men have become increasingly chained to the institutions they have set up, with their commitment to long-term employment and the promotional ladder rigged to seniority. Their wives, on the other hand, have been set free by the development of home appliances and other conveniences, and now their ability and energy is being absorbed by a waiting labor market and a broad range of culturally enriching activities. Not only can they work outside the home, but they have great freedom to decide how, where, and under what terms they will work. The female side of society has become extremely diversified, while the male side, trapped by inertia and peer pressure, has grown more homogeneous.

What ultimately provided Japanese women with increased options, ironically, was their position outside the mainstream of society. While their existence and voices have been pretty much ignored by men in formal arenas, the resulting "inequality" has given women great freedom to act and think as they wish in a surprisingly wide sphere. Although perhaps a dangerous generalization, I believe one is likely to find more truly creative and adventurous women than men in Japan today. Women are the intellectual and economic upstarts of today's society, spending freely and utilizing their energies in diverse ways. Men, meanwhile, remain largely restrained by the old norms and codes of traditional hierarchical society.

Freedom and Equality

The present Japanese Constitution, promulgated in 1946, stipulates equal rights for men and women. Consequently, the problem of sexual discrimination in Japan is one of gaining equal opportunity, not equal rights under the Constitution, as it has been in the United States for example.

Sumiko Iwao holds a Ph.D. from Yale University. She is a professor of social psychology at Keio University's Institute for Communications Research, a member of the Council on National Pensions, and the director of the Japan Institute of Women's Employment.

In Japan equality is not so much the governing principle of democratic   5
society as a tool to be taken up when appropriate. Sometimes there is more
freedom in this approach than in the strictly principled approach. Questions
of fairness and equality are conceived in long-term, multidimensional perspective. Although the husband and wife in a household or the coworkers
in an office may not seem to be treated equally at any particular point in
time, those involved consider the question from a broader perspective. In
facing specific day-to-day situations, Japanese women tend to be extremely
pragmatic; if the advantages and disadvantages balance out in the long run,
people are willing to accept the relationship as fair and equal. The precondi-
tion for achieving this balance, of course, is a long-term, trusting relationship.

The advantages of the "long-term equality" approach are that a flexible
position can be adopted to take into account the complex realities of human
relations, and responses to issues of minor importance can be relaxed and
tolerant. There are some situations in which Japanese women are quick to
demand equality and others where they do not feel it is an important issue.
When they wish to protest against unfair treatment, nevertheless, they are
less likely to opt for a direct confrontation that leaves bad feelings on both
sides than to let the party concerned know indirectly, albeit quite plainly,
that they are unhappy with the situation.

Many Japanese women believe that happiness for both men and women
would be better assured by a model of equality in which men currently
alienated from their families and deprived of culturally enriching pursuits
are given the same freedom, rights, and options in the three main areas of
life (work, family, and leisure) that women currently enjoy. The balance
ultimately maintained in the three areas would depend on the specific needs
and preferences of the individuals concerned.

However, through their less-than-eager pursuit of total equality with
men, Japanese women reveal their awareness that having to bear equal economic responsibility with men does not always serve their best interests. True
equality with men would limit their current options and level of enjoyment of
life considerably, and consequently many Japanese women prefer to evade
the subject.

Below I will consider some of the specific ways in which Japanese
women's lives have changed recently, and the impact of those changes on
society as a whole.

Work as an Option

In the workplace, the number of women has climbed and the range of jobs   10
open to them has widened appreciably. In 1960 most women who worked

Her most recent book is The Japanese Woman: Traditional Image and Changing
Reality *(1993). The essay that we reprint was originally prepared for a lecture presented
in 1991 at the Royal Society of the Arts, London.*

were in the agricultural sector, but today that has changed dramatically. The number in farm jobs has decreased sharply, and there has been a further shift in the economy from manufacturing to services, which are where a majority of today's working women are employed.

Today six out of ten working women are married, and the average length of continuous employment for women has risen to seven years. If we plot the proportion of women who work on a graph, with age as the horizontal axis and percentage employed as the vertical axis, an M-shaped curve emerges. The two peaks of the curve correspond to the age-groups 20–24 and 40–49, and the trough represents the years in between, when many women leave their jobs to give birth and raise children. The distinct M-shaped curve is a striking contrast to the plateau-shaped curve that describes the population of working women in most Western countries where fewer women quit working upon the birth of a child.

The labor market in Japan is tight, and it is expected to grow even tighter in the years to come. Businesses are pinning their hopes on women and retirees to fill the gap. Meanwhile, the number of women who wish to pursue a career has been rising steadily, and the Equal Employment Opportunity Law went into effect in 1986. The legislation, which calls on employers to give women the same opportunities as men in recruitment, training, promotions, wages, and retirement, marked a major shift in emphasis—from protecting working women to ensuring them equality with men. But this has led to a dilemma of sorts. While some women want to pursue a full-fledged career and demand equal treatment with men, the majority of women entering the labor force even today intend to leave their jobs after working four or five years.

The problem is how to provide equal treatment for those who want a career while continuing to offer jobs that meet the needs of the non-career-minded majority. Rather than implement the principle of equality rigidly, Japanese companies have hammered out a realistic solution that accommodates women's diverse goals. Many large companies have begun offering women the choice of two tracks. The Japanese names of these tracks are, literally, "ordinary" and "comprehensive," but I will refer to them as the clerical track and managerial track. The clerical track, which is exclusively for women, does not entail job rotations which involve relocation to another city, but the women joining it are paid less and have fewer chances of promotion than their male coworkers. Women joining the managerial track, meanwhile, receive the same treatment as men, including the possibility of transfers to other locations.

To my mind, it is strange that men are automatically placed on the managerial track. Given the option, at least a few, I am sure, would choose the less demanding clerical track, despite the lower pay. The older generation of males who run Japan's businesses apparently still believe that all men are intent on climbing the corporate ladder. What many of these older men seem not to realize is that young men are changing dramatically too.

In their pragmatic approach to the problem of women's diverse attitudes   15
to work, companies specifically ask women to choose between the clerical
and managerial track when recruiting and then test them accordingly. The
dual-track system should probably be viewed as a singularly Japanese-style
approach in its emphasis on reality rather than principle.

Another point to note is that women's attitudes toward work have
become increasingly diversified. Working women now fall into two main
groups: a small, very talented elite, whose ambitions may run even higher
than men's, and a great mass majority, whose members (though many are
just as talented) do not want to work so hard that it will interfere with their
family responsibilities and enjoyment of nonwork activities.

Japan's remarkable economic growth has been facilitated by the willingness of employees to sacrifice their own interests for the good of the company
and the stoic sense of satisfaction they have gained from actively taking on
more work than they were required to do. For these worker bees, a feeling
of solidarity with their firm and the prospect of moving into a management
post in due time have been sufficient motivation. But today's young men
and women, with their relatively pampered upbringing, cannot be expected
to display the same work ethic.

In a recent opinion poll, the proportion of respondents who said they
like work was over 80 percent for people 40 years of age or older, but the
figure was 10 points lower for females in their twenties and a full 25 points
lower for males in their twenties. The desire to win promotion has always
been weak among women, conditioned by the knowledge that such ambition
will only become a source of frustration. But younger men, it seems, are also
starting to give more priority to job satisfaction than to climbing the corporate
ladder. Younger people today are increasingly unwilling to let work interfere with their private affairs, and they have fewer qualms about refusing
a supervisor's request to work overtime if they have already made other
plans.

Changing Attitudes Toward Work

Until recently most Japanese, whether male or female, used to respond to
inquiries from potential employers about the type of work they wanted to
do with a noncommittal "Anything is fine." Women were afraid that a
specific request would be interpreted as impertinent, and men figured that
even if they were given an assignment they did not like, they would be
transferred to another section in due course, so it was only a matter of
making the most of a temporarily unsatisfactory situation.

But young people today have clear ideas about the type of work they   20
want to do. If they receive an assignment that suits them, they will work like
cart horses, but problems arise if they are assigned to a job they do not like.
In cases like that, men will sometimes quit and women will feel even less
hesitant about leaving. This of course does not apply to the elite of women

professionals. But for the members of the mass majority, who know they are unlikely to be working in the same firm for many years anyway, there is little point in taking the male tack of putting up with an unpleasant job in the hope that things will get better in the future. The growth of employment opportunities for women and the tightness of the labor market have in fact made it easier for women to switch jobs.

Japanese companies generally do not hire people individually to fill particular positions but recruit a new batch of graduates once a year. The members of this group undergo a few months' training and are then distributed among the company's departments. This sort of system is extremely expensive, and employers were previously unwilling to bear the expense of training women, who they presumed would quit within a few years. With the implementation of the Equal Employment Opportunity Law, a growing number of companies have begun providing on-the-job training for women. Such firms may be left empty-handed if the women soon quit, even though a well-trained female work force is a plus for society as a whole.

The differences in men's and women's long-range employment and life goals are at the root of the gap in their attitudes toward work. Women tend to make full use of the benefits to which they are entitled, such as paid holidays, recreational facilities owned by the company, and systems like flextime. In one company that introduced flextime, for example, as long as most of the employees were males, they continued to come in at the regular starting time and stay until after the regular working day was over. But when the number of female employees increased and women began to take full advantage of the system, the men slowly began to follow suit.

Men tend to keep their opinions to themselves at work, because they expect to remain at the same company for many years and assertiveness is not generally conducive to one's prospects for long-term success in a Japanese firm. But women, who know they have the option of leaving, are much more likely to say exactly what is on their minds. The harmonious work environment at Japanese companies has been made possible by the willingness of individuals to suppress their feelings and cooperate with others for the sake of the organization as a whole. But the winds of change are bound to overtake Japanese firms as working women grow in number.

The women of the mass majority hold much shorter-term views of their jobs than men, and their performance is influenced not by the prospects for promotion later on but by how matters stand at present. Their work can be heavily affected by the way their boss treats them. If properly encouraged, they will hustle, but if not they will just sit tight. Bosses who in bygone days were surrounded by young women who anticipated and attended to their every need now have to devote much time and energy to soft-soaping their female subordinates.

After-five gatherings used to be an integral part of company life; they 25 played a key role in bonding and in enhancing group harmony. But they were a source of frustration for women with families, who were torn between the desire not to miss out on the information exchanged during these sessions and the urge to return home to their children. In recent years, however, meetings on important work-related matters have increasingly been scheduled during regular work hours in the face of the growing aversion among young people to intrusions on their after-work hours by their supervisors or associates. Women managers with families are the happiest about this trend.

The influx of married women into the workplace may have a significant impact on management practices. Employees used to work late into the night to get an assignment done, but signs of change are in the making. A certain department store has a policy of changing its displays frequently to attract customers, and for many years it had its employees do the arranging after closing time, which often meant they had to stay very late. But it recently began allowing them to come in earlier in the morning as a way of accommodating the schedules of its female employees. One upshot was that women became able to move into positions of responsibility. Another was the realization among the men at the top that employees could work with undivided attention and get through in a short span of time a task they once had taken hours to complete. In this way, I believe that women's entry into the work force will trigger a reevaluation of the deplorable custom of having men remain in the office until all hours of the night. And if employees show they can work more intently and get assignments done in less time, it may trigger a decline in Japan's long working hours.

The Superwoman Elite

The appearance on the scene of an elite minority of female professionals has had an unmistakable impact on Japanese companies. The members of this group are veritable superwomen, extremely bright and filled with ambition. They present a striking contrast to the mollycoddled young men of their age, who were raised by strong mothers and absentee fathers and tend to be quite pleasant but unenergetic. They are starting, in effect, to climb an uncharted mountain, and nobody yet knows how their ascent will change them and others, what effect their success will have on, for example, their husband's aspirations or their marital relationship.

These trailblazers are filled with confidence and hope, but at the same time they are under a great deal of pressure. They work long hours, achieve impressive results, and win coveted posts. They tend to outperform their male peers even when the latter are also working furiously. Companies are pinning their hopes on these women, and their male coworkers seem to be accepting their success, reasoning that people deserve to be recognized on the basis of their achievements, regardless of their gender.

Companies also know there is an added benefit to hiring women, since they bring a new perspective to an operation formerly run with an all-male mind-set. Until now a variety of firms have sought to give play to the female sensibility in product development, and women—including those of the nonelite mass—have come up with a range of novel ideas, some of which have been turned into successful products. But most products have not turned out so well, since they were conceived only from the standpoint of the consumer and failed to take into account the overall production process. In this regard the proposals of the elite minority are more worthwhile, since they are grounded on an understanding of the entire process in addition to incorporating female sensibilities.

The work ethic of elite professional women and the strength of their   30
commitment to their jobs are akin to those of the middle-aged men worker bees. Deep down these women also feel it is impossible to produce quality work if they do not practically live at their office. They are an invaluable resource for the firm, but are still too few in number to have any major impact on the organization as a whole. In five or ten years, however, as their numbers grow, they will likely become a force that cannot be ignored, and the battle of the sexes for the limited number of top posts may begin.

The main reason that women in general work is financial, most often to pay for children's education or to meet housing loan repayments. The rapid growth in the number of women with money of their own to spend has been a key factor behind higher consumption levels and the establishment of new businesses like housekeeping services. In other words, it has been contributing to the growth of the Japanese economy. But men continue to dominate the workplace. Women have not robbed them of their jobs. While the generational shift in values and life-styles has certainly affected the business world, the increased presence of women in and of itself cannot be said to have produced drastic changes in the workplace yet.

At the same time, an increasing number of women no longer accept the idea that they have to devote themselves simply to enhancing their husbands' efficiency-oriented approach, but want a mate who will play an active role in the home as a partner. Women are also becoming seriously and vocally concerned about the future of the environment and the ecosystem. These trends may eventually result in an economy that does not grow quite so fast but is more humane in its operation.

Expanded Options and Female Roles

Women have changed greatly in many respects, one of the most noticeable being in the quantity and quality of the education they receive. The upsurge in the number of women who have been educated alongside men in the coeducational institutions of the postwar period has resulted in a realization among women that, at least intellectually, they are not inferior. That realization has strengthened their belief in the equality of the sexes.

With their high levels of education (95.3 percent enter high school; 36.5 percent enter college), married women are no longer content to stay at home devoting all their time to keeping house and caring for children. The sharp rise in the number of women who rejoin the work force after their children reach a certain age and the enormous numbers engaged in cultural or academic pursuits attest to this. In recent years more than half of all major literary awards have gone to women, and it may not be an exaggeration to say that the future of Japanese culture lies in the hands of women. All around the country, women are turning their gaze outward, becoming active in areas once dominated by men, such as landscape gardening, architecture, and jobs in international organizations. Many are reexamining the direction of their lives. Some are rebelling against the precept that women should live their lives for others and are resolved to do things that make them happy. Accepting suffering and making sacrifices, formerly considered virtues, are no longer seen by the younger generation as desirable behavior.

The idea of what is "marriageable age" used to hold strong sway over Japanese. Men and women who were still single by their respective marriageable ages (for women the cutoff age was 25) made every effort to find a spouse as quickly as possible. Nowadays the range of options open to women is much wider, and they are in no rush to be led to the altar. Today only about 14 percent of 24-year-old women are married. I recently asked a group of my own students (aged 20–23) what they thought they would be doing in five or ten years. Less than half pictured themselves as married at age 30.

Today the average age of first marriage is up to 25.8 for women and 28.5 for men—one year higher than the respective national averages ten years ago—and in big cities like Tokyo people are marrying even later. In earlier days, when women could not support themselves financially and men were incapable of looking after themselves, people simply had to get married. But today women can easily earn enough to live on. Many single women live at home with their parents, which means that they can use practically their entire salaries on discretionary spending. They may have to endure some parental meddling, but basically they lead lives of total comfort. It takes considerable resolve to leave this for marriage.

Young women today have grown up with all their material wants satisfied, and they are extremely reluctant to forgo their income and freedom. The women of their mothers' generation took it for granted that husbands and wives would start out modestly and pool their efforts to build a better life for themselves. But women in their twenties take comfort for granted, and money occupies a central place in their value systems. They demand that a prospective husband already be earning a substantial sum. Most young men have insufficient incomes to satisfy these women's demands, and so they are rejected as marriage partners.

Japanese women tend to take a highly pragmatic approach to marriage. They consider a proposal from various angles and then make a decision. And they have a rather detailed shopping list, topped by what are popularly referred to as the "three highs," namely the requirements that a husband be

35

highly educated, have a high income, and be physically "high," i.e., tall. In a sense, though, they may be making these demands half in jest, since, as I have said, they are really in no rush to marry.

I should also note two further problems that are keeping people from getting married. One is the gap in attitudes between men and women. Men do not fully grasp the extent to which women have changed, and consequently they are unable to respond appropriately to these changes. The second is a simple matter of demographics. Among people in their twenties and thirties single men outnumber single women by 2.5 million; in Tokyo alone some 500,000 men will be unable to find a spouse.

This situation means that a lot of men are falling by the wayside in   40
marriage. A myriad of matchmaking services have sprung up; about 5,000 are in business today. There are even cases of large companies setting up in-house marriage consultation desks for their male employees, whose long hours at work do not leave them time for dating. Such firms' concern for their employees is commendable and bespeaks the severity of the problem. But this response flies in the face of the attitudes of young men today, most of whom do not want the company meddling in their private affairs.

The situation is even more serious in rural areas. Unlike people with jobs in the city, men with farms depend heavily on their families for help with their work; remaining single is not a realistic option for them. Mayors from rural areas have unsuccessfully combed Japan in search of brides for the men in their villages, and they are now going abroad to Thailand, the Philippines, Sri Lanka, Taiwan, and South Korea. Many women from the Philippines have come to Japan and married men in rural areas, and in such places Catholic masses in Tagalog have suddenly become a fixture of village life. Villagers who once had little contact with people from other parts of Japan are now living and working alongside people from totally different cultures. In this way, Japanese women have inadvertently contributed to the internationalization of Japan's farming communities.

The trend toward marrying later notwithstanding, most women plan to wed eventually. The proportion of women who have been married at least once by age 30 is 63 percent, and by age 35, 88 percent. But their attitudes toward marriage have changed drastically. Traditionally, the ideal was for husband and wife to be like air to each other. This did not mean that the relationship should lack in substance. Rather, it meant that though it was as vital and indispensable as air, it need not be consciously or palpably felt; husbands and wives' mutual affection, devotion, and concern were supposed to be so tacitly accepted and nonverbally expressed that their relationship rested as lightly and unconsciously as air in their daily lives. When we become conscious of the air we breathe, it is a sign of a physical crisis; when the marital relationship had to be consciously dealt with, it was thought, the bond was in danger. At the root of this attitude was the Japanese tendency to trust in long-term relationships. Just like the air they breathe, people took it for granted that their spouses would always be there.

Younger people, particularly women, want more companionship from their spouses. The problem is that in real life, the husband—or in the case of dual-income families, both the husband and wife—works long hours, often faces long commutes, and simply does not have much time to spend with the spouse. Married couples find it difficult to respond adequately to the need for companionship even before children are born and virtually impossible once a baby enters the picture. After that the household begins to revolve around the children, and this situation generally continues until the children enter college or go out to work. Incidentally, both men and women in Japan view it as desirable for a mother to stay at home looking after the children until they begin elementary school.

Emotional and Economic Autonomy

In nearly all families, the husband is responsible for living expenses even if the wife works, as do 70 percent of women in their forties. As a general rule, the husband hands over his earnings to his wife, and she takes charge of the household accounts. About 70 percent of women responding to a recent survey knew exactly how much money their husbands made, and another 25 percent said they had a general idea. The same survey revealed that only 18 percent of men know exactly how much their wives earn, while 46 percent have a general idea. Men seem quite content to let their wives spend or save their earnings as they see fit.

Since women hold the purse strings, they are in a position to cover   45
the household expenses with their husbands' salaries and use their own earnings for things like the children's educational expenses, which are 40 percent higher in two-income families, as well as for their personal social expenses or savings. Perhaps husbands imagine that their wives' incomes are negligible, or maybe they just want to continue believing that they are the family's sole provider. Japanese women are clever, and they know that their husbands' ignorance about their incomes means greater freedom for themselves.

Women's freedom is enhanced by their husbands' tendency to entrust them with everything from control of the family finances to the children's upbringing and education, contacts with relatives, and anything else that they find bothersome. One reason is that men spend so little time at home. Some wives who see their husbands very little refer to them as "boarders." Men explain their absence from home as a necessary part of their labor of love for their families. They work until late at night and spend their weekends on the golf course with clients—all the while claiming that they would much rather prefer not to—"for the sake of the family."

Most Japanese men feel that as long as their wives have seen to the children and housework, they have no reason to complain about whatever else they may do during the day, whether it be working, studying, or socializing. Women plan their daily schedules on their own, only taking when their husbands and children will be home into account. While their menfolk are tied to their jobs, wives are free to take part in various activities. Japanese women once described the ideal husband as one who was *healthy and out of the house,* but recently women's activities have reached such a pitch that they dream of a husband who is *healthy and at home*—that is, looking after the house (and children) while they are out.

What I wish to draw attention to here is the fact that women do not depend on their husbands for emotional support when making decisions. They have a surprising degree of autonomy and freedom in their lives. Japanese women by no means want to be like men, spending inordinate amounts of time at the office and leading culturally impoverished lives. They know that with their wide circle of friends and freedom to work, raise children, pursue a hobby, join a volunteer group, or simply have a good time, they are far better off than men.

However, this setup does not provide for communication between husbands and wives. The root of the problem lies not only in a lack of time but in the deep-rooted belief among the Japanese that people should not need to express their feelings verbally to family members and close friends. In particular, men expect their wives to be attentive to their moods and to be able to read their minds. It does not work the other way around, however; men do not try to or expect to be able to understand their wives' feelings implicitly. To make matters worse, silence in a man was traditionally considered a virtue. In the international arena, problems often get blown out of proportion because the Japanese do not provide a suitable or adequate explanation for their stance. The prototype of this communication gap can be seen in Japan's husband-wife and parent-child relationships.

Women who spend little time with their husbands, communicate with them even less, and share with them only a long-term trust that the other person will always be there will, after twenty or thirty years of marriage, establish independent life-styles totally suited to their respective needs. Such relationships run smoothly until it comes time for the husbands to retire. For their part, men feel they have toiled diligently for the sake of their wives and children and understandably expect to be rewarded for their efforts in retirement. But women by this time have a full schedule that leaves no room for their husbands, and they are not happy to have their freedom suddenly intruded upon by a spouse who sits around the house all day but is incapable of doing any housework.

If a wife and husband have a common interest, there is a good chance that they will be able to work things out, but if not, the wife's unhappiness will only intensify. Women in relationships of this sort deridingly refer to their husbands as "oversized garbage," implying that they are objects that have outlived their usefulness and now only get in the way. The most recent appellation is *"kyofu no washi zoku"* (the "take-me-with-you terrors"). This term conveys the horror women feel when their husbands insist on accompanying them everywhere and spoil what would otherwise have been enjoyable outings.

Having worked with men my whole life, I know firsthand the sort of relationship they have with their work, and it saddens me to think this is the destiny of the worker bees who have sacrificed their own happiness to build up the country's economy. So it is out of sympathy that I would urge Japanese men to strike a balance between work and their private lives, cultivate friendships and interests outside the workplace, and pay more attention to what women are thinking, feeling, and doing. Finally, they must learn to take care of themselves and be able to stand on their own two feet.

Any such change on the part of men may mean less freedom for women. But even if husbands and wives draw closer together, they are too pragmatic about human relations to adopt the American ideal, whereby couples must share both their happiness and their sorrow, provide total fulfillment as lovers and friends, and on top of this constantly learn from each other and mature together. The Japanese believe that expecting too much of a spouse will only put a strain on the marriage and eventually lead to its demise. They feel that the relationship between husband and wife should be the most relaxed of any. Trying to know each other too well can only make the other person's flaws too obvious and increase the chances of divorce.

Getting back to family finances, when men realize that the affluence women are enjoying is made possible at their expense, they may begin to demand that their wives shoulder part of the household expenses. And once a wife's earnings are considered indispensable to the running of a household, women will no longer be free to quit their jobs at will. In that sense, Japanese women today may be enjoying a golden age of freedom.

Perpetrators of Change

Japan's divorce rate is a low 1.29 persons per 1,000 population, but public opinion polls reveal a complete turnaround in Japanese attitudes toward divorce. In 1972, seven out of ten people felt that even if a couple was not happy together, they should not get divorced. In 1987, fifteen years later, six out of ten felt that such a couple should divorce. In most cases the wife initiates the proceedings.

In Japan the number of divorces among couples married only a short time has been falling, but divorces among couples married fifteen years or more are on the rise. The increase among older couples is partly due to the strain that a husband's retirement puts on the marriage, particularly now that postretirement life expectancy is so long. The increasing number of women earning a living is, without doubt, one factor behind the rising divorce rate and will probably contribute to its continued upswing in the future.

As women have come to enjoy a wider range of activities, they have begun to harbor doubts about having large families and being tied down to child-rearing for many years, particularly when they will not have the support of an extended family. Many couples have actually given up on the idea of having several children after calculating the costs of educating them. Reports of the growing destruction of the global environment are causing some to decide against having any children at all. Women, moreover, are beginning to feel that there is more to life than just raising children, and they are well aware of how very hard it is to juggle work and family responsibilities, thanks to firsthand accounts from those who have continued working even after the birth of a child.

The natural outcome has been a plunge in the number of children women bear. The average recently fell to 1.53, provoking considerable alarm and leading to the passage of a child-care leave law this past spring in the National Diet. Even though the national legislature is dominated by men who have always regarded child-rearing as the exclusive domain of women, it passed without dissent a bill that provides both fathers and mothers with child-care leave. This remarkable development may be taken as an indication that Japanese men are now feeling something close to panic at the idea that the nation may be on the road to extinction.

The decline in the number of children is expected to have serious repercussions. Already some kindergartens and elementary schools are closing down due to the lack of pupils. At the national level the labor market is expected to grow even tighter, and the finances of the national pension system will come under heavy strain.

The trend toward fewer children may also take its toll on the emotional 60 health of the people. In small families, parents tend to be overbearing, overprotective, and to have inflated expectations of their children. Many people have noted the unhealthy bonds that develop between mothers and children if the fathers are seldom at home. Some young men, it seems, are saddled with a "mother complex"; even after marriage they cannot free themselves from their emotional dependence on their mothers. Fewer children will only exacerbate these problems.

Industries catering to children that offer everything from kiddie jewelry to educational services are thriving on the weaknesses of today's indulgent parents. Since many women have incomes of their own, they are easily tempted to spoil their children with material goods, and some items that were formerly considered luxuries are now seen as virtual necessities. This has forced mothers without incomes to go out to work and created a vicious cycle of sorts, causing the cost of raising a child to spiral.

Meanwhile, the average life expectancy of Japanese women has risen to nearly 82 years, the highest in the world, and the question of how to remain independent and active in old age has become a topic of deep concern. Today women can expect to live thirty years after their youngest child leaves home, and they know that they may not be able to rely on their children to look after them later in life. Given that women on average live five years longer than men and tend to be younger than their spouses, men can generally count on their wives to take care of them in old age. But women cannot afford that sort of complacency; they are going out to work and developing hobbies to remain self-sufficient and active in their old age.

Women have the potential to change men's attitudes toward work and lay waste to the "company man" ideal. But they have yet to produce significant changes among middle-aged men. Men's failure to understand the mind-set and problems of women is part of the perception gap between the sexes that prevails throughout Japan today. They simply do not have the time to step back from their jobs and rethink the direction of their lives. Women, by contrast, keep up with new developments, organize study groups, and are seriously concerned about how to lead a satisfying, full life in their old age. Their broad-based perspective only serves to widen the gap between the sexes.

Armed with their varied experiences, women are setting forth to find an identity for themselves as individuals. The phrase "finding oneself" has recently been getting a lot of press. The movement to amend the civil code so that husbands and wives can keep their own surnames is one manifestation of this trend. Under the present law, couples must choose either the husband's or the wife's surname upon marriage, and in 98 percent of the cases it is the husband's name that is chosen. Women protest that by adopting their husband's name, they are giving up an integral part of their identity. But men argue that for married couples to have separate names would only cause confusion. Basically they seem not to understand why women should make a fuss over such an issue.

Some women have established a niche for themselves as grass-roots political activists. Individual women are generally unable to get together the huge sums of money needed to win an election. To overcome this obstacle, a movement has evolved to win seats in local assemblies for candidates who stand as proxies for women's groups associated with consumer cooperatives. A large number of women won election in this spring's nationwide local government elections, attesting to the strength of this movement.

The strength of these women lies in their conviction that they have the power to change society, and they have already started to put their ideas to work. They are quite unlike most Japanese, who tend to view politics as part of an inaccessible world that has nothing to do with themselves. While their efforts do not always meet with success, they are continuing to press ahead. I believe that women, through their sheer determination to change what they can around them and with their concern for social issues like preserving the environment, may be the hope for tomorrow's Japan. Now, it is men's turn to change.

Thinking About the Text

1. What is Iwao's thesis? How well does she support it with evidence? How effective is her tone?

2. In paragraph 18 Iwao says that Japanese women forty and over "like work" more than either men or women in their twenties do. She suggests that the change reveals a new attitude in a new generation. But suppose someone said that common sense suggests that, in the past as well as in the present, older (and presumably established) people probably "like" their jobs better because young people are (1) unaccustomed to day-long routines and (2) probably doing the more onerous jobs for less money. Drawing on your experience (including what you see and hear around you), do these objections to Iwao's statement ring true? Explain.

3. Iwao gives an example (para. 26) of how the entry of women into the marketplace improved the conditions for men. What examples (or counter-examples) can you cite, either from firsthand experience or from your reading and your conversations?

4. Reread Iwao's final paragraph two or three times, and then evaluate it *as a final paragraph*. Do you think it provides an effective ending? Why, or why not?

5. Iwao's essay and the preceding essay by Kazuko Watanabe (p. 171) were written at about the same time, and both comment on the condition of Japanese women today. In what ways are they similar, and how do they differ?

Thinking About Culture

6. In her second paragraph Iwao suggests that women have recently been "set free by the development of home appliances," whereas men are "increasingly chained to the institutions they have set up. . . ." To what degree, if any, can this statement be said to apply to men and women in the United States?

7. In Japan a two-track system is available to women but not to men; Iwao suggests that the new generation of male workers may also prefer a two-track system (paras. 13–14). What differences, if any, are there in the career options available to men and women in the United States? How are these differences created?

8. Iwao describes the unhappy relationship that exists between some retired couples (paras. 50–51). If you have seen such a relationship, consider whether Iwao's analysis adequately explains the causes for this unhappiness. If it doesn't, offer your own analysis.

9. Do you find Iwao's capsule description of "the American ideal" (para. 53) accurate? If not, in what ways is it inadequate? Incidentally, *is* there an American ideal in our multicultural society? You may want to discuss the potential for multiple models in *Japan* as well.

10. See paragraph 64 for Iwao's brief summary of the views of men and

women concerning a woman's married name. What are your views on the issue—and why? Incidentally, if a woman retains her birth name after she marries, she is in all likelihood retaining her *father's* name. Should this fact distress women who retain their birth name in an effort to maintain their identity?

11. The women Iwao interviewed and described are middle class, with some college or university experience. Consider the relevance of social class to women's opportunities in America; then extrapolate these findings to construct the Japanese case. What impact do you think social class has on the options of Japanese women?

12. Iwao says that the traditional Japanese ideal in a marriage was for the husband and wife "to be like air to each other" (para. 42), and she goes on to explain the simile. To what degree does this simile describe your own idea of marriage? (You may want to discuss the strengths and limits implicit in such a marriage.)

Karl Taro Greenfeld

Marriage? Girls Just Wanna Have Fun

Rika, the lead character in *Tokyo Love Story,* a popular TV drama, lives in a spacious studio apartment in a trendy neighborhood. She dresses in designer outfits, is dedicated to her job, and enjoys an active social life. She also enjoys an active sex life.

The drama's portrayal of the young, single, liberated career woman reflects a change in attitude from previous generations, when the ideal was for young unmarried women to live with their parents.

Today, many have their own homes or cohabit with lovers. But by their late twenties they succumb to societal, financial, and familial pressures and begin dreaming of nuptial bliss.

Japan is in the throes of a sexual revolution with built-in obsolescence. Any claims of bedrock feminism are belied in the course of interviews with women approaching thirty.

It is singles night at Gold. Young men in suits and ties drink and exchange business cards with their female counterparts. Michiru Hamada, twenty-seven, smoking a long, thin cigarette, sits at a table in the nightclub's

5

Karl Taro Greenfeld, who is Tokyo correspondent for a New York journal, The Nation, *wrote this article for* Japan Times *in 1992. (The names of individuals in the story have been changed to protect their privacy.)*

roped-off VIP lounge overlooking the dance floor. Intermittently, a flickering strobe light makes her vodka and Sprite glow.

Michiru, whose boyfriend is not ready to settle down, has come to the club looking for someone to marry. She attended Keio University, one of Japan's most prestigious private schools, and is an assistant editor in a publishing company.

Michiru considers herself neither chaste nor promiscuous. Her attitude toward sex is not Second-Avenue-Manhattan-circa-1978 liberal; it is having-my-own-prescription-for-birth-control-pills liberal. Asked how many men she has slept with, she responds without hesitating, "Nine."

She continues: "I like sex, maybe more than my boyfriend. Actually, definitely more than my boyfriend. I have been seeing him for two years. I met him at my old job at the Leo Burnette Advertising Agency. I love him, I guess. But even if he was interested, I wouldn't want to marry him. He's too young."

Michiru has lived for most of those two years with her boyfriend Arao in Azabu-Juban, a neighborhood undergoing the Tokyo equivalent of gentrification: rice cake and kimono stores closing, Benetton and Alain Mikli boutiques opening. The couple have shared the cost of practically everything: the rent, the thirty-two-inch Toshiba Bazooka television, their double futon.

Worlds Apart

Michiru's parents still think she is a virgin. "They have no idea I live with   10 a man," she laughs, stirring her drink. "They could not imagine me doing something like that."

Her parents live in rural Ibaraki. They sell tea, a lucrative business. "I will never tell them about Arao," she says. "They are old. They are from another world. I live in two worlds. In many ways I am two people."

Michiru ticks off the time-honored arguments for marriage: "I am tired of dating. I want security. I want to have children before I am too old. I want someone who will always be with me. And I don't want to work.

"As long as he has a future, he doesn't have to be handsome," she says. "Well, I suppose I hope he is, but it's not necessary. In college, I didn't care about marriage so much, and when I got out of school what mattered was to have fun. But now, look around. Who wants to do this her whole life?"

Michiru is not atypical. The majority of Japanese women are wary of becoming old maids. By age thirty, 83 percent are married. The difference in this regard between today's single woman and yesterday's is that the fear of being left on the shelf takes hold later. The mean age of marriage for women has risen from twenty-two in 1949 to twenty-seven in 1992.

The generation gulf, or break with previous practice, is most strongly   15 manifested between the ages of twenty and twenty-five, and narrows considerably past twenty-seven. The idea of youthful sexual freedom, besides being quite novel in Japan, is less sinister than in the West because AIDS is spreading more slowly. As of 1990, the Ministry of Health and Welfare reported a total of 316 cases. Indeed, AIDS containment would seem possible, since 83 percent of the population already uses condoms as a means of birth control. They are available at convenience stores, from traveling saleswomen, or at vending machines.

The reason for the omnipresence of condoms, though, has little to do with disease control. The Ministry of Health and Welfare simply refuses to allow the dissemination of contraceptive pills, except if prescribed for gynecological purposes. And even when doctors take advantage of that loophole, the pill they prescribe has higher doses of estrogen than the safe "mini-pill" available in the United States. Thus, while the lack of an attractive and easily obtainable alternative to condoms could be slowing the spread of AIDS, it is cited by some women as an obstacle to true liberation.

Short-Term Feminists

Nevertheless, the feminist movement, or what there is of it, is embraced by young women casually. The tradition of young women living at home until they marry has essentially given way to a few years of freedom.

"Their life-style may be feminist—for a short time," says Asahi Ito of the Pacific Asia Resources Center, who is herself a confirmed feminist. "They live independently, self-sufficiently, take on lovers, and have relationships based on equality. But the consciousness is never there. That is why suddenly, at age twenty-seven or twenty-eight, they can marry into a traditional, oppressive family environment."

Kazumi Kirishima is twenty-eight and has had four abortions. "The first at nineteen, then at twenty-four, twenty-five, and twenty-six. The first time was OK. I didn't mind so much. By the third, I felt bad. Guilty. I can't explain why I didn't care for the man. I didn't care about the baby. I just felt guilty," she explains.

Kazumi used the pill very briefly. The prescription was obtained through a woman doctor who her boss introduced her to. She didn't like the pill because she gained weight. She prefers an improvised rhythm method, but these days she is simply abstaining. "My life-style," she says, "doesn't allow for it."   20

Kazumi works as a hostess, pouring drinks for businessmen who need a place to talk outside the home and office. She earns $64,000 a year and pays $1,200 a month rent for her one-bedroom apartment. She is saving as much as she can for plastic surgery. Although an attractive woman, she has decided that "for real self-confidence and security" she needs to change her face.

"Then I can go to Germany or America, or perhaps stay here, and find a husband. I began thinking about it when my friend got married. She looked so happy. It's sad growing old alone."

Kazumi boasts she has slept with between fifty and one hundred men—

she says she doesn't remember the exact number. She lost her virginity at fifteen and dropped out of high school that same year. Her mother is dead. Her father drives a truck. "My father agrees with whatever I do," she says. "He is always very positive. He knows about my plastic surgery idea."

"I never thought about marriage before. It just never occurred to me. Never before I was twenty-seven. Gradually, over the past year, I dream about it more and more."

By age twenty-six, even well-educated Japanese working women have   25
already run into the "pin-striped curtain," that barrier keeping them off the fast track as most men annually take another lap. On average, women's salaries are only 52 percent of their male counterparts' (as opposed to 72 percent for American women).

A career woman in Japan, therefore, finds her options narrowing quickly.

Big corporations, the conventional route to success in this country, actually encourage women to get married by their late twenties on pain of banishment to a life as a tea-pouring "office lady."

"I watched men advance whom I knew weren't as good as me," says Noriko Furuse, who now runs her own women's employment service. "I began to hate them and hate the company. So at thirty I started my own company."

Because of Japan's lean social security payments, the outlook for an independent businesswoman or retired single woman without a good pension plan is grim.

Japanese social security guarantees annual payments of only $5,800.   30
Without additional corporate retirement benefits, this is a paltry sum in an expensive city like Tokyo. In her early twenties it may be possible for a woman to ignore such realities; in her late twenties financial exigencies dictate marriage.

Parental Pressure

Parental pressure to marry is still a regular part of most young women's lives, too.

Rie Karube, twenty-eight, has no money problems. Her family is renowned for banking and manufacturing petrochemicals. She drives a Mercedes-Benz 190 between her parents' house and the dry cleaner. She doesn't shop for clothes; the women in her family have been using the same Shibuya seamstress for three generations.

Last year, Rie was engaged to marry her longtime boyfriend, Takao, a rising young executive at a major Japanese airline and scion of a wealthy Kyushu samurai family. She began dating him while a freshman at Sophia University. He was the only man with whom she had ever had sex.

Until last year. At the advertising agency where she worked as a planner and coordinator, she met Mako, a young account executive who had grown up overseas. The attraction was immediate and mutual.

"Other men had shown interest in me since I met Takao," Rie says as   35
she steers the car around a traffic circle. "But Mako was the first one I knew
would be trouble. We were in his tiny office—he was young but he had his
own small wood-paneled office. He asked me out immediately. He wasn't
shy." And sex with Takao had become dull.

She began an affair with Mako in July and the marriage was scheduled
for October.

"I said I loved Mako," Rie says. "But looking back I think it was
mainly sexual. I don't like thinking about it anymore. There is something
embarrassing about the whole thing.

"Part of the reason the affair seemed so intense, I think, was all the
wedding pressure. From my family. From Takao's family. Everybody wanted
us to get married."

Doing the Right Thing

"When Takao asked me I said yes because it seemed like the right thing to
do. It was like an alarm clock had gone off in my father's head when I turned
twenty-seven, so it was time to send out invitations and then gifts. It was as
if the only thing that mattered was the wedding and not me, the person
getting married."

During the affair with Mako, she felt she mattered. Because nobody   40
else knew, that relationship seemed pure compared to the overwrought and
complex negotiations leading up to marriage.

"I refused to talk to Mako about the preparations. He would ask me
why I wanted to get married. I was never able to answer him," Rie says. "I
told Takao I didn't want to marry him and he just said I was nervous. I
tried to talk to my father about postponing the wedding. He refused to talk
to me. They acted like I was a fool. I guess I was getting married because so
many of my friends were. Everybody seemed to have decided it was the right
thing to do. Takao's family and my family would make a good match. But
Takao and I—who cared about that?"

As arrangements for the wedding proceeded, including a weekend trip
to Fukuoka, Kyushu, so both families could meet to discuss the preparations,
Rie's liaison with Mako became more intense. "I sneaked out of the room
to call him from the hotel lobby every hour."

Takao had always worn condoms. Mako didn't. Rie soon thought she
was pregnant.

After a bitter argument with her parents about canceling the wedding,
she rear-ended a taxi and was hospitalized for three days with a neck injury.

Her father and Takao both came to visit, and laughed when she said   45
she didn't want to marry.

"When I found out I wasn't pregnant, I was so happy," she says. "It
would have been terrible to have Mako's baby while I was married to Takao.
The day I left the hospital I went over to Mako's apartment. It was early in
the morning. I rang the buzzer. He answered the door but wouldn't let me

in. He didn't say why, except that someone was there with him. That was all."

During their first giddy week together, Rie had asked Mako if he would come to her wedding party. They were in his tiny office when she asked. He laughed and said he would bring a date. She kissed him and handed him a note saying she loved him. It was just like high school.

The wedding took place at a Tokyo hotel on November 1, 1991. Mako was not invited.

Thinking About the Text

1. What is Greenfeld's attitude toward the young women he describes? Cite specific passages from the text to justify your opinion.

2. Might Greenfeld's first paragraph apply also to almost any popular American TV drama? What about the second paragraph? And the third?

Thinking About Culture

3. Does Michiru (paras. 5–13) strike you as rather like, somewhat like, or very unlike a fair number of young women whom you know? In short, could she be an American of your acquaintance? What similarities and differences do you see?

William R. LaFleur

Abortion's Place in Society: The Case of Japan

Bright Futures and Dark Pasts

Abortion is a deeply debated issue in America, but not necessarily so in every culture. In our own society it often seems that religious issues are at the center of the arguments about abortion. In Japan, by contrast, religious institutions seem—at least today—to accept that abortion is a matter for personal decision. Beyond that, many Buddhist temples provide rituals

---

William R. LaFleur teaches culture and religion at the University of Pennsylvania. His most recent book is Liquid Life: Abortion and Buddhism in Japan *(1993). This essay discusses abortion in Japan, especially in the context of Buddhism.*

through which women who have had abortions and their partners can express their grief and resolve some of the guilt they may feel. If we look at how abortion has come to be dealt with in Japan we have an opportunity to open our eyes to some very interesting—even instructive—possibilities in terms of how to deal with this difficult, vexing problem.

A good place to begin is with some things we can say about the Japan of today. People in other countries frequently report that they find a number of admirable, enviable features in Japanese society. Although there are surely exceptions, Japanese people for the most part are well-fed, hard-working, in good health, enjoying a life-style conducive to longevity, free to live without fear of violent crime, possessors of the world's highest literacy rate, good savers, and financially able to travel extensively both within Japan and abroad.

No one, of course, knows the future. Paul Kennedy, however, in his *Preparing for the Twenty-First Century,* has made some highly informed and intelligent guesses. One of these is that, of all the world's nations, "the Japanese are the people least likely to be hurt by gross and direct damage from global overpopulation, mass migration, and environmental disasters. . . ."[1] In preventing mass immigration the Japanese, as everyone can readily tell, are greatly helped by being an island-nation. Furthermore, by being tight-knit socially and pretending that they are racially uniform, they make entry into their society extremely difficult.

What I wish to call attention to here, however, is the prediction that Japan will not suffer much in the future from *overpopulation.* Although Japanese cities today are densely populated, Kennedy's prediction is that the number of Japanese is not likely to grow very much. In this, Japan contrasts strikingly with other nations that are densely populated now (China and India) or are likely to become so in the future (Mexico and many nations in Africa). Japan, Kennedy claims, will be advantaged by the fact that it will have what is called "zero population growth." It will be able to concentrate on further economic growth rather than on feeding an ever-expanding population. In the twenty-first century, nations will likely be harmed rather than enhanced if their populations are burgeoning.

Behind the statistics concerning Japan's fairly happy present and its relatively bright prospects for its future lies, however, what some might judge to be a deep, "dark" story. The details of this are as follows. Most Japanese couples today have an average of two children.[2] Today's Japanese feel that family planning helps them maximize the available resources for their children. This personal, concrete experience of positive benefits coming as a

5

---

[1] Paul M. Kennedy, *Preparing for the Twenty-First Century* (New York: Random Books, 1993), p. 138.

[2] The fullest account of birth control methods in Japan is Samuel Coleman, *Family Planning in Japanese Society: Traditional Birth Control in a Modern Urban Culture* (Princeton, NJ: Princeton University Press, 1983).

result of close family planning, in fact, reaches back more than two centuries. Between 1721 and 1846 the population leveled out into a "plateau"—at a time when China's, for instance, doubled within even less time.

The "dark" part of this story begins to emerge, however, when we note that this happened at a time when "natural" killers such as war and pestilence were only minimally present and when what we think of as contraceptives were not available. How then did so many Japanese during this period come to recognize the positive benefits of close reproductive planning? We can only conclude that this happened during a time when the only methods for restraining family growth were through abortion and infanticide.[3]

The "Return" of Children

One of the striking features of this earlier period is that, even when they felt it necessary or desirable to practice family planning through so drastic a means as infanticide, the people who did so felt compelled to refer to what had been born as a "child." And when abortion was the chosen method they seem not to have hesitated to refer to the fetus as "life."

To us this may seem peculiar. We in the modern West tend to avoid words like "child" or "life" to refer to someone or something that will be denied a normal entry into our world. But for the Japanese of some centuries ago when infanticide was still common and for those today who have resorted to abortion, use of the word "life" did not, and does not, seem inappropriate.

The reason for this is interesting and important. A difference between the religious views of the Japanese and those common in the West goes a long way to explain what is happening here. In medieval Europe, as the research by John Boswell shows, many people regulated the size of their families by disposing of unwanted children by abandoning them on the steps of churches or foundling homes.[4] The majority died. Sometimes the mortality rate was more than 90 percent. But at least the parents, it appears, felt less guilty than if they had actually "assisted" in the death that came to these children. The death of abandoned children had been, they assumed, God's will.

The people of medieval Japan felt otherwise—in part because they had rather different religious beliefs. Since they were Buddhists they held that death is only a *temporary* removal from this world. They believed that, at least in most cases, when a human being died he or she would be reborn later as a human with an altogether different face, name, and set of relatives. The idea of what is often called "reincarnation" was a firm part of the

10

---

[3] For sources on this and other aspects of abortion in Japan, see my *Liquid Life: Abortion and Buddhism in Japan* (Princeton, NJ: Princeton University Press, 1993).

[4] John Boswell, *The Kindness of Strangers: The Abandonment of Children from Late Antiquity to the Renaissance* (New York: Pantheon Books, 1988).

religious world of medieval Japan and even today still has a lingering power in Buddhists' thinking about what happens after death.

What are the implications of this? One is that the "child" who by direct human action is prevented from entry into our world is not so much killed as it is "returned." Japanese have used exactly such a term. It is returned, that is, to the realm of the gods and Buddhas—that is, the place from which it had been in the process of making an exit by moving through the uterus of a woman. Abortion, then, is a way through which this fetus is sent back again to the realm of the gods and Buddhas—to await a time when it may come into our world as a *wanted* child. That is, it is hoped that the aborted "child" will be able later to come to parents more ready to receive, appreciate, and care for it. Perhaps it might even come to the same set of parents, but next time when they are more ready for the child in question.

Making Apologies

It would be an error, however, to conclude from this that the Japanese of the past or present who had recourse to abortion did so with an untroubled conscience or without a sense of guilt. There is abundant evidence that this is not the case. There may be compelling reasons for abortion—both for the welfare of the mother and even for the fetus thought of as being put "on hold" until able to be reborn into a more welcoming context. That is, the abortion may be thought necessary and unavoidable. Nevertheless, the physical interruption of the ordinary gestation process is regarded by most Japanese as a troubling and guilt-inducing act.

And this guilt is thought to be there, even when not overtly recognized, in women who have had an abortion and probably also in their mates who made them pregnant. To recognize that guilt is also to begin a process to deal with it in a positive fashion. That is, since the common conception is that the aborted fetus is, in fact, a "child" who is forced by abortion to go back to the land of the gods and Buddhas until a more propitious birth-time, it is felt that the parent or parents of such a child—called a *mizuko*, or "child of the waters," in Japanese—should make an apology to the deceased fetus and pray for its well-being wherever it may be. After all, it was surely wronged by "parents" who had created a pregnancy when they should not have done so. Moreover, it was at least in part to convenience them that the *mizuko* had been sent back to the realm from which it had come.

Japanese society is one in which making an appropriate apology is much more important than in America. People will sometimes make an apology for some acts when it is not even certain that they were responsible for them. Even in legal contexts the making of an apology has a large role in Japan. This is because there it is commonly assumed that apologies are oil on the machinery of interpersonal relationships. They make them run more smoothly and prevent them from getting stuck. And this applies in the case of abortions as well. Even when, in cases like these, the person receiving the apology is no longer in the same world as the maker of the apology, it is thought appropriate to do so.

Over the past few decades Buddhist temples have come to include rituals of such apology within the list of services they provide. Such temples often include places where people can make their apology to a *mizuko* through a small image which becomes the focus-point. The image is one of Jizo, a strong but compassionate godlike figure who, at least in the belief of many Japanese people, makes it his business to take special care of deceased children or fetuses in their journeys beyond this world. Jizo is a child's guide through places traversed beyond our world. He is the protector en route to the time and place where that child will be reborn into our world. Jizo is often sculpted in such a way that infants are portrayed as held in his arms or hanging on to the hem of the robes he wears. Persons who go to these special memorial sites for *mizuko* will often place there items having to do with children: dolls, toys, pinwheels, rattles, pacifiers, and the like.

Disagreements

There are, both in Japan and in the West, some persons who are critical of these practices.[5] They claim, for instance, that since temples collect a fee when they provide space and a Jizo image to persons wanting to make apology to an aborted fetus, this is a kind of "guilt money," something that should not be at all necessary. Others claim that even the compulsion to make an apology is a relic of the thinking of a bygone era, not necessary if men and—especially in these cases—women were truly modern and liberated. Why, they ask, should it be necessary for women in the late twentieth century to still feel guilty for their decision not to continue a pregnancy?

The responses to objections such as these are varied. Studies to date of the psychological benefits of performing rituals of apology to *mizuko* suggest such benefits are probably real. Women seem to feel much better after having literally "*done* something" to apologize and make amends to the child they did not feel able to bring into this world. The acts of giving money to the temples and using up some of their "free" time to pay visits—sometimes making pilgrimages, in fact—to the memorial sites seem to result eventually in a feeling of relief and a cleansing away of the feeling of guilt over an abortion.

Westerners, especially if they are convinced that abortion is sinful in almost every instance, object that the Japanese have gotten too accustomed to a high abortion rate. In their view Japan is an overly tolerant society in

[5] A generally critical essay is "*Mizuko kuyo:* Notulae on the Most Important 'New Religion' in Japan," by R. J. Zwi Werblowsky, *Japanese Journal of Religious Studies* 18.4 (December 1991): 295–354.

these matters. The response to this objection, however, might be that Japan has in fact been moving up the moral curve. As already noted, in centuries past the need for some kind of "family planning" made people—especially if they were poor or already had too many children—feel compelled to commit infanticide. This was what above was called the "dark story" behind Japan's success. But infanticide is now extremely rare in Japan; it has been replaced by abortion. Moreover if, as trends indicate, the ever more efficient use of contraceptives makes even abortion less and less necessary, Japan over recent centuries will have shown a remarkable advance in moral sensitivities and moral practices on this matter.

Critics of abortion in America sometimes refer to what is called the "slippery slope"—that is, an inevitably downward trend in morals. In this context it is meant to suggest that, against the objections of the Roman Catholic Church, once contraceptives were legalized, the legalization of abortion—at least in the United States—came soon after with the Supreme Court's decision in 1973. But that is not all. The theory is that, with this legalization, it can be expected that people will sooner or later develop a tolerance for infanticide. According to this view the trend is strictly from bad to worse.

Here, however, is where Japan offers an interesting counterexample.   20 What we know of the history and present practice there shows a pattern of moving to practices that are less and less objectionable—from infanticide to abortion and from there to contraception. What we might even call movement *up* the so-called slippery slope seems to have been the case in Japan. At least it shows that there is nothing necessary about a downward plunge.

In the final analysis, however, those in Japan who feel that abortion should be legalized and readily available to women state that the well-being of the child is also served by this. With their belief that even a fetus whose development in the womb is forcibly interrupted will return to this world at a better time and place for it to be born, many Japanese see this as best not only for the mother but also, in the long run, for the child itself. And this, in fact, fits into a rather common view in Japan that every child ought to be a *wanted* one—by at least one of its parents.

Since members of most religious communities and institutions in Japan agree with this, they clearly feel free to see abortion as morally permissible when thought necessary or preferable. In this view it is better both for individual children and for the society as a whole to make sure that children who are born are children who are desired. Then they will tend to get the care, attention, and education they deserve. In this view the society which regards every child as worthy of such care is one following a preferred moral course.

We in the West may need to face the fact that this perhaps, is, itself an important element contributing to what Paul Kennedy has described as the fairly bright prospects for Japan in the twenty-first century. And in this sense Japanese thinking and practice with respect to abortion gives us both pause and a way of seeing the whole problem from a distinctly different point of view.

Thinking About the Text

1. Examine paragraphs 19 and 20, and see if you agree with LaFleur's logic. If you don't agree, explain why.

2. Do you think LaFleur is advocating the Japanese view? Severely criticizing it? Presenting it impartially? Or doing something else? Support your answer with evidence.

Thinking About Culture

3. In a discussion of the nature of apologies in Japan, LaFleur says that an apology (in this case, to a fetus) "is thought appropriate" even when "the person receiving the apology is no longer in the same world as the maker of the apology" (para. 14). Is such behavior comparable to a Hebrew, Christian, or Moslem prayer for forgiveness? Or are there essential differences?

4. Prepare a report on Jizo, the godlike figure described in paragraph 15. Useful starting points for research are June Kinoshita and Nicholas Palevsky, *Gateway to Japan* (1992); John M. Rosenfield and Elizabeth ten Grotenhuis, *Journey of the Three Jewels* (1979); and Stephen Little, *Visions of the Dharma* (1991).

Chapter 6

Growing Older

Even the title of this chapter, "Growing Older," is an indication of a mind-set about age: Americans generally do not want to think that they are growing "old," but one can get away with saying "older." Some have seen the status and condition of the elderly in Japan as a model for America: Surely, they reason, with a Confucian code of social ethics, a seniority-based system of respect, Japanese older people are well cared for, valued, and happy. With a traditional family system that includes care for dependent elderly in the extended family home, with excellent national health care, and a high rate of personal savings contributing to security in old age, what could be bad about being old?

Despite these supportive conditions, the social value placed on seniority in Japan is being sorely tested now. One indication is the creeping euphemization of "old age": As in America, there are now new words meant to take the sting out of being called older, such as "senior citizen," "golden years," "silver seats" (seats set aside for the elderly on public transportation, some-times—but not always—yielded up by the young when an older person boards), "age of fruition," and the like. If being old were still a good thing, one imagines that such terms would not be needed.

A few years ago, a plan was developed to establish luxurious residences for the elderly in places like Colombia, Argentina, Australia—places with warmer climates, ample space, and a less-expensive standard of living than in Japan. This project, called the "Silver Columbia," received a very bad press, as the Japanese concerns that planned it were accused of trying to export the elderly rather than trying to give them a better life offshore. Perhaps it was a rather benign idea, giving the elderly a kind of resort life at lower cost, rather like communities in Florida serving American elderly. But it was not carried out.

Indeed, as David W. Plath (p. 210) notes, the problem of caring for the elderly will not soon disappear. Japan is becoming a "graying society"; in the first quarter of the twenty-first century, the proportion of people over sixty-five years of age will approach 25 percent. As the number of babies born is diminishing very rapidly (the birthrate is now 1.46 per household), the burden of care, both actual physical care and funding for the population of elderly, will fall on a smaller and smaller cohort of young people.

Longevity in Japan has grown in this century to an average life span of 78 for men, 82 for women, the highest in the world. There are now record numbers of elderly and new designations of categories of elderly: young elderly, who are 60 to 70; elderly between 70 and 80; and old elderly starting at 80 years of age. Because of improved health conditions, there is now a record number of centenarians, persons over 100 years of age. In September there is a special holiday, "Respect for the Elders Day," on which newspaper editorials extol the wisdom of the old, encourage the young (particularly daughters-in-law) to care for them, and exhort government to provide public services for them.

Such editorials may indeed be a response to changing conditions for the elderly: They wouldn't be needed if the respect and care were a given. Family life in Japan has changed. Twenty years ago, about 90 percent of the elderly lived with their children, whereas now about 65 percent do so. Most of the rest live alone or in nursing-care facilities. Daughters-in-law, once relied on for the care of the elderly, now work outside the home, and find it difficult to be available, even if they want to help. In a recent survey, the words "duty" and "obligation" are used when referring to a daughter-in-law's responsibility, and they express reluctance, or a martyrlike attitude toward the prospect of such care. The elderly too resist being dependent, and most say they would like to be on their own as long as possible. As with the aging father in Kazuo Ishiguro's short story (p. 234), they now rely more on their own daughters than on daughters-in-law, a real change from the past, when a son's wife was the preferred caretaker, since the custom of primogeniture meant that parents would normally live with a son rather than a daughter.

Retirement age is young in Japan; in large organizations it is between 52 and 55. Retirement then is clearly not related to the condition of being elderly, and in fact a retired person usually gets a second and third job, since, with delayed childbearing, parents in their fifties are still likely to have high expenses for a child's college years and marriage. Even without such expenses, however, older people want to be active, as Cathy N. Davidson (p. 215) discovered. It is important, they say, to have an *ikigai,* a "reason to live," meaning a hobby, a passion for a sport, a commitment to a cause or a public service project, if they are truly retired from work. The consumer leisure industries, anticipating a boom among retired and elderly populations, have expanded to include a wide variety of activities. Overseas travel is popular, and tours are arranged to suit the needs of older people. Sports are popular, such as "gate ball," a kind of croquet, in which older people engage in national tournaments or just play in local public parks. Study groups, to learn a foreign language or read classical Japanese texts together, are also formed. Elderly may also be active in consumer movement groups, environmental organizations, or volunteer groups to help handicapped children or other causes.

It is the older elderly, those who have become dependent physically or mentally, who are a concern. If families cannot or will not take care of them, government agencies must. Daughters-in-law are now beginning to object to the old tradition of compulsory care, and some young women say they will not marry into a family where there is likely to be a need for this. Where care is a family concern, the older person is living longer, and is often in a state of complete dependency for a longer period than ever before, as medical care keeps people alive, though dependent, much longer. While there are some respite-care institutions, such as senior day-care centers, allowing families to have some time off from constant care, and there are some services for elderly who live on their own, such as hot-meal deliveries, visiting bath-care services, and home-visit volunteers, the burden still is on the family, even as attitudes, among the elderly and among the young, are changing.

Americans too, in spite of our belief in independence and our emphasis on the nuclear family, live increasingly in three-generation households for at least some periods of their lives. We imagine that most elderly are in nursing homes and retirement communities, such as the one described by Diana Bethel (p. 219); but with an increase in the percentage of elderly, a low rate of construction of such institutions, and continuing economic decline, we find families picking up the slack. As in Japan, it is daughters and daughters-in-law who provide most of the care, and often with great difficulty, for many are working women with families who depend on their income. Family ties, then, are stronger than ever, in spite of myths of "granny dumping" (leaving elderly at hospitals and nursing homes).

The old legend in Japan of *Obasuteyama* (Throwing-away-granny Mountain) is fiction, not fact, though some have recently invoked it with an opposite meaning to its original intent. The old story goes that to be extremely filial, a son should take his elderly parent, after the age of seventy, to the top of a particular mountain and there abandon him or her to the good and virtuous death by exposure. The older person, in the story, looks forward to this as the right and proper thing to do, and prepares special clothing and a straw mat. Of course, the story has many modifications, including the filial son, torn between duty and love, who runs back up the mountain wanting to bring the parent down again, but finds the parent already dead with a blissful smile on her face. Now we find the elderly complaining of being tossed around, not tossed out, as sons and daughters may take turns caring for their parents, a few months here, a few months there. More commonly, however, a parent will reside with one child.

Social change, changing family life, working women, and recessionary economies have changed the conditions of the elderly in both America and Japan. Most important however are the implications of the coming "elderly boom" as baby boomers reach old age. With the "baby bust" as the caretaker generation, whom will the elderly turn to?

Explorations

1. In order to deal with difficult realities, we sometimes create euphemisms that help us take the sting out of a problem. In this chapter on the elderly, the terms "silver" and "gold" refer to old age. What euphemisms can you think of in current use, and what effect do they have? Why is it so hard to say "old" in America today?

2. In your family, have you had experience with the care of the elderly? Have you lived with an older relative? Who takes (took) care of this person? How do (did) the younger relative feel about the care? How did the older relative feel about being cared for?

3. In Asian societies, it is conventional to talk about an ideal of "filial piety." What does this mean, and do you know if there is any parallel in American culture?

David W. Plath

Old Age and Retirement

In all industrial societies more and more people are in their later years of life; how best to provide for their well-being has become a serious issue. Japan's situation is acute because of the dramatic rise in longevity since 1950, the practice of retiring long-term employees at age 55, and the lagging development of pension plans and old-age income supports. Programs for the aged now have a high priority in government spending. But the percentage of old persons is expected to double in Japan before the end of this century. Unless reforms are instituted, old age may become a chronic social malady.

Population Change

Japan is famous for having had the world's fastest rate of economic growth since 1950. During the same period Japan also has had the world's most rapid rise in longevity. Average life expectancy at birth in 1950 was about 60 years, and in 1977 it was 73 years for males and 78 years for females.

With declining fertility, each year fewer persons are added, proportionately, to the lower age brackets of the population. The over-60 stratum is

David W. Plath, a member of the Department of Anthropology at the University of Illinois, is the author of numerous articles on aspects of Japanese life. This essay originally appeared in the first edition of the Kodansha Encyclopedia of Japan *(1983).*

growing more rapidly than any age stratum under 60. Until the middle of the twentieth century only about 1 out of 20 Japanese was over age 60. Today the figure is more than 1 in 10, by the year 2000 it will be 1 in 5. And while the gender ratio remains nearly equal under age 60, women over 60 have begun to outnumber men about 5 to 4. Furthermore, by age 65 some 3 out of 5 women—but only 1 out of 5 men—are without a spouse. The problems of old age will increasingly become problems of widowhood.

Mass aging is without precedent in Japan. Coupled with other trends in modern mass society—toward urban residence, paid employment, extended schooling, smaller family units—it is impelling change in many institutions, requiring a reconsideration of the idea that care for the aged is primarily a family task.

Traditional Themes

Japan's premodern ethic called for selfless sacrifice for one's parents, support   5
for them in old age, and respect for elders in general. Political and religious leaders sermonized on these ideals, particularly during the Edo period (1600–1868), when most fiefs held an annual ceremony to honor those of advanced years.

How well the ethic was practiced at home the rest of the year we do not know. Old people who were hale or judicious, those who were wise or who could act as guardians of life's mysteries, probably could command respect or attention. This may not have been true for the frail, the senile, the incapacitated, or those who had no living kin. There long have been traditions about "sudden death prayers" *(pokkuri ojo)* in which old people feeble or desperately ill pray for a quick and painless demise. Many tales and dramas have recounted the story of *obasute* in which useless old people are taken to a mountain *(yama)* and left to die. (A mountain in Nagano bears the name Obasuteyama° today.) There is no evidence that the senile ever have been routinely abandoned in Japan. But the lesson is that even elders might not merit unconditional support when they cease to be an asset to community or family.

These themes remain vital today. Popular religions continue to preach filial piety. The civil code holds children legally responsible for the welfare of aged parents. The annual ceremony for honoring the elders was revived as a national holiday in 1963. And in public opinion polls the great majority of people agree that one should care for parents as a "natural" matter of decency and affection.

On the other hand some temples report a growing number of "sudden-death" petitioners over the past decade. Contemporary literature continues to use the story of Obasuteyama, as in Shichiro Fukazawa's prize-winning 1956 short story "Narayama-bushi ko" ("The Oak Mountain

---

Obasuteyama: Literally, "Mt. Abandoning-old-woman." [Editors' note]

Song"). Films and fiction take up the issue of who should tend the senile, as in Sawako Ariyoshi's best-selling novel *Kokotsu no hito* (1972, *A Man in Ecstasy*). And (assuming that suicide is a measure of willingness to voluntarily abandon life) Japanese have one of the highest ratios of old-age suicide in the world.

Work and Retirement

Traditionally one entered old age in the sixtieth year of life. That year sees one full cycle *(kanreki)* of the East Asian zodiac, so the signs again are the same as they were the year one was born. Some people today celebrate *kanreki* privately. In the past some also took the occasion to withdraw from positions of leadership in family or community.

In premodern Japan, retirement was compulsory at a fixed age (usually   10 60) only for *samurai.* For most people it could be a gradual process. They could hand over control of the family enterprise to the next generation and continue to work as long as they were willing or able. The successor—typically the eldest son—in turn would offer shelter and support in old age.

With the decline of family enterprise, in modern times most workers are subject to mandatory retirement. Age 55 was taken as Japan's Rubicon early in the twentieth century—reasonable in light of life expectancy then. Now it seems too early. Most firms and bureaus terminate employment to-day at 55; in some the age is between 55 and 60. Women often are obliged to retire earlier than men, although the practice has been ruled unconstitutional.

Most countries do not set retirement so early, or if they do, then pension benefits begin immediately upon retirement. But in Japan payments under employees' pension programs do not begin until age 60, or those under the National Pension (Kokumin Nenkin) program until 65. All aged Japanese are eligible for income support under one or another of a complex of welfare and pension systems. But only 1 person in 5 currently can draw benefits at levels comparable to those in other industrial nations. Furthermore, at age 55 most Japanese men must support a wife, at least 1 in 3 has dependent minors, and 1 in 3 has dependent parents.

Not surprisingly, most workers retired at 55 seek reemployment. Even in their late 60s some 7 out of 10 Japanese men and 4 out of 10 women are working, more than double the number in other industrial economies. In the 1970s programs were established to retrain older citizens and help them find jobs. Some local governments began "senior citizen enterprises" *(koreisha jigyodan)* to expand job opportunities. At 55, top-level executives or administrators may find new positions of equivalent pay, status, and security. Most retirees can find jobs only in small workshops that offer them less security and lower wages than the positions they vacated.

Government spokesmen call for raising the retirement age, but business-men and legislators have hesitated. And until the so-called pension strike of

April 1973 the labor unions focused their annual spring struggle campaigns upon the issue of increased base pay, not improved treatment for older workers.

Social Services

Japan has been energetically building new medical services and social pro-   15
grams for its aged. Compared with North Atlantic nations, Japan lags in social-service spending for all age-groups: in 1970 some 6 percent of the gross national product versus 11 percent in the United States and 21 percent in Sweden. But locally and nationally more and more of the annual budget is being channeled into programs for old people.

Since 1973 all medical care has been free for persons 70 years and older. For those under 70 the National Health Insurance pays 70 percent of medical costs; some municipalities pay the remaining 30 percent for persons between 65 and 70. In addition, all Japanese over 65 are entitled to a free comprehensive medical examination each year. In the United States, by contrast, Medicare and Medicaid together cover less than half of the medical expenses incurred by persons over 65.

Senior citizen clubs and centers—for recreation, sports, and study— can obtain government subsidy if they enroll more than fifty members. The first such center made its debut in Tokyo in 1953. A quarter century later, there were 100,000 clubs across the nation, with half of the population over 60 as members. "Colleges for the Aged" *(rojin daigaku)* offer education programs in many cities and prefectures. Other programs of many sorts are being tested. These include day-care centers, foster care, home helpers, meal delivery, telephone visiting, and free use of special equipment for the bedridden. But as yet these programs are available only in a few locales.

Housing policy continues to assume that offspring will provide sheltered care for old people needing it. Japan has no retirement communities, and market surveys find little enthusiasm for the concept. However, migration of younger people to the cities has made virtual old-age communities out of numerous villages, particularly in the southwest. Some housing projects allow priority to old persons wishing to live near their offspring, but no public housing has been built with the special needs of the elderly in mind. (A few private apartment buildings cater to retirees.) And there appears to be a shortage of institutions equipped to serve those who have no kin or who require nursing care.

Buddhist temples traditionally offered refuge to the destitute, including the aged and bereft. But the first facility specifically for the aged *(yoroin)* was opened in Tokyo in 1895 by Christian missionaries. Old-age homes and nursing care homes now number nearly a thousand. But they can accommodate less than 1 percent of the aged in Japan, in contrast to 5 to 8 percent in other industrial nations. Estimates are that 9 out of 10 chronically ill and bedridden old people in Japan must be tended at home by their offspring.

This places upon more than 300,000 families a burden that many people believe should be shared by society at large.

Family Solidarity

The problem may not be that filial values or family solidarity have become   20
weak. Rather, in preindustrial times the frail elderly were so few in number and died so soon that they probably were a minor burden upon most families. That burden has grown to where it calls the values into question because of the strain they place upon family solidarity.

Japan is said to suffer less from family "breakdown" than other modern nations. But the difference may be more apparent than real. With regard to the aged it is pointed out that 7 in 10 old people in Japan are living with offspring, in contrast to 2 or 3 in 10 in North Atlantic countries. But in Japan "living with offspring" is defined as residing in the same housing compound. Two married adult generations in a Japanese household will strive to maintain separate quarters, meals, routines, and budgets so as to dampen conflict. Conversely, in the West the majority of old people residing apart from children are within a short distance of at least one child. It may be that despite differences in residence, old people elsewhere in the industrial world are in contact with children about as frequently—and have as much potential for family solidarity—as do those in Japan.

Prospects

On balance, old persons have a smaller package of welfare benefits in Japan than in northern Europe, though perhaps not much less than in the United States and vastly more than in the Third World. The quality of life in old age, however, is not easy to evaluate without cultural bias. Norms of filial respect may provide old Japanese with compensations not available in the West.

Issues of income support and social services seem sure to grow more serious as the old-age population expands. "Senior power" only began to find a voice in Japan early in the 1970s. But as future generations of Japanese enter old age, they will be better educated, more attuned to political action, and probably will demand a greater share in the benefits of an industrial economy.

Bibliography

Ariyoshi, Sawako. *Kokotsu no hito* (1972).

Fukazawa, Shichiro. "The Oak Mountain Song." Trans. John Bester. *Japan Quarterly* 4.2 (1957).

Koza: Nihon no rojin. 3 vols. Kakiuchi Shuppan, 1972.

Nasu, Soichi. *Teinen: Gojugosai no shiren.* 1972.

Niwa, Fumio. "The Hateful Age." Trans. Ivan Morris. *Modern Japanese Stories* (1961).

Palmore, Erdman. *The Honorable Elders: A Cross-Cultural Analysis of Aging in Japan.* 1975.

Plath, David W. "Japan: The After Years." In *Aging and Modernization.* 1972.

———. "Ecstasy Years: Old Age in Japan." In *Pacific Affairs.* Fall 1973.

Seikatsu Kagaku Chosakai. *Rogo mondai no kenkyu.* 1966.

Sparks, Douglas. "The Still Rebirth: Role Discontinuity and Retirement." In *Adult Episodes in Japan.* 1975.

Tokyo Metropolitan Institute of Gerontology, Sociology Department. *Selected Bibliography of Social Gerontology in Japan: 1960–1973.* 1974.

Thinking About the Text

1. In paragraph 20 Plath suggests that the problem of caring for the elderly "may not be that filial values or family solidarity have become weak." Do the reasons he gives strike you as plausible? Why, or why not?

2. You may not be in a position to evaluate the accuracy of Plath's article, but you *can* evaluate the degree of its clarity and other aspects of its style. How would you rate it as a piece of expository writing? Why?

3. If possible, read one of the suggested readings Plath cites at the end of his article, and prepare a summary of it. If none of these sources is available to you, from a bibliography, such as the *Readers' Guide to Periodical Literature* or the *Academic Index,* locate and summarize a recent article on old age.

Thinking About Culture

4. Do you think retirement should be compulsory at any specified age? (Persons required to retire would of course, as in Japan, be permitted to work at new jobs if they could find employers, or they might become self-employed.) What are your reasons?

5. Following Plath's headings where possible ("Population Change," "Traditional Themes," etc.) write an account (though of course much shorter) of old age and retirement in the United States.

Cathy N. Davidson

The Old Woman in the Bath

As soon as I arrive in Shirahama with the members of the Japanese Women's Studies Society, I realize that this is not going to be a typical three-day vacation by the sea. Instead of being shown to my room, I'm shown to *our*

In 1980 Cathy N. Davidson, a professor of English who now teaches at Duke University, made her first visit to Japan, where she taught English at a women's university. Later she made three additional visits, all of which she describes in her engaging memoir, 36 Views of Mount Fuji (1993). The selection we reprint (with a title of our own) comes from a chapter called "Typical Japanese Women."

room, a gigantic tatami° room. Except when we're at the beach, I'm told, this is where we will be meeting during the day and sleeping at night, all fifteen of us. Now we need to hurry to take our bath together because our dinner will be served in this room in an hour and a half.

"You've had a Japanese-style bath before, haven't you?" Kazue-san asks a little nervously as we head down the hall to the women's bath.

"Oh, of course," I shrug off her comment.

Of course I haven't, but I'm not about to give that away. I know the basics from the guidebooks: Wash thoroughly *before* you get into the bath; make sure never to do anything to spoil the communal, clean bath water. I figure I can wing it on the details.

We undress in a small anteroom and fold our clothes neatly into baskets   5 on the shelves. We walk into the bath with our tiny white terry washcloths. Along one wall is a row of faucets for washing, with drains in the sloping tiled floors. On the other side is the mosaic-tiled bath, as blue as the sea, beneath a cascade of tropical plants.

I've seen naked women before in showers in various gyms in America, but the mood in this Japanese bath is entirely different. I've never seen people more comfortable with their bodies. There are twenty-five or thirty women in the room, our group plus a group of *obasan* (grandmothers) here on vacation from the countryside and some members of an Osaka teachers' association having an annual meeting. The oldest woman is probably close to ninety; the youngest is three. The mood is quietly happy, utterly relaxed.

We sit naked on low wooden stools, soaping ourselves with the terry washcloths, rinsing with red buckets filled from the taps and poured over the body. The conversation is lulled, languid, like the water, like the steamy air.

I finish washing my entire body and notice that most of the women from my group are still soaping a first arm. I slow down, going back again over my entire body, washing and washing, the soapy cloth, the warm water, the joking talking laughing atmosphere, the bodies. The women in my group are now washing a second arm. I slow down again, deciding I will try to do it right this time, Japanese-style, concentrating on a leg. I baby each toe, each toenail, each fold of flesh, noticing for the first time in years the small scar on the inside of my ankle, a muffler burn from a motorcycle when I was a teenager. I'm fascinated by this ritual attention to the body, so different from the brisk Western morning wake-up shower. When I finish (again) and go to shampoo my hair, I see that most of the women in my group are still scrubbing. I give up. It must take practice. I have never seen such luxuriant pampering of bodies.

The bath is a revelation for another reason. I read once that a one-hour bath has the same physiological effect as four hours of sleep. Maybe this is how the Japanese do it, I think, a ritual stop in the otherwise frenetic day.

---

tatami: Thick pallets covered with rice-straw matting. The pallets fit together to form the floor in traditional rooms. [Editors' note]

As I watch these women soaping their bodies with such slow concentra-   10
tion, it is almost impossible for me to remember what they are like most of
the time, raising families, working full-time, responsible for all of the household chores and the household finances, as busy as any American women
I've ever met.

I tell this to my friend, Kazue-san.

"It's hard to be busy when you're naked," she says smiling. "It looks
too silly!"

I find myself laughing. Everywhere around me are the bodies of typical
Japanese women, every one different, every one alike.

"May I help you wash your hair?" Kazue-san asks, as I struggle to pour
some water over my hair from the little red plastic bucket.

"Please let me!" interjects one of the *obasan* who has been watching   15
me for several minutes. She is very old, probably in her seventies or even
eighties. Standing, her face comes even with mine as I sit on the tiny stool.
Her body is bent over, almost parallel to the ground. Kazue-san says she's
probably crippled from malnutrition during the war years and the chronic
lack of calcium in the traditional Japanese diet as well as from bending to
plant and harvest the rice crop every year.

"I bet she still works in the fields," Kazue-san whispers in English, and
I smile back into the old woman's smiling face. Her hair is pure white, her
face covered with spidery lines, but her eyes are absolutely clear, sparkling.
The old woman introduces herself, bowing even more deeply. Her name is
Keiko Doi. I'm too self-conscious to stand up so I introduce myself sheepishly,
trying to bow as low and respectfully as I can without getting up from my
little stool. The other old ladies in the bath are watching us. They seem
abashed by Doi-san's forwardness, but they also look thoroughly delighted.
One of the old ladies says you can never tell what Doi-san will do next. She
is their ringleader, a real character.

"She has no shame!" one of the grandmothers says half critically, half
affectionately of the mischievous Doi-san.

"Too old for shame!" Doi-san retorts, and the other old lady starts
laughing so hard I'm afraid she might hurt herself. She pulls up a stool and
sits down next to us, watching intently, still unable to stifle her laughter.

Doi-san squeezes shampoo into her hand and then rubs her palms
together briskly. She's a pro. She massages the shampoo into my hair, the
thick pads of her fingers making circles against my scalp. Then she lays one
hand on my head, and starts clapping up and down on it with the other
hand, making a sound like castanets as she works her hands over my head.
It feels great. After about ten minutes, she chops with the sides of her hands
over my head, my neck, and my shoulders, a kind of shiatsu massage.

I think I could die at this moment with no regrets. I feel about four   20
years old and totally at home, this tiny grandmother massaging my back and
shoulders, my scalp and forehead. "Do you like this?" she keeps asking. "Is
this comfortable?"

Yes, yes.

The other old ladies are cutting up, making jokes, and Doi-san douses one of them with a bucket of water. The woman douses back, and someone else flips at Doi-san with a washcloth. Kazue-san says we've run into a group of eighty-year-old juvenile delinquents. She's never seen anything like this in her life, and she tells Doi-san, jokingly but admiringly, that she's the most outrageous old lady of them all. In English, I start calling Doi-san the "Leader of the Pack."

"Shuuush!" Doi-san admonishes us to stop talking English to one another. She hands me a cloth to put over my eyes and motions to her friends. Each fills her bucket and comes to stand in a circle around me. They take turns; one pours a full bucket over my head like a waterfall. I take a breath, then the next bucket comes. The water is exactly the right temperature.

When they finish, I just sit there for a while, feeling cleaner than I've ever felt in my life.

The old ladies can't stop laughing, and several of them are slapping   25 Doi-san on the back, chiding her for her outrageousness, but also beamingly proud of their brazen friend.

I ask Doi-san if I may wash her hair but she refuses. Now, she commands, I must soak in the bath. It's time for me to relax.

I say that I can't take water as hot as most Japanese, and one of the strangers already in the bath motions me to a place beside her where the water, she says, is coolest. I lower myself slowly, allowing my body to adjust to the heat.

When I look around, Doi-san has disappeared. The rogue and her octogenarian gang from the countryside have all departed. A new group of bathers is coming in. They look startled at first to see me, a *gaijin*,° but then go about their business. They are probably high school or junior high school girls, many of them still at the last stages of chubby adolescence, utterly unself-conscious about their nakedness.

"That was her," Kazue-san whispers, absolutely deadpan, as she slips into the water beside me.

"Who? What do you mean?" I ask, puzzled at first, then skeptical as   30 Kazue-san smiles impishly.

"Why, the typical Japanese woman," she teases. "Doi-san. I think you finally found her."

Thinking About the Text

1. "Too old for shame!" one of the old ladies says (para. 18). Sei Shonagon, whose thousand-year-old exasperated description of a lover's departure we quote on page 130, listed among "hateful things" not only the conceited lover but also the uninhibited actions of some old people:

gaijin: Foreigner. The word is short for *gaikokujin,* or "person from another country." [Editors' note]

An elderly person warms the palms of his hands over a brazier and stretches out the wrinkles. No young man would dream of behaving in such a fashion; old people can really be quite shameless. I have seen some dreary old creatures actually resting their feet on the brazier and rubbing them against the edge while they speak.

Do you think that Davidson is sentimentalizing the old people she met? That is, do you find them convincing? Why, or why not?

2. Davidson is a professor at Duke University. If she were teaching at your school, would you (having read this essay) be interested in taking a course with her? Why, or why not?

Thinking About Culture

3. Although few if any people would say that the bath in the United States is pretty much the same as the bath in Japan, can a case be made that, in the United States, bathing is—or can be—much more than just a matter of cleaning the body? How does the idea of communal soaking strike you? Do you think that being naked in a tub with others might (or in fact does) put you into a state of community and that the experience can be psychologically important? In fact, have you ever engaged in a comparable experience in a hot tub or whirlpool bath?

4. Does nudity itself, say in a locker room, even without the presence of a bath, contribute to a sense of camaraderie otherwise scarcely attainable? (The Japanese say that *hadaka no tsukiai*—companions in nudity—are the closest friends.)

5. In your library do some research on the bath in ancient Roman times, and compare it with the Japanese bath or with contemporary American bathing practices.

Diana Bethel

Alienation and Reconnection in a Home for the Elderly

Japanese perceive institutions for the elderly as both a blessing and a curse. The demographic, socioeconomic, and cultural changes that come with modernization undermine the traditional Confucian ethic of filial piety which

Diana Bethel wrote this article when she was a Ph.D. candidate in anthropology at the Center for Japanese Studies at the University of Hawaii, Manoa.

sanctions family care for aging Japanese. Increased longevity, urbanization and migration of young people from the country to the city, an increase of women (the traditional caretakers of the elderly) in the work force, crowded housing conditions, and regional economic hardship have made it difficult for many Japanese families to care for their older members (Maeda 1983). Yet despite this decreasing capability, expectations for family care remain strong.

The dread with which the Japanese elderly view institutionalization reflects the social stigmatization of this deviant fate combined with a fear of the old-age home as unfamiliar and even alien. These fears are well grounded, because institutions, by their nature, strip newcomers of their identities, autonomy, social roles, material possessions, and a sense of place in a familiar social universe (Goffman 1961; Tobin and Lieberman 1976). This chapter examines the lives of residents of the Aotani Institution for the Elderly, located in a rural area of central Hokkaido, and identifies the ordinary features of everyday life such as food, clothing, furniture, and spatial organization that residents use to establish a familiar domestic space in an unfamiliar institutional environment.

The Aotani Institution for the Elderly is a social welfare institution whose requirements for admission include a minimum age of sixty-five and an inability to live at home because of decreasing physical strength or mental acuity, economic hardship, or difficult social circumstances (Ministry of Welfare 1985). An applicant must be relatively healthy and able to manage daily affairs. Meals are prepared on site by cooks and served in the common dining hall. Residents who become too sick or frail or exhibit abnormal behavior are sent on to other institutions or must return to their families.

Most Aotani residents are grateful to be in the institution because it is warm in winter, boasts modern indoor plumbing, and has staff on duty twenty-four hours a day. Living in such an institution (especially a social welfare institution), however, is dissonant with cultural norms and sets up a psychological dilemma that every resident must resolve in the struggle to adapt.

The trauma of residents' institutionalization comes from being thrust into an environment that is not only impersonal and unfamiliar but also foreign. As it happens, a Christian Englishwoman and her congregation founded the first institution for the elderly in Japan, known as St. Hilda's, in 1896 (Ogasawara 1986). Before that time, the elderly poor and infirm with no family support were placed in poorhouses along with orphans, the sick, and vagrants.

The founding of St. Hilda's marked the recognition that in a modernizing Japan, social welfare institutions would be needed to address the special needs of older people. As this awareness grew, more homes for older people were established. The number was drastically reduced during World War II, when many of them in the major cities were burned or totally destroyed.

Since the war, the number of institutions for the elderly has increased dramatically. In 1963 there were only 690, but by 1984 this figure had grown to 2,814 (Ministry of Welfare 1985). Each year approximately one hundred more homes are built. Clearly, a need exists for this alternative to family care, and increasing numbers of older people and their families are making use of it. This change in tradition and attitude has brought about a corresponding increase in discussion about institutions and care for the elderly. But as cultural norms lag behind social reality, resistance to the idea of institutionalization remains strong.

The architecture, schedule, food, and loss of familiar furniture and belongings when they enter the facility contribute to residents' difficulty in adjusting. The facility, with its poured concrete construction, dining hall set with tables and chairs, staff dressed in white uniforms, and rigidly structured routines, is the epitome of an unnatural, alien, Western life-style.

Newcomers to Aotani are stripped of familiar reminders of their pre-institutional lives through the restriction—because of space limitations— against bringing bulky items and too many belongings. They must give up all worldly possessions except for those that will fit into the small closet assigned to them. No personal furniture is allowed. Even the cherished family *butsudan* (Buddhist altar) must be disposed of or entrusted to one's children. In its place, the institution provides its own Buddhist altar in which memorial tablets of deceased family members may be placed together with those of other residents.

Residents must adjust to a new way of life determined by the schedule of the institution, which now sets the rhythms of their lives. Waking, eating, and going to bed are all precisely regulated. Without exception, all able residents must rise with the 6:00 A.M. wakeup music and be in bed by the 9:00 P.M. "lights out." Mealtimes are at 8:00 A.M., 12:00 P.M., and 5:00 P.M., and residents are always expected to be present unless they have notified the staff otherwise.

The staff at Aotani have organized meals into tightly structured rituals   10 that are orchestrated by work groups made up of residents. Prior to each meal, those assigned to dining hall duty set the tables and bring food from the kitchen, a process that also provides an opportunity for residents to socialize.

Residents who gather outside the dining room chat as they wait for the music that signals permission to enter the dining room. A staff member sometimes attempts to shoo them away, berating them for waiting "like animals at feeding time." She says, "What will visitors think when they see you crowding around the dining hall entrance? They'll think we never feed you!" Though the residents scatter obediently, a few minutes later, without fail, they begin to drift back toward the cafeteria entrance.

Suddenly, the music begins and waiting residents pour into the dining room. They sit patiently in their assigned seats at their tables until a staff woman announces "*Itadakimasu!*" (Let's eat!) As if runners on their mark, residents take up their chopsticks and begin eating. Because only fifteen minutes are allotted for a meal, slow eaters hurry to avoid being left behind when the staff woman dismisses them with *"Gochisosama deshita!"* (Thank you for the meal). In unison, residents rise from their seats, holding their emptied dishes, and proceed hurriedly to the kitchen counter to stand in line. Each dish is deposited in its designated collection pot for the cooks to wash.

The rigorous schedule is part of the tradition of institution life and is designed to make the management of approximately eighty older people go as smoothly as possible. All residents must adhere to the schedule, whether they like it or not, or face eviction from the home. The rationale for the strict daily schedule is the traditional philosophy that one must lead an orderly and disciplined life *(kisoku tadashii seikatsu)*. The staff's need to run mealtimes efficiently contributes to the residents' sense of being confined and manipulated.

The one-taste-fits-all cafeteria cuisine is a frequent source of contention between residents and food providers. The administration attempts to determine the residents' food preferences, but dissatisfactions inevitably arise. Though residents look forward to mealtimes as the high points of their day, some are picky and refuse to eat unfamiliar foods. Mrs. Sasaki explained that eating "is our only enjoyment" *(tatta hitotsu no tanoshimi)*, so residents are naturally particular about what they are served. Most of the cuisine is Japanese, modified somewhat by the young dietician's westernized palate. Conflicts sometimes arise because of the desire of these elderly people for more familiar fare. This difference in food preferences between residents and staff mirrors differences in food tastes in intergenerational households among grandchildren, parents, and grandparents. Often the only solution at home is to cook two separate menus, one for the younger generations, based on meat and "new" dishes, and one for the older generation, based on fish and traditional dishes.

The dietician's job is stressful because she must listen to complaints   15
and try to balance diverse and often-conflicting demands. Generally residents do not like food they have never eaten before or have eaten only rarely during their childhood. They have no taste for newfangled foods such as spaghetti, hamburgers, ketchup, sauces such as curry, or creamed dishes poured over rice. When curry or creamed sauces are served, some request only the plain rice served with them. Most residents, who rarely had the chance to eat eggs during their youth, avoid them now. Others avoid cold foods such as Jell-O, ice cream, or sodas because it "chills" their bodies *(karada ga hieru kara)*.

Although residents have some input in making up the menus, they have to eat what is served—unless they can come up with something they like better from the local food stores. But because buying food for meals soon becomes expensive, most residents strike a happy medium by eating the basic foods offered in the cafeteria, such as rice and miso soup, and sampling the side dishes, then supplementing their meal with more appetizing traditional and familiar fare, either before or after their cafeteria meal.

The fact that the first institution for the elderly in Japan was founded by a foreigner has become obscure historical trivia, but a sense of foreignness is nevertheless associated with institutions. The Japanese term *rojin homu* (institution for the elderly) reveals an ironic foreign nuance. In an attempt to distance postwar institutions from the image of the earlier *yoro-in* (asylum for the elderly), a new name was chosen—*rojin homu,* which combines the Japanese word for old people and the English word for home. The term was intended to impart a bright, pleasant, Western image of a modern facility to combat the dark, depressing, and shameful image of the early poorhouses and social welfare institutions for older people.

The sense of foreignness that pervades the home arises also from the notion that the need for such facilities is an inevitable side effect of attitudes imported from America after World War II. It is common knowledge, residents assert, that Americans treat their elderly very poorly. In Japan, they insist, institutions for the elderly are out of place and should not even exist, because Japanese feel a strong sense of responsibility toward family members.

Narratives of Institutionalization

At the core of the Japanese code of social conduct is the Confucian ethic of filial piety, according to which children must honor and obey their parents. The Japanese ideal calls for aging parents to live with their eldest son and his family, surrounded by attentive and respectful grandchildren. Institutionalization represents a failure to achieve this ideal. The sense of social stigma associated with this failure can produce acute psychological discomfort in the institutionalized elderly.

Obasuteyama ("the mountain on which grannies are abandoned") is a Japanese legend that has been revived as a commentary on a new social problem (Fukazawa 1964; Imamura 1983; Plath 1972). The term *Obasuteyama* is frequently used by residents as a nickname for homes for the elderly to call attention to the shameful treatment of aging parents by their ungrateful children. According to this legend, in days past in some places in Japan, older people who had outlived their usefulness and were a burden on the productive members of the community were taken by their children deep into the mountains and left to die of starvation and exposure. No evidence of this practice has been discovered, but the numerous references in early Japanese literature and folklore indicate that the myth has been around for a long time.

The legend of Obasuteyama takes on new relevance for the institutionalized Japanese elderly. Residents refer to the story to express their sense of shame, isolation, and abandonment in the impersonal environment of the institution. Residents feel not only that they have been denied their rightful place among family but that others view them as objects of pity or scorn.

The *seken* (the social circle of "others") is a powerful arbiter of social opinion and self-worth. It is composed of relatives, neighbors, and friends who one feels have the power and right to judge one's social behavior. An influential social sanction is the fear of *seken no me*, the "eyes of others," the ever-watchful guardians of proper social conduct and accepted social morality who can indicate their disapproval simply by "showing the whites of their eyes" *(shiroi me de miru)*.

Mr. Matsumoto reports that after he and his wife moved to Aotani, they dared not tell any of their friends. Mrs. Iwasawa had planned on moving from her son's family to a small apartment nearby for a few years before moving into the institution. This way, she thought she could avoid giving the impression that her son had sent her to an old-age home and thereby relieve him of the embarrassment this would cause. Mrs. Iskikawa entered Aotani against the advice of her children and relatives. She now regrets her decision because it caused her son so much embarrassment and shame that he cannot even raise his head in front of relatives. She says they all criticize him unmercifully for sending his poor old mother to such a place. Mrs. Kagawa avoids visiting friends and relatives because she says they will think that she has come to ask for charity and will feel obliged to give her something.

This sense of consternation, shame, and loss of face in the eyes of their neighbors, friends, and relatives causes residents of Aotani to withdraw from their old social networks and to isolate themselves inside the institution, where everyone shares their humiliation.

The social stigma of being in an institution must be neutralized if residents are to accept and adjust to their new lives in the home. Residents feel compelled to create narratives that explain their situation as something other than deviant. To do so, they draw on the legend of Obasuteyama as well as on their own social analyses of postwar Japanese society.

Obasuteyama provides a vehicle for describing the painful and unacceptable experience of being institutionalized. It allows residents to objectify their emotional trauma and perceptions of stigmatization. Residents identify with the old woman who is left on Obasuteyama. The very word carries a loaded emotional charge reflecting the perception that such a fate is a shocking transgression of the ethic of filial piety. As they realize that others share similar feelings, they begin to identify their problem as a recognizable category of suffering. By shifting the focus from the individual to a generational and societal level, they gain social recognition as victims sharing a common fate—a fate given a name and social reality by the legend of Obasuteyama.

Through this shared narrative, residents begin a healing process toward restoring their feelings of self-worth and social acceptability. Identification with the Obasuteyama motif serves as a face-saving strategy of social absolution—designed to convince themselves as well as others of their moral integrity and innocence in spite of their deviation from social norms.

The motif also becomes a vehicle to express otherwise unacceptably bitter and even hostile sentiments. It allows residents to vent indirectly anger and moral indignation at being abandoned, to acknowledge publicly (among peers) their feelings of victimization, and to elicit indirectly sympathy for themselves while focusing blame on their offspring who they feel have abdicated their social and moral responsibility.

Residents also use folk analyses of postwar Japanese society to explain how they have ended up in a home for the elderly. In their sociological analyses, the root of the problem is readily identified as the moral degeneration of the Japanese character, a degeneration explicitly or implicitly associated with a loss of traditional Japanese values and the influence of the West. "Children never committed suicide when we were young," residents marvel as they shake their heads in disbelief. Mrs. Oshima proclaimed, "These days children even kill their own parents," referring to an incident in which two sons went berserk and beat their parents to death with baseball bats.

The cause of the problem, they agree, began with the abolition of the   30 family system after the war. They are quick to explain that Japan has been contaminated by American ideas about individualism and democracy. Mrs. Kayashima explains that

> before the war, the family system was very strong. The authority of the father and mother was absolute. If they said something was white, even if you knew it was black, you had to say it was white. It wasn't the place of children to question their parents. This was all the more the case if you were a young daughter-in-law. After the war things turned topsy-turvy [*yo no naka ga hikkurigaette shimatta*]. New ideas from America, like democracy and freedom, led to the destruction of the family system. Now, newly married couples are registered separately on their own family register. They aren't included in the family register of their parents, so the ties between children and parents have grown weaker. Each person now is a separate entity [*ikko, ikko no ningen*] who has little responsibility and obligation to their parents.

Mrs. Miyake adds:

> That's why Japanese older people are abandoned, just like American old people. "*Demokurashii*" has become a creed of selfishness. Young people think they need only satisfy their own desires and ignore their social responsibilities to others. The concept of freedom has been interpreted as selfishness [*Jiyushugi wa katteshugi toshite toraeteiru*].

Residents see themselves as the innocent victims of the foreign influences and resulting social changes that have shaken the foundations of Japanese society. They feel that since the war and Occupation period, young people have not been properly taught about commitment and social obligations because of American reforms. Mrs. Oda feels that people should strive to become virtuous, upright human beings who fulfill their obligations to others. One of the main obligations individuals incur in this life is toward their parents, who have sacrificed for many years to raise them. Reciprocally, care of parents in their old age is the duty of children. Referring to a Buddhist proverb, she says people who lack a sense of obligation and thankfulness toward others are no better than ignorant beasts. Thus, children who refuse to take care of their aging parents, and instead place them in institutions, lack moral integrity.

By mixing ad hoc social analysis with folktales, residents create a new master narrative that redirects social stigma and shifts the shame for their institutionalization from themselves to their children and to the moral decline of Japanese society. According to this narrative, the foreign concepts of democracy and freedom have undermined Japanese morality and created the need for institutions—foreign and alien to Japanese experience—to hold abandoned elderly.

Reclaiming Alien Territory

Upon entering the institution, much to their surprise, newcomers discover a thriving community of residents busily engaged in day-to-day routines. They gradually abandon their dark preconceptions as they begin to participate in and gain some degree of social satisfaction from interacting with peers in this bustling society. Familiar social patterns are reconstructed and enhanced by sharing familiar foods, organizing space in familiar ways, and maintaining such traditional practices as gift giving.

New residents are placed in a room with two or three other residents; this group becomes their primary social unit in the home. Roommates help to integrate the new residents by serving as guides to this new life. Given the authoritarian structure of institutional life, newcomers soon discover that their main source of support is other residents. Though caregivers may be sympathetic to their wants and needs to a degree, their ultimate responsibility is to enforce the rules that keep institutional life running smoothly. Residents thus seek out friends and acquaintances who help make life bearable and even pleasant and enjoyable. They seek out commonalities with others based on gender, age, and time of admission to the facility.

The lack of privacy demands a major adjustment from residents, even though group living in a crowded context is not an unfamiliar experience for most Japanese (Caudill and Plath 1966). In prewar homes for the elderly, eight or ten residents slept in the same room, men and women together. At Aotani, the rooms are segregated by sex, and the maximum is four people per room, allowing just enough space for each person's bedding at night.

In recent years, ideas about the rights of the individual and the value of privacy have entered the mainstream social welfare philosophy through those who have observed successful systems in Europe or the United States.

Policies for new facilities for the elderly now dictate only one person per room. Where this new scheme is already in effect, however, social workers are reporting that isolation and withdrawn behavior are unfortunate by-products of increased individual privacy.

Residents attempt to remake the physical space of the institution by recreating a social environment consistent with their preinstitutional lives. By doing so, they ward off intolerable depersonalization.

Residents' living quarters are tatami° rooms, in contrast to the public areas of the facility. This context structures the kinds of interactions that develop in the room. A process of negotiation occurs as roommates carve out their own niches and reach agreement on the use of public space in the room. Enjoying food and drink facilitates a feeling of sociability and sharing. The small low folding table that is set up in each room during the day draws residents into a shared social space.

Some institutions have only Western-style rooms (*yoshitsu*) and furnishings, including a chair and small table which residents use when not sleeping or resting. These Westernlike settings, however, are less conducive to social interaction. Although not without problems, tatami-style living seems to allow more flexibility to create shared space. This Japanese feature of the Aotani facility provides a context for familiar patterns of interaction to emerge.

Gender differences are patterned in the ways men and women recon-   40
struct their familiar social environments. For women, a primary objective is to create a warm, domestic environment in their rooms, one that draws friends and neighbors. Serving tea and food is an essential feature of creating an amiable context for social relationships. In the rural communities of earlier years, extending hospitality was considered neighborly behavior. In the institution, these same familiar patterns resurface as women construct new social networks.

The idiom of domesticity is acted out in the serving of tea and light snacks, in pickling small quantities of vegetables or beans, and, in Mrs. Maekawa's case, in making her own plum wine. Most of the women also wear the customary long-sleeved apron, the symbol of the housewife, even though they have no kitchen in which to cook.

Aotani respects and observes the important custom of providing sustenance to family ancestral spirits. The institution's Buddhist altar, the central feature of the traditional Japanese household, is located at the head of the large dining hall. In the early morning, ladies who chant sutras together place at the altar small offerings of freshly cooked rice received from the cooks. Residents who want a more intimate atmosphere in which to commune with their deceased family sometimes set up makeshift altars in their rooms.

---

tatami: Thick pallets covered with rice-straw matting. The pallets fit together to form the floor in traditional rooms. [Editors' note]

Though modest because of institutional restrictions, the altars include pictures of deceased family members decorated by flowers the residents have grown in their own garden plot on the grounds of the facility (Plath 1964).

In one room, a picture of the imperial family graces a central position of the small altar. The past emperor Hirohito was seen by most residents as an age-mate, as someone who had lived through the same history, suffering through the high points as well as the tragedies of this century along with them. He symbolized the prewar family and its espoused authority structure and virtues of social obligation.

Because mealtime at Aotani is not a pleasant occasion, the informal sphere provides an alternative for relaxation and socializing. Rooms become an environment in which residents can enjoy foods they like, at their leisure, in the company of friends. By engaging in the familiar social roles of giving and receiving, they gain the satisfaction of creating a hospitable atmosphere, of serving food graciously, and of being honored as a guest and expressing appreciation for the food.

Good hostesses make sure their tables are set with appealing appetizers 45 and snacks to offer roommates as well as guests, one source of which is leftovers from mealtime. In the short time allotted for meals, many residents are not able to consume all the food on their plates. Because many of the older people at the home have either ill-fitting dentures or few of their own teeth, the food is sometimes too hard for them to eat. They consider it a waste to throw away leftovers of especially delicious foods and often smuggle these tidbits out of the dining room. This is against the rules, but residents manage to slip food into their pockets or into small plastic containers they sneak in and out of the cafeteria.

In the home, food has great value as currency in the reciprocal relationships of gift giving. For those of limited economic means, food from the dining hall allows them to establish their own social exchange networks among the residents. Social etiquette requires that frequent visitors occasionally bring some kind of refreshment for the people whose room they are visiting in order to maintain reciprocity. A food gift sent by family is shared with friends and neighbors in repayment for previous gifts and kindnesses.

Another source of food treats for the communal table is market day, an eagerly awaited event held three times a week by a local store that brings foods to sell to residents. The less mobile ones are thankful for this service, especially during the winter months when most residents refrain from venturing outside on the icy, snow-covered streets. Upon hearing the announcement of the store's arrival, they stream out of their rooms toward the dining hall to buy rice crackers, pickled vegetables, and other teatime treats. Some residents wait in the dining hall to assure themselves first pick of the store's selections.

Social interaction outside the room links individuals to the larger home society. Each hallway is a mini-neighborhood, and those living in adjacent and nearby rooms are neighbors. Visiting patterns reveal an active social life based on these networks. Thus, the Western architecture of the facility is transformed into a familiar, traditional Japanese neighborhood.

Neighbors try to maintain good relationships for sociability's sake as well as for mutual aid in times of emergency. The custom of gift giving helps establish and maintain these social relationships. When Mrs. Kotake came to the home, she brought a big box of grapefruit with her to share with roommates and neighbors in the tradition of *muko sangen, ryo donari* (literally, "three across and both sides"). This custom suggests that one establish and maintain relationships with neighbors living on either side of one's house and in the three houses across the street. Mrs. Kotake initiated reciprocal relations of gift giving in her new environment to establish herself in the social networks of the home. This Japanese custom is one strategy that residents use to domesticate the home and to resist the alienation and foreignness of the institution.

In rooms that are centers of interaction, one woman usually dominates social activity. Mrs. Miyamoto, for example, commands the respect of her roommates and neighbors. She is the oldest woman in the room and takes charge of making and pouring tea for her roommates and visitors. At her invitation, roommates, friends, and neighbors drop by.

Mrs. Miyamoto and her roommates are a lively group of conversationalists, and friends enjoy their company. Their table is always set with tea, rice crackers, and other delicious tidbits to welcome friends and neighbors from other rooms. For some guests, their visit to Mrs. Miyamoto's room will be the second or third stop of their morning rounds to say hello to friends. During the prime visiting periods in the morning—before breakfast and again before lunch—friends and neighbors gather to chat, exchange information, and snack on premeal appetizers. These times extend the brief and regimented dining period.

When guests drop by, they draw aside the curtain over the doorway and announce their visit by saying "Excuse me!" (*Ojamashimasu* or *Gomenkudasai*), as if entering a household. They are then invited into the private, domestic space of the room. They take off their slippers in the small entryway (*genkan*) and step up into the tatami room (shoes are not permitted to be worn in the facility). The hostess then pours a cup of green tea for her guests and offers them the choicest of the snacks arrayed on the small table.

Turning institutional hallways into mini-neighborhoods allows women to expand their domestic spheres by developing familiar visiting relationships between "room households." These social networks, based on sharing food and hospitality, set the tone for a homelike atmosphere in an otherwise impersonal space.

The socializing patterns of male residents in the home differ markedly from those of female residents. Whereas most female roommates socialize over tea in their rooms, male residents rarely do. Some men may drink tea in their rooms, but they rarely do so with their roommates. If roommates happen to be drinking tea at the same time, each pours his tea from his own teapot and remains in his part of the room, interacting very little with the others. Social tea drinking for most of these men is not an activity they would initiate.

In contrast to the female residents who socialize over tea and refresh-   55
ments in their rooms, male residents tend to interact more in public spaces—on the benches in the hallway, in the lounge, or on the grounds outside the facility. Their socializing often revolves around smoking cigarettes or drinking or activities that require little verbal interaction, such as watching television or playing checkers or Chinese chess (shogi). The younger men generally make friends more easily and are more talkative. This is a point of contention with some of the older men, who resent the glib younger men's stealing the limelight.

Some men who enjoy drinking tea, but do not want to go to the trouble of making their own, depend on females to provide the context for socializing. They visit the rooms of female friends to drink tea and eat pickled vegetables or sweets. In some cases, these friends are also their girlfriends. Mr. Sakashita visits Mrs. Tanaka's room quite often to drink tea and read the newspaper (they are "going steady"). Mrs. Tanaka's room is a favorite spot for several of Mr. Sakashita's friends, also.

Mrs. Yamamoto also entertains male visitors. She and her roommates socialize with the men while the men play hanafuda (a card game), in which the stakes are beans. Although the women rarely play a hand themselves, they take the supportive roles of banker (keeper of the beans) and audience. The men feel comfortable going to the room of Mrs. Yamamoto and her friends, who are tolerant of their drinking as they play cards.

According to the staff, heavy drinking is one of the major problems among the men in the institution. The staff do their best to discourage drinking, even to the point of holding a happy hour (banshaku no jikan) daily between 4:00 and 4:30 P.M. in the hope of controlling how much the men drink. Women are not prohibited from attending, but only men show up. This drinking period was established to curb drinking by limiting alcohol consumption to one time and place during the day and to make it a violation for residents to store or drink alcohol in their rooms.

The daily quota of alcohol is predetermined, so the caregivers pass out each man's chosen beverage, already poured. The staff women attempt to recreate the ambience of the drinking places the men like to frequent. They put up one red lantern similar to those in front of public drinking establish-ments, with the words "Old Folks Home" written on it. It is a symbol that the staff women hope will reproduce an atmosphere conducive to drinking and merrymaking. They play enka (popular ballads) and encourage the men to sing along with the new karaoke (musical accompaniment) tapes. By providing a substitute to rival the bars in town, they hope to restrain the men's urge to drink during unapproved periods.

In spite of staff attempts to create a fun drinking situation, complete   60
with sing-along videos and lively conversation, something is lacking. The

socializing customarily involved in the drinking ritual is absent—there is no opportunity for drinking buddies to pour drinks for one another, no competing to pick up the tab, and no potential for drinking too much. The artificial and restrictive setting is but a pale imitation of drinking spots in the outside world.

Men are not supposed to drink beyond the confines of the institution, but once outside they are no longer within the administration's reach. On such outings they walk to town, drink their fill, then return to the home. They also like to bring liquor back with them and to relax with it in the privacy of their rooms. During the winter they can conceal small bottles in their coats as they walk past the front office and into the facility. In the warmer months, they must recruit a sympathetic accomplice who is beyond suspicion to bring in the forbidden liquor. Women friends often assist.

Among alcohol-drinking men and their networks, prohibited liquor is a prized item of social exchange and friendship. Conspiring to bring in liquor undetected gives the men a sense of competence and satisfaction in regaining control of their lives. It provides a thrill and stimulating tension in the uneventful and feminized daily life of the home. Given the restricted lifestyle they are forced to lead in the institution, resistance to authority is an affirmation of their autonomy and masculinity. It thus is not surprising that heavy alcohol consumption is common.

Both male and female residents use food and drink as a means to recreate the social spheres with which they are familiar and to establish continuities between their previous and present lives. The female residents are able to create a more satisfying environment for themselves and their friends that permits the expression of neighborhood patterns of social interaction, while the male residents socialize on less intimate terms in public spaces and use liquor as a social lubricant and excuse to get together. Thus, food and drink are the tools of social exchange that help create the ties binding social relationships. Through establishing satisfying and ego-enhancing social relations, residents recover a sense of their own worth and agency.

For both men and women, being institutionalized, confined, and disciplined by people almost half their age presents a profound insult and creates an overwhelming sense of powerlessness. Defying authority in devious yet innocuous ways is one means of self-assertion. Through strategies to procure food and drink, residents have created networks of conspiracy and resistance.

The importation of Western products and life-styles has immeasurably improved the quality of life for Japanese older people. Indoor plumbing, electricity, gas, and kitchen appliances are but a few examples. Yet, one import—institutions for the elderly—has been accepted with mixed feelings by those directly affected—the residents. Though generally satisfied with their daily lives in the institution, in their darker moments they blame notions of democracy and freedom, also imported from the West, for creating a need for such facilities. The perception of alienness of institutions for the aged stems from historical fact as well as from a folk analysis of morality and social change in postwar Japan. From the perspective of their years, residents view (post)modern Japanese society as a ghastly orgy of depraved consumerism and loss of humanity—and see themselves as the hapless victims of this moral degeneration—by the very fact of their institutionalization.

Yet refusing to dwell on self-pity, they resolutely reclaim the institutional environment from the threat of alienation, the stigma of deviance, and numbing depersonalization. Familiar patterns of social interaction—visiting, gift giving, and spending leisure time—are reconstructed through the use of such traditional and commonplace aspects of material life as food, clothing, and furniture. A cohort effect makes this social reconstruction possible through the concentration of same-age peers who have experienced similar histories and share similar philosophies, cultural values, and rural working-class backgrounds.

Residents of the home represent a segment of the population that is least enthusiastic about the adoption of Western goods, ideas, borrowed words, and life-styles. Having lived through nearly a century of social change in Japanese society, they struggle to retain the traditional and familiar so as to avoid feeling like strangers in their own land.

Even as the outward trappings of foreign culture are adopted, the content reveals distinctly Japanese meanings. In the old-age home we see a Western-looking facility, but an inside look reveals a resilient continuity with a Japanese past. Residents' resistance to the alien and unfamiliar and their corresponding striving toward recovery and reconstruction of community are a microcosm of modern Japanese society.

References

Caudill, William, and David Plath. 1966. Who sleeps with whom? Parent-child involvement in urban Japanese families. *Psychiatry* 29 (4):344–366.

Fukazawa, Shichiro. 1964. *Narayamabushiko* (Ballad of Narayama). Tokyo: Shinchosha.

Goffman, Erving. 1961. *Asylums.* Garden City, N.Y.: Anchor.

Imamura, Shohei (producer). 1983. *Narayamabushiko* (Ballad of Narayama). Tokyo: Tohei Films.

Lebra, Takie Sugiyama. 1979. The dilemma and strategies of aging among contemporary Japanese women. *Ethnology* 18:337–353.

———. 1984. *Japanese women: Constraint and fulfillment.* Honolulu: University of Hawaii Press.

Maeda, Daisaku. 1983. Family care in Japan. *Gerontologist* 23 (6):579–583.

Ministry of Welfare. 1985. *Rojin fukushi no tebiki* (Handbook of social welfare for the elderly). Tokyo: Ministry of Welfare, Social Affairs Division, Section for Social Welfare for the Elderly.

Ogasawara, Yuji. 1986. *Ikiru: Rojin homu 100 nen* (To live: One hundred years of homes for the elderly). Eds. Zenkoku shakai fukushi kyogikai (National Association of Social Welfare Organizations) and Rojin fukushi shisetsu kyogikai (Association of Welfare Institutions for the Elderly). Tokyo: Tosho Insatsu Kabushikigaisha.

Plath, David. 1964. Where the family of God is the family: The role of the dead in Japanese households. *American Anthropologist* 66:300–317.

———. 1972. Japan: The after years. In Donald O. Cowgill and Lowell D. Holmes (eds.), *Aging and modernization,* 133–150. New York: Appleton-Century-Crofts.

Rohlen, Thomas P. 1978. The promise of Japanese spiritualism. In Erik H. Erikson (ed.), *Adulthood,* 129–147. New York: W. W. Norton.

Tobin, Joseph J. 1987. The American images of aging in Japan. *Gerontologist* 27 (1):53–58.

Tobin, Sheldon, and Morton Lieberman. 1976. *Last home for the aged.* San Francisco: Jossey-Bass.

Thinking About the Text

1. What passages did you find most compelling in Bethel's essay? Why?

2. Bethel refers to the "uneventful and feminized" daily life of the home (para. 62). What evidence of a "feminized" environment do you note in the essay? What assumptions about femininity does Bethel seem to subscribe to?

3. In paragraph 8 we learn that residents of Aotani can bring to the institution only the few things that will fit into a small closet. If you are familiar with the workings of a comparable institution, what possessions may a resident bring? In what ways do residents compensate for what they must leave behind? Can you imagine, by the way, what *you* would take?

Thinking About Culture

4. Bethel mentions "the mountain on which grannies are abandoned" (para. 20). What legends have you heard about the ways in which one culture remote from your own treats the elderly? Can you recall when you first heard these legends? How much credence do you (or did you) give to them?

5. Paragraphs 14 and 15 touch upon the different food preferences of the old and the young. In your family, is it evident that persons over, say, sixty have different tastes from those under, say, thirty-five? If so, how do you account for the differences?

6. In her first paragraph Bethel says, "Cultural changes that come with modernization undermine the Confucian ethic of filial piety." You may want to do a bit of research—for example, in an encyclopedia—concerning the Confucian ethic of filial piety, but the sentence itself tells you that in Confucian thinking children are to honor and obey their parents. The question: What "cultural changes that come with modernization" might serve, in the United States as well as in Japan, to undermine "filial piety"?

7. Paragraphs 54 and 55 make the point that the men and the women socialize in conspicuously different ways. In your experience, perhaps at work or

in a dormitory, have you observed comparable distinctions by gender? If so, describe them.

8. What generalizations can you offer about American attitudes toward old age, and about our treatment of the elderly? For instance, is there a big gap between what we say (e.g., "The old are treated with respect") and what we do?

9. A majority (something like 68 percent) of Japanese over the age of sixty-five live the remainder of their lives in the household of their grown children. The comparable statistic for the United States is far lower—though it is increasing. Why do you suppose relatively few Americans live with their children? For instance, do you relate it to a sort of frontier mentality, with its insistence on independence?

10. Do you think that your ideas about the duties of grown children to their elderly parents are about the same as the ideas of your parents (or grandparents)? Set forth your ideas, and, if they differ, the ideas of your seniors.

Kazuo Ishiguro

A Family Supper

Fugu is a fish caught off the Pacific shores of Japan. The fish has held a special significance for me ever since my mother died after eating one. The poison resides in the sex glands of the fish, inside two fragile bags. These bags must be removed with caution when preparing the fish, for any clumsiness will result in the poison leaking into the veins. Regrettably, it is not easy to tell whether or not this operation has been carried out successfully. The proof is, as it were, in the eating.

Fugu poisoning is hideously painful and almost always fatal. If the fish has been eaten during the evening, the victim is usually overtaken by pain during his sleep. He rolls about in agony for a few hours and is dead by morning. The fish became extremely popular in Japan after the war. Until stricter regulations were imposed, it was all the rage to perform the hazardous gutting operation in one's own kitchen, then to invite neighbors and friends round for the feast.

At the time of my mother's death, I was living in California. My relationship with my parents had become somewhat strained around that

---

Kazuo Ishiguro was born in Japan in 1954, and at the age of six was brought by his parents to England, where he continues to live. Of his stories and novels he has said, "I try to put in as little plot as possible." In 1989 his novel The Remains of the Day *won the prestigious Booker Prize in England. The short story reprinted here was first published in 1990.*

period and consequently I did not learn of the circumstances of her death until I returned to Tokyo two years later. Apparently, my mother had always refused to eat fugu, but on this particular occasion she had made an exception, having been invited by an old school friend whom she was anxious not to offend. It was my father who supplied me with the details as we drove from the airport to his house in the Kamakura district. When we finally arrived, it was nearing the end of a sunny autumn day.

"Did you eat on the plane?" my father asked. We were sitting on the tatami° floor of his tearoom.

"They gave me a light snack."   5

"You must be hungry. We'll eat as soon as Kikuko arrives."

My father was a formidable-looking man with a large stony jaw and furious black eyebrows. I think now, in retrospect, that he much resembled Chou En-lai,° although he would not have cherished such a comparison, being particularly proud of the pure samurai blood that ran in the family. His general presence was not one that encouraged relaxed conversation; neither were things helped much by his odd way of stating each remark as if it were the concluding one. In fact, as I sat opposite him that afternoon, a boyhood memory came back to me of the time he had struck me several times around the head for "chattering like an old woman." Inevitably, our conversation since my arrival at the airport had been punctuated by long pauses.

"I'm sorry to hear about the firm," I said when neither of us had spoken for some time. He nodded gravely.

"In fact, the story didn't end there," he said. "After the firm's collapse, Watanabe killed himself. He didn't wish to live with the disgrace."

"I see."   10

"We were partners for seventeen years. A man of principle and honor. I respected him very much."

"Will you go into business again?" I asked.

"I am . . . in retirement. I'm too old to involve myself in new ventures now. Business these days has become so different. Dealing with foreigners. Doing things their way. I don't understand how we've come to this. Neither did Watanabe." He sighed. "A fine man. A man of principle."

The tearoom looked out over the garden. From where I sat I could make out the ancient well that as a child I had believed to be haunted. It was just visible now through the thick foliage. The sun had sunk low and much of the garden had fallen into shadow.

"I'm glad in any case that you've decided to come back," my father   15
said. "More than a short visit, I hope."

"I'm not sure what my plans will be."

---

tatami: Thick pallets covered with rice-straw matting. The pallets fit together to form the floor in traditional rooms.   **Chou En-lai:** Chinese communist leader (1898–1976). [Editors' notes]

"I, for one, am prepared to forget the past. Your mother, too, was always ready to welcome you back—upset as she was by your behavior."

"I appreciate your sympathy. As I say, I'm not sure what my plans are."

"I've come to believe now that there were no evil intentions in your mind," my father continued. "You were swayed by certain . . . influences. Like so many others."

"Perhaps we should forget it, as you suggest."   20

"As you will. More tea?"

Just then a girl's voice came echoing through the house.

"At last." My father rose to his feet. "Kikuko has arrived."

Despite our difference in years, my sister and I had always been close. Seeing me again seemed to make her excessively excited, and for a while she did nothing but giggle nervously. But she calmed down somewhat when my father started to question her about Osaka and her university. She answered him with short, formal replies. She in turn asked me a few questions, but she seemed inhibited by the fear that her questions might lead to awkward topics. After a while, the conversation had become even sparser than prior to Kikuko's arrival. Then my father stood up, saying: "I must attend to the supper. Please excuse me for being burdened by such matters. Kikuko will look after you."

My sister relaxed quite visibly once he had left the room. Within a few   25
minutes, she was chatting freely about her friends in Osaka and about her classes at university. Then quite suddenly she decided we should walk in the garden and went striding out onto the veranda. We put on some straw sandals that had been left along the veranda rail and stepped out into the garden. The light in the garden had grown very dim.

"I've been dying for a smoke for the last half hour," she said, lighting a cigarette.

"Then why didn't you smoke?"

She made a furtive gesture back toward the house, then grinned mischievously.

"Oh, I see," I said.

"Guess what? I've got a boyfriend now."   30

"Oh, yes?"

"Except I'm wondering what to do. I haven't made up my mind yet."

"Quite understandable."

"You see, he's making plans to go to America. He wants me to go with him as soon as I finish studying."

"I see. And you want to go to America?"   35

"If we go, we're going to hitchhike." Kikuko waved a thumb in front of my face. "People say it's dangerous, but I've done it in Osaka and it's fine."

"I see. So what is it you're unsure about?"

We were following a narrow path that wound through the shrubs and finished by the old well. As we walked, Kikuko persisted in taking unnecessarily theatrical puffs on her cigarette.

"Well, I've got lots of friends now in Osaka. I like it there. I'm not sure I want to leave them all behind just yet. And Suichi . . . I like him, but I'm not sure I want to spend so much time with him. Do you understand?"

"Oh, perfectly."   40

She grinned again, then skipped on ahead of me until she had reached the well. "Do you remember," she said as I came walking up to her, "how you used to say this well was haunted?"

"Yes, I remember."

We both peered over the side.

"Mother always told me it was the old woman from the vegetable store you'd seen that night," she said. "But I never believed her and never came out here alone."

"Mother used to tell me that too. She even told me once the old woman   45 had confessed to being the ghost. Apparently, she'd been taking a shortcut through our garden. I imagine she had some trouble clambering over these walls."

Kikuko gave a giggle. She then turned her back to the well, casting her gaze about the garden.

"Mother never really blamed you, you know," she said, in a new voice. I remained silent. "She always used to say to me how it was their fault, hers and Father's, for not bringing you up correctly. She used to tell me how much more careful they'd been with me, and that's why I was so good." She looked up and the mischievous grin had returned to her face. "Poor Mother," she said.

"Yes. Poor Mother."

"Are you going back to California?"

"I don't know. I'll have to see."   50

"What happened to . . . to her? To Vicki?"

"That's all finished with," I said. "There's nothing much left for me now in California."

"Do you think I ought to go there?"

"Why not? I don't know. You'll probably like it." I glanced toward the house. "Perhaps we'd better go in soon. Father might need a hand with the supper."

But my sister was once more peering down into the well. "I can't see   55 any ghosts," she said. Her voice echoed a little.

"Is Father very upset about his firm collapsing?"

"Don't know. You never can tell with Father." Then suddenly she straightened up and turned to me. "Did he tell you about old Watanabe? What he did?"

"I heard he committed suicide."

"Well, that wasn't all. He took his whole family with him. His wife and his two little girls."

"Oh, yes?"   60

"Those two beautiful little girls. He turned on the gas while they were all asleep. Then he cut his stomach with a meat knife."

"Yes, Father was just telling me how Watanabe was a man of principle."

"Sick." My sister turned back to the well.

"Careful. You'll fall right in."

"I can't see any ghost," she said. "You were lying to me all that time."   65

"But I never said it lived down the well."

"Where is it then?"

We both looked around at the trees and shrubs. The daylight had almost gone. Eventually I pointed to a small clearing some ten yards away.

"Just there I saw it. Just there."

We stared at the spot.   70

"What did it look like?"

"I couldn't see very well. It was dark."

"But you must have seen something."

"It was an old woman. She was just standing there, watching me."

We kept staring at the spot as if mesmerized.   75

"She was wearing a white kimono," I said. "Some of her hair came undone. It was blowing around a little."

Kikuko pushed her elbow against my arm. "Oh, be quiet. You're trying to frighten me all over again." She trod on the remains of her cigarette, then for a brief moment stood regarding it with a perplexed expression. She kicked some pine needles over it, then once more displayed her grin. "Let's see if supper's ready," she said.

We found my father in the kitchen. He gave us a quick glance, then carried on with what he was doing.

"Father's become quite a chef since he's had to manage on his own," Kikuko said with a laugh.

He turned and looked at my sister coldly. "Hardly a skill I'm proud   80 of," he said. "Kikuko, come here and help."

For some moments my sister did not move. Then she stepped forward and took an apron hanging from a drawer.

"Just these vegetables need cooking now," he said to her. "The rest just needs watching." Then he looked up and regarded me strangely for some seconds. "I expect you want to look around the house," he said eventually. He put down the chopsticks he had been holding. "It's a long time since you've seen it."

As we left the kitchen I glanced toward Kikuko, but her back was turned.

"She's a good girl," my father said.

I followed my father from room to room. I had forgotten how large   85 the house was. A panel would slide open and another room would appear. But the rooms were all startlingly empty. In one of the rooms the lights did not come on, and we stared at the stark walls and tatami in the pale light that came from the windows.

"This house is too large for a man to live in alone," my father said. "I don't have much use for most of these rooms now."

But eventually my father opened the door to a room packed full of books and papers. There were flowers in vases and pictures on the walls. Then I noticed something on a low table in the corner of the room. I came nearer and saw it was a plastic model of a battleship, the kind constructed by children. It had been placed on some newspaper; scattered around it were assorted pieces of gray plastic.

My father gave a laugh. He came up to the table and picked up the model.

"Since the firm folded," he said, "I have a little more time on my hands." He laughed again, rather strangely. For a moment his face looked almost gentle. "A little more time."

"That seems odd," I said. "You were always so busy."   90

"Too busy, perhaps." He looked at me with a small smile. "Perhaps I should have been a more attentive father."

I laughed. He went on contemplating his battleship. Then he looked up. "I hadn't meant to tell you this, but perhaps it's best that I do. It's my belief that your mother's death was no accident. She had many worries. And some disappointments."

We both gazed at the plastic battleship.

"Surely," I said eventually, "my mother didn't expect me to live here forever."

"Obviously you don't see. You don't see how it is for some parents.   95 Not only must they lose their children, they must lose them to things they don't understand." He spun the battleship in his fingers. "These little gunboats here could have been better glued, don't you think?"

"Perhaps. I think it looks fine."

"During the war I spent some time on a ship rather like this. But my ambition was always the air force. I figured it like this: If your ship was struck by the enemy, all you could do was struggle in the water hoping for a lifeline. But in an airplane—well, there was always the final weapon." He put the model back onto the table. "I don't suppose you believe in war."

"Not particularly."

He cast an eye around the room. "Supper should be ready by now," he said. "You must be hungry."

Supper was waiting in a dimly lit room next to the kitchen. The only   100 source of light was a big lantern that hung over the table, casting the rest of the room in shadow. We bowed to each other before starting the meal.

There was little conversation. When I made some polite comment about the food, Kikuko giggled a little. Her earlier nervousness seemed to have returned to her. My father did not speak for several minutes. Finally he said:

"It must feel strange for you, being back in Japan."

"Yes, it is a little strange."

"Already, perhaps, you regret leaving America."

"A little. Not so much. I didn't leave behind much. Just some empty   105
rooms."

"I see."

I glanced across the table. My father's face looked stony and forbidding
in the half-light. We ate on in silence.

Then my eye caught something at the back of the room. At first I
continued eating, then my hands became still. The others noticed and looked
at me. I went on gazing into the darkness past my father's shoulder.

"Who is that? In that photograph there?"

"Which photograph?" My father turned slightly, trying to follow my   110
gaze.

"The lowest one. The old woman in the white kimono."

My father put down his chopsticks. He looked first at the photograph,
then at me.

"Your mother." His voice had become very hard. "Can't you recognize
your own mother?"

"My mother. You see, it's dark. I can't see it very well."

No one spoke for a few seconds, then Kikuko rose to her feet. She took   115
the photograph down from the wall, came back to the table, and gave it to
me.

"She looks a lot older," I said.

"It was taken shortly before her death," said my father.

"It was the dark. I couldn't see very well."

I looked up and noticed my father holding out a hand. I gave him
the photograph. He looked at it intently, then held it toward Kikuko.
Obediently, my sister rose to her feet once more and returned the picture
to the wall.

There was a large pot left unopened at the center of the table. When   120
Kikuko had seated herself again, my father reached forward and lifted the
lid. A cloud of steam rose up and curled toward the lantern. He pushed the
pot a little toward me.

"You must be hungry," he said. One side of his face had fallen into
shadow.

"Thank you." I reached forward with my chopsticks. The steam was
almost scalding. "What is it?"

"Fish."

"It smells very good."

In the soup were strips of fish that had curled almost into balls. I picked   125
one out and brought it to my bowl.

"Help yourself. There's plenty."

"Thank you." I took a little more, then pushed the pot toward my
father. I watched him take several pieces to his bowl. Then we both watched
as Kikuko served herself.

My father bowed slightly. "You must be hungry," he said again. He took some fish to his mouth and started to eat. Then I, too, chose a piece and put it in my mouth. It felt soft, quite fleshy against my tongue.

The three of us ate in silence. Several minutes went by. My father lifted the lid and once more steam rose up. We all reached forward and helped ourselves.

"Here," I said to my father, "you have this last piece."   130

"Thank you."

When we had finished the meal, my father stretched out his arms and yawned with an air of satisfaction. "Kikuko," he said, "prepare a pot of tea, please."

My sister looked at him, then left the room without comment. My father stood up.

"Let's retire to the other room. It's rather warm in here."

I got to my feet and followed him into the tearoom. The large sliding   135
windows had been left open, bringing in a breeze from the garden. For a while we sat in silence.

"Father," I said, finally.

"Yes?"

"Kikuko tells me Watanabe-san took his whole family with him."

My father lowered his eyes and nodded. For some moments he seemed deep in thought. "Watanabe was very devoted to his work," he said at last. "The collapse of the firm was a great blow to him. I fear it must have weakened his judgment."

"You think what he did . . . it was a mistake?"   140

"Why, of course. Do you see it otherwise?"

"No, no. Of course not."

"There are other things besides work," my father said.

"Yes."

We fell silent again. The sound of locusts came in from the garden. I   145
looked out into the darkness. The well was no longer visible.

"What do you think you will do now?" my father asked. "Will you stay in Japan for a while?"

"To be honest, I hadn't thought that far ahead."

"If you wish to stay here, I mean here in this house, you would be very welcome. That is, if you don't mind living with an old man."

"Thank you. I'll have to think about it."

I gazed out once more into the darkness.   150

"But of course," said my father, "this house is so dreary now. You'll no doubt return to America before long."

"Perhaps. I don't know yet."

"No doubt you will."

For some time my father seemed to be studying the back of his hands. Then he looked up and sighed.

"Kikuko is due to complete her studies next spring," he said. "Perhaps   155
she will want to come home then. She's a good girl."

"Perhaps she will."
"Things will improve then."
"Yes, I'm sure they will."
We fell silent once more, waiting for Kikuko to bring the tea.

Thinking About the Text

1. How would you describe the attitude of the son toward the father at the end of the story? Is this attitude the same as at the beginning of the story?

2. In a sense, not much happens in this story. If the story nevertheless held your interest, how might you account for its power?

3. John Updike, esteemed not only as a novelist but also as a writer of short stories and as a literary critic, has specified what he wants from a story:

> I want stories to startle and engage me within the first few sentences, and in their middle to widen or deepen or sharpen my knowledge of human activity, and to end by giving me a sensation of completed statement.

What do *you* want from a story? To what extent does Ishiguro's story meet your criteria?

4. Retell the story from Kikuko's point of view. You may wish to draw on the information on women presented in Chapter 5.

Thinking About Culture

5. The father considers Watanabe to be a man of principle. The daughter considers him to be "sick." How do you view Watanabe? Explain your response.

6. Describe a conflict that involves attitudes toward elderly parents. For instance, the older people may have ideas about how they should be treated, and these ideas may differ from those of their mature children. Or the mature children in a family may themselves have different ideas about their responsibilities toward infirm parents or grandparents.

7. If you were in Japan and a Japanese friend invited you to dine in a *fugu* restaurant, what would you say?

Chapter 7

The Meaning and Practice of Work

In what has been a sometimes heated "trade war" mood, American and Japanese work habits have been stereotyped or mythologized as, on the one hand, lazy, and, on the other, productive and committed (or workaholic). In fact, although Japanese workers work about 225 hours more per year than Americans, most observers, like Ian Buruma (p. 246), agree that they don't work harder. Many workers appear to be underemployed on the job: White-collar workers may have a desk and title but no real tasks; blue-collar workers may "sit on the bench," only partially active. Office workers often kill time by reading comics or sitting in nearby coffee shops. Many say that they return to the office before 5:00 P.M. to begin the real work, partly because it is customary not to leave the office before the boss does (who must set a good example), and partly because one can collect overtime pay for work done after hours.

While American workers overall are less well prepared educationally, they are actually more likely to be productive during their work hours. A Japanese foreman, however, can count on new recruits being able to work on complicated production problems and to use graphs, charts, and sophisticated mathematical formulas, whereas his or her American counterpart can scarcely be sure of workers' basic literacy.

The real differences in work are not seen in hours or productivity, however, but in the way work is structured and the *feel* of the workplace as well as in the meaning of work in a person's life. Jeannie Lo (p. 263) provides a firsthand account of life in a Japanese factory.

First, occupation, work, or career are closely tied to schooling. While American schools seem to offer unlimited options for a hardworking young person to get ahead, in fact they "track" or "stream" children by ability and interest so that a twelve-year-old's future, as worker or professional, is usually already apparent. Japanese secondary school students are also already in gear for their future occupational lives. If a teen has passed the test for admission to a high-ranking academic high school, it is a sign that he or she will make it into college, and into a good one, thus assuring a good job (or a good marriage). If high school will be the last educational experience (and there are vocational and trade schools as well as general academic high schools), then the school will help to place the student in a job. Usually there are close ties between employers and schools that act as conduits for a stream of reliable workers. Those in college are job-seeking by the junior year and some companies even recruit undergraduates early, a practice called *aotagai*, or "picking the rice while it is still green in the field."

Schooling relates to work in other ways as well. Children are taught that there is a right way of doing things and that mastery of both content and method is a necessary precursor to innovation and creativity. Being wholehearted about your work, or "sincere," is a very important attribute, taught early in school. Quality thus has its moral aspects, as well as being a concrete work goal.

While work is a necessity of life and part of a contractual relationship between the worker and the organization, it is also a kind of spiritual exercise, or so the observers of *seishin kyoiku*, or "spiritual education," would state. The training of new recruits through a special program of physical, social, and meditative exercises is sometimes arranged by a company to help socialize and integrate workers, especially white-collar *sarariman* ("salaryman," a Japanese-English word coined to describe the white-collar wage worker). The article by Bill Powell, Hideko Takayama, and John McCormick (p. 274) compares the lives and motivation of two "salarymen," one American, one Japanese.

Such training, as well as the ongoing training of workers on site, is a big investment, based on the assumption that the workers will be committed to the company for the duration of their work careers. Indeed, workers in such companies say they seek long-term security over immediate gain, as Sony Corporation founder Akio Morita says in the excerpt from his book on page 258. However, the practice of what is called in Japan "permanent employment" is limited usually to only the largest companies and may be changing as workers now tend to make somewhat shorter-term commitments and change jobs more frequently in a new, slightly more American-looking pattern.

Commitment, however, is not just a contractual matter; and for the most part, worker involvement is very high. Companies try to involve all workers in quality and productivity, and the system of "quality control" devised by the American W. E. Deming is one such method of top-down, bottom-up encouragement for monitoring and innovating production. In fact, quality control circles made up of workers from all levels in a plant are more popular in Japan than in America, though some American managers are "repatriating" this concept.

In Japan, government and business leaders are (as always) interested in security and predictability, and are now concerned about several phenomena that may portend change or decline. One is the tendency among young workers to choose *non*permanent employment positions—in fact, to choose to be *furita,* or "freeters," meaning freelance workers who job-hop frequently. Leaders feel that, rather than finding the meaning of life in the work itself, as the first post–World War II generation was said to do, such people put work second to personal satisfactions obtained elsewhere. Japan is far from a leisure-oriented society, though at least one government agency is devoted to encouraging Japanese workers to use their leisure time fruitfully in hobbies, stimulating leisure goods industries. Indeed, hobbies are as intensely pursued as the work goals of most so-called corporate warriors.

Japanese managers and planners are also concerned about the diminishing pool of young male workers, prized by recruiters, and now must seek employees from groups marginalized or ignored in the past, such as women and retirees—or employ foreign workers to fill the gap. Preferring women in this case, they are beginning to have to make adjustments in the workplace, such as offering flexible schedules for women with family commitments and improving the conditions at work. Similarly, those who hire retirees must make some changes to accommodate their needs.

American workers in such fields as finance, insurance, and law may be at least as driven as young Japanese in white-collar work, and blue-collar workers in the "rust belt renaissance" taking place in such formerly depressed areas as the automobile industry are certainly as committed as their Japanese counterparts. And certainly work is seen as a necessity in both countries. But the nature of the workplace and the messages of spiritual, as well as temporal, commitment, do have a different ring in Japan.

Explorations

1. If you have had a job, even a part-time job, how did you feel about the work? What were your relationships with employers and coworkers like? How would you contrast this experience with that of a Japanese worker as described here?

2. Americans often think of white-collar, "salaryman" work as typifying all of Japanese labor. Actually, only one-third of the labor force in Japan works in such environments. You should also consider the diversity of work experiences in America. Choose two occupations to contrast in America, and compare them in terms of required skills, job security, commitment, pay, and other rewards. You may want to consider the following comment by economist John Kenneth Galbraith:

   > Clearly the most unfortunate people are those who must do the same thing over and over again, every minute, or perhaps twenty to the minute. They deserve the shortest hours and the highest pay.

3. Few women in Japan enter a managerial track, and as we saw in Chapter 5, those that do see a glass ceiling above them, a limit to their advancement. Compare American women entering an executive track, and if you can, interview some young recruits as to their options and futures on the job.

Ian Buruma

Work as a Form of Beauty

Do the Japanese really work harder than everybody else? They, as well as most experts trying to explain the Japanese phenomenon, certainly think so. Myself, I sometimes wonder. The Japanese do have a work ethic, not unlike the Protestant one, expressed in such clichés as: We Japanese don't work to live, we live to work, unlike foreigners who. . . . But ethics in Japan can seldom—if ever—be separated from aesthetics. Work is a form of beauty, in the sense that it matters less what one does than how one is seen to do it. Japanese, more than any other people I know, have made work into a spectacle, if not a fine art.

There is a yearly festival that clearly illustrates this. Among the most celebrated heroes of the common man in Edo were the firemen. Flamboyantly tattooed with dragons—a beast associated with water in Japan and thus with firefighting—these noble tough guys were sent to put out the "Flowers of Edo"° by displays of derring-do. They would climb to impossible heights on bamboo ladders, passing heavy buckets of water along a human chain with great acrobatic skill. These once indispensable skills have since been replaced by more modern methods, but they are still practiced every year at the firemen's festival in Tokyo. The ladder-climbing, bucket-juggling, death-defying acts are literally a circus of work.

The aesthetic approach to work, exemplified by the brave firemen, is still a feature of the factory floor, too. Factory—and office—walls are usually festooned with gracefully written Chinese characters poetically expressing the company philosophy. Typical would be something like: Work is the essence of the human spirit; spirit is the essence of harmony. But such slogans aside, it is in the ways of the workers themselves that a traditional aesthetic can be seen.

Flowers of Edo: Edo is the old name for Tokyo; "flowers" refers to the fires that were a constant danger in oil-heated homes constructed of wood, paper, and straw. [Editors' note]

Ian Buruma, cultural editor of the Far Eastern Economic Review *in Hong Kong, is the author of several books on Japanese culture. This essay was published in 1986.*

The president of a Japanese ball-bearing company once said in an interview that in his factory it took exactly four seconds to grind a ball bearing fifteen millimeters in diameter. He was not joking: watching a Japanese assembly line is like watching a ballet performance: Every body movement has been worked out to achieve utmost efficiency; every tool can be reached with minimum effort. Not just that: Everything is calculated to allow the worker to accomplish the maximum amount of work in one continuous movement. (Anyone who has seen a sushi chef in action, putting rice and fish together with the utmost speed, grace, and economy of movement, will know what I mean. It is a perfect illustration of how function and beauty merge in Japan, to become indistinguishable.)

This does not mean that the Japanese work harder than other people.   5 Despite the often rather theatrical insistence on working overtime—to show dedication rather than for any practical reason—time wasting is endemic to Japan's vastly overmanned companies. People will spend hours reading comic books rather than break the taboo of leaving before the boss. But there does seem to be an attention to detail and good workmanship, which is often lost in the West. While nineteenth-century methods and a remarkable degree of inefficiency still persist in such institutions as banks or the construction business, industries geared to export are models of productivity. So, while on one hand it takes an army of carpenters and roof builders an endless amount of time to build an ordinary house, motorcycles, TV sets, and cameras roll off assembly lines at almost unbelievable speeds. What is more, they are likely to have fewer flaws than similar products elsewhere.

Traditional approaches to work partly explain why. Company loyalty, discipline, and, that magic word, consensus—all these qualities have been fostered in Japan for centuries. Military discipline and loyalty were part of the samurai ethic; the necessity for consultation and consensus-forming was part of village life.

Some of these attitudes can be seen in modern companies, often under a Western guise. Perhaps the most celebrated attitude toward the Japanese working system—seen especially in such books on the "economic miracle" as Ezra Vogel's *Japan as Number One*—is "quality control," actually based on an American idea, imported in the 1950s. Workers are encouraged to participate in the process, not just by checking, but through constantly improving the quality of products and the efficiency with which they are produced. A type of letterbox is to be found at the end of all assembly lines, in which workers are asked to deposit suggestions and criticisms, which are discussed weekly at "quality control meetings." Bright ideas do sometimes make their way to the top and are even occasionally implemented. During the early 1970s it was still common to find slips of paper attached to Japanese products with the names of the workers and controllers responsible for that particular camera or gadget. Thus, a note of humanity was introduced in an otherwise rather faceless production process.

The advantage of such participation is that it makes a dull job more interesting; instead of a sulky work force agitating for longer teabreaks, Japanese workers, ideally, feel that they are involved in the achievements of their companies and take pride in them. There is a tradition in Japan—and in China—of mass-production craftsmen, not on the scale of modern factories, of course, but of large potteries, printing firms or kimono makers. Japanese have always excelled at highly skilled crafts aimed at a huge market.

Worker participation also appeals to the traditional ideal of consensus: Decisions are not made by one man at the top, but as a result of long consultations in which everybody's voice is heard. Of course it does not always work this way in reality, especially in so-called one-man companies led by tough self-made entrepreneurs. But the important thing is that people have the feeling they are not just nuts, bolts, or, more to the point these days, digits.

The Japanese love for uniforms is another aspect of the aesthetic work 10
ethic. Uniforms help to foster a collective identity. But apart from that, the work one does ought to be visibly identifiable. Filmmakers wear sunglasses; artists wear berets—the sort of thing painters sported in Montmartre; salarymen wear suits. Even leisure—so often a form of work—has its uniforms: Sunday afternoon hikers wear alpine gear; photo enthusiasts wear safari jackets. All this, so there can be no mistake about what people are up to; it is also an expression of the Japanese belief that once form has been established, substance will follow. The best, most extreme, and thus not entirely typical example of this aesthetic approach in industry is Fanuc Ltd., the world's largest maker of digital machine tools. Company management has the idea that yellow is the color most conducive to high performance. Consequently, everything in the factory, from the machines to the workers' uniforms, is bright yellow.

This aesthetic approach to work is the strongest continuous tradition linking old Japan and the world of high technology. A crucial element is the way work aesthetics is taught. The most common Japanese methods are both old and surprisingly uniform. They are based on a Zen-like ideal of cultivated intuition, honed by endless repetition. This ideal is most romantically expressed in the example of Zen archery. To master the "Way of Archery," said the monks of the Edo period (1603–1868), one had to become one with one's bow. The arrow thus shot would automatically hit the target. What was meant is that the discursive mind, rambling and random, gets in the way of total concentration. To reach the ideal state of readiness one must empty the mind: In other words, stop thinking and you shall find.

The process of acquiring this intuitive technique is based upon a special relationship between master and pupil, a relationship Westerners—and many modern Japanese—like to call "feudal." Whether this is apt or not, such relationships are still very common in Japan, especially in arts and crafts.

Rather than theory, however, I would like to offer some examples. They are imaginary examples and so, to put the ideas across, somewhat caricatural.

But each in its own way represents the aesthetic ideal. I shall start with a modern craftsman: a photographer.

Since childhood, Kazuo Ito had wanted to be a photographer. Through a friend's introduction he was taken on as a second assistant by a famous fashion photographer, whom Ito calls *sensei* (master). Professional photographers, like painters, writers or anybody else successful enough to have apprentices *(deshi)* are usually called *sensei*.

Ito lives in a small room at the master's studio. As an apprentice, his 15 duties are without limit. The first thing he does in the morning is make coffee for the first assistant, who comes in at eight. He then polishes lenses, gets the equipment ready, tests the light batteries, anything, as long as he looks busy when the master comes in. Like the daughter-in-law in a traditional household, Ito gets up before everyone else and goes to bed after everybody is asleep.

The assistant is rarely told directly what to do. He has to anticipate the wishes of his superiors. If an order has to be given, it means Ito is already too late. If he guesses wrongly, he is yelled at, not by the master himself, but by the first assistant. This is part of the learning process. Nothing is explained, nothing is explicit. Ito is taught the ropes like a circus monkey, by watching his trainer carefully: Right merits a pat on the head (if he's lucky), wrong elicits a humiliating scolding. A slight shake of the head means he has to light the photographer's cigarette; a short grunt means adjust the umbrella on the top light.

Ito is paid the equivalent of one hundred dollars a month, but stays at the studio rent-free. His meals, wolfed down during work, are also paid for by the master. His own money goes toward drinking on Saturday nights with other photographers' assistants. He has been known to get into scrapes, but the master always takes care of the damage. The master has taken the place of Ito's father, in a way, and his indulgence has to be paid for by total obedience during working hours. Ito does not enjoy himself especially, but realizes that his present hardship is a necessary initiation into the life of a photographer. He is proud of his capacity to suffer through it, and consoles himself with the idea that one day he will be called master too.

Such methods do not foster the kind of individual initiative thought to be indispensable to creative work in the West. Indeed, the Japanese have a reputation for being imitators, technically polished imitators, but copycats nonetheless. Of course, mimicry is the essence of learning everywhere, but Japanese appear to carry it to extremes. Leaving the romantic matter of unique individuality aside, this stereotypical view of the Japanese is not entirely accurate. A wise Japanese—I forget who—once put it this way: Only when everybody wears exactly the same kimono can one detect true individual differences. Acting in the Kabuki theater comes about as close as one can get to this aesthetic.

Becoming an actor of female roles *(onnagata)* in Kabuki had not been a matter of choice for Ayame. He was born into a Kabuki actor's family, and he learned the rudimentary steps of traditional dance as soon as he could walk. His grandfather would move his hands and feet for him, over and over again, until he could do it himself. In his early teens his slender build, graceful movement, and high-pitched voice made the specialization in female roles an obvious choice. The only male roles he subsequently played were those of effeminate young lovers, the type Japanese matrons, for some reason, have always idolized.

Ayame was preparing for his grand entrance as an Edo-period courtesan. He had applied his makeup in a style unchanged since the play was written. While waiting for his cue, he sipped from a cup of green tea, supplied by one of his apprentices, who watched his every move. As with the photographer's assistant, a Kabuki apprentice is rarely told anything directly. He must learn intuitively, as it were. To get it wrong, in the olden days, meant a severe beating. 20

When he stepped onto the stage, the audience applauded loudly and members of a professional claque, seated in various parts of the auditorium, called out his stage name. His gracefully stylized walk and the coquettish movement of the eyes reminded connoisseurs of his grandfather, also a famous *onnagata*, who acted in the style of *his* father, a celebrated nineteenth-century actor.

Ayame's disciples were looking at him intently from backstage. One day the best of them might, with luck and hard work, emulate his master's technique to perfection. He would have to be so much like him that he could wear his style like a skin. That would not be enough, however. True mastery lies in the way one's own skin comes almost imperceptibly peeping through the master's. Only then can one be said to control the style and not vice versa. There are only a few people left who could recognize the new skin, but that does not in any way diminish its greatness.

The repetitive zeal with which Japanese go about honing their skills makes them seem obsessed with form, with mechanics rather than content. A rather touching example of this is the first reaction of Japanese audiences to moving pictures: They turned round their chairs to watch the projector, a source of much more fascination than the images flickering on the screen. Added to their reputation as copycats is their image as robots. This, too, is missing the point. The preoccupation with style does not necessarily mean the lack of a soul; just as Japanese do not feel that good manners make a human being less "real," "himself," "natural" or whatever term one wishes to use for that elusive inner core of man. Style, in the postromantic West, is largely an extension of man's ego; traditional style in Japan—and China, for that matter—is more a transformation of the ego: To acquire a perfect technique, one eliminates, as it were, one's individuality, only to regain it by transcending the skill. This new individuality is not the expression of one's real private life, but an individual interpretation of something already there and thus in the public domain.

Private life in Japan is just that: private. An artist or, for that matter, a waitress is not expected to reveal his—or her—private "self," but his public one. The borderline between public and private worlds is much clearer in Japan than it is in the West (as in China, many Japanese houses have walls around them). Thus, the public self is not seen as a humiliating infringement on the "real" self. Of course, in certain periods, Japanese artists have rebelled against this division and the rigidity of style by going to the opposite extreme: Writers of the "natural" school saw it as their vocation to burden the reader with the minutest details of their private lives. One key, I think, to the public aesthetic is the skill of an elevator girl.

Yoko Sato is nineteen and she is being trained to be an elevator girl   25 in a department store. She lives at home with her parents but needs the extra money she earns to buy clothes and go to discos on Saturday nights. It's hard being an elevator girl for, as Yoko is ceaselessly told, she is the face of the store. If she does something wrong or displeases a customer, the company loses face.

Yoko does not much enjoy the lectures on company loyalty or philosophy written in fussy Chinese characters by the owner of the store, who likes to expound at length on the uniqueness of his firm. Still, Yoko learned all the lines by heart and recites them every morning with her colleagues. It may be a lot of boring nonsense, but this is the way things are done, and Yoko wants to do a good job.

The voice and bowing lessons are a little more interesting. Yoko always prides herself on being a good mimic—her imitations of the pompous section chief make her friends laugh. The perfect elevator girl's voice is high-pitched, on the verge of falsetto, and seeming to bubble over into merry laughter, without actually doing so. This is not an easy effect to achieve and it takes hours of drilling. Yoko's name was called out by the teacher, asking her to come forward. She was told to speak the following lines: This lift is going up, this lift is going down; and again: this lift is going up . . . and again. Her pitch was too low and her delivery not quite sprightly enough. The teacher told her to practice at home.

Bowing lessons are a more mechanical exercise. An inventive young engineer in the design department devised a bowing machine. It is a steel contraption a bit like those metal detectors through which one must pass at international airports. An electronic eye, built into the machine, registers exactly the angle of the bow and lights flicker on at fifteen degrees, thirty degrees, and forty-five degrees. The teacher of the bowing class explained that the "fifteen bow" was for an informal greeting to colleagues. The "thirty bow" was appropriate for meeting senior members of the store, and the deepest bow essential when welcoming clients, shoppers, and other visitors. Much of the average day of an elevator girl is spent at a perfect forty-five degree angle.

Yoko does not find this in the least humiliating, or even dull. Learning a skill like this is a challenge, and she is eager to get it just right. The girls were lined up in front of the machine and one by one, like pupils at a gymnastics class, they walked up to make three bows. Yoko missed the first one by several degrees; the disapproving noise of an electronic buzzer told her so. She blushed. The second, thirty degrees, she got wrong again, by inches. Determined to get it right the next time, she bent down, back straight, fingers together, and eyes trained on the floor about three feet from her toes—the light flashed, she did it, a smile of contentment spread across her face.

This is an extreme—though in Japan by no means despised—example of the insistence on form and of the way it is taught. The training of elevator girls also points to another constant factor in Japanese attitudes to work: form in human relations. The importance of etiquette and ritual in Japanese work is vital. When male bosses tell their female staff that serving tea, bowing to clients, and other such ceremonial functions are as necessary as the jobs usually reserved for men, they are only being partly hypocritical. To be sure, many men would feel threatened if too many women encroached on their traditional domains. It is much safer to insist that women should stick to the home after marriage or, in the case of unmarried "office ladies" (OLs), stick to making tea or other ceremonies. But, at the same time, Japanese do attach far more importance to such decorative functions than Westerners tend to do; and they genuinely feel that women do them best. Although some Western tourists might find the artificial ways of elevator girls grating, humiliating, or, at best, quaint, Japanese feel comfortable with them and indeed miss such service when it is not provided.

Men, too, spend much of their time on the rites of human relations. Although Japanese have a strong sense of hierarchy, decisions are based upon at least a show of consensus. This makes it difficult to take individual initiatives, and passing the buck is therefore a national sport. Consensus, as indeed all forms of Japanese business, is built on personal relations. These relations are based on mutual obligations: If I do this for you, you do that for me. Such favors are rarely expressed directly and relations take much time and effort to cement. This is where most salarymen—the middle-ranking samurai of today—come in. Because there are so many salarymen and so many relations to cement, many hours are spent in coffee shops during the day and bars and restaurants at night. This may seem inconsequential or even parasitic to the Western mind. It certainly does not make for efficiency. But just as the trade of rugs in the Middle East cannot proceed without endless cups of tea, the coffee shop workers are the backbone of the Japanese miracle. Let us turn again to an example.

Every table at the Café L'Étoile, a coffee shop in the Ginza, was occupied. Through the thick screen of cigarette smoke one could just discern Kazuo Sasaki, a young employee of one of the largest advertising companies. He was exchanging *meishi* (name cards) with three men from a small public relations firm. All four of them studied the cards carefully, made polite

30

hissing noises and sat down. Sasaki ordered his tenth cup of coffee and lit his thirteenth filter-tipped cigarette.

His order was taken by a uniformed young waiter who yelled out the command to another waiter, who shouted it to another link in the chain. The effect was highly theatrical—a spectacle of work, as it were. This particular gimmick was unique to L'Étoile and new waiters were drilled endlessly until they got it just right.

So much of Sasaki's day was spent meeting people in coffee shops that it was easier to reach him at Café L'Étoile than at his office. He has been working for his company for four years. His main job is to delegate commissions taken by his company to smaller companies, who then often delegate them to even smaller firms.

Business was not much discussed at Café L'Étoile. It would be indelicate to come directly to the point. Instead, Sasaki had become expert at discussing golf handicaps—the nearest he got to a golf course himself was one of those practicing ranges where one spent hours hitting balls into a giant net. He also had an endless supply of jokes about last night's hangover, or jocular comments on his client's sexual prowess. He always knew the latest baseball results and could talk for hours about television programs. On those rare occasions when an eccentric client insisted on talking about politics or books, Sasaki was at least a good listener. He has, in short, the social graces of a very superior barber.

In a country where so much depends on social graces, this is not to be despised. It is, I think rightly, argued that human relationships in Japan transcend abstract ideals of right and wrong. This is not true, for instance, in the Judeo-Christian tradition, where God is the final arbiter, in whose eyes we shall be judged. To commit perjury in a Japanese court, to protect one's boss, is the moral thing to do. Loyalty transcends a mere law. (This was proven several times during the long case against former Prime Minister Kakuei Tanaka).[1]

This principle permeates working relationships at every level of Japanese society. It explains, for example, the workings of the Japanese underworld. The underworld in Japan, though not necessarily respectable, is in many ways an overworld. Gangsters have their jobs to do, just like milkmen or prime ministers. Their roles in society, though, again, not respectable, are acknowledged. An often told story is about a man who woke up one night to find a *dorobo* (thief) going through his wallet. According to this tale, the man let him be, for a thief has to make a living too.

Tetsu Yamazaki is a *yakuza* (gangster). He prefers another term for his trade, however: *ninkyodo* (The Way of Chivalry). This sounds more traditional, more in keeping with Yamazaki's image of himself. Like many of his

[1] In 1983, Tanaka was convicted of bribery and of violating foreign exchange law for his role in the 1970s Lockheed scandal. See also p. 337n. [Editors' note]

colleagues, Yamazaki likes to dissociate himself from the common criminal who, alas, has begun to predominate in the Japanese underworld.

Yamazaki, *oyabun* (boss, or literally father figure) of his gang, Yamazaki-gumi, was expecting the local police chief for tea. This official had a habit of dropping in at the Yamazakigumi headquarters for afternoon chats. He kept abreast this way of the latest underworld gossip and in exchange for a good tip, he let Yamazaki carry on with his operations—within traditionally and mutually understood limits, of course. Extortion, protection rackets, prostitution were all right (somebody had to do those jobs), but physical violence against innocent people was not. Extortion, to name one occupation, does not always work without at least the threat of violence; but that fine line could always be worked out between gangster boss and policeman. The police chief was a reasonable man and Yamazaki, when necessary, a generous one.

The policeman arrived. He took his shoes off at the door and was loudly greeted by bowing young mobsters with crew cuts. He was ushered into the main room, where he made an informal bow to Yamazaki, who bowed in return. The boss, dressed in a green, pin-striped suit, a yellow shirt, red tie, and diamond clip, barked an order. A young mobster bowed, and slipped noiselessly into the kitchen, from where he emerged five minutes later with two cups of tea. 40

The police chief, after discussing the weather and inquiring after Yamazaki's golf handicap, asked a question about a recent murder case. He knew which gang was involved. He also knew that the boss of that gang was in debt to Yamazaki. Yamazaki himself was in some trouble over an amphetamine bust. So the police chief asked if perhaps Yamazaki could persuade his fellow boss to hand over the murderer, and then the amphetamine case could be forgotten.

Yamazaki thought this was a reasonable proposition and called up his friend. He told him what was up and asked him to hand over the man as a personal favor. Now, the "murderer" did not have to be the man who actually did it. It is an old Japanese—and Chinese—tradition that underlings take the full rap for crimes committed by their superiors. Unlike plea bargaining in the United States, where offenders get lesser punishments for cooperating, the Japanese system actually allows innocent people to substitute for the real culprits. These "innocents" are obliged to do this out of loyalty to their bosses. It is, in short, their duty.

There is something in it for the substitute, however, for after he gets out of jail there will be certain promotion waiting for him. The man will be happy, the murderer—a senior in the gang hierarchy—even happier. The police will have done their duty and Yamazaki will be off the amphetamine hook.

Their work concluded, the two men promised to meet again soon and the police chief took his leave. Next, Yamazaki received a magazine reporter who wanted to know about traditional customs of the *yakuza* world. The boss was in his element here, as he liked to hold forth on the noble traditions he upheld. He was the heir of Kunisada Chuji (a legendary nineteenth-century Robin Hood type of gangster). If it weren't for men like him, who took care of their boys and taught them the ways of chivalry, the streets of Japan would no longer be safe. The good *yakuza* still understood the Japanese code of honor, forgotten by the young who were corrupted by communist schoolteachers and foreign fashions. Leftists were selling Japan out to the foreigners and it was his duty, as a *yakuza* of the old school, to stop this from happening. When asked about the nobility of extortion, violence, and amphetamine trafficking, Yamazaki got quite indignant: Only bad mobsters engage in such practices; good *yakuza* had nothing to do with it; he was a protector of the poor, just like Kunisada Chuji; why, if the reporter wanted to have proof of this, he could call the local police chief: He knew all about it.

Human relations based on hierarchy are a comfort to many, especially   45
in a highly competitive world. In most Japanese companies seniority counts for more than competence and, ideally, one's job is forever assured. This works best for mediocrity—which, for face-saving reasons, is rarely exposed—and worst for talented mavericks.

Talent, being highly individualistic and thus socially troublesome, is not always highly regarded in Japan. Hard work and skill, especially in the sense of dexterity *(kiyo)*, are the two qualities Japanese pride themselves on as a people. The traditional Japanese stress on refining and miniaturizing everything—the Korean critic Yi O Ryong argues that this is the key to Japanese culture—may explain the modern success in transistor, microchip, or camera making. But although manual dexterity, the appearance of consensus, and the discipline—not to say docility—of the Japanese rank and file account for some of Japan's success story, no country can succeed without talented mavericks. Despite the Japanese saying that nails that stick out must be hammered in, there are those odd, talented exceptions, even in Japan, who refuse to be hammered in. Though sometimes respected, such people are rarely liked. The great Japanese filmmaker Akira Kurosawa, known in Japan as The Emperor, is a case in point. He is undoubtedly one of the greatest artists of the century, but Japanese critics have consistently tried to pull him off his pedestal, often in snide personal attacks. He has consistently refused to toe the social line; he has neither masters nor pupils; the ritual of human relations is less important to him than his talent. He is, in short, a loner, as is almost every truly gifted man or woman in this collectivist society.

But the creative force in Japan comes from these loners. They tend to come to the fore mostly in periods of social instability. The immediate aftermath of World War II seems to have been especially congenial to nonconformist entrepreneurs. Akio Morita, founder of Sony, Konosuke Matsushita of Matsushita, and Soichiro Honda, the grand old man behind the motor cars, immediately come to mind. The interesting thing about such creative oddballs is that once they make it to the top, they almost invariably become traditional masters, laying down the rules for the young to follow. They are more than teachers of technical skills or business methods, in the manner of such figures as Lee Iacocca. In fact, they conform more closely to the image of the classical Confucian sage, concerned with ethics and moral philosophy rather than technique. Matsushita wrote a kind of bible, expounding his philosophy; and Honda's autobiography has an equally lofty tone.

Recently the enormous success of high-technology industries has spawned a new generation of mavericks—whiz kids, laying the paths to Japanese versions of Silicon Valley. Such people are especially interesting as they combine the old Japanese penchant for miniature refinement and uncommon individualism. They often get their start in research and development departments of large companies, but proceed to break with the time-honored tradition of company loyalty to start their own firms. According to an official at the Ministry of International Trade and Industry there are now about five thousand "highly innovative" small companies with the potential to emerge as future Sonys or Hondas. No doubt their leaders, too, will one day write their books and become masters.

Although the difference between artists and craftsmen has never been as clear in Japan as in the postromantic West, there have always been mavericks in the arts as well. But those who do not follow masters often pay a heavy price. The number of suicides among Japanese writers in this century cannot be a mere romantic aberration. Such artists, like the gung-ho entrepreneurs, also thrive in times of unrest. The turbulent early nineteenth century produced such highly eccentric playwrights as Tsuruya Namboku and artists such as Ekin, who rejected every traditional school and persisted in a highly individualistic style. Two famous eccentric geniuses of our own time are Kurosawa and the author Yukio Mishima (1925–1970), Japan's most celebrated twentieth-century novelist, who ended his life at forty-five in a dramatic suicide.

Creative loners are by no means limited to men. In some periods of 50 Japanese history women had more freedom to express themselves than men, paradoxically because they had less freedom to engage in other public pursuits. Perhaps the greatest period for Japanese literature was the Heian (794–1185), particularly the tenth century, when the *kana* syllabary, a truly indigenous script, was developed. While educated men—virtually restricted to the aristocracy—still wrote in literary Chinese, talented women expressed themselves in the vernacular; the obvious example being Murasaki Shikibu (978–1015/31?), the author of *Genji monogatari (The Tale of Genji)*. One of the greatest writers of modern Japan was also a woman: Higuchi Ichiyo (1872–1896), who lived and died—very young—at the end of the nineteenth century. Both women wrote mostly about loneliness—a common theme in literature and a usual fate of writers anywhere, to be sure, but especially in Japan, where isolation from the common herd is particularly keenly felt.

So originality and creativity do exist in Japan. But they are all too often stifled by the pressure to conform. It takes tremendous courage to continue on in one's individual course. Let us be thankful for those few who do. But while such gifted eccentrics are rarer than in countries where individualism is fostered, there is an advantage to the Japanese preference for skill over originality. In places where everyone wants to be a star, but mediocrity necessarily prevails, there is a disturbing lack of pride in an ordinary job well done. In Western Europe there is even a perverse tendency to be proud of sloppiness. Japan may have fewer Nobel Prize winners than, say, Britain, but to see a shop girl wrap a package or a factoryworker assemble a bike is to see routine work developed to a fine art. This, the lack of Nobel Prizes not withstanding, may be Japan's grandest tradition.

Thinking About the Text

1. Buruma quotes a wise Japanese as saying, "Only when everybody wears exactly the same kimono can one detect true individual differences" (para. 18). What does this mean, and do you agree with it? Whether or not you agree, explain the idea to someone who doesn't grasp the sentence. And while you are at it, explain the relevance of the idea to the topic of the essay—work.

2. Explain in your own words the contrasting notions of style in the East and West, referred to in paragraph 23.

3. Explain Buruma's final sentence, taking into account the entire essay.

4. What do you think of this essay as a piece of expository writing? What is skillful or unskilled about it? (You might devote your analysis to one paragraph, or to a group of paragraphs such as 32–35, on Mr. Sasaki's day at the café, or 37–44, on the gangster Yamazaki.)

Thinking About Culture

5. Buruma says (in para. 1, and then develops the idea in later paragraphs) that in Japan work can seldom be separated from aesthetics: "It matters less what one does than how one is seen to do it." Does such a conception play any role in the United States? If so, what examples can you give?

6. In paragraphs 26–30 Buruma discusses the training of an elevator girl. He says that "Yoko does not find [her training] in the least humiliating, or even dull." You probably have not been trained to operate an elevator in a department store, but have you ever gone through training that is at least somewhat similar to Yoko's? If so, how did you respond to such training? Did the culture in which you grew up prepare you to accept such training, or did it instill in you values that conflict with it?

Akio Morita

Attitudes Toward Work

Japanese attitudes toward work seem to be critically different from American attitudes. Japanese people tend to be much better adjusted to the notion of work, any kind of work, as honorable. Nobody would look down on a man who retires at age fifty-five or sixty and then to keep earning money takes a more menial job than the one he left. I should mention that top-level executives usually have no mandatory retirement age, and many stay on into their seventies and even their eighties.

At Sony we have mandatory retirement from the presidency at sixty-five, but to utilize their experience and knowledge we keep former executives who have retired as consultants. We provide them with office space and staff, so that they can work apart from the day-to-day affairs of the company, at Ibuka Hall, a building located five minutes away from the headquarters building. From time to time, we ask them for advice and they attend conferences and other events as representatives of Sony. Many of those people who retire from managerial jobs find executive positions in smaller companies or subsidiary companies of Sony where their managerial experience and skill are needed and valued.

Workers generally are willing to learn new skills. Japan has never devised a system like the American, in which a person is trained to do one thing and then refuses to take a job doing anything else—and is even supported by government funds while he looks for a job that suits his specific tastes. Because of Japan's special situation, our people do not have that luxury. And our unemployment rate lately has not reached 3 percent.

One old style of management that is still being practiced by many companies in the United States and by some in Japan is based on the idea that the company that is successful is the one that can produce the conventional product most efficiently at cheaper cost. Efficiency, in this system, becomes a god. Ultimately, it means that machinery is everything, and the ideal factory is a perfectly automated one, perhaps one that is unmanned. This machinelike management is a management of dehumanization.

But technology has accelerated at an unparalleled pace in the past few   5

In May 1946, a young engineer named Akio Morita and a few friends gathered in a burned-out building in Tokyo, where they founded a new company, Tokyo Telecommunications Engineering Corporation. Later the company became the Sony Corporation, and in 1976 Morita became chairman and chief executive officer. In Made in Japan *(1986), written in collaboration with Edwin M. Reingold and Mitsuko Shimomura, Morita describes the history of Sony. We reprint an excerpt, which we have entitled "Attitudes Toward Work."*

decades and it has entailed digesting new knowledge, new information, and different technologies. Today, management must be able to establish new business ahead of its competitors, rather than pursue higher efficiency in manufacturing conventional products. In the United States and Europe today, old-fashioned low-level jobs are being protected while the new technologies are being neglected.

More important, an employee today is no longer a slave to machinery who is expected to repeat simple mechanical operations like Charlie Chaplin in the film *Modern Times*. He is no longer a beast of burden who works under the carrot-and-stick rule and sells his labor. After all, manual labor can be taken over by machine or computer. Modern industry has to be brain-intensive and so does the employee. Neither machinery nor animals can carry out brain-intensive tasks. In the late sixties, when integrated circuits had to be assembled by hand, the deft fingers of Asian women were greatly in demand by U.S. companies. As the design of these devices became more and more complicated, along came more sophisticated machinery, such as laser trimmers, which required not deft fingers but agile minds and intelligence. And so this upgrading of the workers is something that every country will have to be concerned about, and the idea of preserving old-fashioned jobs in the modern era does not make sense. This means educating new employees and reeducating older employees for new challenges.

That is not all. At Sony we at times have scientists participate in sales for a while because we don't want our scientists to live in ivory towers. I have always felt they should know that we are in a very competitive business and should have some experience in the front lines of the business. Part of the training program for graduates who enter Sony as recruits fresh out of university includes a program where nontechnical persons undergo a month of training at a factory and technical persons work as salespeople in a Sony shop or department store, selling our products.

Japanese labor practices are often called old-fashioned in today's world, and some say the old work ethic is eroding in Japan as it has elsewhere, but I do not think this is inevitable. As I see it, the desire to work and to perform well is not something unnatural that has to be imposed on people. I think all people get a sense of satisfaction from accomplishing work that is challenging, when their work and role in the company are being recognized. Managers abroad seem to overlook this. People in America, for example, have been conditioned to a system in which a person sells his labor for a price. In a way, that's good because people cannot coast; they know they have to work to earn their money or be fired. (I also think the way Americans make their children do work to earn their allowance is a fine idea; in Japan we often just give the money without requiring anything of our children.) In Japan we do take the risk of promising people job security, and then we have to keep motivating them. Yet I believe it is a big mistake to think that money is the only way to compensate a person for his work.

People need money, but they also want to be happy in their work and proud of it. So if we give a lot of responsibility to a younger man, even if he doesn't have a title, he will believe he has a good future and will be happy to work hard. In the United States, title and job and monetary incentives are all tied together. That is why, if a young person has a big job, management thinks he has to have a big salary. But in Japan we customarily give raises each year as employees get older and more experienced in the company. If we give an unusually high salary to one person, we cannot continue to give him annual increases indefinitely. At some point, his salary will have to level off, and at that point, he is likely to get discouraged. So we like to give the same sort of raise to all. I think this keeps our people well motivated. This may be a Japanese trait, but I do not think so.

I believe people work for satisfaction. I know that advertisements and   10
commercials in the United States seem to hold up leisure as the most satisfying goal in life, but it is not that way in Japan yet. I really believe there is such a thing as company patriotism and job satisfaction—and that it is as important as money. It goes without saying that you must pay good wages. But that also means, of course, that the company must not throw money away on huge bonuses for executives or other frivolities but must share its fate with the workers. Japanese workers seem to feel better about themselves if they get raises as they age, on an expectable curve. We have tried other ways.

When we started our research laboratory, we had to go out and find researchers, and because these people had more education and were, naturally, older than our normal new employees we decided they should have higher wages, equivalent to U.S. salary levels. One suggested plan was to put them under short-term contract, say three years, after which we would decide whether to renew or not. But before we decided on this new pay scheme, I asked the new employees whether they would prefer the more common system of lower pay to start, but with yearly increases, or the three-year contract at a much higher wage.

Not one of them asked for the American-level salary. Everyone opted for long-range security. That is why I tell the Americans I meet that people don't work only for money. But often when I say it, they respond, "Yes, I see, but how much do you pay the ones who really work hard?" Now this is an important point. When a worker knows he will be getting a raise each year, he can feel so secure that he thinks there is no need to work hard. Workers must be motivated to want to do a good job. We Japanese are, after all, human beings, with much in common with people everywhere. Our evaluation system is complex and is designed to find really capable persons, give them challenging jobs, and let them excel. It isn't the pay we give that makes the difference—it is the challenge and the recognition they get on the job.

My eldest son, Hideo, may not be the best example of the typical Japanese worker, but he has an interesting and, I think, typical view of work in Japan. He has studied in Britain and the United States, and all his life he wanted to work for Sony. He went to work as an Artists and Repertory man at the CBS-Sony record company on the urging of Norio Ohga. He and I felt that for him to come directly into Sony headquarters would be wrong, because of the family connection and the overtones of nepotism. So he was proving himself at CBS-Sony. He worked with foreign and local artists and became famous and successful in the record industry in Japan. He worked very hard, from about noon until three or four o'clock in the morning, doing his regular office business during the day and then dealing with musicians after they finished their work. Hideo doesn't drink, and so it was hard for him to sit around the Tokyo discos and bars with these rock stars, drinking Coca-Cola while they relaxed with whiskey in the wee small hours of the morning. But it was important for him to do this, and although he could have gone on a long time resting on his laurels, he took stock of himself on his thirtieth birthday and made a decision.

As he put it, "In the record business, there are many people in their late thirties and early forties wearing jogging shoes and white socks and jeans and T-shirts to the office. I looked at those guys and said, I don't want to be like that when I am forty or forty-five. This business is fine and I have been successful, and I have no reason to leave it. If I keep this job, I thought, I might end up being a top officer of CBS-Sony, but I didn't want to see myself at fifty coming into the office at one o'clock in the afternoon in jogging shoes and white socks saying 'Good morning.' I felt I had to prove to myself after seven years in the record business that I could work from nine to five, like ordinary people."

He was assigned to the Sony accounting division—quite a change, you   15
might think, from the artistic side of the record business—and some might have wondered whether he could make it or not, but I believed he could. His attitude is very Japanese, despite his international upbringing:

> All jobs are basically the same. You have to apply yourself, whether you are a record A&R man, a salesman on the street, or an accounting clerk. You get paid and you work 100 percent to do the job at hand. As an A&R man, I was interested and excited and happy, but naturally as long as you are satisfied with your work and are using your energy, you will be happy. I was also very excited about the accounting division. I found out something new every day, struggling with a whole bunch of invoices and the payment sheets, the balance sheet, the profit and loss statement, and working with all those numbers. I began to get a broad picture of the company, its financial position and what is happening day to day and which way the company is heading. I discovered that that excitement and making music at the studio are the same thing.

In the late sixties a European Commission internal memo on Japan was leaked, and a great stir was created because it referred to the Japanese as "workaholics" who live in "rabbit hutches." There is no doubt that inadequate housing is a major problem in Japan, and nobody could deny that the Japanese are probably the hardest working people in the world. We have many holidays in Japan, but only about the same number as the United States. We do not give long summer vacations, even to our schoolchildren.

At Sony we were one of the first Japanese companies to close down our factory for one week in the summer, so that everybody could take off at the same time. And we long ago instituted the five-day, forty-hour week. The Japan Labor Standards Act still provides for a maximum forty-eight-hour workweek, though it is soon to be revised downward, and the average workweek in manufacturing is now forty-three hours. But even with up to twenty days of paid vacation a year, Japanese workers managed to take fewer days off and spend more days on the job than workers in the United States and Europe.

It was only in 1983 that banks and financial institutions began to experiment with the five-day week, closing one Saturday a month, and eventually the whole nation will move closer to the five-day week. Still, International Labor Organization data show that Japanese work longer weeks and have fewer labor disputes than workers in the United States, the United Kingdom, France, or West Germany. What I think this shows is that the Japanese worker appears to be satisfied with a system that is not designed only to reward people with high pay and leisure.

At Sony we learned that the problem with an employee who is accustomed to work only for the sake of money is that he often forgets that he is expected to work for the group entity, and this self-centered attitude of working for himself and his family to the exclusion of the goals of his coworkers and the company is not healthy. It is management's responsibility to keep challenging each employee to do important work that he will find satisfying and to work within the family. To do this, we often reorganize the work at Sony to suit the talents and abilities of the workers.

I have sometimes referred to American companies as being structures like brick walls while Japanese companies are more like stone walls. By that I mean that in an American company, the company's plans are all made up in advance, and the framework for each job is decided upon. Then, as a glance at the classified section of any American newspaper will show, the company sets out to find a person to fit each job. When an applicant is examined, if he is found to be oversized or undersized for the framework, he will usually be rejected. So this structure is like a wall built of bricks: the shape of each employee must fit in perfectly, or not at all.

In Japan recruits are hired, and then we have to learn how to make use of them. They are a highly educated but irregular lot. The manager takes a good long look at these rough stones, and he has to build a wall by combining them in the best possible way, just as a master mason builds a stone wall. The stones are sometimes round, sometimes square, long, large, or small, but somehow the management must figure out how to put them together. People also mature, and Japanese managers must also think of the shapes of these stones as changing from time to time. As the business changes, it becomes necessary to refit the stones into different places. I do not want to carry this analogy too far, but it is a fact that adaptability of workers and managements has become a hallmark of Japanese enterprise.

When Japanese companies in declining or sunset industries change their line of business or add to it, workers are offered retraining and, for the most part, they accept it eagerly. This sometimes requires a family move to the new job, and Japanese families are, again, generally disposed to do this.

Thinking About the Text

1. In paragraph 3 Morita offers a brief view of what he takes to be the American system. Does it ring true to you? Why, or why not?

2. What do you think of the analogy involving brick and stone walls? First, does it ring true? Second, if you think it does ring true, do you think that one system is clearly preferable to the other? Explain.

3. Morita states that "technical persons" (e.g., scientists) are expected to spend some time working "as salespeople in a Sony shop or department store" (para. 7). Should American companies adopt this system? What might be the advantages and disadvantages?

4. In his characterization of Japanese workers, does Morita seem to be taking into account both men and women? Explain.

Thinking About Culture

5. Does the salary system commonly used in Japan, which Morita explains in paragraph 9, make sense to you? Would you choose to work for a company with such a system, in preference to a company that tied together title, job, and money? (Reread paras. 9–12 in preparation for responding to this question.)

Jeannie Lo

A Day in the Factory

The day for factory women begins around 6:00 A.M., or perhaps a bit earlier if they have been assigned to early morning cleanup duties in the company women's dormitory. Women who commute from the far reaches of Aichi Prefecture must start even earlier.

Jeannie Lo conducted the research for her book, Office Ladies, Factory Women *(1990), as a participant-observer, working in the Brother Typewriter Company factory in Nagoya, Japan. The book grew out of an undergraduate honors thesis that she wrote while attending Harvard University.*

Summers in Nagoya are so unbearably hot that many dorm residents leave the door to their room open to let a breeze in through the sliding doors off the veranda, and they sleep in the main room instead of the tiny, cramped bedroom. With my door open, I woke up at 6:00 sharp every morning to the voices of the sweepers outside my door and the sounds of women cleaning the toilets.

By 6:05 I was up. I turned on the television set to listen to the weather report while I washed my face. When I did laundry in the morning I got up much earlier and rushed to the laundry room with a load in my arms. I usually met bright-eyed dormmates chattering away on the weather or work as they did their ironing or their laundry. The dormitory head always came minutes before 6:00 to open the doors to the laundry rooms and kitchens. Of the six washing machines, five were rather primitive tubs that merely spun the clothes around. The clothes had to be removed and wrung out in a side compartment after each wash or rinse. I later discovered that this type of washing machine is typical in Japan, despite the fact that many households are now investing in "American-style" large automatics. There was one automatic machine in the dorm, but no one used it because it did not work very well and left a soapy film on the clothes.

Laundry was an ordeal. The machines were small and could wash only about six articles of clothing at a time, so the women ended up doing laundry three days a week. It took about forty-five minutes to do the wash. Then we had to hang the wet clothes on clotheslines to dry. Laundry is considered women's work. The men's dormitories, in contrast, are equipped with working automatic washing machines on every floor, saving time and effort. By the time I finished my laundry, it was usually 7:00. Running back and forth between my room and the laundry room, I took some time out to boil water for tea and iron the Brother uniform that had been lent to me.

At 7:00 I went to breakfast with many of the other girls in the dormitory. The breakfast menu was not terribly exciting. Since the opening of the Aoi dormitory doors to women employees in 1980, the cafeteria maids have served a set breakfast of rice, a small packet of flavored *nori* seaweed, white miso soup, pickled turnips, and low-grade green tea. The exceptions were Tuesdays, when we were allowed a raw egg to put into our rice, and Sundays, when we ate the dormitory's version of a Western breakfast: one slice of buttered toast and some green tea.

Microwaves in the rear of the dining room were an added convenience. Women who did not enjoy raw eggs could microwave them. People were also allowed to buy food outside of the dormitory and prepare it in these ovens. To save money, some did not go to the dining hall in the morning but made breakfasts of boiled noodles in the tiny kitchens on their floor or in the large kitchen on the first floor, or ate bread in the factory dining hall before the loudspeaker sounded for the lines to start up.

In any case, breakfast at the dormitory was not very social. Most women wandered in alone or with one other person, ate breakfast quickly, and then left for their rooms to change into their work clothes. Certain groups did eat together, though. Women on company athletic teams joined for breakfast promptly at 6:00 when the dining halls opened. They ate the general fare plus a special diet of yogurt and other foods that would help their performance in practices. They also got a raw egg from the dining hall every morning. These women always sat together, with the younger workers bringing the food and serving it to the senior workers. The team kept its own refrigerator in the dining room, stocked with fruit, dairy products, and meat or fish to flavor the rice. The women cut their hair short and often poked each other in the ribs, laughing and telling one another that they looked like "handsome young men." Yet they carried themselves with pride. The other employees respected them and expressed no jealousy. A factory woman living in the dormitory explained, "The handball players work very hard in their practices and games. They deserve the special treatment."

The rest of the female workers came downstairs to the dining hall in waves. The second rush of people came at 6:30. They were the early risers, the women chosen to do that morning's dormitory chores, and the factory women. The plant started up at 8:00, but the downtown offices (in the center of Nagoya) opened at 9:00. The third group came in between 7:00 and 8:00. These were team members who had to jog or do special training exercises before breakfast. The joggers ate quickly and were allowed a quick shower before going off to their jobs.

After breakfast, we returned to our rooms and changed into uniforms. Then we went to the reception area in front of the dormitory management's office and turned our nameplates, hanging on a big board on the wall, from the black-lettered side over to the red-lettered side, indicating that we had left the dormitory for the day. We left through a side door into the foyer lined with rows of numbered boxes. There we traded our dormitory slippers for street shoes. This foyer served as a midway point between the reception area and the outside world. The factory women changed into comfortable cloth shoes to work on the line while the OLs° changed into heeled pumps or other leather shoes. The factory was a seven-minute walk from the dormitory. The women usually left by 7:40. At the front entrance off Horita Street the guard who sat by the gate smiled widely and bowed a friendly "Good morning" to the workers who passed into the faded concrete building. Brother has many different plants throughout Aichi Prefecture and Japan; the one at the Mizuho complex consists of eight weather-worn gray glass-and-concrete buildings. The workers inside these structures build typewriters, word processors, and sewing machines, products that are immediately packed up and shipped to many different parts of the world.

The workers entered the plant and walked to their designated areas.   10

OLs: office ladies, a term used for women workers whose chief function is to pour tea for male workers. [Editors' note]

By 7:50 the locker rooms were filled with young women and men. The men's locker room was on the first floor in the first room off the main entrance. Women working on the typewriter and word processor lines used the locker room on the third floor, off a semiprivate hallway away from the lines. The lockers were a personal space for the workers, filled with each person's belongings. Many women left makeup cases and boxed lunches there until lunchtime. Some factory women spent the early morning, part of their lunch hour, and late afternoon after work at their lockers touching up their faces to look their best for factory work or for a date.

Men and women who had commuted to work changed into their company uniforms: men into tan cotton shirts and pants and women into blue polyester-blend skirts and shirts with the company logo sewn onto the sleeves. The uniforms for the women look like airline stewardess uniforms from the 1950s, or the "uniforms worn by female gas station attendants," in the words of the woman whose locker was next to mine. They are actually an improvement over the solid blue polyester skirts and shirts worn five years ago. Many of the young OLs wore the shirts tucked into their skirts to accentuate their figure; the older ones, more modest, wore less makeup and their shirts out of their skirts.

The locker rooms buzzed with gossip and small talk about daily lives, about what a co-worker was planning to do on the weekend or who she was dating, or about whether mandatory overtime work would be imposed that day. Some high school girls who did part-time work in the factory during their summer vacations came in their school uniforms—navy-blue sailor suit dresses. The factory was short about a hundred workers and had resorted to hiring students on summer vacation for part-time labor.

After changing, some women hurried off to the cafeteria for a quick cup of coffee before beginning work. Others walked leisurely to their workplaces to sit and relax for five minutes before beginning another tiring day on the line. At 7:55, the music for stretching and the morning exercises played over the loudspeaker. The popular program known as "radio exercise" has been broadcast every morning since the 1930s without fail. A woman's voice counts off the exercises in clear Japanese in the foreground of bright music. At Brother, the older men stood and stretched their flanks, arms, and back muscles, twisting and turning their torsos. They started their day the same way every morning, setting into motion the muscles that they used to lift the packages onto trucks day after day. These men smiled and stretched as they brushed off the remnants of morning weariness and bade hello to the people entering the workplace. Sometimes the young engineers found exercise time all too amusing and just flapped their arms and gawked at passersby.

The young women who worked on the lines were indifferent to the music, and none of them did the stretching. The stragglers were changing; the rest spent their last minutes of freedom adjusting their hair and makeup, or drinking their coffee. Most people were positioned on the line about one or two minutes before the work began. They ate candy and gossiped. Early morning was a very social time. At 7:59 A.M., a recording of church bells sounded over the public address system; with the chimes, the workday began.

There were four lines in operation on my floor: a robot line and three "human" lines. The robot line made two thousand typewriter bodies a day. The robots worked tirelessly, 24 hours a day, 7 days a week, 365 days a year, and were highly efficient. There was one male engineer who inspected this line regularly and stood by to ensure that there were no breakdowns. The products of the robot line were then sent over to three human lines: a main line, a subline, and an office typewriter line. The human lines, less than perfect in comparison, worked only eight to nine hours a day and did all of the simple motions that required judgment, like spreading grease, inserting springs, applying labels, and testing machine functions. I was assigned to the subline.

Although mass production usually began exactly at 8:00, it was delayed some mornings for five or ten minutes. One of the managers, Iwasaki, gave pep talks on Mondays and Tuesdays. We stood on the line, next to our workbenches, facing him. He seemed to hope that the cheer he spread would foster a greater sense of loyalty to the group and result in higher productivity for the rest of the week. He usually began by relating the news of the company. In one speech, Iwasaki talked about a companywide athletic competition in a nearby prefecture, some engineers who were visiting from the United Kingdom, and finally about sticking it out on the line and giving our "100 percent." Some of the women on the line looked indifferent to his appeals, averting their eyes and staring at the floor as he spoke, but others listened attentively and smiled in appreciation. They were ready to begin work. Iwasaki radiated a paternal message with his kind words. He was a soft-spoken man who seemed to be concerned with our well-being. He stressed the importance of safety and teamwork, restating the message of the "safety first" signs that were posted by all of the elevators and on the factory walls. Iwasaki beamed: He was silently yet unmistakably proud of the women on the line. What this meant to them, I did not know for sure.

His speech ended at 8:10. The women were silent throughout it and remained so afterward. We then put on our white cotton gloves, which were a testimony of the kind of work we did on the line. (Within three hours, our gloves were perforated, and completely soiled with black grease. We covered the parts of the gloves where the fingers poked through with cotton finger replacements.) When we finished putting our gloves on, Tomita, one of the two senior workers responsible for our group's production, turned on the loading machine at the beginning of the line. The machine loaded one typewriter chassis onto the line every twenty seconds and emitted a loud BUZZ! at the end of each of these intervals to tell us that we should be starting on the next typewriter. There were now typewriters in various stages of manufacture down the line. Tomita yelled down the line to tell all that work had begun: "It's going!"

We immediately began to work on the typewriter body in front of us.

Many of the women on the line had built Brother typewriters for over a year. Their duties in the typewriter manufacturing process had become second nature to them. Typewriter models varied from year to year, but the motions performed on the line did not change significantly. The senior workers guided the junior workers through the small changes in procedure. But most of the women ended up doing the same kind of work as before. During the summer of 1987, we built AX "intelligent" typewriters. These machines were similar to many other kinds of typewriters built previously on the line, except they contained computer hardware. Most of the complicated word-processing function add-ons had already been installed by the robot line the day before.

As the typewriters came down the line, we jumped to action. The silence of the early morning factory was broken by the series of buzzes, clicks, and rumblings from steel parts sliding from one place to another on the robot assembly line, and by the deafening whir of electric screwdrivers bolting typewriter parts together. The experienced women performed sets of five small actions every twenty seconds. These consisted, for example, of accurately inserting, positioning, and screwing in typewriter parts, cleaning installed sections, inserting springs, spreading grease over certain areas, or checking typewriter functions. I was amazed at the speed with which these women performed their tasks. Aiko, whom I watched intently, could accurately type out the entire keyboard, test the superscripting, subscripting, and correcting functions as well as fit a plastic cover over the mechanism, all within twenty seconds. She typed as fast as a trained secretary; over five years, the keyboards had become second nature to her.

When I first entered the factory in June 1987, Kojima, one of the factory   20
managers, explained the entire typewriter manufacturing process to me and immediately set me to work installing motors into special holders to be bolted later into the typewriter chassis. I put together about five hundred of these motor-and-holder units, making many mistakes, taking the units apart, and redoing them. Factory work was much more challenging than I had expected. Matsuda and Tomita, the senior workers on the line, taught me how to use the magnetized electric screwdriver properly to pick up screws and set them into place effortlessly.

Matsuda and Tomita had special functions on the line as the designated senior workers. They oversaw the line and were responsible for flawless production. They listened to the workers' complaints and problems and tried to help them. They also taught the factory workers new techniques and made sure that they mastered them. These women have gained much respect during their years in the factory. They came to work in the Nagoya factory after graduating from junior high schools in different cities in Kyushu, one of the southern islands of Japan. They had worked on the line for fifteen years and could fix a typewriter in a matter of minutes. Most women who join the line learn the fundamentals of building typewriters from them and are assigned two or three tasks on the line. Later, the senior workers work them up to the usual five or six tasks depending upon their performance.

The senior workers have seen a great turnover of women on the line. Many workers come to the factory for a year or two before they quit for marriage or other reasons. They are constantly being replaced by fresh crops of young women. The senior workers also oversee the training of young salarymen who work on the factory lines for two weeks as part of their freshman company training, and OLs who are transferred to the factory when the lines are short of laborers. The company justifies these transfers by the policy that employees must all work for the greater good of the company. The workers choose the company, not the job, when they come to Brother. All newly hired employees look to senior workers for assistance. Many of the women identified with Tomita and Matsuda and talked to them about their personal lives as well as about the fundamentals of using a screwdriver.

I was placed on the line on my second day. First, I was given the small jobs of greasing and setting springs into tiny openings of the typewriter chassis. The motions took me about fifteen seconds. Sachiko and Mieko, the women who stood at my sides, completed five motions in seventeen seconds. Sachiko straightened and inserted a typewriter head mechanism into the chassis, screwed another metal part onto the body, and inserted two springs into the back roller. Mieko adjusted the settings of two of the key mechanisms, drilled in the roller, and washed it in strong-smelling cleaning fluid. I was astounded at their speed.

Every day at 9:00, the Chimney Sweep song from "Mary Poppins" played over the loud speaker. It was a signal to the factory women to sit down and rest for exactly sixty seconds. The line paused for a minute. This minute, which passed all too quickly, gave some relief from standing. We could collect our thoughts while we sat on the benches waiting for the buzzer to sound and the line to start up again. Promptly at 9:01, the interrupted flow of typewriters down the line restarted, and it was production as usual.

Some mornings, however, things did not run like clockwork, and we had more time to complete our assembly line tasks. Sometimes there just were not enough parts available to manufacture the daily quota of typewriters, or the robot line did not run as smoothly as expected. Then, Tomita would interrupt the flow of typewriters, screaming down the line, "Hold it!" We finished the typewriter we were working on and did not pass it to the next person until we heard her yell "Next!" and the buzzer sounded again.

At 10:00, a tune from the "Nutcracker Suite" played over the loud-speaker, signaling our ten-minute coffee/bathroom break. We turned off the fluorescent lamps above our workbenches, and the senior workers switched off the main assembly line power. Women marched in droves to the ladies' room or the cafeteria. Some remained at their benches, ate candy, and continued the discussions they had begun early that morning. At 10:08, "Camptown Ladies" played over the loudspeaker, indicating that it was time to return to our workbenches. The line started up again at 10:10, when another loud buzz sounded. We had another one-minute break at 11:00 A.M.,

25

after which time dragged until noon. We unanimously agreed that these were the longest fifty-nine minutes in the day. Mieko and Sachiko marked the minutes until noon, yelling encouragement to the women nearby: "Just thirty minutes until lunch time!! Only twenty minutes more! Stick it out!" We reminded ourselves that we would be rewarded with a forty-minute sit-down lunch if only we could stick it out until noon.

Finally, "Camptown Ladies" blasted again over the intercom. The lines stopped. We turned off the lamps at our workbenches and walked in groups to the sinks at the sides of the room to scrub with detergent the black grease that had smeared our hands and gloves during work. We draped our gloves, smelling of kerosene, over the wooden benches by the line and walked to the cafeteria.

The factory cafeteria was a large, dingy green room in the southern part of the factory. Workers entered from one end, passed a series of vending machines selling anything from coffee to instant Chinese noodles, and proceeded to the other end of the room to one of the small company-run stores or hot-lunch stalls. The food was not very tasty, but it was inexpensive and filling, and we enjoyed the chance to sit.

Lunchtime at the cafeteria was a social time, as I came to understand it. It was the only time that men and women could actually speak to each other, although few took advantage of this opportunity. Workers stood in long or short lines, depending on which lunch they wanted. The men usually opted for the B-lunch, which consisted of miso soup, a bowl of rice, salad, tofu with ginger and miso flavorings, and fried meat or seafood. Women usually chose to eat small sandwiches from the company store, thick noodles in broth, or the A-lunch, a cold boxed lunch of boiled rice, fried vegetables, and fried meat. There was an unconscious division of the sexes even in the cafeteria lines. And at 350 yen ($2.80), the B-lunch was more expensive and more filling than the A-lunch, which cost 250 yen ($2.00), or the small sandwiches at 80 yen ($.64) each. Most women ate lightly and had ice cream or candies for dessert.

Other options chosen by both sexes were curried rice, boiled eggs, and rice balls with seaweed or fish, sold at the store on the far end of the dining hall. The store also sold ice cream, candy, sandwiches, and pastries during working hours. It was unmanned, and purchases were made on an honor system, with the worker slipping money into a slot in the money box. The older women who ran the food services set out large pots of tea on the long dining hall tables for the rest of the workers.

Factory women carried their trays of food to the long dining hall tables, where the same groups sat together every day. Unlike office workers, factory workers at Brother rarely socialized with the people in their work sections. Some had come to Brother by introduction from friends or relatives and ate with them. Most ate with friends from other work groups.

As at breakfast, women on teams ate together. Three-quarters of the women's softball team worked in the Mizuho factory, and they usually ate in a large group at one long table. Sometimes they invited me and some male engineers to eat with them. These women took enormous pleasure in questioning me relentlessly on the appearance and actions of American men, and in poking fun at the young male engineers, for anything from how they looked that morning to their bachelor status. Once, Hiromi, a young catcher on the team, teased a designer in the sewing machine division: "Yamada-san, you look very handsome today. Do you have a date?" Flattered, he bought ice cream for the team members at his table.

Lunch was the time to relax and to forget about the stresses of work. The men smoked cigarettes. The women made small talk with the men at the tables, but the differences between the sexes were apparent. People sat in their chairs or wandered about outside of the dining hall. Sometimes women from the advertising division would come to the cafeteria to hand out joke computer-dating surveys that humorously matched men and women to unlikely people in the company. Michiyo, a young typewriter inspector, expressed dismay at finding herself paired up with a fifty-year-old married factory administrator in the sewing machine division.

The fun lasted until 12:35 when "Camptown Ladies" played over the loudspeakers once again. In neat formation, the Mizuho workers carried their trays to the bins near the entrance to the cafeteria and put their dishes and chopsticks in tubs of soapy water. Then they walked back to their respective workplaces. At 12:40, bells chimed over the public address system. Tomita-san yelled "It's time" and flipped the power switches to restart the flow of typewriter bodies down the line. We worked until our one-minute sit-down break at 2:00. At 3:00, we got another ten-minute coffee break. One hour before quitting time, Tomita stopped the line, assembling us for a ten-minute general cleanup of the area. The women worked in pairs to carry the trash out to the dumpster, sweep the floors, and wipe down the workbenches with turpentine. These actions promoted general camaraderie and teamwork. Working quickly with a partner meant that you had that much more time to rest until the line started up again. Cleanup was a welcome time since it meant that quitting time was approximately an hour away.

Most days we were allowed to leave the factory at 5:00. Everyone, 35 however, was required to do overtime work when the company was short of workers or needed to produce more than the usual number of machines. We sometimes worked overtime four or five times a week when there was heavy demand, and occasionally we even worked on Saturdays and Sundays. During the early weeks of production of the AX-26 typewriter, the women did overtime about five times a week and worked full nine-hour days on both Saturday and Sunday.

The factory administrators did not force workers to do overtime or to work on weekends, but no one ever voiced a complaint. Factory workers did not consider overtime requests to be unreasonable or unusual. It was understood that they would ungrudgingly work the extra hours if the company needed them, and they did receive compensation for the extra hours they put in. The closest thing to a complaint was when women called the overtime policy "selfish" on the part of the company, but they continued to work with the same fervor and retained the same commitment to their jobs that they had during periods of normal production.

The lives that women led after hours varied. One worker was a mother. She had to pick her children up from the sitter's home, clean house, do the shopping, and cook dinner. Overtime work was especially hard on her. Other factory women returned to their dormitories to eat dinner or watch television, knit or talk to friends, do their laundry, and prepare for bed. Others went to night school to get nursery-school teaching certification or high school diplomas so they could eventually leave the line and do work that was less physically demanding and more intellectually challenging. The women who competed on sports teams were excused from overtime and went straight to the Brother sports grounds or gymnasium after 3:00 to practice for three or four hours before they returned to the dormitory for dinner, bath, and bed.

Factory women went out with their work sections once or twice a month to eat at an inexpensive restaurant or bowl a few games. One day, I went with the women on my line to a self-serve octopus pancake restaurant where we sat around a big table and made octopus pancakes and other dishes. Each serving cost 400 yen ($3.20). In the restaurant, everyone listened intently to Mako's explanation of the best way to make the pancakes and then tried it. Mako, a vivacious girl, dominated the conversation with talk about bowling and her crazy boyfriend, the fisherman. Afterward, we had ice cream and bean jam at the local Sugakiya, a fast-food restaurant serving Chinese noodles, soft ice cream, and other desserts.

On special occasions, the women went in large groups to an inexpensive pub where they could quaff a couple of beers or lemon sours, have dinner, and talk and laugh in loud voices, away from the company of men. At 9:00 P.M., the women who lived in the dormitory left, with ample time to spare for their 9:30 curfew. The other women took the trains back to their homes in various parts of Aichi Prefecture.

Most nights, however, the factory women did not go out. They returned   40 to the dormitory and were the first ones to soak in the bath when the shower and bath room opened at 7:00. Mieko told me that it was very important to "remove my fatigue" with a nice long soak. After the bath, the women sat in their rooms eating sweets and drinking tea with their roommates. They usually watched television—quiz programs, suspense dramas, music programs—whatever was popular at the time. Bedtime came around 11:00 P.M., or much later if the conversation was good or if one became engrossed in a piece of knitting.

I have described a typical day in the life of a factory woman, but not all days are really like this. The lives of the women are unique, and not everyone lives in the dormitory. Women have different roommates or different relationships within the company. . . . The differences in work experience are small, however. Women shift bench positions on the line every six weeks, or sometimes when a fellow worker calls in sick, but their work content does not change much. They experience the same breaks every day, see the same coworkers, and listen to the same announcements and music piped in over the public address system.

The content of the work is of little consequence to the factory woman. It does not matter to her whether she drills in a normal head mechanism for a student typewriter or a computerized one for an intelligent word-processing typewriter. The end result for the factory woman is the same. She will use a screwdriver to attach one piece of metal to another, and another tool to adjust the springs.

The few things that affect the factory woman are the seasons and the relationships formed with different members of the workplace. The summers are hot and humid, and the factory becomes infested with microscopic mites that creep into their stockings and bite their legs as they stand on the line. Some women resort to spraying insect poison on their legs to kill the bugs. In the winter the mites disappear. The late spring and autumn bring unceasing rains and gray weather, making the factories appear gloomier and more unpleasant than usual.

Relationships within the workplace have much to do with a factory woman's outlook. Some girls remain cheerful despite the long hours and the monotony. They quickly become favorites in the workplace, lifting everyone's spirits. Factory work is not merely a physical drain but also a mental and spiritual one. It takes only about two weeks for most bodies to get used to the work and the eight hours of standing; but factory women, unlike OLs, find it hard to identify with their work group. They have few opportunities to speak to others in the group, and there is little intellectual stimulation. Frequently the workers actually run out of things to think about.

The work renders the women somewhat helpless. On my line one of the floor supervisors came by, smiled, and patted the women on their bottoms while they worked. When this happened to me, I was infuriated and felt completely powerless. I was working on a typewriter body at the time, and there were machines flowing down the line. The women told me that the supervisor often did that kind of thing, and they could do nothing but ignore it when it happened.   45

The on-line experiences for men and women are basically the same except for these incidents of harassment. There were only two men, in their late forties, on my line. They packaged and inspected typewriters at the far end. These men, who were not considered by the women to be part of their group, kept to themselves and had little contact with anyone except the senior workers. Despite the similarities in jobs, men receive more benefits than women do. They get monetary compensation when they marry and when they have children. Women do not. Men can be promoted to the position of factory supervisor if they show ambition and work hard enough. Women can become senior workers on the line and gain more responsibilities, but the position of "senior worker" is not official or company-ordained. It comes only with seniority and ambition.

Women usually resort to talking about men and marriage while they work on the line. This, in fact, is their favorite topic. It gets their minds off the work and onto their dreams of a brighter future. For most, marriage and husbands will be their eventual ticket out of the monotony of factory work. Some will stay on the line indefinitely. Many of the women told me that they wanted to marry as soon as possible, to enter into the security of married life. They wanted to end their days at the factory.

Thinking About the Text

1. What does Lo's tone tell you about her attitude to the women in the plant compared with her attitude toward the plant managers and owners?
2. In what ways does Lo's account of women in a Japanese factory square with Kazuko Watanabe's (p. 171) and Sumiko Iwao's (p. 180) accounts of women's positions in Japan in Chapter 5?

Thinking About Culture

3. If you have ever worked on an assembly line in a factory, compare your experience with Lo's. Do you think that managers of American factories can learn anything from Lo? If so, what?
4. How do you think automation affects American workers? Can you think of points of comparison with the Japanese case as here described?
5. Lo describes the "Japanese love of uniforms." What is your perspective on the experience and effect of wearing uniforms?

Bill Powell, Hideko Takayama, and John McCormick

Who's Better Off?

This is a tale of two countries that could not be more different—and two men who once were very much alike.

By the end of the 1980s, the United States and Japan were headed in opposite directions. With increasing budget and trade deficits, the United States seemed a nation in decline—sluggish, complacent, and unable to cut

This article, written with the assistance of Shigeo Shimoda in Tokyo and Tom Hazlett in Evanston, Illinois, originally appeared in Newsweek *on March 22, 1993.*

it in a world where competitive standards were set in Tokyo. Japan, by contrast, was the country that would inherit the earth, its relentless ascension driven by the quality of its products, the discipline of its work force and its government's fiscal sobriety. The friction turned acrimonious and personal. Japanese officials last year dismissed U.S. workers as slouches, ill equipped for the global marketplace. As one politician put it: "U.S. workers are too lazy. They want high pay without working."

Today's headlines tell a different story. Japan is in crisis, its economy in its steepest postwar slump. Suddenly there is talk of downsizings and the unraveling of a social contract at the core of Japan's success: In return for loyalty and ceaseless hard work, Japan Inc. guaranteed a job for life. The United States, by contrast, is growing briskly. As Japan's economy contracted in the fourth quarter last year, America's surged by nearly 5 percent.

Yet one dilemma unites the two countries. The U.S. recovery Bill Clinton inherited will evaporate if it fails to make new opportunities for displaced or disenchanted workers. The payoff would be an adaptable work force, quick to seize opportunities. At the same time, Japan's work force, too, must adapt. The fabled salaryman who toils in return for a lifetime job may be at risk amid Japan's slump. Is the likelihood of a trim, flexible work force ascendant in America but fading in Japan? Has the U.S. worker who boldly charts his own career eclipsed the Japanese worker whose marriage to the company now leaves him vulnerable? Who, now, is better off?

For a year *Newsweek* has tracked the lives of two contemporaries, one   5
Japanese and one American. Tokyo's Shigeo Shimoda, forty-eight, has worked most of his adult life for Matsushita Electric Industrial Co. Ltd., one of Japan's most powerful firms and the maker of Panasonic products. Tom Hazlett, forty-eight, of Evanston, Ill., abandoned corporate life before it could abandon him: He started his own business. Each man's path—one rigid but secure, one fraught with anxiety—violates the other's mind-set. These are their stories.

Shigeo Shimoda: The Company Man

They hear the talk of crisis now, the men and women of the second sales department of the Panasonic industry sales office. THE DAY OF THE MASS UNEMPLOYMENT AGE HAS ARRIVED, read a recent headline in *The Yomiuri Weekly*, a popular magazine. The Japanese economy is in tatters, and the bad news just keeps getting worse. Late last month Shigeo Shimoda, the general manager of the department, sat in his living room at home watching television when the startling news came: Akio Tanii, the president of Matsushita, had suddenly and unexpectedly resigned, his thirty-six-year career over in a blink. Lifetime employment in Japan, it turns out, isn't necessarily for everybody. The question now is, is it for anybody?

Huge companies—like Matsushita—know that they are too bloated to be as fiercely competitive as they once were. Suddenly, something has to give, and many in Japan have begun to wonder: Is Japan's "salaryman" finally going the way of William H. Whyte, Jr.'s long-lost Organization Man in America—betrayed, ultimately, by the cruelties of market economies?

Shigeo Shimoda insists he doesn't spend time worrying about it. He is, as usual, much too busy. Shimoda is a forty-eight-year-old father of two sons, Kentaro, twenty-one, and Keisuke, eighteen. Born the year World War II ended, he is a product of Japan's postwar miracle. Like so many others of his generation, he went to work for a giant Japanese company as a young man and hasn't stopped since. Ask Kentaro, now a college student in Tokyo, what his father's hobby is and he responds simply, "Work."

For twenty-three years now, Shimoda has worked for Matsushita Electric Industrial Co. Ltd., arguably the archetypal Japanese company. Conservative, disciplined—in many of its plants the workers still do morning calisthenics—the company now employs 242,000 people worldwide and churns out products under names like Panasonic and Technics. Today, Shigeo Shimoda is a department manager, or *"bucho,"* with two main responsibilities: He sells an array of electronics products like computer chips and cathode-ray tubes to a range of foreign industrial companies; then he makes sure those customers keep coming back for more. In the United States, a management consultant once said, "The customer is always right." In Japan, he could say, "The customer is God." Keeping God happy is Shimoda's primary responsibility.

FIERCE LOYALTY

He has been doing so, in one guise or another, since 1970, when he first   10
joined Matsushita. He had spent two years at a small trading company in Tokyo, where he met a young "office lady" who would become his wife. Soon after, he jumped at a chance to join a company that had powered Japan's postwar economic miracle, and he's never looked back. Salarymen of Shimoda's generation, after all, do not job-hop. They are loyal. He is, his wife, Naomi, says matter-of-factly, *"kaisha ningen . . .* such a kaisha ningen."

Kaisha ningen means a company man. In the 1970s, when Japan was desperately trying to overcome the effects of two oil shocks, the white-collar worker came to be known as *"moretsu sarariman"*: the fierce salaryman. Shimoda's two boys were born in the early '70s, but working as a junior manager in the company's import department, he rarely saw them awake. "My husband used to come in long after the children went to bed," his wife recalls. "He was good enough to call in and tell me that he did not need supper. But when he called it was usually 10 or 11 in the evening." Naomi, as all good Japanese wives are supposed to do, would wait, sitting up in the tiny living room of their one-bedroom suburban Tokyo apartment.

In Japan, the company man does what the company wants—and so does his wife. In September of 1980, Shimoda sat in the bath after returning home late one evening, chatting with his wife—"It was the only time we could talk usually," she recalls. "What," her husband asked that night, "do you think about moving to Germany?" Naomi had never been outside Japan in her life. She thought first, she says, about her children. Where would two young Japanese boys go to school in Germany? But a salaryman's wife, too, is kaisha ningen. "I just said I was happy for him," she says.

The following January, Shimoda was traveling all over Western Europe, scouring it for products Matsushita could import back to Japan. It was a time of intensifying trade disputes between Japan and the West, and his company "felt great pressure to do something to relieve the trade imbalance," he recalls. It wasn't easy. While Matsushita flooded the world with consumer electronics, it sent back, thanks to Shimoda, lots of Italian tomatoes. During their ten years in Frankfurt, his wife says, he was on the road one-third of the time. And when he wasn't traveling, he would come back after 10 almost every night to their suburban home. "Unlike other families who say they could get away from the hectic salaryman's life once they were outside Japan, ours got even worse," says Naomi.

It is easy, in the West, to misunderstand this kind of life. Can any Japanese man who leads it really care much about his family? To most Japanese the equation is entirely different; in Japan you lead this kind of life because it provides a sense of security. And you do worry about the consequences. For children, the disruptions an overseas assignment can cause are universal, of course. Shigeo Shimoda's eldest son, Kentaro, then nine, attended his first class in a German school three days after arriving, speaking not a word of the language. But for the children of Japan's salarymen there are dilemmas that are acutely Japanese as well.

In Japan, at the age of fifteen almost everyone takes the single most   15 important test of their lives: a high school entrance exam that, as Shimoda puts it, "can determine your future to a very great extent." Do well and you get into a good high school, and that greatly increases your chances of getting into an elite university. And once in an elite university, passage to an elite company, like Matsushita, is all but assured. Mess it up, though, and you're in trouble. There are no second acts in Japanese life.

Shimoda's two sons attended a Japanese school once a week during their early years in Frankfurt. But as they grew up in Germany, becoming fluent in the language, their parents knew there was going to be a problem. "They were quite behind in their Japanese education since they had no chance to learn science or mathematics in Japanese," Shimoda recalls. He tells the story for a reason: In corporate Japan, tireless work and loyalty do bring rewards beyond a steady paycheck. One day, on a visit back to Tokyo, he met with a "consultant" from the Matsushita personnel department. What high schools was he interested in for his son? "Matsushita people then went down to the school and talked to the teachers and administrators on our behalf," Shimoda says. Kentaro, eager to return, left Frankfurt in 1987 to attend a well-regarded Kyoto high school, where he lived in a school dormitory.

Tough Times

Four years later the parents followed. Shimoda had saluted, gone to Germany and done what was asked of him. In the process, he had caught the eye of one of Matsushita's European managers, Hiroshi Takagi. When he was named director of industrial sales in Tokyo, Takagi wanted Shimoda as one of his managers, partly because he knew he would work hard. In March 1991 Shimoda proudly took his new position in Matsushita's office in central Tokyo. He sat in Japan's open offices, where a *bucho* always sits: back to the windows, facing the people he manages.

But when the Shimodas returned, Japan's notorious "bubble economy"—the frenetic speculation that drove up land and stock prices to outrageous levels—had collapsed. It wasn't clear, however, how bad the aftershocks would be. Tokyo still acted rich—particularly to an expatriate couple just returning home after ten years. "I looked at the prices in stores as if they were an illusion," says Naomi Shimoda. Prime Minister Kiichi Miyazawa would give a speech calling on Japan to become a "life-style superpower." He meant that men like Shimoda should be able to knock it off and take a rest once in a while.

It was a nice thought. But by the middle of last year it became obvious to Shimoda and his colleagues that the good times were gone. Orders from his major customers, like General Electric, had stagnated. For his younger subordinates who are not yet managers, there was an ironic result: They were working less. But that also meant they earned less from overtime, which in good times can account for nearly 30 percent of an average office worker's paycheck.

Matsushita managers who are at Shimoda's level earn the equivalent of about $120,000 per year (an amount that goes a lot farther in the United States than it does in Japan). They are not eligible for overtime. It is part of the ethic of Japanese offices that when times are tough, managers toil longer than ever. Shimoda today leaves his new house—built in part with money borrowed from the company—just before 8. He does not get home much before 11. "Our main concern now is how to increase sales," Shimoda says.

Shimoda and thousands of others like him are now doing the things that are standard operating procedure when the economy slows. Business entertaining—usually four nights a week—is no less frequent, but far less profligate. He now shuns pricey "hostess bars." The customer still gets to take a taxi home after a night of drinking. But Shimoda takes the subway with the other tipsy salarymen.

The subject of the recession, he concedes, comes up in the office often. "We joke, 'you're next, you're next'." But gallows humor this isn't. Shimoda simply doesn't consider the possibility that he, an aging middle manager in

20

a company that needs to cut costs, could become a victim. "I have never imagined or thought of myself being in that position," he says with a smile.

That, in the end, is why Shimoda and his family put up with a lifestyle that seems so alien to Americans. It is why the salaryman works so hard—because in hard times, he expects his loyalty to be returned. It is a faith that doesn't exist anymore in corporate America. Who today at any American company—even the strongest like Intel—would dare say, as Shimoda does: "There is a sort of mental contract between a company and the employee in Japan. I thought once of leaving Matsushita. When the economy was very strong here I thought I could start a business importing European products into Japan. But I thought of what my late father would have said to me. He would have asked, what had I returned to the company? The company has invested a lot in me. It has trained me." It is an inordinate amount of faith, and corporate Japan knows that it can't be easily trifled with. But it is a faith that, recession or no, may not be sustainable in the long run.

Will there be *kaisha ningen* a generation from now? Only the children of today's company men—now getting their first whiff of hard times—know for sure. On a recent Sunday afternoon, Shigeo Shimoda puttered in the small garden in back of his house, something that is, by Tokyo standards, an extraordinary luxury. His sons don't look forward to Sundays, because it's usually cleanup day. "This is the house we all worked so hard to build," Shimoda will say with an enthusiasm that bewilders them. "Let's take care of it!" Kentaro, now a college student studying law, has heard it before. "My father," he says, "is a very diligent and serious man. He is a typical Japanese man. He does what is considered right. Some people say he is a successful businessman working for a top corporation. But do I want to be like him? I think to be a salaryman is the best way if you want to have a stable income, and a stable life." He hesitates. "But for now, I am not sure if I would choose to be one of them."

Tom Hazlett: The Wages of Freedom

The headquarters of Hazlett Associates fills the small, third-floor bedroom of a house in Evanston, Ill. In less prosperous times, the answering machine chirped a message recorded by Tom Hazlett's wife, Jan, giving callers the impression that Tom had an employee. Today there is less desperation. If Hazlett happens to be gulping lunch in the kitchen when clients call, he can grab another of the household's five phones. The Hazletts' three kids then fall silent. Given the shared perils of the last few years, even six-year-old Ellie knows that customers aren't impressed by an executive-search firm that plays the TV loud.

For fifteen years, Tom Hazlett made his way up the rigging of corporate America. Like Shigeo Shimoda, he thrived as the organization man, eventually landing a $90,000-a-year job at an advertising agency. But he wasn't content.

The loyalties that bound people and their companies were coming unglued; today's valued veteran was becoming tomorrow's layoff victim. So Hazlett, seduced by the American notion that being your own boss is best, did what Shimoda never would: He quit his job.

ROLAIDS AND MAALOX

Six years later, Hazlett's gamble seems to have paid off. But it hasn't been easy. He has survived stress attacks and washed down Rolaids with Maalox. To help, Jan began a new career, struggling to sell real estate in the depths of the U.S. recession. When the family's future seemed bleakest, Jan tried to cheer up Tom with a greeting card, a wry advertisement for "Ed's Dump and Croissants." Inside she scribbled, "There are always opportunities." She wasn't wrong. Tom Hazlett's story is a cautionary tale for would-be entrepreneurs. But it's also a glimpse of what's possible in a culture that thrives on personal risk.

Hazlett grew up in Evanston, just west of Northwestern University on Lake Michigan. At the age of eight he worked himself out of his first job, collecting used clothes hangers; the manager of College Cleaners, unable to use the bulging wagonloads Hazlett delivered daily, stopped paying him. After high school he moved on to Amherst College in Massachusetts. For the class of '66 the game plan was simple: You parlayed your education into a lifetime niche, usually with a big corporation or professional firm. After a tour as a naval officer, Hazlett picked up an M.B.A. at Northwestern and took a job in Cincinnati marketing Vanish toilet-bowl cleaner for the Drackett Co.

Tom had met Jan before he moved. She was artsy, more spontaneous. He was quiet and methodical, so much so that Jan called him "P-Squared," for Perfect Person. But he also had integrity and wit. They married in 1973 after her dad warned Tom that Jan had no head for money. She did, though, have the entrepreneurial bent of her father, who owned a dental lab in Indianapolis. She'd heard the sermon as a little girl at the dining-room table: Start your own business.

Hazlett didn't think much about that. He eventually landed at Needham, Harper & Steers, a Chicago ad agency whose triumphs included handing McDonald's the slogan "You deserve a break today!" Needham took care of its own—so much so that when a life-threatening viral disease hobbled Hazlett for six months, his paychecks never stopped. Part of him cherished that paternalism: Had he been working solo, he and Jan might have been wiped out.

But like others whom the threat of death slaps to their senses, Hazlett came back changed. He had less stomach for the office politics and memos. The 1980s preached personal fulfillment, and Hazlett needed a dose. He considered leasing a seat on the Chicago Board of Trade, where the pits sprouted young millionaires. But that was too bold. He jumped instead to Tatham-Laird & Kudner, another blue-chip Chicago agency, where he ran

30

major accounts for the likes of RJR Nabisco. Hazlett stayed for five years, eventually becoming a partner. But by the end, corporate life was unbearable. Even today Hazlett gropes to explain why. It wasn't any one incident. He was a misfit, a mentor who developed younger talent at a time when agencies were turning to star systems. His habit of stepping aside to let subordinates deliver the major presentations they had prepared earned some murmurs of disapproval from his superiors.

Jan, watching the frustration build, parroted her father's sermon: Go into business for yourself. At the same time, he couldn't pick up *Business Week* without seeing some wunderkind in red suspenders. He got star-struck. If others could do it, why not Tom Hazlett? So late in 1986, with a $145,000 mortgage and his third child only a month old, Hazlett quit corporate America and joined a small sales-promotion firm, sure he could become a part owner.

But in all his careful calculations he had overlooked his greatest weakness. Because he didn't know how to sell himself without the corporate trappings, he didn't attract as much business as he'd hoped. It was as if his lifelong preparation—the right schools, the right companies—had suddenly abandoned him. "I had only paid lip service to the possibility of failure," he says.

So he decided to quit and switch careers altogether. The onetime mentor who enjoyed bringing subordinates along would take up executive search, a field that had always interested him for its emphasis on people. He learned the business by working at two small Chicago firms. But by late 1990 the corporate bloodbath he had barely escaped was hurting the search industry. The firms that had wanted him no longer needed him. Hazlett, reasoning that a nation with 2,000 struggling search firms could use one more, set up shop.

"COOL" MATCHMAKER

The Hazletts were now on their own. Jan was trying to jump-start a career   35
in real estate. Tom flooded the mails with announcements of his new business. He positioned himself as the cool, investigative matchmaker who would work intensely on a small number of searches. For months Hazlett didn't have a client. Independence quickly became a blessing he could barely endure. He would awaken at 4:30 A.M., frantic for someone to offer him a job, yet confident that with the nation's economy so miserable, no one would bother. At night, after the kids went to bed, he and Jan would try to sort it out.

With both income streams slowed to a trickle, they seemed to be balancing the checkbook every hour. They sold their house and moved to the one they're now renting. They also slashed spending: A week at a friend's house in Wisconsin replaced skiing vacations to Colorado. Still they continued to deplete their reserves. As the noose tightened, Jan couldn't shake questions unthinkable back when Tom was an organization man. Will our kids sell apples on the street?

Jan, at least, could flee to a busy broker's office. Tom worked alone, sitting in the third-floor office, sifting through a rising tide of résumés. With time—a commodity in alarmingly plentiful supply—he honed his sales pitch: I'm not like the big search firms. You're looking at the person who will do the work—which usually starts with about a hundred telephone calls. Some jobs trickled in. Greg Jiede, general manager of TeleAmerica, a marketer, needed an account executive. Hazlett risked Jiede's ire by rewriting the job description and requirements. But Jiede liked all four of Hazlett's finalists and hired one of them.

As his business blossomed, Hazlett's workday lost the rhythm of his years as a salaryman. Telephone calls now start as early as 6 A.M. and alternate with correspondence, searches of databases, and trips to Chicago's Union League Club, an exclusive enclave that is his surrogate office. More calls dribble into the evening; the toughest involve telling job finalists that they were just that. At night he spends another solitary stretch, organizing the next day. His foes are the casual telephone chat and the extra cup of coffee over the sports section: If he doesn't discipline himself, no one will.

The rhythms of the Hazletts' family life have changed as well. Old roles have begun to reverse: As Jan's career pulls her away from the house, often, it is Tom who drives the morning car pool, starts dinner, and hangs up Ellie's wet swimsuit. At times he's envious of Jan. "There's a collegial nature to her office that I miss," he says. But Hazlett enjoys the new responsibilities; his children are more a part of his life than before. Still, balancing work and home hasn't grown any easier. "I made the decision that my family is my top priority," he says. "But sometimes I feel guilty. When I'm driving Jeff to soccer practice, should I be making more phone calls?"

Guilt aside, the future looks bright. Hazlett's goal is at least a dozen searches a year; right now he's working on seven, and the rebounding U.S. economy should bring more. After a dismal 1991, the couple's income last year approached the salary Tom abandoned in 1986. This year they should easily exceed it. Still, Tom's business isn't as stable as he wants. "I can't yet say it's irretrievably panned out," he says.

The closest Hazlett comes to the silken safety net beneath his Japanese counterpart, Shimoda, is a new support group of eight businessmen, all refugees from corporate America. They meet monthly and call themselves the Lost Boys. They talk out one another's dilemmas and swap names of potential clients. It's not like life at Matsushita, but then, neither is the personal pride Hazlett brings away from each lunch. "I know my business is starting to grow—and it's *my* business," he says. "If I correctly understand the Japanese, this is the essential difference in our mind-sets. I am alone. I've hit a couple of walls, but I'm not going to stop until I get through the next one. Not now."

Until recently, Shimoda's way looked like a key to Japan's economic surge. Now that rigidity may hamstring its ability to recover. Meanwhile, Hazlett's rocky, but successful, transition shows the adaptability Americans

40

must display if they're to remake the U.S. economy for the twenty-first century. Over the long haul, which country will benefit most? Perhaps the one that combines the best traits of both men: retaining some sense of corporate loyalty, without losing the courage to take risks.

Thinking About the Text

1. Does the opening paragraph—a single sentence—gain your interest? What rhetorical devices are Powell, Takayama, and McCormick using?

2. In paragraph 30 we are told that Tom Hazlett's employer, an advertising agency, "took care of its own—so much so that when a life-threatening viral disease hobbled Hazlett for six months, his paychecks never stopped." Nevertheless, not many years later Hazlett "jumped" (para. 31) to another advertising agency. Assuming that the company had continued to treat him fairly, do you think he owed it to the company to remain rather than to move to a competitor? (Consider not only this particular case, whose details we know nothing about, but also the general idea.)

3. Write a similar narrative, though of only 500–750 words, sketching the histories of two approximately comparable people who live different kinds of lives.

4. Do the authors present the two men (and the two systems) impartially, or do you think that the article as a whole favors one? Explain.

Thinking About Culture

5. In the next-to-last paragraph the writer speaks of Hazlett's "personal pride" and quotes Hazlett: " 'I know my business is starting to grow—and it's *my* business,' he says." Hazlett's pride is understandable, but can we argue that someone might take comparable pride in being part of a large business? After all, we can take pride in our families, in our schools, in our religions. We hear, for instance, professional military people say that they are proud to serve in their country's armed forces. Can you conceive of taking comparable pride in a business?

Chapter 8

Leisure and Entertainment

Researchers and officials at Japan's Leisure Research and Development Center, a government agency, have been working day and night to get people to take more time off from work and spend that time (and money) on recreational activities. These efforts have not borne much fruit, despite the growing number of leisure attractions—some of which are described by Gayle Hanson (p. 288). Corporate employees still hesitate to take more than a few days of vacation at a time, rarely use the full two weeks allotted them, and when they do have time off, tend to spend it prone, watching television and sleeping.

In spite of these unpromising conditions, the Japanese entertainment industry is very big business indeed. One need only look to Tokyo Disneyland—as Pico Iyer (p. 307) does—to behold a nation hungry (and willing to pay lavishly) for fun. Spectator sports such as baseball and *sumo* are very popular, and a new phenomenon, the J League (soccer), has led the field in the past two years, promising to be bigger than baseball. Baseball, introduced in Japan in 1935, hit its stride after World War II, and now games are as highly attended, and players as lionized, as in America. Baseball teams are usually sponsored by major companies, as in the Hanshin Tigers and the Yomiuri Giants (railway and newspaper companies), and the Yakult Swallows and Nippon Ham Fighters (manufacturers of health foods and pork products). The two pro baseball leagues, the Central and the Pacific, play their annual "Japan Series" at about the same time as the American World Series, in October—and the whole country watches.

There are some differences between American and Japanese baseball, and these are encountered with varying degrees of amusement and discomfort by the many American players hired by Japanese teams. Michael Shapiro's article (p. 300) highlights these features, such as the omnipresent bunt, the games that end in ties, and the fact that, as the American humorist Dave Barry has said, "the game [is] somewhat less exciting than the cheerleaders." Cheers, by the way, reach their peak of excitement in such lines as "Storm clouds penetrated by balls to the star of victory! O

Giants with honorable name—Grow! Our Team! Brave and heroic! Giants! Giants! Go! Go! Heroes!"

Baseball and other spectator sports in both America and Japan create expert audiences, participant-observers who pride themselves on their extensive, and ever-expanding, knowledge of the players and of the history of the sport. These lay authorities know that being a spectator need not mean being passive. Baseball promotes active membership in fandom, and this involves a notion of regionalism, of local identity, even now when the teams have long since abandoned the idea of local recruitment of players. Loyalty can be invoked on a national level as well, as baseball has become a sentimental icon of America, along with apple pie, the flag, and Mom.

The long, hot baseball games of summer are in striking contrast to the ceremonious, but dramatic, seconds-long bouts of traditional wrestling called *sumo*. No one knows when *sumo* began in Japan, but it has been on the scene for at least 2,000 years. It seems more like a ritual than a sport, and its competitions and passions are played out in the context of a very rigid, feudal hierarchy. A few years ago, when a young star unaccountably struck his master, he was forced to resign and after a long series of discussions, Japan Sumo Association officials decided that this transgression was ultimately their responsibility and themselves took pay cuts for "allowing" such a flagrant flouting of the sport's Confucian code of respect and obedience to occur. (Clyde Haberman examines this incident in Chapter 11, "Notions of Nation," on p. 409.)

What happens in a *sumo* match? Oversimplifying: not much. Two very large men, often tipping the scales at 400–500 pounds, square off in a round ring, stomp and lunge at each other, trying to get the other to step or fall out of the ring. They can grab, shove, lift, and hit—almost anywhere—and the moves are well known by fans, who call out approvingly in the few seconds it takes for one man to fell the other. The rankings are front-page news all over Japan, and the leading wrestlers in the top division become popular heroes, even idols for young women. One of the most popular *sumo* wrestlers was recently engaged to the leading soft-porn model superstar, and their relationship was very much a public affair. It was called off, however, and one of the reasons cited was that the young woman would be too much of a distraction to the wrestler's dedication to the art of *sumo*.

The world of mass sports in Japan changes rapidly, in spite of the fact that *sumo* (and other ancient sports, including traditional archery) persist in their popularity. The J League, Japan's first professional soccer league, begun in 1993, is a stunning example. Soccer now overshadows baseball among young people, who are fans and increasingly players. In 1992, for example, about 7,000 teams participated in the soccer equivalent of the Little League, compared with 3,000 in Japan's Little League baseball. J League tickets are all but impossible to get, selling out far in advance of games. Fans seem pleased with the fast pace, which makes soccer games far more exciting than baseball. Young soccer players tend to exhibit their individuality in odd hairstyles and even pierced ears, while baseball teams seem to homogenize their players. And of course, marketing (as in America) supports the craze; caps, flags, towels, and other logo-emblazoned gear sell well.

Other leisure activities are more regularly part of people's lives, not requiring much planning or time, or incorporated into work life as nearly compulsory after-hours recreation. For example, visits to bars and restaurants, part of the enormous *mizu shobai* (water trade) industry, are important aspects of the corporate, white-collar worker's life. There are, as June Kinoshita and Nicholas Palevsky (p. 310) describe, a range of after-hours clubs and bars, varying by style and cost. The role of the bar hostess is particularly important in soothing the cares of the businessman who is a regular at her bar, puffing up his ego, and impressing his colleagues and clients. Such hostesses, especially at the high-class bars, are not necessarily prostitutes, but entertainers, in a continuum with the more refined and traditional art of the *geisha*. *Karaoke* bars are also popular places allowing participants to perform songs accompanied by recorded music and be applauded, no matter how unskilled they are. (Anne Allison's study on p. 314 provides a close look into the world of hostess clubs and *karaoke* bars.)

For cheaper, less time-consuming relief and escape, comic books and television are very popular. Comic books reach nearly everyone; there are comics *(manga)* targeted at small children and comics targeted at graying businessmen. Most feature action and fantasy and appear weekly. The hottest selling weekly, *Shonen Jump,* sells up to five million copies per week and is noted for its action strips drawn by star cartoonists, who have their own fan clubs, like pop singers.

There are girls' *manga,* filled with romantic fantasy and humor, and boys', filled with action and sports. Some *manga* are very violent, even by American standards, and some are pornographic. In recent years, grass-roots "mothers' groups" have lobbied to restrict publishers from, if nothing else, the cover display of pornographic contents in *manga*.

The most popular leisure activity reported among working adults is sleeping or watching television. As Mark Schilling reveals (p. 324), the television set, in many Japanese homes, is always on as long as someone is at home. Daytime soap operas ("home dramas") are very popular, and not just among housewives. There is one that consistently grabs top audience ratings: the 8:15 A.M. dramatic series (repeated at noon), which runs for six months to a year. It is always a well-acted, compelling tearjerker, often historical, but usually set in this century, and often the lead character is a woman. Variety shows with singers, outrageous hosts, and other performers, including Japanese-speaking foreigners (called *gaijin tarento,* or "foreign talent"), are very popular. At the end of the year, many top singers and performers, divided into two teams (like the teams of a school sports day), compete in a spectacular face-off of singing and dancing to determine the year's best. And of course, there are cartoons, not just for children, but including sitcom family cartoons, as well as action and science-fiction cartoon shows. TV fare, in other words, is not all that different from the American television menu.

Shopping comes in second, after couch-potato activity, as a use of leisure time. In cities, the central shopping districts are often made into pedestrian malls on Sundays by closing the streets to vehicles. This allows large numbers of families, groups of friends, and couples on dates to mill about—not necessarily with shopping in mind. As we will see in Chapter 9, consumer industries are aware of the entertainment aspect of shopping, and department stores are attractive and stimulating places to spend time.

The simple reduction of work hours will not send more people to the beaches in summer or on long ski vacations in winter. The leisure industries are persistent and successful at marketing state-of-the-art equipment for such activities and even creating the environments themselves. Recently, the world's only year-round, indoor ski slope was created in the Tokyo area, complete with snowmaking machines and chair lifts, and Wild Blue Yokohama features a variety of indoor waves simulating the South Seas and other locales for swimming. But the more time-limited and less-expensive leisure pastimes—such as *sumo*, baseball, and soccer—provide excitement and a cathartic release, a sense of "event" for spectators as well as a reason for spending a little of their savings on something to remember their free time by.

Explorations

1. What spectator sports do you follow? Christopher Lasch, an American historian, notes that "players not only compete; they enact a familiar ceremony that reaffirms common values." What common values are exhibited (or reaffirmed) in the sports that interest you?

2. An American was once told by a Japanese bar hostess that "Americans hate performing *karaoke*; they are so worried that they will do badly—but Japanese don't care at all." Why might this be true?

3. Americans are said to "work to live," while a common stereotype about Japanese is that they "live to work." Explain these generalizations and enumerate how these statements may be true or untrue for different segments of each population.

Gayle Hanson

Japan at Play

Outside the biannual Tokyo Motorcycle Show, the *bosozoku*° boys buzz through the streets like a swarm of mosquitoes. All red-leather jumpsuits and attitude, they gun their Yamahas and Kawasakis, the better to instill fear and admiration in the throng around the exhibition hall.

Makoto Matsushita isn't buying any of it.

"Rice burners," he says with scorn, taking the final pull on an Asahi World Beat beer and crushing the can with his boot heel. "Damn rice burners." His half-dozen companions laugh in agreement, and it's easy to see why. Lined up at the curb are six of the finest looking Harley-Davidsons that ever left stateside.

"Oh, Japanese bikes are better than Harleys," Matsushita claims with a sly grin. "But with a Harley-Davidson you are getting more than a motorcycle. What you're getting is freedom."

There's a lot of talk in Tokyo about the "big one," the mother of all earthquakes that will shake this city to its foundations. The truth is, a whole lotta shaking is already going on. You can see the shock waves in the Chanel-suited techno-geisha flexing her charge cards in the Ginza's ultrachic boutiques, the samurai-salaryman locked in nightly combat in the pachinko° parlors, the Harley-Davidson fans rhapsodizing about freedom, and the Tokyo Disneyland enthusiasts flocking to partake of American fantasies—in sum, all the Japanese who have decided that life is about spending and not just saving, playing and not just working.

It's as though after forty years of corporate calisthenics, during which Japan pumped its way to the top of the international money markets, the nation has stopped at the watercooler to ask itself, "Are we having fun yet?" Japan is hurtling toward the twenty-first century with one eye on the plunging stock market, an ear tuned to the cacophonous sounds of rap, and both hands grasped around the handlebars of a Harley-Davidson sportster.

And on this front of the trade wars, at least, America has achieved a partial victory. For when it comes to learning the fine art of fun there's little sweeter to the Japanese than the words "made in the U.S.A." Japan today is still sumo and sushi,° the sublime elegance of the tea ceremony and the haunting melody of the samisen.° But it is also Paris couture, Italian shoes

5

bosozoku: Bikers.   **pachinko:** Pinball gambling machines.   **sushi:** Rice seasoned with vinegar, then shaped and topped with fish or seaweed.   **samisen:** An instrument resembling a banjo. [All notes are the editors'.]

Gayle Hanson is a staff writer for Insight on the News *magazine, where this article appeared on April 27, 1992.*

and California cuisine, Mickey Mouse and McDonald's McChao, L. L. Bean and Levi Strauss, an island nation where the Blues Brothers and Brooks Brothers collide in a pressure-cooked stew flavored with distinctly American seasonings.

That's not to say that everyone embraces this cultural miscegenation, or that tradition-bound Japan is throwing off its kimono in favor of sweats. But a new generation raised in the affluence of the seventies and eighties is asking unprecedented questions about the individual cost of national success.

Atsuki Onaga's work is play. Well, at least the study of it.

On the ninth-floor offices of the government-funded Leisure Research   10
and Development Center, Onaga and his colleagues have spent the past two decades monitoring the rise of a leisure culture in Japan. Their task is to assist both the public and private sectors in understanding the myriad ways the population seeks to entertain itself.

As befits their edict, the center's staff members take a more leisurely approach to their work than the average Japanese salaryman. There's not a blue suit in sight at playtime central, and Onaga himself has an impish grin that belies the enormity of his think tank's task.

"We began in 1972," he says. "The Ministry of International Trade and Industry and fifty private companies got together and decided to fund the center. At the outset we knew that the most pressing need for the future was to teach the Japanese how important leisure is."

The goal was set with the recognition that as Japan prospered, disposable income would increase. In 1973 the center began what was to become an annual survey of leisure activities. The survey asks some 4,000 residents age fifteen and over their attitudes toward leisure and how they spend their free time. Not surprisingly, in twenty years there has been an enormous shift in attitudes toward work and play.

"It was very difficult at the start," says Onaga. "As a culture we have been oriented toward work. But the realization came that we were working far more than other countries. And we knew that we would have to reduce our work hours. But there has been a lot of resistance. Particularly at first. When we went to corporations and talked to them about reducing work hours they would agree and say it was a fine idea. But the employees didn't want to stop working. We realized that we basically had to change the minds of the people."

In 1987, when Onaga visited the United States to study working condi-   15
tions, he was surprised to find that many U.S. corporations were familiar with Japan's problem. "I was amazed at how much they knew," says Onaga. "They were aware that we don't take paid holidays and vacations even when they are due us. But they also understood that many Japanese were eager to make as much money as possible because their life-style was so low." Unspoken by Onaga is the fact that many U.S. businesses, and the U.S. government, were all for increased Japanese leisure on the theory that this would eventually

mean Japan would consume more American goods and export fewer of its own, hence lowering the U.S. trade deficit.

After Onaga returned home, the center recommended to the government a fundamental change in Japanese habits. Its advice: Stop working so hard. The proposal became law and the workweek was officially shortened from forty-eight to forty hours. "In 1988," says Onaga, "we began the move to a two-day weekly holiday one week, alternating with a one-and-a-half-day break." Translation: Japan discovered the weekend.

How much the directions from the top have changed the hours people actually work is an open question. About half of Japan's large corporations have adopted the plan, according to Onaga, and by the end of the decade all will have complied. But workers are still free to impress their bosses by staying past the official hours. Still, Onaga is optimistic. "Naturally we found at first that young guys and girls wanted more free time than money," he says, laughing. "But things have changed dramatically in the past two years and now even the middle-aged businessman wants to live freely." By the end of the decade, he says, "we hope to have one day off for every two days worked."

Even discounting for the enthusiasm of officials whose job it is to promote leisure, Japan is clearly no longer the nation of workaholics that once loomed ominously in the American imagination. But by the same token, it's equally clear that old habits die hard. The distinction between leisure and work is sometimes a slippery one in Japan. Leisure, from a certain point of view, is just another market, to be studied, sized up, and mastered through strategic plans. Onaga, for example, says fears that Japan's economic bubble is bursting have slowed leisure developments at least temporarily, and that has caused some concern at the center.

"You can't just have people sitting around and watching television or doing nothing," he says. "Such inactivity can lead to social problems and unrest. What people need are meaningful and healthy activities in their lives. We have to think about developing a field for play so that all the population, and not just the wealthy, have access to leisure facilities. We have begun that process but it won't be completed until the twenty-first century."

And what does Onaga himself do for leisure-time relaxation?

"I work," he says slyly.

20

It's a Sunday afternoon at Tokyo Disneyland. Whether the rides qualify as Onaga's meaningful and healthy activities is not clear, but the people are lined up to find out—the wait is more than two hours for Space Mountain, just under two hours for Big Thunder Mountain.

The pizza line is an hour long, but the Party-Gras parade is only minutes away. Thousands of onlookers line the streets as a surreal vision floats into focus. Hundreds of elaborately costumed American and Japanese youths are dancing through Tomorrowland in a conga line. The music is Brazilian samba. The lyrics are Japanese. Only the chorus and characters seem familiar.

And then they appear, lighter than air and wafting above the crowd in all their inflatable glory. First Minnie Miranda, Carmen's rodent cousin, dances into sight, a fruit-topped hat perched precariously on her head. Seconds later Mambo Mickey pops into view, doing what appears to be a solo version of the lambada. It just goes to prove that when you rule the kingdom you can party all the time.

This is a cat and mouse story. The mouse is Mickey, and the cat is his   25
Japanese cartoon counterpart—a warm and fuzzy, white-furred critter called Hello Kitty, whose name, face, and perky ears can be seen from one end of Japan to the other in comic books, on television, and on merchandise ranging from bubble bath to backpacks.

This is also the tale of two theme parks, Sanrio Puroland and Tokyo Disneyland, home to the cat and mouse, and the background to a larger battle for the hearts, minds, and yen of the fun-seeking Japanese public.

It has been said that the opening of Tokyo Disneyland in 1983 was the single most important cultural event in late twentieth-century Japan. From his patch of reclaimed land in Tokyo Bay, a mere eight miles from the city's center, the little black mouse roars with a voice that has echoed through every stratum of Japanese society. Theme park fever has spread to even the most isolated regions of the country. But nobody has caught the mouse, or even come close.

The first thing to know about Tokyo Disneyland is that it is owned— lock, stock, and Goofy's ears—by a Japanese real estate conglomerate, the Oriental Land Co., in essence a franchise that must pay annual monetary homage to the home office in Burbank, Calif. The rides, shows, and parades, however, all have their origin at Disney headquarters. If the Japanese provide the yen that run the machine, the blueprints were drawn by Americans. Naysayers claimed that the Japanese would never be drawn to so foreign a notion of fun, but the skeptics, quite obviously, were wrong.

"We had our first 10 million visitors within less than a year of opening," says Toshiro Akiba, a senior officer with Tokyo Disneyland. "That's even better than they did at Disney World during their first year. We hit 100 million visitors last year. So we are definitely doing very well."

Visitors to Tokyo Disneyland spend an average of $75 for the three   30
T's—tickets, trinkets, and treats—plus the opportunity to wait in line for hours, stroll through a litter-free environment, and hobnob with some of celluloid's most notable characters. With some 15 million visitors a year, the numbers quickly reach the size beloved by accountants, bankers, and investors. So it's little wonder that the Japanese have jumped on the theme park bandwagon with a vengeance. In 1990 there were more than two hundred permits pending for park developments across the country. But not everybody has the magic touch.

On the surface Shintaro Tsuji would appear to have such a touch. The septuagenarian founder of Japanese media giant Sanrio Ltd., Tsuji not only had the yen to build a theme park, but as the creator of Hello Kitty he appeared to be in the running for the title of the Japanese Walt Disney.

Sanrio broke ground in 1987 for its indoor theme park (designed by an American company, Los Angeles's Landmark Entertainment Group). In December 1990, Puroland threw open the doors. But the crowds have yet to materialize; in its first year, 2.2 million people visited the park sixty miles from Tokyo.

Despite the disappointing launch, Sanrio executives are putting on a happy face. "What we tried to do here was create a fun environment that was like a festival," says Managing Director Makoto Sato. "When you look at Disneyland, the theme is America; what we wanted for Puroland was the theme of communications. We also didn't want to rely too heavily on things we had created in the past, like Hello Kitty. We were looking for something new. But after the park opened we realized we needed more of a blend."

The communications theme of the park is not communicated particularly well. There is only one major ride, the Puroland boat trip, a water cruise through a land peopled by bobbing elves and reeking of various artificial scents. There are several theater shows, including a heart-stopping 3-D computer-animated journey into time and space; the film is less than five minutes long, though, with a twenty-minute introduction. And Puroland's attempts to create an aura of fantasy are doomed by first impressions— visitors descend into its depths on an escalator. Is this a shopping mall? Well, yes, in a manner of speaking.

Among the changes Sato envisions is an increased profile for Hello   35
Kitty and other Sanrio cartoon characters. With the confidence that only deep pockets can provide, Sanrio will spend several years tinkering with Puroland, adding more rides and interactive amusements that the company hopes will attract a larger audience including more teenagers.

If Puroland doesn't share the same level of success as Disneyland, both parks share a similar challenge—attracting the elusive audience of teenage males. Puroland is a haunt for young families; Disneyland's audience is made up largely of young women, some of whom manage to drag their boyfriends along.

In their quest for the yen of young men, both parks might learn a lesson from Namco's Wonder Eggs, a small entertainment center that opened in February on the outskirts of Tokyo. Designed around an open plaza, the center in some ways harks back to the small amusement parks that used to dot America's seaside cities.

There is something for everyone in the family, including carnival games, carousels, and fast-food stands. There are also attractions that are peculiarly Japanese, including a photo booth where young women can have their pictures taken in a variety of wedding gowns.

But the biggest draw at this fledgling interloper is the arcade of virtual reality games, the hottest concept since video games invaded and gobbled up the pinball market. The best of them provide the thrills of genuine adventure and none of the risks. The only thing you stand to lose playing Sim-Road is your lunch.

Sim-Road is the first arcade race game to use a real automobile. Players   40 and their passengers sit inside a Mazda Miata and pit themselves against a winding racecourse that is projected on the three wraparound screens that surround them. The course is demanding in the extreme, with hairpin turns that could destroy the confidence of Grand Prix drivers.

"It is unbelievable," says young Yoshi Takahora, who tumbles out of the red sports car after a particularly harrowing run. His girlfriend, Yukiko, who went along for the ride, looks slightly less enamored. "It is too exciting," she says.

Wonder Eggs may not have the midnight thrills of Disney's Space Mountain, but it does have its own variation—a dark journey into a land of demons, where patrons shoot monsters with laser guns. The number of direct hits is displayed on computer screens in the cars that ferry combatants through the abyss. There are no prizes except the satisfaction of knowing you've beaten the devil.

And there's more. Road Race allows video race car drivers to go head-to-head, with a commentator calling the action for spectators watching on an overhead television monitor. Phantomers, another group game, offers competing players the opportunity to shoot 3-D electronic images. Who needs cartoon characters when you can zap space aliens with stun guns, or a reasonable facsimile.

After only a month Wonder Eggs was a virtual hit. On a sunny weekday afternoon there were thirty- to forty-minute lines at the most popular games. Of course, this gives the girlfriends plenty of time to try on that veil, while their young swains battle enemies from outer space or go once around the track at Le Mans.

Namco has also found a unique way to monitor the popularity of its attractions. Unlike Disneyland, which prides itself on the fact that there are no vending machines inside its gates, the entire ticketing system at Wonder Eggs is computerized and automated.

As visitors wend their way from attraction to attraction they insert a pass into a ticket machine that immediately deducts the cost of each game or ride and notes the time it was used. This gives the folks at Namco plenty of opportunity to finetune their game business while counting the profits.

So let this be a warning to the cat and mouse. The word is out. The Eggs have hatched.

Aaron Narikiyo probably doesn't fit the Japanese government's notion of a leisure development. For one thing, his capital requirements are minimal—just enough for some jewelry, American clothes, and grease for his hair. "Aaron Narikiyo," says Kosuzu Mao, his manager, "is the No. 1 Elvis impersonator in Japan."

Bleached blond and dressed in blue silk, with Colonel Parker's° attitude

---

Colonel Parker: Elvis Presley's manager.

if not his appearance, Mao tosses her head toward the corner of the lounge to indicate a shadowy profile: "He'd really like to sing tonight, but . . . I just don't know if he's got enough time. He really should be going."

It's after midnight in Pub Elvis, a fourth-floor joint in Tokyo with all the familial ambience of a basement rec room. That is, if the family in question consisted entirely of rabid Elvis Presley fans. Mirrors, memorabilia, and an impenetrable cloud of cigarette smoke provide the atmosphere.

The government counts dining out, which includes drinking and dancing out, as the No. 1 leisure activity in Japan, where there is one restaurant for every four citizens. The market caters to all tastes, as is evident at Pub Elvis.

Suddenly, there he is. The King. Elvis-san.

Narikiyo wears an American flag shirt and hefts a bottle of Bud. His heavy bracelets jangle as he proffers a hand weighted with jewelry. He runs his fingers through a glistening pompadour; dimples punctuate his ever-so-shy smile. "Very pleased to meet you, little lady," he drawls.

He is speaking Japanese with a Memphis accent. No, it's English with a Japanese accent and Memphis attitude. Whatever. He can walk the walk and talk the talk.

"We'd like to do a little song for you," he says, nodding to include his dapper backup singers, Kenji Koyama and Hiroshi Ishikawa. "We'd like to sing 'Burnin' Love.' "

The room parts as the three men make their way to the microphone. Under the glare of the spotlight, Elvis Narikiyo and his boys belt out the tune in perfect synchronization with a videotape of the Ur-Elvis on an overhead screen. The crowd is transported. The entire audience jabs fists in the air and shouts the chorus in unison: "A hunka hunka . . ."

The song ends. The video screen goes dark. Narikiyo saunters back through his fans. "Thank you," he tells one and all. "Thank you very much."

While another sing-along Elvis croons "Love Me Tender" in the background, Narikiyo divulges his tale. "I fell in love with Elvis when I was just a kid," he says. "I was thirteen years old [in 1968] and loved the music. He has so much feeling he is like a god to me. I even named my daughter Lisa."

He pauses, sips, sighs. "On the day Elvis died I was with some friends and we were sitting around playing guitars and singing his songs. Someone walked in the room and said the King was gone. Well, we just sat there for the rest of the night playing his music — 'Hound Dog,' 'Blue Suede Shoes.' "

Seven years after Presley's death Narikiyo took up the King's mantle, mastering every nuance. It's not a living — Narikiyo admits to a day job as an art teacher — but it's clearly his passion. He tells of his planned August foray to Graceland to honor the fifteenth anniversary of Presley's death. He's already performed successfully in Hawaii — manager Mao hands around candid snapshots capturing him in midperformance, white suit glowing against a background of orchid plants and palm trees. And he hopes he'll get the chance to strut his stuff during his visit to Memphis.

As for Colonel Mao, well, she sees America as one big Pub Elvis, ripe and ready for the arrival of Nippon's heir to the throne. "You know," she says, "he is exactly the same size as Elvis. His chest measurement is the same. His waist is the same. There's only one thing . . . his legs are shorter."

The pub's patrons eagerly advance their own opinions about the King, pop music, and America in general. "I was in high school when Elvis made his big comeback," says forty-four-year-old Miyazaki Yoshi, a financial analyst who by his own reckoning comes to Pub Elvis three or four times a week. "But I like the early Elvis the best. He was a warrior then, like a samurai. He had great, great power. But Elvis was not the greatest American pop singer," he adds, staring intently. "The greatest American pop singer was Connie Francis."

"No, no," another voice chimes—and the debate takes off.

Japan sees American images, hears American music, and plays American games, but it does so through its own set of filters. A debate about the relative merits of Connie Francis and Elvis Presley makes perfect sense in Tokyo, where the aesthetic nuances of a teacup can enliven hours of discussion.

Many Japanese are obsessed with their idea of America in the Eisenhower era. From the dozens of black-jeaned young men who dance intricate routines to rockabilly music blasting out of loudspeakers each Sunday in Yoyogi Park, to the denizens of Pub Elvis, their identification is also touching. They may work sixty hours a week, but on their weekends they long to identify with the rebel spirits of Marlon Brando and James Dean. If General Motors truly wants to sell cars to the Japanese, they'll build replicas of 1959 Caddies.

But not everyone is looking back. Miles and generations away from the Pub Elvis, in the heart of Roppongi, Tokyo's nightclub district, the Bronxification of a generation of young Japanese is proceeding apace. In the basement of a nightclub called Droopy Drawers, amidst megadecibels and smoke machines, M. C. Muro and the Krush Posse hold sway, scratching and rapping their way through a tune called "Concrete Jungle."

The rhymes are untranslatable, but not the sentiments. The dance floor throbs with individuals whose only partner is the reflection in the wall-sized mirror. Up in the deejay's booth, Muro raps while D. J. Krush and D. J. Go scratch sounds and sample riffs from the LPs spinning on twin turntables. After the conclusion of "Jungle," they segue into "Heisei Period,"° a postmodern anthem about the materialism of young Japanese. As the audience gives itself over to the rhythm, the politics of the song seem subsumed by the beat.

"Often it seems as though they do not understand the meaning of the lyrics," Krush comments afterward. "We hope someday to make them understand."

M. C. Muro is a Buddha-faced twenty-two-year-old who fronts the group and writes the lyrics. Krush, at twenty-seven, is the elder statesman.

Heisei Period: "The Age of Peace" (the name of the period beginning with the reign of the present emperor).

Reared on the soul sounds of James Brown, he sees the posse's rap as political but distinct from that of U.S. rappers.

"We are very interested in doing political music," he says. "But because of the difference in American and Japanese cultures, we say different things. For example, discrimination and racism are not the problems here they are in America. And Japan, compared to America, is a very safe country. People are happy here and have everything they need so we take that situation and talk about that. We rap about there being too much happiness and too many material goods around us." 70

With one record under their belt and a weekly gig hosting a cable television program called *Funky Tomato*, Krush Posse seem to be on the brink of major success. Their shows are packed. But while intrigued by the possibility of success, they are ambivalent, as might be expected from foes of commercialism suddenly threatened by commercial glory.

"Break dance was very big for a while and then the record industry people got a hold of it and pffft . . . it was gone," says Krush. "At the moment Japan is in the middle of a dance boom, and we would like to make a rap boom from that. Something that wouldn't be just another trend."

The guys would also like to tour the United States, and look forward to the day when they can get down with the homeboys on their home turf. Asked how they plan to get their message over on the mean streets of New York, the answer is obvious to them. "The first thing I'll do is pick up a microphone and start to rap," says Muro.

Young dreams have a way of disappearing in the haze of middle age. Do they ever see themselves becoming Krush Posse Salarymen?

"Never," says Krush, laughing. 75

The stereotype of the Japanese salaryman, the economic worker bee whose only waking thought is improving the hive, is only partly justified. Sure, there are millions of blue-suited men who travel hours on the train each day in order to work long hours at their jobs. But plenty of their counterparts can be found in Westchester, N.Y., or Grosse Pointe, Mich., Chicago, or L.A., anywhere around the globe, in fact, where capitalism reigns and a young guy with get-up-and-go is trying to do just that.

The operative word is "guy." Japan remains a country in which the majority of women of working age do not pursue careers outside the home after marrying. View the salaryman's life-style—long hours at the desk followed by songfests and drinking bouts—through the same lens as a college fraternity or fraternal club and it is considerably less foreign.

The Japanese are ambivalent about their salarymen. On the one hand, the popular culture now recognizes the concept of overwork, once a foreign notion. Indeed, *karoshi*, death from overwork, is the buzzword of the nineties in Tokyo. On the other hand, there are fears that this leisure thing could be carried too far—that the secret of Japan's success may be endangered as the self-sacrificing, single-minded careerist becomes an object of pity or ridicule, rather than an ideal to admire and emulate.

When Japanese politicians accuse American workers of being lazy and without a work ethic, they may not simply be scoring political points with the voters. Laziness in their own work force is a growing fear. As the nation's leisure culture develops, what will happen if it's too successful and the salarymen break out of lockstep uniformity?

A stroll through downtown Tokyo on a pleasant spring afternoon will catch countless workers on so-called off-time napping in the sun. If it's raining, they'll be in the local pachinko parlor. It might be the middle of the afternoon, but there are plenty of salarymen pouring hundred yen pieces (about 75 cents) into machines with names like "Panic" and "Halloween." If pachinko looks like the ultimate in mind-numbing activity, like the cliché of the salaryman it is more complicated than it first appears.

A sort of vertical pinball machine, pachinko was invented in the United States and brought to Japan in the 1920s. It may be the most popular mass entertainment in Japan. Official estimates, which everyone assumes are deliberately low, are that more than 30 million people play pachinko and that the industry rakes in hundreds of millions of dollars a year.

When the ball bearings bounce down through the pegs the right way, the machine pays off in more ball bearings. These can be redeemed for tickets, which, in theory, are exchanged for detergent, lighter fluid, or other products.

Actually, however, there is a thriving secondary market of cash payments for the tickets. It's technically illegal to trade the tickets for cash, but this particular national pastime has been going on for decades. The closest equivalent in the United States would be slot machines.

"Pachinko may be listed as the fourth-most-favorite form of entertainment," says a government official who asks to remain unnamed, since officially the game is not supposed to be that popular. "But at least part of the time that people say that they are out dining in restaurants or going for drives in the country [the top two entertainments]—well, they're probably playing pachinko."

A district called Kabuchiko, to the side of Tokyo's commercial hub, has been the center of Japan's adult-oriented entertainment since the fourteenth century. Hawkers and hookers are everywhere, as are high school girls out for a night on the town and sweethearts meeting for quick couplings in the district's many pink-painted love hotels. With a quick turn around the corner it is possible to leave the wonders of this modern Babylon behind.

A few steps away are narrow side streets where one- and two-story buildings lean into each other as though for support. The air is acrid from the open-air charcoal grills of tiny restaurants, their counters open to the street. It is here that many salarymen come to drink after work. And it is on one such street that each night, Monday through Thursday, a guy known variously as "the professor" and "Dr. Pachinko" stops after 9 to wind down before heading home. At a local restaurant his reputation precedes his arrival.

"He's been playing for thirty years," offers Akira Kimura, an electrical engineer. "He's been on a winning streak for the past thirty days. If you want to know anything about pachinko he's the one to ask."

"Right," chimes in a voice from the other end of the counter. "He's the professor. The professor of pachinko."

When the professor finally does make an appearance he's a half hour later than usual. Everyone knows he's just spent four hours at the machines, but no one asks whether he's won or lost. It is assumed that he just redeemed his winnings at the tiny pay-off window up the alley. To ask him straight-out would be impolite.

He is stoop-shouldered and shy and his right hand trembles from   90
gripping the game control. He orders iced tea mixed with the volatile Japanese vodka called *shochu* and smiles. The other patrons collectively relax. They sense he's been victorious.

His titles turn out to have double meaning—during the day he works at a large university. "I've been able to send both of my children to Boston," he admits with an inkling of pride after being questioned about his winnings.

The bashfulness he exhibits when it comes to personal matters disappears when he is asked about the art of the game. He whips out pencil and paper, the better to diagram playing strategies.

"You must always pay attention to the position of the top nail," he says jabbing his illustration for emphasis. "And you must watch the shape of the nails."

A request to watch him in action is denied. Nor will he reveal which parlor he plays in, except to say it is a small one.

However, he is willing to give general advice. "Never play on Friday,"   95
he cautions. "There are too many people."

Pachinko can be seen as a microcosm of Tokyo itself. Both are mind-bending environments with sights and sounds layered thick enough to jar all but the most focused concentration. Both demand the ability to function in crowds and a subtlety of reflex. And each reveals its true nature only after the penetration of a carefully constructed surface.

While the pursuit of golf, mostly played on three-decker driving ranges, may have more cachet, pachinko remains the quintessential salaryman's game.

To spend several hours amid the noise of thousands of cascading steel balls, a relentless rock-and-roll soundtrack, and chain-smoking enthusiasts is to understand that leisure has many definitions.

Even as many Japanese embrace the growing culture of leisure, there are those who find the whole subject distasteful, particularly the older generations whose sweat built the postwar boom. They distrust the notion of time frittered away in the pursuit of personal pleasure.

At the same time, like parents everywhere, they hope their efforts will   100
make life easier for their children.

Yoko Okada is not a typical Japanese woman. Fifty-seven and married with three children, she helps her husband run a construction company and the Mini Pub, a restaurant they have owned for five years.

"I work three jobs," she says proudly. "I am a housekeeper, construction company owner, and businesswoman. I really don't have much time at all."

Though she dreams of a round-the-world trip after her retirement, she has difficulty envisioning a life without work.

"I really don't think that giving people an easy life is too good an idea," she ventures. "Taking it too easy is spiritually wrong. I am very concerned when I look at the young today, because if you don't work at your utmost, you are looking for trouble. Today people want to work on impulse, only when they feel like it." Okada's eldest daughter is married, the youngest helps out with the restaurant, and her son is learning to be a ski instructor.

"When I came down from Hokkaido thirty years ago," she says, "if I   105
hadn't worked hard I wouldn't have survived. The reality today is that people who worked incredibly hard, who did nothing but save, have kids who are only screwing around. And it's because the parents give them money and freedom. Parents aren't used to spending money on themselves, so they save and spend money on their children.

"There is a story about the samurai," she adds. "It is said they could be satisfied from a meal made from what they picked from their teeth. Spiritual nourishment was more important in the past. But I think the Japanese people are beginning to question whether the high standard of material living is all that we need."

In an odd way, Harley-Davidson enthusiast Makoto Matsushita believes the same thing. "Thirty-two years ago, I lived on a dirt road in the country-side," he recalls. "One day I was sitting at home and I heard an incredible sound. Someone told me that it was the famous Harley-Davidson motorcycle. From that day forward I made it my focus and my dream. Someday I would own a Harley-Davidson and I would drive it across a long straight road in the U.S.A."

Matsushita realized his dream two years ago on an eighteen-day ride from Anchorage, Alaska, to New Orleans. Asked to describe his experience, he cracks a broad grin.

"It was great fun," he responds. "I never had so much fun."

Thinking About the Text

1. The Leisure and Research Institute, we are told by its spokesman Atsuki Onaga in paragraph 12, seeks "to teach the Japanese how important leisure is." How important *is* leisure—and why is it important? Suppose you met someone who was so dedicated to his or her work—perhaps a lawyer, a potter, a tennis coach, or whoever—that this person preferred working over going to movies or sporting events, or even to taking vacations. What would you say to this person?

2. Onaga is quoted as saying, "You can't just have people sitting around and watching television or doing nothing. . . . Such inactivity can lead to

social problems and unrest" (para. 19). Explain why you agree or disagree. If you agree, what sorts of problems, and what kinds of unrest might be produced?

3. According to Onaga, Japan needs to develop "a field for play so that all the population, and not just the wealthy, have access to leisure facilities" (para. 19). Are there such facilities in your neighborhood? If so, what are they? Who makes use of them? Do you use them, and, if you don't, why not?

4. In paragraph 22 we learn that Tokyo Disneyland is popular. If you have ever visited a theme park, would you characterize the activities as "meaningful and healthy"? Explain.

Thinking About Culture

5. Paragraphs 48–61 discuss an Elvis impersonator. If you have ever seen such a person, describe the impression made on you. Try to explain why impersonating Elvis is such a popular industry.

6. "Taking it too easy is spiritually wrong," a Japanese woman says in paragraph 104. "I am very concerned when I look at the young today, because if you don't work at your utmost, you arc looking for trouble." Can you imagine an American saying this? Explain why, or why not, and explain why you agree or disagree with the speaker.

7. From the pastimes described in Hanson's essay, select one that seems especially Japanese and explain why it could or why it could not be successfully transplanted to the United States. If you think it would not be popular, explain why, and describe how, if altered, it might become popular.

Michael Shapiro

A Whole Different Ball Game

The most predictable thing about the Japanese all-star baseball team's unpredictably strong showing against the Americans this fall was the inevitable question about what in Japan is called "the real World Series."

Michael Shapiro, a freelance writer, lived and worked in Tokyo until he returned to the United States in 1989. His articles on baseball have appeared in the New York Times *and* Sports Illustrated. *He has also published a book on the topic,* In the Land of the Brokenhearted. *The article we reprint appeared in the* Japan Society Newsletter *in June 1989.*

For decades the Japanese baseball establishment has spoken of the day—always distant—when the nation might be ready to take on the Americans in a contest for global baseball supremacy. This talk often died quickly when the American all-stars, weary from the long season at home but enticed by all the money being offered by Japanese sponsors, came over to throttle the best of the Japanese.

Two years ago New York Mets manager Davey Johnson brought over an especially powerful team that took all but one game from the Japanese, and in the process beat them by the sort of lopsided scores reminiscent of the prewar years, when Babe Ruth came to play and sat in the outfield under an umbrella, convinced that no Japanese could hit the ball out of the infield.

Same Rules, Different Game

This fall Sparky Anderson's American side left town a winner, but barely so. The final game ended in a scoreless tie. The Japanese did what they were not expected to do: They pounded Los Angeles Dodger pitcher Orel Hershiser, which no American team had come close to doing in the closing months of the season; their pitchers overwhelmed some of America's best hitters; and the Japanese batters came from behind, beating the Americans in the late innings—a time when Japanese teams of the past were certain to fold. From that surprising showing emerged the obvious question: What would happen if they played for real? The Americans would win, and not just because they are bigger and stronger.

That the Americans would triumph tells a good deal about the nature of two very different games in two very different societies. The baseball played in America is not the baseball played in Japan. The Japanese play *Japanese* baseball. The rules are the same, as are the distances between the bases and the number of balls and strikes. But the games are different. What the Japanese have done in the past fifty years with the most quintessentially American game is nothing short of remarkable. They have refitted it for local consumption—as they have been adept at doing with most everything that has ever come into the country. They have seized upon the elements of the game that celebrate what Japan wishes to celebrate in itself. 5

The Japanese are good at baseball in almost every way, save one: failure, or rather the willingness to fail. Because failure has been all but eliminated from the game Japan has devised for itself, that game is doomed to being second best when the tall and sandy-haired fellows come to play.

My conclusion is based on four years of observation and upon the tutelage of, among others, Leon Lee, Leron Lee, and Randy Bass, Professors Emeritus of Japan's College of Hard Knocks: the academy of foreign ball players. Some 250 Americans have come to play in Japan. Many have gone home richer but with nervous stomachs, the latter a condition induced by long seasons spent asking themselves, "Why?"

(1) "Why does the umpire tell me that he must give some assistance

to the weak Japanese pitcher and call balls in the dirt strikes against me?"
(2) "Isn't a strike a strike and a ball a ball?" And, (3) "Why does the manager
say, 'I want to get away from the rational theory of baseball and try other
things,' after calling for a pitch out with the bases loaded and two men out,
thereby walking in a run?"

The answer to the second is no. The answer to the first and third is:
because he did. It is an answer frequently heard and seldom satisfying. Only
when a player learns to accept it can he begin being comfortable playing
baseball in Japan.

The Lee brothers spent, respectively, ten and eleven years playing in   10
Japan. Bass, a slugger, succeeded as no American ever has at the Japanese
game. It was they who were sought out by the newly arrived foreigners, eager
to know what to expect and how to react. The advice was always the same:
Forget everything you ever thought baseball should be; you're in Japan now.
Though not a player I nevertheless took my place at my mentors' knees.
And then, when the lessons were done, I looked again at ballfields that had
seemed very much like those I'd seen at home. But when I looked a second
time I saw that the form had changed and the game taking place before me
was only superficially like the one I'd left behind.

Lesson One: Honne *and* Tatemae,
or the Truth You Mean
and the Truth You Say

There is one pitcher in Japan who throws baseballs at people's heads. His name
is Osamu Higashio. Until his retirement at the end of the past season, he had
hit some 150 batters during his long and distinguished career. No one else had
even come close. But more significant than Higashio's insistence upon declaring
the outside part of the plate his (and woe betide the batter who invaded his
space) was his willingness to confess to his penchant for aiming an occasional
pitch at the man at bat. Higashio, a wiry man with a quick smile, was blunt, in
the way that country people in Japan often are. What he said and what he did
were one and the same. And in that he was alone.

Japan's baseball is built upon the premise that what the nation lacks
in speed and size it makes up in will. Baseball people call this "Fighting
Spirit." So crucial is "fighting spirit" to the Japanese definition of the game
that there are even drills to hone it. The most notorious of these was the
dreaded "Thousand Ground Ball Drill" in which the victim stood in the
infield and fielded a thousand grounders in rapid succession. Often he would
fall to the ground, gasping. That is when the coaches would begin aiming
batting balls at him. Oxygen was often required when the drill was done.

"Fighting spirit," however, represents the *tatemae* of Japanese baseball,
the truth that is stated. It is rare to see a Japanese player display such spirit
on the field, such as sliding hard into second base to break up a double play,

or barreling into a catcher to dislodge the ball from his mitt. That sort of behavior would not do in a small and narrow country where people live on top of one another. But because the inclination toward aggression exists in the human heart, Japanese players are taught to talk about aggressive play a lot, although never actually displaying it.

Only Higashio threw at people's heads. That was his place, just as it was Shigeo Nagashima's to be Japan's Babe Ruth (not Sadaharu Oh. Oh hit the home runs; Nagashima was the star) and just as it is for Hiromitsu Ochiai to be the bad boy of the game. Everybody knows that Ochiai will brag and practice when the mood suits him and demand a lot of money from his bosses. But only Ochiai can do that. Japan is filled with surrogates—the violent teenagers of "Be-Bop High School" movies, the insulting wiseguy TV comics—who can do what people would like to do but which society deems unacceptable.

It is not acceptable to play baseball aggressively. But it is good to talk   15
about it. That way the nation can celebrate its considerable will and noses do not get bloodied. A few years ago an American named Tim Ireland came to play second base for the Hiroshima Carp (who, incidentally, are not named for seafood but for a company, like all the other teams). Ireland was a marginal player with little power. But he did have "fighting spirit." The problem with Ireland's "fighting spirit" was that he meant it. His was "fighting spirit" of the *honne* variety. No one told him that he was not supposed to slide into infielders with spikes flashing. He lasted two years and never quite understood that the truth you state does not necessarily have to be the truth you mean.

Lesson Two: The Way of Baseball, or Form over Content

In Japan there is a way to hold a bat. Actually, this varies by team. The Nippon Ham Fighters generally bat one way and the Yakult Swallows another. The batters might hold their hands high, or might stretch their hands out over the plate just before the pitch is delivered. While in America young hitters are reminded to seek a zone of comfort in the batter's box—"get comfortable up there, son . . ."—Japanese rookies spend a lot of time learning to bat like everyone else.

They spend hours in batting practice, and when they are not at practice, they are swinging a bat at the air. Before they go to sleep at night, rookies take a few hundred practice swings. The idiosyncratic major league batting styles that American boys grow up trying to imitate—"Look at me Dad, Stan Musial, just like a corkscrew!"—are seldom, if ever seen in Japan. (For an exception, see Lesson One, under Ochiai, the designated rebel, whom mothers do not encourage their sons to emulate.)

Form, be it in the arrangement of flowers or the manipulation of a sword, is central in Japan where learning is accomplished by observation and imitation. Consistency is a virtue. And practice perfects consistency.

Saying that Japanese baseball teams practice is like saying that Donald Trump makes deals.

They practice for two hours a day during the season—when Americans are loosening up in the field and taking batting practice; and they practice when the season is done—when the Americans are either playing winter ball in the Dominican Republic or going to banquets. When it is too cold to practice in Japan they practice in Hawaii or Arizona. That is called pre-spring-training training. Spring training follows. Then comes the season. Practice in Japan is interrupted only by games.

"Doing," Not Playing, Baseball

Practice affords a player the chance to sharpen skills in the manner his coaches see fit. There are not a lot of errors in a Japanese baseball game. The men in the field have handled more grounders and fly balls than there are people at Kamakura beach on a Sunday in August. Practice ensures a measure of predictability, which is a satisfying feeling for the people of a thin archipelago spread across a fault line and subject to the whims of the typhoons and tidal waves. What cannot be made predictable is lamented; but that which can is rehearsed until it is perfected. Games matter in Japan, but not nearly as much as practice does. A player can be benched or sent to the farm team for having a bad practice. Coaches supervise practice, watching for lapses, noting consistency. There is no room for error in practice, no allowance for saving one's best for the game. Victory is all well and good but unless it comes appropriately—through the correct application of the accepted principles of performance—then it is rendered hollow. 20

Willie Stargell, the Pittsburgh Pirates Hall of Famer, used to talk of the necessity of seeing baseball as a game. You don't work at baseball, he would say. You play it.

Not so in Japan, where the operative word is *suru*, to do. You *do* baseball like you do work and you do schoolwork. If you fail at work your boss will get angry, and you will let your workmates down. If you fail at schoolwork you will not get into a good college, and you will let your parents down. If you fail at baseball you let down the team that hired you, the manager who played you, the teammates who befriended you, and the fans who adored you. And so you do not fail. You practice until you get it right. And once you get it right you keep practicing to make sure you do not slip.

No one said it was supposed to be fun.

Lesson Three: Better to Bunt
Than Not to Bunt

The operating principle in American baseball is called the "Big Bang Theory," a philosophy advanced and extolled primarily by Earl Weaver, the great

Baltimore Orioles manager. The theory dictates that the winning team will score more runs in one inning than the loser will score in all nine. To that end it is necessary to play for the big inning—to achieve the "big bang." This means risk. It means not surrendering outs on sacrifice bunts. It means taking the chance of hitting into a double play with a man on first, but also of advancing that man to third with a base hit, having two men on base and maybe scoring a bunch of runs.

The operating principle in Japanese baseball is "a run at a time." When   25
a man reaches first the next man, with less than two out, will always bunt, thereby sacrificing himself, surrendering an out in the interest of moving the baserunner that much closer to home. The Japanese are fine bunters.

They have practiced bunting. They can move a runner from first to second every time. They can take part in the creation of a single run. For a long time I wondered why some manager didn't just start playing for the "big bang" and tell his men to swing away. My tutors disabused me of this idea. If one team did that then the harmony would be broken, the harmony that comes when the game is played predictably. Teams know what to expect from one another. If one team was to break from the field and play by different rules, it might win. But then everyone else would, in a sense, lose.

Everyone bunts. With less than two men out. Always. Just as everyone cheers when the designated cheerleaders (you can spot them in their uniform shirts and caps, white gloves and wooden clappers) instruct them to cheer. Everyone sings the same songs—"You're tough and strong and wild with the number 45 on your back . . ."—and refrains from offering gratuitous comments on the quality of a particular fellow's play—"You stink, you bum!" Japanese baseball's pleasure is a shared experience, on the field and in the stands.

Seizing the Moment, Paying the Price

The confluence of these lessons came for me one afternoon in the Yokohama Stadium, where I sat next to Leon Lee, the younger of the two Lee brothers. Young boys were clamoring for his autograph and Leon politely told them, in Japanese, "Later, please." The Baltimore Orioles were in town for an exhibition series, and Leon and I were anxious to watch.

In truth, the game was not much of a contest. The Americans were scoring, seemingly at will. But in an unspectacular moment the elements of "fighting spirit," predictability, and form came together in a way that would exemplify why Japanese baseball is good for Japan, but not when Japan wants to beat America.

The Oriole batter hit a hard bouncing ball toward first base. The   30
Japanese first baseman locked his eyes on the ball. And then for a brief moment, he froze. He watched the ball and Leon could see—and helped me to see—that he was trying to remember what he had been taught to do

and what he had practiced to do with a ball bouncing just the way this ball was bouncing.

The problem, however, was that the ball was bouncing unusually, which is inevitable in a game played with a round ball, cylindrical bat and on a sloping playing surface. So there he stood, at first, waiting. The runner was a speedy man, and the first baseman would have to charge the ball to catch him at the bag. But to charge the ball would have meant risking flubbing the play. And so he waited for the ball to come to him, seemingly calculating that the longer it took to travel, the more familiarly it might bounce.

The ball reached him just as the runner reached first. The first baseman caught the ball. In the American context of the game that would not have mattered because the runner was safe. But in Japan the first baseman had not failed. He had not dropped the ball. He would not incur the wrath of his manager. He was safe to play another day.

The problem is that baseball is a game of motions repeated in seeming monotony. And then, at a key juncture in the game, something a little different happens. A ball bounces unusually; a curve ball does not break sharply enough, even though it looks like a ball. And it is those moments that must not only be seized, but conquered. The team that can squeeze an advantage from them is the team that wins.

So dismiss the home runs and the strike outs that strength provides. Think of the subtler moments. Because that is where America will beat Japan in baseball, today and tomorrow.

Of course none of it matters, not when compared to the price Japan   35
would have to pay to beat the Americans. They'd have to adjust their game to the Americans' game—setting players free to trust their instincts, letting them risk the failure of the muffed play, letting them *play*.

But then the game would lose its essential quality: It wouldn't be Japanese baseball anymore.

Thinking About the Text

1. Do you find Shapiro's comparisons effective? Reread his essay, noting the structure and the use he makes of comparison and contrast.

2. Characterize Shapiro's attitude toward the Japanese. Point to specific passages to support your opinion.

3. In paragraph 16 Shapiro suggests that American batters are encouraged to find their own style whereas Japanese players learn a traditional style. Does your own experience confirm the comment about coaching in this country? Or do coaches seek to get rid of the bad habits that inexperienced players think of as their style?

Thinking About Culture

4. Shapiro argues that Japanese baseball differs from U.S. baseball. If you are familiar with a comparable difference—let's say between South American soccer and U.S. soccer—describe and analyze the differences.

5. "Japanese players are taught to talk about aggressive play a lot, although never actually displaying it," says Shapiro (para. 13). How different is this from sport here? You might argue that although there are a few roughnecks, on the whole American players do not behave aggressively. Or else argue that, as some commentators have suggested, American audiences like to see violence. Or argue that the degree of aggression depends on the sport.

6. Shapiro's thesis is that the baseball games are different because the cultures are different. If you are familiar with a culture other than that of mainstream America, explain how the culture reveals itself in a sport or in some other leisure activity.

7. The concepts of *tatemae* and *honne*, or "appearance" and "reality," have been incorporated into Japanese baseball (see "Lesson One," paras. 11–15). Is this distinction peculiarly Japanese, or can you find examples in American sport and society?

8. Shapiro remarks that the Japanese have "seized upon the elements of the game that celebrate what Japan wishes to celebrate in itself" (para. 5). What elements of the game have Americans seized on to celebrate American life? Write an essay in which you compare baseball to some other American sport, in order to identify the elements of American life that each of the two sports "celebrates."

Pico Iyer

In the Land of Mickey-San

"It's as if we're taking the seeds offered from across the sea and cultivating them into our own Japanese garden," the long-beaked cartoon crane explains to the audio-animatronic figures of a little girl and her brother. "Culture doesn't just come; it develops slowly, richly. Generation after generation has

---

Pico Iyer was born in Oxford, England, in 1957, was educated in England and America, and has traveled extensively, especially in Asia. His books include Video Night in Kathmandu *(1988) and* The Lady and the Monk *(1991). He is an essayist for* Time *magazine, where this selection appeared in January 1988.*

to digest and refine these marvelous influences." The message may seem a little heavy for an amusement park, but the audience in the country's first revolving Carousel Theater is all ears. As the stage revolves, the sagacious bird launches into a lecture on the virtues of isolationism. Finally the Feathered One concludes, "People are like dreams," a huge red sun rises above the stage, and all the flesh-and-blood visitors to the Meet the World pavilion are ushered next door into a kind of epilogue to the show: a National Panasonic model of the ideal Japanese home of the future, featuring four members of a robot-simulated family, plus dog, attending to their own techno-gadgets. Tokyo Disneyland is not your average theme park.

Outside the pavilion's twenty-one-TV lobby, a kimono-clad granny is being photographed in Goofy's welcoming embrace. White-collar workers in blue blazers and dark ties are shuffling around the lines for the world's only Cinderella Castle Mystery Tour. A girl in a warm-up jacket that reads IT IS ARGUED THAT DOUBLE SUICIDE IS THE SUBLIME CULMINATION OF LOVE placidly sips melon juice. Nothing disturbs the clean blue air except high tinkling cries of "*Kawaii!*" (Isn't it cute!) "Look," coos an extravagantly chic young mother to her three-year-old son, dapper in black leather pants, while his leather-jacketed father records the scene on videotape. "Look over there at Mickey-san!"

In a country where ritual is often the closest thing to religion, Mickeysan's Imperial Palace has in less than five years become something of a national pilgrimage site. In 1987 roughly one million schoolchildren, who would previously have been taken to Japan's great historical sites, were brought to the park. Last week, as people across the nation gathered at shrines to usher in an auspicious New Year, Tokyo Disneyland stayed open for thirty-six straight hours, serving as a kind of alternative temple. By day's end 200,000 votaries had observed the country's most important holiday at its favorite playland.

All this may seem a far cry from Walt Disney's original conception. But in a deeper sense, it may be its ultimate realization. For if the Disney parks of Florida and California offer squeaky-clean visions of a perfect society, the Disneyland that flourishes in Tokyo is even cleaner and more utopian. Yet even as the Japanese version reproduces virtually every feature of its American models, it turns them into something entirely Japanese. Melvin, Buff, and Max, the antlered commentators at the Country Bear Jamboree, speak in the grave basso profundos of Kurosawa samurai. Alice in Wonderland has Oriental features. Frontierland has been turned into Westernland ("The Japanese don't like frontiers," explains a park official), and Main Street has become the World Bazaar.

The central icon of this singular faith is, inevitably, Mickey Mouse, whose unfailing perkiness and elder-statesmouse status (recently celebrated in a seventeen-day fifty-ninth birthday party) assure him success in a culture that has respect for old age and a soft spot for the cute. The little fellow's image is everywhere in Japan—on Mitsubishi bankbooks, in framed photos within Zen temples, even on Emperor Hirohito's wristwatch. "Mickey Mouse is an actor," explains the slogan on the cover of a Mickey Mouse diary, "and as such he can do anything; he can play any role."

One role he definitely plays is to support another of Japan's driving principles: pleasure as big business. Foot-high dolls of his consort Minnie in kimono go for more than $60 in Tokyo Disneyland, and the number of ice creams sold there in a single year would, if piled up, reach fourteen times as high as 12,388-foot Mount Fuji.

In the end, though, what most distinguishes Tokyo Disneyland from its American forebears is its user-friendly audience. There are no screeching infants along its spotless walkways and no teenagers on the make. At closing time, after soft neon and colored lights have turned the place into a lovely fairyland, there is no frantic rush for the gates. Elegant secretaries and college boys in shirts bearing the vaguely anarchic slogan CIVIL RIGHT FREAK YOU KNOW UNIVERSITY EDUCATION stand in orderly lines until sweetly smiling cheerleaders lead the crowd forward in regimented squads.

So when the daily Parade of Dreams Come True culminates in a refrain of "Tokyo Disneyland is your land . . . ," the line makes sense in more ways than one. Here, after all, is a flawlessly clean, high-tech, perfectionist model of the flawlessly clean, high-tech, perfectionist society. Small wonder, perhaps, that a couple of years ago, when a group of Japanese were asked what had given them the most happiness in life, more than half mentioned not marriage or family, nor work or religion or love, but simply, and inevitably, Disneyland.

Thinking About the Text

1. Is there any sentence in the essay that serves as a thesis sentence? If so, what is it? If not, formulate a sentence that you think gets at the heart of the essay.

2. How would you characterize Iyer's attitude toward his subject? Admiring? Good-natured? Condescending? . . . (These one-word characterizations are mere examples; one word may, of course, not be adequate to characterize his attitude.) Do you find *implied* rather than explicit perspectives in his essay? Explain.

Thinking About Culture

3. Make a list of the ways that, according to this essay, Tokyo Disneyland resembles the American Disney parks, and make another list of the ways in which it differs. What do you make of these similarities and differences?

4. Describe an American amusement park or theme park (not a Disney park)

as a visitor from another culture might describe it. You may want to draw on your reading in this book to imagine how a Japanese person might describe the park in a letter to home. Or you may want to see it from the perspective of Horace Miner (p. 29).

June Kinoshita and Nicholas Palevsky

A Guide to Water Worlds

Onsen

For Japanese bathing enthusiasts the search for the ultimate bath is something in the nature of a religious quest. That *yu*, hot water, is held to have divine powers is best demonstrated by remote shrines, such as Yudono-san (Bathtub Mountain), where a hot spring is regarded as the god incarnate. Volcanic activity gives rise to thousands of *onsen* (hot springs), but popular legends often ascribe hot springs to miracles worked by famous ascetics and priests. Kobo Daishi (774–835), in order to succor the sick, supposedly created many of Japan's most famous hot springs by striking the ground with his magic staff. During the war-torn Middle Ages, certain onsen called *kakushi-yu* (hidden hot water) were used by military generals as camp hospitals. An injured warrior was supposed to make his way secretly to the agreed-upon spring where, with the aid of the beneficial waters, he could recuperate to fight again.

Many rustic onsen, deep in the mountains, are set up purely for medicinal purposes. At these *tojiba*, elderly people and convalescents can stay for a few dollars a night, living in simple lodgings and preparing their own food. Depending on the mineral content of the water—iron, sulfur, radium, and the like—the springs are thought to have a salutary effect on a wide range

June Kinoshita, an editor at Scientific American, *and Nicholas Palevsky, both fluent in Japanese, wrote* Gateway to Japan *(1992), an extremely interesting and useful guidebook to Japan. After discussing* onsen *(hot springs), Kinoshita and Palevsky discuss* mizu shobai *("the water trade," a figurative term for the world of bars and other evening sources of pleasure). This world of pleasure in turn is connected to "the floating world" (*ukiyo*), a term applied to the world of entertainment, especially the world of sex. The spoken word* ukiyo *allows for a pun, since it can also mean "the fleeting world," "the transient world" of Buddhist thought, a term easily applied to the world of pleasure. (The written words are not identical, however, since the first character differs.)*

We have given a single title to this extract of two consecutive entries from Gateway to Japan, *one on hot springs and the other on the sexual aspects of "the water trade."*

of conditions, including skin diseases, gout, and rheumatism. People stand under waterfalls of hot water or sit in wooden steam boxes with their heads sticking out. Patients with internal ailments drink large amounts of the health-giving water. Certain onsen are paired, and alternating between them is considered particularly effective for certain ailments.

Many *tojiba* are located in beautiful, isolated areas. A few even lack electricity: They use the soft light of oil lamps. These lodges cater to hikers, skiers, and nature lovers, and may consist of a series of thatched huts and old wooden buildings. Meals consist of trout caught in nearby streams and *sansai* (mountain greens) gathered from the mountains. These inns generally boast a *rotemburo,* an outdoor bath, usually in some particularly idyllic spot. Here, in the midst of nature, is where the communal essence of the bath is most strongly felt. Young women may not bathe outside in broad daylight— grannies are out night and day—but late in the evening mixed groups bathe, sing, and drink sake, which is floated from person to person in little cypress tubs. In the summer, a broiled trout often flavors the sake tub. You may also encounter sake in which *mamushi,* a poisonous snake, is pickled; this elixir is said to increase sexual potency.

ONSEN CITIES

This sense of communality—near-sacred in Japan—appeals to schools, company groups, sports clubs, and circles of friends who take an onsen vacation together not only for enjoyment, but also to enhance group solidarity. The usual choice is not an isolated spring, but a famous onsen mecca, such as Atami or Beppu. These groups can be seen strolling around the town, dressed in matching *yukata.*° Onsen vacations are also great favorites of couples, especially those seeking anonymity. A typical hotel in a large onsen town, however, may not be the best place to find a quiet, undisturbed evening; large groups use the huge halls of these places for *enkai:* banquets, often attended by *geisha* or "companions," which start off quite formally but don't end that way. These too are considered exercises in group cohesion: Any unpleasantness—and most of the later part of the evening—is usually forgotten by morning. Hang-overs, and any other lingering sense of uncleanness, can be soaked away in the baths, which remain open around the clock.

The baths themselves are for the most part exuberant souvenirs of the   5
Japanese Everyman's first encounters with affluence in the 1960s. There are sand baths, baths in cablecars, baths in caves, multistory variety bathhouses, and vast "jungle baths" filled with water slides, tropical plants, pavilions, waterfalls, Buddhas, and white plaster Cupids.

yukata: A cotton robe. [All notes are the editors'.]

Sex, Fantasy, and the "Water Business"

The term *ukiyo,* or "floating world," is derived from a Buddhist belief about the impermanence and futility of material existence. (In Japanese, the word "floating" can mean "fleeting.") In his *Tales of Ise,* the courtier Narihira finds in this pessimistic worldview a vivid sense of beauty:

Most wonderful when	*Chireba-koso*
they scatter—	*Itodo sakura wa*
The cherry blossoms.	*Medetakere*
In this floating world,	*Ukiyo ni nani ka*
does anything endure?	*Hisashikarubeki*

By the early Edo period, the term *ukiyo* came to refer to the fashionable and hedonistic pleasure quarters. These "nightless cities" consisted of brothels, teahouses, and bathhouses, all engaged in prostitution. The *ukiyo-e,* or "pictures of the floating world," depicted actors and courtesans—demure, willow-waisted women, often in not-so-demure poses. The officially sanctioned districts, such as Yoshiwara in Edo, Shimabara in Kyoto, and Shinmachi in Osaka, were surrounded by a large wall and gate.

SOAPLANDS

When the priest Nisei Shonin revived Kobe's Arima Onsen as a place of worship and healing in the twelfth century, he built twelve temple hostels, and within each temple he installed two women, called *yuna,* or "hot-water women," to wash pilgrims. These bathhouse girls soon drifted into prostitution. Later, the bathhouse girls of Edo achieved great notoriety when the authorities tried to outlaw them. What had happened was inevitable, since the bath is a primal physical experience that naturally leaves the bather in a hedonistic mood. Prostitutes and "onsen geisha" are still an integral, if partially hidden, part of the onsen scene. (. . . Classical geisha . . . are not prostitutes. . . .)

The connection between bathing and sex is so strong that, although prostitution was outlawed in 1958, the institution persists quite openly in "soaplands," where the action centers around a bubble bath. These are tolerated partly because both the bath and what comes after are thought to have therapeutic value. Large "soapland cities" exist in Sapporo, Kawasaki, Gifu, and Shiga-ken, to name only the most famous. Soaplands used to be called *toruko,* or *toruko-buro* (Turkish baths), but were renamed soaplands, supposedly because of a misunderstanding involving a taxi driver, the Turkish ambassador, and a toruko named Embassy. In response to protests by the Turkish government, these establishments across the nation agreed, on a set day, to change their names from *toruko* to the less offensive "soapland."

FANTASY

Such names as Embassy, Palace, and Dreamland are often used not only for soaplands but also for *pachinko* (pinball) parlors, *kissaten,*° and "love hotels," lodgings that offer bargain hourly rates because of the rapid turnover of their clients. All these establishments offer theme decor; love hotels offer fantasy beds and baths in addition to a fanciful exterior. The most famous, a Disneyland-type castle named Emperor that towers over the Meguro section of Tokyo, was a bit upstaged by the opening of a real Magic Kingdom outside Tokyo in 1984. Pension lodgings, often decorated to evoke rural American themes, have become popular. Wholesome or sleazy, these various establishments offer an escape from the humdrum of everyday life, although perhaps less effectively than the primal succor of the bath or the elegant repose of a fine *ryokan.*°

In modern Japanese society, nighttime entertainment has become big 10 business. Such quaint terms as "hot-water girls" and "floating world" have given way to the cold, utilitarian *mizu-shobai,* or "water business." Although soaplands are included in this term, by far the most common mizu-shobai institutions are *sunakku* ("snacks"), hostess bars, and cabarets, which offer liquor and female companionship. These range in size from huge Tokyo cabarets, where hundreds of hostesses circulate among tables according to a computerized dispatching system, to tiny sunakku run by one woman behind a counter; dozens of the latter type of establishment can be fitted into a single building.

Added to the hostesses' flirting is some of the motherly understanding you may encounter in your ryokan maid; one of the hostess's objectives is to help the customer forget the aggravations and injured dignity of the day. If men come in a group, she will help them cement social or business relationships by keeping the party convivial. In a smaller club, there is no better way to emphasize shared sentiments than with *karaoke:* Individuals stand up and sing a tune, accompanied by a recorded soundtrack. (The word literally means "empty orchestra.") "Yesterday" and "My Way" are often available for foreign guests. Video disks supply bouncing-ball lyrics and visual accompaniments, usually soft porn or soft-focus landscapes.

Thinking About the Text

1. Write a brief guidebook entry to Tokyo Disneyworld, based on the information in the essays by Pico Iyer (p. 307) and Gayle Hanson (p. 288).

2. Write a guidebook entry to some part of your neighborhood—for instance to golf courses, places of worship, health clubs, bowling alleys, pizza parlors,

kissaten: Coffee shops.   *ryokan:* Inn.

or colleges. Alternatively, if you are aware of anything in the United States that is somewhat comparable to an *onsen,* write an entry for an American guidebook.

Thinking About Culture

3. The discussion of *onsen* emphasizes the "sense of communality" (para. 4). Would you say that there is a comparable sense of "communality," or community, in American health clubs or gyms, or perhaps in some high school clubs, or in fraternities and sororities? Explain.

4. Look at a mainstream, general guidebook to the United States, or to any part of the country, and see if it says anything about sex. If it does, compare the tone of the discussion with the tone of Kinoshita and Palevsky. If it says nothing about sex, what does that tell you?

Anne Allison

The Hostess Club: A Type of Routine

When men enter the hostess club in the company of other men, what they do there reflects their two objectives: to get away from work and to have a good time together. The first objective stems from what is generally said to be the great stress and strain of being a working man in Japan. Hours are long, demands are rigorous, and one is discouraged from complaining. When a man walks into a bar or club at the end of the day, he does so to release and let go, position himself in a place that looks different from the workplace, and participate in activities that are self-indulgent and carefree.

Achieving the second objective, enjoying oneself in the company of co-workers or business relations, requires that the relaxation promote business and strengthen work ties. Most Japanese believe that how men relate to one another outside the office foretells how they will behave inside. The hostess club provides customers with a common, more egalitarian ground than is possible at the office.

The activities of a hostess club—the drinking, talking, joking, flirting, singing—serve to both break down and build up; they dissolve the structure

Anne Allison is an assistant professor of cultural anthropology at Duke University. This report of her research in a Tokyo hostess club is from her book Nightwork, *published in 1994.*

that operates outside and create a new one. The first is the more apparent. The customers drink, loosen up, and talk about things that will be forgotten or seem unimportant the next day. As simple and undirected as these activities appear, however, there is also the agenda of uniting the men. Talk should rarely be divisive, and drinking should lead men not to solitary contemplation but to an effusiveness rarely displayed elsewhere. For the evening to be considered successful this double platform must be maintained; the men get away from work, and they get together in ways essential for work.

Membership

The person heading for Bijo will be first greeted by a man in a tuxedo who opens doors and parks cars for the entire building. To the guest's right is an elegant *kissaten* (coffee shop) on the first floor; to his left, a fancy Western disco down a mirrored flight of stairs to the basement; and on the vertical roster a list of all the bars and clubs in the building. As he enters the open foyer, the customer encounters his own image reflected in the mirror covering the whole back wall. As he rides up in a small elevator encased in mirrored door, walls, and ceiling, his gaze is inevitably directed toward himself.

Having been presented immediately with three motifs of the *mizu-shobai* domain—service (from the attendant), glitter (from the ambience of the building), and self-reflection (from real mirrors), the customer alights on the sixth floor with only two doors to choose between: one to Bijo and the other to a bar specializing in bourbon. The door to Bijo is open, and one of the three male employees (the manager and waiters) monitors it to keep out men who are not members and to greet those who are. Addressed by name, unless he is a newcomer, the customer is immediately welcomed into a familiar setting, shown into the club, and quickly seated, most likely in "B" room. He is greeted by all the employees in a position to do so with an *"Irashai mase"* ("Please enter"), a standard greeting to private visitors and to customers in general in Japan, in restaurants, stores, small businesses. The Mama and other hostesses may also greet the customer with a nod, although their attention will be focused on their charge of the moment.

Typical of hostess clubs, Bijo services a "members-only" clientele. Potential members, introduced and recommended to the club by a member, undergo an informal interview with the Mama. The Mama exchanges *meishi* (business cards) with the prospective member and calls him the next day to make the offer definite. If he is interested, she will then turn over any subsequent practical and financial aspects of membership to the manager, thus fostering the pleasant, though hardly realistic, impression that a member's relationship with the Mama is personal rather than financial.

Another standard practice of hostess clubs is the "keep bottle" system, which requires members to purchase bottles of liquor from the club and to keep them at the club. Whenever the member visits, the bottles are brought out and the liquor is served. Some clubs require that bottles be consumed and new bottles purchased within a limited time. Bijo, however, either too classy or too expensive to adopt this policy, allows bottles to remain untouched for months in the service closet, where they are neatly stacked and dusted. Each bottle is marked with the customer's name, providing both a sign system of the status of the individual customer, based on the cost of his bottle (Chivas Regal, for example, is the most expensive, as everyone knows), and a substantiation—even reification—as they stand together in the service closet, of a male community established through common membership.

Service by Males

Having ordered and paid for a bottle in advance, a member will be seated and then, usually without a word being spoken, his bottle will be brought out promptly, always accompanied by glasses, ice, mineral water, and a snack for each guest. The man who has served him up to this point—a waiter or the manager—will usually prepare to pour him the first drink and then, only at this point, hesitate and ask as confirmation, "Is mizu wari (scotch and water, the favorite drink at Bijo) all right?" Proceeding to fill the glass, the waiter exemplifies a level of service that will continue to be prompt, efficient, and unsolicited all evening.

From this moment on, a waiter will speak only to answer questions or verify commands. He will not ask for food or drink orders but will take an order for food if summoned by a guest (or, more commonly perhaps, by a hostess in the name of the guest) and will bring out new supplies of bottled water and ice whenever he sees they are needed. His service seems to consist of foreseeing and responding to the customer's unspoken needs. Indeed, once his initial task of seeing the guest through the preliminaries is completed, his presence is practically effaced by that of the more commanding hostess. This inconspicuousness, however, has a symbolic value.

The male employees, with their silence, sobriety, and submissiveness, contrast most sharply with the mizu-shobai women. The waiters rank lowest of all those employed at the club; they work the longest hours, are kept the busiest, and treat customers the most politely.[1] Standing as though on guard, they smile rarely and laugh less, seldom showing any expression of emotion.

If one were to ask a customer what it is about the waiters that enhances the time he spends at the club, he would probably answer, "Nothing in particular" or simply say that the waiter expedites service. Waiters are noticed, in fact, only in their failure to go unnoticed. That is, if an ashtray is not emptied, a fresh

[1] At Bijo there were always between four and five male employees: the manager, one or two waiters called "boys," a piano player referred to as sensei, and a cook who goes by the anglicized "cook" and remains unseen in the kitchen. In rank, the cook is perhaps higher than the waiters. The manager, also higher though possibly superseded by the rank of the piano player, is paid a salary only slightly higher than most of the veteran hostesses despite the longer hours and greater responsibility. The waiters at Bijo work from about 4 P.M. to 12:30, compared to hours of about 7 to 11 P.M. or midnight for the hostesses.

bottle of water not delivered, or the request for a song not conveyed to the piano player, then a customer's attention is distracted from whatever is happening at his table as he is forced to call on the waiter to correct the lapse. When the service provided by the waiter is at top form, however, the customer's needs are attended to almost telepathically. What the waiter is paid for, in other words, is responsiveness without presence. It is in order to be symbolically absent that he functions silently, without facial expression.[2] The customer does not want to see him, so the waiter makes himself unseen.

Drinking

The speed with which the setups for drinks are delivered is an indication of the significance given to drinking. It is expected and even required at hostess clubs. The Japanese male who does not drink here, in fact, is considered odd, unsociable, somewhat unmasculine, and almost un-Japanese. Alcohol goes hand in hand with the relaxing atmosphere of the nightlife; not only does it break down the barriers between men as quickly as possible, but it also dissolves barriers within the individual.

This function of alcohol—loosening the glue of a social order that is generally glued tight—is appreciated by far more than the businessman out to have a good time. Rules and expectations are burdensome in Japan, and women drinking alone, housewives drinking together at home, and students drinking in groups all seek a release from the various obligations of Japanese society. The behavior that accompanies the drinking—throwing up, urinating in public, dancing on train platforms, falling asleep stretched out on the seat of a train, making passes at or otherwise insulting someone normally shown respect, speaking openly about things that usually go unsaid—all such behavior is for the most part excused (yet more so for males than females).

Like insanity in the United States, drunkenness in Japan grants one an immunity from acts or behavior committed "under the influence." This was particularly true in prewar Japan, when even the charge of murder would not be leveled if the perpetrator had been drunk at the time. Today's laws are somewhat more stringent, including penalties for driving after more than one drink. Yet socially there is still a blind spot. How people behave when they are drunk is overlooked because, it is believed, drink changes behavior, and drunken behavior should not be judged by the usual standards.[3] The

---

[2] The case with the manager is a bit different, he being more visible in his role as managerial bookkeeper and stand-in host when the hostesses and Mama are busy.

[3] According to some studies, Japanese are genetically more sensitive to alcohol than other racial groups and react strongly to even a small amount of alcohol. Reporting on such a study, *National Geographic* has also stated that the rate of alcoholism in Japan is 4 percent of drinkers—statistically half the rate in the United States ("Alcohol, the Legal Drug" by Boyd Gibbons [February 1992]). In my experience in Tokyo I observed that drunken behavior can occur after one sip, and have been told that alcoholics are few in Japan because everyone makes it to work the next day. If cultural constructions affect the definition of alcoholism, it is difficult to compare the rates of alcoholism between Japan and the United States.

Western praise for those who "can hold their liquor well" misses the point in Japan, where many drink to achieve the freedom and the chance to act irresponsibly that come with drunkenness. The tendency is to drink hard, to get drunk, and to act drunk even when the drinking has just begun. (A parallel is the activity at American college "mixers.")

In the hostess club this logic of drink makes good sense. Tired of the 15 rules and rituals that control their actions during the day, men use alcohol regularly, almost fiercely, after hours. With drink as an umbrella, they are protected and indulged. Thanks to the social blind spot, what they do will be excused, what they say overlooked. With a drink, they can let their feelings loose, vent a long-harbored resentment, even cut a boss to the quick; it will all be forgotten next day. But the catharsis of their remarks and behavior builds relationships that will continue in the months and years ahead.

Talking: Banter and Breast Talk

The rules, boundaries, and key components of the talk within hostess clubs are tacitly understood. The talk should be unstructured chatter about things so insignificant that they need not be recalled later. Such forgettable conversations build a commonality among men.

Conversation, I mean to suggest, is not so much a pleasure in and of itself as a means to an end. Not dissimilar in this regard to the other activities at the club, it is often undertaken with a nervous hesitation that belies the gaiety it seeks to express. Supposedly idle conversation will begin spontaneously as soon as the first drink has been poured; in fact, the members of a party will often shift in their seats while waiting for an appropriate remark from a brave volunteer. At such a time, each moment of silence seems like an eternity.

It is at this point that the hostess is assigned a table, and her arrival will be greeted with a sigh of relief. She will ward off a silence that could threaten the evening's objectives, launching the conversation so necessary to recreation. To smooth the conversational path between men is, in fact, a primary function of hostesses, according to most of the men I spoke with.

Although the hostess participates in the conversation, she often becomes its subject, as in the following instance. Four customers (Hamano, Agata, Mori, and Yamamoto, all from the same division in the same company) were in the club, and for about an hour I served as their sole hostess. The atmosphere was jovial and lighthearted, and the talk consisted of playful put-downs, directed primarily at Hamano, the highest-ranked among them, sexual banter about me, sometimes addressed to me, and rambling, seemingly insignificant chatter.

Hamano, speaking in English to me and his colleagues, was teased for 20 incorporating Japanese words: "You *to* [and] me are going to Tokyo, *ne* [isn't that so]?" Because Hamano must conduct at least some of his business in English, his companions found this very amusing.

I was asked to guess the ages of the men, a common game in the hostess club, and I answered seriously forty-six, forty-five, fifty, and then jokingly thirty for Agata, who seemed the oldest, about sixty. Only one verified my estimate, while Hamano and Agata kept joking back and forth that actually their ages were reversed. Again, all laughed at this ploy.

References to sex were constant. . . . Hamano said to me, *"oppai okii"* (your breasts are big), and then started talking to Agata about the kind of woman he liked. Agata told me that Hamano liked big-breasted women even if they were not pretty; Hamano denied this, saying that he liked pretty women even with small breasts like mine (though earlier he had said mine were big). He declared that some women have bodies of three dimensions, sketching out three increasingly large curves in the air, starting at the chest, moving to the stomach, and ending at the hips. . . .

Though puzzling at first, considering the repetitiousness and regularity of such comments, the exaggeration of the response, I came to understand, resulted less from the content of what was said than from the fact that it was said at all. Though blatant reference to female flesh, particularly breasts, is not infrequent in Japan, it triggers in the hostess club an emotion and attitude that men are waiting to let loose. Something of the forbidden, the freedom, the frivolity that the nightlife is agreed to represent, breast talk becomes a signal that the time for play has just begun. More effective than the suggestion that propriety should be abandoned for the night—the popular phrase *"Bureiko shimashoka?"* (Should we dispense with rank, regimen, courtesy?)—a statement like "Your breasts are more like kiwi fruit than melons" is the act of abandon itself. When issued by the highest-ranking member of the party and greeted with laughter, the statement signals the men's endorsement of this abandon and their acceptance of a flippancy and familiarity in their language during the evening.

Speaking of a hostess's breasts is one example of talk that falls into a wider convention of pointing to, discussing, or making fun of something—or more likely, someone—that all men present can relate to on a fairly equal basis. Such references, often sexual, frequently carry the weight of authority that men have as customers and that women must yield to in their status as hostesses. Bijo's hostesses would be laughed at and ridiculed for such perceived weaknesses as lack of beauty, old age (in their thirties), having an unpleasant singing voice, making mistakes when playing the piano (one hostess played), ineptness in servicing, being part of the nightlife with its implied dirtiness, and failing to display great interest in or knowledge of the world. Remarks of this nature were often pointed and brief—"Where did you learn to play piano—in kindergarten?" "How old are you, grandma?" and "I suppose a comic book is as much as you can read." Rarely delivering these barbs with any overt intention of being rude, the men would sit back and laugh, sure that the talk was appropriate to the place and confident that they controlled what was said and how judgment would be passed. . . .

Talking: Insult, Joke, and Pretense

Men use praise and insults to talk to hostesses about themselves. In a party   25
of men, for example, the conversation may be something like "Hisao's good
in English." "No, Nobu's the one who's better. He's a real playboy." "No,
Kazuo is the one who's the playboy; Nobu's a real big shot." "No, Chitoshi's
the one who's *erai* (prestigious)." Usually the building up or praise of men
(to one another) is done in terms not used for evaluation during the day
(that is, at home or at work). Being *josei ni motte iru hito* (good with women;
having a lot of women) is typical, as are comments on how good a drinker,
golfer, singer, and so on, a person is. In this vein, everything said and
responded to at the club is in the realm of "happy time." No one gets angry
and everyone is mutually supportive.[4]

Men, nevertheless, also engage in mutual put-downs. Typically they
are playful and are taken to be anything but serious. Two men were discussing
their own sexual prowess or lack of it. Sato told me that Miyoshi started out
by having sex seven times a night, decreasing to four times on the second
date, three times on the third, once on the fourth, and after that being no
good at all. He, in comparison, could do it four times a night but only once
a month. Then he charged that Miyoshi, in fact, only did it once a month
too, and Miyoshi replied that it was once a month to his *wife*. Sato counted
up Miyoshi's girl friends: Sachiko, Reiko, Keiko, and two others. Miyoshi
interjected that Sachiko was the only one, that she was his ideal woman, and
that Sato could talk about her all he wanted to but he'd never met her.
Keiko, he said, was another story: She's in love with Miyoshi, but Miyoshi
is not in love with her. Sato said that it was just the reverse.

These men were colleagues in the same company and division and
seemed to be of about equal standing. Criticism among such "friends," they
told me, was simply a form of compliment. In the repartee among men
many strategies are used, in addition to compliment and insult, to juggle,
homogenize, and reconfirm male relations positively. One is to introduce
everyone as "friends"—*tomodachi* or "homo"*dachi* as one put it (denied,
laughingly, by his mates)—while refraining from articulating the true nature
of the relationship. Two men in their forties told me the unlikely story that
they were brothers and that the third member of their party, a man in his
fifties, was their father. Subsequently the older man assumed the role of the
biggest lecher *(sukebei)* among them, the common pattern between a superior
and inferiors.

Men hesitate during club conversation to identify themselves in terms
of business. At a club of white-collar members, one customer told me he

---

[4] For example, I saw one man become increasingly drunk and slovenly while other members
of his group did not. He started blubbering, falling off his chair, spilling his drink, and trying
repeatedly to touch the penis of the man sitting next to him. No one said anything or in any
way appeared uncomfortable.

was a bartender at the *Boeicho* (Defense Department). When I asked another, who had told me of traveling to Brazil and about ten other countries that year, what his work was, he answered that he had been "chasing girlfriends." Two other times when I asked the question, I received no answer. Still another, in conversation alone with me, would talk generally about work—how he had worked until he came to the club that night, how work was his hobby, and so on—yet say only that his business was *sabisu-gyo* (service industry).

Pretense, preferably absurd, is a common ploy along these lines as well. Men often claim that they are *yakuza* (gangsters), for example. Joking about nationality and heritage is also prevalent. Many customers would introduce themselves or their colleagues to me as being other than Japanese. One claimed that his companion was descended from head hunters in New Guinea and another said he was descended from Scandinavians. Such absurd assertions were routinely met with a roar of laughter. When the claims were less ridiculous, however—as when one man alleged that his companion was a Korean—the laughter from the others was equally loud but the reaction from the one so depicted was a hearty and immediate "No, no, no, I'm a pure Japanese!"

In the hostess club there is little talk of the office, infrequent mention   30 of home (specifically of wife and children), and no comment of a critical nature that is not disguised by laughter and much joking. The unspoken rule is to avoid anything that could be construed as "serious." But there are exceptions. On occasion, business may be discussed briefly. As one customer told me, for the hours spent "bullshitting," five minutes may be relegated to business. And if it's a deal that is being aimed for (in contrast to the pure entertainment of coworkers going out drinking, for example), the five minutes may make the rest of the evening worthwhile. . . .

Singing

The somewhat illusive relationship between the serious and the light in hostess-club conversations is perhaps best exemplified by the rather recent phenomenon of singing in clubs, which represents both a break from discourse and a commonality with it. Providing, it is said, an activity by which the Japanese can enjoy themselves, it can also, I have observed, entail a considerable amount of anxiety and serious preparation.

Called generically *"karaoke,"* the system is to provide accompaniment to which the customer (or the Mama, a hostess, or a piano player) will sing the words of a popular song.[5] The singing is meant to be a performance and, even in one-counter bars, will be done into a microphone. During the

---

[5] The accompaniment is usually a cassette system in smaller bars—from which comes the word *karaoke*—and a "live" piano and player in larger clubs such as Bijo.

performance the room quiets down, and at the end of it there is applause. Lyrics are provided in books organized by *minyo*, or folk songs; *enka*, modern Japanese songs; American songs; and so on. The selection of a song is often attended to with as much care as its execution.

In Bijo the piano player starts playing at 7:30 P.M. and will occasionally sing along with his music. The Mama or a hostess may be asked to sing, and soon the customers begin to participate. A standing microphone is placed to one side of the piano, along with the accoutrements of music stand, spotlight, and a demarcated circular area to stand in. Because the tables are located a fair distance away from the microphone, this area virtually becomes a stage. The customer's singing a song, therefore, becomes an occasion, unlike the casual outbreaks of song in an American bar.

Characteristically, a customer must be urged at length by the Mama, a hostess, or his companions to sing. He will first resist, saying variously that he's *hazukashii* (shy), *umakunai* (not good), *heta* (bad), *saitei* (the pits), or *onchi* (tone deaf). Eventually he will give in, singing at least once and perhaps a second song or, later, another song to the more or less attentive room.

One customer explained that this activity, which became popular only in the 1980s, developed when the traditional split between nighttime women of culture *(geisha)* and women of sex disappeared. Now, he said, there are very few *mizu shobai* women trained in the arts, so the men have had to take over the singing. Another said simply that men can talk only so long. Singing gives them something else to fill their time on their night out.

Others stressed that when a member of their party sings they immediately feel closer to him. *Karaoke* allows a presentation of oneself through which certain barriers between men can be surmounted. To this end it was implied that how well one did mattered far less than simply doing it. Such sociologists as Tsurumi have argued that the worse one sings, in fact, the better.[6] To suggest a kinship of men based on inability, however, is fallacious. Though it is true that even a poor singer is applauded by a surprising number of the people in the room, and even those who are mediocre are routinely said to be good (*umai* and *jozu*), it is also true that every man wants to be good and that the really proficient singers are recognized for being precisely that.

All men are expected to sing while out drinking with buddies at night; it is *shoganai* (inevitable). To not sing, particularly if other members of one's party have already done so, is viewed as unfriendly and distancing. To sing, therefore, becomes a sign and a promoter of camaraderie.

Singing is also a reflection of the individual. And for this reason some men practice and perfect their numbers. Many fall into what the Japanese refer to as *wan pa-tan* (one pattern), performing always the same song but

[6] Tsurumi made the point during a lecture on Japanese social behavior given to recipients of Japan Foundation Fellowships at the Japan Foundation in 1982.

at least with the assurance that repetition has given them. Others will plow through the song books at length, discussing with their table what might be most appropriate to their particular voices. Singing is thus approached with a seriousness and self-consciousness not matched in conversation. And the assumption is that everyone wants to, and should, do well. A hostess who had recommended that a predominantly "one pattern" customer try a song she thought would be flattering advised him, after he sang it rather poorly, to buy a cassette of the song and practice it repeatedly for at least two weeks.

Some of the men will play up to the audience during their performances, looking directly at faces or crooning to females (hostesses). Many will try to let the mood of the song (particularly the folksong) take them over, closing their eyes and coming close to tears at the inevitably sad lyrics. Nearly all who sing are attentive to the words, timing, and demeanor. Those who are not are considered sloppy and are not accorded the supportive applause at the song's end. I saw this happen only a few times, with men who were very drunk, once with a young and impatient customer, and most often with foreigners who had misinterpreted the construction and rules of the activity. As a hostess told a customer to be "serious" when he started hamming it up while singing a duet, to be untalented is excusable but to be excessively casual is inappropriate and in bad taste.

This singing, it should be noted, is not as easy as might be imagined.   40
In addition to the appreciable anxiety of singing in front of a crowd, which includes one's coworkers, boss, and sometimes clients, is the fact that the songbooks provide only the words, not the melody. Since many of the songs are stylized, with fancy accompaniment in between, the singer, to avoid blunders, must know not only the tune but the form in which it is usually performed. For all of these reasons—the need to be fairly serious, to perform as well as possible, to be familiar with the arrangement of the selection, to just get up and do it in the first place—men are often visibly nervous as they walk up to the microphone. One man, always breaking into a sweat that he would anxiously pat at with a handkerchief, admitted that singing like this was nerve-racking. The accomplishment was, however, cathartic, and the release he shared with his companions helped produce a greater relaxation for the members of his party.

Thinking About the Text

1. In your own words, summarize Allison's principal discoveries about the hostess club. What conclusions do you draw about the "routine"?

2. Kinoshita and Palevsky provide a brief guidebook description of hostess clubs in the "Fantasy" section of "A Guide to Water Worlds" (p. 310).

How would Allison respond to this description? How might she describe a hostess club in one or two paragraphs?

Thinking About Culture

3. Allison stresses the functional aspects of white-collar workers' relaxation in hostess clubs. Can you think of comparable situations and explanations in the United States? How are they different, and how are they the same, as those in Japan?

4. What Allison describes as "breast talk" would be considered sexual harassment in the United States. Or would it? Discuss context and attitudes toward such "talk."

5. Reread the section on drinking. Would this behavior and its consequences be regarded as pathological in the United States? Consider the role alcohol plays in social life in the United States, and your experiences with "social drinking" among young people. Compare it with alcohol's role in Japan as Allison describes it.

6. If you have ever visited an American club or restaurant with *karaoke* entertainment, describe how it differed from the Japanese *karaoke* as described by Allison. Think of another context in which amateur public singing is encouraged and expected in the United States, and analyze it as Allison might.

Mark Schilling

What's Hot on Japanese TV

By their own admission Japanese are *terebi ningen,* a people glued to the tube. Despite a workaholic reputation, the average Japanese spends nearly four hours a day planted in front of the set.

And what is that average Japanese person watching? In Tokyo, he or she would probably be tuned into a program on the five commercial networks or the two channels—one general, one educational—operated by public broadcaster NHK. Cable and satellite channels exist, but their share of the viewing audience is still small—1 percent of the total.

Also, the program would probably be Japanese. Although Japanese love

---

Mark Schilling, a freelance writer and translator, has lived in Japan since 1975. This essay appeared in a magazine aimed at American teachers of courses in Japanese culture.

foreign movies on TV—every network has its own weekly foreign film theater—they rarely take to foreign shows. "Dallas" flopped spectacularly in Japan in the early '80s—the only major TV market in the world where the series failed to hit. "Cosby" lasted all of one season. "Teenage Mutant Ninja Turtles" disappeared down the sewer after a few weeks on NHK's Satellite Two channel. And despite a determined marketing campaign by a local TV distributor, "The Simpsons" never made it to the air.

Instead, viewers are likely to be tuned in to *"Chibi Maruko-chan"* ("Little Miss Maruko"). Set in the Japan of the early '70s, this animated series relates the adventures of the title character—a sweetly obnoxious third-grade girl who might be Bart Simpson's Japanese cousin. Last year *"Chibi Maruko-chan"* soared to the top of the ratings, scoring as high as 39.9—a record for an animated program. The show also produced a hit theme song that sold two million copies and won an award for Record of the Year. By the end of January, *"Chibi Maruko-chan"* had subsided to 34.4 in the Tokyo area, still good enough for third place.

The top show that month, however, was NHK's broadcast of the final   5
day of the year's first professional sumo tournament. The rating, a spectacular 39.5 in Tokyo, was no fluke: In the past year sumo has emerged as Japan's most popular spectator sport, outclassing even the perennial favorite, baseball.

Two main reasons are the Hanada brothers, who are on their way to becoming the top sumo stars of the '90s. Sons of a popular former champion and nephews of a former grand champion, Takahanada and Wakahanada are sumo royalty who have earned their crowns with a rapid ascent up the sport's tough ranking ladder.

In January the younger of the two, nineteen-year-old Takahanada, won his first top division tournament—the youngest wrestler ever to accomplish that feat. When he stepped up to receive his trophy from his uncle, who was serving his last tournament as head of the Japan Sumo Association, TVs in every *ramen* and *yakitori°* joint in the country were tuned in.

The second-ranked show that week was *"Kimi no Na wa"* ("What's Your Name"). The story of a poor girl who struggles to be reunited with the boy she met during a Tokyo air raid, *"Kimi no Na wa"* first ran on NHK radio for two years, beginning in April 1952, and became a major hit. The show was the basis for a film starring Sada Keiji and Kishi Keiko that topped the box office chart in 1953.

"Kimi no Na wa" is also the latest NHK series to fill the 8:15 to 8:30 A.M. time slot, six days a week. Scheduled for half- to one-year runs, these series are known as *tokei gawari* (literally, "in place of a clock"), for the little digital clock that clicks off the seconds in the corner of the screen. The clock, which the nation's *sarariiman* ("salarymen") and *OL* ("office ladies") use to

---

ramen and **yakitori:** Noodles and grilled chicken, the standard fare at many inexpensive restaurants. [Editors' note]

time their morning dash for the train, is an important reason why almost any series in this slot garners high ratings.

Some, however, do better than others: *"Oshin,"* a 1983 series about a young girl who succeeds in business against great odds, became the highest-rated *tokei gawari* ever, scoring in the 60s. It also became a national phenomenon, discussed endlessly on talk shows and in weekly magazines. The show's influence even extended to sumo: A wrestler who became grand champion after a long struggle with diabetes was dubbed the *Oshin* grand champion. By that measure, *"Kimi no Na wa"* has had but indifferent success.

Another NHK hit for January was *"Nobunaga."* This historical drama portrays a year in the life of Oda Nobunaga, a sixteenth-century warlord who encouraged the spread of commerce and Christianity—and dealt ruthlessly with his enemies. It is the thirtieth NHK *taiga dorama* (literally, "big river drama")—lavishly produced yearlong series that usually center on a famous historical figure. Appearing in the 8:00 to 8:45 Sunday night time slot, *taiga dorama* have become a Japanese viewing habit.

But they can flop: One such failure focused on the struggles of Japanese Americans during World War II. The sight of Japanese actors trying to impersonate *nisei* (second-generation Japanese Americans) and speak "native" English strained the credulity of even normally tolerant Japanese viewers. Also, the series' examination of the wrongs perpetrated against Japanese Americans in the United States—and by Japan against its Asian neighbors—did not appeal to the older and largely conservative *taiga dorama* audience. *Taiga dorama* soon returned to the distant past, leaving controversial themes behind.

One show that has stirred up absolutely no controversy in its twenty-three-year run is *"Sazae-san."* An animated series about the misadventures of the title character—a twenty-three-year-old housewife who lives with her three-generation family in Tokyo—*"Sazae-san"* is the Japanese equivalent of the bland-but-comforting American family sitcoms of the '50s and '60s. Although ostensibly set in the present—the electrical appliances the family uses are all recent models made by sponsor Toshiba—its atmosphere is that of the high-growth era of thirty years ago.

Every show consists of three episodes based on a comic strip by Machiko Hasegawa that ran in the *Asahi Shimbun* for twenty-three years. Hasegawa, however, hasn't drawn a new one since 1974. The show's producers keep recycling the ones they consider suitable for TV—about half of the 6,000 newspaper strips. If viewers have tired of *Sazae-san*'s sameness, they have yet to show it by changing channels; the program has been in the top ten since its 1969 premiere, often occupying the number one slot.

But the number one show for 1991 was *"Kohaku Utagassen"* ("The Red and White Song Contest"). A three-hour song competition between a red (women's) and white (men's) team that is shown every New Year's Eve on NHK, *Kohaku* has long been the top showcase for Japanese pop talent and a holiday tradition.

In recent years, however, younger fans of everything from rap to heavy metal have turned away from the show's heavy diet of Japanese pop and sentimental ballads, causing *Kohaku*'s ratings to slip. At one time, there was even talk of canceling the show, but NHK decided to revitalize it instead with infusions of foreign sounds (Paul Simon) and genres (opera). Reviews and results have been mixed: The 1991 *Kohaku*'s rating—53.0 for the final segment—was mediocre for a show that once scored in the 80s.

The most popular program category, however, is not animation or drama or music, but information, which includes everything from sober-sided NHK news shows to hot springs "documentaries" hosted by young—and occasionally unclothed—female MCs. One igniter of the information boom was "News Station," an evening news show on Fuji TV hosted by Hiroshi Kume.

A former comedian, Kume brought a rapid-fire delivery and razor-sharp wit to the news. His off-the-cuff comments outraged rival newscasters, who denounced the show as mere "entertainment," but delighted viewers, who welcomed Kume's informal candor. After its 1988 debut, the show topped the ratings and inspired a host of imitators. Even NHK, the leading exemplar of the good-gray news style, began to lighten up. But "News Station" is still the leader in its 10:00 P.M. time slot and Kume-san seems settled in for a long, successful run. It's as though Jay Leno decided to shoot for Dan Rather's job instead of Johnny Carson's—and got it. Japanese TV is different.

Thinking About the Text

1. Having read Schilling's article, what generalizations would you venture about Japanese television? Have any other selections in this book contributed to shaping your generalizations? Explain.

2. In paragraph 13 Schilling says that a certain television program "is the Japanese equivalent of the bland-but-comforting family sitcoms of the '50s and '60s." If you have some idea of these American programs, describe the type, as specifically as possible.

3. Speaking of TV news in the last paragraph, Schilling mentions "the good-gray news style." Exactly what do you think he means by this term? Which newscasters in American TV fit this description? Are there any who do not? If there are, what styles do they exemplify?

Thinking About Culture

4. Paragraphs 11–12 concern *taiga dorama*—lavishly produced historical dramas made for TV. Do we have such things on American television? If so,

what are they? And, to the best of your knowledge, to whom do they appeal?

5. To what extent do Schilling's comments fit American television? Of course you would have to change the names of the programs, but how much else would you have to change? Be as specific as possible.

6. In the final paragraph Schilling implies that we can hardly imagine Jay Leno in Dan Rather's job. Can you realistically imagine it? If not, why not?

7. In paragraph 3 Schilling lists several very popular American television shows that unexpectedly flopped in Japan. Draw on your reading in this book and your knowledge of those shows to speculate on why they failed to engage the Japanese.

Chapter 9

The Cultural Meanings
of Consumption

In both the United States and Japan in the post–World War II era, relative affluence spurred the creation of a large consumer market, the proliferation of product development, and widespread advertising encouraging everyone to believe they need or want the items and life-style displayed. The media—for instance, the *New York Times,* the "Oprah" show, and even the advertisements in magazines and on television shows—are an integral part of this created culture of style and material goods and are themselves "consumables."

In both Japan and the United States, magazine advertisers particularly target youth markets. These audiences share interests in clothing, music, sports, and other leisure activities, but the products they buy are national, not international. In Japan, Japanese rock music, for example, is preferred over exports from the United States, and to be "correct," trendy clothing must be Japanese, even if it imitates the Seattle grunge or urban hip-hop looks popular in America.

One aspect of Japanese culture that especially supports the burgeoning consumer industries is the custom of gift giving, which Harumi Befu examines in this chapter (p. 333). Of course, Americans too give gifts, both spontaneously and individually—and more ritually, for birthdays, weddings, at religious holidays like Chanukah and Christmas, and at holidays invented by marketers, such as Mother's Day and Father's Day.

The meaning of gift giving is ultimately perhaps the same in both cultures: a reaffirmation of a relationship, a binding together of affection and obligation, a continuity of reciprocity. The outward manifestations are a little different.

Most American gift giving is individualistic and personal. The exception is the corporate gift to clients, which in both countries tends to generic uniformity (whether it is a desk pen set with the company logo in America or a beautifully wrapped box of dried seaweed in Japan). In America, personal gifts are supposed to relate specifically to the recipient's desires and character. Probably, when we give a gift, we try to find an object that the recipient

329

would very much like to have but would not buy for himself or herself, perhaps because it would seem too self-indulgent. Indeed, this kind of gift also exists in Japan, between family members at birthdays, or close friends, with attention to the recipient's personal tastes and secret wishes, but usually gift giving does not follow this pattern.

In Japan, several occasions necessitate gifts: midsummer, New Year's, and end-of-year gifts to a wide range of acquaintances, family, and official or business contacts; gifts for funerals, births, marriages, and other rites of passage; and less formal gifts to the sick or to friends and colleagues upon one's return from travel.

Money is often an appropriate formal gift for such occasions as funerals and weddings, but the bills (cash only) must be new and the presentation envelope a special one with appropriate decorations. An American equivalent can be found in banks, which at Christmastime furnish a folded card with a cutout that accommodates a crisp new bill, to be given to the letter carrier, or to anyone whose tastes the giver does not presume to know. In Japan money is also (less formally) given to children at gift-giving times. Marketing agencies say that children "have six pockets," filled by two sets of doting grandparents and one set of parents. Children thus have substantial savings or disposable income. While older generations who experienced scarcity and hard times might still practice thrift, for the younger set, there is no message of restraint and no sense of "sin" in spending.

Children and youths are the targeted audience for music sales, whether in compact discs (which are also available for rental) or taped albums, and sheet music. Popular-music promoters depend on this market segment, which enjoys the music, emulates and admires the performers, and above all, buys constantly. The teen "idol"—a singer or group of singers—is created by such a promotion agency with the audience in mind. Such performers are invariably cute, young, and often dressed to look even younger, and they sing bouncy, or wistful, rather than sexy or torchy songs. Well-organized fan clubs encourage their admirers into adoring purchases of "idol" goods, items ranging from tissue packet covers to clothing emblazoned with the star's image, sold in special "idol" shops in major cities.

These stars are not born but made. Talent searches by promotion agencies across Japan select trainees who are then put through a long course of preparation, including physical exercise, vocal training, and lessons in stage presence. When the moment is ripe, their debut ushers in about two years of stardom, until their star falls and another's rises, on cue.

There are close ties, of course, between the promotion agencies, teen-magazine editors, and market-research think tanks, and one product of this connection was the finding that adolescent girls tend to cluster in groups of five to seven close friends. This data led promoters to create boy singing groups in similar numbers, on the theory that then, each girl in a circle of friends would have an idol of her own in the group's favorite team, minimizing competition, and maximizing the sale of idol items.

As Donald Richie (p. 360) points out, music is also a private entertainment, and the Sony Walkman became a hit in Japan (and elsewhere) because it permits the private enjoyment, in public, of one's individual choices of music, and, like the comic book, a source of solace and release (and privacy) on the crowded city streets, buses, and trains. Now that cellular telephones are becoming popular as well, a new portable form of electronic entertainment and "connection" is almost as visible on the streets.

The sale of such new products is amplified by the practices of gift giving, with the result that consumer industries are motivated to create new gift-giving holidays, such as Christmas and Valentine's Day. In Japan Christmas is primarily a social, even a romantic occasion rather than a family or religious holiday, as we see in Anne Pepper's essay (p. 345). (Whether it is primarily a religious holiday in the United States is also much in doubt.) The celebration of Christmas focuses on giving presents to children, having a decorated cake, and for the twenty-something set, having a very special night on the town—a collection of festive attributes with no particular focal image or meaning beyond the general message of being with, and giving to, the people you care for. Marketing experts have gotten into the act, of course, and manufacturers have created not only Christmas decor, cards, and the infamous (nearly inedible, but gorgeous) Christmas cake, but also the idea of giving gifts to mark the day. Since Christmas has become *the* romantic holiday, more popular than Valentine's Day, among the young, the most coveted items on a young woman's list for Santa are red roses, Tiffany rings and heart pendants, and especially a night in a posh hotel with dinner, floor show, and chilled champagne in the room. Since dinner and room reservations are sold out (and paid in full) six months ahead, some young men reserve rooms not knowing who their dates will be. Those who can't get reservations for Christmas Eve are called "Christmas refugees." Recently, however, alternative or recession "chic" has made it trendy to have a "home party" instead, even potluck, quite shameful according to traditional hosting principles, which demand that everything be supplied by the host.

Valentine's Day is another such gift-constructed holiday, though usually not as pricey. Similarly "managed," in this case by chocolate and card companies, Valentine's Day is an occasion for young women to purchase chocolates and cards for men. This custom has extended beyond the need to buy for one's significant other: *Giri-choko*, or "obligation chocolates" are required for male colleagues and bosses as well. But the reciprocity principle is served here too, for on March 14, one month later, young men must give a "return gift" on White Day—usually white chocolate, white flowers, or even white lace lingerie. (On p. 350, Elizabeth Andoh makes clear that this sort of "Japanification" of imported practices is not limited to holidays.)

But it does not take a holiday to get people to purchase in Japan. Indeed, shopping is the number one leisure activity for most young people— and adults as well, as we noted in the previous chapter. Even after the shops are closed, Japanese merchandising makes it easy to buy, for nowhere are vending machines more prevalent and diverse. As James Sterngold (p. 357) notes, these machines, most often outdoors and easily accessible, sell everything, literally: From hot hamburgers and liters of whiskey to videocassettes and fresh flowers, all consumption needs are served. In public baths you can get fresh underwear from a machine, and, of course, you can get a health profile and horoscope from computerized machines. For a time recently, according to David E. Sanger (p. 354), slightly used women's panties were also packaged and sold through vending machines to men interested in such items.

Shopping is more than purchasing. Downtown shopping areas are closed to traffic on Sundays, and strolling with friends or family is itself pleasant recreation. Department stores do more than direct sales: All have restaurant complexes; some have cultural centers, theaters, galleries, and concert halls; and the largest also offer adult education courses (and day care for participants' children). Perhaps nowhere in the world has consumption, relatively free from puritanical restraints on materialism, developed such an encompassing culture of its own as in Japan. Urban areas, as David Sanger describes them, seem like giant markets of trustworthy and attractive goods, playful and convenient places, rather than threatening places where *caveat emptor* is the guiding principle.

Explorations

1. Gift giving is both a ritual and a personal act in America, as well as in Japan. What occasions in America require more or less predictable, if not totally ritualized, gifts? Which require very personal ones? What do you think is the meaning of the increasingly popular "gift certificates" or gifts of money in America? How do you react to such a gift?

2. Do you enjoy shopping at a mall? Is it an activity you do with friends? How would you compare the shopping mall activity of American teenagers to the shopping activities of their parents or grandparents? What about shopping activities among different ethnic groups? or differences in the ways men and women shop?

3. Compare the description of the marketing of popular music to young teens in Japan to the equivalent, if you think there is one, in America. How do musicians become popular in America? Describe the different types and identify the segments of the population to which they appeal.

Harumi Befu

Gift Giving

Gift giving in Japan involves elaborate rules and is part of a larger system of social exchange. Gifts may be brought each time a visit is made and are usually exchanged on other specified occasions. An average Japanese family probably gives or receives a gift at least once a week, and the money spent on these gifts constitutes a substantial portion of the family budget. Usually gifts are presented to a family as a unit and rarely exchanged within the family.

There are several major gift-giving seasons during the year: the New Year (*otoshidama* given to children), the end of the year (*seibo* gifts), and the midyear (*chugen* gifts). Significant stages in human life such as birth, coming of age *(seijin),* and marriage, as well as funerals and partings require gifts. Gifts are given to the sick or victims of fire or other disasters as encouragement *(mimai),* or are given as souvenirs for friends, relatives, and others after even the shortest trip (see *miyage*), and for happy celebrations (see *shugi*). On formal occasions gifts are wrapped in heavy white paper decorated with a special tie *(mizuhiki),* and on joyous occasions they are wrapped with a symbolic ornament *(noshi).* When money is given as a gift, as it often is, the bills must be clean and crisp and enclosed in a special money envelope *(noshibukuro),* sold at stationery stores. On inauspicious occasions, such as funerals, the tie is gray and white or black and white, while on happy occasions the tie is usually red and white.

Traditionally gifts in Japan had religious or magical significance. Foods and liquor were offered to the gods on the altar and then eaten in a banquet called *naorai,* so that by sharing the god's food, one acquired some of the god's spirit and power. Edible gifts given by a healthy person to the sick were believed to have, upon being consumed, the magical power of helping to restore health. These religious and magical qualities are seldom remembered or appreciated now. Gifts are often given out of a sense of obligation and in turn require a return gift *(kaeshi).* It is not unusual for people to keep lists of gifts received in order to be able to give a return gift of the exact value. Gifts given to a superior, such as *seibo, chugen,* or to a teacher or a person to whom one is indebted, do not require a return gift.

Gifts given before services are rendered *(hizatsuki)* are an advance expression of thanks, brought for example when one begins lessons in traditional arts like the tea ceremony. When asking for an unusual or substantial favor of a person one has not been formerly acquainted with, an advance

---

Harumi Befu, a professor of anthropology at Stanford University, has written on many topics, including Japanese social structure and internationalization. We reprint an article that originally appeared in an encyclopedia of Japan.

gift (*meishigawari;* literally, "in place of name card"), often of considerable value, is given. Only a thin and tenuous line separates gifts expressing genuine thanks from those with ulterior motives, better classed as "bribes." Actually most gifts simultaneously express one's gratitude or respect, serve material ends, and fulfill important social obligations.

Thinking About the Text

1. Compare Befu's concise essay on gift giving with Millie R. Creighton's various comments on gift giving (p. 334). What different things did you learn about gift giving—in Japan and in general—from the two selections?

Thinking About Culture

2. Befu's essay originally appeared in the nine-volume *Kodansha Encyclopedia of Japan.* (Befu's article will give you a good idea of what this work is like.) Pretend there were a comparable *Encyclopedia of the United States.* Write an essay (750–1,000 words) entitled (like Befu's) "Gift Giving."

3. If you are thoroughly familiar with another culture, write an essay, titled "Gift Giving," for an encyclopedia devoted to that culture.

4. Does your family have any special gift-giving habits you observe, such as the exchange of joke presents, on certain days? If so, consider the "history" of those habits—who started them, and why? How much of a tradition have they become? In what context do they take place? What function, or functions, do they serve?

5. Are there gifts one "expects" to receive on certain occasions? For example, some children of affluent parents might expect to receive a car when they graduate from high school. What is the meaning of such a gift, say, contrasted with a small surprise gift given between friends?

Millie R. Creighton

Japan's Department Stores: Selling "Internationalization"

Once, while walking to Isetan Department Store to conduct research interviews, I stopped to listen to the words of the then current pop hit that accompanied the video being shown on Studio Alta's huge screen overlooking

Millie R. Creighton, a professor of anthropology at the University of British Columbia, is especially interested in the anthropological analysis of Japanese department stores. This essay originally appeared in the November 1989 edition of the Japan Society *Newsletter.*

the bustling east gate intersection of Shinjuku's commercial district: "We are living in a material world." Reflecting on these words I remembered why, as an anthropologist, I had been drawn to a study of Japan's major urban department stores. In our modern and very material world where consumerism is viewed as a route toward self-expression, identity, and communication, stores do more than proffer goods for sale; they serve as a mirror of society, reflecting a culture's values, the nature of social relationships, the expected behavior of individuals in various roles. Through their packaging and presentation of goods and services retailers sell consumers the opportunity to create themselves and define others.

Department stores have a major role in helping the Japanese create "themselves." Because of their high-ranking niche in Japan's retailing world, department stores offer customers status, prestige, and respectability; they have the capacity to create consumer trends, fashion waves, and even national customs. These stores function as guardians and preservers of all that is considered traditional Japanese culture. They have also had a major role in "internationalizing" Japan in the sense that they have been instrumental in introducing and disseminating foreign ideas, holidays, and of course, merchandise throughout the country. In their efforts to sell, department stores have attempted to adapt all of these foreign imports, creating for them meaning in the Japanese context. One way that retailers create a place for foreign goods and customs in Japanese life is by emphasizing the contrast between Japanese goods, customs, or even people, with those from outside. During my research, I discovered that the role of department stores in year-end *(Oseibo)* or midyear *(Ochugen)* gift exchanges, in the adoption of foreign holidays or merchandise, and recently in establishing special liaison centers for foreigners tends to reinforce the distinction between "Japanese" and "foreign"—a distinction that helps shape Japanese identity.

Oseibo and Ochugen

The French sociologist Mauss° theorized that throughout the world the bonds of social life are woven through the exchange of gifts and that social gift giving is not truly voluntary but an obligation. People are tied together by the obligation to give, to receive, and to repay. Many Japanese traditions involve the exchange of gifts given according to precedent and the nature of the social ties involved. Department stores have a higher status in Japan than specialty or discount stores, making them the appropriate places to buy such gifts because the prestige of a store's wrapping paper is often more important than the actual item given. Department stores also play a large role in establishing gift-precedent and instructing givers and receivers in such precedent.

Among these practices the twice-yearly gift-giving customs of Oseibo

---

Mauss: Marcel Mauss, author of *The Gift: Forms and Functions of Exchange in Archaic Societies* (1967), originally published in French in the 1920s. [All notes are the editors'.]

(year-end gifts) and Ochugen (midyear gifts) are conceptualized by the Japanese as "very Japanese" even though they are believed to have been introduced
from China in the Tokugawa period.° These were easily adapted to Japan's
agricultural separation of seasons since the transition to the New Year and
the marking of midyear had great religious significance. Seasonal gift giving
at these times was first a means of expressing support among family groups
tied together in cooperative agricultural labor. The role of department stores
grew as the exchanges became more stylized and as the emphasis changed
from simple to "glamorous" or prestigious gifts.

Watching Ochugen or Oseibo promotions and sales at department   5
stores is like seeing Japanese patterns of social behavior transcribed into
material form. The one-way flow of gifts from those in lower-ranking positions to their superiors clearly reflects the rank-consciousness and hierarchical
pattern of Japanese social relationships. Individual feelings such as affection,
intimacy, or friendship have little to do with selecting gifts or who is to
receive them. Instead, concepts of indebtedness, *giri* or social obligation, and
the desire to be well cared for by people in responsible positions define who
gives gifts to whom. The emphasis placed on families giving presents to the
man's superiors within his company reflects the shift from village-based
agricultural communities to an urban "salaryman" culture. The principle of
"matching the face with the price" means the price paid for a gift must be
consistent with the receiver's status. For example, company employees must
not only give gifts to their superiors; they must make sure that the division
head gets a more expensive present than the section head and, of course,
the face of the company president has the most expensive price-tag of all.

Foreign countries had hoped to increase their sales of exports to Japan
with the increasing value of the Japanese yen and the resulting decline in consumer prices for these goods on the Japanese market. However, in the case of
obligatory gift giving the principle of "matching the face with the price" implies
that lowering the price of an item will not necessarily enhance its salability.
Even before the shift in exchange rates, Fields *(From Bonsai to Levi's)* described
how the importers of Johnnie Walker Black attempted to increase their sales
in Japan by reducing the scotch's shelf price. They succeeded in reducing the
price but as a result dramatically reduced sales of the whiskey. The popularity
of Johnnie Walker Black as an obligatory gift resulted partly from its glamour
as a "foreign" whiskey and partly from its famous brand name. Its popularity
was also due to the fact that everyone knew it sold for 10,000 yen.

Gift Consultants

In addition to their high status among retailers, department stores have the
advantage in obligatory gift sales because their gift prices are standardized,

---

Tokugawa period: 1603–1867, during which the *shogun* Tokugawa family ruled most of
Japan.

unlike discount stores where the prices may vary and the same gift sets may sell for considerably less. Department stores reinforce their advantage by offering numerous gift-giving services such as free delivery and hand-inscribed calligraphy greetings to accompany the wrapping, in addition to the largest selection of gifts. Unlike many other types of retailers, department stores also offer extensive gift-consulting services that are considered especially important for the new bride. Gifts are often socially defined as going from a man to his male superior, but it is usually women who do the actual selecting, purchasing, and sending of gifts (writing their husband's name on the accompanying form as the sender). This can be a confusing task for young wives, and department store consultants come to their rescue by clarifying who they, or their husbands, are indebted to and for how much. Recently department stores have also begun to send consultants to foreign businesses in Japan, hoping to increase sales by "educating" foreigners in the principles of Japan's semiannual gift customs.

Many Japanese express regrets about the contemporary nature of the gift-giving practice, and every year large numbers of housewives reveal in national polls that they would like to stop buying the gifts. Some social critics are concerned that since these customs are now largely removed from their original community context, they are used primarily for career or political advancement. Givers openly expect their superiors or those in power to repay by taking good care of them. At its extreme form this might take on the aspect of a bribe—similar to giving money or valuable information to executives, administrators, or lawmakers in hopes of a favorable outcome—and pave the way for a Lockheed or Recruit type scandal.°

Others simply feel that the custom has become so stylized it has lost all meaning and human sentiment. Ads try to induce a sense of heartfelt sincere emotion with slogans such as "*Magokoro o komete, okurimasu* (Send gifts, enclosing one's genuine heart)." But what Mauss pointed out about gift giving universally, many Japanese housewives feel: The gifts are not truly voluntary, but obligatory.

Department stores promote a few trendy or unusual gifts each year   10 such as packages of arctic ice for midsummer gifts, or year-end gift certificates entitling recipients to helicopter rides for *hatsumode*—the first shrine visit of the year. But for the majority of customers, the gift consultants advise a "safe" item such as a gift set of food, a bottle of alcohol, or a box of soap—items that are always acceptable and of a clearly recognizable price. These gifts are devoid of personal connotations but laden with clearly understandable social meaning. The expression of individuality and personal senti-

---

Lockheed or Recruit type scandal: The Lockheed scandal involved Japanese businessmen and politicians who received bribes and kickbacks for the purchase of Lockheed-manufactured planes by a Japanese civil airline. The Recruit scandal resulted from the president of that employment agency's giving money (not as a direct bribe, but as a kind of political lubricant) to politicians to gain entree to powerful circles and become an insider.

ment in gift selection is not ignored by department stores but has been allocated to Western holidays.

Adopted Holidays

Japan has often been characterized as a borrower. Many Western gift-giving holidays were incorporated into Japanese life, with a great deal of help from department store advertising and sales promotions. The influence of the West gave rise to greater individualism and an increased desire for self-expression. Contradictions between Japanese and Western values were avoided by preserving traditional Japanese values and customs on Japanese holidays, while allocating individualism and self-expression (even romantic love) to adopted Western occasions. Gifts that reflect the personality of the giver, or that express a personal feeling for the recipient are not really appropriate for Oseibo or Ochugen, but were promoted by department stores as wonderful for Christmas or birthday gifts. The new Western holidays provided some structure to gift giving but remained less stylized. These gifts did not have to be a set price, were not restricted to certain items, and could even be handmade by the giver. The decision to give such a gift could also vary from year to year.

Department stores helped popularize many of the foreign customs either by giving them an initial boost or by tying them to existing Japanese symbolism. For Mother's Day, many department stores set up tables at the exits and entrances of train stations. Store employees give commuters printed cards to address to their mothers. The stores provide the cards and pay the postage fees. Department stores managed to link Father's Day to existing Japanese associations of men with alcohol. Falling in June, Father's Day became the perfect occasion for the opening of summer beer gardens on department store roofs.

Christmas is seen by the Japanese as a foreign holiday, in contrast to New Year's, which is embraced as the most important and most characteristically "Japanese" event of the year. It is somewhat puzzling that Christmas could remain so popular given its contrasting image to *Oshogatsu*, which occurs only one week later. However, it is quite possible that the celebration of Christmas as a "foreign" holiday helps assure that New Year's customs do not face pressure to change with waves of fashion, thus enhancing the role of Oshogatsu as a national symbol of Japanese heritage. Many Oshogatsu customs derive nostalgic value from past New Years remembered from childhood or imagined from Japanese history. Games involving shuttlecocks, kites, and spinning tops are strongly associated with New Year's, and are displayed or given to children year after year. The same New Year's treats known as *Osetchiryoori* are also found attractively arranged each year in layered lacquered boxes. Department stores conform their New Year's sales to these expectations with displays of shuttlecock paddles (most of which are very glamorous and not intended for children to actually play with), classes on making Osetchiryoori for the full-time homemaker and popular sales of prepacked Osetchiryoori feasts for working women who don't have the time. The symbolic association between Oshogatsu and Japanese nationality is evident when one sees a large poster in a department store basement food floor that glamorously depicts typical Osetchiryoori offerings with the large bold-faced caption, "*Nihon no Dento, Nihon no Oshogatsu* (Japanese Tradition, Japanese New Year's)."

The first of January in Japan is clearly not a day for eating hamburgers, cake, and soft ice cream, nor an occasion to give children video games, baseball bats, or Barbie dolls. Yet modern Japanese children want these things, just as adults sometimes want to give presents based on personal inclinations not tied to concepts of giri or relationships between groups. As well as providing an occasion to give personalized gifts, Christmas in Japan highlights the favorite items of contemporary children. The custom of eating Christmas cakes is widespread and the sale of toys skyrockets. Department stores report that toy sales for December are three times any other month, with December 25 regularly the highest selling day of the year for the toy department.

The adoption of Christmas has created an occasion for providing the favorite playthings and foods for children—items that may change from year to year with popular trends. In contrast, New Year's or Oshogatsu habits are preserved and reenacted each year. Christmas allows an occasion that emphasizes individualized gifts, personal friendships, and relations within the nuclear family. Oshogatsu and the associated custom of Oseibo emphasize the household as a unit, relationships between households, gift giving according to social obligation, and foods or pastimes designated as part of Japan's cultural heritage.

15

Valentine's Day: A Man's World

Valentine's Day, another "imported" holiday, was initially brought to Japan by the chocolate industry, but retailers played an enormous role in popularizing it. As part of their promotional attempts, department stores set up displays of St. Valentine's birthplace (Terni, Italy), established "Valentine post offices" promising a February 14 delivery, and offered classes on *tezukuri* (hand-made) chocolates. In Western countries the day is marked by the mutual exchange of sentimental gifts among romantic couples; in Japan it is a day for women to give chocolates to men. One Japanese man stated that this twist was responsible for its success, claiming that the men never would have given the presents to begin with, which would have made the women embarrassed to do so. However, since the men were never expected to give presents, women could do so without the fear of seeming silly. The giving of obligatory chocolates, known as *giri-choko* (obligation chocolate) is now also part of the Valentine's Day tradition in Japan. The flow of giri-choko follows established precedent, women give and men receive. Female office workers give all of their male coworkers giri-choko as a means of showing gratitude.

Normally women are expected to be even more reserved than men, and expected to act particularly reserved (even shy) in their relations with men. Valentine's Day is an exception and many Japanese consider it the one day of the year women and girls are allowed freedom of personal expression. A spokesperson for one department store said, "This is the only day girls can express their feelings very openly."

Since Japan's Valentine's Day is frequently presented as an occasion releasing women from normally restricted behavior, I would like to present an alternative, and somewhat contrasting, interpretation. Instead of freeing women, it is possible that Valentine's Day as practiced in Japan acts to reinforce a traditional female social ideal that presents women as inferior to and dependent on men. Western-style sweets (chocolates) are the designated gifts for Valentine's Day. Sweets are associated with women in Japan, and sweet things are symbolic of dependency. (The word for dependency relationships, *amae*, is strongly associated with the word for sweet, *amai*.) For traditional gift-giving practices, such as Oseibo and Ochugen, people of inferior status give gifts to the superiors they rely on. If projected to Valentine's Day this would imply that women (the givers) are considered inferior to their husbands and boyfriends (the receivers).

The giri-choko custom likewise suggests that female office workers are viewed as ranking lower than their male colleagues. Far from an opportunity for free personal expression, many women now feel compelled to give the chocolates for fear they would be considered lacking manners if they did not. One woman once complained that when she and several friends at work exchanged Christmas presents, they were scolded by their supervisors and told not to engage in such playful activity on company time. However, there were no complaints when the same women gave giri-choko to their male colleagues on Valentine's Day. The fact that the giri-choko practice is indulged by companies and widely engaged in by women suggests that, despite the passage of Japan's Equal Employment Opportunity Law, the traditional image of status inequality between the sexes still persists in corporate practice and in the minds of many company executives and employees, both male and female.

Domesticating Foreign Merchandise

Throughout their history, Japanese department stores have played an active role in the importation of foreign goods. In order to popularize foreign items they have frequently had to teach people how to use them. In order to aid the transition to foreign-style clothing for daily wear, the stores became educators, employing specialists to teach consumers how to put on the strange foreign garments with zippers and buttons rather than the familiar ties or obi. Reflecting the belief that it is never too late to learn, some stores such as Isetan still have designated sales areas designed for elderly women who have never worn anything but kimono. Specially trained employees assist their elderly clientele in learning how to put on Western-style clothing for the first time. In many cases, however, the role of the department store is now being reversed. It strives to maintain the existence of kimono by employing kimono teachers to instruct Japanese customers in how to wear the traditional costume.

In addition to clothing, department stores have had a major role in introducing the Japanese to many foreign foods. Free samples on the basement food floor are intended to encourage people to develop new tastes. Employees give meal suggestions or teach their customers how to make foreign foods. Sometimes they devise means of making foreign foods more palatable to Japanese tastes, such as suggesting that yakitori sauce be substituted for dressings like sour cream or cheese sauces, which many Japanese find unappetizing.

The image of foreign goods, habits, or institutions is often altered when they are redefined for the Japanese. In the United States, Sears has a "down-home" reputation, the average person's store. Seibu Department Store brought Sears to Japan, establishing a special "Sears corner" in their own stores and distributing catalogues devoted to the sale of Sears merchandise. In Japan, Sears was introduced through a department store, so it had prestige. Sears was foreign, so it was "classy." Having been transformed for its Japanese customers, Sears now represents elegance, flair, and elitism. Like Fiorucci, Dior, and Calvin Klein, Sears is another famous "brand name" for Seibu's shoppers.

Blue-Eyed Department Store Employees

Japanese department stores have long provided customers with a contrast between goods and customs thought of as Japanese or foreign. Recently they have capitalized on the Japanese interest in foreign countries by giving customers the foreigners themselves. Seibu began this trend in 1985 when it opened the first Foreign Customers' Liaison Office in its Yurakucho branch store. The staff, all of whom could speak Japanese, consisted of foreigners from several different countries. Similar offices have since been opened in many department stores. Foreign customers are promised that they will be served from a foreign rather than Japanese perspective, and that they will not have to cope with the Japanese language while shopping. These offices will also help foreigners (*gaijin*) deal with land agents, find schools for their children, interpret Japanese laws—in short, give advice on any issue about life in Japan. Some stores initiated clubs that foreigners can join such as Isetan's "I Club." Many stores that did not yet have specific foreign service counters began to employ foreigners for special exhibits. In 1986, I and two other American women worked as guides for Takashimaya's annual Exhibit of Japanese Tradition (*Nihon no Dentoten*).

Department stores advertise that their new services and special offerings for foreigners are helping to "internationalize" Japan by making life easier for foreign residents and by giving foreigners a chance for regular company employment. Some store personnel believe that Japanese-speaking foreign clerks or guides send a new message to Japanese customers. A Japanese manager for the original foreign service center told me that Japan's poor success at "internationalization" was because many Japanese have a "gaijin complex," involving the conviction that foreigners can never learn to speak Japanese or fit in to Japanese daily life. He believed the presence of foreign clerks fluent in Japanese would help disprove this conviction.

The special services have helped open new employment options for   25
foreigners (department stores were the first companies in Japan to employ foreigners as regular members of their permanent employment staffs) and have greatly assisted many foreign residents trying to cope with the complexities of living in Japan. However, these foreign services can sometimes add to the frustrations of foreigners in Japan. First, these special services may actually reinforce a "gaijin complex" by emphasizing the "differentness" of foreigners. For some Japanese the existence of foreign liaison centers simply reaffirms their beliefs that most foreigners can't learn the Japanese language or customs after all, and therefore require special help just to go shopping. Television and newspaper reports of department store events for foreigners often stereotypically exaggerate their differentness, i.e., by calling them "blue-eyes," or by focusing on their ineptitude with Japanese customs. For example, while working at Takashimaya, I was interviewed on one news program while the television screen showed only my feet—sticking out of too-tight Japanese *geta*.° In another instance a television broadcast of our participation in the exhibit focused on the fact that one of the three foreign guides did not know how to eat Japanese *soba*° noodles correctly.

Gaijin Kimono

Furthermore, the special services are often a disadvantage to foreigners hoping for a Japanese experience, as the following example shows. While living in Japan I knew a West German woman whose primary interest in Japan was the tea ceremony and who studied under a Japanese teacher. Before leaving Japan she decided to buy a custom-made *yukata* from a reputable department store. She had a fair ability in Japanese and found it much easier to discuss certain topics such as kimono in Japanese than in English, which for her was a difficult foreign language. Unfortunately, the employees insisted on speaking English to her (now often considered a standard "service" for foreigners). The yukata was finally ordered but was a shocking disappointment when it arrived. Kimono for women are normally cut longer than floor length, then folded and tucked around the midriff. This is a complicated process, but helps fit the kimono to the female form. Unknown to this buyer,

---

geta: Wooden clogs.   **soba:** Thin noodles made of buckwheat.

the store had recently introduced a new "gaijin kimono" cut at floor length and not folded before placing the obi. My acquaintance says store employees never asked her if she wanted a "gaijin kimono"; since she was not Japanese, they simply decided to make it that way. What she wanted was an authentic Japanese yukata to use in her tea study.

This example reflects a major potential problem of special services for foreigners that department stores should try to avoid. Namely, the stores should not try so hard to treat foreign customers as foreigners, thereby eliminating what is authentically Japanese about the shopping experience. Most people do not travel halfway around the world hoping to be treated exactly as they were "back home." For most foreign tourists and residents in Japan, the thrill of visiting a Japanese department store derives largely from the differences.

Department stores should also not assume that *all* foreign shoppers desire the same goods or treatment. Many foreign residents come to Japan as company employees or family members who would be happy to speak with department store clerks in their native language rather than struggle with Japanese, and grateful for the store services that help them adjust to their new living environment. In contrast, there may be other residents who were brought to Japan by their companies, for military service, etc., but who hope to learn as much about the country as possible before their stay ends. Many of these may be interested in special classes or clubs for foreigners now being started by some department stores that teach Japanese cooking, language skills, the art of bonsai, etc. Finally, there are foreign residents who have lived in Japan for years and have long since adopted a very Japanese life-style, are fluent in the Japanese language and accustomed to Japanese habits. These foreigners will find it frustrating (perhaps offensive) when a clerk responds in English to their questions in Japanese. They will not have pleasant feelings toward a store that sends them a modified kimono, or in any other way assumes they do not want the same treatment as Japanese. In the 1980s Japanese retailers began to notice the differences among Japanese customers and switched their sales strategies from an emphasis on the masses to appealing to distinct market segments. It is time for stores to realize that foreigners do not uniformly have the same desires either.

Blurring the Lines of Demarcation

Throughout their history, Japan's large retailers, its department stores, have catered to Japanese consumers' desire for Japanese traditions and their equally strong interest in foreign countries. In department store offerings, as in Japanese society as a whole, it is often the contrast between Japanese and foreign goods, customs, or traditions that helps shape Japanese identity. *Washoku* (Japanese cuisine) contrasts with *yooshoku* (Western cuisine), *yama-tokotoba* (words of Japanese origin) with *gairaigo* (words of foreign origin),

Nihonjin (Japanese) with *gaijin* (foreigners). In many cases, when foreign goods or holidays were adopted, they were adapted, redefined, and given a specific role or place in Japanese life. Western-style clothing was adopted for everyday wear, while kimono were reserved for occasions such as weddings, age-marking ceremonies, or Oshogatsu that emphasize a Japanese heritage. Foreign holidays were defined as occasions for individualistic expression in contrast to many Japanese occasions.

Now, as Japan struggles to "internationalize," the question is: "What role will foreigners have in Japanese life and society?" Perhaps the presence of foreign employees in department store operations will enable Japanese customers to see foreigners as people, and not just as "different." I hope the new services for foreigners will help integrate them into Japanese life, not further demarcate them from Japanese.   30

Thinking About the Text

1. Briefly summarize each part of Creighton's essay (there are nine of them; an introduction and eight subsequent parts marked with headings). Which sections engaged your interest most? Why?

2. According to Creighton, "department stores have a major role in helping the Japanese create 'themselves' " (para. 2). What does it mean to say that a store can help people to create themselves? If you think any American stores play such a role, explain how.

Thinking About Culture

3. On what occasions in the last year did you give a gift? If possible, compare two occasions, one in which you gave a gift that in substantial measure expressed your personality or the recipient's, or both, and another in which you gave a gift that was more conventional. How do you account for the difference? Was it determined by the holiday, your relationship to the recipient, or some other factor?

4. In her first paragraph Creighton says that stores "serve as a mirror of society, reflecting a culture's values [and] the nature of social relationships. . . ." Evaluate this statement, with reference to at least one large store that you are familiar with. (The store may serve a particular ethnic clientele.)

5. In paragraph 21 Creighton says that, in Japan, foreign foods are sometimes adapted to Japanese taste. If you are familiar with an ethnic cuisine, explain to what extent it is adapted in the United States. For instance, is the American version less spicy? How Mexican is the food at Taco Bell? How Chinese is canned chow mein?

Anne Pepper

Christmas in Japan

"Let's Santa!" screams the headline of a trendy Tokyo magazine as December approaches.

In a country that has enthusiastically adopted Halloween and Mother's Day along with Buddhist and native Shinto festivals, it's not surprising to find Christmas on the holiday calendar as well. When December comes, the great Ginza emporiums rival Bloomingdale's or Harrod's in the lavishness of their Christmas decorations. Christmas carols fill the air, impeccably decorated trees enchant tired shoppers, Santa Clauses smile—and bow—at passers-by. Seeing all this, one might think that Christmas in Japan differs little from Christmas in the West.

But like most foreign phenomena that have become part of the local culture, Christmas in the land of the rising sun has been given a Japanese twist. With scarcely 1 percent of the population being Christian, few think of it as a religious holiday; it is primarily a social occasion. Christmas Eve, rather than Christmas Day, is the time to celebrate, since December 25 is a normal workday in Japan.

Though Christmas has long been on the calendar, the Xmas phenomenon really took off in Japan during the flush days of the bubble economy, when marketing wizards outdid themselves coming up with new ways for people to spend their money. Christmas was a natural. Everybody knew there was a holiday called Christmas, but few were inclined to pull out all the stops until retailers, the hospitality industry, and the mass media pointed the way.

As a result, in the late 1980s Christmas became the trendiest holiday on the annual calendar. To a newly affluent generation of Japanese, it was marketed as an occasion to go on a spending spree and have a romantic night on the town. A date on Christmas Eve, done properly, could cost a man an entire month's salary. Tokyo's toniest hotels were the place to take a girl if you really wanted to impress her. The more famous the hotel, the more famous would be the entertainer doing the dinner show. Formal dress was required by most hotels to attend these shows: tuxedos for men, long dresses for women. The meal would be continental, with numerous courses and frequent changes of wine. Champagne for the really extravagant spenders, or, if the man had reserved a room for overnight, he might have arranged for a bottle of iced champagne to be waiting upstairs after the show.

The other essential element of such an evening was the Christmas gift

5

Anne Pepper is a freelance writer based in Tokyo. This essay originally appeared in 1993 in an English-language journal published in Japan, called Mangajin.

which the young Romeo was expected to present to his fair maiden. Lest there be any doubt as to what might be a suitable gift, all he had to do was look in one of the popular magazines for suggestions. Jewelry ranked high on the list—not just any jewelry, but particular items from prestigious stores. Tiffany's was a sure winner, so much so that long lines of young men formed outside the Tokyo branch of Tiffany's after the December issue of certain magazines hit the stand. One year, Tiffany's was wiped clean out of a particular ring, leaving legions of dejected Romeos to settle for second best.

To be sure that a Christmas Eve reservation was secure at a leading hotel, bookings were made several months in advance. In many cases, the reservation was made even before the young man knew who his date for the evening would be. Christmas Eve became the most important night of the year to have a date—no self-respecting single in Japan would admit to spending the evening home alone. To help unattached young men and women find a date for the most romantic night of the year, department stores and other institutions started arranging get-acquainted parties in advance of the Christmas season. Hotels, protecting themselves from last-minute cancellations should a young man not be able to find a date for Christmas Eve, required that advance reservations be paid in full.

How is Christmas celebrated now that the economic bubble has burst? Conspicuous consumption is out, and a do-it-yourself Christmas is in. As usual, the popular magazines, having heralded the new trend, give plenty of tips for how to bring it off successfully. Instead of going to a fancy dinner show at a hotel on Christmas Eve, go to a Christian church and watch the service. (After this advice was published, regular worshippers were sometimes disconcerted by flashbulbs going off in the middle of the service.) Then rent a *karaoke* box° and sing with friends. Clothing should be informal and Christmas presents and decorations should be handmade. One magazine goes so far as to recommend eating Christmas Eve dinner at McDonald's.

But most suggest what is called in Japanese a "home party." "Buy table games your friends can play at home," advises one weekly. A department-store publication proposes throwing a potluck dinner, and asking friends to bring something—a radical departure from traditional Japanese concepts of hospitality. "Serve sparkling wine instead of champagne," and "Buy your prepared Christmas Eve dinner at a Seven-Eleven," are some other ideas finding their way into print.

Entertaining at home has been the exception rather than the rule in   10
postwar Japan, with its rabbit-hutch-size living quarters, but with the advent of the recession, the mass media has cast its approval on a cozy Christmas Eve at home. The warmth of the mood, they suggest, makes for a more genuine Christmas than a stuffy evening at a hotel.

---

karaoke **box:** A small room or freestanding dumpster-size unit, which can be rented by the hour. See Anne Allison's description of *karaoke* on p. 321 (especially para. 32). [Editors' note]

The big hotels, undaunted, decided that if they couldn't feed people Christmas dinners on the premises, they would prepare complete meals that can be heated and served at home. For an extra fee, the dinners are delivered to the customer's doorstep.

Christmas is now so widespread that every retailer who can figure out an angle has gotten in on the act. The Kentucky Fried Chicken chain had a leg up on other merchants, because standing in front of every one of their stores is the jovial, pot-bellied likeness of Colonel Sanders, looking for all the world like a life-sized Santa Claus. In December, a red suit and hat complete the transformation.

KFC also got a boost from the fact that chicken has become a popular Christmas dish in Japan, partly because few homes have ovens large enough to accommodate a turkey or goose. KFC's Christmas Party Barrels are snapped up so fast on December 24 that the chain does five times its usual volume on that day, to the tune of over 2 billion yen.

As for the dessert, there is no choice. Everyone in Japan knows that on Christmas Eve it is proper to serve a Christmas cake. They know this because bakeries throughout the country are filled with beautifully decorated cakes bearing a Santa Claus figure and a Christmas greeting spelled out in Japanese or English. In the late afternoon on December 24, piles of these cakes are displayed on tables out on the sidewalk, to catch the eye of fathers—or mothers—returning home.

Any cakes unsold are worthless on the 25th, and this has given rise to   15
a slang phrase in Japanese. "Christmas cake" refers to a woman who has reached the age of twenty-five without finding a husband.

The sale of Christmas trees has become such big business that American growers would like to get in on the action. They hope to entice Japanese into forsaking plastic trees for fir ones. But before this can happen, the growers will have to scale down their trees to the small size of most Japanese homes. One importer has suggested that the Americans develop a miniature fir similar to a bonsai tree.

The popularity of home parties doesn't mean that the streets are silent on the 24th. Christmas Eve dinner cruises are now in vogue. Since the late 1980s, Tokyo and other big cities on the water have been served by small ships that are essentially floating restaurants. They have romantic names such as *Symphony* or *Lady Crystal,* and feature Western—especially French— cuisine.

Japan's top-of-the-line passenger cruise ship, the *Asuka,* was first launched during the bubble economy. It offers several overnight "Christmas Cruises" in December, with cabins ranging from 41,000 yen to 200,000 yen° per person. From December 21–27, the ship makes a week-long Christmas cruise to Kyushu costing 264,000 yen to 1,200,000 yen per person. In Kyushu, the destination is Huis Ten Bosch, an authentic Dutch-style village complete

---

41,000 yen to 200,000 yen: Roughly $400 to $2,000. [Editors' note]

with canals and a full-scale copy of the royal palace. The hotels and restaurants at Huis Ten Bosch boast of offering the most authentic European Christmas in Japan.

For those who can't afford a cruise, but who want to get out and do something spectacularly different with a date on Christmas Eve, a helicopter ride at twilight is sure to impress.

Another "in" place to take a date on Christmas Eve is Tokyo Disneyland. 20
TDL stays open late on December 24, and is always mobbed with dating couples. When the park closes for the evening, they head for one of the nearby resort hotels, where, naturally, a reservation has been booked well in advance.

The idea of a fun-filled *"ibu"* has captivated not only Japan's swinging singles. Since married women rarely get an opportunity to go out on the town with their husbands, some have seized on Christmas Eve as an occasion to insist that hubby take them out. This gives them a chance to dress up in their best Western finery—a chance that doesn't come along very often. And if hubby can't be corralled for a Christmas night celebration, a group of matrons might dress up and go out on their own.

Perhaps hubby is out entertaining clients, for Christmas Eve is also an ideal occasion to arrange something special for important corporate contacts.

The present emperor was born on December 23, and custom has it that an emperor's birthday shall be a national holiday. This has been a great boon to the Christmas industry, because it puts people in a holiday mood the day before Christmas Eve. It has also been a plus for the travel industry. On years when December 23 falls on a Friday or Monday, they can offer longer than usual Christmas getaways. Holiday packages to Southeast Asia, Micronesia, and even Hawaii are snapped up eagerly by single travelers, especially young working women. Christmas travel offers them very good value for money, whereas travel a week later, during the New Year holidays, carries a peak-season surcharge.

About the time the bubble economy collapsed, a new type of urban leisure park appeared in Japan, and these are proving immensely popular with singles on a date. All are going after the Christmas trade by grafting Santa Claus and special holiday events onto their usual attractions. Wild Blue Yokohama's main attraction is a mammoth indoor pool where people can swim and surf, and a twenty-meter-wide screen rises above the pool for a knock-out show of sound, light, and water. Add Christmas to this show and the result is a lot of entertainment for a reasonable sum of money. The biggest of these indoor ocean parks, down south in Miyazaki, will celebrate its first Christmas with a Santa-in-the-tropics theme.

As interest in big-ticket Christmas themes has declined, consumers are 25
spending more for basic elements such as cards and flowers. As a result, Japan may now have the most elaborate Christmas cards in the world. They talk, they sing, they play music—powered by tiny electronic devices so slim that they can be easily mailed. Other Christmas cards incorporate a present:

calendars, the old standbys, have been replaced by telephone cards and book certificates. For that someone special, a Christmas card may contain a compact disc.

Times, indeed, have changed, if someone special gets a compact disc instead of a dinner show. And for those couples who want a romantic Christmas Eve in 1993, the newest "in" thing to do this year is drive at night across the recently opened Rainbow Bridge over Tokyo Harbor and look at the city lights across the water.

How about the kids? Seventy percent of Japanese children between the ages of six and ten say that they believe in Santa Claus. Small wonder, for in Japan, Santa Claus is not likely to let them down.

The array of toys at stores such as Kiddyland is mindboggling, as are some of the prices. Sophisticated electronic gadgetry runs into sums too steep for a child's wallet. Doting grandparents, their own childhood marred by wartime deprivation, are heavy spenders. These grandparents are likely to have come from large families—six, eight, or even ten children—and having so few grandchildren makes them more likely to up the amount spent per child.

Two years ago, when the first new baby in a generation was born into the Imperial family just before the onset of the Christmas season, the toy industry joyfully started promoting what they hoped would become a new tradition: Baby's First Christmas. They introduced stuffed animals that play Christmas carols, Christmas tree ornaments depicting a tiny doll in a cradle, and even teddy bears emblazoned with the logo "Baby's First Christmas."

Christmas celebrations in Japan will no doubt continue to evolve, but only time will tell if the excesses of the late 1980s will ever again be part of a Japanese *Kurisumasu*.   30

Thinking About the Text

1. Did Pepper's essay hold your interest? Why, or why not?

2. Do you think the final paragraph ends her essay effectively? Explain.

Thinking About Culture

3. It is certainly odd that Christmas is celebrated in a country where the Christian population is only about 1 percent, but, when you think about it, some aspects of the celebration of Christmas in the United States are also odd. What, after all, has Santa Claus to do with the birth of Jesus? And why the yule log, the Christmas tree, the wreath with holly? Why, in fact, is Christmas celebrated on December 25, since the New Testament

gives no clue about the date of the birth of Jesus? Consult a reference work—an encyclopedia is probably a good place to begin—in order to find out the answers to these questions.

4. In the United States, different ethnic communities celebrate Christmas in different ways. If you are familiar with a Christmas celebration that would surprise a white Anglo-Saxon Protestant, write a description of it.

Elizabeth Andoh

The Japanification of American Fast Food

When my daughter, Rena, was growing up in Tokyo in the 1970s, we lived in Ogikubo, a short walk from the train station. On her way to and from kindergarten we would pass through the old marketplace, a maze of alleys with stalls selling household gadgets and food. Just beyond was our local Seiyu *depato* (department store), snugly set into a block of fast-food restaurants. Among the *ramen* noodle shops were McDonald's, Mister Donut, Kentucky Fried Chicken, and Baskin Robbins, known as *sate wan* ("31") for the thirty-one flavors of ice cream it supposedly sold, although Rena and I counted only ten flavors.

At the time, the Japanese menus at these "American" restaurants were not significantly different from their true American counterparts on the other side of the Pacific, although there were some Japanese peculiarities. The most frustrating of these for Americans was not being able to order according to personal preference. Hamburgers *always* came with mustard, ketchup, *and* onions. Drumsticks and wings *always* outnumbered breasts (the Japanese think that dark meat is tastier than white meat). This never seemed to bother Rena's Japanese friends, who ate the burgers and chicken as served. To the horror of all those watching, Rena would pick off the onions, one by one. She did learn to like dark meat chicken, however.

For the first five or six years of operations in Japan, most American food outlets followed a similar approach: They began with a very selective, fairly "authentic" and conservative menu, presented and priced to meet Japanese expectations. At this introductory stage, the very "foreignness" of the food seemed stylish and appealing to the Japanese.

Elizabeth Andoh is the author of An American Taste of Japan, *a cookbook with recipes that integrate Japanese ingredients and culinary philosophy with American eating habits. She has lived in Japan for many years, periodically returning to the United States, where she gives cooking classes. This selection appeared in her feature column "A Taste of Culture" in the magazine* Mangajin.

By the late '70s, however, interesting hybrid variations began to crop up. Mister Donut introduced *an* ("sweet bean paste") as an alternative to jelly in its donuts, and "31" offered *matcha* (a kind of green tea) and *ogura* ("sweet red bean") ice cream. This was more than just the coincidental borrowing of an indigenous flavoring to make American donuts and ice cream appeal to the Japanese. For such hybrid foods to survive, and thrive, they must satisfy some deeper cultural "logic."

In Japan elaborate sugar and rice flour confections have been consumed   5
with tea (both ceremonial *matcha* and the more ordinary *sencha*) for centuries. Since many of these tea cakes are filled with sweet bean paste, *an*-filled donuts make sense to the Japanese. Similarly, the Japanese have enjoyed *kaki-gori* (shaved ice drizzled with sweet syrups) for a very long time. In fact, there are tales told of transporting huge blocks of ice from the mountains to satisfy the noble appetites of the Shogun in the eighteenth century! Since one of the most popular *kaki-gori* flavors is *Uji Kintoki* (*Uji*, the name of a place near Kyoto famous for its tea, refers to the tea-flavored syrup on top, and *kintoki* refers to the sweet red beans on the bottom) it's not surprising that the Japanese came up with this flavor for ice cream.

Recent additions to the Mister Donut menu follow a similar pattern of adaptation and assimilation. A Japanese turn-of-the-century snack that continues to be enjoyed today is called *daigaku imo,* or "University Potato." The name refers to the students who first popularized this snack consisting of chunks of fried sweet potato, glazed in a honeylike syrup and sprinkled with black sesame seeds. In the fall of 1992, Mister Donut introduced a new line of muffins. What do you think the most popular flavor was, particularly among college kids? You guessed it, sweet potato with black sesame!

This type of functional adaptation is not limited to sweets by any means. McDonald's, which began operations in Japan in the summer of 1971, has been selling its french fried potatoes without ketchup to the Japanese public from the start (most Japanese think ketchup is too messy for finger food). Last fall they decided to spice up their fries by offering customers a choice of four different seasoned salts: *nori* (a kind of seaweed), curry, barbecue, and Mexican. I couldn't get statistics from the company to either confirm or deny my hunch that the most popular flavor was *nori,* but I do know that most children brought up in Japan, regardless of their nationality, adore *nori*-flavored potato chips and *senbei* (rice crackers).

In addition to the functional adaptation of ingredients and cooking techniques, there is another important factor in the process of culinary acculturation: ritual association. In other words, the Japanification process requires that American foods find a cultural niche in some Japanese ceremony or event. In this respect, Kentucky Fried Chicken was the first, and arguably the most successful, American transplant in Japan. From the start in the fall of 1970, the joint venture of Pepsico and Mitsubishi Trading Company seemed to understand and appreciate the dietary quirks and marketing challenges of Japan. They immediately expanded their menu to suit local rituals.

The first major accommodation was the introduction of roast chicken at Christmastime.

Those of you with a quizzical expression on your face right now probably have not lived in Japan within the past twenty years. While those of you who are chuckling softly remember burnished brown chicken legs, tied decoratively at the "ankle" with silver foil and red ribbon, that would appear during the month of December at KFCs throughout Japan. In the Japanese scheme of things, Christmas is a secular holiday and the menu consists of roast chicken legs and *dekoreshon keki* (cake with gobs of decoratively piped buttercream). The fact that this Japanese ritual *(Kurisumasu)* originated in a foreign land makes it only more "logical" for the Japanese to celebrate it with foreign foods.

In the cross-cultural culinary business, sometimes indigenous foods get repackaged, too. Last year, Nihon KFC transformed Hokkaido salmon, which is usually salted and savored in grilled chunks, into a fried fish sandwich, similar to McDonald's popular Filet-o-Fish.   10

Market pressure to remain responsive to food fashions often produces strange, multicultural hybrids. Perhaps the most ridiculous, by American thinking, was the brief popularity of Nihon KFC's *tira misu,* a gooey puddinglike confection inspired by the Italian dessert that goes by the same name.

More important to the Japanification process than mere food fads, though, was Nihon KFC's efforts to incorporate deeply rooted Japanese culinary practices into their "American" menu. The most significant of these was the introduction last fall of toasted riceballs as a replacement for biscuits with their fried chicken.

Indeed, Japan KFC seems to be coming full circle in the acculturation process, with the creation of a subsidiary to produce and sell their version of *yakitori* (chicken grilled on skewers). And, their PR people tell me, the next move will be to open a Japanese-style boxed lunch shop near their headquarters in Ebisu. This experiment is scheduled to begin in November of this year.

Similarly, McDonald's Japan recognized the importance of rice when it introduced two types of *kare raisu* ("curry rice," white rice served with a thick curry-flavored gravy): beef and chicken. Although the origins of this thoroughly Japanese dish might have been in the subcontinent of India more than a hundred years ago, the currently popular dish bears little, if any, resemblance to true Indian curries. Japanese curry rice is, however, a cheap, convenient meal for harried housewives and mothers, students cramming for exams, and salaried bachelors.

A further indication of the Japanification of McDonald's is the less publicized fact that, in their shop near the Imperial Hotel in Tokyo, miso soup is available from 7 to 9 A.M.   15

Americans living in Japan often speak wistfully of the original fast-food chains, not understanding that their compatriots across the Pacific are equally responsible for similar changes to Japanese food in the United States. Just fifteen years ago the avocado was inspiring a new kind of sushi, the California roll, and fresh shiitake mushrooms were being cultivated in America to join other types of "wild" mushrooms in continental-style soups and sauces.

More significantly, the service and presentation of Japanese food in the United States have changed to accommodate American eating habits: Soup is brought to the table at the beginning of the meal, and single pieces of *nigiri-zushi* (the familiar ovals of vinegared rice with slices of fresh fish) are served. The custom in Japan is to serve soup at the end of the meal, and, due to an unfortunate culinary pun, *nigiri-zushi* are traditionally served in pairs (one piece, *hito kire*, can also mean "to cut a man down").

With all these mutations and hybrids, what is "real" Japanese food anyway?

Thinking About the Text

1. Andoh and Anne Pepper (p. 345) each briefly comment on the "Japanification" of Kentucky Fried Chicken. If you find the comments of one writer on the subject to be more interesting and thought-provoking than the other's, explain why.

2. Andoh's article is reprinted from *Mangajin* ("comic-book people"), a magazine that covers contemporary Japanese popular culture and literature and is aimed at those teaching and learning Japanese. Several other selections in this book are reprinted from *Mangajin*, including those by T. K. Ito, Virginia Murray, and R. U. Loveless (p. 139), Mark Schilling (p. 324), and Anne Pepper (p. 345). Taken together, what do these articles suggest about *Mangajin?* What does it seem to assume about its audience? What does it want them to know? How does it inform them? How would you describe its style? Does it remind you of any American publications?

Thinking About Culture

3. If you are familiar with the Americanization of any ethnic or foreign food, describe and explain the changes.

4. Are there certain foreign or ethnic foods that you especially like, and others from the same cuisine that you strongly dislike? If so, how do you explain your responses?

5. A small Japanese boy, traveling with his parents in Hawaii, called out with relief when he saw the golden arches of McDonald's: "Look! They have Japanese food here!" Discuss the question of the "universalization" of certain foods. For instance, is pizza Italian or American or global?

David E. Sanger

Tokyo's Tips for New York

Japan is getting its comeuppance these days, and getting it hard. Its industries, it turns out, are not as invulnerable as everyone thought. Its political system is even more corrupt than everyone thought. And even its venerable bullet trains, which symbolize efficiency and technology, suffer from quality-control troubles.

But in managing the chaos of urban life, Japan remains the world champion. After six years in New York and nearly six in Tokyo, I never cease to be amazed at how well Japan's capital works—and how few of its lessons seem to leave its shores. Herewith, a list of ideas from the streets of Tokyo that America would do well to import.

1. Subway and Bus Machines

You can buy a subway ticket in Tokyo with a 10,000 yen bill, the equivalent of $90. The machine will just spit out your $1.30 ticket, and $88.70 in change. No big deal.

On the buses, there is no need to dig deep for coins or tokens. The machine, which looks much like the ones on New York City buses, only about half the size, can readily take the equivalent of $10 bills or make change for coins. It's simple, quick, and easily armored, and it vastly reduces stress.

2. Gun Control

Japan has a simple rule when it comes to handguns: They are prohibited.   5
That may explain why the Japanese police report that Tokyo had a grand total of eight gun-related murders in 1992, just about what New York has in two days. Japanese are permitted to own as many rifles and shotguns as they please, but the licensing requirements are stiff, and the firearms must be stored in a locked cabinet. Violators receive heavy jail sentences. The results are striking: People walk their dogs at 1 A.M. without fear. In short, if you take gun control seriously, it can be done.

3. Obasans

Every block in Tokyo has at least one of these—stern neighborhood ladies, about as smiley as the Terminator, using their deadly stares to make sure

---

David E. Sanger is the Tokyo bureau chief of the New York Times. *This short article appeared in the* New York Times Magazine *in 1994.*

you package your garbage correctly and leave it in the proper place for collection. (As foreigners living in a largely Japanese neighborhood, our household garbage gets special scrutiny. But our neighbors give us a break, viewing our absence of training in this regard as one of those many cultural handicaps—along with a lack of appreciation for *natto*, a particularly potent fermented bean dish—that are beyond our control.)

To make life easier for the street monitors, the city just imposed a requirement that garbage be placed in clear bags, a way of ensuring that the burnables and recyclables are not mixed. Privacy advocates protested, but the fact is that the old ladies know what is in your garbage anyway. They see all.

4. Canned Coffee

Forget about the Handycam and the next-generation memory chip: Japan's biggest technological advances are in its vending machines. On almost every street corner you can find one that serves hot and cold drinks, including a vast array of canned coffees. The idea may sound off-putting, but the coffees actually taste great. More important, the machines assure that coffee is available anywhere you may be hanging around: train stations, bus stops, building lobbies. Each machine serves it hot or cold. Best yet, America already owns the technology. The maker of one of the most popular canned coffees here, called "Georgia," is Coca-Cola.

Vending machines in general are so popular in Japan that some people worry they are on the verge of becoming a social menace. For years you have been able to buy everything from T-shirts to condoms through streetside machines. But recently the police began to crack down on entrepreneurs who sold slightly used girls' panties via machines. Men with a passion for such goods were paying $40 each until the police moved in.

5. School Uniforms

When I first arrived in Japan, the Prussian-like school uniforms that boys and girls begin wearing in junior high school seemed to me to embody everything that was wrong with Japanese conformism. But I have come to appreciate the subtle benefits. The uniform helps make students feel they belong, putting everyone on the same team. Teachers say it helps discipline, creating a vaguely military air in the classroom. In America, no doubt, this rule would run afoul of civil liberties groups, and maybe it should. But given our math scores and theirs, it is worth a try.

10

6. The Electronic Train

Walking onto one of Tokyo's new commuter trains at rush hour, you are greeted by one of the flat-panel, liquid-crystal television screens that are placed over every door. In English as well as Japanese, they announce the current stop and the next one—interspersing a bit of news hot off the wires, stock prices, and, inevitably, a few commercials. No unintelligible announcements from the conductor.

7. Kobans

One of the secrets of Japan's low crime rates, the Japanese insist, is the humble *koban,* a usually flimsy police shack. It may not look imposing, but it is the ultimate form of community policing. Every neighborhood has one, often right by the subway entrance or bus stop. Kobans mean never having to wonder where the cops are—they are in their little booth, watching. They are equipped with maps to help the lost, the confused, and the drunk. Granted, for the mean streets of New York some modifications may be necessary; bullet-proof kobans, for one.

8. Required Parking Spaces

Before you can buy a car in Tokyo, the police come to your house—not to make sure you have a license, but to measure your parking space. No space, no Toyota. This is how Japan avoids alternate-side-of-the-street parking rules. Some will argue that requiring a parking space excludes poor people from owning cars. They may be correct. But it also assures that cars can navigate the city streets without weaving around double- and triple-parked cars.

9. Automatic Taxi Doors

Imagine this the next time you hail a broken-down cab in midtown: A sleek, dent-free taxi pulls up and the driver opens the rear door with the press of a button on the dashboard. If you are juggling packages and a briefcase, there is no need to find a free hand. The driver, who speaks the nation's official language, is wearing white gloves. The seats are covered with white slipcovers, cleaned nightly.

And in a city virtually without street names, the drivers know every   15
nook and cranny—or will hop out of their cabs to ask shopkeepers. A few have even equipped their cabs with navigation equipment, which includes an electronic map that shows the shortest way from where you are—a bobbing "X" determined by satellites—to where you are going. True, it costs $5.50 as soon as the door pops closed. But here's the best part: Unless you ask, drivers won't tell you their life stories.

Thinking About the Text

1. Sanger's article, from the *New York Times Magazine,* is meant to entertain as well as to inform. Write a comparable piece, listing several—nine, if you can think of them—good ideas that ought to be put into practice in

America, or (if you want to think small but smart) in your school. These ideas may in fact be realities that you have heard exist elsewhere, or they may be your own inventions.

Thinking About Culture

2. Perhaps you can think of reasons why some of the ideas Sanger reports won't work in the United States. Sanger himself cites possible objections to school uniforms (para. 10). If you can think of objections, state them.

James Sterngold

Why Japan Is in Love with Vending Machines

Vending machines are everywhere in this supposedly tradition-bound country, dispensing nearly all of life's necessities, and many of the frills.

In addition to the usual train tickets, soft drinks, and cigarettes, Japan's colorfully turned-out machines dispense jewelry, fresh flowers, frozen beef, rice, whiskey, hamburgers, pornographic magazines, videocassettes, and batteries. From bustling urban intersections to the most bucolic rural lane, there is sure to be a humming box to satisfy a consumer's needs for a few coins.

If you need a date, a vending machine will provide leads on prospects. If you are sightseeing and have forgotten a camera, a machine sells throwaway cameras. If you visit a public sauna and want to feel fresh afterward machines there sell underwear. On your way to an appointment and forgot your business cards? A company is developing a machine that will print them out instantly.

Vending machines are common in the United States, of course, but they have not achieved the same importance as marketing tools. Japan has about 5.4 million of the machines, almost the same number as in the United States, but for half the population. And each Japanese machine produces on average twice the sales volume as its American counterpart. A total of more than $45 billion in goods was sold through Japanese vending machines last year.

"They are a reflection of the pace of life today," said Stephen Marvin, 5 a stock analyst here at Jardine Fleming Securities. "People would prefer just grabbing something from a machine and running."

James Sterngold regularly writes about Japan for the New York Times, *where this article appeared in January 1992.*

In a nation where retailing methods have often been described as a reflection of the people's unique social character, the trend represents a deep change in habits. For generations, the formula for reaching consumers in Japan was said to require lavish attention and lots of personal service. Japan had so many small neighborhood shops, it was said, because they provided the sense of intimacy and trust consumers demanded.

But convenience is proving to be more attractive than the supposed comforts of dealing with a shopkeeper who is like an old family friend.

The popularity of vending machines also shows how difficult many Japanese find reconciling their age-old devotion to elaborate courtesies with their increasingly harried lives.

In a nation where every social encounter—at work, at home, at the store—is still governed by obligation and ritual, many prefer to drop a couple hundred yen into a machine than deal with a person. In fact, some experts suggest that this is a more important reason for the proliferation of vending machines than their mere convenience: Many Japanese consumers simply feel more comfortable dealing with a machine, contrary to their garrulous reputation.

"Because of traditional attitudes it can be psychologically awkward to   10 walk into a shop and buy something small, like a pack of cigarettes, and then just leave," said Paul Hasegawa, head of the international division of I&S, a large advertising company. "So if you're embarrassed, you buy things you don't really need. You can't just rush off if you're in a hurry. A machine is easier. It may sound odd to you, but that's the way Japanese people think."

Not Just a Quirk

But the vending machine is more than just another quirk in a quirky land. The willingness of consumers to pour their coins into these increasingly high-technology devices offers a glimpse into how shrewd marketers are capitalizing on changes in their society. And many shopkeepers have embraced the trend to get around a host of restrictions they normally face. With rents sky high and labor in short supply, vending machines create more shelf space and run twenty-four hours a day, needing only to be refilled from time to time.

This untraditional means of distribution also happens to be one of the most intensely competitive businesses in the country. Beverage companies, which account for nearly half of all vending machine sales, use the devices as weapons in an unceasing battle for market share and the attention of consumers. They provide the machines to merchants for free or charge little, since the aim is to seize a location.

Mr. Marvin said the vending machine manufacturers themselves earn little profit from sales of the bulky boxes because of the competition. And the price of 100 yen—about 80 cents—has not budged in a decade.

Vending machines have insinuated themselves into just about every nook in the Japanese landscape. The traditional *shotengai*, or shopping street, still exists, even in crowded Tokyo, with the neighborhood fish shop, greengrocer, tofu shop, and perhaps a barber and a couple of noodle shops. But increasingly these small merchants can be found behind banks of vending machines, where those who have no time or interest in swapping the latest gossip can be in and out in a flash.

"They're all out there for a reason," said T. Burke McKinney, director   15 of marketing for Coca-Cola Japan, which operates more vending machines, some 760,000, than any other company here. "The real issue is the Japanese life-style. People are demanding the convenience."

Japanese commonly commute up to four hours a day and work unusually long hours. Government efforts to persuade them to ease up have largely had the effect of encouraging people to stand in ever-growing lines to play golf on weekends or take their place in expressway tie-ups leading to resorts.

In fact, the hectic pace has made long coffee breaks a thing of the past for many Japanese. So the Ueshima Coffee Company developed a canned coffee drink with a special lining to preserve the flavor.

Nobuhiro Shirakawa, an official of Otari Inc., which makes machines that sell bouquets of fresh flowers, said his company's devices let young men avoid the embarrassment of having to admit to shopkeepers that they were buying something nice for a sweetheart, an unaccustomed gesture in Japan.

Bashful Natures

And for men and women who are shy about courtship, there are vending machines to make the introductions. A man can pay the equivalent of a few dollars to have his particulars—including the kind of car he drives—printed on strips of paper that are dispensed to women who put a few coins into the machine seeking a date.

Japanese vending machines also benefit from the country's electronic   20 expertise. Among the latest innovations: solar machines to reduce electricity use; machines that use small elevators to deliver items at chest height; machines fitted with point-of-sale computers that automatically radio headquarters with details on sales, inventories, and whether the mechanisms are functioning properly.

Perhaps the most important innovations are turning the devices into a medium for advertising. Some companies are experimenting with the installation of video screens to deliver messages with their products.

"We are only just beginning to scratch the surface of what advertising potential the machines have," said Mr. McKinney of Coca-Cola. "We've already got some 700,000 ministores out there. Why not 700,000 communicators?"

The profusion of vending machines has not been without criticism. Some protest that the machines make it easy for underage youths to buy alcohol and cigarettes. The legal drinking age in Japan, though rarely enforced, is twenty years old, and although Japanese machines can do a lot of things, they do not yet check for proof of age.

The United States is unlikely to follow Japan's lead in providing so many machines, which usually have a plastic front, for a simple reason.

"Can you see one of these things lasting in Dallas or Jacksonville or   25 New York?" Mr. McKinney asked.

Indeed, Japanese vending machines are significantly safer from crime. "We're not worried about bandits here, as I think you are in the United States," said Takashi Kurosaki, an official of the Japan Vending Machine Manufacturers' Association. "The companies have virtually no losses due to vandals or thieves."

Thinking About the Text

1. For what reasons is Japan in love with vending machines, according to Sterngold? Based on other readings in this chapter, can you imagine other reasons?

Thinking About Culture

2. Among the items available from Japanese vending machines and unavailable (to the best of our knowledge) from American vending machines are fresh flowers, whiskey, hamburgers, pornographic magazines, and business cards. If you had money to invest, would you invest it in machines that would distribute any of these in the United States? Explain.

3. In paragraphs 9 and 10 Sterngold explains that one reason for the popularity of the vending machines in Japan is that they allow a customer to avoid exchanging required pleasantries with a shopkeeper. Might this factor operate also in the United States? Explain.

Donald Richie

Walkman, Manga, *and Society*

Among the most successful new products in consumer-minded Japan is the Walkman. This device, for those few who may not know it, is a set of earphones wired to a portable radio and/or cassette-player. [While Panasonic, Sanyo, Nippon, Sony, and others manufacture versions of the cassette player,

---

Donald Richie, a former curator of film at the Museum of Modern Art in New York, has lived most of his life in Japan. This essay, originally published in 1985, comes from his 1993 recent collection of essays, A Lateral View. Other essays by Richie appear on pages 63 and 133.

Sony's trade name "Walkman" has almost become the generic term for the device.]

As the name indicates, it is not to be used in the privacy of the home; it is to be used in public, specifically while walking, or at least moving.

Its benefits, according to the advertisements, include: putting one's time to good use by using foreign-language tapes; rendering one's journey agreeable by listening to music; informing and educating oneself by catching up with the latest news, cooking programs, etc.

The hype is thus toward both self-improvement and pleasure, and it is these positive elements of Walkman which are stressed by the manufacturers and by any user you may interrupt to ask.

Looking at the myriads of walkmen and walkwomen, however, a   5
thought occurs. Is it not possible that the negative benefits are greater than the positive? Does not the true popularity of Walkman lie not in what it puts into the ears but what it keeps out?

The thought occurs for two reasons. First, I have never interrupted a language or cooking lesson. Rather, Walkman users are subjecting their ears to a very high-decibel combination of pop/rock/*enka.*° Secondly, if my negative-input theory is correct, then Walkman constitutes a parallel to the uses to which another consumer item, the *manga,* is put.

Manga are enormously popular comic strip books in Japan. Dozens of weekly and monthly published titles are sold in hundreds of thousands of copies. Though the manga may be "read" in private, its public consumption is remarkable. Any train, any subway, any park bench is filled with those whose eyes are glued to their opened manga.

Here the hype stresses no self-improvement. Indeed, with such success assured there is no need for manga advertisement. And in any event with a context so fatuous and complacent on one hand, so violent and salacious on the other, any suggestion of self-improvement would be ludicrous.

Instead, we are told that manga are entertaining. At least this is what I am told when I interrupt a reader's pleasure to ask. Manga are *omoshiroi* (interesting), I am informed. This is a palpable falsehood, no matter how sincerely voiced. One day, however, after much fruitless research and several direct snubs, when I was thus occupied in disturbing people, I received an answer that opened new depths. Manga, I was told, is a kind of portable television: It occupies, pleasantly enough, the brain while one is doing something else—sitting, standing, waiting.

The connection is made. Manga is to the eyes as Walkman is to the   10
ears. Both are attractive for entirely negative reasons. Their salient quality is not input but, as it were, output. They both, like television, exclude.

And what is it that they so successfully exclude? Why, life itself. The others standing, sitting, squeezed; the urban crush and the urban clutter and clatter; rural emptiness, rural sprawl; an environment both packed and empty.

---

enka: Modern Japanese songs, usually about romance or a broken heart. [Editors' note]

The manga offers an absolutely inconsequential visual world which excludes and is preferred to the real one. The Walkman offers an aural world of equal inconsequentiality which veils both cacophony and stillness. Both Walkman and manga offer not only a substitute but also a secession.

The result is an alternate world, one which—given the popularity of both Walkman and manga—is preferred. One might say that users are audiovisual dropouts in that the aim of the devices is the exclusion of the real world. At the same time, however, such use is not only retreat. However pathetic, the results are that an attempt is being made to find a more habitable place.

One thinks of a parallel with the West—drugs. By comparison, Japan has only a minimal drug problem, but the manga/Walkman effect does approximate the results of certain drug use: Reality is in both cases veiled and, for addicts, the engendered false world is preferred. Another parallel, both manga and Walkman are addictive: The alternate "reality" is so much more pleasant. As with certain combinations of uppers and downers, a peaceful equilibrium is possible.

To say that Walkman and manga are only a fashion among the young answers no questions and seems to beg the one it suggests. Fashion is, by definition, the future. And, even in its most extreme manifestations it rises from need. Also, fashion is criticism—it can have meaning only when defined against an "unfashionable" status quo.

In the continuing popularity of Walkman and manga (and pachinko°   15 as well) it is possible to detect an implicit criticism. This can be seen as an answer by society to the activities of those who turned the country so madly consumerist, who willfully "developed" nature to its present state of despoilation, and who have so thoroughly taught that the acquiring of wealth is the highest aspiration.

Not that the developers and the money-grubbers were not always within this society (and any other as well); rather, that in contemporary Japan these have come to assume greatest control. And there is but a thin difference between the man who (for aesthetic reasons) moves a rock a few centimeters this way, a bamboo grove a few centimeters that, and one who (for economic reasons) moves the rock entirely away and cuts down the bamboo grove. In both there is no respect for any original integrity. In both there is an insistence that the hand of man—specifically the hand of the Japanese man—forms. It is simply that the premises are different: In the landscape artist the aim is aesthetic gain; in the developer the aim is financial gain.

A form of criticism long favored in Japan is silence. One refuses to respond—the criticism is all the stronger for being unvoiced. One would like to believe this invisible criticism is there, right there: The Japanese younger generation—closed, eyes preoccupied, ears plugged, all senses sealed.

---

pachinko: Pinball gambling. [Editors' note]

Thinking About the Text

1. Richie's thesis is stated most directly in paragraph 11: Walkman excludes "life itself." Do you believe this thesis? And, if you do, is this necessarily a bad thing? Explain.

2. Richie suggests (para. 13) that in the West a parallel to Walkman is drugs, which also allow a person to live in a "false world." But why can't one equally say that when one goes to a concert or to a museum or to a sporting event one enters a "false world"? Your thoughts about the appropriateness of extending Richie's view to these activities?

3. In paragraph 13 Richie says that Walkman is "addictive." Given your own familiarity with users of Walkman, do you seriously accept Richie's assertion that it is addictive? Explain.

4. Compare Richie's comments on *manga* with those of James Fallows in Chapter 1 (p. 16). Whose remarks do you find more enlightening (or at least convincing)? Why?

Thinking About Culture

5. Richie's final point is that the use of Walkman may represent a criticism of society. Putting aside the question of the soundness of his diagnosis of Japanese youth, do you think his idea can be applied to youth in the United States? Explain.

6. The Japanese comic book industry is the largest in the world. If you have any interest or expertise in American comic books or graphic novels, track down comparable Japanese *manga* and analyze similarities and differences. (For example, you may want to compare Keiji Nakazawa's *Barefoot Gen*, a Japanese *manga* about the bombing of Hiroshima, with Art Speigelman's *Maus*, an American graphic novel about the Holocaust.)

Chapter 10

Delinquency, Crime, and Punishment

To an American police officer, a Japanese city seems like heaven; to a Japanese tourist, American urban areas are frightening. There is little disagreement over where social order and safety are greater.

Japanese are particularly aware of problems in American life since the murder of teenager Yoshihiro Hattori in Baton Rouge, Louisiana, in October 1992. Each time a Japanese visitor is killed in the United States (5 in every 100,000 murders in America are of Japanese), the media in Japan underline the inherent dangers of travel to the United States: the rate of private gun ownership, the assumption that a stranger is a danger, the need to watch out for life-threatening violence. Hattori, a high school exchange student, rang the wrong doorbell in a middle-class suburban neighborhood as he looked for a Halloween party. He was killed by the homeowner "protecting his property," and when that homeowner was found not guilty, the reaction in Japan was of incredulity. One result was the creation of special lessons in "survival English" available to those traveling to the United States. The list of vitally important words and phrases includes "Duck!," "Freeze!," "Back off!," "Hands up!," "I've been shot!," "My wife has been raped!," and the like.

The editorial from the *Mainichi Daily News* (p. 393) included here lists a number of cases of shootings of Japanese visitors to the United States and laments that "a great and good nation like America" should have such a dangerous weak point as a "lawless arsenal of guns among the citizens."

Japan's high degree of public order is not won through the availability of guns as protection or deterrent—even criminals rarely use guns, though increasingly, they own them, an aspect of the "internationalization" of crime, as the article by Mark Schreiber (p. 386) shows.

Law-abiding citizens are, however, unhappy about the presence of *yakuza*, or members of organized crime "families." As Walter L. Ames (p. 379) describes them, they are members of a well-governed, hierarchical system involved in managing gambling, prostitution, and much of the *mizu shobai* (bars, strip joints, and other aspects of the "water trade" or nighttime entertainment). Gang leaders, however, may justify their activities by saying, as one did, "The police take care of citizens by day; we are the nighttime police." These gangsters are both renegade heroes and civic nuisances. As "Robin Hood" figures they are not so convincing, although they are heroes to some working-class youth. The *yakuza* receive little public interest, so long as their criminal impact is not directly experienced by many ordinary people. Only when there is internecine violence affecting innocent bystanders and property owners—or when an eminent politician is shown to have *yakuza* ties—does the public protest.

Even *yakuza*, however, are subject to the pressures of social cohesion and convention. When one gang member and his family moved into a new house in a middle-class, non*yakuza* neighborhood in Osaka a few years ago, the neighbors were upset, and with the police developed an "only in Japan" strategy: The women of the neighborhood agreed to snub the *yakuza* house-wife in the shopping district, playgrounds, and other public places, and the children did the same to the *yakuza* children in school. After a few months of this ostracism, the *yakuza* family gave up and moved out, and the police had not appeared at all.

In Japan, while a few older people may sigh that life is not what it once was, urban experiences are relatively benign and even desirable. Young people see the city, particularly Tokyo, as the hub of their cultural universe; small children safely ride the subways alone, even returning late from lessons in the evening; and a woman does not need to look over her shoulder, walk only on brightly lit streets, or carry Mace. Most street crime is seen in dubbed American movies. Youth crime is relatively low, though a high-profile concern, as Merry I. White points out (p. 367).

But there are problems nonetheless. Though these are not related to racial tensions or to a decline in public services, they have become more visible, especially in the early 1990s. Urban problems in Japan include home-lessness, though the numbers are miniscule compared to data in the United States. Further, in Japan the homeless are usually men and occasionally women but never children. (In the United States, the fastest growing group of homeless is children.) On the other hand, as Edwin M. Reingold indicates (p. 373), street violence is nearly nil as police keep a protective eye on the neighborhoods they serve from the neighborhood *koban*, or police box from which they take ambulatory surveys of the neighborhood, give directions, help lost children, and the like. The most often cited problems of life in the city are, relatively speaking, more inconveniences than mortal risks: health-destroying work hours and stress; crushing commuter crowds (on the very efficient and predictable public transit systems); cramped living quarters; and the isolation of the elderly from their families.

American commentators would probably choose these problems over the ones they see in their cities. In both the United States and Japan, major cities are seen as the creative centers of change and the source of energy and sophistication. New York and Tokyo still attract visitors; still are the focus for novelty, fashion, and art; and still, like Paris for the French, are defining cultural experiences. They contain the intense distillation of their culture's values, opportunities, and problems—nice places to visit, and some even like living there!

Explorations

1. What are your opinions on crime in America? For example, what do you think are the principal causes of crime, what do you think about imprisonment and the prison system, what do you think about the death penalty? You may want to focus on particular types of crime to give shape to your response.

2. What are your experiences with "juvenile delinquency"? Who were the "juvenile delinquents" in your community? How did they act, how did they dress, how did they get the reputation? Did (or do) you consider yourself, or any of your friends or relatives, a "juvenile delinquent"?

3. What is the crime rate like where you live? Perhaps you moved recently to attend college; compare your present views on crime with those before you moved. What sort of precautions do you take to protect yourself? When you travel, what sort of precautions do you take? How have you been affected by media coverage of crime? By the experiences of your peers?

4. Has any friend or family member been a victim of a violent crime or felony? Interview this person to find out what his or her reactions were, what precautions the victim now takes, and what, if anything, the victim feels should have been in place, in terms of police protection or other sources of public safety, to prevent it.

5. What is your opinion on guns and gun control? That is, where do you fall on the continuum from those who are second-amendment absolutists (no regulation of guns whatsoever) to those who think only the police and military should be allowed access to guns? Explain and justify your position.

Merry I. White

Over the Edge: Delinquency and Other Teen Social Pathologies

Friendship affiliations in Japan, as in the United States, can cross the line into peer-pressured bad behavior, even perhaps into delinquency. Bad behavior—in the form of the testing of adult and institutional limits—is not, however, encouraged or exaggerated by the availability of drugs and the accompanying acceleration of juvenile crime rates seen in most American cities. Juvenile crime rates in Japan are low—so low that the number of juvenile arrests for one year in Osaka, the second largest city in Japan, is the same as that for one day in New York. The total of juvenile crime cases processed by the police in 1988 was 193,000. The total of juveniles from thirteen to twenty-one years of age involved in stimulant drug use in the same year was 1,273 persons; and in the following year—1989—the total number dropped. Hot-rodders are frequently arrested for a range of crimes, from assault and robbery to extortion and homicide, and these youth are a special category in police records. The number of young people arrested has declined every year since 1983.

Hankoki, or the "rebelliousness of adolescence," is seen mostly as a deviation, not a normal attribute of youth. One researcher, however, noted that one function of the *sempai-kohai* relationship may be to help the teen "pass from the rebelliousness of *hankoki* to the acceptance (of one's position in society) characteristic of a more mature person." In this study, the researcher quoted a teenager who said that the worst thing a *sempai* could say to a *kohai* is *"rei shinakatta yo"* (you broke with etiquette). The relationship is then a peer-based mechanism of control.[1]

When such controls have no effect, or when problems have different causes, Japanese youth tend more toward "acting in" than toward "acting out," suffering more from personal pathologies rather than contributing to social disorder. Acting-in leads to psychiatric symptoms, among which the most prevalent is school refusal (truancy) due to bullying or to psychosomatic symptoms.[2] These are a subject of great concern but what Japanese officials

---

[1] Katrina Merritt, "The Success of the Japanese Educational System: The Role of the Peer Group in Promoting Student Motivation and Achievement," Undergraduate Senior Honors Thesis, East Asian Studies, Harvard University, April 1992, p. 54.

[2] Suzanne Vogel, personal communication.

Merry I. White, whose essay on Japanese education appears on page 95, is an associate professor of sociology at Boston University and an associate in research at the Edwin O. Reischauer Institute of Japanese Studies, Harvard University. This selection is from her book The Material Child: Coming of Age in Japan and America *(1993).*

worry about more is that acting *out* may be on the rise: The ratio of juvenile to adult offenders has increased to the point where juveniles now account for 57.4 percent of all suspects questioned or arrested. And the average age of delinquents has dropped every year for the past decade. Seventy percent of first offenders are now between thirteen and fifteen. Most second offenders were under ten at the time of their first detainment.

The picture of juvenile crime is a complicated one. The offenders come from a wide range of family backgrounds. Eighty percent of those held in juvenile homes were from middle- or upper-middle-class families. Ikuya Sato sees the largely middle-class motorcycle-gang members as adolescents seeking escape from boredom and a chance for *play*, rather than as alienated dropouts from a class-bound system.[3] Many children arrested for various crimes report that the thrill of risk-taking led them on: Interviews with the delinquents said their lives are more oriented to friends than to parents, and more to relationships with friends of the opposite sex who apparently goaded them to commit crimes.[4] Many are urged into teen prostitution this way: 60 percent of juvenile arrests are of females involved in some form of sex trade. And yet there is also a strong indication that crimes among some juveniles are also related to economic issues: About one-third of arrested youth are jobless and out of school, between the ages of fourteen to nineteen.

Even among those who have not been led to crime, some young people report a tendency to be pushed to antisocial, or "cool," behavior: 5

> People conform a lot at my age (fifteen). But in a funny way. It doesn't look good to get too earnest about school events such as the cultural festival, or be too wholehearted about the clean-up brigade: You look foolish. What looks good is to duck out of such things, even though everyone knows that it is good to do the right thing.

Some find just sticking out in gaudy attire or the adjusted school uniform is enough to give them the thrill of being on the edge. Slightly aberrant activity, or just slightly antiestablishment demeanor is one thing, but a sixteen-year-old girl reports that she's at some risk to do more than avoid goody-goody behavior, however mild the risk may look to an American:

> My bad point is that I am easily influenced by my friends. I don't have a strong will of my own. I could easily become delinquent. My friends recently asked me to smoke with them, but since I had as a small child taken a vow, I said no. . . . But in things I don't care much about, I just follow the others.

---

[3] Ikuya Sato, *Kamikaze Biker* (Chicago: University of Chicago Press, 1991), p. 220.

[4] "Children and Crime" editorial, *Yomiuri Shimbun,* October 21, 1990.

Many teens smoke (fewer than in the United States, where 1 million teens take up the habit every year), but more problematic for social order is teen drinking. The Japan National Citizens' Association on Alcohol Problems reports, in its 1990 survey of thirteen- to eighteen-year-olds in Tokyo, that half were "habitual drinkers" and 56 percent had had their first drink before the end of elementary school. Peer pressure is of course at work here, along with the general availability of beer, wine, whiskey, and *sake* in sidewalk vending machines. Teens also spend (20 percent spend over 6,000 yen per month on average) in bars and at *karaoke* boxes,° where bring-your-own is the rule and where there is a definite lack of monitoring. Children of hard-drinking fathers can scarcely ignore this role model and even young teens, in an unguarded moment, can tell you their *own* favorite brands: "My beer is Asahi Dry and my whiskey is Suntory White—Oops, what am I telling you!" (a sixteen-year-old high-school student, Chiba Prefecture).

The reporting of alcohol use in both countries is problematic, but interview material in the United States shows similar patterns. Half of all thirteen- to eighteen-year-olds in the United States are habitual drinkers, with most of them drinking at least once a week, and half a million drink more than five drinks at a sitting. The rate for young teens has dropped slightly, but it is very common for thirteen-year-olds to have a drink. Five percent of eleven-year-olds, for example, regularly attend drinking parties, 61 percent before the end of high school. As in the Japanese study of delinquency, the American study of teen drinking associates alcohol consumption with alienation and lack of parental supervision. Most of these young people come from middle-class homes, but most are alone at home for many hours of the week. Analysts further say that parental drinking habits as well as peer group drinking are key influences. More important, hard drugs and even marijuana are becoming much less acceptable among American teens, so that alcohol is a replacement.[5]

Drug use is, as any newspaper reader knows, epidemic in America, but Japan has been far more successful in antidrug enforcement. Dealers, smugglers, and users are arrested. There is aggressive involvement in international drug-control operations. Another difference lies in the drugs of choice: In Japan, amphetamines are popular, rather than cocaine, heroin, marijuana, and psychedelic drugs. But a drug culture is slow to form and there are strong social taboos against drug abuse—excluding, of course, alcohol and smoking, which are approved.[6] *Karaoke* boxes again are one focus for the

---

karaoke boxes: Small rooms or free-standing dumpster-size units, which may be rented by the hour, for groups to sing with electronically enhancing equipment. [Editors' note]

[5] Report on Teen Alcoholism in the United States, *Yomiuri Shimbun*, November 1990.

[6] "Japan is successful in containing the drug problem" in *Japan Times*, International Weekly Edition, September 1990.

campaign against all substance abuse by children, for in these private rooms, smoking, drinking, and glue-sniffing are said to be frequent activities.

There has been an increase in delinquent behavior among teenage girls. Their crimes of choice appear to be shoplifting and prostitution. Girls are more frequent repeaters: Girls commit another crime within six months of being released from juvenile detention homes and boys within a year.[7]

So-called playful delinquency[8] includes shoplifting and—to some extent—prostitution, engaged in by schoolgirls eager for a thrill and pocket money. Swiping an unlocked bicycle is a favorite sport of some middle-school boys. Defying the police for the thrill of it is part of the pattern of delinquency of the *bosozoku,* or motorcycle gangs. Gang membership often emulates participation in adult *yakuza* crime families, with a hierarchical system led by a boss, and rituals of entry and loyalty. Stealing and extortion are often part of the activities of such a group, as are "dare" crimes, in which more junior members of the group are exhorted to prove their stuff by performing a crime.[9]

The problems of teenagers, as noted above, more often turn them in on themselves rather than out into the community. School problems, especially bullying and hazing, may create intolerable pressure and even lead in some cases either to violence by the oppressed child, or suicide. Violent crimes are rare, overall, but there is some evidence of violence increasing in schools (against teachers, as well as classmates) and at home (against adult relatives, particularly mothers). Suzanne Vogel notes that where an American child might run away from home if problems become too great, Japanese *parents* have been known to leave the home to the violent or problematic high-schooler, who has thrown them out.[10] The discussion of suicide in Japan usually relates it to academic pressure and the potential for failure in the rugged ladder toward the university, but statistics belie this, showing that the higher levels are actually in the twenty to twenty-four age-group beyond the age of examination hell.[11]

Remembering that overall the rates of juvenile pathologies and crime are relatively low in Japan, and that deviant-behavior data in general tends to include such violations as those of school regulations—perming one's hair or affixing colored stickers to one's bookbag[12]—places Japanese delinquency in perspective for Americans; but Japanese educators, parents, and social commentators are far from pleased with relativity: They are concerned that any rise in the incidence of problems in any sector of the juvenile

10

---

[7] White Paper on Crime, Ministry of Justice, 1990.

[8] Tsukasa Kitajima, "The Rise in Juvenile Delinquency," *Japan Echo,* vol. 9, special issue, 1982.

[9] Sato, op. cit.

[10] Suzanne Vogel, personal communication.

[11] Heisei Gannenchu no Jisatsu no Gaiyo, Report on Suicide in 1989, National Police Agency, Tokyo, 1990.

[12] Rosey Clarke, "The New Japanese Teenager," *Winds,* September 1985, pp. 23–30.

population may foretell problems for the future of a generation, and thus for society at large.

The Tokyo Metropolitan Police recently offered parents and teachers a guide to visual indicators that a child might be "going bad," as shown in the accompanying illustration. (See p. 372.)

This kind of publicity resembles American advertising campaigns aimed at parents, listing signals that children may be taking drugs. In the United States, many such ad campaigns focus on encouraging parents to talk with their children, about drugs and the danger of AIDS. Similar U.S. campaigns are aimed at the children, themselves. 15

There are larger questions related to the relationship of teen and parent, in terms of friendship and illicit behavior, that inform the contrast between American and Japanese adolescence. At the beginning of this chapter, we noted that American adults are suspicious of teen association, while there is in Japan the notion that children alone or together are not naturally inclined to disobedience or uncontrolled antisocial behavior but are rather inclined naturally and by early training to prosocial behavior. We saw in the discussion of schooling that discipline in the early years of school is rare, and that what would appear to an American to be chaos, rules. Children are certainly expected to be energetic and physical, and to need to use their energies, but the assumption is that children want to do what is right, and confrontation is not necessary, since intentions are good. Parents, too, feel that children do not by nature want or need to oppose them, that "breaking of the will" is not a tenet of child-rearing.

Further, age-appropriateness is so strong a value even among delinquent groups, that most rule-breakers are pressured by their peers to "graduate" and settle down to an ordinary life once they have come of age, at twenty.

In America, the conflict between the understanding that children are born naturally good and the notion that given the opportunity, they will misbehave, leads to contradictory parental signals, the contradiction reinforced as well by our philosophic and political ideologies encouraging freedom of choice and the rights of the individual—which, pushed to the extreme in parent-child confrontations, leads to even greater gaps between beliefs and practices in child-rearing, discipline, and guidance.

Thinking About the Text

1. Based on your other reading about Japanese youth (in this book or elsewhere), do you find any of White's statistics and facts on Japanese juvenile delinquency surprising? Explain. If you find yourself wanting to know more about some topics or statistics White brings up, do some research on it. You may want to start by checking out some of the sources she cites (in the footnotes accompanying her selection).

The Tokyo Metropolitan Police Office asks:

Do You Know How Your Children Dress?

Female

1. Light makeup with false eyelashes, eye shadow and lipstick or lipgloss
2. Magnetic earrings
3. Turned-up collar
4. Open jacket with red T-shirt underneath
5. Intentional cigarette burn scar to show toughness
6. Slovenly long skirt with unironed pleats
7. Colored pantyhose
8. Blow-dried hair or straight permanent brushed back
9. Shaved eyebrows
10. No school badge
11. Decorative medal
12. Rolled-up sleeves
13. Large safety pin
14. Ring
15. Keyholder with disco membership card
16. Quilted bag with change of clothes and small candy tin for holding cigarettes
17. Sneakers or deck shoes

Male

18. Forelock
19. Small mustache (if one can be grown)
20. Bright colored T-shirt (usually red)
21. Chain bracelet
22. Beat-up empty school bag
23. Closely shaved hair around temples
24. Shaved eyebrows
25. No school badge
26. Decorative medal
27. Rolled-up sleeves
28. Intentional cigarette burn scar to show toughness
29. Ring
30. Oversized jacket, not too long
31. Long trousers almost covering the feet
32. Black enamel shoes (only gang leaders are allowed to wear these)

This illustration and list is from a police brochure on how to tell a juvenile delinquent when you see one.

Thinking About Culture

2. Americans tend to associate juvenile crime with low income and disadvantage. Why do we make this correlation, and why might it not pertain in Japan?

3. Some Americans say petty crimes are part of the natural developmental process associated with adolescence. If there are signs of this in the case of Japan, what are they?

4. On page 372, White includes a poster from the Tokyo police that is supposed to help Japanese parents determine whether or not their children are juvenile delinquents. Try the same exercise focusing on American teens: Either make a list of characteristics or draw a poster with labels. Compare your results with those of your classmates. How do the juvenile delinquents they describe differ from and resemble yours? To what do you ascribe the differences and similarities?

Edwin M. Reingold

Common Crime, Common Criminals

Despite the depredations of the *yakuza,*° Japan's crime rates for the more common offenses are still the lowest among industrialized nations. There are probably no cities elsewhere in the world where a lone citizen can walk the streets at night without fear of being mugged, raped, or killed. Except for the gangs, the use of firearms is miniscule, even in bank robberies, of which there are few. A desperate police officer, heavily in debt to usurious *yakuza* moneylenders, recently robbed a bank in Osaka, but he used a toy pistol instead of his service weapon.

This anecdote, however, does not gainsay the surge in serious crime— kidnapping, torture, and murder, not just the traditional intimidation of classmates—by juveniles. As the good life beckons to those with money and as more women are moving into the workplace, many children are left alone to grow up with baby-sitters. Fathers working late hours rarely see their children, and there is little familial socializing except on holidays. While this situation is similar to that of the modern upwardly mobile Western family,

---

yakuza: Gangsters. [Editors' note]

Edwin M. Reingold has been a journalist for more than forty years, reporting from Japan since 1969, when Time *magazine first assigned him there. This selection is from his book* Chrysanthemums and Thorns: The Untold Story of Modern Japan *(1992).*

it is fairly new to Japan. Critics say that traditional familial and group restraints on antisocial behavior are collapsing at a time when affluence and leisure time are on the increase.

There is a detectable increase in cocaine addiction and trafficking as more and more Japanese travel abroad. Cocaine brings at least three times the world price in Japan, which may explain why the amount confiscated by police leaped from 13.6 kilos (about 30 pounds) in 1989 to 70 kilos (about 155 pounds) in the first half of 1990 and is rising. Police say there may be connections between the gangs and Colombia's Medellín Cartel. Some of the cocaine seized in the port of Kobe was taken from Colombian ships, and Latin Americans have been arrested in connection with the seizure. There is no official tolerance for or leniency toward illegal drug use in Japan—marijuana is viewed as a hard drug—and first offenders are given stiff sentences. The former Beatle Paul McCartney, his wife, and four children were once detained at Narita Airport when he was found to have 219 grams (about a half-pound) of marijuana in his possession. He had come with his entourage of fifty musicians and eleven tons of equipment for a nationwide tour. McCartney was interrogated for eight hours—his wife and children were released—and then thrown into a Japanese jail overnight. Japanese papers carried front-page photos of McCartney the next morning, handcuffed and roped together with other suspected miscreants as he was taken to court. It was just the kind of case the police were pleased to get: Treating a celebrity as they would a common drunk or addict sent a sobering message to the drug users of the nation, young and old, famous or not. McCartney was expelled, and the long anticipated tour cancelled.

Ethnocentric Japanese authorities often refer to the rise of drug offenses unfairly as the Americanization of crime, or the American disease, brought about by the exposure of Japanese youth to Western films, music, and pop culture. Local origins of the problem are not admitted. It is still quite common for a foreigner who reports a crime to be told that the perpetrator was most likely another foreigner. This feeling was given some highly publicized credence a few years ago, when a seemingly respectable American student was found to have been the cat burglar who had preyed successfully on a central Tokyo neighborhood. The Japanese remember the Vietnam War, when American servicemen visiting Japan were one conduit for narcotics from Southeast Asia.

But contemporary Japanese fiction of the period depicts a homegrown, 5 as well as GI-induced, source of drugs. The chemically produced methamphet-amine ("speed") drugs are said to be the province of the *yakuza*, as well as much of the smuggled cocaine and heroin, now that the number of American servicemen has dwindled.

In most crime categories, like murder, rape, and robbery, Japanese figures are much lower than those in the West. But at least one kind of criminal seems to stymie the efficient Japanese police. It is the pickpocket, a breed that infests the train stations of the nation, whose arrest rate was a disappointing 25.9 percent. Many of these are freelance dips unconnected with organized crime. The police reported that the famed *Tokaido Shinkansen,* or Bullet Train line segment between Tokyo and Osaka, is a particularly ripe venue for pickpockets. Of 163 cases aboard the trains in the September-November period of 1989, only two arrests were made.

There are plenty of theories as to why most other crimes are so low. For one, it is generally agreed that the lack of handguns among ordinary people has a lot to do with it. It is just more difficult to kill somebody with a sword, unless one is practiced and adept at it, than with a handgun. Gangsters prefer guns, but daggers and swords are used frequently by nonprofessionals. The lack of ordinary weapons has led to some bizarre crimes. During the Occupation era, one Masamichi Hirasawa strode into a bank, identified himself as a health inspector, and announced that he had been sent to administer a preventative dose of medicine for a raging disease. He mixed up a lethal cocktail, which the submissive bank staff obediently quaffed. As twelve of them died in agony, he walked off with the money. He was caught and spent the rest of his life in jail.

One can't overlook, as a crime prevention tool, the presence everywhere of the local uniformed police. They maintain small substations in every neighborhood and, like old-fashioned beat cops in the West, know every household and every person in the neighborhood. The police aren't perfect, as we have seen, but there is no doubt that they are a deterrent.

Police routinely set up traffic roadblocks to make sobriety tests. They sometimes shove an alcohol detector wand into the car and ask the driver a question. As the motorist breathes onto the sensitive part of the instrument, it determines whether alcohol is present. The police, who take traffic accidents very seriously, confiscate the driving licenses of drinking drivers.

Legitimate auto-body shops will not repair a damaged car, I discovered   10
to my annoyance, without a police report detailing the damage and how it was caused. One Sunday I had inadvertently backed into a concrete-and-steel utility pole while leaving the home of an artist in the Aoyama district of Tokyo. The rear bumper was dented, and I sent the car for repair the next day. But the body shop would not touch it until I had taken the police to the scene of the accident, where they could match up the scratches and determine that there was no other damage for which I should be held liable.

Auto accidents of all kinds are taken seriously. The Ichihara Prison, not far from Tokyo, was established in 1969 just for traffic offenders. Almost all of the inmates have had a previous traffic offense of some kind. About a third have been convicted of negligent homicide; about half, of driving under the influence of alcohol. The average sentence is nine and a half months. During that time, the inmates take driving aptitude tests, analyze traffic accidents in classes, undergo driving simulation, have psychological discussions about right living, attend "introspection therapy" sessions, and watch documentaries, some of them heart-rending stories of the victims of traffic accidents. New inmates are housed in a semiopen dormitory, to make sure they don't decamp at night, and after a period are moved to an open dormitory. When it is time for prerelease orientation, they move into the "Dormitory of Hope." During their stay the inmates are subjected to lectures on self-control and accountability. There is also a "Monument of Atonement" at which the inmates can pray and seek expiation.

Prisoners held in standard prisons for felonies are given much harsher treatment. They have little privacy and few privileges. But amid a spare life of discipline they are nevertheless given counseling and job training. The death penalty still applies and about two persons a year are executed by hanging, but the government does not reveal any information about the condemned prisoners, not even the number executed.

Japan has a trial-by-jury law, but it has been in suspension since 1943. In the meager twenty years during which juries heard cases in Japanese courts, exactly 25,192 cases were tried. Only 484 cases actually went to jury deliberation. In many cases, defendants plea bargained, pleaded guilty, or were persuaded to waive their right to a jury's deliberation. But with the acquittal rate running 17 percent, the authorities became restive and abandoned the system. Under the jury law, certain crimes, such as political activities proscribed by the Peace Preservation Law, were not subject to jury trial. The court was free to change the members of the jury at will and, most significant, the court was not bound by the verdict of the jury. The prevailing sentiment among the populace is that the system is stacked against the suspect. It hasn't eliminated crime in Japan, but certainly plays a part in keeping most people on the safe side of the law.

Even so, skeptics suggest that the Japanese authorities underreport crime and that Japan is not the law-abiding place it seems to be. Much of the extortion and strong arm activities of the gangs is not reported, but every year there are suicides—sometimes committed by whole families— hopelessly in debt to *yakuza* moneylenders. When the late photojournalist W. Eugene Smith was beaten and nearly killed by hired hoodlums for documenting the plight of the sufferers of corporate pollution in Minamata, it was no shock to most Japanese. This kind of intimidation by hired brutes on behalf of companies and even political figures is not unusual.

Yet if the incidence of crime seems different in Japan, and it is, it also   15
strikes the observer that the nature of the criminal is somewhat different from the Western stereotype. The swaggering gangster, often portrayed in films as a kind of Robin Hood, is a popular stereotype, and ordinary citizens give him a wide berth. The world of *mizu shobai*, literally the "water business," or the saloon and nightclub world, is shot through with shady characters, fast-buck sharpers engaging in illicit activity such as illegal gambling, prostitution, confidence games, and extortion. It is a world few foreign visitors penetrate, or wish to.

Foreigners encounter simpler crimes. Charles d'Honau, an American businessman then living in Japan, arrived home one evening to find a Japanese man rifling through the family possessions. Having heard similar tales from foreigners and Japanese alike, and having been warned against doing any violence to the intruder, d'Honau ordered the criminal to stop and then commanded him to take a seat and wait until the police arrived. The burglar bowed, then resignedly took his seat until the police arrived to take him away. No force was used; it is widely understood in Japan that injuring a burglar is as much a case of battery as it would be to assault a person at random on the street, even if it occurs in your own living room.

Ordinary law-abiding Japanese do not normally sleep with guns or other weapons at hand. Traditional Japanese house construction is so flimsy that breaking and entering would be a misnomer. Some Japanese never lock their houses, and in traditional homes, it is customary for a visitor to enter the *genkan,* or foyer, to announce his or her arrival. But in today's modern, faceless, reinforced-concrete apartment blocks with fireproof metal doors, locks are used. The modern Japanese, now blessed with a plethora of worldly goods—computers, pianos, stereos, giant-screen televisions—but fated to live in cramped quarters, have plenty of things to be stolen. But Japanese footpads are selective. Even in Japan's sprawling cities, really conglomerations of distinct neighborhoods, disposing of stolen goods is a problem. It is also difficult to conceal anything from the alert eyes of the police.

Professor Eiichi Kato, who spent nineteen years with the Ministry of Home Affairs, many of them watching public officials for evidence of having received bribes, says nothing escapes the eyes of neighbors and the police in Japan's neighborhoods. Some 15,000 police substations blanket the country and constantly check on who is in what house, what their normal habits are, and provide what some call twenty-four-hour protection (others call it spying). Whatever it is called, it is unlikely that a criminal could pull a truck up to a house, as is sometimes done in the United States, and matter-of-factly haul away the contents. Thievery from warehouses and distribution channels is another matter, and goods that "fell off the truck" can be found being traded in some Japanese back-street markets. Footpads robbing someone's home look for cash, credit cards, and signature seals with which money can be withdrawn from bank accounts.

Perhaps the Japanese craving for new goods accounts for the discriminating taste of Japanese burglars. Used goods are not desired, and in fact, the scrapping of old appliances and furniture helps to keep the wheels of the industry turning. The periodic collection of such goods, called *sodai gomi,* or "rough trash," yields a bonanza for many poor Japanese and foreigners, who cruise the streets inspecting what well-off Japanese throw away. And at parties it is not unusual for a host or hostess to show off what pieces of furniture or what television or stereo and accessories were picked off a neighborhood *sodai gomi* pile.

Having spent more than a decade living and traveling in Latin America [20] and Africa before coming to Japan to live, my family had never had the experience of being burglarized, except for one bungled attempt in Nairobi. But on a warm spring night in Tokyo, coming home earlier than expected,

I noted a light in the bedroom as we entered the apartment. I was about to say something to my wife or the children about wasting energy when I caught a glimpse of a small person darting past the bedroom door. Remembering the experience of d'Honau and others, I shouted—in what language I cannot remember—and ran to the bedroom, only to see the person disappearing through the open balcony door with a pocketful of cash. He left behind the jewelry because of the difficulty of fencing it, the police said later. The room was a wreck, clothing spilling out from every drawer. When the police arrived they fingerprinted all ten fingers of every member of the family, thoroughly blackened all the possible points of contact with a tenacious powder, but never found the burglar, one of the rare ones to get away.

Little cases of burgled cash notwithstanding, the arrest rate in Japan fits the expected pattern—higher than any other country's. Japan has an arrest rate that averages around 98 per 100 homicides, versus about 70 in the United States, 81 in Great Britain, 83 in France, and 94 in West Germany. In the case of robbery, larceny, and theft, Japan's police are far ahead of their counterparts in the West. They make 78 arrests per 100 robberies, versus 26 in the United States, 23 in Great Britain, 25 in France, and 46 in West Germany. Japanese police make an arrest in 56 of every 100 larcenies, compared with a rather anemic 17 arrests in the United States, 30 in Great Britain, 16 in France, and 29 in West Germany.

Thinking About the Text

1. What do you think Reingold would say are the principal reasons for the low crime rate in Japan?

2. In paragraph 2 Reingold reports the belief that the rise in crime may be related to the affluence achieved by men working longer hours and by the increased number of women entering the work force. Does this make sense to you? Explain.

3. Reingold, Merry White (p. 367), and Walter Ames (in the next selection) all write about delinquency and crime in Japan. How would you characterize their individual attitudes to the Japanese? Cite specific passages to support your characterization. Whose essay do you find most convincing? Why?

Thinking About Culture

4. Do you think that the sort of treatment the Japanese police gave to Paul McCartney (para. 3) would have had any particular effect on Americans if the episode had taken place in the United States? Explain.

5. In paragraph 10 Reingold says that auto-body shops require a police report

before they will repair a damaged car. In your opinion, is this an idea that we should import? Explain.

6. Reingold mentions (para. 18) that in the United States, but not in Japan, a burglar can pull a truck up and haul away the contents of a house. *Why* can this occur in the United States?

Walter L. Ames

Yakuza *and the Police*

While doing anthropological field research in Japan for my doctoral dissertation, I had many opportunities to observe police interaction with *yakuza* (gangsters). I was struck by the remarkable cordiality between the two and the general openness of Japanese gangs. I will give a few examples.

Police officials in Okayama prefecture told me that a large gangster funeral would soon be held and arranged for me to attend. On the appointed day, I went to a large Buddhist temple in Okayama City with a detective from one of the nearby police stations. Five or six large American luxury cars with license plates from various prefectures in western Japan were parked directly in front. Black and white striped funeral bunting was draped on the wall surrounding the temple courtyard, and the diamond-shaped symbol of Japan's largest gangster syndicate, the Yamaguchi *gumi* (gang), to which the local gang belonged, hung over the gate into the courtyard. Thousands of rings of artificial flowers donated by small businesses, bars and cabarets, city assemblymen, and citizens lined the inside of the courtyard. Hundreds of gangsters from all over western Japan in dark suits, closely cropped hair, all wearing black arm bands and lapel pins declaring the names of their gangs, filled the courtyard. Dozens of gangsters, just arriving, met with loud shouts of greeting from the others in the courtyard.

A number of police officers stood across the street from the temple entrance watching the gangsters congregate. Most said hello to the police, and several of the gangsters from local gangs approached the police officers and jokingly commented that they had parked their cars in parking lots so as not to get parking tickets. The police knew the gangsters by name and bantered with them. One of the policemen asked the gang leaders standing by the gate if I might go inside to watch the funeral, explaining I was a

Walter L. Ames has a Ph.D. in anthropology from the University of Michigan and a degree from Harvard Law School, where he was affiliated with the East Asian Legal Studies program. This article, drawn from his dissertation ("Police and Community in Japan"), originally appeared in a newsletter issued by the Japan Society of New York.

student from America. I was then ushered into a courtyard and led to the main temple building where I watched the ceremony surrounded by the top gangster bosses from western Japan. After the ceremony, gangsters with arm bands stood at the intersections near the temple and directed traffic as the other gangsters left, while the police continued to watch from nearby.

And I saw similar examples of such openness and cordiality on other occasions. I went with police officers for casual visits to gangsters' offices (storefront headquarters of local gangs with signs in front bearing the name of the gang and its syndicate affiliation). I also accompanied the police official responsible for gangster affairs in Okayama prefecture to the opulent homes of several gang bosses; while I interviewed a boss, he chatted amiably with underlings in another room. The interrogations of arrested gangsters which I sometimes glimpsed in the police station invariably involved constant joking. I even witnessed a brawl in a restaurant between gangsters of the same local gang during which the police merely tried to restrain the two fighting factions until the gang boss arrived to actually settle the dispute. The police officers called many of the gangsters by name during this incident.

The police keep records on gangsters. Every police box and police station is equipped with a book that lists all of the gangs in the area, their members, and carries organization charts indicating who is linked through fictive kinship bonds to whom, histories of the gangs, their major sources of income, and sometimes even photos of the gang members. Police officers say that this kind of detailed information on gangs is necessary in order to avoid being "ridiculed" by the gangsters during interrogations.

The openness of Japanese gangs and their relationship to the police often baffle Western observers, and can only be understood when notions of American Mafia are dismissed from the mind and Japanese gangsters and police are seen in their own historical, cultural, and ideological contexts. Their cordiality does not necessarily imply corruption, as it might between American gangsters and police, and should not be confused with friendship because definite tension exists between police and gangsters. Japanese relationships which are characterized by incessant joking are usually marked by potential hostility. Police and gangsters find it mutually advantageous to maintain rapport and to enhance it by a facade of cordiality. A complete rupture in the relationship would be counterproductive for both parties. This nucleus of goodwill and understanding seems to remain even when the police must severely crack down on a gang after a major incident.

The rapport between police and gangsters stems in part from the fact that police and politicians have used gangsters throughout Japan's modern history to help maintain social order, especially to counterbalance the burgeoning strength of leftists. It has only been since around 1960 that Japan's ruling circles have begun to worry about the increasing power of gangs, especially the large nationwide syndicates, and have taken steps to suppress them. Yet, the overlapping traditional conservative ideals of gangsterism with the ideology of police officers and ruling conservative politicians still fosters a degree of sympathy and attraction toward the world of gangsters.

What Are Gangsters?

Gangs per se are not illegal in Japan and have operated openly for centuries. Gangsters traditionally have been called *yakuza,* a word synonymous with gambling—taking its meaning from the worst possible hand in the Japanese card game of *hanafuda.* The lowest score is twenty, which is the sum of eight *(ya),* nine *(ku),* and three *(za).* The term connotes the sympathetic notion that gangsters are losers in society, affiliating with gangs because of their unfortunate circumstances. Yakuza are also referred to as *bakuto,* which means literally a gambler. A yakuza is not just any gambler or rough, but one who has formed a fictive parent-child *(oyabun-kobun)* or brother-brother *(kyodaibun)* bond through a formal ritual closely paralleling the Japanese marriage ceremony. At the core of gangs are the intense and binding patron-client relations that tie the members together in formal bonds of obligation and indebtedness.

Forms of address based on Japanese kinship terminology are used within gangs. A gang boss is referred to as the *oyabun* (literally, parent role) of the gang, and is called *oyaji* (father) when addressed by his underlings or *ojiisan* (grandfather) after he retires. The boss refers to his followers as *kobun* (literally, child role) or *wakaimono* (youngsters), the chief of whom is the *wakagashira* (head youngster). When a gangster collects his own followers within the larger gang of the *oyabun,* an *ikka,* or "one room within a house," is formed. If he gathers sufficient followers, he forms a *bunke* (branch household) outside the original gang yet closely affiliated and subordinate to it. The gangster then becomes the oyabun of his own subgang. When a bunke is formed, the sign in front of the gang office with the name of the gang on it usually declares the gang's bunke status and the name of the main gang or *honke* (main household). The *honke-bunke* terminology used by gangs is borrowed from kinship terms traditionally used to designate household relationships in farm villages and in certain urban commercial settings as when a shop opens a branch run by a former apprentice.

Edo period (1600–1868) firemen *(machi hikeshi)* are usually thought of as the spiritual predecessors of today's yakuza. There were forty-eight machi hikeshi gangs located in Edo in the early eighteenth century with a headman leading each group. Under the headman were various followers linked in patron-client relationships and ranked in a similar manner to modern gangsters. Machi hikeshi worked as carpenters and plasterers on high-scaffolding construction jobs, a common occupation among modern yakuza as well, and mobilized as fire fighters only when fires occurred. When there was a fire, the machi hikeshi gang boss quickly decided the main goal for the extinguishing efforts and the gang's standard bearer (each gang had

10

its own distinctive standard and *happi* coats) would climb to the roof of the target building and wave the standard furiously as a focal point while the gang members tore down the surrounding buildings and pumped water on the fire. For the sake of the gang's honor, he was never to descend, even if the fire began to consume the building. If several gangs arrived at the scene at the same time, they would usually fight each other to determine which would have the glory of raising its standard. The open display of gang symbols by modern gangsters on their arm bands, lapel pins, funeral bunting, office signs, and even gang flags probably stems directly from the machi hikeshi gangs of Edo. The honor and fame of the gang is the most important consideration.

A fascinating aspect of gangster lore that receives frequent attention, especially in movies, is *jingi,* or the code of morality and highly formalized words and actions of greeting peculiar among gangsters. Jingi entails care and protection from the oyabun for his gang members and absolute loyalty by the kobun to their boss. If a gangster is disloyal or causes trouble for his gang, it has traditionally been considered proper according to the code for him to cut off a joint of his finger to show repentance. Gangsters also have their bodies tattooed—sometimes the entire body from the neck down and from the elbows and knees up—to demonstrate manliness by stoically enduring the pain of application. Because of the social stigma accompanying tattoos in Japan, they also signify a resolve never to abandon gangster life. The code of loyalty and the extremely honorific greetings of gangster jingi are said to closely resemble the morality and conduct of samurai on the battlefield. This is of significance because the Japanese police trace their spiritual ancestry to the feudal samurai.

Social Origins

Gangsters are drawn almost exclusively from the lowest levels of Japanese society, strata that are subject to severe prejudice and social and economic discrimination. I was told by reliable sources that up to 70 percent of the gangsters in western Japan are of formerly outcaste (*burakumin*) origin. Ethnic Koreans and Chinese, also targets of prejudice, join gangs in lesser numbers. Gangsters were not always heavily of outcaste origin, however; during the Edo period, most yakuza came from among lower-class samurai, farmers, artisans, and petty merchants fallen on hard times. In the Meiji period (1868–1912), the new gangsters were mainly from the fallen samurai class or desperately poor farmers, fishermen, miners, stevedores, and other laborers. Burakumin, Koreans, and Chinese began to join gangs in increasing numbers only after World War II.

Gangsters today tend to come from poor or single-parent families. They are often rejected by society as youths because of criminal activities, making it difficult to secure employment when they get older. Gang leaders have remarked in interviews with journalists that in Japanese society the gangs alone are willing to give a fair chance to teenagers who have no education, no money, no family background. Gangs offer an income and a feeling of security within the group for the isolated and lonely.

Certain aspects of the gangster subculture probably stem from attempts to compensate for their low social status. For instance, the manners of gangsters are usually impeccable when dealing with people they respect. When I visited the home of a gangster boss in Okayama, the boss and his immediate kobun came out to my car to greet me when I arrived (a favor usually reserved for only the most honored guests in Japan), and then formally escorted me to my car after the interview. Several of the gangsters even stopped traffic so I could leave easily. While I was chatting with the boss in another room of his home, one of his underlings shined my shoes, which I had removed.

Gangsters are very concerned with "face," and a gangster's power is   15 directly related to his reputation. One of the bosses I interviewed bragged that he is nationally known and said that when he goes to the National Diet building in Tokyo, the guards recognize him, salute, and allow him to go inside, drink coffee and chat with the Dietmen. Although this may be an exaggeration, it shows the longing of gangsters to be recognized and accepted by society. The surprising openness of Japanese gangsters, in sharp contrast with the secretive nature of the American Mafia, probably stems from their desire for fame. The Japanese saying that "face is more powerful than money *(okane yori kao ga kiku)*" is taken to heart by yakuza.

Gangsters tend toward ostentatious display, possibly as a way of compensating for social inferiority. Gang bosses have a penchant for expensive foreign automobiles, and one gang boss estimated that up to 70 percent drive such cars. A Lincoln Continental, a favorite gangster car, had a base price of $26,500 in Okayama in early 1975. Gangsters also prefer flashy clothes and often wear colorful Hawaiian shirts, dark glasses, black shirts with white ties, or other unusual clothing.

Sources of Income

Gangs engage in both legitimate and illegitimate activities to earn money. Members of one of the smaller gangs in Okayama prefecture entertain at bars in the city by singing and playing guitars, and several of the gangsters are said to be so good that the police once had them give a musical performance while they were incarcerated in the police station jail. Other local gangs specialize in loan sharking or construction subcontracting. Some gangsters sell items such as picture frames to restaurants and bars or work as common day laborers to earn additional income. The wives, parents, or other relatives of many gangsters, and sometimes the gangsters themselves, run small restaurants or bars.

Gangs collect money from a wide variety of illegal activities. Most gangs have income from skimming money from bars, restaurants, and pachinko° halls as payment for not disrupting business or handling any problems that occur at the establishments. Gangs also use threats to collect debts for a fee (serving as *jidanya,* or "makers of compromise"), deal in stimulant drugs and pornography, and engage in gambling. There are no Okayama gangs that specialize in prostitution, as many gangs in Osaka are said to do, but individual gangsters may form some sort of a pimp relationship with bar hostesses to support themselves.

Officials note that gangs are changing their methods of illegal operations as Japanese society and economy change. They are relying more on sophisticated "crimes of intellect" which are harder to detect than extortion or threats, and are thus becoming more like the American Mafia. Large syndicates have connections with some movie companies, and are involved in casino and cabaret management in Korea, Taiwan, Hong Kong, the Philippines, Singapore, and Thailand. A Tokyo-based syndicate is said to be operating a prostitution hotel and massage parlors in Hawaii which cater to Japanese tourists. Gangsters are also beginning to operate as *sokaiya* ("stockholders' meeting specialists"), by buying a few shares in a number of corporations and extorting money from the companies by threatening to disrupt their stockholders' meetings, or by offering to smooth the proceedings by intimidating dissident stockholders in exchange for a sizable payoff from the management. This is in keeping with the practice of corporations before the war to hire gangsters to help solve labor disputes by intimidating strikers.

Shared Values

A certain folklore has grown up around gangsters and many Japanese identify positively with the values expressed in gangsterism. Gangsters represent the traditional Japanese core values of *giri* (obligation) and *ninjo* (humaneness). They describe their world as that of *ninkyodo,* or the "way of chivalry." Famous gangsters of the Edo period, such as Kunisada Chuji (1810–1850) and Shimizu no Jirocho (1820–1893), are the subjects of popular stories and movies extolling their Robin Hood–like images of protecting the weak of society against powerful tyrants and unjust government officials. Gangsters traditionally shared the tenet of not bothering "citizens under the sun (people in normal society)," isolating themselves in the shadows of society and dealing only with people who sought out what the gangs had to offer. Gangs have long been tolerated by citizens and police because they were not perceived as a threat; they were seldom involved in street crime. Attraction to gangster ideals and the glamorous, masculine, physical gangster image is not limited

20

---

pachinko: Pinball gambling machines. [Editors' note]

to any particular segment of society, but seems to be most pronounced among the lower working classes.

Thinking About the Text

1. If this essay held your interest, reflect on why that might be so. You may find it useful to return to the essay and annotate passages that you found engaging. What made them so? Unusual facts and details? Ames's analysis and interpretation of those facts and details? His writing style? Explain.

2. In paragraph 6 Ames says that we must dismiss "notions of American Mafia." Exactly what notions do you have of the Mafia? Are they incompatible with what Ames says of Japanese gangs in his first six paragraphs?

3. In his final paragraph Ames mentions that some earlier Japanese gangsters now have Robin Hood reputations. Which, if any, earlier American gangsters have such a reputation? How deserved is the reputation?

Thinking About Culture

4. In paragraph 7 Ames says that the police use gangsters "to help maintain social order." Is this practice known in the United States? If so, what is its American form?

5. Ames comments on "the overlapping traditional conservative ideas of gangsterism with the ideology of police officers" (para. 7). What does he mean? To what degree do you think the statement can be applied to the United States?

6. Judging from what you read in newspapers and magazines, and see and hear on TV, are American gangs (including those of young people) highly organized, and do they have certain ideals and codes? If you are familiar with this material, explain it to an outsider.

7. In paragraph 10, Ames says that firemen during the Edo period are usually "thought of as the spiritual predecessors of today's *yakuza*." If the topic interests you, do some research on the history of firefighting in the United States, considering such issues as class, ethnicity, and community.

8. Watch a classic American gangster film such as *Little Caesar* (1930), *Public Enemy* (1931), or *Scarface* (1932), paying more attention to how the gangsters are represented than to the story. These films were made for a mass audience; what do they say about gangsters to the American public who paid to see them? Report on your findings. You may want to also consider more recent American gangster films, such as the *Godfather* movies. A further possibility would be to track down American films that deal with the *yakuza* in some way (for example, *The Yakuza* [1975], directed by

Sydney Pollack and starring Robert Mitchum, or *Black Rain* [1989], directed by Ridley Scott and starring Michael Douglas) to examine how the *yakuza* are represented.

Mark Schreiber

A Nation Without Guns

On a Monday evening in June, 1993, acerbic TV personality "Beat" Takeshi provided viewers of *TV Tackle* on Tokyo's Channel 10 with another example of his bizarre brand of entertainment: a montage of news clips about Japanese murdered while abroad. The scene shifted from Cambodia to Beijing, to Manila, and to Baton Rouge. Each news clip was interspersed with the art deco image of a rotating globe, while in the background the rasping voice of Louis Armstrong was heard singing "What a Wonderful World."

When the montage of a dozen-plus murders was over, Takeshi solicited remarks from his panel of celebrity guests. "Well," they sighed in unison, "at least Japan is safe."

However complacent such a response may seem, it was sincere. In an increasingly agitated world, Japan is seen, from inside and outside, as exceptionally fortunate to enjoy a relative absence of both violent crime and serious social unrest.

As inhabitants of a small island nation with cramped urban living conditions and their own share of social and demographic problems, the Japanese see their society's freedom from violence as one area in which they compare very favorably with other countries. In the "Survey on Social Awareness," conducted by the prime minister's office in December 1992, subjects were asked, "What facet of Japan or being Japanese gives you the greatest sense of pride?" The country's high degree of public order led all other replies by a wide margin and was cited by 49.4 percent of respondents. Even among those who voiced pessimism about Japan's future, only 11 percent feared a decline in public order more than anything else.

Japan owes much of the orderliness of its society, of course, to such   5
factors as a highly homogenous population, deep-rooted family ties, a strong tradition of obedience to authority, full employment, and, in more recent years, the perception among close to 90 percent of the Japanese that they belong to the middle class.

Mark Schreiber, a resident of Japan since 1965, is a columnist for Intersect, *an English-language magazine published in Japan. We reprint an adaptation of one of his* Intersect *essays.*

Perhaps even more significantly, Japan does not have many guns. The purchase of hunting rifles and shotguns is subject to extremely tight controls, and their use is strictly regulated. Possession of handguns, except by Japan's police and armed forces, is illegal. These stringent gun laws are energetically enforced. In the words of a spokesman for the National Police Agency's Firearms Control Office, "We believe the people of Japan recognize the rigid enforcement of gun laws as being one of the main factors contributing to this country's high level of social order."

The gun-related crime that does occur is nearly all tied to the activities of criminal gangs. But even that is relatively scarce, as the 1992 White Paper on the Police shows: In 1991, the latest year for which figures were available, firearms were used in only seventy-four murders and twenty-two robberies in all of Japan. The statistics show an indifference—amounting to disdain in many cases—toward guns on the part of Japan's criminals, not to mention its average citizens.

Why didn't guns ever become popular in Japan? Akira Kawada, vice president of the National Police Academy and ICPO-Interpol's vice president for Asia, believes that aversion has deep cultural and historical roots. "In the old days, the samurai used to say *'Tobidogu o tsukau no wa hikyo'*—the use of flying objects is unfair," Kawada explains with a smile. "It means you have to fight face-to-face, that using things like bullets and arrows is cowardly.

"Then there is the matter of Japan's old class system, in which only the samurai were permitted to own weapons. From the end of the sixteenth century, for almost three hundred years until the Meiji Restoration [in 1868], there were practically no guns in Japan. So ordinary citizens knew nothing about them. I think this mentality persists."

Family Business

Despite the disapproval with which they seem to be viewed, guns, hunting, and target shooting still comprise a legitimate field of commercial enterprise. Shugo Hamada, thirty-four, is the fourth-generation proprietor of Hamada and Son, Ltd., a company founded in 1895 and one of seventy-two establishments in the Tokyo metropolitan area licensed to deal in firearms and ammunition. The shop attracts foreign customers as well as Japanese, and is identified by an English-language sign that reads "Guns and Rifles." 10

Inside, along with hunting garb, books, videos, and assorted paraphernalia, is a large glass wall case with some two dozen guns, carefully secured with a chain. Curious passers-by sometimes come in to gaze at the guns— rather to Hamada's exasperation.

"Most people have never seen or touched a gun in their lives," Hamada says. "I've thought about putting up a sign marked 'Museum' outside and charging people admission."

He is rueful about the effect that the sight of real guns can have. "There's one question I've been asked so many times that it's starting to drive me nuts. That's when people ask me, 'Could I actually take one of these and kill somebody?' "

The trade's prospects do not look good. Although people have more free time now, the number of gun users continues to fall. Hunting, and with it the opportunities for gun use, is on the decline in Japan. One reason is the red tape involved in keeping a gun.

"The other reason is the aging of the gun population," Hamada points   15
out. "Many hunters are in their fifties and sixties, or even older. As they give up the sport, they're not being replaced by the younger generation, which has had fewer chances to be involved with guns."

Innocents Abroad

The relative safety which the people of Japan enjoy at home is not without its drawbacks. Many of them see their unfamiliarity with guns (and violent crime in general) as a serious handicap when they travel abroad.

This perception was tragically bolstered in October 1992 by the fatal shooting of Yoshihiro Hattori, a sixteen-year-old exchange student, in Baton Rouge, Louisiana. Invited to a Halloween party, Hattori knocked on the door of the wrong house. The owner emerged with a large-caliber pistol and ordered Hattori to "freeze." Hattori, whose English was only fragmentary, clearly did not understand the command; when he failed to halt, he was shot in the chest at almost point-blank range.

Hattori's killing outraged Japan, and when a jury unanimously acquitted the man who had shot him the controversy was rekindled. Petitions circulated in Japan calling for stricter gun control in the United States netted at least 1.6 million signatures. And while the Ministry of Foreign Affairs refrained from direct involvement beyond offering a statement of regret, the Ministry of Transport (which oversees Japan's civil aviation) responded with the publication of a booklet for overseas travelers entitled "A Collection of Phrases for a Safe Journey," which includes such expressions as "Freeze!" "Back off!" and "Hands up!"

An International Role Model?

Japan's low crime rate and criminal justice system have attracted the attention of numerous foreign scholars. While virtually all outside observers acknowledge that gun control prevents crime, opinions are divided over whether the Japanese example can serve as a model for other countries.

Perhaps the most ambitious study of gun ownership by civilians is a   20
470-page book by David B. Kopel, a Colorado lawyer. Entitled *The Samurai, the Mountie and the Cowboy*, the book considers whether the gun control laws of other democracies might be successfully adopted in the United States. The first chapter, which reviews the status of guns in Japan, is entitled "No Guns, No Gun Crime."

Citing studies by criminologists that point to a corollary between state sponsorship of violence and individual violence, Kopel notes that "Japan's model of governmental disarmament is repeated at the broadest levels of society." He writes that "Japan's police have little interest in using or glamorizing guns." Off-duty police are obliged to leave their pistols in the station, unlike the United States, where "heavy reliance on guns [by the police] serves, intentionally or not, to legitimize a similar attitude in the rest of the population." In Japan, not even prison guards carry guns.

According to *The Japanese Police Establishment,* by Ralph J. Rinalducci, Article 7 of the Police Duties Execution Law states a police officer may only use his weapon if he has reasonable grounds to do so—e.g., to apprehend a criminal or prevent his escape, to protect other persons, for self-defense, or to suppress resistance to his official duties. Consequently, police officers rarely fire or even draw their weapons in the line of duty.

L. Craig Parker, Jr., of the University of New Haven's Division of Criminal Justice, visited Japan in the early 1980s as a Fulbright scholar and later published *The Japanese Police System Today: An American Perspective.* After approximately one month of field study, Parker writes, "Having asked the question perhaps fifty times, I stopped inquiring directly about police use of firearms. One officer stated that when he had been called to a bank robbery in progress, in which the person inside was suspected of being armed, he had drawn his weapon but not used it."

While gun control advocates in the United States criticize the lax restrictions that make guns accessible to criminals, Kopel chooses to acknowledge their function as an effective and probably necessary deterrent to crime. He writes, "Unlike Japanese, Americans are not already secure from crime, and are therefore less likely to surrender their personal means of defense. The extensive network of social controls, which is the foundation for Japanese gun control, does not exist in the United States."

Kopel's greatest reservation about the Japanese system is not about the   25 laws per se, but about the power of the police. "To an American . . . concerned about civil liberties," Kopel states, "the breadth of Japanese police powers is horrifying." He contends that, without abrogating the Bill of Rights, America could not give its police and prosecutors extensive Japanese-style powers to enforce severe gun laws effectively. He concludes that, instead of attempting to plant Japanese law in American soil, "a more realistic gun policy must consider guns in the context of American culture."

Parker's study tends to support Kopel's conclusion, noting that "while a stronger federal gun control law could make a serious dent in felonious crime, without a quasi-national police force it would be difficult to implement the law."

The general consensus, then, is that Japan's gun laws work because they are applied in Japan. But while such laws function almost ideally among those who choose to obey them, such is not necessarily the case for those who make up Japan's criminal underground. Yet even here, some maintain that guns are probably far less of a problem than they could be if it were not for the apparent preference to shun gunplay.

Armed and Dangerous

Will Japan remain essentially gun-free? That depends on the only segment of society with the potential to commit mayhem with firearms: organized crime. The *yakuza*, Japan's criminal underworld (referred to in official documents and the mass media as *boryoku-dan,* or "violent groups") have for some years been moving into Southeast Asia, the United States, and other areas where guns are relatively easy to obtain.

The controversial 1986 book *Yakuza,* by David Kaplan and Alec Dubro, quotes a police official as saying, "We are convinced that literally every yakuza owns or carries a handgun even on the streets, an entirely different situation from the past." This statement has often been reiterated. There are 56,600 official gang members in Japan. Yet, in 1992, there were only 222 incidents involving the firing of illegal handguns. And most of those bullets struck objects, not people.

Recent developments, however, give more cause for concern. Most   30
disturbing is the sharp rise in the seizure of guns from non–gang members. In 1992, 26.1 percent of the 1,450 handguns police confiscated were taken from ordinary criminals, compared to only 7.6 percent for the previous year's 1,032 seizures.

Police Academy Vice President Akira Kawada agrees this phenomenon is disturbing. "When members of organized crime use guns among themselves, ordinary citizens don't worry so much," Kawada says. "But since there has been some leaking [of armed violence] into the general population, people are starting to feel concerned."

The number of handguns seized by authorities in 1992 was the highest since 1987. Much of the rise can be attributed to the emergence of a new source: mainland China. The *Mainichi Shimbun* newspaper noted that in the three years since China emerged as a supplier of illegal handguns in 1989, it has eclipsed the United States in this trade.

Also, at least several hundred thousand foreign workers are believed to have entered Japan on tourist visas with the intention of working illegally, attracted by the high value of the yen and the shortage of blue-collar labor. While most of them seek only to engage in honest toil and send their earnings back home, others have become involved in drugs and prostitution.

The boldness of foreign criminals is even starting to intimidate the yakuza. *Shukan Asahi,* a popular weekly magazine, quoted a Japanese gang boss as saying, "Nobody in my group would even think of shooting a cop. But these foreigners all carry knives, even the girls, and think nothing about walking around packing a pistol as well. They have nothing to lose, so they're not afraid of anything—that's what scares us the most."

With Japan becoming increasingly subjected to so-called *kokusai-ka*   35 (internationalization), the potentially volatile nexus of foreigners, crime, and guns clearly has the authorities concerned. But these concerns have yet to manifest themselves in radically new approaches.

"Until now, in their ordinary operations, the Japanese police were not so good in penetrating the foreign community," Kawada says. "Over the past one or two years, they have tried to expand their contacts and develop sources of information in the underground.

"Foreign criminals do not yet have their own base of operations here. That means they are probably getting some assistance from organized crime. This might mean they are discouraged from using guns by the Japanese. But if they ever come to the point that they can operate by themselves, this might change.

"If we maintain the same tactics as in the past," Kawada warns, "then maybe we will fail."

Not a Right but a Privilege

It may be exaggerating to say that guns in Japan have been regulated into nonexistence, but not by much. According to the law, the bearing of arms is not a right but a privilege. Would-be gun owners must prove they can be trusted with a lethal weapon. The law permits adults to possess any number of shotguns and rifles, but the conditions under which they can do so are exacting, and the relevant legislation is scrupulously enforced. You can own a gun and shoot it, at the permitted times and places. But if there's an accident, or if, as a result of careless storage, the gun is stolen and used to commit a crime, you can face penalties almost as severe as those facing the criminal.

The rigid enforcement of Japan's gun laws is supported by the vast   40
majority of the population who, having no experience with firearms them-selves, tends to perceive them in a negative light. Because the law works, and works well, the average citizen does not feel threatened or intimidated by his gun-owning neighbor. Thus both sides can be said to have achieved a reasonable *modus vivendi* in which guns do not cause society to become polarized. In the Japanese scheme of things, this may be the greatest measure of the law's success.

Thinking About the Text

1. The essay could have begun with the fourth paragraph. What function(s), if any, do the first three paragraphs serve?

2. In paragraph 16 Schreiber suggests that the Japanese lack of familiarity with guns is a "drawback" because it leaves the Japanese tourists unprepared for the violence they may find abroad. Can one seriously suggest that a

little more violence in Japan would be a good thing because it would help to prepare Japanese tourists?

Thinking About Culture

3. Americans have the freedom, codified in the Second Amendment to the Constitution, to own and use guns, but this constitutional amendment was passed in times very different from the present. Some Americans advocate stricter gun controls than now exist, even after the February 1994 passage of what is called "the Brady Bill." Find an American editorial in a newspaper or magazine (perhaps published around the time the Brady Bill was passed) that opposes gun regulation, and prepare a response to it from a Japanese point of view.

4. Schreiber specifies several "factors" that contribute to "the orderliness of [Japanese] society" (para. 5). Reread the paragraph and consider which (if any) of the specified factors are also part of American life. Then, thinking further about the orderliness he refers to, ask yourself if you would be willing to abrogate the Bill of Rights (see para. 25) in order to achieve something like this orderliness.

5. More about orderliness and rights: Ordinarily the police can search us only if they have a reasonable suspicion. But when we get on an airplane all of us are frisked and our luggage may be searched. Why—since we have given the authorities no grounds for suspicion—do we put up with this infringement on our liberty? If the answer is that we do so in order to be safe, that is, safe from a terrorist on the airplane, why might someone not argue that, similarly, we should all give up guns in order to be safe from guns?

6. In paragraph 18 Schreiber tells us that at least 1.6 million Japanese, outraged by the acquittal of the killer of Yoshihiro Hattori, the Japanese high school student in Baton Rouge, signed a petition calling for stricter gun control in the United States. Can you imagine signing such a petition if an American student were killed abroad in a country that did even less than we do to control guns? If not, why not? Would it be because you think it is not appropriate to tell other countries how to govern themselves? Because you think it would be pointless? Or for some other reason?

7. In his next-to-last paragraph Schreiber says that if a gun plays a role in an accident, or is stolen and used in a crime, the owner can face severe penalties. Given what he has told us of Japanese society, does this seem to you to be—for the Japanese—reasonable? Do you favor such legislation in the United States? Why, or why not?

A Gun Tragedy Again

Once again, Japanese students in the United States were shot. This time, the tragedy occurred in Los Angeles. The victims, Takuma Ito and Go Matsuura, had been in California for some time studying filmmaking, inspired by renowned director Steven Spielberg. Senseless bullets dashed their high hopes. The remarks of their fathers, made after confirming the death of their children and televised across the Pacific, that the youths "were deeply in love with America" heightened our sympathy.

Previously, two Japanese students were shot in the United States: the "Halloween shooting" of Yoshi[hiro] Hattori, an exchange high school student, in Baton Rouge, Louisiana, in October 1992, and Shoichi Kuriyama, who became the victim of an apparent mugger in San Francisco in August last year.

More than 2 billion guns of all kinds are in the possession of private citizens in the United States. Of the more than 20,000 murders taking place every year there, over 60 percent are committed [with] guns. The prevalence of firearms to this extent among the citizenry is indeed peculiar to the United States.

What do the Americans themselves think of this state of affairs? According to a poll taken jointly by *Time* magazine and CNN last December, more than 70 percent of the people support stringent control and registration of guns. At the same time, however, more than 70 percent are opposed to a total ban on the possession of handguns.

The survey points to a self-contradictory public opinion, which calls for stricter gun control on the one hand, and adheres to the freedom of possessing handguns for self-defense on the other. This explains the difficulty in bringing about effective gun control.

President Bill Clinton announced that he would seek licensing of gun possession following the shooting rampage in the Long Island, N.Y., commuter train last December and directed Attorney General Janet Reno to conduct a study. In addition, Clinton pledged to place top priority on anticrime measures, including gun control, in his State of the Union message this year.

In late February the Brady gun control legislation came into force which

5

This selection is a March 31, 1994, editorial from the English-language edition of a Japanese newspaper. Prompted by recent killings of Japanese students visiting the United States, it alludes to the shooting of sixteen-year-old Yoshihiro Hattori in Baton Rouge in 1992; for more on this incident, see the essay by Mark Schreiber (p. 386, especially paras. 16–18).

obliges gun dealers to set a five-day waiting period for the investigation of a new purchaser of a gun before the weapon is handed over.

The inadequacy of this system is obvious, as the law is aimed at only new purchasers. If such a society of guns is to be reformed at all, it is mandatory to institute a control system to significantly cut the lawless arsenal of guns among the citizens.

Nowhere in the community of advanced countries can people obtain and possess antipersonnel guns as openly and freely as in the United States. This is quite abnormal, a point the Americans should reflect upon much more seriously.

Although we are not given to preaching human rights and other lofty ideals of what's good for humanity, we may be entitled to offer the Americans a piece of advice on gun control: A total, flat, unconditional ban on handguns and other antipersonnel firearms among the citizens, as enforced in this country, is the only answer. Unless they are resolved to seek this end, shedding once and for all their obsession with the constitutional amendment guaranteeing "the right to bear arms" and the nostalgia for the period where guns were the law, Americans can never hope for a society where citizens could stroll, go shopping, or walk a dog in the middle of the night without fear of being mugged and murdered. 10

We should remind our youths who seek to study in the United States that they may do so at the risk of their life. Authorities, both Japanese and American, might help, by providing the present and prospective students with detailed information and guidance on how to ensure their personal safety while in the United States.

It is indeed a pity that a great and good nation like America should have such an Achilles' heel.

Thinking About the Text

1. In paragraph 10 the authors say that "a total, flat, unconditional ban on handguns and other antipersonnel firearms among the citizens, as enforced in this country, is the only answer." Putting aside your own possible objections to gun control, and putting aside the unlikelihood that such a ban could be adopted here, do you believe that a total ban is in fact the only way to substantially reduce the number of deaths from guns? Support your position with reasons.

2. You have just read an editorial, and from your reading of newspapers you are probably familiar with what might be called the conventions governing newspaper editorials. Assume that you are the editor of an American newspaper and that you have seen the *Mainichi Daily News* editorial. Write your own editorial for your newspaper, taking off from the *Mainichi* essay. You may rebut it, or recommend it to American readers, or update it. In

short, you may adopt whatever point of view you wish, but remember that you are writing an editorial for a newspaper. *Alternate possibilities:* Yoshi Hattori's parents collected more than a million signatures urging the United States to eliminate private ownership of handguns. They presented the petition to the American ambassador in December 1992. Write an editorial responding to this petition, or write the note that the ambassador might be imagined to have written in response to the petition.

Thinking About Culture

3. In paragraph 10 the authors call on Americans to shed "their obsession with the constitutional amendment guaranteeing 'the right to bear arms.' " Do we ever shed our constitutional rights? For instance, do we do so when we agree to prohibit false advertising (an apparent limitation of the right to free speech)? Do we do so when we submit to a metal detector and a pat-down at the airport?

4. Why do you suppose so many Americans oppose gun control? Is the reason a wholesome dislike of government interference, an inheritance from frontier days and ways of thinking? a love of hunting? or some other factor?

Chapter 11

Notions of Nation

In elementary schools across America, children learn about the U.S. Constitution, the Bill of Rights, the structure of government, and the long list of presidents. They also learn American political history, from the creation of a democratic state to the wars of empire and defense of the "more perfect union." They learn that our driving ideologies have been more inclusive and less dictatorial and exclusive than those of many modern states.

In Japan, schoolchildren learn of the origins of Japan in the union of two powerful gods, they learn of the long, unbroken line of emperors descending from Jimmu Tenno in the seventh century B.C., according to legend, to the present emperor, Akihito. They learn the history of feudal society, of the courts and warriors, and (occasionally) of the lives of ordinary farmers and tradespeople. "Modern" Japan in school texts begins with the opening of the country to the West in mid–nineteenth century and proceeds through modernization and industrialization to World War II and the creation of a postwar democracy.

The cultural principles governing society's structure ("rule by law," "equality," "hierarchy," etc.) create premises for actual institutions (such as Congress or Parliament, the judicial system, or bureaucracies) but not the structures themselves. The gap between principle and human realities is often fairly great. Clyde Haberman's article (p. 409) describing the revolt of a young *sumo* wrestler illustrates the gap mostly strikingly, as *sumo* is one of the most traditional of feudal hierarchies remaining in Japan. The attempt to make the ideal forms fit actual needs produces such things as the "back-door" route (using connections, nepotism, greasing palms, etc.) that many politicians on both sides of the Pacific use to facilitate action. Young executive wannabes too know that the corporate ladder is not so climbable as the meritocratic principles would indicate and that, without the "right connections," progress up the rungs is nearly impossible.

What we learn in school of democratic processes, wars, and guiding foundation principles is not all there is to know, of course. American children learn about equality and diversity in practice, as they become aware of ethnic, racial, and class differences. Japanese children similarly learn about hierarchy and fairness, homogeneity and personal identity, classlessness and economic disparity.

In Japan, the understanding of this discrepancy between real and ideal has produced its own "principle of the gap," or the paired concepts of *tatemae* and *honne*, or appearance and reality. For nearly every stated ideal way of behaving, it is understood (at least tacitly) that there may be a very different reality or human need. Relationships, such as the hierarchical ones of family, school, and workplace, might have to appear to obey the prescribed forms of loyalty, deference, obedience, and so on, but underneath, there may be quite a different way of relating.

For example, a junior student might need to defer publicly to a senior in an activity club, but in private might be quite assertive and in control. In public too, a woman might need to appear self-sacrificing, but in private might be a rampant hedonist. These contrasts are of course known in American experience too, but we like to think we are more consistent, and we go to great lengths to avoid the sin of hypocrisy.

According to Chie Nakane (p. 400), "traditional" structural premises are actually postwar phenomena and are rapidly changing. These include:

1. A person identifies with a social group first—a frame—rather than with his or her personal attributes.

2. A collectivity orientation governs everyone, even the leader.

3. Hierarchies are fair and meritocratic, allowing juniors to move up to senior status, prerogatives, and responsibilities by age.

4. These structural ideals are supported by a social ethic which (based on Confucian principles) gives moral weight to knowing your place and serving the relationships and institutions.

By stepping outside these principles, breaking through the *tatemae* (ideal) to the *honne* (reality) or at least revealing the *honne* more publicly, several groups in Japan have made waves and are perhaps affecting the range of the acceptable.

Hierarchy is only one social principle that is being tested. Similarly, the notion of homogeneity, that Japan is populated by one people with one culture, has been assaulted. A Japanese child does *not* encounter a "multicultural environment"—the American mixed salad, or mosaic, or bouillabaisse, which has made it difficult to discern a unitary "America." In order to create a coherent nation-state, Japanese leaders of the Meiji period (1868–1912) created the premise of homogeneity and unity of custom and purpose out of a number of fairly diverse regional cultures. There is, then, no intrinsic celebration of diversity in Japan. Indeed, many observers feel there is definite denial of the obvious distinctions that exist, accompanied by equally definite labeling of those who stick out obtrusively.

Even Japanese Americans whose grandparents or great-grandparents all came from Japan find it hard to be seen as Japanese in Japan, and sometimes experience a strange identity crisis. The standards of behavior and the high profile of strangers have made Dorinne K. Kondo's (p. 412) experience in Japan revealing of the limits of acceptance even among people who are extraordinarily welcoming and hospitable.

Being more markedly "other," then, bears even greater problems. Japan never experienced massive immigration. Centuries ago, Koreans were brought to Japan to practice crafts such as potterymaking, but not in large numbers. More recently, as Susan Chira (p. 428) describes, during the Japanese occupation of Korea, Koreans were conscripted and brought to Japan as labor during the Second World War. Postwar Korean migrants came to improve their economic conditions, but few in any generation have achieved citizenship or mainstream occupational success.

William Wetherall (p. 419) describes the conditions of the Ainu, an indigenous group who are very few in number; there remain only about 10,000 with Ainu blood and there are almost no pure-blooded Ainu. They are thought to have first lived on the main island of Honshu and to have been pushed north to Hokkaido when other Asian mainlanders from Korea and China came to settle Japan. The Ainu are hunter-gatherers and did some cultivation as well. There remain small villages, mostly established for tourism, where traditional Ainu ways of life are on display.

Another racial group lives in Okinawa, with very different artistic traditions, language, and social customs, but these people are much more assimilated into Japanese culture than are the remaining Ainu. There is, however, currently a revival of Okinawan folklore as part of a movement to improve conditions in Okinawa, where poverty, joblessness, broken families, and disease are far more prevalent than in the rest of Japan.

The most publicized "other" group in Japan is the *burakumin*. These are people whose origins are somewhat obscure, but who are said to be the outcaste community formed during the Tokugawa era (1600–1868) because their occupations as leatherworkers, butchers, and scavengers brought them into contact with the polluting influence of death. The *burakumin* (literally, "people of the hamlet"), shunned by the wider society, tended to live in isolated, very poor communities. Their children began to attend school and to take mainstream jobs only in this century, and even now there are problems of discrimination in hiring and marriage.

In a notorious speech of a few years ago, the then prime minister, Yasuhiro Nakasone, connected American educational and production problems with the low levels achieved in school by black and Hispanic children. This remark was seen on both sides of the Pacific as a racist statement, but apparently Prime Minister Nakasone intended only to say that a diverse society has problems that a "homogeneous" one does not.

Finally, social class is a relatively unattended concept in Japan. While there is indeed a much narrower income gap in Japan than in other advanced industrial societies, and while surveys reveal that most people (up to 90 percent) assign themselves a middle-class identity, still there are people who can't make it.

Just as in 1950s America an image of the suburban middle-class family dominated media and advertising, in Japan today it is assumed that "most people" correspond to an image. Simply put, it is an urban white-collar family, a father, mother, and perhaps two children, in a single-family house if they're lucky, or usually a smaller condominium or apartment. They'll have all the modern conveniences, as well as top-of-the-line electronic items such as a TV and VCR, an audio system, and a family computer. In this model, Mother is at home baking bread in her fancy new electric breadbaker, and Father is polishing his expensive golf clubs. This middle-class life was, of course, never available to everyone, but it is even less evident today in the realities of a recession and new choices for individuals, particularly women.

James Fallows (p. 431) describes a Tokyo slum that demonstrates that it isn't choice or even especially a recession that keeps some people from the fruits of society. The inhabitants of Sanya are indeed stark exhibits of what it means to have fallen through the cracks. They have missed out on the positive side of hierarchy, homogeneity, and classlessness and are ignored or blamed for their own condition.

Blaming the victim is not only a Japanese practice, as the continuing debate over welfare practice in the United States demonstrates, and our own blinders and confusion over the realities of differentness are instructive to note even in a climate of "politically correct" celebration of diversity.

The contradictions between ideology and reality are evident not only in a later-developing society like Japan whose leaders had to create modernity, democracy, and stability rather precipitously, but also in places like America where the founding ideologies were "modern." The gap between ideal and real is another commonality.

Explorations

1. As an exercise with your classmates, make a list of traits you associate with America and Americans. You may want to finish a series of sentences beginning with "America is . . ." and "Americans are . . ." Do you note the outlines of any cultural myths about America—what Americans are, or what they believe (or are expected to believe) about themselves?

2. America is often described as a "classless society"; still, do you think

of yourself as belonging to a particular class? If so, which one: upper, middle, or lower? Do you further categorize yourself? For example, if you think of yourself as "middle class," do you make a further distinction among "upper middle," or "lower middle," or even "middle middle"? Why do you categorize yourself as you do—what history, aspirations, possessions locate you in a particular class? What do people in other classes have or believe that set them apart from you?

3. Reflect on your ethnic group. Where are your ancestors from? How do those in your ethnic group refer to themselves, and does it differ from what those not in your ethnic group call your group? What does your ethnic group value? What are the stereotypes about your ethnic group? In general, do you identify strongly with your ethnic group, or do you try to differentiate yourself from it? Explain.

4. While Japan appears to be a relatively homogeneous country in terms of race, foreign (usually Caucasian) models are popular in fashion and diversity. (Mannequins in clothing shops are almost always Caucasian.) What might this popularity represent, and are there any parallels in American fashion and advertising?

5. Recently, Japanese school texts have been the subject of criticism for not treating Japan's role as an aggressor in World War II and for not acknowledging, for example, the exploitation of Korean women as "comfort women" forced to provide sex for Japanese soldiers during the war. What similar "convenient" lapses were, or are, there in American texts?

6. Consider the American ideal of equal opportunity. What does it mean in the abstract, and how is it implemented in practice? Find examples of successful and unsuccessful implementation.

Chie Nakane

Hierarchy in Japanese Society

In any society, individuals are gathered into social groups or social strata on the bases of attributes and frame. The way in which these underlying factors are commonly weighted bears a close reciprocal relationship to the values

Chie Nakane, a professor of anthropology and a member of the Asian Institute at Tokyo University, is the first woman to have been awarded tenure at a major Japanese university. This selection is from her book Japanese Society *(1970).*

that develop in the social consciousness of the people in the society. For example, the group consciousness of the Japanese depends considerably on the immediate social context, or frame, whereas in India it lies in attribute (most symbolically expressed in caste, which is fundamentally a social group based on the ideology of occupation and kinship).

The ready tendency of the Japanese to stress situational position in a particular frame, rather than universal attribute, can be seen in the following example: When a Japanese "faces the outside" (confronts another person) and affixes some position to himself socially, he is inclined to give precedence to institution over kind of occupation. Rather than saying, "I am a typesetter" or "I am a file clerk," he is likely to say, "I am from B Publishing Group" or "I belong to S Company." Much depends on the context, of course, but where a choice exists, he will use this latter form.

In group identification, a frame such as a "company" or "association" is of primary importance; the attribute of the individual is secondary. The same tendency is found among intellectuals: among university graduates, what matters most, and functions the strongest socially, is not whether a man holds or does not hold a Ph.D. but, rather, from which university he graduated. Thus, the criterion by which the Japanese classify individuals socially tends to be one of institutional affiliation rather than universal attribute. Such group consciousness and orientation fosters the strength of an institution, and the institutional unit (such as school or company) is in fact the basis of Japanese social organization.

The term *kaisha* (company) symbolizes the expression of group consciousness. Kaisha does not mean that individuals are bound by contractual relationships into a corporate enterprise, while still thinking of themselves as separate entities; rather, kaisha is "my" or "our" company, the community to which one belongs primarily and which is all-important in one's life. Thus, in most cases, the company provides the whole social existence of a person and has authority over all aspects of his life; he is deeply emotionally involved in the association. The sort of reasoning involved here, that Company A belongs not to its shareholders but rather to "us," is carried to such a point that even modern legal arrangements must compromise in the face of this strong native orientation. I would not wish to deny that in other societies an employee may have a kind of emotional attachment to the company or his employer; what distinguishes this relation in Japan is the exceedingly high degree of the emotional involvement. It is openly and frequently expressed in speech and behavior in public as well as in private, and such expressions always receive social and moral appreciation and approbation.

The resulting system of lifetime employment has advantages for both   5
employer and employee. For the employer, it serves to retain the services of skilled workers against times of labor shortage. For the employee, it gives security against surplus labor conditions; whatever the market circumstances, there is little likelihood of the employee finding better employment if he leaves his job. The system has, in fact, been encouraged by contradictory

situations—a shortage and a surplus of labor. Here is demonstrated a radical divergence between Japan and America in management employment policy: A Japanese employer buys potential labor for the future, and an American employer buys labor immediately required. According to Japanese reasoning, any deficiencies in the current labor force will be compensated by the development of maximum power in the labor force of the future; the employer buys his labor material and shapes it until it fits his production need. In America, management buys ready-made labor.

The characteristics of Japanese enterprise as a social group are, first, that the group is itself familylike and, second, that it pervades even the private lives of its employees, for each family joins extensively in the enterprise. These characteristics have been encouraged consistently by managers and administrators since the Meiji period. And the truth is that this encouragement has always succeeded and reaped rewards.

A cohesive sense of group unity, as demonstrated in the operational mechanisms of household and enterprise, is essential as the foundation of the individual's total emotional participation in the group; it helps to build a closed world and results in strong group independence or isolation. This inevitably breeds household customs and company traditions. These in turn are emphasized in mottoes that bolster the sense of unity and group solidarity and strengthen the group even more.

Consciousness of "them" and "us" is strengthened and aggravated to the point that extreme contrasts in human relations can develop in the same society, and anyone outside "our" people ceases to be considered human. Ridiculous situations occur, such as that of the man who will shove a stranger out of the way to take an empty seat but will then, no matter how tired he is, give up the seat to someone he knows, particularly if that someone is a superior in his company.

These characteristics of group formation reveal that Japanese group affiliations and human relations are exclusively one-to-one: A single loyalty stands uppermost and firm. There are many cases of membership in more than one group, of course, but in these cases there is always one group that is clearly preferred while the others are considered secondary.

In the foregoing discussion it has been shown that a group where   10
membership is based on the situational position of individuals within a common frame tends to become a closed world. Inside it, a sense of unity is promoted by means of the members' total emotional participation, which further strengthens group solidarity. In general, such groups share a common structure, an internal organization by which the members are tied vertically into a delicately graded order.

A functional group always consists of heterogeneous elements, and their vertical relation becomes the actuating principle in creating cohesion among group members. Because of the overwhelming ascendancy of vertical orientation, even a set of individuals sharing identical qualifications tends to create differences within it. As this is reinforced, an amazingly delicate and intricate system of ranking takes shape.

There are numerous examples of this ranking process. Among lathe operators with the same qualifications, differences of rank exist which are based on relative age, year of entry into the company, or length of continuous service; among professors at the same college, rank can be assessed by the formal date of appointment; among commissioned officers in the former Japanese army, the differences between ranks were very great, and it is said that, even among second lieutenants, distinct ranking was made on the basis of order of appointment.

Ranking-consciousness is not limited merely to official groups but is found also among writers and actors—that is, groups that are supposed to be engaged in work based on individual ability and should not therefore be bound by any institutional system. A well-known novelist, on being given one of the annual literary prizes, said, "It is indeed a great honor for me. I am rather embarrassed to receive the award when some of my *sempai* [predecessors or elders] have not yet received it."

A Japanese finds his world clearly divided into three categories: *sempai* (seniors), *kohai* (juniors), and *doryo*. *Doryo*, meaning "one's colleagues," refers only to those with the same rank, not to all who do the same type of work in the same office or on the same shop floor; even among doryo, differences in age and year of entry or of graduation from school or college contribute to a sense of sempai and kohai. These three categories would be subsumed under the single term "colleagues" in other societies.

Once established, vertical ranking functions as the charter of the social   15
order, so that whatever the change in an individual's status, popularity, or fame, there is a deeply ingrained reluctance to ignore or change the established order. In this kind of society, ranking becomes far more important than any differences in the nature of the work. Even among people with the same training, qualifications, or status, differences based on rank are always perceptible. Because the individuals concerned are deeply aware of their existence, these distinctions tend to overshadow and obscure even differences of occupation, status, or class.

In Japan, once rank is established on the basis of seniority, it is applied to all circumstances and to a great extent controls social life and individual activity. Seniority and merit are the principal criteria for the establishment of a social order, and every society employs these criteria, although the weight given to each may differ according to social circumstances. In the West, merit is given considerable importance, while in Japan the balance goes the other way. In other words, in Japan in contrast to other societies, the provisions for the recognition of merit are weak, and the social order is institutionalized largely by means of seniority.

In everyday affairs a man who is not aware of relative ranking is not able to speak or even to sit or to eat. When speaking, he is always expected to be ready with differentiated, delicate degrees of honorific expressions appropriate to the rank order between himself and the person he is addressing. The expressions and the manner appropriate to a superior are never to be used to an inferior. Even among colleagues, it is only possible to dispense with honorifics when both parties are very intimate friends. The English language is inadequate to supply appropriate equivalents in such contexts, but behavior and language are intimately interwoven in Japan.

The ranking order that produces delicate differentiations between members of a group develops firm personal links between superior and subordinate. Such relationships form the core of the system of a group organization. A group structure based on a vertical line of this strength is demonstrably different from one based on a horizontal line.

Most Japanese, whatever their status or occupation, are involved in *oyabun-kobun* (boss-subordinate) relationships. The oyabun-kobun relationship comes into being through one's occupational training and activities and carries social and personal implications, appearing symbolically at the critical moments in a man's life. The oyabun often plays the role of the father, and it is by no means exceptional for him to play an even more important role.

It is said that the greatest battle weakness of the former Japanese army [20] was the disruption that ensued when a platoon leader was killed. A platoon that had lost its organizational pivot because of the death of its lieutenant easily degenerated into a disorganized mob, committing gross errors of judgment. In the British and American armies there is no such disruption; a substitute platoon leader quickly steps out from the ranks, and control of the platoon continues undisturbed until there is only one soldier left.

Herein, then, lies the supreme importance of the role of the leader: He is both the holder of legitimate status and the outstanding personality, able to synthesize the members and suppress antagonisms among them. Even though a leader's absence from his men is only temporary, it may give rise to increased antagonisms among them. Legitimacy is based on seniority (not necessarily of age but of years of service in the group); the most senior man is also very probably the man who is highest in rank after and most closely linked with the leader, since the group hierarchy is formed according to the order of entry into the group. If there is more than one man in such a position, the most senior in age would become the first candidate for succession to the leadership.

Whatever their size, Japanese groups share common structural characteristics. Regardless of the size of the whole group, the functionally effective core is fairly small, usually of one or two dozen members. This is a size that enables each member to have direct contact with all the others, which can be organized on two or three levels, including the leader on the top level. Thus, members on the lowest level do not stand too far (i.e., through too many levels) from the leader. The ideal type of effective group is organized on two levels, with all members linked directly to the leader. When a group becomes larger, with an increased number of levels, the effectiveness of the entire system tends to decrease, and a functional core develops at each level.

These factors contribute to inefficiency of organization, in the matter of poor communication from the lower sectors to the top and between sections. However, such inefficiency is perhaps more than balanced by the extreme efficiency of communication from the top to the lowest level. Indeed, the swiftness by which the members of a group can be mobilized from the top in Japan is not paralleled in any other society. The secret of such swift action and the source of the high level of group energy seems to lie in the nature of the core of group organization, based on the relationship between two immediately linked men. The golden rule is that the junior man should invariably carry out any order from his immediate superior, for this immediate link between the two men is the source of the existence of the junior man in the organization. Hesitation or refusal constitutes a violation of the system, even if the execution of the order takes a man outside his assigned role, for what is important is the working of the vertical system, rather than the nature of the work or the formal assignment of roles. The prompt acceptance of an order by a junior predisposes his senior in his favor, and the accumulation of such give-and-take contributes to the mobilization of the entire group.

However, at the same time this highly involved relationship between the two men entails the phenomenon of "the creation of groups within a group" (*tochu to o tsukuru* in Japanese)—the sectionalism from which Japanese organizations regularly suffer. This precludes horizontal relations. It is difficult for a horizontal link or balanced cooperation between sections to function in Japan. The equal balance of powers between peers or collaboration between two equally competing groups is almost nonexistent in Japanese society, for when there is more than one faction within a group one will dominate. The existence of equally competing powers is a most unstable situation in Japan; stability always resides in imbalance between powers where one dominates the others.

A de facto coalition of equally strong factions is unlikely in Japan, for one of the factions is always invested with disproportionate weight. On this basis the leader mediates between opposing factions in order to arrive at group consensus, and will appeal to the weaker faction to concede its point "for the sake of my face"—that is, for his standing and reputation; and if the leader's face is saved, so is that of the opponent. Given such group structure and the use of emotional appeals, the majority opinion readily emerges. Thus, though the issue itself may never be subjected to logical examination, the group can reach agreement to act on a generally accepted decision. General agreement prompts readiness to act, and if a recalcitrant minority adamantly resists concession, radical action might finally be taken by which this minority could be made outcasts from the group.

From the above discussion two negative characteristics of group structure can be deduced: first, that the group is always under the risk of internal fission, and second, that it has the crucial external weakness of not permitting cooperation between groups. On the positive side, when the group is functioning at its best, great power and efficiency can come from concentrating and mobilizing its members' energies, since the ties binding individuals are emotional and stable. It follows, however, that efficiency is open to impairment through ambitions that upset the balance of power.

It is demonstrable that the informal hierarchy and the factions that develop among a group's members overlap and supersede an institution's formal administrative organization. In firmly established institutions, such as long-founded companies and governmental organizations, the instability and disintegration of informal groups are well compensated for by the institutional frame itself. Even when the informal hierarchy is deformed or destroyed, individual members still remain within the frame. Even while its efficiency is lowered, the group can preserve itself by means of the formal administrative organization. The institutional frame fulfills the important function of keeping the members together, whatever factions are found within it. Since members are classified primarily by the institution, whatever internal rivalries they may feel, they realize that they are all in one boat racing with other boats. It goes without saying that the degree of effectiveness of an institutional frame (the coherence of its members) is heightened when the institution itself possesses wide prestige and an important role in the society.

The overall picture of society resulting from such interpersonal (and intergroup) relations is not that of horizontal stratification by class or caste but of vertical stratification by institution or group of institutions. The construction of social groups based on vertical organization stresses their unitary aspects and brings about numerous vertical schisms within the society. Even if social classes like those in Europe can be detected in Japan, and even if something vaguely resembling the classes that are illustrated in the textbooks of Western sociology can also be found in Japan, the point is that in actual society this stratification is unlikely to function. It does not really reflect the social structure. In Japanese society, it is really not a matter of workers struggling against capitalists or managers but of Company A ranged against Company B. The protagonists do not stand in vertical relationship to each other but instead rub elbows from parallel positions. The organization of unions in Japan, their ideals, and the peculiarities to be seen in the union movement cannot be understood without this kind of analysis. The antagonism and wrangling between management and labor in Japan is unquestionably a "household" problem, and though their basic divergence is the same as it is the world over, the reason it cannot develop in Japan into a problem intimately and powerfully affecting society as a whole lies in the group structure and the nature of Japanese society.

Competition takes place between parallel groups of the same kind, and the prize in the race is the rating. A common Japanese reaction may well take the form, "Their rating is higher than ours, so . . ." Among governmental organizations, the ranking is known in an informal way, though in a manner sufficiently overt for those closely concerned. The Finance Ministry stands out at the top, and the Education Ministry, for example, is placed considerably lower. Generally, earlier entrants (those having a longer history) have the higher ratings, but the fact that rating can be changed through the acquisition of additional political and economic power and influence is a primary factor in whipping up the race.

The ranking order among institutions is likewise of immediate concern to individuals, in that individual status and prestige go according to this ranking as well as according to the individual's rank within each institution. Even typists and drivers take pride in belonging to a company with a high ranking, for they are able to feel superior to typists and drivers employed by lesser-ranked companies, even though they receive the same pay. The Japanese are not so much concerned with social background as with institutional affiliation. Since the hierarchy of each field is so clearly perceived and widely known, and since the hierarchy within individual institutions also extends beyond the institution, taken together they offer a fairly distinct picture into which an individual can be fitted. 30

The building of a hierarchy based on the ranking order of institutions is further complicated by the tendency for a set of institutions to be organized in the manner of the inverted V, in just the same way as individuals form a group. It is usual, for example, for a large business firm or industrial plant to attach to itself a considerable number of affiliated and subordinate companies, many of which are called its "child companies." The nature and degree of the relationships between parent company and child company vary considerably. A child company may be created by separating a part of the original company, or by investing a part of the capital of the latter; or an independent smaller company may establish a parent and child relationship with a large one. Personnel and finance may be transferred from the one to the other. However, some child companies have a considerable degree of independence from the parent company and an autonomy not found in the case of, for example, an American subsidiary company. Indeed, there are examples of a child company which develops and becomes so successful that it reaches a status comparable to that of its parent company. On the other hand, a child company may be closely tied to the parent company, forming one distinct hierarchical organization with it and the other companies affiliated at various levels. Such a case is usually centered on a large company, say, with more than 10,000 employees—at the lowest level there may be a very small enterprise consisting of the members of a single family.

Clusters of this kind, which exist in all business sectors in Japan, are at their most pronounced in such fields as automobile production and the building industry. Toyota Motor Corporation, one of the largest automobile enterprises in Japan, is a convenient and telling illustration. Centered on Toyota Motor Corporation are twelve companies known as the Toyota Group. These companies are closely linked with Toyota Motor Corporation through activities or business such as sales, exports, production of parts, and supply of materials.

An examination of the interinstitutional relations in any such group reveals the operation of the same structural mechanism as exists in the single institution—immobility, both within and between groups. For this reason, a group, on whatever level, is organized vertically and keeps its solidarity and exclusiveness. For the same reason, any element built into the body of the group is virtually unexchangeable. Thus, the one-to-one, single-bond affiliation, solidly fixed, contributes to the maintenance of order in the overall structure of society. It is not a simple matter of "loyalty," for the structure of the group is significant. A society having this type of social organization does not spontaneously put its resources into a pool from which every group can take supplies whenever they are needed. In this system of organization, therefore, a group tends to develop self-sufficiency so that it can function by itself. Otherwise, it would not survive.

Thinking About the Text

1. Summarize Nakane's chief points about the structure of Japanese society. In the context of other selections you have read in this book, does anything she says surprise you?

2. Nakane is a Japanese sociologist analyzing Japanese society. Read or reread a selection by one of the following Japanese authorities commenting on Japanese society: Ikuo Amano (p. 109), Sumiko Iwao (p. 180), Akio Morita (p. 258). Are its generalizations about the Japanese in keeping with Nakane's comments? Does Nakane's perspective clarify or change your reading of the selection?

3. Nakane contrasts the idea of "attribute" with the idea of "frame" as ways in which individuals are identified. How do you identify yourself? By one or the other? Or by a combination of the two?

Thinking About Culture

4. Is a sense of group unity, as Nakane describes it, exclusive to Japan? Cite some instances (such as a football team) in America, of such group unity, and compare and contrast these to the Japanese case. How is a sense of group identity formed and enforced? You may want to approach this question from the perspectives of both someone inside a group and someone outside a group.

5. Are there hierarchies in American society similar to those described by Nakane? Are we organized around age and gender as hierarchical principles or by other qualities?

6. In a culture emphasizing cohesion, unity, and harmony, how is competition handled?

Clyde Haberman

Wrestler Fails to Keep Hold on Honorable Past

In the highly structured, rigidly disciplined, virtually feudal world of Japanese *sumo* wrestling, there had never been anything like it.

In response, the Japan Sumo Association, with about as much ceremony as it takes to hurl someone from the ring, cast out from its midst an excitable young man named Futahaguro, who had enjoyed the highest rank— *yokozuna*, or grand champion.

His tumble from grace spoke volumes about *sumo* and its hierarchical traditions. More significantly, it said a good deal about Japan itself and its values.

Futahaguro's sin was that he possessed a wicked temper, and displayed it in particularly nasty style last Sunday by kicking the eighty-eight-year-old head of his supporters' group and then shoving and injuring his master's wife.

A Breach of Decorum

It was, *sumo* elders agreed, an unspeakable breach of decorum, and so they   5
accepted his forced resignation Thursday, the first time such a disgrace had befallen any of the sixty-two wrestlers who have held the rank of *yokozuna* over the last three hundred years.

Even Futahaguro, a much-troubled man of twenty-four years, agreed that he had gone too far.

"The fact that I undermined the title of *yokozuna* was bad not only for me but for society as a whole," he said at a news conference.

The Japanese have constructed a society where displays of temper are considered as unseemly as stepping on a *tatami* straw mat with one's shoes on. It simply isn't done. And if it is done, the offender had better expect to lose considerable face, whether or not he is right on the substance of the matter.

For him to compound the sin by attacking his elders is anathema.

"I have never heard of such an incident before," said Tatsunami, master   10
of the *sumo* "stable" that includes Futahaguro. He is also the man whose wife had been pushed. "He lifted his hand to his master. Even I have things that I cannot forgive."

Clyde Haberman, a journalist, has spent several years in Japan. This article originally appeared in the New York Times *in January 1988.*

On Every Front Page

The enormity of this event for Japanese was reflected in the news coverage. The story was on the front page of every major national newspaper. It led evening news broadcasts. One sports newspaper devoted three full pages to the episode.

A big reason for the attention was the obvious fact that Futahaguro, whose real name is Koji Kitao, held the loftiest rank in a sport that has a rich history deeply rooted in the national religion of Shinto.

To outsiders, *sumo* may appear to be nothing more than a contest between two outsized men with low centers of gravity, trying to shove each other out of a circular ring in matches that routinely last only a few seconds. But to millions of Japanese, it is a reflection of their national traditions and myths, a vestige of a more honorable past when *samurai* held sway and everyone knew his place.

There was simply no room in that world for a young man like this *yokozuna*, who belligerently proclaimed his differences with his stable master. Judging from man-on-the-street comments carried in newspapers and on television, many Japanese seemed to view Futahaguro as the embodiment of a modern generation that has become, in their eyes, too prosperous, too independent, too selfish.

Too Much Pressure

His story, though, can also be regarded as the bitter tale of a young man   15
who had too much pressure forced upon him.

Many *sumo* experts believe he never should have been promoted to the top rung in the first place, for he had never won a tournament. In fact, he is the first *yokozuna* ever to have retired without a single tournament victory under his thick brocaded belt.

But he was promoted nonetheless in August 1986—a young giant, standing 6 feet, 6 inches tall and weighing 345 pounds—because the Sumo Association felt that more *yokozuna* were needed to maintain fan interest.

Futahaguro, who until then had fought under the name of Kitao, seemed to fill the bill. But he never really got going.

Despite a stellar runner-up performance in the fifteen-day November tournament, one of six held each year, he seemed to be in over his head. Partly because of his perceived shortcomings, the association promoted two other wrestlers to *yokozuna* in recent months.

Junior Wrestlers Complained

His troubles revealed themselves in October, when he roughed up some of   20
the seven junior wrestlers who, in accordance with tradition, serve as his personal attendants. One of them reportedly suffered ear damage from a

Futahaguro blow. Six of the seven walked out on him, saying he was too cruel, and three later quit the sport entirely.

This incident was allowed to pass. But the fight last Sunday was considered unforgivable.

As he quarreled with Tatsunami, the stable master, the young wrestler grew progressively angrier. In the process, he kicked Keizo Bando, elderly chairman of the Futahaguro Supporters' Association, who was on hand. Then, he swung out at Tatsunami's wife, Chieko, as she approached him from behind, knocking her into a sliding door and injuring her left hand.

Shouting an epithet, he stomped out and said he would not return.

Outburst Sealed His Fate

Although he reportedly apologized by phone to the stable master, his outburst had irrevocably sealed his fate, and the Sumo Association accepted his written resignation, formally tendered by Tatsunami.

He still disagreed with his master, Futahaguro told reporters. "I thought   25 I wouldn't be able to follow him any longer in pursuing my *sumo* career," he said.

But Tatsunami felt that more was at stake. The stable master says, "Even though he may have the highest rank, total selfishness is not allowed. *Sumo* people must live together in a group."

To many Japanese, the same could be said for the entire nation, and any disruptions of group harmony can have broad consequences. Futahaguro was not the only one to pay for the misadventure.

The directors of the Sumo Association reprimanded the stable master for having been negligent in supervising his young wrestler. And for good measure, they cut their own salaries by 20 percent for three months, to show that they, too, bore responsibility.

Thinking About the Text

1. Recast Haberman's article as a case study by Chie Nakane (p. 400). What details would you emphasize? What sort of analysis would you provide?

2. Consider Haberman's last paragraph. What is the underlying idea of responsibility here? Is there evidence of this in American society?

Thinking About Culture

3. Haberman observes that the episode he writes about "said a good deal about Japan itself and its values" (para. 3). In a recent newspaper or newsmagazine find an episode, from the field of sports, entertainment, or

business, that you think says a good deal about the United States and its values, and explain why the episode is revealing.

4. Choose an American celebrity to be the subject of a "case study in American values." Consider not only what the celebrity does and says, but also how he or she became a celebrity, and what the celebrity seems to represent to other Americans.

Dorinne K. Kondo

On Being a Conceptual Anomaly

As a Japanese American,[1] I created a conceptual dilemma for the Japanese I encountered. For them, I was a living oxymoron, someone who was both Japanese and not Japanese. Their puzzlement was all the greater since most Japanese people I knew seemed to adhere to an eminently biological definition of Japaneseness. Race, language, and culture are intertwined, so much so that any challenge to this firmly entrenched conceptual schema—a white person who speaks flawlessly idiomatic and unaccented Japanese, or a person of Japanese ancestry who cannot—meets with what generously could be described as unpleasant reactions. White people are treated as repulsive and unnatural—*hen na gaijin,* strange foreigners—the better their Japanese becomes, while Japanese Americans and others of Japanese ancestry born overseas are faced with exasperation and disbelief. How can someone who is racially Japanese lack "cultural competence"?[2] During my first few months

---

[1] Edward Said, *Orientalism* (New York: Pantheon, 1978). The issue of what to call ourselves is an issue of considerable import to various ethnic and racial groups in the United States, as the recent emphasis on the term "African American" shows. For Asian Americans, the term "Oriental" was called into question in the sixties, for the reasons Said enumerates: the association of the term with stereotypes such as Oriental despotism, inscrutability, splendor, exoticism, mystery, and so on. It also defines "the East" in terms of "the West," in a relationship of unequal power — how rarely one hears of "the Occident," for example. Asian Americans, Japanese Americans included, sometimes hyphenate the term, but some of us would argue that leaving out the hyphen makes the term "Asian" or "Japanese" an adjective, rather than implying a half-and-half status: i.e., that one's loyalties/identities might be half Japanese and half American. Rather, in the terms "Asian American" and "Japanese American," the accent is on the "American," an important political claim in light of the mainstream tendency to see Asian Americans as somehow more foreign than other kinds of Americans.

[2] Merry White, *The Japanese Overseas: Can They Go Home Again?* (New York: Free Press, 1988). Offers an account of the families of Japanese corporate executives who are transferred abroad and who often suffer painful difficulties upon reentering Japan.

Dorinne K. Kondo teaches anthropology at Pomona College. The selection presented here is from her book, Crafting Selves: Power, Gender, and Discourses of Identity in a Japanese Workplace *(1990).*

in Tokyo, many tried to resolve this paradox by asking which of my parents was "really" American.

Indeed, it is a minor miracle that those first months did not lead to an acute case of agoraphobia, for I knew that once I set foot outside the door, someone somewhere (a taxi driver? a salesperson? a bank clerk?) would greet one of my linguistic mistakes with an astonished "Eh?" I became all too familiar with the series of expressions that would flicker over those faces: bewilderment, incredulity, embarrassment, even anger, at having to deal with this odd person who looked Japanese and therefore human, but who must be retarded, deranged, or—equally undesirable in Japanese eyes—Chinese or Korean. Defensively, I would mull over the mistake of the day. I mean, how was I to know that in order to "fillet a fish" you had to cut it "in three pieces"? Or that opening a bank account required so much specialized terminology? Courses in literary Japanese at Harvard hadn't done much to prepare me for the realities of everyday life in Tokyo. Gritting my teeth in determination as I groaned inwardly, I would force myself out of the house each morning.

For me, and apparently for the people around me, this was a stressful time, when expectations were flouted, when we had to strain to make sense of one another. There seemed to be few advantages in my retaining an American persona, for the distress caused by these reactions was difficult to bear. In the face of dissonance and distress, I found that the desire for comprehensible order in the form of "fitting in," even if it meant suppression of and violence against a self I had known in another context, was preferable to meaninglessness. Anthropological imperatives to immerse oneself in another culture intensified this desire, so that acquiring the accoutrements of Japanese selfhood meant simultaneously constructing a more thoroughly professional anthropological persona. This required language learning in the broadest sense, mastery of culturally appropriate modes of moving, acting, and speaking. For my informants, it was clear that coping with this anomalous creature was difficult, for here was someone who looked like a real human being, but who simply failed to perform according to expectation. They, too, had every reason to make me over in their image, to guide me, gently but insistently, into properly Japanese behavior, so that the discrepancy between my appearance and my cultural competence would not be so painfully evident. I posed a challenge to their senses of identity. How could someone who *looked* Japanese not *be* Japanese? In my cultural ineptitude, I represented for the people who met me the chaos of meaninglessness. Their response in the face of this dissonance was to *make* me as Japanese as possible. Thus, my first nine months of fieldwork were characterized by an attempt to reduce the distance between expectation and inadequate reality, as my informants and I conspired to rewrite my identity as Japanese.

My guarantor, an older woman who, among her many activities, was a teacher of flower arranging, introduced me to many families who owned businesses in the ward of Tokyo where I had chosen to do my research. One of her former students and fellow flower-arranging teachers, Mrs. Sakamoto, agreed to take me in as a guest over the summer, since the apartment where I was scheduled to move—owned by one of my classmates in tea ceremony—was still under construction. My proclivities for "acting Japanese" were by this time firmly established. During my stay with the Sakamotos, I did my best to conform to what I thought their expectations of a guest/daughter might be. This in turn seemed to please them and reinforced my tendency to behave in terms of what I perceived to be my Japanese persona.

My initial encounter with the head of the household epitomizes this   5
mirroring and reinforcement of behavior. Mr. Sakamoto had been on a business trip on the day I moved in, and he returned the following evening, just as his wife, daughter, and I sat down to the evening meal. As soon as he stepped in the door, I immediately switched from an informal posture, seated on the *zabuton* (seat cushion) to a formal greeting posture, *seiza*-style (kneeling on the floor) and bowed low, hands on the floor. Mr. Sakamoto responded in kind (being older, male, and head of the household, he did not have to bow as deeply as I did), and we exchanged the requisite polite formulae, I requesting his benevolence, and he welcoming me to their family. Later, he told me how happy and impressed he had been with this act of proper etiquette on my part. "Today's young people in Japan," he said, "no longer show such respect. Your grandfather must have been a fine man to raise such a fine granddaughter." Of course, his statements can hardly be accepted at face value. They may well indicate his relief that I seemed to know something of proper Japanese behavior, and hence would not be a complete nuisance to them; it was also his way of making me feel at home. What is important to note is the way this statement was used to elicit proper Japanese behavior in future encounters. And his strategy worked. I was left with a warm, positive feeling toward the Sakamoto family, armed with an incentive to behave in a Japanese way, for clearly these were the expectations and the desires of the people who had taken me in and who were so generously sharing their lives with me.

Other members of the household voiced similar sentiments. Takemi-san, the Sakamotos' married daughter who lived in a distant prefecture, had been visiting her parents when I first moved in. A few minutes after our initial encounter, she observed, "You seem like a typical Japanese woman" (*Nihon no josei, to iu kanji*). Later in the summer, Mrs. Sakamoto confided to me that she could never allow a "pure American" (*junsui na Amerikajin*) to live with them, for only someone of Japanese descent was genetically capable of adjusting to life on *tatami* mats, using unsewered toilets, sleeping on the floor—in short, of living Japanese style. Again, the message was unambiguous: My "family" could feel comfortable with me insofar as I was—and acted—Japanese.

At first, then, as a Japanese American I made sense to those around me as a none-too-felicitous combination of racial categories. As fieldwork progressed, however, and my linguistic and cultural skills improved, my informants seemed best able to understand me by placing me in meaningful cultural roles: daughter, guest, young woman, student, prodigal Japanese who had finally seen the light and come home. Most people preferred to treat me as a Japanese—sometimes an incomplete or unconventional Japanese, but a Japanese nonetheless. Indeed, even when I tried to represent myself as an American, others did not always take heed. For instance, on my first day on the job at the confectionery factory, Mr. Sato introduced me to the division chief as an "American student," here to learn about the business and about the "real situation" (*jittai*) of workers in small enterprise. Soon it became clear that the chief remembered "student," but not "American." A week or so later, we gathered for one of our noon meetings to read from a pamphlet published by an ethics school. The owner came, and he commented on the theme of the day, *ketsui* (determination). At one point during his speech, he singled me out, praising my resolve. "If Kondo-san had been an ordinary young woman, she might never have known Japan." I stared at my shoes, my cheeks flaming. When the exercise finished, I hurried back to my work station. Akiyama-san, the division head, approached me with a puzzled expression on his face. "*Doko desu ka?*" he asked. (Where is it?—in other words, where are you from?) And after my reply, he announced loudly to all: "She says it's America!"

My physical characteristics led my friends and coworkers to emphasize my identity as Japanese, sometimes even against my own intentions and desires. Over time, my increasingly "Japanese" behavior served temporarily to resolve their crises of meaning and to confirm their assumptions about their own identities. That I, too, came to participate enthusiastically in this recasting of the self is a testimonial to their success in acting upon me.

Conflict and Fragmentation of Self

Using these ready-made molds may have reduced the dissonance in my informants' minds, but it served only to increase the dissonance in my own. What occurred in the field was a kind of fragmenting of identity into what I then labeled Japanese and American pieces, so that the different elements, instead of fitting together to form at least the illusion of a seamless and coherent whole—it is the contention of this book that selves which are coherent, seamless, bounded, and whole are indeed illusions—strained against one another. The war was not really—or only—between Japanese and American elements, however. Perhaps it had even more to do with the position of researcher versus one of daughter and guest. In one position, my goal had to be the pursuit of knowledge, where decisive action, independence, and mastery were held in high esteem. In another, independence and mastery of one's own fate were out of the question; rather, being a daughter meant duties, responsibilities, and *inter*dependence.

The more I adjusted to my Japanese daughter's role, the keener the 10
conflicts became. Most of those conflicts had to do with expectations sur-

rounding gender, and, more specifically, my position as a young woman. Certainly, in exchange for the care the Sakamotos showed me, I was happy to help out in whatever way I could. I tried to do some housecleaning and laundry, and I took over the shopping and cooking for Mr. Sakamoto when Mrs. Sakamoto was at one of the children's association meetings, her flower-arranging classes, or meetings of ward committees on juvenile delinquency. The cooking did not offend me in and of itself; in fact, I was glad for the opportunity to learn how to make simple Japanese cuisine, and Mr. Sakamoto put up with my sometimes appalling culinary mistakes and limited menus with great aplomb. I remember one particularly awful night when I couldn't find the makings for soup broth, and Mr. Sakamoto was fed "*miso* soup" that was little more than *miso* dissolved in hot water. He managed to down the tasteless broth with good grace—and the trace of a smile on his lips. (Of course, it is also true that although he was himself capable of simple cooking, he would not set foot in the kitchen if there were a woman in the house.) Months after I moved out, whenever he saw me he would say with a sparkle in his eye and a hint of nostalgic wistfulness in his voice, "I miss Dorin-san's salad and sautéed beef," one of the "Western" menus I used to serve up with numbing regularity. No, the cooking was not the problem.

The problem was, in fact, the etiquette surrounding the serving of food that produced the most profound conflicts for me as an American woman. The head of the household is usually served first and receives the finest delicacies; men—even the sweetest, nicest ones—ask for a second helping of rice by merely holding out their rice bowls to the woman nearest the rice cooker, and maybe, just maybe, uttering a grunt of thanks in return for her pains. I could never get used to this practice, try as I might. Still, I tried to carry out my duties uncomplainingly, in what I hope was reasonably good humor. But I was none too happy about these things "inside." Other restrictions began to chafe, especially restrictions on my movement. I had to be in at a certain hour, despite my "adult" age. Yet I understood the family's responsibility for me as their guest and quasi daughter, so I tried to abide by their regulations, hiding my irritation as best I could.

This fundamental ambivalence was heightened by isolation and dependency. Though my status was in some respects high in an education-conscious Japan, I was still young, female, and a student. I was in a socially recognized relationship of dependency vis-à-vis the people I knew. I was not to be feared and obeyed, but protected and helped. In terms of my research, this was an extremely advantageous position to be in, for people did not feel the need to reflect my views back to me, as they might with a more powerful person. I did not try to define situations; rather, I could allow other people to define those situations in their culturally appropriate ways, remaining open to their concerns and their ways of acting in the world. But, in another sense, this dependency and isolation increased my susceptibility to identifying with my Japanese role. By this time I saw little of American friends in Tokyo, for it was difficult to be with people who had so little inkling of how ordinary Japanese people lived. My informants and I consequently had every reason to conspire to recreate my identity as Japanese. Precisely because of my dependency and my made-to-order role, I was allowed—or rather, *forced*—to abandon the position of observer. Errors, linguistic or cultural, were dealt with impatiently or with a startled look that seemed to say, "Oh yes, you are American after all." On the other hand, appropriately Japanese behaviors were rewarded with warm, positive reactions or with comments such as "You're more Japanese than the Japanese." Even more frequently, correct behavior was simply accepted as a matter of course. *Naturally* I would understand, *naturally* I would behave correctly, for they presumed me to be, *au fond*, Japanese.

Identity can imply unity or fusion, but for me what occurred was a fragmentation of the self. This fragmentation was encouraged by my own participation in Japanese life and by the actions of my friends and acquaintances. At its most extreme point, I became "the Other" in my own mind, where the identity I had known in another context simply collapsed. The success of our conspiracy to recreate me as Japanese reached its climax one August afternoon.

It was typical summer weather for Tokyo, "like a steam bath" as the saying goes, so hot the leaves were drooping limply from the trees surrounding the Sakamotos' house. Mrs. Sakamoto and her married daughter, Takemi, were at the doctor's with Takemi's son, so Mr. Sakamoto and I were busy tending young Kaori-chan, Takemi-san's young daughter. Mr. Sakamoto quickly tired of his grandfatherly role, leaving me to entertain Kaori-chan. Promptly at four P.M., the hour when most Japanese housewives do their shopping for the evening meal, I lifted the baby into her stroller and pushed her along ahead of me as I inspected the fish, selected the freshest-looking vegetables, and mentally planned the meal for the evening. As I glanced into the shiny metal surface of the butcher's display case, I noticed someone who looked terribly familiar: a typical young housewife, clad in slip-on sandals and the loose, cotton shift called "home wear" *(homu wea)*, a woman walking with a characteristically Japanese bend to the knees and a sliding of the feet. Suddenly I clutched the handle of the stroller to steady myself as a wave of dizziness washed over me, for I realized I had caught a glimpse of nothing less than my own reflection. Fear that perhaps I would never emerge from this world into which I was immersed, inserted itself into my mind and stubbornly refused to leave, until I resolved to move into a new apartment, to distance myself from my Japanese home and my Japanese existence.

For ultimately, this collapse of identity was a distancing moment. It led me to emphasize the *differences* between cultures and among various aspects of identity: researcher, student, daughter, wife, Japanese, American, Japanese American. In order to reconstitute myself as an American researcher, I felt I had to extricate myself from the conspiracy to rewrite my identity as Japanese. Accordingly, despite the Sakamotos' invitations to stay with them for the coming year, I politely stated my intentions to fulfill the original terms of the agreement: to stay just until construction on my new apartment

15

was complete. In order to resist the Sakamotos' attempts to recreate me as Japanese, I removed myself physically from their exclusively Japanese environment.

Thus, both the fragmentation of self and the collapse of identity were results of a complex collaboration between ethnographer and informants. It should be evident that at this particular point, my informants were hardly inert objects available for the free play of the ethnographer's desire. They themselves were, in the act of being, actively interpreting and trying to make meaning of the ethnographer. In so doing, the people I knew asserted their power to act upon the anthropologist. This was their means for preserving their own identities. Understanding, in this context, is multiple, open-ended, positioned—although that positioning can shift dramatically, as I have argued—and pervaded by relations of power. These power-imbued attempts to capture, recast, and rewrite each other were for us productive of under-standings and were, existentially, alternately wrenching and fulfilling.

Thinking About the Text

1. If you found passages of Kondo's selection to be particularly interesting or enjoyable, identify them and explain why. If you didn't, explain why not.

2. Reread the passage on page 417 describing what Kondo calls the climax of her "collapse of identity." Have you ever had such an epiphany—in this case, a moment of observing yourself as others see you? Describe it; what did you learn from it?

3. An alternative assignment: Describe to someone of another culture (or ask them to read the passage about) Kondo's "collapse of identity." Interview that person to find out if they have ever had such an epiphany. If they have, report on your findings, describing what, from your perspective, is most interesting about the person's experience.

4. This selection turns on the fact that Kondo is initially assumed to be a native Japanese by those Japanese among whom she is doing anthropologi-cal research. Anne Allison (p. 314) also does anthropological research—in a Japanese hostess bar. Speculate on how Allison's experiences might have been affected had she looked Japanese. Or (drawing on Allison and the selections in Chapter 5) imagine how Kondo's research in a hostess bar might have proceeded.

Thinking About Culture

5. In Kondo's selection as in others (to name just a few: Lo, p. 263; Fallows, p. 16; Bethel, p. 219; Ames, p. 379; Reingold, p. 373; Allison, p. 314) there

is implicit or explicit the problem of participation and observation in the culture one is analyzing. How far can one understand the experience of a person from another culture, or of another gender—or just any other person? Realistically, how much can one expect to learn, and how valid will it be, and what can one do with the knowledge? Draw on your reading in this book and your own specific experiences as you explore these questions with your classmates.

William Wetherall

Ethnic Ainu Seek Official Recognition

The prime minister of Japan steps behind a podium on the stage at the National Theater. The cameras are rolling as he clears his throat and begins his National Founding Day speech on February 11, 1993.

> Today, we celebrate the origins of our country in an antiquity so remote that history records them only in legends. During the past century, Japan, whose government I represent, has been considered a monoethnic state by most of its officials, including at times myself. This year, though, presents us with a timely opportunity to acknowledge, and even extol, our country's racial and ethnic diversity.
>
> The United Nations, parent and guardian of the International Covenant on Civil and Political Rights, which Japan has ratified as a party state, has designated this the International Year of the World's Indigenous People. And so it is fitting that I, on behalf of the state, officially recognize Japan's Ainu citizens as a bona fide native people.

Thus ought to begin a speech that will probably never be made—at least not by Kiichi Miyazawa. Just a few weeks before he became prime minister in 1991, Miyazawa told TV commentator Dave Spector, in a weekly-magazine interview, that Japan was a teamwork, harmony-of-all society that seldom depends on the genius of one person. He claimed this was so because Japan was "a practically monoethnic people."

"At least he said practically," Spector told me, alluding to the time

---

William Wetherall, a scholar of Asian affairs, specializes in minorities. This essay originally appeared in an English-language newspaper, Japan Times, *in January 1993.*

when another prime minister, Yasuhiro Nakasone, had not made even this concession.

At the press conference following the installation of Miyazawa's first Cabinet, in November 1991, a journalist raised doubts about whether Michio Watanabe was an appropriate choice for foreign minister. Watanabe, who had earned a reputation for offending African Americans and other minorities with offhand comments intended as humor, acknowledged that he had received criticism, then said: "Japanese are a monoethnic people, so (we've) got to be more careful (when speaking so as not to offend others)."

Both Miyazawa and Watanabe were parroting the myth of homogeneity espoused by many highly visible Japanese public figures, like Nakasone, who in September 1986 claimed that the United States was a less "intelligent society" than Japan because "in America there are many blacks, Puerto Ricans, and Mexicans." When U.S. minorities and others demanded an apology, Nakasone said that it was easier for Japan to educate and inform its people because it was a "monoethnic state."

Nakasone's characterization of Japan as monoethnic insulted all of the   5
country's minorities, but none more than Japanese of Ainu ancestry. The strongest reaction came from Hokkaido Utari Kyokai (HUK), also known as the Ainu Association of Hokkaido, a social foundation with about 16,000 members, or two-thirds of the roughly 25,000 Ainu counted in a 1986 Hokkaido survey. The largest organization representing Ainu interests, HUK immediately criticized Nakasone's remark as one that "ignored the existence of ethnic minorities in the country."

Giichi Nomura, HUK's charismatic director, broadsided Nakasone in a widely read editorial (*Asahi Shimbun,* October 1986): "Does (he) really think that Japan is a monoethnic state? In Hokkaido there are the Ainu people, and in Okinawa there are residents who have their own history and culture. (There are also) the peoples of North Korea, South Korea, China, and Taiwan who, while maintaining their own life, customs, and so forth, have naturalized in Japan or are engaged in making a living as permanent residents; is (Nakasone) saying that these peoples are the same people as the so-called Yamato° people?"

Nomura called on Nakasone "to recognize the existence of ethnic minorities in Japan, and to sweep away the heretofore erroneous concept of 'monoethnic state' (that is used) toward these ethnic minorities."

Some Ainu wrote letters to Nakasone. In one, an Ainu mother told the prime minister about the discrimination that she and her children continued to face. She wanted Yamato people "who have Japanese nationality just as we do" to understand the plight of Ainu citizens.

"Japan is definitely not monoethnic," she said, and then implored Nakasone to revise his perception. "[We] need," she concluded, "a society

---

Yamato: An ancient name for Japan, especially the Kyoto-Nara region. [Editors' note]

in which the multiple peoples residing in this country [are able to] speak their respective mother tongues, while living together [using] the Yamato tongue as a common language."

In October 1986, in defense of his "monoethnic state" remark, Naka-   10
sone stated that in Japan "there are no ethnic minorities who, as people with Japanese nationality (citizenship), are receiving discrimination."

To this remark he added:

> From reading books by Takeshi Umehara, (I know that) Ainu and the people who came across from the continent considerably fused together. In my case, too, my eyebrows are thick, and my beard is heavy. I think there's a considerable amount of Ainu blood in me.

While Nakasone may have been naive about the political hazards of ill-timed speculation over the roots of his facial hair, his knowledge of Ainu in Japan past and present far exceeded his awareness that Ainu or similar peoples had once inhabited his own ancestral turf in Gunma Prefecture, northwest of Tokyo. In fact, Nakasone had more than just read a book by Umehara, a self-styled philosopher who trespasses on anthropology and is notorious for his romantic views of early Japan.

In late 1985, Nakasone and Umehara had a lengthy discussion about the role of Japan in the flow of world civilization. In the course of their talk, Umehara outlined the strongest theory on the peopling of the Japanese islands, endorsed by anthropologists such as Kazuo Hanihara, with whom Umehara had published a book called *Ainu wa gen-Nihonjin ka* (Are Ainu the Original Japanese?).

According to Hanihara and others, Japanese of Ainu and Okinawan descent represent vestiges of the old Mongoloid peoples that inhabited the Japanese archipelago before the arrival from the continent of new Mongoloid peoples. The Yamato people appear to have come from an amalgamation of these genetically different groups. The mixing was never complete, however, and despite accelerating rates of migration within Japan, there are still regional genetic and cultural differences.

In conversation with Umehara, Nakasone displayed his knowledge of   15
the fact that his own home province was once known by a name that means "the land of people with body hair." He also praised the Ainu bear festival as an example of the kind of appreciation of nature's benevolence that Umehara thinks should be revived in a neoanimistic renaissance, to save Japan and the rest of the world from destruction by "Western" civilization. Through Nakasone's patronage, Umehara was able to build the Ministry of Education's International Research Center for Japanese Studies in Kyoto.

The discussion was published, at government expense no less, in the February 1986 issue of *Bungei Shunju*, one of Japan's most popular monthly magazines. Yet later that year, Nakasone was telling the world that the Ainu people were not a true minority.

Nakasone's "no minorities" flap so incensed some Ainu that they literally marched on Tokyo, decked out in their ethnic regalia, to show the prime minister that his putatively homogeneous country was home to at least one indigenous minority with its own culture, religion, and language. At one rally, an appeal was even read aloud in Ainu.

This second round of Ainu protest focused on HUK's 1984 proposal for a new Ainu law that would recognize their indigenous rights. The present law, called the Hokkaido Former Aboriginal Protection Law, was promulgated in 1899, and has been revised five times, most recently in 1968. Several bills to abrogate this law, without replacing it by a new law, have been opposed by HUK. The present law fails to empower the Ainu people with rights of national self-determination, and thus aids extralegal policies that seek to "terminate" the Ainu as an ethnic minority by "helping" them assimilate.

After Nakasone's flaps, some Ainu representatives and supporters objected to the disparaging wording of the title of the present law. But HUK is opposed to simply renaming the law, and demands instead that the state adopt its proposal for a new law, which among other things would end discrimination, support Ainu culture and language education, restore fishing rights, and promote economic self-sufficiency.

Ainu also want to be included in Japan's negotiations with Russia over   20
the disputed southern Kurils, which Ainu regard as part of their ancestral lands, but the Ministry of Foreign Affairs refuses to recognize Ainu as an indigenous people with proprietary rights.

Freeze the world in the late fifteenth century, about the time that Columbus was preparing to sail for Chipango. The map of the political territory called "Japan" did not yet include Ainu lands such as present-day Hokkaido, or the Kuril Islands (the southern group of which Japan wants "back" from Russia), or the former Japanese colony and erstwhile forty-eighth prefecture of Sakhalin (Karafuto). Nor did "Japan" extend to the Ogasawara (Bonin) Islands between present-day Tokyo and Guam, or to the islands of the Ryukyu Kingdom (now Okinawa) between Kyushu and Taiwan.

In these earlier times, reminiscent of today, the "national government" consisted of an unstable alliance of powerholders who, in their jostling for control, either ignored or used an isolated imperial court. Local strife escalated into provincial wars. Yet the menagerie of largely Japanese pirates who had been menacing the coasts of Korea and China for more than a century were brought under sufficient control to enable more trade between Japan, China, Korea, and the Ryukyu Kingdom.

Some Ainu communities on Hokkaido were defending their homelands from Yamato incursions from the south, while others were migrating northward. The sixteenth century saw Yamato hegemony fully jump the Tsugaru Strait to the islands that became Hokkaido in 1869.

It had taken more than a millennium for Yamato migrants from the south to intermingle with and displace, or invade and conquer, the Ainu-related people who had been living in much of northern Honshu. And it would take another three centuries for the Yamato people to extend their domain to Hokkaido and the Kurils, and to leap the Soya Strait to Sakhalin.

The Ryukyu Kingdom, a tributary state of China during this time, also came under increasing Yamato suzerainty until the 1870s, when it was annexed and prefecturized. Today, the "development" of both Hokkaido and Okinawa, at opposite ends of Japan, continues to be "guided" by a national government agency that amounts to a legacy of Yamato colonialism.

Several territorial disputes with roots in the age of imperialism continue to fester along Japan's international borders. The largest of these disputes is with Russia, over the southern Kurils, or so-called Northern Territories, which were once Ainu lands.

Ainu people were also inhabiting the major islands of the northern Kurils, where they came into contact with Kamehadals and Aleuts. Other Ainu were living on the southern half of Sakhalin, which they shared with the reindeer-breeding Uilta and the originally riverine and coastal Nivkh.

By the mid–nineteenth century, Russia was claiming the northern Kurils and all of Sakhalin, while Japan claimed the southern Kurils and the southern half of Sakhalin. In an 1875 treaty with Russia, Japan ceded its claim to southern Sakhalin for the northern Kurils.

Indigenous inhabitants were given three years to choose a national affiliation. All Aleuts relocated to the Kamchatka Peninsula or the Komandorskii Islands. A few Ainu went to Kamchatka, but the majority remained in the northern Kurils and thus became Japanese.

In 1905, a treaty concluding the Russo-Japanese War awarded southern Sahkalin to Japan. It also gave Japan fishing rights off Kamchatka, which led to an expansion of Japanese canneries on the Siberian mainland. Japanese forces occupied northern Sakhalin in 1920, but were withdrawn in 1925 in return for major oil and coal concessions. The Japanese navy patrolled the Sea of Okhotsk, ostensibly to protect Japan's expanding regional interests.

By the nineteenth century, Ainu and other indigenous peoples were no longer able to defend their lands from Cossack and Yamato invaders. After their lands were colonized by Russia and Japan, they were nationalized. Those who refused to assimilate were regarded as disloyal, while those who assimilated were still disparaged.

In 1884, having failed to persuade the partly Russified Northern Kuril Ainu to move to the southern Kurils, Japan forcefully relocated them to a new village on the island of Shikotan. Numbering barely 100 to begin with, their population rapidly fell as Yamato immigrants came to greatly outnumber them.

Some Northern Kuril Ainu resisted Yamatoization by clinging to their Russian ways. During World War II, practically all Ainu on the Kurils, including the fewer than 50 Northern Kuril Ainu who still lived on Shikotan, were evacuated to Hokkaido.

Southern Kuril Ainu numbered about 2,000 around 1800. By 1900, their population had been reduced to a few hundred by disease and intermarriage, and by emigration and relocation to Hokkaido. In 1946, Soviet surveyors reportedly found only two people who they thought were Ainu. Few former Kuril Ainu—Northern or Southern—survive in Hokkaido. Two evacuated Shikotan Ainu visited family graves on the island in 1964.

The Sakhalin Ainu population, nearly 2,400 before the end of the   35
nineteenth century, was down to fewer than 1,300 by 1940. Practically all of these Ainu were "repatriated" with other Japanese at the end of the war. Only a few Ainu remain on Sakhalin. Sakhalin Ainu who migrated to Hokkaido, and their Hokkaido-born offspring, number about 1,000. Only 13 such Ainu were able to visit family graves on Sakhalin in 1992.

Sakhalin is home to about 3,000 Uilta and Nivkh, and some Nanay, ethnic minorities who are also indigenous to the Siberian mainland. When south Sakhalin was a Japanese colony, Uilta and Nivkh, like Ainu, were "protected" by the government of Japan in ways that forced or pressed them to adopt Yamato names and speak Japanese.

Uilta and Nivkh men and boys were drafted into the Japanese army to patrol the border between north and south Sakhalin and to spy on Russia. Some were killed when Soviet forces invaded Japan's half of Sakhalin at the end of World War II. Others were abandoned by the Japanese army and taken prisoner by the Soviets, who did not treat them well.

A few Uilta and Nivkh POWs elected to settle in Hokkaido when released from Siberian camps. Others returned to Sakhalin, where they shared the fate of nationalized former colonial subjects like Koreans, who fought or labored on Japan's side during World War II, but afterward lost their Japanese nationality and could not receive war pensions.

For more than a century before Nakasone's no-minorities flap in 1986, historians and anthropologists in Japan had considered the Ainu people an indigenous ethnic minority. And in the years leading up to Japan's ratification of the International Covenant on Civil and Political Rights in 1979, most academic and journalistic opinion regarded Ainu as a group that surely ought to qualify as an ethnic minority.

So the claim in the Ministry of Foreign Affairs' 1980 (first) report to   40
the United Nations' Human Rights Committee that "minorities of the kind mentioned in the Covenant do not exist in Japan," could only have been inspired by the "monoethnic state" ideology that still pervades the government, and not on informed historical and anthropological opinion.

Popular reaction to Nakasone's flap, in addition to strong protests from Ainu organizations, forced the government to admit the existence of "the people of Ainu (sic)" in its 1987 (second) report. But the terseness and defensive tone of the admission, which totaled fewer than 100 words and made no mention of discrimination, betrayed the government's familiar reluctance to face the truth.

The government's passivity drew considerable fire from many quarters, but especially from Hokkaido Utari Kyokai, which continued to take its case directly to the United Nations. By way of preparing for the 1993 International Year of the World's Indigenous People, HUK participated in several international meetings on human rights for indigenous peoples.

It took every bit of such global publicity (which works wonders on Japan's thin-skinned Ministry of Foreign Affairs), plus editorial kicks from the domestic press, and not a little urging from civic groups and academic societies, to persuade the government to devote nearly 300 words in its 1991 (third) report on the Ainu minority. This report reiterated the second report, then summarized measures that "the government of Hokkaido" and "the government of Japan" have been taking to improve the living conditions of Ainu people.

The third report, paraphrasing the 1986 Hokkaido prefectural survey of Ainu living conditions, concluded that "the living standard of the Ainu people improved steadily, but the gap between the living standard of the general public of Hokkaido and that of the Ainu has not narrowed as expected. Therefore, the government is endeavoring to improve further the living standard of the Ainu people and to eliminate the difference between the general public and the Ainu. . . ."

The government's multiple personalities are evident in the variety of ways that its different ministries and agencies treat Ainu. Yet all are affected by schools of history and anthropology that reflect statist, if not Yamatoist, attitudes of denial and exclusion.

Though the Ministry of Foreign Affairs finally came around to recognizing Ainu as an ethnic minority, its bureaucrats are hesitant to regard them as an indigenous people. "There is no international agreement on the definition," one official said, as though it were untenable that the government should do the right thing on its own.

Over the years, the Ministry of Foreign Affairs has published some pamphlets in English and Russian on the Northern Territories issue. Such propaganda manages to reveal more than three centuries of "Japanese" knowledge about Sakhalin and the Kuril Islands without mentioning the Ainu people, or otherwise alluding to the fact that Sakhalin and the Kuril Islands had been inhabited by Ainu and other indigenous peoples long before they were "discovered" and then "developed" by Russia and Japan.

The Ministry of Education's National Museum of Ethnology in Osaka displays Ainu artifacts in its "Culture of the Ainu" exhibit. Asked why the Ainu exhibit is outside the "Culture of Japan" exhibit, the museum's resident expert on Northeast Asian indigenous peoples, Kazuyoshi Otsuka, told me that "It is to show ethnic differences."

In a talk at a 1989 Tokyo meeting to consider HUK's new Ainu law proposal, Otsuka fumbled with his labels for citizenship and ethnicity. At times he used "Nihonjin" (Japanese) to mean "Japanese national," but elsewhere he used it to designate himself and other ethnic majorities in contrast with Ainu. Asked from the floor whether he thought that Japan needed an explicit term for the ethnic majority as in China, where majorities are called Han, he seemed uncertain that Yamato should be used for this purpose—even though both Okinawans and Ainu refer to ethnic majorities and their language by words that mean Yamato.

The Ministry of Education's National Museum of Japanese History in Chiba Prefecture has no Ainu exhibits whatsoever. Some are planned, and may be ready in a few years. As to why there were none from the start, an official said: "It is not clear that Ainu were in Japan in early times. Besides, the museum does not attempt to present a comprehensive history of Japan, but takes up only certain topics."

Ainu activists know that they have nothing to lose, and everything to gain, by telling the world their side of the story—the historical and social truths that the government wants kept out of its propaganda.

In less than a decade, HUK and a small number of Ainu individuals have mounted a global campaign that has already pressed the government to recant some of its most cherished contentions. It is only a matter of time before the government agrees that Ainu are an indigenous people.

Such recognition would not itself mean victory for Ainu, unless it legally empowered them, as a nation within a state, to join the government in all domestic and foreign negotiations involving the disposition of lands and resources that belonged to their ancestors.

Loss of absolute power through the democratization of local, especially minority, populations is, of course, precisely what Japan's nearly autonomous bureaucrats fear most. But the alternative may be worse: a reputation as a state so hypnotized by its own myth, and so banal about its evils, that it cannot do what is morally right.

It all comes down to the quality of political leadership in Japan. Nakasone had the will to be great, and a touch of charisma. If he had done as HUK Director Giichi Nomura had suggested, and spoken the simple truth about Japan's ethnic minorities, he might have secured himself a permanent place in history's hall of great world leaders. Instead he chose to remain an unreformed Yamatoist, whose view of humanity was flawed by his misplaced faith in monoethnic ideology.

What Miyazawa said to Dave Spector about Japan not needing "the genius of one person" was tantamount to rationalizing his own inability to lead the country, rather than merely follow the whims of its political and bureaucratic mobs. But he's good at smiling.

In July 1992, after giving a speech before the National Press Club in Washington, D.C., Miyazawa was given two books, one of them titled "The North American Indians." He held them over his head and smiled. Picture Miyazawa, or a successor, waving two or three books, of dozens in print, about Ainu, before the cameras of the world, and smiling.

Maybe before the end of this century, a Japanese prime minister will declare Japan a multiethnic state. Imagine him (or her) announcing in the clear diction that some of Japan's leaders are capable of uttering: "From this day forward, the government of Japan recognizes its Ainu citizens as one of Japan's indigenous peoples. As such, Ainu are to be accorded all the rights due such peoples, as stipulated in the new Law Concerning the Ainu People, which was passed in the Diet today, and goes into effect immediately."

Twenty-five thousand Ainu in Hokkaido, and thousands elsewhere in Japan—if not the millions of other Japanese who, like Nakasone, boast family roots in northeast Japan—would celebrate such a restoration of nationhood. And editorials throughout the world would sigh in relief that Japan, at last, has joined the growing club of influential states that care about all of the people they presume to govern.

Such a positive embrace of an ethnic minority people would be, for   60
Japan, a first step only, but one in the right direction. Next would come Okinawans. Then Koreans and Chinese, and a growing list of others. And who knows but that someday a more enlightened state will be moved to certify the decreasing numbers of Yamato people as a minority.

Thinking About the Text

1. Although some 25,000 people today identify themselves as Ainu, it is believed that only about 200 are pure-blood Ainu. Assuming the accuracy of the figure, does this mean that—despite the speeches and the marches—there is virtually no Ainu population, and that Japan today indeed is monoethnic?

Thinking About Culture

2. In the United States a person who is, say, one-eighth African American is (and has been) considered African American (or in earlier years, Negro or black). Why is this now the case? Why was it the case in the past? Does it make sense? Does "making sense" have anything to do with what is the fact?

3. Imagine you are a Japanese official committed to the idea of a monoethnic Japan. Write a letter in response to Wetherall's article. You may wish to imagine yourself as one of the officials Wetherall singles out in his article. If necessary, draw on other readings in this chapter or book to support your argument.

Susan Chira

They Call Japan Home
but Are Hardly at Home

The narrow streets and small wooden homes look at first like any other Japanese neighborhood. But here and there, telltale signs appear—a sticker on a door with a tiny Korean flag, bolts of brightly colored Korean silk hanging in a shop window, posters of red-cheeked girls in Korean traditional dress, the kimchi pots of spicy pickled cabbage on display in the central market.

This is Ikuno ward, the largest Korean neighborhood in Japan—in Japan, yet forever outside Japan. In a society that prides itself on its cultural and racial homogeneity, there is no room for another ethnic group with its own distinct traditions.

Unlike the United States, Japan has no history of absorbing immigrants, allowing them to embrace a new cultural identity without relinquishing the old. Koreans in Japan continue to remain apart, victims of discrimination in jobs, loans, and housing, subject to taunts and contempt.

"You have to be very strong willed to live as a Korean in this country," said Soon Hee Bae, who first came to Japan fifty-three years ago at the age of eighteen. "Japanese government and society demands that we throw away our traditions and cultural traits and dissolve into Japanese culture."

Most Koreans were originally forced to come here when Japan ruled   5
Korea from 1910 to 1945. Many came as virtual slave laborers, set to work digging canals in Osaka or mining coal. Koreans were then considered Japanese citizens. After World War II, Korea became independent, but Koreans in Japan found themselves stateless.

Few Seek Citizenship

Koreans are allowed to become citizens, but because they believe that doing so means giving up their Korean identity, few apply. Out of the nearly 700,000 Koreans in Japan, only 5,110 became citizens last year. Until a few years ago, Koreans who became Japanese citizens had to take Japanese names; Koreans here still say that naturalization means pressure to renounce their Korean past and submerge themselves in a Japanese present.

Applicants for citizenship must pass an interview, and officials often visit their homes. On such visits, Mrs. Bae said, officials may check to see

---

Susan Chira regularly writes for the New York Times, where this article appeared in February 1988.

whether the family speaks Japanese at home or whether the children attend Japanese or Korean schools.

Koreans who are not citizens face more overt discrimination in schools and when they look for jobs. Sang Sook Choi, the daughter of a Korean pastor, hoped to become a kindergarten teacher. She graduated near the top of her class, but one day her teacher called her in and advised her to seek work in Korean-run schools. If Japanese kindergartens hired a Korean teacher, she explained, parents might keep their children away.

That was more than twenty-five years ago, but little has changed. Her own daughter had the same experience.

"My children did well in school," she said. "I didn't want them to be   10 ashamed of being Korean, and we gave them Korean names. But they always had to be careful not to speak Korean or have a different kind of lunch in their lunchbox, anything that might be a reason to tease them. My son got telephone calls teasing him; his schoolmates wouldn't come over to play. Compared to my childhood, it was a little better. No one would even speak to me at school."

Ikuno ward provides a kind of refuge. It is one of the very few ethnic neighborhoods in Japan. Of the 160,000 people who live there, 38,525 are Korean, according to the ward office.

Koreans living in Ikuno can send their children to any one of several Korean-run schools, where they can learn Korean language and history. They can attend Korean-run churches, be admitted to Korean-run hospitals or shop at markets offering Korean clothing and food. The politics that divide North and South Korea split the ward as well—nearly every institution is affiliated with either the North or the South.

Koreans denied jobs in Japanese companies can turn to Korean-owned businesses. These include construction concerns, real estate agencies, pinball parlors, and bars, but many are small cottage industries.

A Question of Identity

These small factories—many no larger than a garage—line Ikuno's back streets. Here Mrs. Choi and her husband Chol Doo Kim, tend their family business, turning out small plastic parts and toys for larger companies. They work from 8 A.M. to 6:30 P.M., six days a week. They take home about $2,350 a month, slightly less than the average pay for a Japanese family. Others are less fortunate; workers in the ubiquitous sandal-making shops earn about $315 a month from piecework done at home.

As much as economic discrimination, the problem of preserving their   15 identity worries many Koreans in Ikuno, prompting conflicts not only with Japanese society but with their own parents. Like so many first-generation immigrants, Koreans who first arrived in Ikuno felt compelled to fit in. Their children grew up speaking Japanese and using Japanese names. Some are now trying to rediscover their heritage.

"My father always said, 'You are Korean,' but has he ever taught me Korean language or traditions, or told other people his real name?" asked Duk Hwan Kim, the director of a local community center. Mr. Kim helped to organize a community festival featuring Korean dances and music. But no one in his generation—he is now forty—knew the dances or music, so they had to send to South Korea for videotapes.

Su Gil Kim, a twenty-six-year-old filmmaker, and Chun Hae Oh, a music teacher, have decided to raise their young son differently. Even though both speak only limited Korean, they are trying to talk to their son in Korean. They plan to place him in a Korean school, although such schools are not recognized by Japan's Education Ministry.

"Japan is a narrow, exclusive, closed society, and we don't want him to be confined in Japanese society," Ms. Oh said. "This is the place where I've been brought up, so I have affection for it, but I don't consider Japan my homeland."

Thinking About the Text

1. Chira says (para. 6) that Koreans are allowed to become Japanese citizens, but many choose not to do so because they believe it means giving up their Korean identity. For example, they are expected to speak Japanese at home. Does the Japanese position make any sense to you? A related question: Do you think that some minimal competence in English should be required of persons seeking to become naturalized citizens of the United States? Explain.

2. In paragraph 10 a Korean resident in Japan talks about the difficulties of her school days. Would you say that her experiences could not have occurred in the United States? Explain.

Thinking About Culture

3. In paragraphs 16 and 17 Chira talks about persons of Korean background who apparently have little knowledge of Korean traditions but who are eager to regain their heritage. This experience may strike you as familiar. If so, describe a person, or perhaps a family, that has made efforts to regain a tradition. How successful have the efforts been?

4. As a class exercise, try to identify American attitudes toward Korea and Koreans. For example, what sort of news stories (if any) does one see or hear about Korea and Koreans? How is Korea presented in history and geography books? If certain attitudes and beliefs can be identified, discuss how they resemble, and how they differ from, Japanese attitudes to Koreans. (If you are a Korean or a Korean American student, you are in a good

position to help your classmates with this question.) Are these attitudes in any way representative of American attitudes to Asians and Asian immigrants? To immigrants and foreigners generally?

James Fallows

The Other Japan

Not many Japanese are interested in visiting Sanya, but for a foreigner it's a compelling destination. Before I went, I'd heard it described as Tokyo's largest slum. It's not exactly a slum, as Americans understand the term, and its pathologies would barely be noticed in a city with more glaring problems, like Manila. Still, this rare illustration of Japanese social breakdown is in its way as instructive as the country's many and more obvious successes.

The ideographs that make up Sanya's name mean "mountain valley," but it's actually a featureless flatland in the northeast corner of Tokyo, bordered by a crook of the city's major river, the Sumida. Through hundreds of years of Tokyo's history the area has been, as William Wetherall put it in the *Far Eastern Economic Review*, "a repository for the bottom of Japanese society." Japan's rush into modernization began with the Meiji Restoration, in 1868, but in the long preceding era of shogun rule Sanya had been one of Edo's (old Tokyo's) main execution grounds. From the thirteenth to the nineteenth century some 200,000 people are supposed to have been beheaded, crucified, or otherwise put to death there. The ordinary-looking traffic overpass that spans Sanya's main intersection is even now called Namidabashi, "Bridge of Tears." The street it crosses used to be a small river that separated the realm of criminals and outcasts from the city that had expelled them. Here Edo-era families said good-bye to errant relatives about to cross the bridge to the other world. Some people still call the main avenue in Sanya the Street of Bones.

Whether because of the ghosts hovering over Sanya and the blood in its soil, or simply because of the momentum of urban growth, Sanya never developed a "normal" business and residential base like the rest of the city. Even after the executions stopped, it was a refuge for fringe characters, such as worn-out and over-aged prostitutes from the nearby Yoshiwara pleasure

James Fallows, Washington editor for The Atlantic Monthly, *lived in Japan for several years. He is the author of a book about Asia,* Looking at the Sun *(1994), and also of a book about the differences between Japan and the United States,* More Like Us: Making America Great Again *(1990). This selection was an article in* The Atlantic *in April 1988.*

zone, and for Japan's class of outcasts, who performed "unclean" duties, such as leatherwork and handling the dead. About 45,000 people now live within the area commonly referred to as Sanya. Most of them are normal working-class Japanese, but about 7,000 are "flophouse occupants"— derelicts, bums, and casual laborers who live in the many flophouses and shelters of Sanya when they're not living on the streets.

Just how rough and tough today's Sanya seems depends on what you're expecting, which in turn probably depends on whether you're from Japan. On my first visit, in 1986, I went with a Japanese friend who usually comes across as Mr. Cool. As we emerged from the subway station, I noticed that he was suddenly walking with hunched-up shoulders and wearing an apprehensive expression, looking around nervously every few seconds, behaving as most Americans would in a dangerous part of town. Apparently we'd crossed the border into Sanya—I hadn't detected the change myself. A few minutes later, when we were stepping over drunks lying on the sidewalk and passing men urinating woozily against walls, I realized that Sanya was indeed different from the rest of Tokyo. But at the same point it became clear that Sanya is, rather than a slum, what Americans would call a Skid Row or tenderloin district, full of people who are not just poor but also sick, drunk, down-and-out. In specific, it lacks two elements that make true slums, in the United States and elsewhere, so alarming.

The first thing it lacks is families. There are no children in the Sanya flophouses, no teenagers that I saw, and practically no women. Nearly all the inhabitants are full-grown men, usually middle-aged or older, who for a variety of reasons have slipped out of the work-and-family network that holds the rest of the country together. Their stories are of course sad, but there seems to be no chance that they will spawn an even sadder multigeneration "culture of poverty" in Sanya. The absent father is known as the missing member of American slum society: Absent fathers, brothers, and sons are the mainstays of Sanya.

The second classic slum element that Sanya lacks is an air of impending danger. This is not to say that it is a calm or harmonious place. Since 1984 there have been two notorious Sanya-related murders. In one case, a film director working on a leftist documentary about Sanya was stabbed to death there. In the other, a labor activist trying to organize Sanya's residents was gunned down in another part of town. Many of the people on the street have black eyes, visible bruises, oozing cuts. The violence of American slums is mainly visited on other people in the slum, but a lot spills out. Sanya's violence is more completely self-contained. The two killings were politically motivated; they were the work of the *yakuza*, Japan's gangsters, who organize Sanya's main racket—finding day-labor jobs for the derelicts, in return for kickbacks from the daily wage. The *yakuza* often overlap with right-wing Japanese-nationalist groups, and through the 1980s there have been recurrent shoving matches and fights in Sanya between the *yakuza* and leftist groups trying to break the gangsters' hold. The killings are said to have been an extension of this struggle, as the *yakuza* tried to rid their territory of meddlesome do-gooders.

Sanya's residents are always vulnerable to being caught in the political cross fire or robbed or beaten by their neighbors. If they wander out into the rest of the city, they may be attacked by gangs of schoolboys who look for drifters to beat up. (This phenomenon, involving groups of otherwise respectable adolescents, has caused much worried comment in the press, which usually ties it to intense academic competition and to the prevalence of bullying, or *ijime*, in the schools.) But Tokyo's other 10 million people can still lead untroubled, crime-free lives in happy ignorance of the turmoil in Sanya. In the course of three visits the most aggressive behavior I encountered was from a stumbling, palsied-seeming man who draped his arm around me and with beery breath kept shouting, "Okay, Joe! Okay!" into my face.

I should mention a third important difference between Sanya and the worst American slums: The members of Japan's "underclass" are the same race as everybody else. True, Japanese society does contain tangled, castelike barriers of discrimination, especially against ethnic Koreans and the ancient untouchable class once known as *eta* ("filth") and now as *burakumin*, or "hamlet people." Their euphemistic new name comes from the isolated settlements, or *buraku*, in which until about a hundred years ago they were required to live. The *burakumin* are still discriminated against in school and work, as the Burakumin Liberation Research Institute, in Osaka, has documented, and they and Koreans are overrepresented among *yakuza* and Sanya bums. But the attitudes that oppress them can't really be called racial discrimination, since the victims are not a separate race. Japan maintains a meticulous system of birth and family registers, usually in each family's ancestral village; these records, inspected by prospective employers or spouses, make it almost impossible to keep an "undesirable" background concealed. The registers are necessary precisely because other Japanese often can't tell who belongs in what caste by just looking or listening. I'm not sure whether this color-blind caste system is morally better or worse than straightforward color prejudice, but it does remove racial complications from Japan's underclass problem.

These three differences from American and European slums—the lack of children growing up in a culture of poverty, little spillover crime, and the lack of a visible racial minority—help explain why mainstream Japan seems so little concerned about Sanya. If you get on the Chiyoda subway line near the Imperial Palace, you can get off the same train thirty-five minutes later at the Bridge of Tears. As Tokyo distances go, that's right next door, but Sanya might as well be in the South Bronx, or on Pluto, for all the attention its residents get from their fellow Japanese. The best-known relief center in Sanya is run by the Catholic Maryknoll order, and several other churches sponsor volunteers—this in a country that is less than 1 percent Christian. The volunteers at the centers and the donations on which they operate come disproportionately from the United States, Germany, and other foreign countries, not Japan. (In fairness, the Japanese chapters of American-style voluntary or charitable organizations are extremely weak, probably because other forms of organization in the country—family, school, work group—are so very strong.) But in addition to the three obvious factors that account for Sanya's isolation, I got the feeling that there was a fourth— embarrassment—that helped explain why people ended up in Sanya and why everyone else ignored them once they were there.

The man who explained Sanya's meaning to me was Dr. Masahiko Katori. Katori is a psychiatrist whose regular job is as the president of a private mental hospital, but on Fridays he operates a general medical clinic in Sanya, sponsored by the Tokyo government, for token pay. Katori must be successful—he drives a new white sports car and lives in what is for Tokyo a very nice apartment—but you would not instantly deduce that on meeting him. He is a grizzled-looking man of sixty, missing several lower teeth. Most Japanese men pass out business cards on which their institutional rank is specified with minute precision; in conversation they expect to be addressed not as "Mr." but as "Section Chief," "Division Manager," and so on. "Hospital President" Dr. Katori never gave me a card and said only that he worked at a hospital. He talks in a gruff voice, dresses in unconventional combinations of coats and pants, and has taken on some of the flavor of his clientele. "I feel like I'm becoming a kind of alcoholic just by being here," he told me with a melancholy laugh, in a coffee shop on the Street of Bones. "Before I came to Sanya, I could hardly drink half a beer. Now I may drink two or three bottles of whiskey a week. You could say alcoholism is an infectious disease!"

It may sound as if I'm mocking Katori, but that's not my intent. I admire him and what he does. He jokes about becoming an alcoholic, but he crusades tirelessly to get his patients off the bottle. He puts on slide shows, displaying biopsy slides of a cirrhosis-damaged liver; on his clinic walls are comic-book-style posters with tips on how to fend off the tuberculosis and pneumonia that finally kill those whom alcohol has softened up. He speaks about Sanya with a combination of tenderness and dispassion that I haven't encountered in American social workers. Unlike most of his fellow Japanese, he obviously views these bedraggled, dying derelicts as his brothers and feels sympathetic pain when they are hurt. But like most Japanese, and unlike many Westerners in comparable positions, he holds no-nonsense moralistic views about how each person contributes to his own downfall.

As Katori describes it, Sanya is full of people who were not strong enough to survive the collision between an old Japanese principle and the new Japanese life. The old principle, still very much in force, is that dignity comes from performing your duties as part of a group—the family, the company, the team. The new reality is that some duties no longer need to be performed. Technology has eliminated some, and Japan's impending "internationalization" and import liberalization will remove many more.

Japan has tried harder than most countries to preserve traditional jobs, but even it can't preserve all of them forever. The loss of identity that comes with unemployment is hardly unique to Japan, but here it has a special sting, because honorably discharging one's duty matters more in Japan than anywhere else.

"In the old days this used to be an agricultural country," Katori said one time, as he walked me to a small sushi restaurant tucked incongruously amid the flophouses. "During the snow season people would come in from the countryside to find work. They had no way to earn money in the home village, and here they could earn money for the start of the school year [which in Japan means spring]. It was a natural pattern for them to commute from the countryside to the city, then back to the country when the weather was warm."

In Tokyo the natural job for the migrants was day labor on construction, dockyard, and general-labor gangs. Sanya became a center for itinerant day laborers, who spent their nights in the flophouses and their early mornings being mustered into work details by the *yakuza*. (There are similar areas in Yokohama, Nagoya, and Osaka, the one in Osaka being the largest day-labor and flophouse district in Japan.) The golden age of day labor was in the years just before and after the 1964 Tokyo Olympics, when the city went into a frenzy, similar to what Seoul has just undergone, of highway improvement, stadium-building, and general sprucing-up before displaying its rebuilt self to the world. "The people you see here," Katori said one afternoon as we walked through lines of bruised, pulpy-faced patients at his clinic, "they built the Tokyo you see."

He was not just speaking metaphorically. During the pre-Olympic building boom as many as 15,000 day laborers lived in Sanya. Many left when the boom was over and found other places in the great employment-security machine that is modern Japan. Those still in Sanya are the ones who couldn't adapt to anything else—which is why so many are in their fifties and sixties. "The Tokyo Olympics were the root of the problem," Katori said. "There was so much work then, people got absorbed here. They didn't go back home."

The old generation is fast dying out, hastened on by neglect and disease, but Katori claims that migration may be putting a new generation in place. It's a bad time to be a day laborer, because bulldozers now do the job that pick-and-shovel gangs did even at the time of the Olympics. Nonetheless, country people still come to Tokyo, as part of Japan's inevitable adjustment to the outside world. "Many of the people here are from Hokkaido, the coal-mine areas," Katori said. "The mines are closing"—even at 250 yen to the dollar, the price of Japanese coal was out of sight—"and the men don't know what else to do, so they come here looking for work. They are so ashamed. Those who used to mine coal by the ton—now they're supposed to wrap candy with dainty fingers in the candy factories. It's hard for them.

"We are starting to have the regulation of rice production"—that is, the Japanese government is inching away from the enormous subsidies that have kept rice farmers in business—"so people come to the city from the farming regions. There used to be a lot of fishing far from Japan, but now other countries are restricting it, and the fishermen lose their jobs." Japanese whalers are being laid off too, and the papers have reported on whaling villages where everyone is suddenly out of work. "The longshoremen and stevedores in Yokohama lost their jobs when the container ships came. The railroads are going private this year and laying off workers." The shipyards, steel mills, and aluminum smelters are shedding workers too. "We are starting to see a flow into Tokyo because of the strong yen."

To an economist, every one of the changes Katori described would make perfect, obvious, inescapable sense. For Japan to operate energy-eating aluminum mills is insane; for other countries to let Japanese boats fish their waters, rather than catching and selling the fish themselves, is simple neglect of self-interest. Moreover, each of these adjustments (except maybe the whaling one) resembles a painful change that Japan's robust industries have forced on some other country. I'm sure Katori would prefer that Japan not open its protected industries, but unlike some Western counterparts, his point was not that society is to blame. He seemed to be saying instead that society had applied great pressure, by forcing people out of their familiar roles, and under that pressure some people broke.

"These men are mainly from rural areas, traditional backgrounds," he said. "They come hoping for work, but once they come here, they are discouraged. They start to miss their wives and children badly. They are heartsick for their familiar scenes. They tend to feel this ache most at night, and they can't go to sleep because of their worries. For a day laborer, what he fears most is not the hunger or the low wage. What he fears most is not being able to sleep. He knows he must get up very early to get work, and then work maybe in dangerous jobs all day. So to go to sleep he will drink—and drink and drink. In the evening time, you and I think of a drink with dinner. They drink to work tomorrow, but of course the amount increases and after a while they can't work at all."

Eighty percent of the people in Sanya flophouses are alcoholics, Katori said. From looking around, I would have guessed a hundred percent, but he said that the rest were chronic gamblers plus a surprisingly large minority of "sweets addicts," capable of blowing any money they get on candy, in order to gorge. When they can find day labor, they can earn 7,000 to 8,000 yen a day (about $56 to $64), after the cut for the *yakuza*. A night in the flophouse is 750 yen; the rest, Katori said, goes for whiskey, beer, or *shochu* (a harsh spirit made from potatoes). Those with a little money can invest it with the *yakuza*, buying "work stamps" to prove that they've held more jobs than they actually have. Japan offers modest short-term unemployment benefits worth $160 a month to laid-off day laborers, but only to those whose stamps show that they've worked twenty-eight days in the previous two months. The class divide in Sanya is between those still healthy enough for the 1,000 to 1,500 day-labor jobs typically available and those past that stage. Katori said that at a certain point men can no longer afford a flophouse, or would rather use the money to drink themselves to sleep on the streets. Small-time thieves prey on these pathetic men, sticking lighted cigarettes against their wrists to judge if they're comatose enough to be stripped and robbed.

"When they get to this point, it is a kind of chronic suicide," Katori said. "First they were commuting from their home village to the city every few months. Then they were commuting only from the flophouse to the day-labor site each day. Then they commute to the jail, then the hospital. When they can't make money any other way, they have three choices left: becoming thieves, selling their blood, or prostituting themselves with gays. This is disgusting to me. When they don't have jobs, they try to get hit by deluxe cars. Some people have made a specialty out of 'bumper fractures,' breaking the two bones in the lower leg. It's very painful but they do it. Somehow they never get hit by old, cheap cars." Katori said that about ninety people died out-of-doors last year in Sanya, mainly in the winter. The city government's estimate is only half that high, but considering how many of Sanya's men are old and sick, either figure seems low. It is very easy to imagine life ebbing out of those motionless forms.

Alcoholism and unemployment are of course universal problems, but Sanya's plight has a peculiarly Japanese edge. Even Katori, no one's idea of a typical salaryman, described the day laborers' plight through such familiar concepts as group identity, preserving face, stoic self-control. "Their philosophy is, don't look ahead, don't look back, just live for today. When they have money, they will gamble it or drink it. One man, who is now dead, worked for three months on a construction project in Akita Prefecture. The day it was over, he took a taxi back to Sanya." This extravagant gesture, equivalent to taking a taxi from Chicago to New York, used up all his earnings. Katori urges the Tokyo government to build better clinics, he laments the closing of the mines, he wishes other Japanese would pay more attention to Sanya. But finally, he said, the solution is for each individual to resist temptation and do his duty again.

He also offered a Japanese interpretation of why that was so hard. "They would like to go home. There everyone has a place at the table. But after five or ten years they lose their place. They want to come back, but to do it in the daylight—that would be too harsh. Everything would be too clear. So they come back at night. They come to the window and take a look in at the family they have left. But then—they see their reflection in the mirror, and they are too ashamed. They cannot go in and take their proper place again. They have let all the others down."

Thinking About the Text

1. Fallows is a professional writer, and he seems to us to be very good at his job. If you found this essay interesting, examine it and call attention to some of the techniques that Fallows uses. For instance, what function does

his second paragraph serve? (After all, if he had omitted it we would not be conscious of a gap.) Or consider the fact that Dr. Katori dominates the second half of the essay. Why do you suppose Fallows gives him so much space? You might also examine the humble devices (for instance, transitions and repetition) which Fallows uses in order to keep his argument clear. In short, be prepared to discuss some of the rhetorical techniques Fallows uses.

2. In Fallows's essay, "the other Japan" is a slum district of homeless men. But there are other kinds of "other" in Japan—people or groups who are considered "other" than the norm. In this chapter, for example, Dorinne K. Kondo has an experience of being "other," despite her Japanese ancestry. Look back through the book for other selections you may have read that deal with being different, excluded, or outcast in Japan, and try to come up with some generalizations on the topic.

Thinking About Culture

3. Working with your generalizations from question 2, discuss how being an "other" in Japan differs from being an "other" in the United States.

4. In his final paragraph Fallows says that Dr. Katori "offered a Japanese interpretation" of why it is so hard for Japanese derelicts to resist temptation and to do their duty: They see that "they have let all the others down." Does this strike you as especially Japanese, and as something that an American would not be likely to say about the inhabitants of Skid Row? Explain.

5. Has Fallows changed the way you think about American slums and homelessness? Explain.

Appendix: Doing Research

Using Sources

Many people are afraid to write because they fear they have no ideas. We have pointed out that one *gets* ideas by writing; for instance, when you interact with a text by annotating it, your ideas begin to take visible shape, and these ideas stimulate further ideas, especially when you question—when you *think* about—what you have written. But of course in writing about complex, serious questions, nobody is expected to invent all the answers. On the contrary, a writer is expected to be familiar with the chief answers already produced by others, and to make use of them through selective incorporation and criticism. In short, writers are not expected to reinvent the wheel; rather, they are expected to make good use of it, and perhaps round it off a bit or replace a defective spoke. In order to think out your own views in writing, you are expected to do some preliminary research into the views of others.

We use the word "research" broadly. It need not require taking copious notes on everything written on your topic; rather, it can involve no more than familiarizing yourself with at least some of the chief responses to your topic. In one way or another, almost everyone does some research. If we are going to buy a car, we may read an issue or two of a magazine that rates cars, or we may talk to a few people who own models that we are thinking of buying, and then we visit a couple of dealers to find out who is offering the best price.

Take this question: Why did President Truman order atomic bombs be dropped on Hiroshima and Nagasaki? The most obvious answer is to end the war, but some historians believe he had a very different purpose. In their view, Japan's defeat was ensured before the bombs were dropped, and the Japanese were ready to surrender; the bombs were dropped not to save American (or Japanese) lives, but to show Russia that the United States would not be pushed around. Scholars who hold this view, such as Gar Alperovitz in *Atomic Diplomacy*, argue that Japanese civilians in Hiroshima and Nagasaki were incinerated not to save the lives of American soldiers who otherwise would have died in an invasion of Japan, but to teach Stalin a lesson. Dropping the bombs, it is argued, marked not the end of the Pacific War but the beginning of the Cold War.

One must ask: What evidence supports this argument or claim or thesis, which assumes that Truman could not have thought the bomb was needed to defeat the Japanese because the Japanese knew they were defeated and would soon surrender without a hard-fought defense that would cost hundreds of thousands of lives? Moreover, what about the momentum that had built up to use the bomb? After all, years of effort and two billion dollars had been expended to produce a weapon with the intention of using it to end the war. If the argument we are considering is correct, all this background counted for little or nothing in Truman's decision, a decision purely diplomatic and coolly indifferent to human life. The task for the writer is to evaluate the evidence available, and then to argue for or against the view that Truman's purpose in dropping the bomb was to impress the Soviet government.

A student writing on the topic (whether arguing one view or the other) will certainly want to read the chief books on the subject (Alperovitz's *Atomic Diplomacy,* Martin Sherwin's *A World Destroyed,* and John Toland's *The Rising Sun*), and perhaps reviews of them, especially the reviews in journals devoted to political science. (Reading a searching review of a serious scholarly book is a good way to identify quickly some of the book's main contributions and controversial claims.) Truman's letters and statements, and books and articles about Truman, are also clearly relevant, and doubtless important articles are to be found in recent issues of scholarly journals. In fact, even an essay on such a topic as whether Truman was morally justified in using the atomic bomb for *any* purpose will be a stronger essay if it is well informed about such matters as the estimated loss of life that an invasion would have cost, the international rules governing weapons, and Truman's own statements about the issue.

Conducting Field Research

Keep in mind, however, that a source need not be something in print. You may find, for instance, that your topic requires you to conduct some interviews, either to gain factual information that is otherwise unavailable or to learn about attitudes. Usually you will consult experts for the facts and interested laypersons for opinions and attitudes, but bear in mind that experts also operate through the filter of opinion and that "ordinary" people may have facts that experts do not have. Similarly, you are engaged in research if, for example, in the process of gathering information for a paper comparing attitudes toward AIDS in Japan and in the United States, you call the local Planned Parenthood office, or call a national AIDS hotline, or consult your college health center.

Interviewing

Interviews are (especially in the social sciences) an important means of gathering information. By talking with people, you find out the social facts of their lives, their attitudes, hopes, and fears. A good interview produces more than information in the narrow sense; it elicits a portrait, or at least a sketch, of a person's life and views.

Here are some suggestions for conducting an interview.

1. Finding Subject(s) for Interviews.   For the purposes of this text, your interviews might seek to examine personal and social phenomena with which to compare the Japanese material included here. Choosing potential interviewees itself is an art. You should think first: What is it I want to learn about? Who best can tell me? Do I want an expert in the field (of, say, child development), or do I want an ordinary person who can give me a view of her own life?

If the purpose of interviewing is to discover representative attitudes or if you hope to generalize from the experiences of a sample of people, you'll need a critical mass. One or two persons cannot represent a sufficient range of views and experience, and variables such as age, sex, and ethnic background might need to be considered. Of course, for this exercise you will not be assembling a sample of thousands, nor will you be employing standardized questionnaires and surveys to gather background information for the interviews on the sample. For our purposes then, decide which variables are important, choose a small number of people (perhaps as many as ten, depending on your purposes and the number of personal stories you can gather), and talk with them in depth. Remember, for these exercises, depth is usually more worthwhile than numbers.

2. Preliminaries.   Prepare your questions. The interview question list is sometimes called an "interview protocol." Choose simple ways of asking things. You can be general, as in "Tell me something about . . . ," but usually it works better to ask why or how, and to be rather specific, especially at the beginning of an interview. If you are speaking with several people, it may be useful to have them fill out a short biographical form, listing whatever information about them (not too personal) you may think important to weigh against their statements, such as age, sex, family background, and education. If you don't use such a form, ask such questions as part of a warm-up to get the interviewee talking.

Confidentiality is important. You must tell your interviewees that in no way will they be identified in your essay and that any information they give that might lead to identifying them will not be used, or will be disguised. You will most likely use pseudonyms for persons who will be directly quoted, unless they are being interviewed as experts, in which case they are used to being quoted directly (or misquoted!).

3. Location.   *Where* you interview is important, too. Meeting in a busy cafeteria will probably not be conducive to a good interview. On the other hand, experienced interviewers in Japan note that coffeehouses, peaceful quiet nooks away from offices and the hustle of urban life, are the best places. Meetings should be in places where there is little distraction, whether it is the office of a professor, a student lounge, or the person's apartment or home. Be sure that wherever you meet, it is convenient for the person whose help you are getting. Also, if you are taping the interview, choose a place where there will not be disturbing background noise.

4. The Interviews.   Remember that your goal is to engage the interviewee in an interesting conversation that yields the information you need. This doesn't have to be an artificial exchange. Keep in mind that you are talking with a person whose life or ideas or experiences interest you, and remember that your prepared questions aren't sacred: Change them as the conversation develops. Of course, for comparability across all the interviews you are conducting, the same basic matter must be covered in each.

Most people are pleased to be asked to talk about themselves and happy to explain even the most elementary aspects of what they do to an engaged listener. Get engaged!

You have told your interviewees how long the interview will last, approximately: Stick to that time, and at the end (usually no more than an hour, to avoid burnout), thank them and depart. In some cases, if they are interested, you can offer to share the results of your study with them later.

5. Notes and Taping.   Not all interviewees are comfortable with being taped. Moreover, it is not necessarily the best method for you either. If the recorder malfunctions you've lost your record, but more usually, the presence of a tape recorder may make you sloppy, as you figure that the tape will capture everything useful, and an answer you don't understand completely can be sorted out later when you audit the tape. But if you don't get it when you hear it the first time, during the interview, you won't get it later. Also, transcribing interviews off tape is time consuming and boring. Most interviews for your purposes as a student are best taken down in notes during the interview: The slower speed means you have time to think as you write, and so does the interviewee. You can rephrase a question, change the tack, and think up "probe" questions to get closer to the point you want to make. The flexibility helps a lot.

You'll probably want to devise some system of shorthand, to help you write quickly but legibly.

As soon as possible after the interview, and definitely during the same day, sit down with your notes and read them over, filling in gaps from the remembered conversation. Add your own impressions of the person and his or her demeanor, looks, the ambience of the room, whatever will help you later remember the detail of the occasion. You never know what might be helpful.

Writing Up Your Findings

Assemble the interviews and read them all in one sitting. This will help give you the big picture of the data, opinions, and attitudes. Go back to your original notion or hypothesis, the reason you pursued the interviews in the first place, and think, What do I know now that I didn't then? What is the point of all this? What anecdotes illuminate my point?

One social scientist likes to say that once you get to this stage, you should think, What makes all this data "sing"? What gives the story life? What are the counterintuitive surprises here that make it interesting?

In your essays, use the interviews as exemplars, illustrations, and hard data. You may use direct quotations if they are particularly vivid, characteristic, and memorable, but most of your essay, of course, should be your own words. And you may find that your voice will be in a sort of dialogue with those of your informants. Use their words as both expert witness accounts and also as examples of representatives of the population you've decided to write about.

It is considered appropriate to offer copies of the paper to those you've interviewed.

Audience and Purpose

All writers of course must keep their **audience** in mind, not so much when they are getting ideas and drafting, but when they are revising their drafts. During the process of revising writers are always asking themselves such questions as Will this be clear to my readers? and Do my readers already know (and believe) this? The answers to these questions will determine such things as how much summary, how many examples, and even what facts the writer will set forth. Obviously you don't want to bore your writers by telling them at great length what they already know or by explaining an unfamiliar point with far more examples than are necessary.

But exactly who *is* your audience? Sometimes an instructor may specify that you write for a particular audience—a letter to the campus newspaper, or to the city newspaper, or to a member of congress—but most instructors will tell you that your audience consists of your classmates. That is, even though some or all of them may never read the essay, keep them in mind—rather than your instructor—as your readers. Your instructor may happen to be a Chicana female, but your essay will not address that fact. Rather, your essay will keep in mind a more generalized image of a reader—someone who is thoughtful, well-disposed, interested in hearing your views—someone who is pretty much like you but who of course does not have your particular experience.

Doing research is not the whole of a research paper. Your **purpose,** the reason you did the research, ought to be evident in the final paper. Sometimes your purpose may be only to inform your audience, for instance if you are writing a review of research (essentially, brief summaries of what has already been written or said about your topic), but usually your purpose will be both *to inform and to persuade.* Your reader will expect you to sketch the chief views, but your reader will also expect you to have thought about this material and will therefore also expect you to evaluate it and to set forth (with evidence) your own position. In short, your reader will expect you to have thought about the research and to have developed an argument based on your findings. Most businesses today devote an entire section to research and development. That's what's needed in writing, too. The reader wants not only a lot of facts but also a developed idea, a point to which the facts lead. Don't let your reader say of your paper what Gertrude Stein said of Oakland, California: "When you get there, there isn't any there there."

Finding Material in the Library

You already know, of course, that reference works such as *Encyclopaedia Britannica* and *Encyclopedia Americana* can give you some basic information about almost anything, but you may not be familiar with the *Kodansha Encyclopedia of Japan* (1976), a nine-volume work that—although it is now somewhat dated on such matters as economics and politics—is amazingly useful. Looking for something about the abacus or acupuncture? Or about agriculture, or *aikido* (a martial art)? Or—to skip a good deal—something about the *zaibatsu* (giant financial and industrial combines), Zen, or the Zero fighter (the chief fighter plane of the Japanese Imperial Navy in World War II)? For a brief introduction, turn to the *Kodansha Encyclopedia,* where you often will also find suggestions for further reading.

If you are working on a current issue, such as contemporary attitudes toward abortion or AIDS or exhibitions of American artists in Japan, you will want to use one of the many indexes to current periodicals. For example, the *Readers' Guide to Periodical Literature* (1901–) indexes about two hundred popular magazines such as *The Atlantic, Newsweek,* and *Time.* But for deeper coverage you may want to turn directly to the relevant specialized index, such as the *Art Index* (1929–), the *Business Periodicals Index* (1958–), *Education Index* (1929–), the *Film Literature Index* (1973–), or the *Public Affairs Information Service Bulletin* (1915–).

If you want deeper coverage than the *Readers' Guide* offers, and yet not the near-exhaustive coverage of specialized indexes such as those just mentioned, probably the first index to consult, if your library has it is, the *Expanded Academic Index,* a CD-ROM database index of about 1,500 scholarly and general-interest periodicals (in humanities, social sciences, and science and technology) as well as the last six months of the *New York Times*. If you want to find material in newspapers and your library does not use the *Expanded Academic Index*, consult the *National Newspaper Index*, which covers the four most recent years of the *New York Times*, the *Christian Science Monitor*, the *Washington Post*, the *Los Angeles Times*, and the *Wall Street Journal*. There is also an index exclusively devoted to the *New York Times*.

Student Research: An Example

It happens that a student, Doris Berger, was interested in Japanese attitudes toward AIDS. (In another course she had written a paper examining arguments for the compulsory testing of medical workers, and she now wondered if Japan required testing.) This is not a subject that has been much discussed, either in Japanese or in English, but she decided to see what would turn up when she consulted the *Expanded Academic Index*. This index can be approached through the author's name (you can enter a name and see what this person has published in the periodicals), through the title of the article, or through the subject. To search by subject, enter what is called a "keyword"—type on the keyboard whatever word or words you think will define the topic—and the screen will tell you what it has in the index that fits the keyword, or keywords.

Obviously "Japan" is too broad as a keyword—Berger didn't want *everything* the index had on Japan—and "AIDS" is also too broad, given her topic, so she entered two keywords, "Japan" and "AIDS." The idea was to catch any articles that dealt with this combination, and only with this combination. The search immediately produced thirty-six items, many of which were relevant. *Many*, but not all, because the computer, looking for "Japan" and "AIDS," came up with a number of items such as "Japan Aids Auto Manufacturers." Of the twenty or so relevant articles, her library had eight: two in the *New York Times*, two in *Nature*, one each in *Business Week*, *Far Eastern Economic Review*, *Time*, and *U.S. News and World Report*. Her instructor was able to give her one additional article, an account in a newspaper, the *Japan Times Weekly International Edition*. For the relatively brief paper that Berger was writing, these materials (along with some articles about AIDS in the United States, and an interview with a physician, and some conversations with friends) were ample.

Narrowing the Subject to a Topic, Developing a Thesis, and Taking Notes

Since the materials were not too numerous, Berger could photocopy them all without going to great expense. This meant that she could annotate and highlight the information thus copied, and always have it at hand without having to search again for it in the library if she needed to check some detail when she came to draft her essay.

But exactly what was her topic? She had chosen a broad subject—AIDS and Japan—but what would her *topic* be, what slice of the broad subject? She found that Japan does not have any sort of compulsory testing, but she did not find any explanations or arguments for this position. She thought of writing about Japanese attitudes toward persons with AIDS, or about foreigners in Japan with AIDS. Until she at least tentatively chose a topic, she could hardly highlight and annotate the source material. Or, rather, she could mark what seemed to her of special interest, but only after she had browsed through a fair amount could she begin selecting a focus for her paper. She found, as she browsed, that what interested her could be stated as follows: "In Japan AIDS has been publicly discussed only recently." Among the questions that came to mind were these three: "Why was Japan slow in facing the topic?" "Why the recent change?" and "How do Japanese attitudes compare with American attitudes?" (Of course, Berger was also aware of a large question: "Is there an American attitude, or are there many attitudes?") Her tentative answers to some or all of her questions would then provide her with her **thesis,** that is, with her point, the argumentative edge to her essay—for instance that the Japanese are more (or less) tolerant than Americans are, perhaps because of certain religious traditions.

On rereading the material, she jotted down important facts on 3-by-5-inch cards, for instance statistics. She thus had a card with such details as the numbers of cases of AIDS in Japan, derived from several sources, and another card with statistics for the United States. (The reason for using lots of cards, and for putting only closely related material on a single card, is that when you are ready to draft your paper you can move the cards around, in effect organizing and reorganizing your paper before you actually draft it.) She also jotted down a few quotations, phrases or sentences that seemed to her to be especially interesting. She did not, rightly, copy long passages. Rather, for the most part she **summarized,** quoting directly only material that she found she could not abbreviate or material that, because it was put in an especially interesting way, she thought she might quote in her paper. These passages she copied carefully, and she then double-checked to make sure that she had copied the material exactly. Since she had the original at hand, in the photocopy, at this stage she really didn't have to check for accuracy. Such a check is especially important, however, if you are copying material from a library book. Accuracy at this stage will save you the trouble of finding the book later in order to check your quotation.

Why use quotations? Quotations in a finished essay serve two purposes: They add authority, and they provide voices other than your own, giving your reader the pleasure of hearing another voice for a moment or two. Quotations should *not* be used for a third purpose, to pad the paper.

Quoting from Sources

The Use and Abuse of Quotations

When is it necessary, or appropriate, to quote? Sometimes the reader must see the exact words of your source; the gist won't do. If you are arguing that Z's definition of "homelessness" is too inclusive, your readers have to know exactly how Z defined "homelessness." Your brief summary of the definition may be unfair to Z; in fact, you want to convince your readers that you are being fair, and so you quote Z's definition, word for word. Moreover, if the passage is only a sentence or two long, or even if it runs to a paragraph, it may be so compactly stated that it defies summary. There is nothing to do but to quote it, word for word.

Second, you may want to quote a passage which could be summarized but which is so effectively stated that you want your readers to have the pleasure of reading the original. Of course readers will not give you credit for writing these words, but they will give you credit for your taste, and for your effort to make especially pleasant the business of reading your paper.

In short, use (but don't overuse) quotations. Speaking roughly, quotations should occupy no more than 10 or 15 percent of your paper, and they may occupy much less. Most of your paper should present your ideas, not other people's ideas.

How to Quote

Long and Short Quotations   **Long quotations** (five or more lines of typed prose, or three or more lines of poetry) are set off from your text. To set off material, start on a new line, indent ten spaces from the left margin and type the quotation double-spaced. (Some style manuals call for triple-spacing before and after a long quotation, and for typing it single-spaced. Ask your instructors if they have a preference.) Do not enclose quotations within quotation marks if you are setting them off.

Short quotations are treated differently. They are embedded within the text; they are enclosed within quotation marks but otherwise they do not stand out.

All quotations, whether set off or embedded, must be exact. If you omit any words, you must indicate the ellipsis by substituting three spaced periods for the omission; if you insert any words or punctuation, you must indicate the addition by enclosing it within square brackets, not to be confused with parentheses.

Leading into a Quotation   Now for a less mechanical matter, the way in which a quotation is introduced. To say that it is "introduced" implies that one leads into it, though on rare occasions a quotation appears without an introduction, perhaps immediately after the title. Normally one leads into a quotation by giving the name of the author and (no less important) clues about the content of the quotation and the purpose it serves in the present essay. For example:

```
Peter Ouchi provides a clear answer to Dekker
when he says that ". . ."
```

The writer has been writing about Dekker, and now is signaling readers that they will be getting Ouchi's reply. The writer is also signaling (in "a clear answer") that the reply is satisfactory. If the writer believed that Ouchi's answer was not really acceptable, the lead-in might have run thus:

```
Peter Ouchi attempts to answer Dekker, but his
response does not really meet the difficulty
Dekker calls attention to.  Ouchi writes, ". . ."
```

or:

```
Peter Ouchi provided what he took to be an an-
swer to Dekker, when he said that ". . ."
```

In this last example, clearly the words "what he took to be an answer" imply that the essayist will show, after the quotation from Ouchi, that the answer is in some degree inadequate. Or the essayist may wish to suggest the inadequacy even more strongly:

```
Peter Ouchi provided what he took to be an an-
swer to Dekker, but he used the word "homeless"
in a way that Dekker would not have allowed.
Ouchi argues that ". . ."
```

If after reading something by Dekker the writer had merely given us "Peter Ouchi says . . .", we wouldn't know whether we were getting confirmation, refutation, or something else. The essayist would have put a needless burden on the readers. Generally speaking, the more difficult the quotation, the more important is the introductory or explanatory lead-in, but even the simplest quotation profits from some sort of brief lead-in, such as "Ouchi reaffirms this point when he says . . ."

A Sample Essay

The system of documentation Berger used in her paper is the Modern Language Association (MLA) system, set forth in detail in Joseph Gibaldi and Walter S. Achtert's *MLA Handbook for Writers of Research Papers*, 3rd ed. (1988). We explain this system in our discussion of documentation, beginning on page 454.

Doris Berger
Professor Schmalz
English 201
May 5, 1994

Illness and Taboos in Japan:

The Case of AIDS

In the United States we are so used to reading about AIDS and to hearing talk shows with segments on AIDS, in which all sides express themselves strongly, that it is hard to believe that in Japan AIDS is more or less a taboo subject. We might expect it to be a taboo subject with some of the people who are infected, or even with some members of the family, but according to Jonathan Friedland in Japan "many doctors [are] still treating AIDS as a taboo subject" (18). And, again according to Friedland, as late as January 1993 only three Japanese with AIDS had publicly discussed the disease.

According to Rieko Tanaka, writing in the autumn of 1992 in the Japan Times Weekly International Edition, the Health and Welfare Ministry officially recognized 494 people with AIDS, as well as 2,272 who were HIV positive. By the end of the same year, according to James Sterngold, 274 people in Japan had died of AIDS, a majority of them being foreigners. It is difficult, however, to get exact figures, and in any case the official figures may not be accurate. Friedland writes:

> The total number of AIDS patients and HIV carriers in Japan is still small in comparison to other developed countries. According to the Health Ministry, as of October 1992, Japan had 508 AIDS patients and 2,456 people who had tested positively for HIV. Hemophiliacs who contracted the disease from blood transfusions make up about 75 percent of those infected. Compare this to the U.S., a country with

> double Japan's population but roughly 100
> times as many full-blown AIDS patients, and
> the picture may not look so grim. But doctors
> and activists say the official numbers under-
> estimate the total of HIV carriers by as much
> as 10 times. (18)

If, however, the official figures are wrong, the estimates of doctors and activists may also be wrong. In
any case, it is probably true that the number is very
small compared with the number for the United States,
where at least 200,000 people have already died of AIDS.
The relatively small number of Japanese cases may be one
reason why AIDS has not, until recently, been much discussed in Japan.

But there seem to be several additional reasons for
the relative silence in Japan. One is--to put the matter
bluntly--the moral stigma attached to certain kinds of
illnesses in Japan. As was the case in the United
States a generation or two ago, cancer is a word that is
virtually unmentionable, and it is still common for doctors not to tell the cancer patients or their families
what the diagnosis is. Mental illness is another taboo
subject, and so is serious physical disability. This
sort of treatment, according to Shigeo Kaneko, is really
one aspect of a widespread attitude in Japan, summed up
in a Japanese proverb, "The nail that stands up gets
pounded down." Of course, cancer and mental illness
can't be pounded down (that is, made to conform), but by
ignoring such phenomena the Japanese can make everything
smooth and normal, at least in their own minds. In
these cases conformity is achieved, Kaneko says, by not
seeing certain things. People who fit into these groups
are well taken care of, but their diseases often are not
spoken of. (Our own record, of course, is far from

spotless. For instance, to many people mental illness
still carries a stigma, and only in the last few years
have we recognized the needs and the rights of persons
who use wheelchairs or persons who have difficulty
seeing or hearing.)

The person with AIDS in Japan, then, is likely to
be regarded as a nonperson, partly because (being statistically insignificant) he or she is like virtually no
one else, and partly because such a person is seen to be
polluted and therefore is to be avoided and not even
recognized. According to Karen Lowry Miller, in a recent issue of Business Week, "family shame" characterizes the response to AIDS, and "many families will
abandon a relative with HIV, even disallowing burial in
the family plot" (54). Of course, in the United States,
too, persons with AIDS may be regarded as polluted. According to John Harleston, in the minds of many Americans there are two kinds of people with AIDS, those who
are responsible for their condition and those who are
not, or, to put it bluntly, guilty people and innocent
people. The guilty ones are homosexuals, intravenous
drug abusers, and prostitutes; the innocent ones are hemophiliacs (who acquired the disease through a transfu-
sion of contaminated blood) and children who are
infected through their mothers. Of course, not all
Americans draw this distinction, but probably enough do
draw it so that we can say that in this country, as in
Japan, many persons with AIDS are regarded as people to
be shunned. In our country, however, shunning may take
the form of public denunciations, for example by persons
holding signs condemning AIDS, whereas in Japan it seems
to take the form of nonrecognition.

Yet another reason why Japan has been reluctant to
face the problem of AIDS in Japan is the fact that the

disease is somehow regarded as a foreign disease, and
one chiefly limited to homosexuals. The rise in the
number of Japanese cases of AIDS of course has diminished this attitude, but foreign men are still blamed.
It is even thought that women cannot develop or carry
AIDS. When a Japanese prostitute in the port city of
Kobe died of AIDS in 1987, reports Time, the Japanese
were shocked to find that a Japanese woman could harbor
the disease ("Global Affairs" 41).

The number of cases of AIDS in Japan is now large
enough for the government to recognize that AIDS is not
simply a disease of foreigners. According to an article
by James Sterngold in the New York Times, the government
now advertises condoms in subway ads, and, even more remarkable, it urges people to have compassion for persons
infected with the AIDS virus. In Tokyo, according to
Masao Kuriyama, there is a new chain of trendy condom
shops, Condomania, located in fashionable areas, giving
out informational material on AIDS with the colorful
novelty condoms that they sell. The big change came in
1992; although in that year the government spent only
the equivalent of about $16 million for research and ed-
ucation concerning AIDS, it voted to spend five times as
much in the following year, about half for research and
half for education.

Apparently a good deal of education is necessary.
One theme that recurs in several of the reports about
AIDS in Japan is that most Japanese people have very
little knowledge about the disease--presumably because
it is hardly discussed in public. For instance,
Sterngold says that 41 percent believe AIDS can be contracted from a toilet and 62 percent believe that it can
be gotten from a mosquito bite. (Randy Shilts, a journalist who wrote extensively about AIDS, especially in

his book <u>And the Band Played On</u>, perhaps has said the
last word about the possibility of infection from a mosquito bite. Shilts says you <u>can</u> get infected: "If you
have unprotected anal intercourse with an infected mosquito, you'll get AIDS" [432].)

Although according to a letter in the <u>New York
Times</u> (Silva E16) many Japanese still think of AIDS as a
disease of gay foreigners, it seems to be agreed that
Japan has finally come to recognize that AIDS is not
just a foreign problem but is also a Japanese problem.
Japan has for the most part been a more sexually permissive society than the United States has been, and it is
well known that middle-class Japanese men visit Korea,
Thailand, and Manila for sexual tours. Prostitution
districts in these countries are known to harbor many
cases of AIDS, and there is every reason to believe that
many Japanese have contracted AIDS in brothels and have
brought the disease to Japan. As we have seen, the Japanese government has only recently begun to appropriate
substantial amounts of money for treatment and for education. It may be just in the nick of time.

Unlike Japan, the United States has for some years
talked freely about AIDS, and it has devoted considerable financial resources toward research and education,
though not with great success thus far. Whether Japan
will be more successful--now that it is at last facing
the problem--remains to be seen. But surely one thing
is clear: The recognition that there is a problem is a
necessary step if the problem is to be solved.

Works Cited

"Fear of AIDS Chills Sex Industry." <u>U.S. News and World
    Report</u> 16 Feb. 1987: 25.

Friedland, Jonathan. "Fatal Error: Ignorance over AIDS
    Hampers Countermeasures." <u>Far Eastern Economic Re-
    view</u> 7 Jan. 1993: 18-19.

"Global Affairs Are a Bummer." <u>Time</u> 9 Feb. 1987: 41.

Harleston, John. Telephone interview. 6 Nov. 1993.

Kaneko, Shigeo. Personal interview. 10 Nov. 1993.

Kuriyama, Masao. Personal interview. 30 Oct. 1993.

Miller, Karen Lowry. "Japan Finds the Silent Treatment
    Is Poor Therapy." <u>Business Week</u> 22 Feb. 1993: 54.

Shilts, Randy. "Talking AIDS to Death." <u>Esquire</u> Mar.
    1989. Rpt. in <u>Our Times</u>. Ed. Robert Atwan. 3rd
    ed. Boston: Bedford-St. Martin's, 1993. 432-44.

Silva, John L. "Japan Denies It Has an AIDS Problem."
    <u>New York Times</u> 5 Apr. 1992: E16.

Sterngold, James. "Japan Confronts Sudden Rise in
    AIDS." <u>New York Times</u> 8 Nov. 1992: 19.

Tanaka, Rieko. "Sexual Views Must Change to Stem AIDS,
    Doctor Says." <u>Japan Times Weekly International
    Edition</u> 31 Aug.-6 Sep. 1992: 4.

Documentation (MLA Format)

In the course of your essay, you will probably quote or summarize material derived from a source. You must give credit, and although there is no one form of documentation to which all scholarly fields subscribe, the form established by the Modern Language Association (MLA) is widely used. The sample paper beginning on page 449, "Illness and Taboos in Japan: The Case of AIDS," uses the MLA format.

This discussion is divided into two parts, a discussion of citations within the text of the essay, and a discussion of the list of references, called Works Cited, that is given at the end of the essay.

Citations Within the Text

Brief citations within the body of the essay give credit, in a highly abbreviated way, to the sources for material you quote, summarize, or make use of in any other way. These "in-text citations" are made clear by a list of sources, entitled Works Cited, appended to the essay. Thus, in your essay you may say something like this:

```
In discussing racial stereotypes, James Fallows
comes up with a powerful, but highly controver-
sial, formula: "Racial prejudice boils down to
the deeply anti-American message that some
people are born to fail" (120).
```

The citation, the number 120 in parentheses, means that the quoted words come from page 120 of a source (listed in Works Cited) written by Fallows. Without the page headed Works Cited, a reader would have no way of knowing that you are quoting from page 120 of a book called *More Like Us: Making America Great Again.*

Usually the parenthetic citation appears at the end of a sentence, as in the example just given, but it can appear elsewhere; its position will depend chiefly on your ear, your eye, and the context. You might, for example, write the sentence thus:

```
James Fallows thinks that the basis of racial
prejudice is "the deeply anti-American message
that some people are born to fail" (120), but he
does not support this view with hard evidence.
```

Five points must be made about these examples:

1. Quotation Marks. The closing quotation mark appears after the last word of the quotation, *not* after the parenthetic citation. Since the citation is not part of the quotation, the citation is not included within the quotation marks.

2. Omission of Words (Ellipsis). If you are quoting a complete sentence or only a phrase, as in the examples given, you do not need to indicate (by three spaced periods) that you are omitting material before or after the quotation. But if for some reason you want to omit an interior part of the quotation, you must indicate the omission by inserting an *ellipsis,* the three spaced dots. To take a simple example, if you omit the word "deeply" from the quotation, you must alert the reader to the omission:

```
Fallows thinks that "racial prejudice boils down
```

```
to the . . . anti-American message that some
people are born to fail" (120).
```

Suppose you are quoting a sentence but wish to omit material from the end of the sentence. Suppose, also, that the quotation forms the end of your sentence. Write a lead-in phrase, then quote as much from your source as you need, then type three spaced periods for the omission, close the quotation, give the parenthetic citation, and finally type a fourth period to indicate the end of your sentence.

Here is an example. Suppose you want to quote the first part of a sentence that reads, "A sense of place is important even to Americans." Your sentence would incorporate the desired extract as follows:

```
Fallows says that "a sense of place is impor-
tant . . ." (118).
```

Note that it is acceptable to replace the capital A with a lowercase *a*.

3. Punctuation with Parenthetic Citations.   In the examples, the punctuation (a period or a comma in the examples) *follows* the citation. If, however, the quotation ends with a question mark, include the question mark *within* the quotation, since it is part of the quotation.

```
Fallows asks his readers, "But is the connection
between intelligence and success really so nec-
essary and natural?" (153).
```

If, however, the question mark is your own, and not in your source, put it *after* the citation, thus:

```
What answer can be given to Fallows's assertion
that racial prejudice is "deeply anti-American"
(120)?
```

4. Two or More Works by an Author.   If your list of Works Cited includes two or more works by an author, you cannot, in your essay, simply cite a page number, since the reader will not know which of the works you are referring to. You must give additional information. You can give it in your lead-in, thus:

```
In More Like Us, Fallows argues that "a sense of
place is important even to Americans" (118).
```

Or you can give the title in a shortened form within the citation:

```
Fallows argues that "a sense of place is impor-
tant even to Americans" (More 118).
```

5. Citing Even When You Do Not Quote. Even if you don't quote a source directly, but use its point in a paraphrase or a summary, you will give a citation:

```
Race prejudice is based on the idea that some
people by nature can't succeed (Fallows 120).
```

A GOVERNMENT DOCUMENT OR A WORK OF CORPORATE AUTHORSHIP

Treat the issuing body as the author. Thus, you will probably write something like this:

```
The Commission on Food Control, in Food Resources
Today, concludes that there is no danger (37-38).
```

A WORK BY TWO OR MORE AUTHORS

If a work is by *two* authors, give the names of both, either in the parenthetic citation (the first example below) or in a lead-in (the second example below):

```
There is not a single example of the phenomenon
(Smith and Dale 182-83).
```

```
Smith and Dale insist there is not a single ex-
ample of the phenomenon (182-83).
```

If there are *three or more authors,* give the last name of the first author, followed by "et al." (an abbreviation for *et alii,* Latin for "and others"), thus:

```
Gittleman et al. argue (43) that . . .
```

Or:

```
On average, the cost is even higher (Gittleman
et al. 43).
```

PARENTHETIC CITATION OF AN INDIRECT SOURCE (CITATION OF MATERIAL THAT ITSELF WAS QUOTED OR SUMMARIZED IN YOUR SOURCE)

Suppose you are reading a book by Jones, in which she quotes Smith, and you wish to use Smith's material. Your citation must refer the reader to Jones—the source you are using—but of course you cannot attribute the words to Jones. You will have to make it clear that you are quoting Smith, and so, after a lead-in phrase like "Smith says," followed by the quotation, you will give a parenthetic citation along these lines:

```
(qtd. in Jones 324-25).
```

Parenthetic Citation of Two or More Works

```
The costs are simply too high (Smith 301; Jones
28).
```

Notice that a semicolon, followed by a space, separates the two sources.

A Work in More Than One Volume

This is a bit tricky.

If you have used only one volume, in Works Cited you will specify the volume, and so in the parenthetic in-text citation you will not need to specify the volume. All that you need to include in the citation is a page number, as illustrated by most of the examples that we have given.

If you have used more than one volume, your parenthetic citation will have to specify the volume as well as the page, thus:

```
Jackson points out that fewer than one hundred
fifty people fit this description (2: 351).
```

The reference is to page 351 in volume 2 of a work by Jackson.

If, however, you are citing not a page but an entire volume—let's say volume 2—your parenthetic citation will look like this:

```
Jackson exhaustively studies this problem (vol.
2).
```

Or:

```
Jackson (vol. 2) exhaustively studies this prob-
lem.
```

Notice the following points:

1. In citing a volume and page, the volume number, like the page number, is given in arabic (not roman) numerals, even if the original used roman numerals.

2. The volume number is followed by a colon, then a space, then the page number.

3. If you cite a volume number without a page number, as in the last example quoted, the abbreviation is "vol." Otherwise do *not* use such abbreviations as "vol." and "p." and "pg."

An Anonymous Work

For an anonymous work, give the title in your lead-in, or give it in a shortened form in your parenthetic citation:

<u>A Prisoner's View of Killing</u> includes a poll

taken of the inmates on Death Row (32).

Or:

A poll is available (<u>Prisoner's View</u> 32).

AN INTERVIEW

Probably you won't need a parenthetic citation, because you'll say something like

Shirley Evans, in an interview, said . . .

or

According to Shirley Evans, in an interview . . .

and when your reader turns to Works Cited, he or she will see that Evans is listed, along with the date of the interview. But if you do not mention the source's name in the lead-in, you will have to give it in the parentheses, thus:

No whale meat is served in American restaurants

(Evans).

The List of Works Cited

As the previous pages explain, parenthetic documentation consists of references that become clear when the reader consults the list titled Works Cited, given at the end of an essay. (Writers in other disciplines sometimes title this list References, Sources, or Bibliography.)

The list of Works Cited continues the pagination of the essay; if the last page of text is 10, then Works Cited begins on page 11. Type the page number in the upper right corner, a half inch from the top of the sheet. Next, type the heading: Works Cited (*not* enclosed within quotation marks), centered, one inch from the top, then double-space and type the first entry.

An Overview   Here are some general guidelines.

FORM ON THE PAGE

1. Begin each entry flush with the left margin, but if an entry runs to more than one line, indent five spaces for each succeeding line of the entry.

2. Double-space each entry, and double-space between entries.

3. Underline titles of works published independently, for instance books,

pamphlets, and journals. Enclose within quotation marks a work not published independently, for instance an article in a journal, or a short story.

4. In the sample entries below, pay attention to the use of commas, colons, and spaces after punctuation.

ALPHABETIC ORDER

1. Arrange the list alphabetically by author, with the author's last name first.

2. For information about anonymous works, works with more than one author, and two or more works by one author, see below.

A Closer Look   Here is more detailed advice.

THE AUTHOR'S NAME

Notice that the last name is given first, but otherwise the name is given as on the title page. Do not substitute initials for names written out on the title page.

If your list includes two or more works by an author, do not repeat the author's name for the second title but represent it by three hyphens followed by a period and two spaces. The sequence of the works is determined by the alphabetic order of the titles. Thus, Smith's book titled *Poverty* would be listed ahead of her book *Welfare*. See the example on page 461, listing two works by Roger Brown.

For a book by more than one author, see page 461.

Anonymous works are listed under the first word of the title, or the second word if the first is *A, An,* or *The,* or a foreign equivalent. On the following pages, we will discuss books by more than one author, government documents, and works of corporate authorship.

THE TITLE

Take the title from the title page, not from the cover or the spine, but disregard any unusual typography such as the use of all capital letters or the use of the ampersand (&) for *and*. Underline the title and subtitle (separate them by a colon) with one continuous underline, to indicate italics, but do not underline the period that concludes this part of the entry.

Capitalize the first and the last word.

Capitalize all nouns, pronouns, verbs, adjectives, adverbs, and subordinating conjunctions (for example, *although, if, because*).

Do not capitalize (unless it's the first or last word of the title) articles (*a, an, the*), prepositions (for instance, *in, on, toward, under*), coordinating conjunctions (for instance, *and, but, or, for*), or the *to* in infinitives.

Examples:

```
The American Abroad: A New View
On the American Tourist: Toward a New View
On the American Tourist in the Southwest
```

Place of Publication, Publisher, and Date

For the place of publication, provide the name of the city; you can usually find it either on the title page or on the reverse of the title page. If a number of cities are listed, provide only the first. If the city is not likely to be known, or if it may be confused with another city of the same name (as is Cambridge, Massachusetts, with Cambridge, England) add the name of the state, abbreviated (use the two-letter postal code; NJ, not N.J.).

The name of the publisher is abbreviated. Usually the first word is enough (Random House becomes Random), but if the first word is a first name, such as in Alfred A. Knopf, the surname (Knopf) is used instead. University presses are abbreviated thus: Yale UP, U of Chicago P, State U of New York P.

The date of publication of a book is given when known; if no date appears on the book, write n.d. to indicate "no date."

Sample Entries   Here are some examples, illustrating the points we have covered thus far:

```
Douglas, Ann. The Feminization of American Cul-
     ture. New York: Knopf, 1977.
Brown, Roger. Social Psychology. New York:
     Free, 1965.
---. Words and Things. Glencoe, IL: Free, 1958.
Davidson, Cathy N. 36 Views of Mount Fuji: On
     Finding Myself in Japan. New York: Dutton,
     1993.
```

Notice that a period follows the author's name, and another period follows the title. If a subtitle is given, as it is for Davidson's book, it is separated from the title by a colon and a space. A colon follows the place of publication, a comma follows the publisher, and a period follows the date.

A Book by More Than One Author

The book is alphabetized under the last name of the first author named on the title page. If there are *two or three authors*, the names of these are given (after the first author's name) in the normal order, *first name first.*

Gilbert, Sandra M., and Susan Gubar. <u>The Mad-
woman in the Attic: The Woman Writer and
the Nineteenth-Century Literary Imagina-
tion</u>. New Haven, CT: Yale UP, 1979.

Notice, again, that although the first author's name is given *last name first,*
the second author's name is given in the normal order, first name first.
Notice, too, that a comma is put after the first name of the first author,
separating the authors.

If there are *more than three authors,* give the name only of the first,
and then add (but *not* enclosed within quotation marks) "et al." (Latin for
"and others").

Altshuler, Alan, et al. <u>The Future of the Auto-
mobile</u>. Cambridge, MA: MIT P, 1984.

GOVERNMENT DOCUMENTS

If the writer is not known, treat the government and the agency as the
author. Most federal documents are issued by the Government Printing
Office (abbreviated to "GPO") in Washington, D.C.

United States Congress. Office of Technology
Assessment. <u>Computerized Manufacturing Au-
tomation: Employment, Education, and the
Workplace</u>. Washington: GPO, 1984.

WORKS OF CORPORATE AUTHORSHIP

Begin the citation with the corporate author, even if the same body is
also the publisher, as in the first example:

American Psychiatric Association. <u>Psychiatric
Glossary</u>. Washington: American Psychiatric
Association, 1984.

Carnegie Council on Policy Studies in Higher Education. <u>Giving Youth a Better Chance: Options for Education, Work, and Service</u>.
San Francisco: Jossey, 1980.

A BOOK IN SEVERAL VOLUMES

If you have used more than one volume, in a citation within your essay
you will indicate a reference to, say, page 250 of volume 3 thus: (3: 250).
If, however, you have used only one volume of the set—let's say volume

3—in your entry in Works Cited specify which volume you used, as in the next example:

> Friedel, Frank. <u>Franklin D. Roosevelt</u>. 4 vols.
>   Boston: Little, 1973. Vol. 3.

With such an entry in Works Cited, the parenthetic citation within your essay would be to the page only, not to the volume and page, since a reader who consults Works Cited will understand that you used only volume 3. But notice that in Works Cited, although you specify volume 3, you also give the total number of volumes.

A BOOK WITH AN AUTHOR AND AN EDITOR

> Churchill, Winston, and Franklin D. Roosevelt.
>   <u>The Complete Correspondence</u>. 3 vols. Ed.
>   Warren F. Kimball. Princeton UP, 1985.

Note that when the abbreviation "Ed." appears before the editor's name, it stands for "Edited by."

If you are making use of the editor's introduction or other editorial material rather than of the author's work, list the book under the name of the editor rather than of the author, as shown below under "An Introduction, Foreword, or Afterword."

A REVISED EDITION OF A BOOK

> Reischauer, Edwin O. <u>Japan: The Story of a Na-
>   tion</u>. 4th ed. New York: McGraw, 1990.

A TRANSLATED BOOK

> Kato, Shuichi. <u>Form, Style, and Tradition: Re-
>   flections on Japanese Art and Society</u>.
>   Trans. John Bester. Berkeley: U of Cali-
>   fornia P, 1971.

AN INTRODUCTION, FOREWORD, OR AFTERWORD

> Storry, Richard. Introduction. <u>Mirror, Sword,
>   and Jewel: The Geometry of Japanese Life</u>.
>   By Kurt Singer. New York: Kodansha, 1973.

Usually a book with an introduction or some such comparable material is listed under the name of the author of the book (here Singer) rather than under the name of the writer of the introduction (here Storry), but if you are referring to the apparatus rather than to the book itself, use the form just given. The words *Introduction, Preface, Foreword,* and *Afterword* are neither enclosed within quotation marks nor underlined.

A BOOK WITH AN EDITOR BUT NO AUTHOR

Let's assume that you have used a book of essays written by various people but collected by an editor (or editors), whose name appears on the collection.

```
White, Merry I., and Sylvan Barnet, eds.  Com-
     paring Cultures: Readings on Contemporary
     Japan for American Writers.  Boston:
     Bedford-St. Martin's, 1995.
```

If the book has one editor, the abbreviation is "ed."; if two or more editors, "eds."

AN ARTICLE OR ESSAY REPRINTED IN A COLLECTION

Some collections reprint earlier material, such as essays from journals or chapters from books. The following example cites an essay that was originally printed in a book called *Chrysanthemums and Thorns: The Untold Story of Modern Japan.* This essay has been reprinted in a later anthology of essays on Japan, edited by Merry I. White and Sylvan Barnet.

```
Reingold, Edwin M.  "Common Crime, Common Crimi-
     nals."  Chrysanthemums and Thorns: The Un-
     told Story of Modern Japan.  New York: St.
     Martin's, 1992.  Rpt. in Comparing Cul-
     tures: Readings on Contemporary Japan for
     American Writers.  Ed. Merry I. White and
     Sylvan Barnet.  Boston: Bedford-St.
     Martin's, 1995.  373-78.
```

Reingold's essay is from his book *Chrysanthemums and Thorns,* but it has been reprinted on pages 372–377 in an anthology of writings on Japan, edited by White and Barnet. Details of the original publication—title, date, and so forth—were found in White and Barnet's book. Most editors include this information, either in the copyright acknowledgments or at the foot of the reprinted essay; some even cite the original page numbers. If the original page numbers are readily available, you may include them before the reprint information.

Notice that the entry begins with the author and the title of the work you are citing (here, Reingold's essay), not with the names of the editors of the collection or the title of the collection.

A Book Review

Here is an example, citing Weisman's review of Ozawa's book. Weisman's review was published in a periodical called the *New York Times Book Review*.

```
Weisman, Steven R.  "Land of the Setting Sun?"
        Rev. of Blueprint for a New Japan: The Re-
        thinking of a Nation, by Ichiro Ozawa.  New
        York Times Book Review 11 Sep. 1994: 22.
```

If the review has a title, give the title between the period following the reviewer's name and "Rev."

If a review is anonymous, list it under the first word of the title, or under the second word if the first word is *A, An,* or *The*. If an anonymous review has no title, begin the entry with "Rev. of" and then give the title of the work reviewed; alphabetize the entry under the title of the work reviewed.

An Encyclopedia or Other Alphabetically Arranged Reference Work

The publisher, place of publication, volume number, and page number do *not* have to be given. For such works, list only the edition (if it is given) and the date.

For a *signed* article, begin with the author's last name. (If the article is signed with initials, check elsewhere in the volume for a list of abbreviations, which will inform you who the initials stand for, and use the following form.)

```
Daniels, Roger.  "Japanese Americans, wartime
        relocation of."  Kodansha Encyclopedia of
        Japan.  1983 ed.
```

For an *unsigned article,* begin with the title of the article:

```
"Immigration."  The New Columbia Encyclopedia.
        1993 ed.

"Automation."  The Business Reference Book.
        1977 ed.
```

A Television or Radio Program

```
Sixty Minutes.  CBS.  26 Feb. 1995.
```

Articles in Periodicals

The title of the article is enclosed within quotation marks, and the title of the periodical is underlined to indicate italics. Omit the articles *A, An,* and *The* when they begin the title of a periodical.

Some journals are paginated consecutively; the pagination of the second issue begins where the first issue leaves off. Other journals begin each issue with page 1. The forms of the citations differ slightly. First, an article in

A JOURNAL THAT IS PAGINATED CONSECUTIVELY

```
Canan, Penelope.  "Power, Social Process, and
     the Environment."  Journal of Political and
     Military Sociology 21 (1994): 1-11.
```

Canan's article occupies pages 1–11 in volume 21, which was published in 1994. (Notice that the volume number is followed by a space, and then by the year, in parentheses, and then by a colon, a space, and the page numbers of the entire article.) Because the journal is paginated consecutively, the issue number does *not* need to be specified.

A JOURNAL THAT BEGINS EACH ISSUE WITH PAGE 1

If the journal is, for instance, a quarterly, there will be four page 1's each year, so the issue number must be given. After the volume number, type a period and (without hitting the space bar) the issue number, as in the next example:

```
Greenberg, Jack.  "Civil Rights Enforcement Ac-
     tivity of the Department of Justice."
     Black Law Journal 8.1 (1983): 60-67.
```

Greenberg's article appeared in the first issue of volume 8 of the *Black Law Journal.*

AN ARTICLE IN A WEEKLY, BIWEEKLY, OR MONTHLY PUBLICATION

```
Lamar, Jacob V.  "The Immigration Mess."  Time
     27 Feb. 1989: 14-15.
```

AN ARTICLE IN A NEWSPAPER

Because a newspaper usually consists of several sections, a section number or a capital letter may precede the page number. The example indicates that the article begins on page 1 of section D and is continued on a later page.

```
Sterngold, James.  "Japanese Assail U.S. on
     Trade."  New York Times 2 Apr. 1994, sec.
     D: 1+.
```

A Database Source

Treat material obtained from a computer service, such as Bibliographies Retrieval Service (BRS), like other printed material, but at the end of the entry add the name of the service and the identification number of the item.

```
Jackson, Morton.  "A Look at Profits."  Harvard
     Business Review 40 (1962): 106-13.  Bibli-
     ographies Retrieval Service, 1984.  Acces-
     sion No. 621081.
```

Caution: Although we have covered the most usual kinds of sources, it is entirely possible that you will come across a source that does not fit any of the categories that we have discussed. For two hundred pages of explanations of these matters, covering the proper way to cite all sorts of troublesome and unbelievable (but real) sources, see Joseph Gibaldi and Walter S. Achtert, *MLA Handbook for Writers of Research Papers,* 3rd ed. (New York: Modern Language Association of America, 1988).

A Note on Plagiarism

Plagiarism is the unacknowledged use of someone else's work. The word comes from a Latin word for kidnapping, and plagiarism is indeed the stealing of something engendered by someone else. Plagiarism is *not* limited to the unacknowledged quotation of words.

A paraphrase is a sort of word-by-word or phrase-by-phrase translation of the author's language into your language. True, if you paraphrase you are using your own words, but you are also using someone else's ideas, and, equally important, you are using this other person's sequence of thoughts. Even if you change every third word in your source, and you do not give the author credit, you are plagiarizing. Here is an example of this sort of plagiarism, based on the previous sentence:

> Even if you alter every third or fourth word from your source, and you fail to give credit to the author, you will be guilty of plagiarism.

Even if the writer of this paraphrase had cited a source, the writer would still be guilty of plagiarism, because the passage borrows not only the idea but the shape of the presentation, the sentence structure. The writer of this passage hasn't really written anything; he or she has only adapted something. What the writer needs to do is to write something like this:

> Changing an occasional word does not free the writer from the obligation to cite a source.

And the source would still need to be cited, if the central idea were not a commonplace one.

You are plagiarizing if without giving credit you use someone else's ideas—even if you put these ideas entirely into your own words. When you use another's ideas, you must indicate your indebtedness by saying something like "Nakane points out that . . ." or "Japanese department stores, as Creighton mentions, . . ." Nakane and Creighton pointed out something that you had not thought of, and so you must give them credit if you want to use their findings.

Again, even if after a paraphrase you cite your source, you are plagiarizing. How, you may wonder, can you be guilty of plagiarism if you cite a source? Easy. A reader assumes that the citation refers to information or an opinion, *not* to the presentation or development of the idea; and of course in a paraphrase you are not presenting or developing the material in your own way.

Now consider this question: *Why* paraphrase? Often there is no good answer. Since a paraphrase is as long as the original, you may as well quote the original, if you think that a passage of that length is worth quoting. Probably it is *not* worth quoting in full; probably you should *not* paraphrase but rather should drastically *summarize* most of it, and perhaps quote a particularly effective phrase or two.

Generally what you should do is to take the idea and put it entirely into your own words, perhaps reducing a paragraph of a hundred words to a sentence of ten words, but of course you must still give credit for the idea. If you believe that the original hundred words are so perfectly put that they cannot be transformed without great loss, you'll have to quote them, and cite your source. But clearly there is no point in paraphrasing the author's hundred words into a hundred of your own. Either quote or summarize, but *cite the source.*

On the other hand, there is something called **common knowledge,** and the sources for such information need not be cited. The term does not, however, mean exactly what it seems to. It is common knowledge, of course, that Ronald Reagan was an American president (so you don't cite a source when you make that statement), and under the conventional interpretation of this doctrine, it is also common knowledge that he was born in 1911. In fact, of course, few people other than Reagan's wife and children know this date. Still, material that can be found in many places and that is indisputable belongs to all of us; therefore a writer need not cite her source when she says that Reagan was born in 1911. Probably she checked a dictionary or an encyclopedia for the date, but the source doesn't matter. Dozens of sources will give exactly the same information and, in fact, no reader wants to be bothered with a citation on such a point.

Some students have a little trouble developing a sense of what is and what is not common knowledge. Although, as we have just said, readers don't want to hear about the sources for information that is indisputable and can be documented in many places, if you are in doubt about whether to cite a source, cite it. Better risk boring the reader a bit than risk being accused of plagiarism.

Acknowledgments (continued from p. iv)

Ruth Benedict, "The Child Learns" is excerpted from *The Chrysanthemum and the Sword* and appears courtesy of the estate of Ruth Benedict, © 1946 Ruth Benedict.

Diana Bethel, "Alienation and Reconnection in a Home for the Elderly" is reprinted from *Re-Made in Japan,* Joseph J. Tobin, ed., and appears courtesy of Yale University Press, © 1992 Yale University Press.

Ian Buruma, "Work as a Form of Beauty" originally appeared in *Tokyo: Form and Spirit,* Mildred Friedman, ed., and appears courtesy of the Walker Art Center, © 1986 Walker Art Center.

Susan Chira, "They Call Japan Home but Are Hardly at Home" courtesy of *The New York Times,* © 1988 The New York Times Company. Reprinted by permission.

Millie R. Creighton, "Japan's Department Stores: Selling 'Internationalism' " originally appeared in the *Japan Society Newsletter* and is reprinted courtesy of the Japan Society, © 1989 PHP Institute of America, Inc.

Cathy N. Davidson, "The Old Woman in the Bath" originally appeared in *36 Views of Mount Fuji* and is reprinted here courtesy of Dutton Books, © 1993 Dutton Publishing Group. "A Teacher Learns" originally appeared in *36 Views of Mount Fuji* and is reprinted here courtesy of Dutton Books, © 1993 Dutton Publishing Group.

John Elder, "Whale Meat" is excerpted from *Following the Brush* and appears courtesy of Beacon Press, © 1994 Beacon Press.

James Fallows, "The Japanese Are Different from You and Me" appears courtesy of the author, © 1986 James Fallows. First published in the *Atlantic Monthly.*

Karl Taro Greenfeld, "Marriage? Girls Just Wanna Have Fun" appears courtesy of *Japan Times,* © 1992 Japan Times.

Clyde Haberman, "Wrestler Fails to Keep Hold on Honorable Past" appears courtesy of *The New York Times,* © 1988 The New York Times Company. Reprinted by permission.

Gayle Hanson, "Japan at Play" is taken from *Global Changes: Japan and the Pacific Rim* and appears courtesy of *Insight,* © Insight 1992.

Kazuo Ishiguro, "A Family Supper" appears courtesy of the author, © 1990 Kazuo Ishiguro.

T. K. Ito, Virginia Murray, and R. U. Loveless, "Computerized Matchmaking" originally appeared in *Mangajin* and appears courtesy of the authors, © T. K. Ito, Virginia Murray, and R. U. Loveless.

Sumiko Iwao, "The Quiet Revolution: Japanese Women Today" was originally presented as a lecture at the Royal Society of the Arts and appears courtesy of the author, © 1991 Sumiko Iwao.

Pico Iyer, "In the Land of Mickey-San" appears courtesy of *Time* magazine, © 1988 Time Magazine, Inc.

June Kinoshita and Nicholas Palevsky, "A Guide to Water Worlds" originally appeared in *Gateway to Japan: A Complete Traveler's Guide,* June Kinoshita and Nicholas Palevsky, eds., © 1990 Kodansha Institute. Reprinted by permission.

Yoko Kirishima, "Liberation Begins in the Kitchen" was translated by Wayne R. Root and Takechi Manabu and appears courtesy of *Japan Interpreter,* © 1975. Reprinted by permission.

Dorinne K. Kondo, "On Being a Conceptual Anomaly" is excerpted from *Crafting Power, Gender, and Discourse of Identity in a Japanese Workplace* and appears courtesy of the author, © 1990 Dorinne K. Kondo.

Jeannie Lo, "A Day in the Factory" originally appeared in *Office Ladies, Factory Women* and appears courtesy of M. E. Sharpe, © 1990 by Jeannie Lo.

Mainichi Daily News, "A Gun Tragedy Again" originally appeared as an editorial in the *Mainichi Daily News,* © 1994 Mainichi Daily News.

Neil Miller, "In and Out of the Closet" is an excerpt from *Out in the World: Gay and Lesbian Life from Buenos Aires to Bangkok* by Neil Miller and appears courtesy of Vintage Books, © 1993 Vintage Books.

Horace Miner, "Body Ritual Among the Nacirema" is reprinted from *American Anthropologist* and appears courtesy of the estate of Horace Miner, © 1956 by Horace Miner.

Akio Morita, "Attitudes Toward Work" is excerpted from *Made in Japan* and appears courtesy of Signet Books, © 1986 Dutton Publishing Group.

Chie Nakane, "Hierarchy in Japanese Society" originally appeared in *Inside the Japanese System,* Daniel T. Okimoto and Thomas P. Rohlen, eds., and is reprinted courtesy of Stanford University Press, © 1988 Stanford University Press.

Anne Pepper, "Christmas in Japan" originally appeared in *Mangajin* and appears courtesy of the author, © Anne Pepper.

David W. Plath, "Old Age and Retirement" is reprinted from the *Kodansha Encyclopedia of Japan* and appears courtesy of the Kodansha Institute.

Andrew Pollock, "They Eat Whales, Don't They?" appears courtesy of *The New York Times,* © 1993 The New York Times Company. Reprinted by permission.

Bill Powell, Hideko Takayama, and John McCormick, with the assistance of Shigeo Shimoda and Tom Hazlett, "Who's Better Off?" originally appeared in *Newsweek* and is reprinted courtesy of Newsweek, Inc. All rights reserved.

Edwin M. Reingold, "Common Crime, Common Criminals" is excerpted from *Chrysanthemum and Thorns* and reprinted with permission of St. Martin's Press, © 1992 St. Martin's Press, Inc., New York.

Donald Richie, "Introduction to *A Taste of Japan*" is excerpted from *A Taste of Japan* and appears courtesy of Kodansha International, © 1993 Kodansha International. "The Japanese Kiss" and "Walkman, *Manga,* and Society" are excerpted from *A Lateral View: Essays on Culture and Style in Contemporary Japan* and appear courtesy of Stone Bridge Press, © 1992.

Masashi Sada, "The Lordly Marriage Declaration (*Kampaku Sengen*)" was translated by James McLendon and appears courtesy of the publishers of *Kampaku Sengen,* Free Balloon Company, Ltd., and Free Flight Records, Ltd. of Tokyo, © 1979.

David E. Sanger, "Tokyo's Tips for New York" courtesy of *The New York Times,* © 1994 The New York Times Company. Reprinted by permission.

Mark Schilling, "What's Hot on Japanese TV?" originally appeared in *Mangajin* and appears courtesy of the author, © Mark Schilling.

Mark Schreiber, "A Nation Without Guns" originally appeared in *Intersect* magazine, was adapted for the *Japan Society Newsletter,* and is reprinted courtesy of The Japan Society, © 1994 PHP Institute of America, Inc.

Michael Shapiro, "A Whole Different Ball Game" originally appeared in the *Japan Society Newsletter* and is reprinted courtesy of The Japan Society, © 1989 PHP Institute of America, Inc.

Sei Shonagon, "Love in the Tenth Century" is excerpted from *The Pillow Book of Sei Shonagon,* Ivan Morris, trans., and appears courtesy of Oxford University Press, © 1967 Oxford University Press, Inc. Reprinted by permission.

James Sterngold, "Why Japan Is in Love with Vending Machines" appears courtesy of

The New York Times, © 1992 The New York Times Company. Reprinted by permission.

Time, "Let Them Eat Beef" editorial appears courtesy of *Time* magazine, © 1988 Time Magazine, Inc.

Joseph Tobin, "Dealing with a Difficult Child" is excerpted from *Preschool in Three Cultures: Japan, China, and the United States* by Joseph J. Tobin, David Y. H. Wu, and Dana H. Davidson and appears courtesy of Yale University Press, © 1989 Yale University Press.

Alessandro Valignano, Cosme de Torres, and Francesco Carletti, "Reports of the Earliest Western Visitors to Japan" is excerpted from *They Came to Japan,* Michael Cooper, ed., and is reprinted courtesy of The University of California Press, © 1965 University of California Press.

Kazuko Watanabe, "The New Cold War with Japan: How Are Women Paying for It?" appears courtesy of *Ms.* magazine, © 1991 Ms. Foundation. Reprinted by permission. All rights reserved.

Takashi Watanabe, "Young Japanese Confront Social Taboos" appears courtesy of *Nikkei Weekly,* © 1992 Nikkei Publishing.

William Wetherall, "Ethnic Ainu Seek Official Recognition" originally appeared in *Japan Times* and is reprinted by permission, © 1993 Japan Times.

Merry I. White, "Japanese Education: How Do They Do It?" is excerpted from *The Japanese Educational Challenge: A Commitment to Children* and appears courtesy of The Free Press, © 1987 Macmillan Publishing Group. Reprinted by permission. "Over the Edge: Delinquency and Other Teen Social Pathologies" is excerpted from *The Material Child: Coming of Age in Japan and America* and appears courtesy of The Free Press, © 1993, Macmillan Publishing Group. Reprinted by permission.

Shinobu Yoshioka, "Talkin' 'bout My Generation" appears courtesy of *Look Japan,* © 1993.

Index of
Authors and Titles